Lecture Notes in Computer Science 4969

Commenced Publication in 1973
Founding and Former Series Editors:
Gerhard Goos, Juris Hartmanis, and Jan van Leeuwen

Richard Kronland-Martinet   Sølvi Ystad
Kristoffer Jensen (Eds.)

Computer Music Modeling and Retrieval

Sense of Sounds

4th International Symposium, CMMR 2007
Copenhagen, Denmark, August 27-31, 2007
Revised Papers

 Springer

Volume Editors

Richard Kronland-Martinet
Sølvi Ystad
CNRS-LMA
31, Chemin Joseph Aiguier
13402 Marseille Cedex 20
France
E-mail:{kronland;ystad}@lma.cnrs-mrs.fr

Kristoffer Jensen
Aalborg University Esbjerg
Niels Bohrsvej 6
6700 Esbjerg
Denmark
E-mail: krist@cs.aaue.dk

Library of Congress Control Number: 2008931216

CR Subject Classification (1998): H.3, H.4, H.5, H.2, I.2, C.3

LNCS Sublibrary: SL 3 – Information Systems and Application,
incl. Internet/Web and HCI

ISSN   0302-9743
ISBN-10   3-540-85034-1 Springer Berlin Heidelberg New York
ISBN-13   978-3-540-85034-2 Springer Berlin Heidelberg New York

Springer is a part of Springer Science+Business Media

springer.com

© Springer-Verlag Berlin Heidelberg 2008
Printed in Germany

Typesetting: Camera-ready by author, data conversion by Scientific Publishing Services, Chennai, India
Printed on acid-free paper   SPIN: 12448005   06/3180   5 4 3 2 1 0

Preface

CMMR is an annual event focusing on important aspects of computer music. CMMR 2007 was the fourth event in this series and was co-organized by Aalborg University Esbjerg, Denmark (http://www.aaue.dk) and Laboratoire de Mécanique et d'Acoustique, CNRS in Marseille, France (http://www.lma.cnrs-mrs.fr). The conference was held in Copenhagen during 27–31 August, 2007 jointly with the International Computer Music Conference 2007 (ICMC2007).

The first three editions of CMMR were a great success and gathered high-quality papers by prominent researchers from the field of computer music. The post-proceedings of these conferences were published by Springer in the *Lecture Notes in Computer Science* series (LNCS 2771, LNCS 3310, LNCS 3902). The current edition follows the lineage of the previous ones, including the collection of 33 papers specially reviewed and corrected for this post-proceedings volume.

The field of computer music is interdisciplinary by nature and closely related to a number of computer science and engineering areas such as information retrieval, programming, human-computer interaction, digital libraries, hypermedia, artificial intelligence, acoustics, and signal processing. In 2007, CMMR focussed on a challenging theme: "The Sense of Sounds." Defining the notion of *sense of sounds* is intricate, since it refers to a very general concept that can be addressed through a large number of domains (philosophy, cognition, music analysis and musicology, perception, acoustics, signal processing). Nevertheless, this notion is familiar to all of us and our concern can be illustrated by questions like: Why do we easily distinguish a sound produced by a breaking glass from the sound produced by a shock on a metallic structure, although the spectral content of the two sounds is very close? Why do we easily accept the ersatz of a horse's hooves made by a sound effects engineer knocking coco-nuts together? Why do some musical excerpts generate strong emotions? These questions clearly show both the complexity and the pragmatism behind the rather unknown concept of *sense of sounds*. CMMR 2007 mainly addressed this issue from the sound modeling and retrieval point of view, aiming at establishing relations between the structure of sounds and their impact on human beings as well as discussing new progresses in this field. In spite of a growing activity and interest by the international research community for this particular theme, CMMR2007 probably was the first international gathering devoted to this specific topic. It was partly supported by the French National Research Agency (ANR) within the project senSons (www.sensons.cnrs-mrs.fr).

The book is divided into two main chapters dealing with the understanding and the generation of *sense of sounds*. The chapter "Towards the Understanding of Sense of Sounds" addresses theoretical issues related to the perceptual and cognitive aspects of the sounds. Here, we made a distinction between feature extraction and perceptual and cognitive aspects of music, and opened the field to multimodal aspects. In the chapter "Towards the Generation of Sense of sounds," practical issues are addressed and both methods and tools to manipulate perceptual features are described. In addition, some musical applications are presented, showing the close relationship between art and *sense of sound*-related research areas.

We would like to thank the Program Committee members for their valuable paper reports and thank all the participants who made CMMR2007 *"sense of sounds"* a stimulating and unique event. Finally, we would like to thank Springer for accepting to publish the CMMR2007 post-proceedings in their LNCS series.

February 2008   Richard Kronland-Martinet
                                                                  Sølvi Ystad
                                                              Kristoffer Jensen

Organization

CMMR2007 *"sense of sounds"* was jointly organized by Aalborg University Denmark, and Laboratoire de Mécanique et d'Acoustique, CNRS in Marseille, France.

Symposium Chairs

Richard Kronland-Martinet (CNRS-LMA Marseille, France)
Sølvi Ystad (CNRS-LMA Marseille, France)
Kristoffer Jensen (Ålborg University, Esbjerg, Denmark)

Program Committee

Program Chair

Sølvi Ystad (CNRS-LMA Marseille, France)

Members

Mitsuko Aramaki (CNRS-INCM, Marseille, France)
Federico Avanzini (University of Padova, Italy)
Nicola Bernardini (MIUT Italy)
Roberto Bresin (KTH, Stockholm, Sweden)
Chris Chafe (CCRMA, Stanford, USA)
Roger Dannenberg (Carnegie Mellon University, USA)
Amalia De Goetzen (University of Verona, Italy)
Philippe Depalle (CCRMIT McGill University, Canada)
Barry Eaglestone (University of Sheffield, UK)
Ichiro Fujinaga (McGill University, Canada)
Emilia Gomez (Universitat Pompeu Fabra, Spain)
Cynthia M. Grund (University of Odense, Denmark)
Kristoffer Jensen (Aalborg University Esbjerg, Denmark)
Marc Leman (University of Ghent, Belgium)
Richard Kronland Martinet (CNRS, Marseille, France)
Miller Puckette (UCSD)
Xavier Serra (Universitat Pompeu Fabra, Spain)
Tamara Smyth (Simon Fraser University, Canada)
Thierry Voinier (CNRS-LMA, Marseille, France)
Dan Trueman (Princeton University, Spain)
Vesa Valimaki (HUT)
Christophe Vergez (CNRS, Marseille, France)
Gerhard Widmer (University of Vienna, Austria)
Diana Young (MIT Media Lab, USA)

Sponsoring Institutions

Aalborg University Esbjerg, Denmark
CNRS, Laboratoire de Mécanique et d'Acoustique, Marseille France.
French National Research Agency (ANR, JC05-41996, "senSons")
Re-New - Digital Arts Forum, Denmark

Table of Contents

I Towards the Understanding of Sense of Sounds

I-i Perceptual and Cognitive Aspects of Music

Fifty Years of Computer Music: Ideas of the Past Speak to the
Future 1
   John Chowning

Music Cognition: Learning, Perception, Expectations 11
   Barbara Tillmann

Capturing Expressive and Indicative Qualities of Conducting Gesture:
An Application of Temporal Expectancy Models 34
   Dilip Swaminathan, Harvey Thornburg, Todd Ingalls, Stjepan Rajko,
   Jodi James, Ellen Campana, Kathleya Afanador, and
   Randal Leistikow

Musicians Outperform Nonmusicians in Speech Imitation 56
   Barbara Pastuszek-Lipińska

Cognitive Styles and Computer-Based Creativity Support Systems:
Two Linked Studies of Electro-acoustic Music Composers 74
   Barry Eaglestone, Nigel Ford, Peter Holdridge, Jenny Carter, and
   Catherine Upton

The Usability of Music Theory Software: The Analysis of Twelve-Tone
Music as a Case Study 98
   Tuukka Ilomäki

Understanding Emotion in *Raag*: An Empirical Study of Listener
Responses 110
   Parag Chordia and Alex Rae

I-ii Relevant Features in Sounds and Music

The Artistic Play of Spatial Organization: Spatial Attributes, Scene
Analysis and Auditory Spatial Schemata 125
   Gary S. Kendall and Mauricio Ardila

Semiotics of Sounds Evoking Motions: Categorization and Acoustic
Features 139
   Adrien Merer, Sølvi Ystad, Richard Kronland-Martinet, and
   Mitsuko Aramaki

Exploring Perceptual Based Timbre Feature for Singer Identification ...   159
   Swe Zin Kalayar Khine, Tin Lay Nwe, and Haizhou Li

Cognitive Implications of Musical Perception   172
   Adam Lockhart

A Meta-Analysis of Timbre Perception Using Nonlinear Extensions to
CLASCAL   181
   John Ashley Burgoyne and Stephen McAdams

Real-Time Analysis of Sensory Dissonance   203
   John MacCallum and Aaron Einbond

I-iii   Multimodal Perception and Interaction

Multimodal Design for Enactive Toys   212
   *Amalia de Götzen, Luca Mion, Federico Avanzini, and
   Stefania Serafin*

Psychoacoustic Manipulation of the Sound-Induced Illusory Flash   223
   Sonia Wilkie, Catherine Stevens, and Roger Dean

On Cross-Modal Perception of Musical Tempo and the Speed of Human
Movement   235
   *Kathleya Afanador, Ellen Campana, Todd Ingalls,
   Dilip Swaminathan, Harvey Thornburg, Jodi James,
   Jessica Mumford, Gang Qian, and StJepan Rajko*

Between Mapping, Sonification and Composition: Responsive Audio
Environments in Live Performance   246
   *Christopher L. Salter, Marije A.J. Baalman, and
   Daniel Moody-Grigsby*

II   Towards the Generation of Sense of Sounds

II-i   Rule-Based Music Retrieval and Generation

Retrieving and Recreating Musical Form   263
   Ole Kühl and Kristoffer Jensen

Placement of Sound Sources in the Stereo Field Using Measured Room
Impulse Responses   276
   *William D. Haines, Jesse R. Vernon, Roger B. Dannenberg, and
   Peter F. Driessen*

Rule-Based Expressive Modifications of Tempo in Polyphonic Audio
Recordings   288
   Marco Fabiani and Anders Friberg

Exploring the Perceptual Relevance of Inherent Variability of Drum
Sounds 303
  Matthias Rath and Marcel Wältermann

Improving Musical Expressiveness by Time-Varying Brightness
Shaping 313
  Mathieu Barthet, Richard Kronland-Martinet, and Sølvi Ystad

II-ii   AI Approaches for Interactive Musical Systems

NN Music: Improvising with a 'Living' Computer 337
  Michael Young

A Real-Time Genetic Algorithm in Human-Robot Musical
Improvisation 351
  Gil Weinberg, Mark Godfrey, Alex Rae, and John Rhoads

A Musical Framework with Swarming Robots......................... 360
  Yuta Uozumi, Masato Takahashi, and Ryoho Kobayashi

Emergent Rhythms through Multi-agency in Max/MSP 368
  Arne Eigenfeldt

II-iii   Tools and Applications for Composers and Performers

Experiencing Audio and Music in a Fully Immersive Environment 380
  *Xavier Amatriain, Jorge Castellanos, Tobias Höllerer,
  JoAnn Kuchera-Morin, Stephen T. Pope, Graham Wakefield, and
  Will Wolcott*

A Network-Based Framework for Collaborative Development and
Performance of Digital Musical Instruments 401
  Joseph Malloch, Stephen Sinclair, and Marcelo M. Wanderley

The ImmApp: A Digital Application for Immersive Interaction with
Sound Art Archives.. 426
  J. Milo Taylor

BioTools: A Biosignal Toolbox for Composers and Performers 441
  Miguel Angel Ortiz Pérez and R. Benjamin Knapp

Focus-Plus-Context Audio Interaction Design........................ 453
  David Gerhard, Brett Park, and Jarrod Ellis

Maps and Legends: Designing FPS-Based Interfaces for Multi-User
Composition, Improvisation and Immersive Performance 478
  Robert Hamilton

DECONcert: Making Waves with Water, EEG, and Music 487
  Steve Mann, James Fung, and Ariel Garten

Author Index.. 507

Fifty Years of Computer Music: Ideas of the Past Speak to the Future

John Chowning

CCRMA, Department of Music, Stanford University, Stanford, California 94305
jc@ccrma.stanford.edu

Abstract. The use of the computer to analyze and synthesize sound in two early forms, additive and FM synthesis, led to new thoughts about synthesizing sound spectra, tuning and pitch. Detached from their traditional association with the timbre of acoustic instruments, spectra become structured and associated with pitch in ways that are unique to the medium of computer music.

1 Introduction

In 1957, just fifty years ago, Max Mathews introduced a wholly new means of making music. An engineer/scientist at Bell Telephone Laboratories (BTL), Max (with the support of John Pierce, who was director of research) created out of numbers and code the first music to be produced by a digital computer. It is usually the case that a fascination with some aspect of a discipline outside of one's own will quickly conclude with an experiment without elaboration. But in Max's case, it was the beginning of a profoundly deep and consequential adventure, one which he modestly invited us all to join through his elegantly conceived programs, engendering tendrils that found their way into far-flung disciplines that today, 50 years later, continue to grow without end.

From the very beginning Max's use of the computer for making music was expansive. Synthesis, signal processing, analysis, algorithmic composition, psychoacoustics—all were within his scope and all were expressed and described in great detail in his famous article [1] and the succession of programs MUSIC I-V.[1]

It is in the nature of the computer medium that detail be elevated at times to the forefront of our thinking, for unlike preceding music technologies, both acoustic and analogue, computers require us to manage detail to accomplish even the most basic steps. It is in the detail that we find control of the sonic, theoretical and creative forms. And it is through paying attention to detail that we reveal our scientific/engineering insights or our artistic expression—our own voice.

The first examples of computer-generated music produced by Max and by John Pierce at BTL were rich in ideas, including algorithmic composition, novel tuning, matching tuning systems to complementary spectra, imaginative and compelling graphics and visualizations and, soon following, controllers [2]. It is fortunate that

---

[1] For a complete account of Max Mathews' work and publications, see
http://www.ina.fr/produits/publications/collections/collec_11.fr.html.

R. Kronland-Martinet, S. Ystad, and K. Jensen (Eds.): CMMR 2007, LNCS 4969, pp. 1–10, 2008.

these two scientists/engineers—who cultivated a nexus between science and art, and who invited many composers and artists to their laboratories (e.g., Varèse and Cage) to share the possibilities that they saw—were willing to place these nascent musical studies in the public view, confident in the intellectual content of their ideas, which few others could see. Some of their ideas remain as compelling now as they were then and should be "re-viewed" given the enriched domains of application at this 50-year mark.

2 Breakthroughs

The richness of the ideas in these early examples was not matched by the quality of the sounds with which they were expressed. Little was known about some important aspects of perception and the acoustics of musical instruments. Two important composers were invited by Max to work at BTL, both of whom made important contributions in this area in addition to creating compositions: James Tenney and Jean-Claude Risset.

Preceding Max's famous article by a few months was an article by Tenney that described in exquisite detail the program that Max had created [3]. Tenney had been invited by John Pierce and Max to work at BTL beginning in 1961. He had studied with the visionary Lejaren Hiller at the University of Illinois, so he came prepared in matters of programming and stochastic processes in composition. During his three years at BTL he made several important contributions; he created compositions using this new medium, and he wrote in great detail about what he had learned from Max and how Tenney had constructed his compositions. Because he was a composer, Tenney's description of Max's MUSIC IV was from a musical view, and it remains an exemplar of clarity and completeness.[2]

But, important to the points being presented in this paper, he came upon a music-driven question in his compositions using MUSIC IV for which there was no answer, so with Max's guidance, he did a study regarding the *perception* of attack times [3]. The italicization is to draw attention to two points: 1, the fact that from the outset psychoacoustics had been seen by Max as one of the crucial disciplines in the advancement of computer music[3] and 2, that musicians have a particular sensitivity to details of auditory perception.

2.1 Risset Uncovers the Microstructure

There is no doubt that the most important breakthrough in the early days of computer music occurred when Jean-Claude Risset and Max began detailed computer studies in the analysis, synthesis and perception of acoustic instrument tones, culminating in Risset's *An Introductory Catalogue of Computer Synthesized Sounds* [1]. With this work the medium of computer music reached a level beyond Max's correct but

---

[2] His early interest and important contributions notwithstanding, Jim Tenney did not continue in computer music, but rather became a distinguished teacher, performer and composer of acoustic music. He died August 24, 2006.

[3] Max wrote in 1963 "At present, the range of computer music is limited principally by cost and by our knowledge of psychoacoustics [4]."

abstract assertion that computers (coupled with loudspeakers) can produce any perceivable sound. The capability of simulating natural-sounding tones presupposes an understanding of the perceptual relevance of the physical stimuli, only some of which have been "selected" as meaningful by the auditory system.

2.2 FM Synthesis—40 Years

It was forty years ago that this author 'stumbled" upon FM synthesis [4]. The actual date is not known. Not having a scientific or engineering background, I did not have the habit of keeping dated lab notes, but I did keep notes. There is a record of my having visited BTL on December 18, 1967 when I showed the data that I used in my first trials to Max, Risset and Pierre Ruiz and played for them the examples. It was a month or two before, almost certainly late at night, while experimenting with extreme vibrato frequencies and depths that I realized "there is more here than at first meets the ear."

Its discovery was not a purposeful search—that is, stemming from a realization, from looking at the equation, that there might be some interesting experiments to try—rather, it was altogether a discovery of the "ear."

One must remember that while the theoretical potential for the production of rich dynamic sounds with the computer was great, the knowledge required for realizing this potential was meager. Risset's catalogue was in progress and little known outside of BTL. Furthermore, the cost in computer time was enormous, limiting the complexity of synthesis algorithms. Deep into the details of digital reverberation at the time, I was keenly aware of this issue. My "ear" was continually scanning for any sound having internal dynamism, coupled oscillators, random vibrato, etc. That I found it within such a computationally efficient algorithm was certainly partly chance, but then I was also certainly prepared for that chance.

The first experiments were each only a few seconds duration, because of the tens of minutes of compute time on a time-shared system. But they do show that from the outset, all of the essential features were noted that would eventually be developed and used in musical contexts:

- both harmonic and inharmonic spectra could be produced
- a change in frequency deviation (Δf) produced a change in bandwidth of the spectrum
- the spectrum is conserved through the pitch space with a constant ratio of FM frequencies

As it turned out, these parameters of FM synthesis have a remarkable perceptual relevance.

As mentioned above, Risset's study of trumpet tones had a major influence on my own development of FM synthesis. I first heard about this study on the aforementioned visit to BTL in 1967, during which I showed my first experiments in FM synthesis. Risset explained his analysis and re-synthesis of trumpet tones and played some examples. It was not until 1970, however, that I fully appreciated the importance of his discoveries about trumpet tones.

While working on the FM synthesis of percussive sounds, I noted that in nearly all tones of this class the amplitude envelope and the envelope controlling the modulation index were very similar if not identical. I also noted that there was as strong a correlation of the perception of 'strike force' to the modulation index as there was to intensity. I considered other classes of tones where this might be the case, and I remembered Risset's explanation of the "signature" of trumpet tones, some three years previous. With only a few attempts I was able to create credible brass-like tones by simply coupling a single function to the amplitude and modulation index envelopes with appropriate scaling. I realized that this correlation of force or effort (strike force, breath and bow pressure velocity, etc.) to the bandwidth and/or high-frequency emphasis of partials can be generalized to all natural sound and that the parameters of FM synthesis provided a straightforward implementation of this important correlation[4].

Then began a rapid development of FM synthesis[5], and the eventual licensing of the technology by Stanford University to Yamaha—the rest is history.

3 Structured Spectra and Pitch Space

There are two ways in which additive synthesis and FM synthesis have been used that merit emphasis, because they touch upon issues that are important beyond any particular means of synthesis. John Pierce and Max foresaw one way in the early years: the creation of a non-traditional scale that has a structural link to timbre, where the frequency ratios from the scale are used in the construction of the tone's spectra. Karlheinz Stockhausen created a similar relationship between pitch and spectrum in his Studie 1 (1953). Risset, however, used synthesis in a manner not foreseen—a manner imaginative and evocative.

3.1 Constructing Spectra *in* the Pitch Space

The final example in Risset's catalogue stands as a striking advance in computer music, although little recognized and little exploited. It is the first instance where pitch is used to express timbre in the same functional manner that pitch expresses melody and harmony, that is, melody-harmony-timbre all within the pitch space. Pitch is composed sequentially as line and simultaneously as harmony, for which there are rich functional theories, but composing timbre as a collection of partials drawn from the pitch space cannot be achieved with acoustic instruments and falls squarely in the domain of computer music.

The sound potential of any instrument is vast, but limited—the partials that make up an instrument's tone can only be partly modified by performance techniques and devices such as mutes. A clarinet and a violin can play the same pitch at the same loudness for the same duration, but they cannot be made to have the same spectrum through time—the frequency and intensity of an instrument's partials are locked within boundaries defined by its and the performer's physical properties.

---

[4] The ease with which spectral change could be coupled to effort (key velocity) is one of the reasons for the YAMAHA DX7's remarkable success.

[5] The first real-time FM synthesis was programmed on a DEC PDP-15 computer by Barry Truax in 1973, while studying in Utrecht. At Stanford, Bill Schottstaedt developed a particularly powerful form of the algorithm that was used in many compositions for many years.

Risset realized in his timbre studies that in creating natural sounding complex timbres by summing numbers of sinusoids (pure tones) where each sinusoid can have its own independent control over intensity and frequency through time, he had unlocked timbre from any physical constraints. He could create tones that cannot exist in the natural world, complex timbres where the partials themselves are a part of the pitch space. He composed a short pitch sequence that is heard first sequentially in time (melody), then simultaneously in time (harmony), and then again simultaneously with exactly the same pitches but now as partials associated with a single sound source, as shown in Fig. 1. [2].

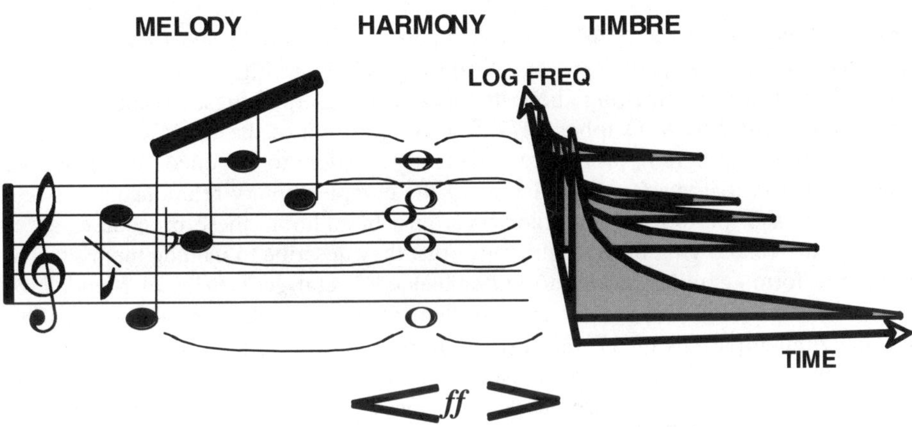

Fig. 1. Pitches become the partials of the gong-like tone, linking timbre to the pitch space in a manner uniquely possible with computers- from *Mutations* 1969 Jean-Claude Risset

Because all of the partials die away in a similar manner, they fuse and are heard as timbre rather than harmony. The timbre is similar to that of a gong, but a gong whose spectrum is imprinted with pitch information, giving the sound an extra-natural structural link to the preceding. Risset's was an altogether new conception, uniquely possible with computers, and beautifully framed in several of his compositions, first in *Mutations* (1969).

3.2 Constructing Spectra <u>*and*</u> the Pitch Space

John Pierce and Max saw early on that using the computer for both control and synthesis could unlock tuning systems from physical constraints, just as Risset had unlocked timbre. Max composed a piece, *The Second Law* that is entirely made up of noise, entirely free of common understandings of pitch, yet expressing pitch. In his *Eight-Tone Canon* (1966)[2], Pierce divided the octave into eight equal steps—the even-numbered steps (equal to the multiples of three in a twelve-step division) and odd-numbered steps each form a diminished seventh chord. But what is interesting about this short piece is that Pierce used tones composed of sums of sinusoids that progress from octave to half-octave to quarter octave, with each iteration of the canon.

Except for the octave, the spectra are inharmonic, but composed of frequencies that are common to the pitch space!

***Stria* (1977.** While the above example is not rich in the sonic sense, it is a compelling and powerful idea that I found especially evocative because of my interest in spectra composed of *ordered* inharmonic partials —some of which are simply produced by FM synthesis. One class of such spectra that I found particularly interesting is based upon carrier-to-modulator frequency ratios (f_c/f_m) derived from the Golden Ratio or $\Phi \approx 1.618$. Remembering Pierce's canon, I conceived a composition in the mid 1970s that is based upon spectra structured in a way that is complementary to the division of the pitch space. The traditional octave is replaced by a pseudo-octave based upon powers of the Golden Ratio (Φ^n) rather than powers of 2, and the spectra are produced by values of f_c/f_m that are also powers of Φ as can be seen in Fig. 2.

After several years thinking about its theoretical underpinnings, I realized *Stria* in the months from July to October 1977. The composition of the work was dependent upon computer program procedures, specially written to produce the enormous amount of data that specified the details of the complementary relationship between pitch space and the ordered inharmonic partials. In addition, these procedures are at times recursive allowing musical structures that they describe to include themselves in miniature form - similar in idea to the embedded fractal geometries of Mandelbrot. From the beginning, *Stria* softly unfolds element by element, overlapping such that the inharmonic partials create increasing spectral density, ordered by ratios of Φ in both time and pitch. The major division of STRIA is at the Golden Section where recursion is used to create enormous acoustic mass. The final section of the composition is the inverse of the beginning, becoming ever less complex until it ends with a fading pure tone.

Stria was first presented on October 13, 1977 at the Centre Pompidou as part of IRCAM's concert series "La Voix des voies" produced by Luciano Berio. The composition is fully described in the Fall and Winter issues of the Computer Music Journal, 2007 [6].

***Voices* v.2 2007.** *Voices,* for soprano and interactive computer, uses the same division of the pitch space and structured spectra as in *Stria*. Again, all the sounds are produced by FM synthesis and all the spectra are generated from ratios based on Φ, as noted above (except for a few instances of voice-like tones that use integer ratios). The formal structure of *Voices* is altogether different, however, and requires a larger set of differentiated sounds than did *Stria*.

The important and initial question was how well would a soprano, both as a performer and as a "sound," fit into this 'artificial' pitch/spectral space, where first, the scale is unfamiliar to the performer and not related to any of the common modes or tunings and second, the partials of sung vowel tones are harmonic and do not share the same spectral distribution? Can one mix such a sonic artifact, totally dependent upon the computer for its existence, with a natural, perhaps the most natural, musical sound, the singing voice?

The music performance problem would seem to be a major hurdle for the soprano. While a single scale step in the 9 step/pseudo-octave division only differs from the

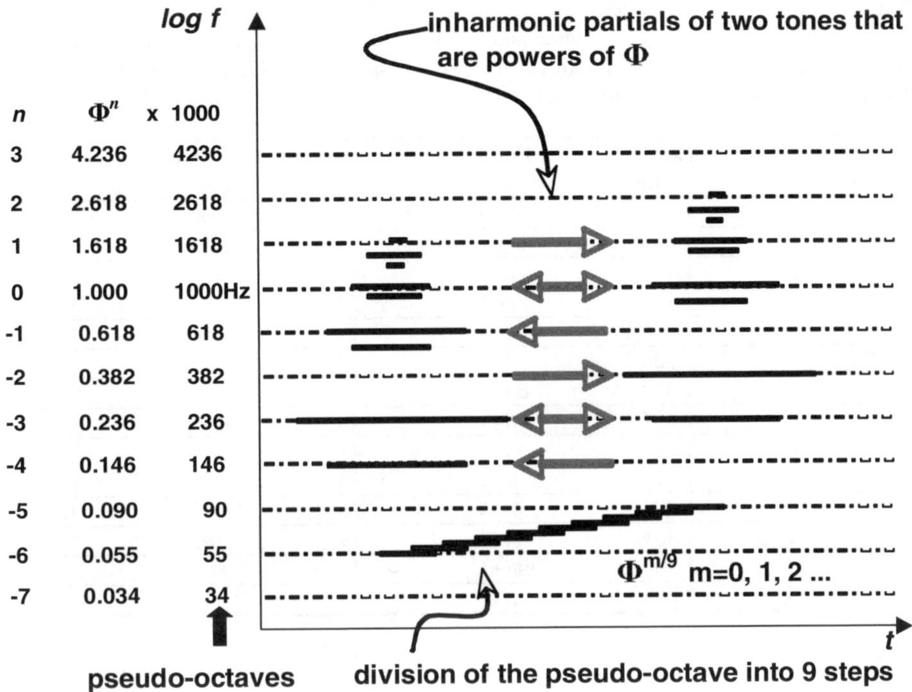

Fig. 2. The pitch space in both *Stria* and *Voices* is based upon pseudo-octaves that are powers of the Golden Ratio Φ, which are further divided into 9 steps. The spectra of tones generated by FM c:m ratios that are also powers of Φ, contain partials that are powers of Φ, here shown at the interval of a pseudo-octave.

traditional semi-tone by 7 cents, the maximum difference in the progression is nearly a quartertone and there are 13 steps in the interval closest to a true octave, as shown in Table 1.

It is my good fortune to have had a soprano[6] at hand with whom I could work during the initial stages of the composition to test my hypothesis: singing in this unusual scale is possible if the structured inharmonic spectra of the accompanying tones are infused with complementary pitch information, since most good performers tune to context. I included in the program (written in MaxMSP) the option for the singer to give herself a cue tone for the current target pitch or the following target pitch. In fact, the option is rarely used since the singer seems to easily tune to the partials of the structured spectra—to the context, as hypothesized.

The other part of the initial question, how well would the soprano sound, having partials in the harmonic series, fit within a context composed of dense inharmonic

---

[6] Maureen Chowning, for whom *Voices* is written, has had experience singing in alternative tunings, e.g. *Solemn Songs for Evening* by Richard Boulanger, written in the Pierce-Bohlen scale.

Table 1. A comparison of the scale used in *Voices*, $\Phi^{n/9}$, with the common tempered scale, $2^{n/12}$, showing the closest scale degree and the difference in cents. The 6th step of the common scale repeats to maintain the proximate *Voices* step and show that it is the 13th step of the *Voices* scale that is closet to a true octave.

n	Voices Scale	Pitch	Cents	Common Scale	n
0	1.000	a		1.000	0
1	1.055	a#(-)	-7	1.059	1
2	1.113	b(-)	-14	1.122	2
3	1.174	c(-)	-22	1.189	3
4	1.238	c#(-)	-29	1.260	4
5	1.306	d(-)	-37	1.335	5
6	1.378	d#(-)	-44	1.414	6
7	1.454	d#(+)	48	1.414	6
8	1.534	e(+)	41	1.498	7
9	1.618	f(+)	34	1.587	8
10	1.707	f#(+)	26	1.682	9
11	1.801	g(+)	19	1.782	10
12	1.900	g#(+)	11	1.888	11
13	2.004	a(+)	4	2.000	12

partials, albeit structured? The somewhat surprising answer: the performer and the listener are unaware of any spectral mismatch. Moreover, one senses an overall pitch coherence that is more like a soprano singing with an acoustic instrument ensemble having harmonic spectra, than singing with idiophones having dense inharmonic spectra such as gongs and bells. There are several possible reasons that there is no overall percept of "out-of-tuneness" or psychoacoustic dissonance.

While the spectra of low tones in *Voices* are often dense, they are selectively dense with partials of a single tone spaced at intervals from large to small (in log frequency), as is the case with the harmonic series. In addition the spectra are composed such that the energy is concentrated around the low order partials (small modulation index). Therefore, whether or not low order partials fall within a critical band is dependent upon the interval of two tones within the pitch space, as is the case with partials in the harmonic series.

Another reason is that the concentration of harmonic energy in typical soprano tones is limited to the low order harmonics, especially the fundamental, which reduces the incidence of strong partials interacting within critical bands.

Finally, there is a third reason, which is somewhat speculative, why there is little psychoacoustic dissonance. Critical band theory is based upon perceptual experiments using stimuli having few variables and partials that are highly stable, quite unlike sounds of the natural listening experience. We know that the auditory system responds to partials in a different way when mediating temporal factors are present such as amplitude envelopes or synchronous micro-modulation (e.g. random or quasi-periodic vibrato).

This internal dynamism brings into play an additional perceptual theory based upon grouping and common fate from the Gestalt laws of perceptual organization. It is a higher-level mechanism (probably not in the peripheral auditory system) that causes partials to fuse or cohere, where individual partials are difficult or impossible to distinguish, and they become identifiable as a source, known or unknown, and segregable within a collection of sources.

It seems that these temporal features, which are intrinsic to our "out of lab" perceptual experience, may reduce the importance of the interaction of individual partials relative to critical bands because the interaction becomes transitory and no longer stable.

Dynamic partials not only animate the sounds of which they are a part, harmonic or inharmonic, but contribute to the surface allure of the larger sound context, leading the ear through time in a complex of detailed multi-dimensional spaces of timbre, location, loudness and—most importantly regarding dissonance—pitch. The pitch space is loosened from its abstract skeletal form by the internal dynamic detail, and accommodates the sound of the soprano, whose fluid expression derives from its own internal dynamism.

4 Conclusion

During the thirty years since composing Stria, I have often wondered whether the integrated spectral tuning and pitch tuning worked because of the particular attributes of the work itself, the manner in which the work slowly unfolds from sparse to dense spectra and having no other spectral forms than those rooted in the Golden Ratio? Is it a pitch/spectrum construct that is unique to the piece?

My experience with *Voices* suggests that it is not. It could it be that these early ideas—Risset's structured spectra, Max's and Pierce's joining of odd tunings with complementary spectra and Max's evolving pitch space in his melodic metamorphoses, can be generally exploited with synthesized sound, with physical-models where the "physical" is infinitely malleable, or even sampled sounds, especially with the availability of new stable high-Q filters [7]. A medium is defined by its distinctive attributes and these ideas are certainly unique to music made with computers.

References

1. Mathews, M.V.: The Digital Computer as a Musical Instrument. Science 142(3592), 553–557 (1963)
2. Goebel, J.: The Historical CD of Digital Sound Synthesis. Computer Music Currents 13, Schott Wergo (1995)
3. Tenney, J.: Sound-Generation by Means of a Digital Computer. Journal of Music Theory 7(1) (Spring 1963), http://links.jstor.org/
4. Chowning, J.: The Synthesis of Complex Audio Spectra by Means of Frequency Modulation. J. Audio Eng. Soc. 21, 7 (1973)
5. Chowning, J.: Composing the Sound Itself, John Chowning Portraits Polychrome,. Nouvelle edition augmentée. Institute national de l'audiovisuel, Paris (2007)

6. Meneghini, M.: An Analysis of the Compositional Techniques in John Chowning's Stria. Zattra, L.: The assembling of Stria by John Chowning: A philological investigation. Baudouin, O.: A Reconstruction of Stria. Dahan, K.: Surface Tensions: Dynamics of Stria. The Reconstruction of Stria. Computer Music Journal 31(3) (2007)
7. Mathews, M.V., Smith, J.O.: Methods for synthesizing very high Q parametrically well behaved two pole filters. In: Proceedings of the Stockholm Musical Acoustics Conference (SMAC 2003) (Stockholm), Royal Swedish Academy of Music (August 2003), `http://ccrma.stanford.edu/~jos/smac03maxjos`

Music Cognition:
Learning, Perception, Expectations

Barbara Tillmann

University Claude Bernard Lyon 1, Sensory Neurosciences, Behavior and Cognition
Laboratory, CNRS-UMR 5020, IFR 19,
50, avenue Tony Garnier, F-69366 Lyon cedex 07, France
btillmann@olfac.univ-lyon1.fr
http://olfac.univ-lyon1.fr/equipe-02.html

Abstract. Research in music cognition domain has shown that non musician listeners have implicit knowledge about the Western tonal musical system. This knowledge, acquired by mere exposure to music in everyday life, influences perception of musical structures and allows developing expectations for future incoming events. Musical expectations play a role for musical expressivity and influence event processing: Expected events are processed faster and more accurately than less-expected events and this influence extends to the processing of simultaneously presented visual information. Studying implicit learning of auditory material in the laboratory allows us to further understand this cognitive capacity (i.e., at the origin of tonal acculturation) and its potential application to the learning of new musical systems and new musical expectations. In addition to behavioral studies on cognitive processes in and around music perception, computational models allow simulating learning, representation and perception of music for non musician listeners.

1 Immersion in Music: What Is the Brain Doing?

In everyday life, we are immersed almost constantly in a musical environment. The development of mp3-players and music-playing telephones has been further enhancing this immersion. In Western culture, most of this music (e.g., classical music, pop, rock, folk, jazz, lullabies) is based on the Western tonal system, even if new musical styles as well as music of other cultures are increasingly present. Most of music listeners are without explicit musical training or practice on an instrument: how is the nonmusician brain process and understand musical structures? The present chapter will focus on perceivers, not composers or performers (see [1, 2] for reviews on musical performance).

Music cognition research has provided evidence that nonmusician listeners have acquired implicit knowledge about the Western tonal musical system, just by mere exposure to musical pieces obeying the rules of this system. The musical knowledge, acquired thanks to the cognitive capacity of implicit learning, influences the perception of musical structures and allows developing expectations for future incoming events. This chapter presents some of the basic regularities of the tonal system and an

R. Kronland-Martinet, S. Ystad, and K. Jensen (Eds.): CMMR 2007, LNCS 4969, pp. 11–33, 2008.

overview of empirical data showing that listeners have knowledge about these regularities and that this knowledge influences music perception (section 2). Particular emphasize is given to studies investigating listeners' musical expectations and their influence on event processing, both auditory and visual, as well as their link to musical expressivity (section 3). Section 4 focuses on the cognitive capacity of implicit learning, which is the basis of tonal acculturation, and how it can be studied in the laboratory with new artificial tone and timbre systems. Section 5 presents how connectionist models can be used to simulate nonmusician listeners, notably for the learning of a musical system, the cognitive representation of this knowledge and its influence on perception. Finally, most music cognition research has studied learning, perception and expectations for music of the Western tonal system. However, the same questions apply to the processing of other musical systems (section 6). To show the generality of the cognitive capacity of learning, knowledge and expectations it is necessary that the research domain overcomes the Western tonal focus and shows comparable phenomenon for other musical systems (see [3]).

2 Tonal Knowledge and Perception of Musical Structures

The overall pattern of results in music cognition research suggests that mere exposure to Western musical pieces suffices to develop implicit knowledge of the tonal system. Just by listening to music in everyday life, listeners become sensitive to the regularities and structures of the tonal system without being necessarily able to verbalize them [4-6]. This acquisition is based on the cognitive capacity of implicit learning (see section 5). The implicitly acquired knowledge influences listeners' music perception, the understanding of musical structures and relations as well as the development of musical expectations (see section 3).

The present section proposes a summary of the Western tonal system underlining its statistical regularities (i.e., forming the basis of musical structures and relations) and reviews some experimental research investigating listeners' tonal knowledge and its influence on perception.

2.1 Some Basic Regularities in Western Tonal Music

Western tonal music can be described as a constrained system of regularities (i.e., regularities of co-occurrence, frequency of occurrence and psychoacoustic regularities) based on a limited number of elements. This section presents the tonal system from the perspective of cognitive psychology and of implicit learning: it underlines the basic regularities between musical events, which appear in most musical styles of occidental everyday life (e.g., classical music, pop music, jazz music, Latin music etc.) and which can be acquired by implicit learning processes.[1]

The Western tonal system is based on 12 pitches repeated cyclically over octaves. Strong regularities of co-occurrence and frequencies of occurrence exist among the 12

---

[1] In addition to these regularities based on the pitch dimension, regularities exist on the time dimension, like the underlying beat allowing listeners to develop temporal expectations about when the next event is the most probable to occur. This chapter focuses on the pitch dimension, but will consider the time dimension in sections 3 and 6.

pitch classes: tones are combined into chords and into keys, forming a three-level organizational system. Sets of 7 tones form scales, which can be either major or minor. For each tone of a scale, chords (e.g., major or minor) are constructed by adding two tones – creating a second level of musical units. Based on tones and chords, keys (tonalities) define a third level of musical units. Keys have more or less close harmonic relations to each other, with the strength of harmonic relations depending on the number of shared tones and chords. The three levels of musical units (i.e., tones, chords, keys) occur with strong regularities of co-occurrence. Tones and chords belonging to the same key are more likely to co-occur in a musical piece than tones and chords belonging to different keys. Changes between keys are more likely to occur between closely related keys than between less-related ones.

Within each key, tones and chords have different tonal functions creating tonal and harmonic hierarchies. For example, chords built on the first, fifth, and fourth scale degrees (referred to as tonic, dominant and subdominant respectively) have a more central function than chords built on other scale degrees. From a psychological point of view, the hierarchically important events of a key act as stable cognitive reference points [7] to which other events are anchored [8]. These within-key hierarchies are strongly correlated with the frequency of occurrence of tones and chords in Western musical pieces. Tones and chords used with higher frequency (and longer duration) correspond to events that are defined by music theory as having more important functions in a given key [5, 6, 9].

This short description reveals a fundamental characteristic of Western tonal music: the tonal functions of tones and chords are depending on the established key context; the same event can define an in-key or an out-of-key event and can take different levels of functional importance (i.e., tonal stability). For example, the C major chord functions as a stable tonic chord in a C major context, as a less stable dominant or subdominant chord in F or G major contexts respectively and as an out-of-key chord in a D major context. For listeners, understanding this context dependency of musical events' functions is crucial for the understanding of musical structures, notably the variety of musical structures that can be created on the basis of the restricted set of twelve pitch classes. Listeners' tonal knowledge is necessary to interpret differently the same sound event depending on the context in which it occurs. Acculturated listeners understand these musical structures in an implicit way.

2.2 Listeners' Tonal Knowledge of Pitch Structures

Numerous research has provided evidence for nonmusicians' tonal knowledge of pitch structures (see [5, 10, 11] for reviews). Nonmusician listeners are sensitive to the context dependency of musical events: they perceive the musical structures and relations between tones, chords and keys (i.e., modulations) (e.g., [12-14]). This knowledge also allows the perception of the underlying harmonic structures as well as the understanding of musical motifs and their variations. Behavioral studies in music cognition domain have provided evidence for this tonal knowledge with a variety of experimental methods. The seminal probe-tone paradigm, which asks listeners to rate how well a given tone fits into a preceding tonal context, showed the perceived context dependency for tones as well as the perceived distances between keys (see [6] for a review). For other subjective judgments, listeners rate the musical material for the degree of perceived similarity, musical tension or completion (e.g., [15, 16]). These judgments of perceived musical tension or completion reflect tonal hierarchy, as described by music theory: stable tones and chords (i.e., with important tonal functions) receive lower ratings of musical tension and were judged to induce more completion than less stable tones and chords. The influence of the perceived pitch structures has been shown also in memory tasks (e.g., [17]) and speeded response time tasks, which will be presented more specifically in section 3.

Experimental research on music perception has to find a balance between the complexity of real musical material and strong experimental control of the used material – leading to the use of simple tone contexts or melodies. One attempt to push the balance in the direction of real material used short minuets to investigate the perception of tonal functions [18]. A minuet is often constructed in two parts, with a first part ending on a half cadence (i.e., with the dominant, a less stable degree) and the second part on an authentic cadence (i.e., with the tonic, the most stable degree). Completion judgments on these parts presented separately showed that listeners perceive the differences in tonal stability of these endings: parts ending on the authentic cadence received higher ratings of completion than did parts ending on the half cadence. Furthermore, results of a musical jigsaw puzzle (i.e., participants had to find, among other choices, the two parts belonging to the same piece and to put them in the correct temporal order) showed that even nonmusician listeners understand these structural markers and their role for the temporal organization of the musical piece.

This overview presents some examples about how we can experimentally access listeners' musical knowledge and study its influence on perception. Tonal knowledge works like a "perceptual filter" and it allows listeners to understand the context dependency of musical events. Listeners interpret musical events with their knowledge about basic regularities of the tonal system, and they develop musical expectations for future events depending on the context. Because of the temporal nature of sound, expectations are taking a central position in music perception: which sounds are most probable to come next and when should they occur?

3 Musical Expectations: Pitch and Time

When presented with a musical context (i.e., the beginning of a melody), listeners develop expectations about future events – what kind of event (tone, chord, timbre) is the most probable to occur next and at what time point. These musical expectations can be linked to sensory features (or surface features), such as dynamic and timbral characteristics, melodic contour and intervals, but also to the repetition of specific notes, note groups or motifs. They can be further linked to the tonal structures of the musical system and thus require listeners' tonal knowledge, acquired by mere exposure to musical pieces obeying this system.

Expectations are part of cognitive functions in general, they are shaping our interaction with the environment and (depending on their nature) facilitate or delay the processing of events. The processing of an expected event is facilitated in comparison to an unexpected or less-expected event. For example, we recognize a familiar face faster in a context, in which it is probable to appear and is thus expected (i.e., our neighbor in front of his house) than in an unrelated context (i.e., on vacation in the mountains). Musical expectations are not only influencing efficiency of processing, but have been attributed a role for musical expressivity. Composers (or improvising performers) fulfill listeners' perceptual expectations more or less early or only partially in the musical piece. Following Meyer [19], playing with musical expectations is at the origin of musical expressivity that is communicated by musical pieces. In the following, we first present experimental research interested in the efficiency of processing for musically expected events and this research line brings us back to musical expressivity and emotion.

Musical expectations have been studied with production and perception tasks. In production tasks, participants hear a musical context (i.e., two tones or the first bars of a musical piece) and were requested to produce the continuation. In Carlsen [20, 21], participants were asked to sing what they felt to be the most natural continuation. In Schmuckler [22, 23], pianists were asked to complete fragments in terms of how they expected the piece would continue. In perception tasks, expectations are investigated by either asking participants to directly judge the "expectedness" of a musical phrase's ending on a subjective scale (from 1 unexpected to 7 expected; [23, 24]) or measuring speed of processing (with the hypothesis that expected events are processed faster than unexpected ones). Production tasks are mainly limited to the investigation of musical experts, while perception tasks allow the investigation of nonmusician listeners. Of particular interest among perception tasks is the priming paradigm, an indirect investigation method of perceiver's contextual expectations. The present section reviews this paradigm and its application to the investigation of tonal and temporal expectations, cross-modal influences as well as schematic *versus* veridical expectations.

3.1 The Priming Paradigm: Studying Nonmusicians' Musical Expectations

The priming paradigm (extensively used in psycholinguistics, see [25]) is an implicit investigation method that studies the influence of perceivers' expectations on the efficiency of perception (i.e., accuracy and processing speed). This implicit investigation method allows probing nonmusicians' musical knowledge without requiring explicit judgments (see [26] for a review).

In this paradigm, a prime context (i.e., a chord sequence) is followed by a target event (i.e., a chord) and the relation between prime and target is systematically manipulated (i.e., musical relatedness as defined by music theory). The hypothesis is that the prime context allows listeners to develop expectations for future events, with more strongly related events being more expected. These expectations then influence event processing, notably processing is facilitated for expected events over unexpected or less-expected events.

Since the priming paradigm is an indirect investigation of the context's influence on event processing, participants are not required to make direct judgments on the relation between prime context and target, but their task focuses on another dimension of the target event. Participants make speeded judgments on a perceptual feature of the target; a frequently used task is based on sensory consonance/dissonance judgments (e.g., [27, 28]), and for this purpose, half of the targets are consonant (i.e., well-tuned, correctly constructed chords), half of the targets are rendered acoustically dissonant (i.e., either by mistuning or by adding out-of-key tones)[2]. In most studies, the manipulated relations between prime context and target event concerned pitch relations for chords (harmonic structures) and tones, but less often temporal relations.

Harmony and Melody. The manipulated pitch relations between prime context and target chord can be relatively strong, contrasting an expected, in-key target (i.e., the tonic) to an unexpected, out-of-key target [26, 33], or more subtle, comparing two chords belonging to the context key. For example, Bigand and collaborators used eight-chord sequences and the last chord defined the target. The target chord acted as either the most important chord of the context key and was supposed to be highly expected (the tonic chord) or a less important chord, supposed to be less expected (the subdominant chord). In order to reduce sensory influences, the target chord's relation to the global context (chords 1 to 6) was manipulated while holding constant the local context (chord 7). The requested consonant/dissonant judgments are more accurate and faster when targets act as tonic rather than as subdominant chords [28, 34]. This outcome, valid for both musician and nonmusician participants, suggests that the processing of harmonic spectra is facilitated for events that are the most predictable in the current key context. Global musical priming effects have been extended to longer contexts (14-chord sequences, [34]) and more severe control of sensory influences [35]. Furthermore, the processing advantage is not restricted to the comparison of tonic and subdominant chords, but processing times reflect the top of the tonal hierarchy: the tonic is processed the fastest, followed by the dominant and then the subdominant [36].

More recently, the musical priming paradigm, which was initially introduced solely for chord processing, was extended to melodic processing: melodies were constructed by pair and differed only by a single note so that the target functioned as either the tonic or the subdominant. Processing times were faster for the related tonic target tone. Using melodies and target tones (instead of target chords) further allowed us to investigate whether musical expectations influence perceptual processes (e.g., detection, pitch processing). In the described melodic material, melodic expectations (based on listeners' tonal knowledge) influenced pitch discrimination, with finer discrimination for the expected tonic tones [37].

Time. Although pitch is the most obvious form-bearing dimension of Western tonal music, regularities in other musical dimensions also contribute to listeners' perceptual experience and may be internalized through similar processes. Beyond pitch, time is a crucial form-bearing dimension in music [38]. Temporal regularities include the organization of event-onset-intervals through time leading to a sensation of meter - a sensation of a regular succession of strong and weak beats superimposed over an isochronous pulse. Temporal regularities also include the temporal patterns of onset intervals creating rhythms that are perceived against the metrical background.

---

[2] When the experimental manipulations contrast related and unrelated target chords, the experimental trials consist of musical sequences with 25% of the trials ending on related consonant chords, 25% on related dissonant chords, 25% on unrelated consonant chords and 25% on unrelated dissonant chords. Additional priming tasks require judgments of temporal asynchrony [29], phoneme-discrimination [30], timbre-discrimination [31] and lexical decision of sung words/nonwords [32].

Temporal regularities have been shown to influence the perception of musical events in many ways, including performance in recognition tasks [28, 39-41], recall [42], completion judgments [40, 43, 44], evaluations of musical tension [15, 45], and musical expectations [24, 34, 40, 46, 47]. To investigate the influence of temporal expectations on chord processing, the priming paradigm was adapted to manipulate temporal structures, notably by opposing regular, isochronous sequences to irregular sequences and by manipulating the temporal occurrence of the last chord [40]. These manipulations are similar to those previously used with subjective judgments [24, 43]. In the priming paradigm, processing was facilitated when sequences were played in a regular, isochronous way in comparison to when played irregularly. In addition, processing was slowed down when targets occurred earlier than expected in comparison to on-time or later than expected.

For music perception, the question is how listeners process pitch and time dimensions together since their combination defines the musical structure of a piece (e.g., [48]). For the respective contributions of tonal and temporal regularities in music processing, two theoretical frameworks have been distinguished [41]. A single-component model [46] predicts interactive interference between the processing of the two dimensions. A two-component model, based on experimental and neuropsychological data, predicts that tonal and temporal structures are processed independently, and the processing of one dimension does not interfere with the processing of the other dimension. The hypothesis, which is currently proposed in music cognition domain, is that independence between the two dimensions occurs at initial stages of processing, but is followed by integration of the two dimensions in later stages of processing, thus leading to interactive influences [40, 41, 49, 50].

3.2 Cross-Modal Influences

Musical expectations based on listeners' tonal knowledge are fast and automatic (see also section 3.3). Their influence is not restricted to the processing of musical features, but influences the processing of linguistic features. In sung material, phoneme-monitoring and even lexical decision performance is influenced by the musical function of the sung target, even if the task does not concern the music [30, 32]. Using the musical priming paradigm, the last chord of 8-chord sequences defined the target and acted either as a strongly expected chord (the tonic) or a less expected chord (the subdominant) [30]. The four tones of each chord were sung with synthetic phonemes (e.g., /di/, /du/, /ki/, /sa:/). Participants decided whether the target was sung on a syllable containing the phoneme /i/ or /u/. Phoneme discrimination was better for strongly expected tonic targets than for subdominant targets. The finding suggests that processing of musical and phonetic information is not independent, but interacts at some stage of processing.

This interaction does not require that syllabic and musical information are combined into the same acoustic signal, but also occurs for spoken syllables that are presented in synchrony to the musical sequences in the contralateral ear [51]. It does not even require to be in the same modality: musical expectations influence visual syllable identification, when the syllables are presented in synchrony to the expected versus less-expected chords [52]. In these cross-modal experiments, participants listen to the musical sequences (ending on related or less-related chords) as background music while making speeded identification judgments on visually displayed syllables. Syllable identification was faster when the simultaneously presented chord was the related tonic chord than when it was the less-related subdominant chord.

Further experiments extended this cross-modal influence to the processing of visually displayed geometric forms [52]. This finding thus suggests that the initially reported data pattern is not specific to music and language, but attentional processes might define a common underlying process linked to expectations and temporal integration. This hypothesis is based on the dynamic attention theory proposed by Jones [53]: musical structures guide listener's attention over time and attentional resources are increased for the tonic chord (i.e., functioning as a tonal accent). These increased attentional resources would thus benefit to the simultaneous visual processing. This finding further suggests dynamic attentional resources that are shared by auditory and visual modalities.

3.3 Expectations and Musical Expressivity

Listeners' musical expectations do not only influence processing speed, but they have been attributed a role for expressiveness and emotion evoked by music [19, 54]. Based on knowledge about musical structures and relations, listeners develop expectations about future events. These expectations are not necessarily directly satisfied, but might be temporarily blocked. From this play between violations, disruptions and resolutions of expectations raise meaningful and expressive moments in music. With this role of expectations in mind, the repeated listening of a musical piece raises "Wittgenstein's puzzle" (as named in [4]): how can a well-known familiar piece be pleasant and expressive when we know exactly what will come next? Together with Jackendoff [55] and Meyer [19], Dowling and Harwood [4] propose to attribute schematic expectations a role at a subconscious level, allowing a violation of schematic expectations even if no surprise occurs at a conscious level (e.g., we remain surprised even if we know exactly that a deceptive cadence will occur).

Musical priming data provide some evidence for the automaticity of schematic expectations and their resistance to 'knowing what to come'. For single-chord contexts, Justus and Bharucha [56] opposed schematic expectations for related targets to veridical expectations for unrelated targets, which had been induced by various experimental conditions. The influence of schematic expectations on target processing was always stronger: musically related targets were processed faster even when unrelated chord pairs occurred more often or were preceded immediately by the to-be-processed target pair. Recently, we investigated with longer musical contexts and finer tonal comparisons in how far the automatic expectations based on listener's schematic knowledge can be influenced by veridical expectations and repetition priming [57]. In two-phase experiments, familiarization with a less-expected musical structure (via repeated processing) did not reverse the response time patterns. Only the exact repetition of the same sequences succeeded in decreasing, but not eliminating the processing cost of less-related targets in comparison to related targets. This behavioral data set on repeated processing of unexpected endings is in agreement with previously reported Evoked-Related Potential (ERP) data on incongruent endings (i.e., strong violations with out-of-key tones). The evoked potential linked to the expectancy violation (i.e., a late positive component peaking around 500-600ms, LPC, see 3.2.2) decreased, but persisted with repeated presentations [58].

The resistance of schematic expectations to veridical expectations provides an important element for our comprehension of musical expressiveness. Expectations for future musical events seem to be developed automatically and are not influenced by the experimental design or previously encountered exemplars. Each encountering of a musical structure seems to be like a new processing that is based on automatically developed expectations derived from tonal schematic knowledge. Lerdahl [59] describes musical forces and motion in musical space as source of musical emotion. He states "a melody or chord progression does not simply follow the inertial path of least resistance. It would be dull and would quickly come to stop unless enlivened by motion away from places that pull it towards rest" (p. 371). The priming data suggest that the tonic chord is a strongly expected event, independently of repetition or context, and that it would represent an attractive resting point. Musical sequences do not directly jump to the most expected events and thus create tension patterns, notably in relation to the tonic as the most stable, central event. The interplay between listeners' automatic schematic expectations and the realization of the musical structures would thus give rise to tension-relaxation patterns, to musical expressiveness and emotion.

4 A Connectionist Model of Nonmusician Listeners: Learning, Representation, Perception

As shown in music cognition research (see sections 2 and 3), listeners have acquired knowledge about the tonal system and its underlying regularities. Different models of mental representation have been proposed for musical knowledge, with parsimonious models based on few dimensions being preferred. Proposed models use geometric configurations ([60]; see [6] for a review), are based on either behavioral data [7, 61] or music theory [62, 63] or use artificial neural networks [11, 64]. The advantage of the artificial neural networks is not only that the model can arise from simple exposition to music, thus simulating tonal acculturation of nonmusician listeners, but also to have the possibility to present experimental musical material to the model in order to simulate the perception of nonmusician listeners.

4.1 A Hard-Wired Representation of Tonal Knowledge

Bharucha [64] proposed a connectionist account of tonal knowledge representation. In the MUSACT model (i.e., *MUSical ACTivation*), tonal knowledge is conceived as a network of interconnected units. The units are organized in three layers corresponding to tones, chords, and keys. Each tone unit is connected to the chords of which that tone is a component. Analogously, each chord unit is connected to the keys of which it is a member.

Musical relations emerge from the activation that reverberates via connected links between tone, chord and key units. This reverberation is comparable to interactive activation processes used in word recognition models to simulate knowledge-driven influences [65, 66]. When a chord is played to MUSACT, the units representing the sounded component tones are activated and activation reverberates between the layers until equilibrium is reached (see [34, 64] for more details). The emerging activation patterns reflect tonal and harmonic hierarchies of the established key: for example, units representing harmonically related chords are activated more strongly than units representing unrelated chords. The context dependency of musical events in the tonal system is thus not stored explicitly for each of the different keys, but emerges from activation spreading through the network. The activation levels are interpreted as relative levels of expectation for future events: the more a chord unit is activated, the more the represented chord is expected and the more its processing should be facilitated. The model's architecture allows the testing of experimental material and the generation of predictions for music perception in human listeners. The model has been tested for a set of musical priming data investigating listeners' musical expectations in short and long contexts. The activation levels of the units representing the target chords in related versus unrelated contexts simulate behavioral data: activation levels were higher for related targets than for unrelated targets (see [34, 64] for details).

The MUSACT model proposes a parsimonious representation of tonal knowledge: tones and chords are presented once and not repeatedly for each tonality to reflect the contextual dependency. The change of an event's tonal function is reflected in the activation pattern, and thus emerging from the network's architecture associated with reverberation and accumulation of activation over time. However, the model is hardwired and based on music theoretic constraints. It does not simulate tonal acculturation processes to show in how far this architecture is also plausible from a learning perspective.

4.2 A Learned Representation of Tonal Knowledge

A strong advantage of artificial neural networks (e.g., connectionist models) is their capacity to adapt in such a way that representations, categorizations or associations between events can be learned. Connectionist models have the characteristic that 1) rules governing the material are not explicit, but emerge from the simultaneous satisfaction of multiple constraints represented by the connections, and 2) these constraints can be learned by repeated exposure. The MUSACT model takes advantage of the first characteristic of connectionist models. In [11], we take advantage also of the second one to simulate tonal knowledge acquisition in nonmusician listeners. For this purpose, unsupervised learning algorithms seem to be well suited: they extract statistical regularities via passive exposure and encode events that often occur together [67-70]. Self-organizing maps [68] are one version of unsupervised learning algorithms that leads to a topological organization of the learned information.

To simulate tonal acculturation, a hierarchical network composed of two self-organizing maps was exposed to short musical sequences (i.e., chord sequences). After learning, the connections in the network have changed and the units have specialized for the detection of chords and keys (the input layer coded the tones present in the input material[3]). The learned architecture is associated with a spreading activation process (as used in MUSACT) to simulate top-down influences on the activation

---

[3] Additional simulations integrating harmonic and subharmonic information [71] to the input pattern lead to different connection patterns, but after reverberation the activation patterns highly correlated with those of the models based on the simple input coding.

patterns. Interestingly, the learned connections and the activation patterns after rever-beration mirror the outcome of the hardwired network MUSACT, which has been conceived as an idealized end-state of implicit learning processes (see [11]).

4.3 Simulating Perception of Tones, Chords and Keys

In order to be compelling, a cognitive model of music perception should not only simulate the internalization of Western pitch regularities via mere exposure, but should also simulate the behavior of listeners after having adapted to Western tonal music. The learned neural network architecture was tested for its capacity to simulate a set of empirical data on music perception. The experimental material was presented to the model[4] and the activation levels of network units were interpreted as levels of tonal stability. The more a unit (i.e., a chord unit, a tone unit) is activated, the more stable the musical event is in the corresponding context. For the experimental tasks, it was hypothesized that the level of stability affects performance (e.g., a more strongly activated, stable event is more expected or judged to be more similar to a preceding event). Overall, the simulations showed that activations in the trained self-organizing network mirror data of human participants in tonal perception experiments. The model succeeded in simulating data obtained for perceived relations between chords [16, 26, 28, 33, 72-74], between keys [14, 61] and also between tones, even if it was trained with chords only and not with melodies [7, 17, 61]. This outcome suggests the level of activations in tone, chord and key units as a single unifying concept for hu-man performance in different perceptual tasks.

A key-finding tool. The activation levels of tone and chord units are used to simulate the perception of tones and chords in tonal contexts. The activation levels of key units can serve as a key-finding tool: without additional calculations, the key is emerging from the overall network activation. The rationale of the simulations for key percep-tion is comparable to the simulations for tone and chord perception: the musical se-quences are presented to the model and the activation levels of the key units are read out. The key unit with the maximum activation represents the key the most strongly induced by the network at that time point. When a F Major chord followed by a G Major chord is presented to the model, the most strongly activated key unit is F Major after the first chord and C Major after the second chord. As predicted by music the-ory, the two-chord sequence instills the C Major key. Note that the model has some independence of the stimulus encountered and inferred the key as an abstract structure (i.e., the C Major chord, the tonic, was not presented). As for this chord pair, it is possible to use the model for longer chord sequences and to track the instilled key over time (see [11] for details). The tested sequences (used by [61] for human listen-ers) are without modulation or contain direct and close modulation *versus* distant and remote modulations. The key-tracking over time by the model can then be compared to the judgments of human listeners. Several similarities emerge: for example, the positioning of the pivot chord in the sequence, the progressive moving through the cycle of fifths or the detection of a key without having heard the tonic yet. In sum,

---

[4] For event sequences, activation due to each event is accumulated and weighted according to recency [64]. The total activation of a unit is thus the sum of the stimulus activation, the phasic activation accumulated during reverberation and the decayed activation due to previous events.

the key layer of the connectionist model reveals an emerging property of key tracking. However, this key-finding tool is currently restricted to major keys. Future developments of the model thus need to include the minor keys to fully allow the exploitation of this emerging property of key-finding.

5   Implicit Learning of Tonal Knowledge and of New Musical Knowledge

Implicit learning processes enable the acquisition of highly complex information and without complete verbalizable knowledge of what has been learned [75]. Two examples of highly structured systems in our environment are language and music. Listeners become sensitive to the underlying regularities just by mere exposure to linguistic and musical materials in everyday life. The implicitly acquired knowledge then influences perception and interaction with the environment. Tonal acculturation is one example of the cognitive capacity to become sensitive to regularities in the environment. Francès [5] was one of the first underlining the importance of statistical regularities in music for tonal acculturation, suggesting that mere exposure to musical pieces is sufficient to acquire tonal knowledge, even if it remains at an implicit level. In music cognition domain, numerous research has provided evidence for nonmusicians' knowledge about the tonal system (see sections 2 and 3).

This capacity of the cognitive system is studied in the laboratory with artificial material containing statistical structures. For the auditory domain, implicit (or statistical) learning studies use structured material that is either based on artificial grammars (i.e., finite state grammars) or artificial language systems (i.e., [76-79]). The present section gives two examples with artificial structures using musical timbres and tones. Section 6 presents the application of the implicit learning approach to contemporary music, thus getting closer to ecologically valid material to which we are exposed.

5.1   Influence of Acoustic Similarities on the Learning of Statistical Regularities: Implicit Learning with Timbral Structures

Most implicit learning studies using auditory materials have focused on the statistical regularities and applied a random attribution of the sounds to the sequences. Some studies consider the acoustical characteristics of the sound, such as prosodic cues in verbal material [79-81] or acoustical similarities in non-verbal material [82]. The goal is to test whether the relation between the statistical regularities and regularities inherent to the material could influence learning: conflicting information might hinder statistical learning, while converging information might facilitate learning. Notably, tonal acculturation might represent a beneficial configuration: musical events appearing frequently together are also linked acoustically since they share (real and virtual) harmonics.

To investigate whether convergence with acoustical features represent a facilitatory or even necessary condition for statistical learning, Tillmann and McAdams [82] systematically manipulated acoustical similarities between musical timbres so that they either underline the statistical regularities of the timbre sequences, contradict these regularities or are neutral to them. The statistical regularities were defined as in artificial language studies (see [79]). Based on a restricted set of elements (syllables or here musical timbres), groups of three elements define units (three syllables define artificial words, three timbres define timbre-triplets). These units are chained together in a continuous sequence without silences in between. The transition probabilities between elements inside a unit are high, while transition probabilities between elements crossing units are low (i.e., a unit can be followed by one of the six other units)[5]. If listeners become sensitive to these statistical regularities, they should be able to extract the triplets of timbres from the continuous sequence, just as listeners are able to extract words from a syllable-stream of an artificial language (e.g., [79]). In [82], the sequences were constructed in such a way that the acoustical dissimilarities between timbres potentially created perceptual segmentations that either supported (S1) or contradicted (S2) the statistical regularities or were neutral with respect to them (S3).

To manipulate the acoustical similarities/dissimilarities, musical timbres were selected from the timbre space defined by [83]. Timbre is a multidimensional set of auditory attributes that is based on temporal and spectral features of sounds (cf. also [84-86]). Based on perceived dissimilarity judgments, a multidimensional analysis revealed a three-dimensional spatial structure in which the synthesized timbres were placed and the distances between timbres reflect the perceived dissimilarities among them. For example, the horn timbre is close in space to the trombone timbre (both brass instruments), but is distant from that of the vibraphone (a percussion instrument). For S1, the timbres of the triplets were chosen in such a way that the distances between adjacent timbres inside the triplets were small, but the distances between the last timbre of any given triplet and the first timbre of all other triplets (across boundaries) in the sequence were large. For S2, the distances between timbres inside the triplets were large, but the distances between timbres of two successive triplets (across boundaries) were small. For S3, mean distances between timbres inside the triplets were equal to mean distances between timbres of two successive triplets. In S1, the triplets were thus defined by statistical cues and by abrupt acoustical changes between triplets. In S2 and S3, the triplets were only defined by statistical cues, while in S2 the acoustical similarities were out of phase with the statistical boundaries. For the three sequences, the transition probabilities inside the triplets and across triplet boundaries were identical, and the same set of timbres was used.

The experiments consisted of two phases: an exposition phase and a testing phase. In the learning group, participants first listened to the continuous timbre sequence without being told about the triplets. In the testing phase, participants had then to distinguish statistical units from new units. This test performance was then compared to a control group that was lacking the exposition phase and was directly working on the test phase. The comparison of test performance between learning and control groups allows estimating the amount of learning as well as the initial biases influencing the responses without prior exposition.

The data of the learning group in comparison to the control group revealed no interaction between sequence type (S1, S2, S3) and amount of learning: performance increased by the same amount for the three sequences. After exposure, participants

---

[5] The transition probability of B given A is calculated as the frequency of the pair AB divided by the absolute frequency of A [79].

were better in chosen the existing triplets over other associations of three timbres. Additionally, performance reflected an overall preference for acoustically similar timbre triplets (in S1) over dissimilar timbre triplets (S2). This outcome extends previous data from the domain of implicit learning to complex nonverbal auditory material. It further suggests that listeners become sensitive to statistical regularities despite similarities or differences among the acoustical surface characteristics in the material. The surface characteristics only affected grouping and overall preference bias for the different materials.

This data set suggests that tonal acculturation does not necessarily need the convergence between statistical and acoustical regularities. Supporting evidence can be found in acculturation to Arabic music, which is lacking the convergence between statistical and acoustic features [87]. Together with the implicit learning study on twelve-tone music ([88]; see section 6), the data emits the rather encouraging hypothesis about the possibility to learn regularities of new musical styles independently of acoustical features.

5.2 Implicit Learning of Regularities of an Artificial Tone System: Grammaticality Judgments and Tone Expectations

The seminal studies by Reber [77] used artificial grammars to study implicit learning processes. A finite state grammar and a restricted set of letters were used to create letter strings. In a typical experimental setting, participants are first exposed to stimuli that are based on a finite-state grammar, without being told about the grammatical structure. After exposure, participants are informed about the stimuli's grammaticality and are required to classify novel sequences as grammatical or ungrammatical. Performance is generally above chance-level, without (or only little) verbalizable knowledge of the regularities underlying the letter sequences.

For the adaptation of this paradigm in the auditory domain, the letters of the artificial grammars are replaced by sine waves [76], musical timbres (e.g., gong, trumpet, piano, violin, voice in [89]) or environmental sounds (e.g., drill, clap, steam in [90, 91]). The basic experimental design remained the same as in the original studies using letters. In Altmann et al. [76], for example, letters were translated into tones (i.e., generated with sine waves) by using a random mapping of tone frequencies to letters (e.g., the letter M became the tone C), and participants' performance was as high when trained and tested with letter strings as with tone sequences. These studies provided evidence that implicit learning processes also operate on auditory sequences and that the simple exposure to sequences generated by a statistical system allows participants to distinguish sequences that break the rules.

In two recent studies, we used an artificial grammar with tones (i.e., creating tone sequences) and tested implicit learning of these regularities with a) explicit, direct grammaticality judgments and b) an adaptation of the priming paradigm to investigate whether musical expectations can be developed with the newly acquired knowledge. The novelty of our approach was to test listeners with new grammatical items that were opposed to ungrammatical items containing very subtle violations. Notably, the tones creating the ungrammaticality in the sequence belonged to the tone set of the grammar and they respected frequency distributions of tones, bigrams, and melodic contour (i.e., as defined for the grammatical sequences). For these tone structures, participants' grammaticality judgments were above chance-level after an exposure phase. This outcome suggests that listeners became sensitive to the regularities underlying the used artificial grammar of tones [92].

In a second study, we combined implicit learning and priming paradigms to investigate whether newly acquired structure knowledge allows listeners to develop perceptual expectations for future events [93]. Participants were first exposed to structured tone sequences (based on the artificial grammar), and made then speeded judgments on a perceptual feature of target tones in new sequences. The priming task was adapted from musical priming research (see section 3 and [94]) and required participants to judge whether the target tone was played either in-tune or out-of-tune. Most importantly, the target tone either respected the artificial grammar structure or violated it by creating subtle ungrammaticalities (as in [92]). In this priming task, grammatical tones were processed faster and more accurately than ungrammatical ones. This processing advantage was not observed for a control group, which was lacking the exposure phase to the grammatical tone sequences. This finding suggests that the acquisition of new structure knowledge allows listeners to develop auditory expectations that influence single event processing. It further promotes the priming paradigm as an implicit access to acquired artificial structure knowledge studied in the lab. A recent extension of this experimental approach showed similar cross-modal influences as had been observed for the musical material (see section 3.3): response times for visual syllable identification were faster when a grammatical tone was played at the same time than when a tone was played that created an ungrammaticality.

These studies with artificial tone structures imitate the phenomenon of tonal acculturation inside the lab: Nonmusicians acquire implicit knowledge of the Western tonal system by mere exposure to musical pieces obeying this system. The beneficial influence of auditory expectations on the processing of expected events can arise after short exposure to a structured tone system in the laboratory. Based on this finding, we make the hypothesis that musical expectations and their influence on processing efficiency can also occur after exposure to new musical systems (e.g., the twelve-tone music tested by [88], see section 6). Furthermore, the experiment using timbres presented above [82] further suggests that these processes might occur independently of acoustical surface characteristics and their combination to statistical regularities of the musical system.

6 Learning, Perception and Expectations in Other Musical Systems

Listeners who are familiarized to the music of their culture do not perceive a disorganized superposition of sounds or groups of sounds, but they perceive coherent melodic lines, they develop expectations and anticipate possible continuations and endings of a musical piece. Research in music cognition analyzes how listeners succeed in these processes, and aims to specify listeners' knowledge about the musical system, its acquisition, structure and influence in perception and performance.

Most research on music perception and cognition has focused on the Western tonal musical system of the 18th and 19th centuries. And even if the principal regularities of this system are used in a variety of musical styles (classical music, pop, folk, jazz etc.), this represents a restriction that needs to be redressed. Notably, a more general theory of music perception and cognition requires studying the hypothesis about learning, perception, knowledge and expectations also for other musical systems and listeners [3, 95]. Regularities between musical events also exist in other musical systems (e.g., Indian or Arabic music) and cultural learning and familiarity to these systems lead to auditory experiences different from those of naive listeners.

This section presents some research studying cognition and perception of musical systems from other cultures and of new musical systems. The overall results point out that the acculturation processes also apply to other musical systems: listeners acquire knowledge about their musical system (or to a new musical system) by mere exposure and this knowledge influences perception of musical structures. Even if these findings suggest the generality of the processes underlying learning and perception of music (and are rather encouraging for creators of new musical systems), research on musical systems other than the tonal system remains rather rare up to now. For contemporary music, one example of a perceptual investigation has been realized on a piece by Roger Reynolds (The Angel of Death). The perception of its musical structures has been investigated by a series of behavioral experiments, contrasting also the composer's intent to the listeners' understanding (see Special Issue of Music Perception, 2004, Vol. 22 (2)).

Perception of pitch regularities in other musical systems. The probe-tone paradigm has been used to investigate perception of scale structures in Balinese music [96] and Indian music [97]. As in the original studies on Western tonal music [61], a context was followed by one of the possible tones and listeners rated how well this tone fits into the preceding context. Both studies compared the perception of the scale structures by naïve listeners and by acculturated, native listeners. For Indian music, for example, the data patterns of both groups of listeners showed sensitivity to the sensory information present in the context. However, only the Indian listeners (but not the North American listeners) showed the perception of fine-graded musical features that were independent of the tones presented in the context [97]. This outcome can be interpreted in terms of musical knowledge that Indian listeners have acquired by mere exposure, while American listeners were missing this acculturation process.

Converging evidence has been reported with segmentation tasks for Arabic music: both Arabic and European listeners use salient surface features for segmentation (i.e., pauses, register changes), but only Arabic listeners use cues based on subtle modal changes [87]. Finally, differences between novice and expert listeners have also been reported for Finnish spiritual folk hymns and North Sami yoiks [98, 99].

Learning and perception of time structures. Numerous research conducted with Western listeners (i.e., Western European and North American listeners) have shown that perception and production of weakly metric rhythms is less accurate than perception and production of strongly metric rhythms (e.g., [100, 101]). Simple integer ratios in general are easier to perceive than complex ratios [102], leading to the hypothesis of more complex cognitive processes necessary for the processing of complex ratio (e.g., 2:3) *versus* simple ratio meters (e.g., 1:2).

However, Hannon and Trehub [103] recently showed the importance of acculturation in the perception of metrical patterns. Meters with simple ratio predominate in Western music, while meters with complex ratio are common in other musical cultures, as for example Macedonian music. While North American adults showed weaker performance for the complex-meter patterns than the simple-meter patterns, Macedonian and Bulgarian adults performed equally well with both patterns. The hypothesis of the importance of exposure (versus the complexity of processing or cognitive predisposition for simple meter processing) received further support by additional infant experiments: 6-month-old North American infants performed equally well for both metric patterns, thus being able to process even complex patterns. However, by the age of 12-months, North American infants performed like North American adults with a bias for simple patterns [103, 104]. In contrast to adults, this bias of infants was reversible with simple training by exposure to complex patterns, thus suggesting some sensitive period for the acquisition of temporal structures. In sum, this example on temporal perception illustrates the pitfalls of Western-focused research and the importance of testing the perception of other musical systems for both naïve and native listeners.

Simulating learning and perception of other musical systems. Artificial neural networks have been used for the simulation of the learning and perception not only of Western tonal music, as exposed above, but also of other musical systems. Krumhansl et al. [98, 99] used self-organizing maps to simulate melodic expectancies by experts of North Sami yoiks versus experts of Finnish folk songs or Lutheran hymns. Different models were trained on the different systems and their predictions for yoiks were compared with behavioral data obtained for human listeners with various expertise.

Two further examples of the use of connectionist models to simulate learning of knowledge and its influence on music perception have been proposed by Bharucha and Olney [105]. A connectionist model (i.e., an auto-associative net) is trained with Indian *rags* (those used in the study by [97]). After learning, the network fills in missing tones of the scale and the authors make the link to faster processing of expected events (i.e., tones of the activated scale pattern). In addition, a trained connectionist model can serve to simulate the perceptual filter or bias created by the knowledge of one musical system on the perception of another system: A connectionist model is first exposed to the regularities of Western tonal music. Once learning has occurred, an Indian *rag* is presented to the model. The simulations show that the model assimilates the *rag* to the learned major and minor keys. The model thus shows the assimilation processes of Indian structures to the Western schemata learnt previously.

Implicit learning of regularities in new musical systems. Tonal acculturation is an example of implicit learning processes on material encountered in everyday life and leading to nonmusicians' implicit knowledge about the Western tonal musical system. The few studies on the perception of music of other cultures by native listeners suggest similar acculturation processes for exposure to music of other cultures (on both pitch and time dimensions). Implicit learning research studies the strengths and limits of this cognitive capacity in the laboratory with artificial material. Bridging the gap between complexity of real life learning and artificiality of experimental material, Bigand and collaborators [88] investigated the implicit learning of twelve-tone music in the laboratory. This atonal musical system is based on a tone row, the ordered arrangement of the 12 tones of the chromatic scale (forming a basic rule of 12-tone musical grammar initially proposed by Schoenberg [106], 1941). One piece of music is based on one row and its possible transformation. Historically, the proposition of this tone system that broke with the concepts of tonal structures and hierarchy has led to considerable debate about whether listeners can understand these new structures. The researchers have brought this question into the lab with the implicit learning paradigm. First, listeners were exposed to musical pieces composed with a specific 12-tone row. In the test phase, participants listened to new excerpts presented by pair and had to select the excerpt that "was composed by the same composer". More specifically, one excerpt was based on the same row as in the exposition phase, and the other excerpt on a different row. Participants (musicians and nonmusicians) performed above chance in this test, even if they were very uncertain of their responses. Moreover, a control group, which had been exposed to excerpts based on both rows, did not differ from chance. This experiment suggests that the listeners became sensitive to the specific atonal structures in the exposure phase despite the complexity of the material [88].

References

1. Palmer, C.: Sequence memory in music performance. Current Directions in Psychological Science 14, 247–250 (2005)
2. Repp, B.H.: Sensorimotor synchronization: A review of the tapping literature. Psychonomic Bulletin & Review 12, 969–992 (2005)
3. Stevens, C., Byron, T.: Universals in music processing. In: Hallmam, C.T. (ed.) Oxford Handbook of Music Psychology. Oxford (2008)
4. Dowling, W.J., Harwood, D.L.: Music Cognition. Academic Press, Orlando (1986)
5. Francès, R.: La perception de la musique, 2nd edn. Vrin, Paris (1958)
6. Krumhansl, C.L.: Cognitive foundations of musical pitch. Oxford University Press, New York (1990)
7. Krumhansl, C.L.: The psychological representation of musical pitch in a tonal context. Cognitive Psychology 11(3), 346–374 (1979)
8. Bharucha, J.J.: Anchoring effects in music: The resolution of dissonance. Cognitive Psychology 16(4), 485–518 (1984)
9. Budge, H.: A study of chord frequencies. Teacher College (1943)
10. Bigand, E., Poulin-Charronnat, B.: Are we all experienced listeners? Cognition 100, 100–130 (2006)
11. Tillmann, B., Bharucha, J.J., Bigand, E.: Implicit learning of tonality: a self-organizing approach. Psychol Rev. 107(4), 885–913 (2000)
12. Hébert, S., Peretz, I., Gagnon, L.: Perceiving the tonal ending of tune excerpts: The roles of pre-existing representation and musical expertise. Canadian Journal of Experimental Psychology 49, 193–209 (1995)
13. Bartlett, J.C., Dowling, W.J.: Recognition of transposed melodies: a key-distance effect in developmental perspective. J. Exp. Psychol. Hum. Percept. Perform 6(3), 501–515 (1980)
14. Cuddy, L.L., Thompson, W.F.: Perceived key movement in four-voice harmony and single voices. Music Perception 9, 427–438 (1992)
15. Bigand, E.: Perceiving musical stability: the effect of tonal structure, rhythm, and musical expertise. J. Exp. Psychol. Hum. Percept. Perform 23(3), 808–822 (1997)
16. Bharucha, J.J., Krumhansl, C.L.: The representation of harmonic structure in music: hierarchies of stability as a function of context. Cognition 13(1), 63–102 (1983)

17. Dowling, W.J.: Scale and contour: Two components of a theory of memory for melodies. Psychological Review 85(4), 341–354 (1978)
18. Tillmann, B., Bigand, E., Madurell, F.: Local versus global processing of harmonic cadences in the solution of musical puzzles. Psychological Research/Psychologische Forschung 61(3), 157–174 (1998)
19. Meyer, L.B.: Emotion and Meaning in Music. University of Chicago Press, Chicago (1956)
20. Carlsen, C.: Musical expectancy: Some perspectives. Council for Research in Music Education 71, 4–14 (1982)
21. Carlsen, C.: Some factors which influence melodic expectancy. Psychomusicology 1(1), 12–29 (1981)
22. Schmuckler, M.A.: The performance of global expectations. Psychomusicology 9, 122–147 (1990)
23. Schmuckler, M.A.: Expectation in music: Investigation of melodic and harmonic processes. Music Perception 7, 109–150 (1989)
24. Schmuckler, M.A., Boltz, M.G.: Harmonic and rhythmic influences on musical expectancy. Percept Psychophys 56(3), 313–325 (1994)
25. Neely, J.H.: Semantic priming effects in visual word recognition: A selective review of current findings and theories. In: Besner, D., Humphreys, G.W. (eds.) Basic processes in reading: Visual word recognition, pp. 264–336. Lawrence Erlbaum, Mahwah (1991)
26. Tillmann, B.: Implicit investigations of tonal knowledge in nonmusician listeners. Annals of the New York Academy of Sciences 1060, 100–110 (2005)
27. Bharucha, J.J., Stoeckig, K.: Reaction time and musical expectancy: priming of chords. J. Exp. Psychol. Hum. Percept. Perform 12(4), 403–410 (1986)
28. Bigand, E., Pineau, M.: Global context effects on musical expectancy. Percept Psychophys 59(7), 1098–1107 (1997)
29. Tillmann, B., Bharucha, J.J.: Effect of harmonic relatedness on the detection of temporal asynchronies. Perception & Psychophysics 64(4), 640–649 (2002)
30. Bigand, E., et al.: The effect of harmonic context on phoneme monitoring in vocal music. Cognition 8(1), B11–B20 (2001)
31. Tillmann, B., et al.: Influence of harmonic context on musical timbre processing. European Journal of Cognitive Psychology 18, 343–358 (2005)
32. Poulin-Charronnat, B., et al.: Musical structure modulates semantic priming in vocal music. Cognition 94, B67–B78 (2005)
33. Tillmann, B., Bigand, E., Pineau, M.: Effects of global and local contexts on harmonic expectancy. Music Perception 16(1), 99–117 (1998)
34. Bigand, E., et al.: Effect of global structure and temporal organization on chord processing. Journal of Experimental Psychology: Human Perception and Performance 25(1), 184–197 (1999)
35. Bigand, E., et al.: Cognitive versus sensory components in harmonic priming effects. Journal of Experimental Psychology: Human Perception and Performance 29(1), 159–171 (2003)
36. Tillmann, B., et al.: Tonal centers and expectancy: facilitation or inhibition of chords at the top of the harmonic hierarchy? Journal of Experimental Psychology: Human Perception & Performance (in press)
37. Marmel, F., Tillmann, B., Dowling, W.J.: Tonal expectations influence pitch perception (in press, 2007)

38. McAdams, S.: Contraintes psychologiques sur les dimensions porteuses de formes en musique. In: McAdams, S., Deliege, I. (eds.) La musique et les sciences cognitives, pp. 257–284. Bruxelles, Mardaga (1989)

39. Boltz, M.G.: The generation of temporal and melodic expectancies during musical listening. Perception & Psychophysics 53, 585–600 (1993)

40. Tillmann, B., Lebrun-Guillaud, G.: Influence of tonal and temporal expectations on chord processing and on completion judgments of chord sequences. Psychological Research 70, 345–358 (2006)

41. Peretz, I., Kolinsky, R.: Boundaries of separability between melody and rhythm in music discrimination: A neuropsychological perspective. Quarterly Journal of Experimental Psychology 46A, 301–327 (1993)

42. Boltz, M.G.: Some structural determinants of melody recall. Mem Cognit 19(3), 239–251 (1991)

43. Boltz, M.G.: Perceiving the end: Effects of tonal relationships on melodic completion. Journal of Experimental Psychology: Human Perception and Performance 15, 749–761 (1989)

44. Palmer, C., Krumhansl, C.L.: Independent temporal and pitch structures in determination of musical phrases. J. Exp. Psychol. Hum. Percept. Perform 13(1), 116–126 (1987)

45. Bigand, E.: The influence of implicit harmony, rhythm and musical training on the abstraction of "tension-relaxation schemes" in a tonal musical phrase. Contemporary Music Review 9, 128–139 (1993)

46. Jones, M.R., Boltz, M.: Dynamic attending and responses to time. Psychological Review 96, 459–491 (1989)

47. Dowling, W.J., Lung, K.M., Herrbold, S.: Aiming attention in pitch and time in the perception of interleaved melodies. Percept Psychophys 41(6), 642–656 (1987)

48. Lerdahl, F., Jackendoff, R.: A generative Theory of Tonal Music, vol. 368. The MIT press, Cambridge (1983)

49. Peretz, I., Morais, J.: La musique et la modularité. In: McAdams, S., Deliege, I. (eds.) La musique et les sciences cognitives, pp. 393–414. Bruxelles, P. Mardaga (1989)

50. Pfordresher, P.Q.: The role of melodic and rhythmic accents in musical structure. Music Perception 20(4), 431–464 (2003)

51. Hoch, L., Tillmann, B.: Effect of tonal relatedness on spoken syllable identification to the contralateral ear (manuscript in preparation)

52. Escoffier, N., Tillmann, B.: The tonal function of a task-irrelevant chord modulates speed of visual processing. Cognition (in press)

53. Jones, M.R.: Dynamic pattern structures in music: Recent theory and research. Perception and Psychophysics 41, 621–634 (1987)

54. Meyer, L.B.: On rehearing music. In: Meyer, L.B. (ed.) Music, the arts and ideas, pp. 42–53. Chicago University Press, Chicago (1967)

55. Jackendoff, R.: Musical parsing and musical affect. Music Perception 9, 199–230 (1991)

56. Justus, T.C., Bharucha, J.J.: Modularity in musical processing: the automaticity of harmonic priming. J. Exp. Psychol. Hum. Percept. Perform 27(4), 1000–1011 (2001)

57. Tillmann, B., Bigand, E.: Musical priming: Schematic expectations resist repetition priming. In: 8th International Conference of Music Perception and Cognition. Evanston, Chicago (2004)

58. Faita, F., Besson, M.: Electrophysiological index of musical expectancy: Is there a repetition effect on the event-related potentials associated with musical incongruities? In: Third International Conference for Music Perception and Cognition, ESCOM, Liege (1994)

59. Lerdahl, F.: Two ways which music relates the world. Music theory spectrum 25, 367–373 (2003)
60. Shepard, R.N.: Geometrical approximations to the structure of musical pitch. Psychol. Rev. 89(4), 305–333 (1982)
61. Krumhansl, C.L., Kessler, E.J.: Tracing the dynamic changes in perceived tonal organization in a spatial representation of musical keys. Psychol. Rev. 89(4), 334–368 (1982)
62. Lerdahl, F.: Tonal pitch space. Music Perception 5(3), 315–349 (1988)
63. Lerdahl, F.: Pitch-space journeys in two Chopin Preludes. In: Jones, M.R., Holleran, S. (eds.) Cognitive bases of musical communication, APA, pp. 171–191 (1991)
64. Bharucha, J.J.: Music cognition and perceptual facilitation: A connectionist framework. Music Perception 5(1), 1–30 (1987)
65. McClelland, J.L., Rumelhart, D.E.: An interactive activation model of context effects in letter perception: Part 1. An account of basic findings. Psychological Review 86, 287–330 (1981)
66. Seidenberg, M.S., McClelland, J.L.: A distributed, developmental model of word recognition and naming. Psychological Review 96, 523–568 (1989)
67. Grossberg, S.: Some networks that can learn, remember and reproduce any number of complicated space-time patterns. Studies in Applied Mathematics 49, 135–166 (1970)
68. Kohonen, T.: Self-Organizing Maps. Springer, Heidelberg (1995)
69. Rumelhart, D.E., Zipser, D.: Feature discovery by competitive learning. Cognitive Science 9, 75–112 (1985)
70. von der Malsberg, C.: Self-organizing of orientation sensitive cells in the striate cortex. Kybernetic 14, 85–100 (1973)
71. Parncutt, R.: Harmony: A psychoacoustical approach. Springer, Heidelberg (1989)
72. Krumhansl, C.L., Bharucha, J.J., Kessler, E.J.: Perceived harmonic structures of chords in three related keys. Journal of Experimental Psychology: Human Perception and Performance 8, 24–36 (1982)
73. Patel, A.D., et al.: Processing syntactic relations in language and music: an event-related potential study. J. Cogn. Neurosci. 10(6), 717–733 (1998)
74. Tekman, H.G., Bharucha, J.J.: Implicit knowledge versus psychoacoustic similarity in priming of chords. Journal of Experimental Psychology: Human Perception and Performance 24(1), 252–260 (1998)
75. Seger, C.A.: Implicit learning. Psychological Bulletin 115, 163–169 (1994)
76. Altmann, G.T.M., Dienes, Z., Goode, A.: Modality independence of implicitly learned grammatical knowledge. Journal of Experimental Psychology: Learning, Memory, and Cognition 21(4), 899–912 (1995)
77. Reber, A.S.: Implicit learning of artificial grammars. Journal of Verbal Learning and Verbal Behavior 6, 855–863 (1967)
78. Reber, A.S.: Implicit learning and tacit knowledge. Journal of Experimental Psychology: General 118, 219–235 (1989)
79. Saffran, J.R., Newport, E.L., Aslin, R.N.: Word segmentation: The role of distributional cues. Journal of Memory and Language 35(4), 606–621 (1996)
80. Thiessen, E.D., Saffran, J.R.: When cues collide: use of stress and statistical cues to word boundaries by 7- to 9-month-old infants. Developmental Psychology 39(4), 706–716 (2003)
81. Johnson, E.K., Jusczyk, P.W.: Word segmentation by 8-month-olds: When speech cues count more than statistics. Journal of Memory and Language 44(4), 548–567 (2001)

82. Tillmann, B., McAdams, S.: Implicit Learning of musical timbre sequences: statistical regularities confronted with acoustical (dis)similarities. Journal of Experimental Psychology: Learning, Memory & Cognition 30, 1131–1142 (2004)
83. McAdams, S., et al.: Perceptual scaling of synthesized musical timbres: Common dimensions, specificities and latent subject classes. Psychological Research 58, 177–192 (1995)
84. Grey, J.M.: Multidimensional perceptual scaling of musical timbres. Journal of the Acoustical Society of America 61, 1270–1277 (1977)
85. Krumhansl, C.L.: Why is musical timbre so hard to understand? In: Nielzen, S., Olsson, O. (eds.) Structure and perception of electroacoustic sound and music, pp. 43–54. Excerpta medica, Amsterdam (1989)
86. Samson, S., Zatorre, R.J., Ramsay, J.O.: Multidimensional scaling of synthetic musical timbre: perception of spectral and temporal characteristics. Canadian Journal of Experimental Psychology 51, 307–315 (1997)
87. Ayari, M., McAdams, S.: Aural analysis of Arabic improvised instrumental music (tagsim). Music Perception 21, 159–216 (2003)
88. Bigand, E., D'Adamo, D.A., Poulin, B.: The implicit learning of twelve-tone music. In: ESCOP 2003, Granada, Spain (2003)
89. Bigand, E., Perruchet, P., Boyer, M.: Implicit learning of an artificial grammar of musical timbres. Cahiers de Psychologie Cognitive/Current Psychology of Cognition 17(3), 577–600 (1998)
90. Howard, J.H.J., Ballas, J.A.: Acquisition of acoustic pattern categories by exemplar observation. Organization, Behavior and Human Performance 30, 157–173 (1982)
91. Howard, J.H.J., Ballas, J.A.: Syntactic and semantic factors in the classification of nonspeech transient patterns. Perception & Psychophysics 28(5), 431–439 (1980)
92. Poulin-Charronnat, B., Tillmann, B., Perruchet, P.: Implicit learning of artificial grammar of tones: direct and indirect judgments (manuscript in preparation)
93. Tillmann, B., Poulin-Charronnat, B.: Auditory expectations for newly acquired material: Combining implicit learning and priming paradigms (manuscript in preparation)
94. Tillmann, B., Marmel, F.: Testing musical expectations at various positions inside a chord sequence: An adaptation of the musical priming paradigm (manuscript submitted for publication, 2007)
95. Stevens, C.: Cross-cultural studies of musical pitch and time. Acoustical Science and Technology 25, 433–438 (2004)
96. Kessler, E.J., Hansen, C., Shepard, R.N.: Tonal schemata in the perception of music in Bali and in the West. Music Perception 2, 131–165 (1994)
97. Castellano, M.A., Bharucha, J.J., Krumhansl, C.L.: Tonal hierarchies in the music of North India. Journal of Experimental Psychology: General 113, 394–412 (1984)
98. Krumhansl, C.L., et al.: Cross-cultural music cognition: cognitive methodology applied to North Sami yoiks. Cognition 76(1), 13–58 (2000)
99. Krumhansl, C.L., et al.: Melodic expectation in Finnish spiritual folk hymns: Convergence of statistical, behavioral, and computational approaches. Music Perception 17, 151–195 (1999)
100. Povel, D.-J., Essens, P.J.: Perception of temporal patterns. Music Perception 2, 411–440 (1985)
101. Keller, P.E., Burnham, D.K.: Musical meter in attention to multipart rhythm. Music Perception 22, 629–661 (2005)
102. London, J.: Hearing in time. Oxford University Press, New York (2004)
103. Hannon, E.E., Trehub, S.E.: Metrical categories in infancy and adulthood. Psychological Science 16, 48–55 (2005)

104. Hannon, E.E., Trehub, S.E.: Tuning in to musical rhythms: Infants learn more readily than adults. Proceedings of the National Academy of Sciences of the United States of America 102, 12639–12643 (2005)
105. Bharucha, J.J., Olney, K.L.: Tonal cognition, artificial intelligence and neural nets. Contemporary Music Review 4, 341–356 (1989)
106. Schoenberg, A.: Style and idea: Selected writings of Arnold Schonberg. Farber and Farber, London (1941)

Capturing Expressive and Indicative Qualities of Conducting Gesture: An Application of Temporal Expectancy Models

Dilip Swaminathan[1], Harvey Thornburg[1], Todd Ingalls[1], Stjepan Rajko[1], Jodi James[1], Ellen Campana[1], Kathleya Afanador[1], and Randal Leistikow[2]

[1] Arts, Media and Engineering, Arizona State University, USA
[2] Zenph Studios Inc, Raleigh, NC, USA
sdilip@asu.edu

Abstract. Many event sequences in everyday human movement exhibit temporal structure: for instance, footsteps in walking, the striking of balls in a tennis match, the movements of a dancer set to rhythmic music, and the gestures of an orchestra conductor. These events generate prior expectancies regarding the occurrence of future events. Moreover, these expectancies play a critical role in conveying expressive qualities and communicative intent through the movement; thus they are of considerable interest in musical control contexts. To this end, we introduce a novel Bayesian framework which we call the *temporal expectancy model* and use it to develop an analysis tool for capturing *expressive* and *indicative* qualities of the conducting gesture based on temporal expectancies. The temporal expectancy model is a general dynamic Bayesian network (DBN) that can be used to encode prior knowledge regarding temporal structure to improve event segmentation. The conducting analysis tool infers beat and tempo, which are indicative and articulation which is expressive, as well as temporal expectancies regarding beat (*ictus* and *preparation* instances) from conducting gesture. Experimental results using our analysis framework reveal a very strong correlation in how significantly the preparation expectancy builds up for staccato vs legato articulation, which bolsters the case for temporal expectancy as cognitive model for event anticipation, and as a key factor in the communication of expressive qualities of conducting gesture. Our system operates on data obtained from a marker based motion capture system, but can be easily adapted for more affordable technologies like video camera arrays.

1 Temporal Expectancy and Human Movement

In everyday human movement, be it walking footsteps, the striking of tennis balls during a match, the movements of a dancer set to rhythmic music, or the gestures of an orchestra conductor, *the occurrences of future events are highly informed by the occurrence times of past events*. We consider this as the defining property of *temporal structure*. From this definition, event sequences lacking temporal structure must be Poisson processes [32], which have independent, exponentially distributed inter-event times. With a Poisson process, any event's occurrence is "maximally surprising" as it does not depend

R. Kronland-Martinet, S. Ystad, and K. Jensen (Eds.): CMMR 2007, LNCS 4969, pp. 34–55, 2008.

on the elapsed duration since previous events.[1] Poisson processes have a rich history in electroacoustic music, for instance they are used extensively by Xenakis [45] to specify the formal structure of sparse textures of sound. Sparse textures are built up from *rare* events [45]; which from the listener's standpoint are conceptually identical to events which are *unexpected* due to lack of temporal structure: if an event is considered "rare" by a listener, the structurally similar past events are no longer in that listeners memory.

On the other hand, when one *observes* temporally structured movement, the fact that the occurrence of the next event is highly informed by the occurrence times of past events naturally induces an *expectancy*, a strong feeling of *anticipation* that this event is about to occur. We hypothesize, moreover, that an important process by which a performer builds up *tension* is the sustaining or gradual heightening of this anticipation over prolonged periods. Consider a hypothetical movie scene, where a killer stalks his victim in a forest and the victim is alternately running and hiding behind trees, trying desperately to survive, yet the inevitable is soon to come. Our anticipation is sustained by ominous, swelling music, and rapidly shifting camera views from increasingly odd angles. In this example, the filmmaker runs the entire gamut of multi-modal feedback and also relies heavily on long-term narrative structures. However, in many situations such tension can be built up through bodily gesture alone.

The idea of expectancy has received much attention in the music cognition literature [24,30,4,15]. One central theme in these efforts is that the subsequent *realization* or *circumvention* of expectancies involving melodic or harmonic structures is a fundamental component of the listener's affective response [24,30]. Another central theme in these efforts has addressed expectancies with respect to higher-level semantic elements in music. Some of these studies have used an ERP paradigm, focusing on demonstrating N400 effects, which are a well-established marker of semantic expectancy [20]. These studies demonstrate that listeners generate expectancies with respect to the meaning of memorized melodies [25] and more generally to linguistic semantics associated with melodies, both emotive and non-emotive [34]. A third central theme in these efforts has been temporal expectancies, especially as a means to the perception of rhythm [31,9,23,17,46]. For instance the pioneering work of Povel and Essens' [31] reveals that in the perception of temporal patterns, humans generate a hierarchical clock for which durations are governed by the pattern's distribution of accents. Since the state of the clock indicates when it is about to reset, this model provides at least an implicit encoding of temporal expectancy. Desain [9] and Zanto et al. [46], among others, extend this work, as they reveal specific neurological mechanisms behind the generation of temporal expectancies. Furthermore, Jones et al. [17] and McAuley [23] have observed direct effects on how different expectancy patterns can influence listeners perception of duration and meter.

While the music cognition literature is rich in theories regarding temporal expectancy and its role in music perception, relatively little attention has been paid to parallel structures in movement perception. Within the gesture literature there has been a recent surge in interest in semantic expectancies on the part of observers. Like the research on

---

[1] The standard, *homogeneous* Poisson process which is what is usually meant has the additional consideration that event times are identically distributed i.e, the event process evolves at a constant rate [32].

semantic expectancies, much of this research has used ERP methods, focusing on demonstrating N400 effects, which have been linked to semantic processing more generally. This research provides evidence that observers generate expectancies with respect to the meaning conveyed by gestures that accompany speech, and its relation to the meaning of the co-occurring speech [33,1,43,44,14]. The role of semantic expectancies in gesture perception is also supported by evidence using an eye-tracking paradigm [10]. Only recently have researchers begun to ask questions about how movement-based expectancies and musical expectancies relate. Hagendoorn [12] has reviewed neurological mechanisms underlying movement-based expectancies, hypothesizing that the elicitation, realization, and circumvention of these expectancies each play similar roles in dance perception as they do in music perception.

For the purposes of developing gestural control interfaces for musical expression, the aforementioned research is interesting, however there are still some unanswered questions. Three crucial areas that remain unexplored are 1) the specific effects of temporal expectancy in the perception of human movement, 2) the role of expectancies in how the *performer* perceives his/her own actions, and 3) how the expectancies of observer and performer combine during performance. For instance, what role might expectancy play in movement or (gesturally controlled) music improvisation? We hypothesize that just as music composers or improvisers seem to be aware of their potential to craft emotion in their "audience," so too are those who move. Hence, the role of expectancy in gestural control for musical expression must therefore be situated within the *communicative intent* underlying expressive movement.

Other aspects of communicative intent in expressive movement have been well-studied, for instance the Laban Movement Analysis (LMA) system [11] concerning *Body*, *Effort*, *Shape*, and *Space* has been familiar to the dance and kinesiology communities for over 80 years. However, the present lack of computational frameworks conformable to low-cost sensing technologies has prevented extensive application of LMA to gestural control of interactive music systems. We hypothesize that the aspects of temporal expectancy considered by our framework relate most closely to the LMA *Effort* qualities of *Time*, *Weight* and *Flow* [11]. Indeed, a recent study concerning Effort qualities for movement synthesis and character animation [38] shows that these qualities are fully observable from timing information alone without considering the content of the gesture. However, Time, Weight, and Flow give only a coarse, qualitative description of the timing information latent in any particular gesture or full-body movement sequence. The temporal expectancy framework, by contrast, reveals an explicit mechanism for modeling event anticipation on the part of the observer and the performer. Hence, temporal expectancy and LMA should be considered as complementary rather than competing paradigms. Systems based around temporal expectancy can only augment the expressive possibilities of systems based around LMA, and vice versa.

As such, we are developing a conducting gesture analysis tool based on the induction of temporal expectancies from human movement. Our efforts will enable musical expression to be more tightly coupled to the performer's communicative intent. A more complex interplay between performer and instrument may also arise as the instrument can be programmed to induce sympathetic expectancies in the performer, to subvert the performer's intentions, or to cultivate situations where complex temporal structures emerge from the hybrid nature of the interaction. Our initial realization concerns conducting gesture, due to the rich set of associations which couple expressive gesture to expressive musical form. Conducting gesture conveys both *indicative* and *expressive* attributes of the music, for instance *timing* (beat, tempo, and meter); *dynamics* (crescendo/diminuendo, accents); *articulation* (legato/staccato/marcato/tenuto) and *phrasing* [19,41]. As we will show, much of this information is largely conveyed via temporal expectancies.

To this end, we propose a fully integrated Bayesian framework for the joint induction of a) temporal expectancies regarding *ictus* (beat) and *preparation* (sub-beat), as well as b) fundamental expressive and indicative musical attributes from conducting gestures, namely *beat*, *tempo*, and *articulation*. This framework as well as computing temporal expectancies concerning ictus and preparation positions, incorporates them as a source of *prior knowledge* to aid the induction of musical attributes[2]. We use a feature set consisting only of the magnitude velocity and direction of the conductor's baton relative to shoulder position. We note that dynamics in these features are *invariant* to the presence of specific spatial patterns. Features are currently extracted using a marker-based motion capture system from Motion Analysis Corporation. However, they may also be readily computed using low-cost video camera arrays, as suggested by the state of the art regarding body kinematics recovery from video [27,40,26,39,5].

Computational conducting gesture analysis has proven quite challenging. The vast majority of current systems are rule-based [41,28,19] and assume standard spatial patterns which correspond to various meters (3/4, 4/4, etc.) However, experienced conductors often evolve highly personal styles which do not always follow these patterns [21]. Nevertheless both orchestra and audience seem to have little trouble inducing timing, articulation, dynamics, phrasing, and other expressive qualities from the gesture, even if they are only peripherally aware of the conductor's motion [41]. This is partly due to reinforcement from the music and foreknowledge of the score; however, few would argue that the conductor's role in managing this process by conveying critical information via bodily gesture is anything less than central. Hence, a major speculative hypothesis of this paper is that conductors convey musical attributes not directly through the standard patterns, but by inducing temporal expectancies in viewers through trends in features such as magnitude velocity and direction which are a) invariant to specific spatial patterns and b) intelligible through peripheral awareness. Experimental results (Section 4) yield substantial evidence confirming this hypothesis, especially those regarding the conveyance of articulation through the temporal expectancy regarding the preparation event.

The rest of the paper is organized as follows. Section 2 discusses the general temporal expectancy model originally introduced in [36,37], Section 3 discusses in detail the various computational models developed for the conducting gesture analysis application, and Section 4 shows results and highlights a case study exploring the effect of staccato and legato articulation on all temporal expectancies considered.

---

[2] Expectancies regarding sub-beat positions turn out to be highly informative regarding articulation; see Section 4.

2   General Temporal Expectancy Model

Before giving the mathematical details of our modeling approach, we must define what is meant by temporal expectancy in the context of a Bayesian framework. Furthermore, the definition must agree with our definition of temporal structure as described in Section 1; namely, that temporal structure is evident if the tendencies for new events to occur depend on the occurrence times of previous events. Bayesian *posterior temporal expectancy* is defined as the posterior probability that a new event will occur in the next time instant, given all features observed up to and including the current time. Via Bayes rule, the posterior expectancy incorporates these observations along with prior knowledge from temporal structure. To encode this prior knowledge, [37] defines a *prior temporal expectancy*, which is the conditional probability that a new event will occur in the next time instant, given all past event occurrence times. Hence, our use of the Bayesian posterior temporal expectancy is entirely consistent with the afore-mentioned definition of temporal structure: *any* temporally structured event sequence will generate an informative (non-uniform) prior temporal expectancy and thus influence the posterior temporal expectancy, which models the belief that a new event is about to occur.

The *temporal expectancy model* is a general Bayesian framework for representing temporal expectancies and fusing them with multimodal sense-data to improve event segmentation and temporal structure inference. It is a statistically optimal framework that enables a *joint* approach for event segmentation and temporal structure inference, rather than the usual two-stage approach where events are detected in the first stage and are presented as inputs to another algorithm for identifying temporal structure separately [7,13]. Such a joint approach proves to be effective from an *estimation-error* perspective, as the inherent fusion of anticipatory prior knowledge concerning subsequent events with raw sense-data observations, improves the detection of these events and estimation of their locations even under high noise conditions. An accurate estimation of event times in turn improves our estimates of the unknown parameters of the temporal structure. These improvements are amply demonstrated in a study done by some of the present authors [37].

2.1   Probabilistic Model

The fundamental temporal expectancy model is represented by a *switching state-space model*(SSM). The corresponding directed acylic graph (DAG) [3] is shown in Fig. 1 with clear and shaded nodes representing hidden and observed variables respectively.

In Fig. 1, variables are defined as follows.

- T_t encodes unknown parameters of temporal structure. In a quasi-periodic case, T_t may encode the mean period in frames between event times.

---

[3] A DAG [29] is a graphical representation of a factorization of a joint probability distribution into conditional distributions. If a DAG consists of nodes $X_{1:N}$, the corresponding factorization of $P(X_{1:N}) = \prod_{i=1}^{N} P(X_i|Pa\{X_i\})$, where $Pa\{X_i\}$ are the parents of X_i. For instance, in Fig. 1 $P(T_{t-1}, T_t, \tau_{t-1}, \tau_t, M_{t-1}, M_t, S_{t-1}, S_t, Y_t) = P(T_t|T_{t-1})P(M_t|T_t, \tau_{t-1})P(\tau_t|M_t, \tau_{t-1})P(S_t|M_t)P(Y_t|S_t)$.

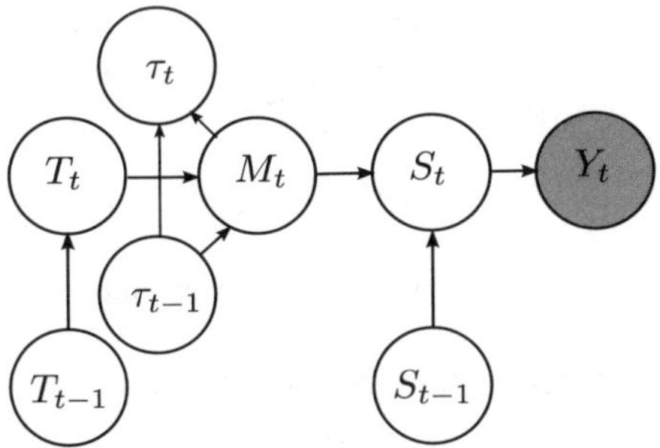

Fig. 1. Single time slice directed acyclic graph of the fundamental temporal expectancy model. Observed variables are shaded; hidden variables are unshaded.

- τ_t encodes the elapsed duration since the previous event.
- $M_t \in \{1, 0\}$ where 1 indicates that an event occurs at frame t. It is not required that event occurrences be synchronous with frame times, hence the actual occurrence time can lie between frames $t - 1$ and t.
- S_t denotes the *state* following the dynamic law influenced by M_t. It can be a discrete, continuous, or mixed random variable.
- Y_t indicates the *observation* and can be modeled as a noisy version of the state.

To complete the description of the fundamental temporal expectancy network we need to specify $P(T_t|T_{t-1})$, $P(\tau_t|M_t, \tau_{t-1})$, and $P(M_t|T_t, \tau_{t-1})$.

If the temporal structure parameters do not vary with time, then ideally $P(T_t|T_{t-1}) \triangleq \delta_{\{T_t = T_{t-1}\}}$ i.e., $P(T_t|T_{t-1})$ concentrates impulsively on the event where $T_t = T_{t-1}$. However, in most practical cases temporal structure may vary continuously $(T_t \approx T_{t-1})$. For example, in a tempo tracking application with T_t encoding the tempo period we specify

$$\log T_t \sim \mathcal{N}(\log T_{t-1}, \sigma_T^2) \tag{1}$$

to express on average a proportionate tempo change of σ_T per frame, where $\sigma_T \ll 1$.

To specify $P(\tau_t|M_t, \tau_{t-1})$, we define $\tau_{0,t} \triangleq \max(0, \sup\{1 \leq s \leq t : M_s = 1\})$; i.e., the last frame for which $M_t = 1$. If $M_t = 1$, the event actually occurred in the interval $(\tau_{0,t} - 1, \tau_{0,t}]$. We assign the actual occurrence to the midpoint $\tau_{0,t} - 1/2$, to best mitigate time quantization errors induced by assigning onsets to frame boundaries. Hence $\tau_t = t - (\tau_{0,t} - 1/2)$, which can be written as

$$\tau_t = (1/2)\mathbf{1}_{\{M_t=1\}} + (\tau_t - 1)\mathbf{1}_{\{M_t=0\}} \tag{2}$$

In order to specify $P(M_t|T_t, \tau_{t-1})$, we define a hypothetical random variable L as the current inter-event time between previous and subsequent events. If $M_t = 1$, i.e., a new event has occurred between times $t - 1$ and t, then $L \in (\tau_{t-1}, \tau_{t-1} + 1]$. Therefore,

$$P(M_t|T_t, \tau_{t-1}) = P(L < \tau_{t-1} + 1|L \geq \tau_{t-1}) \tag{3}$$

$$= \frac{\int_{\tau_{t-1}}^{\tau_{t-1}+1} P(L|T_t)dL}{1 - \int_0^{\tau_{t-1}} P(L|T_t)dL} \tag{4}$$

$$= \mathrm{Haz}(\tau_{t-1}) \tag{5}$$

where $\mathrm{Haz}(\tau_{t-1})$ the denotes the *hazard rate* [32]. To model quasi-periodic structures, which are evident in conducting gestures as well as rhythmic dance movements, footsteps in walking, etc. we specify

$$\log L \sim \mathcal{N}(\log T_t, \sigma_L^2) \tag{6}$$

where T_t denotes the inter-event period without jitter, and σ_L specifies the amount of jitter.

We can also model very different kinds of temporal structure. For instance, many event processes occur in "bursts", such as web queries, stock trades, blog visits/comments and so forth. Recent work by Barabasi et al [3] has characterized inter-event times associated with these processes by *power- law* distribution i.e.,

$$P(L|T_t) = C(T_t)l^{-T_t}\mathbf{1}_{l\geq 0} \tag{7}$$

where $T_t \in (1, 2)$; $C(T_t)$ ensures $\int_0^\infty P(L|T_t) = 1$. Here, T_t encodes the exponent of the power-law dependence. These distributions are *heavy-tailed*, which means large gaps in activity are interleaved with brief "burst periods", where many events occur in a short interval.

2.2 Prior and Posterior Temporal Expectancies

Recall that within a Bayesian framework, we had defined the *prior temporal expectancy* as the conditional probability that a new event will occur in the next time instant, as a function of temporal structure parameters and states. As well, we defined the *posterior temporal expectancy* as the posterior probability that an event will occur in the next time instant, given all the past sense-data observations up to and including the current time instant . Mathematically, we can express these expectancies as follows.

We define the prior temporal expectancy as

$$\gamma_0(t|T_t, \tau_{t-1}) \triangleq \quad P(M_t = 1|T_t, \tau_{t-1}) \tag{8}$$

which represents the prior belief that an event will occur at frame t given τ_{t-1} and T_t. The prior expectancy is not a single number, but an entire distribution, a *function* defined over all possibilities of past event occurrences and occurrence times. The prior expectancy is *fused* with raw sense-data observations implicitly to estimate the event occurrence $M_t, t \in 1 : N$.

The predictive posterior temporal expectancy is defined as

$$\gamma(t) \triangleq P(M_t = 1|Y_{1:t-1}) \tag{9}$$

$$= \int_{\tau_{t-1}, T_t} \gamma_0(t|T_t, \tau_{t-1})P(T_t, \tau_{t-1}|Y_{1:t-1}) \tag{10}$$

It represents the belief that an event will occur at frame t after observing past data $Y_{1:t-1}$. Hence, γ_t models the immediate *anticipation* that an event is about to occur, given all past sense-data observations.

We have developed a general framework for representing temporal expectancies and using them for jointly segmenting and inferring temporal structure from event sequences. A practical application of this framework is demonstrated by developing a conducting gesture analysis tool, for which we need to develop explicit models for M_t, S_t, Y_t. For instance, we include ictus and preparation onsets present in a conducting stroke by expanding $M_t \in \{'O1','C1','O2','C2'\}$: where $'O1'$ and $'O2'$ denote onsets of ictus and preparation respectively. $'C1'$ denotes the continuation part of the stroke from ictus to the preparation and $'C2'$ denotes the part of the stroke from preparation to the onset of the next ictus. Now, we need probabilistic models to explain the influence of M_t on the observed noisy magnitude velocity ($Y_{V,t}$) and direction ($Y_{\theta,t}$) of conducting motion which we proceed to develop.

3 Computational Models for Conducting Gesture Analysis

In this section, we describe all the computational models involved in building the conductive gesture analysis tool, which include an augmented temporal expectancy model for ictus and preparation instances, as well as a model for the observed conducting gesture itself. To begin with, Section 3.1 discusses how event occurrences (ictus; preparation) influence the dynamics of observed magnitude velocity and direction trajectories of conducting gestures based on a novel construct, the *hypotrochoidal model*. The process of conducting is enmeshed in a complex feedback loop comprising the conductor and the orchestra. The conductor adapts his/her body kinematics in response to the performance of the orchestra similar to the process of a servo mechanical loop. A complete model that accounts for all the above factors does not exist (to the best of our awareness) and may be quite difficult to construct. Presently we use the hypotrochoidal model which conforms to *observed tendencies* related to the standard spatial forms, which for instance models the cusp-like behavior associated with the ictus. The algorithm used to normalize the 3D motion of the conductor and thereby extract the magnitude velocity and direction trajectories is given in Section 3.1. Sections 3.3, 3.4 make use of informal *maximum entropy* techniques in order to model in a probabilistic sense, the largest typical set of spatial trajectories which conform to the observed tendencies. Section 3.5 describes the induction of temporal expectancy for conducting gestures based on the fundamental temporal expectancy model and Section 3.6 integrates all previously described dynamic models into a single probabilistic model which fuses features across magnitude velocity and direction to jointly infer beat, tempo, and articulation.

3.1 Hypotrochoidal Model

We now consider how beat positions manifest as tendencies in either magnitude velocity or direction. While experienced conductors may eschew the standard spatial forms, we hypothesize that these tendencies are at some level rooted in the spatial forms; i.e. beats manifest as "cusp-like" behavior. To model such tendencies in magnitude velocity and direction which generate these cusps, we first a) derive *constraints* from a general class of idealized forms called a *hypotrochoid*, and then b) apply *maximum entropy criteria* to construct dynamic probabilistic models given these constraints [16,22]. This maximum

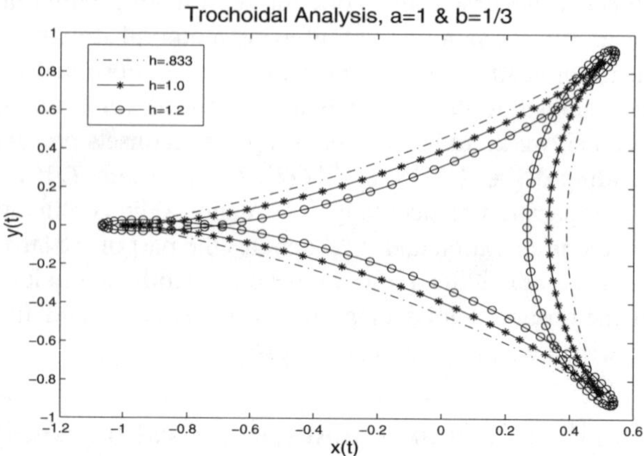

Fig. 2. Synthesized hypotrochoids

entropy approach allows us to model the largest possible typical set of actual conducting gestures which conform to the given constraints.

A hypotrochoid is a spatial curve with the following parametric equations [42]:

$$
\begin{aligned}
x(t) &= (a - b)\sin(t) - h\sin\left(\frac{a-b}{b}t\right) \\
y(t) &= (a - b)\cos(t) + h\cos\left(\frac{a-b}{b}t\right)
\end{aligned}
\tag{11}
$$

Fig. 2 shows a graph for $a = 1$, $b = 1/3$, and $h \in \{0.833, 1.0, 1.2\}$. The ratio b/a determines the number of segments, while h controls nuances of the cusps. When $h < 1$ cusps become smoother and when $h > 1$ they develop loops. Since loop behavior is more natural in the context of conducting gestures we target values of h slightly above 1.

Now we consider what trends in magnitude velocity and motion direction features are implied by the hypotrochoidal model. These features are computed as follows.

$$
\begin{aligned}
\text{Magnitude velocity}: V(t) &= \sqrt{\dot{x}(t)^2 + \dot{y}(t)^2} \\
\text{Motion direction}: \theta(t) &= \tan^{-1}(\dot{y}(t)/\dot{x}(t))
\end{aligned}
\tag{12}
$$

Fig. 3 displays graphs of these features using $a = 1$, $b = 1/3$, and $h = 1.2$.

To analyze the conducting gestures, we focus on the 3D motion of the baton, as monitored by the motion capture system. We handle the natural variations in orientation and scale by normalizing the motion to a standard planar kinesphere.

3.2   Normalization of Conducting Gesture

The standard planar kinesphere can be interpreted as a simple bounding box within which the conductor's motion is confined to, projected, and analyzed in 2D. To normalize the conducting gesture to the kinesphere, we fix the shoulder of the conductor as the

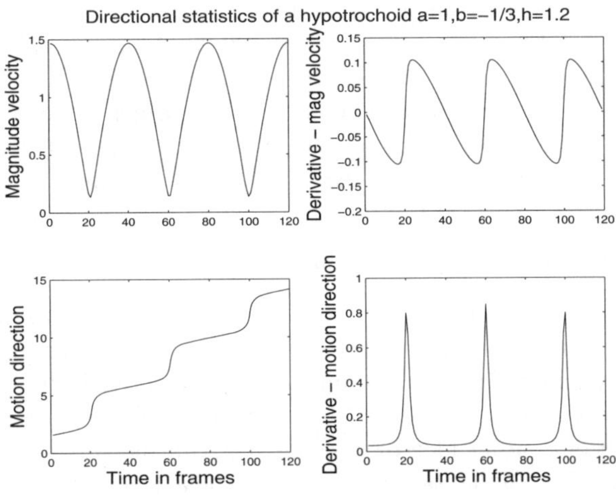

Fig. 3. Magnitude velocity and motion direction trajectories for synthesized hypotrochoid

origin, with y-axis passing through the shoulder and pointing up. We then estimate the plane $Ax + By + Cz = 1$ that fits the cloud of points of the baton motion over time using recursive least squares; then we find the point of projection (X_o, Y_o, Z_o) of the origin $(0, 0, 0)$ onto this plane. The spherical coordinate equivalents of (X_o, Y_o, Z_o) is computed as (R_o, A_o, B_o), where R_o is the radius and A_o, B_o are the spherical angles. We pre-transform the coordinate system such that the center direction maps to $(1, 0, 0)$ and the transformed 3D observation at time t (X_t, Y_t, Z_t) is converted to spherical coordinates (R_t, A_t, B_t).

We then generate a bounding box whose edges are determined by a fading maximization technique i.e.,

$$B_t^a = \max(\alpha \cdot B_{t-1}^a, |A_t|)$$
$$B_t^b = \max(\alpha \cdot B_{t-1}^b, |B_t|)$$

$$(13)$$

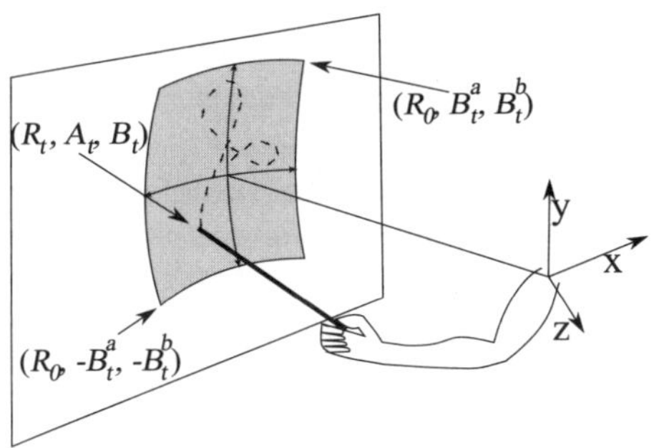

Fig. 4. Normalization of the conducting gesture using the kinesphere algorithm

and normalize the the spherical angles A_t, B_t by B_t^a and B_t^b respectively. The corners of the box are given by $(R_o, \pm B_t^a, \pm B_t^b)$ converted to Cartesian coordinate equivalents. The normalized spherical angles namely $A_t^N = A_t/B_t^a$ and $B_t^N = B_t/B_t^b$ give the normalized 2D coordinates of the conducting motion, which we use to calculate the magnitude velocity and directional angle features using (12). Fig. 4 shows how the conducting gesture is normalized using the kinesphere algorithm.

3.3   Modeling Trends in Magnitude Velocity

From Fig. 3, we observe that the magnitude velocity of the wrist motion starts at a minimum (close to zero) at the cusp (ictus) and increases to a maximum at the midpoint (preparation). Correspondingly, the magnitude velocity derivative remains positive at the ictus, becomes zero at the preparation and becomes negative before the next ictus.

Consistent with our earlier idea of expanding M_t to include $'O1', 'C1', 'O2'$ and $'C2'$ modes, we see that all the four M_t modes are clearly evident from the magnitude velocity trajectory of a single stroke. These modes are diagrammed in Fig. 5. The influence of magnitude velocity modes on the noisy magnitude velocity observations is modeled as a SSM, for which Fig. 6 shows the DAG.

In Fig. 6 $Y_{V,t}$ denotes the observed magnitude velocity; V_t the inherent magnitude velocity and A_t the "first order difference" of V_t. That is, $P(V_t|V_{t-1}, A_t)$ concentrates deterministically on $V_t = V_{t-1} + A_t$. In order to specify $P(A_t|A_{t-1}, M_t)$ we first summarize the observed tendencies in A_t under different modes in Table 1.

$P(A_t|A_{t-1}, M_t)$ is then developed by encoding the tendencies in Table 1 using Jaynes' principle of maximum entropy [16]. Let us first consider continuation modes. From Table 1 we have $A_t > 0$ for $M_t ='C1'$ and $A_t < 0$ when $M_t ='C2'$. Furthermore, we expect some continuity of A_t; i.e. $A_t \approx A_{t-1}$, which can be controlled by $E|A_t - A_{t-1}|^2 < \sigma_A^2$. Putting these constraints together and using the methods specified in [8], we can solve for the maximum entropy dependence in closed form.

$$A_t \sim \mathcal{N}^+(A_{t-1}, \sigma_A^2), \quad M_t ='C1'$$
$$A_t \sim \mathcal{N}^-(A_{t-1}, \sigma_A^2), \quad M_t ='C2' \tag{14}$$

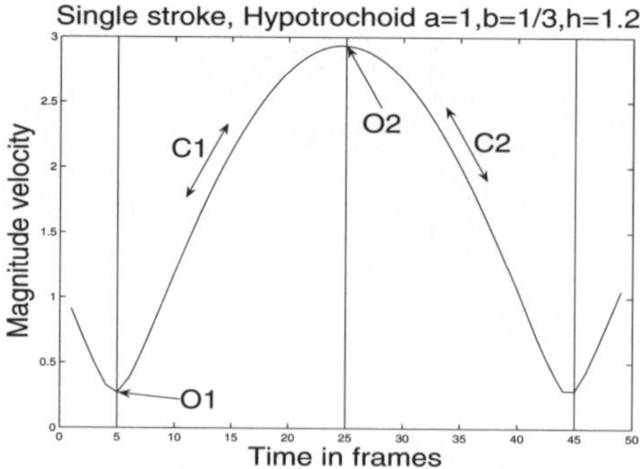

Fig. 5. Single stroke of magnitude velocity with various M_t segments

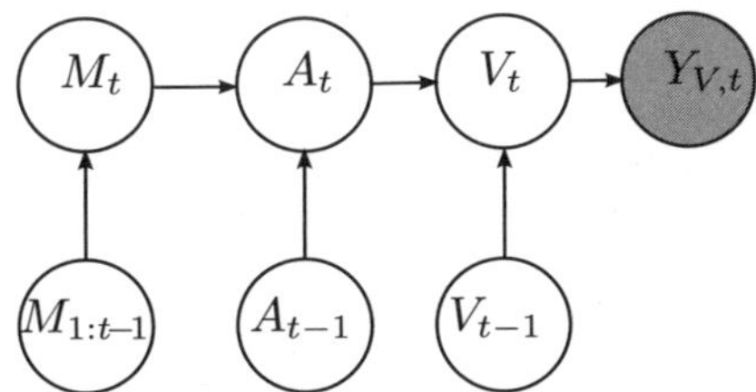

Fig. 6. Magnitude velocity: Single time slice DAG

Table 1. Magnitude velocity modes and corresponding tendencies observed in A_t

Mode M_t	Observed tendencies in A_t
$'O1'$	$A_t > 0,\ A_t \neq A_{t-1}$
$'C1'$	$A_t > 0,\ A_t \approx A_{t-1}$
$'O2'$	$A_t < 0,\ A_t \neq A_{t-1}$
$'C2'$	$A_t < 0,\ A_t \approx A_{t-1}$

where $\mathcal{N}^+$ and $\mathcal{N}^-$, respectively, are Gaussian distributions truncated to be positive and negative, sharing the mean A_{t-1} and variance σ_A^2. At the ictus and preparation, we do not constrain $A_t \approx A_{t-1}$; instead we allow for sudden changes in dynamics, weakly constraining $A_t \approx A^{(1)}$ (for $M_t =' O1'$) and $A_t \approx -A^{(2)}$ (for $M_t =' O2'$), where $A^{(1)}, A^{(2)} > 0$ are nominal values; i.e.

$$
\begin{aligned}
A_t &\sim \quad \mathcal{N}^+(A^{(1)}, \sigma_{A,1}^2), \quad M_t =' O1' \\
A_t &\sim \ \mathcal{N}^-(-A^{(2)}, \sigma_{A,2}^2), \quad M_t =' O2'
\end{aligned}
\tag{15}
$$

Finally, via $P(Y_{V,t}|V_t)$ we model the observed velocity as the actual velocity plus zero-mean Gaussian noise: $Y_{V,t} \sim \mathcal{N}(V_t, \sigma_{Y,V}^2)$.

3.4 Modeling Trends in Motion Direction

From the hypotrochoidal model, we also observe the ictus through a rapid (not necessarily abrupt) change in the direction of motion; during the rest of the stroke the direction changes much more slowly. We call the region of rapid change just succeeding the ictus the *transient region*, and assume that the latter ceases before the preparation.

As shown in Fig. 7 we do not observe preparation through motion direction data. Hence, we model $M_t \in \{'O','T','C'\}$ and specify the corresponding SSM using the DAG shown in Fig. 8. Here $M_t =' O'$ corresponds to the onset of the ictus; $M_t =' T'$ the remainder of the transient region, and $M_t =' C'$ the continuation, or remainder of the stroke. We let θ_t model the inherent direction of motion, ω_t the inherent derivative of θ_t, and $Y_{\theta,t}$ the observed direction.

Similar to magnitude velocity, the inherent motion direction is driven by its derivative; i.e. $P(\theta_t|\theta_{t-1}, \omega_t)$ concentrates deterministically on $\theta_t = \theta_{t-1} + \omega_t$. This derivative is large during onset and transient regions; otherwise small. Similar maximum

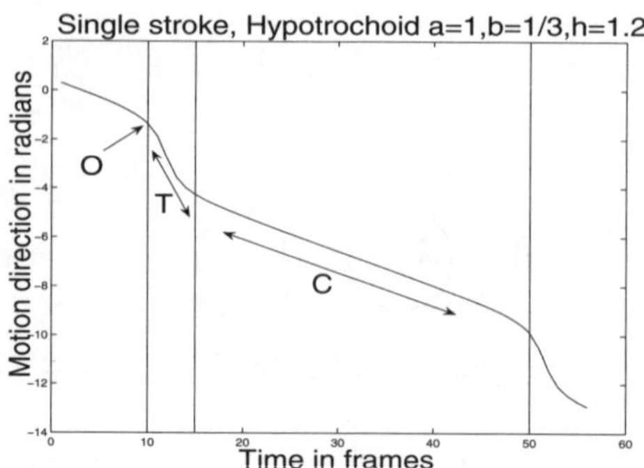

Fig. 7. Single stroke of motion direction with all M_t segments

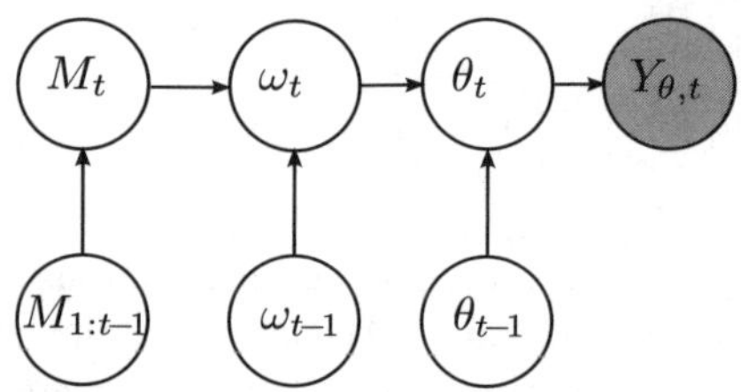

Fig. 8. Motion direction : Single time slice DAG

entropy arguments as those used for the magnitude velocity model apply here, as well; hence we have for $P(\omega_t|\omega_{t-1}, M_t)$:

$$P(\omega_t|\omega_{t-1}, M_t \in \{'O','T'\}) = \mathcal{N}(0, \sigma_T^2)$$
$$P(\omega_t|\omega_{t-1}, M_t ='C') = \mathcal{N}(0, \sigma_C^2)$$

(16)

where $\sigma_T \gg \sigma_C$. Finally, we model $Y_{\theta,t}$ as θ_t plus zero-mean Gaussian noise: $Y_{\theta,t} \sim \mathcal{N}(\theta_t, \sigma_{Y,\theta}^2)$.

3.5 Temporal Expectancy Model for Conducting Gestures

Let us now turn to modeling temporal structure via $P(M_t|M_{1:t-1})$. In most musical circumstances it is safe to assume, at least locally, that the temporal structure of beat onsets is quasi-periodic [6], with a tempo period that changes slowly over time. The fundamental temporal expectancy model discussed in Section 2.1 can be used to model the dependence $P(M_t|M_{1:t-1})$ as first-order Markov by introducing additional variables concerned with the underlying temporal structure. The DAG of the temporal expectancy network used for modeling the more complex temporal structures found in conducting gestures is shown in Fig. 9. Here, T_t encodes the tempo period similar to that of the model proposed in Section 2.1, whereas other variables encode information specific to conducting gestures. For instance, $\alpha_t \in \{'L','S'\}$ denotes the type of articulation expressed at time t namely *legato or staccato*, and anticipating the fusion of

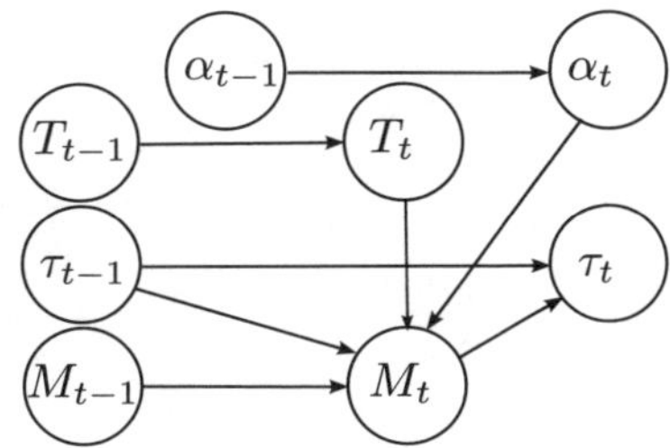

Fig. 9. Single time slice DAG of temporal expectancy model for conducting gesture

Table 2. Behavior of timer variables and computation of elapsed durations under different modes

M_t	$\tau_{1,t}$	$\tau_{2,t}$	$\tau_{ictus,t}$	$\tau_{prep,t}$
$'O1'$	$1/2$	$\tau_{2,t-1}$	$\tau_{1,t}$	$\tau_{1,t} + \tau_{2,t}$
$'T1'$	$\tau_{1,t-1} + 1$	$\tau_{2,t-1}$	$\tau_{1,t}$	$\tau_{1,t} + \tau_{2,t}$
$'C1'$	$\tau_{1,t-1} + 1$	$\tau_{2,t-1}$	$\tau_{1,t}$	$\tau_{1,t} + \tau_{2,t}$
$'O2'$	$\tau_{1,t-1}$	$1/2$	$\tau_{1,t} + \tau_{2,t}$	$\tau_{2,t}$
$'C2'$	$\tau_{1,t-1}$	$\tau_{2,t-1} + 1$	$\tau_{1,t} + \tau_{2,t}$	$\tau_{2,t}$

magnitude velocity and direction features (Section 3.6), we consider M_t as the *union* of all previously described modes; i.e. $M_t \in \{'O1,' T','C1','O2','C2'\}$ as defined in Table 3. In order to compute elapsed durations since the most recent ictus, $\tau_{ictus,t}$ and the most recent preparation, $\tau_{prep,t}$ we propose the use of *dual timer* variables, namely $\tau_{1,t}$, $\tau_{2,t}$ and hence, $\tau_t \in \{\tau_{1,t}, \tau_{2,t}\}$. The joint distribution for the SSM in Fig. 11 factors as per the DAG.

Now we specify the individual distributions implied by the DAG (Fig. 9). As we expect instantaneous tempo deviations to be proportional to the current tempo period, $P(T_t|T_{t-1})$ follows $\log T_t \sim \mathcal{N}(\log T_{t-1}, \sigma_T^2)$, following (1). The timers $\tau_{1,t}$ and $\tau_{2,t}$ evolve deterministically according to the second and third columns of Table 2; i.e.; both $P(\tau_{1,t}|\tau_{1,t-1}, M_t)$ and $P(\tau_{2,t}|\tau_{2,t-1}, M_t)$ concentrate deterministically on these possibilities.

$P(\alpha_t|\alpha_{t-1})$ encodes the assumption that articulation changes infrequently across time; i.e.

$$P(\alpha_t|\alpha_{t-1}) = (a)1_{\{\alpha_t \neq \alpha_{t-1}\}} + (1-a)1_{\{\alpha_t = \alpha_{t-1}\}} \tag{17}$$

where $a \ll 1$. Finally, $P(M_t|M_{t-1}, \tau_{1,t}, \tau_{2,t}, \alpha_t, T_t)$ is used to encode the prior temporal expectancy, which we now discuss.

Since all expectancies considered (ictus; preparation) depend only on the elapsed duration since the previous ictus ($\tau_{ictus,t}$, given by the fourth column of Table 2), we may encode the prior temporal expectancy via $P(M_t|M_{t-1})$. A state transition diagram for $P(M_t|M_{t-1})$ with transition probabilities as functions of α_t, $\tau_{ictus,t}$, and T_t is shown in Fig. 10. Here there are essentially three expectancies to consider: ρ_{ictus}, the expectancy for the next ictus; ρ_{prep}, the expectancy for the preparation, and ρ_{C1}, the expectancy for the end of the transient region.

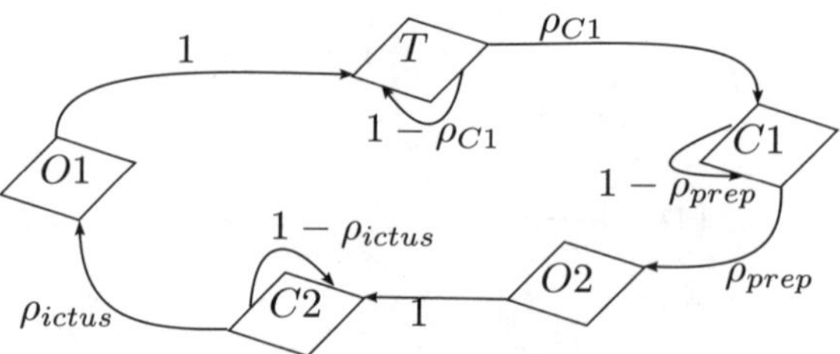

Fig. 10. Fusion: Mode transitions

The ictus expectancy ρ_{ictus} is induced by the quasi-periodic structure of the beat pattern, which depends on the tempo but not on the articulation. We model the inherent elapsed duration between ictii using a random variable L; $\log L \sim \mathcal{N}(\log T_t, \sigma_{\tau,1}^2)$, similar to (6). The probability that a new ictus will occur at time t, given that time $\tau_{ictus,t-1}$ has elapsed since the previous ictus, is the same as the probability $L < \tau_{ictus,t-1} + 1$, given that $L \geq \tau_{ictus,t-1}$. Hence $\rho_{ictus} = \mathrm{Haz}(\tau_{ictus,t-1})$, following (5).

We expect that the preparation expectancy, ρ_{prep}, depends on both tempo and articulation. Nominally the preparation should occur halfway between ictii; however, under staccato articulation depending on the orientation of the conductors hand, the preparation can occur much earlier or later than the midpoint. We model the corresponding elapsed-duration variable,

$$\log L \sim \begin{cases} \mathcal{N}(\log(T_t/2), \sigma_{\tau_L}^2), & \alpha_t =\,'L' \\ \mathcal{N}(\log(T_t/2), \sigma_{\tau_S}^2), & \alpha_t =\,'S' \end{cases} \tag{18}$$

where $\sigma_{\tau_S} \gg \sigma_{\tau_L}$ expresses the much greater deviations attributed to staccato articulation ($\alpha_t =\,'S'$). Then, using similar arguments used for ρ_{ictus} we specify $\rho_{prep} = \mathrm{Haz}(\tau_{ictus,t-1})$ according to (5).

Finally, considering the length of the transient region, we do not explicitly model its dependence on tempo or articulation because we expect it to be very short. Ideally under $h = 1$ for the hypotrochoidal model (Section 3.1), the transient region should have zero length; however under more practical conditions, we expect this region will persist for one or two frames (at a nominal rate of 20 fps). We specify $\rho_{C1} = 1/2$ to model an expected duration of two frames.

3.6 Fusion of Magnitude Velocity and Motion Direction Features with Temporal Expectancy Model

To jointly estimate beat, tempo and articulation as well as infer posterior temporal expectancies regarding ictus and preparation from observed magnitude velocity and motion direction features, we fuse the aforementioned probabilistic models for inherent magnitude velocity (Section 3.3, Fig. 6) and motion direction (Section 3.4, Fig. 8) trends with the prior temporal expectancy model developed above (Section 3.5, Fig. 9). Fig. 11 shows a single time-slice of the resultant DAG. We must remap the mode definitions for the magnitude velocity and motion direction modes for the inherent feature trajectory

Table 3. Correspondence between fusion modes and velocity, motion direction modes

M_t fusion	M_t mag. velocity	M_t motion dir.
$'O1'$	$'O1'$	$'O'$
$'T1'$	$'C1'$	$'T'$
$'C1'$	$'C1'$	$'C'$
$'O2'$	$'O2'$	$'C'$
$'C2'$	$'C2'$	$'C'$

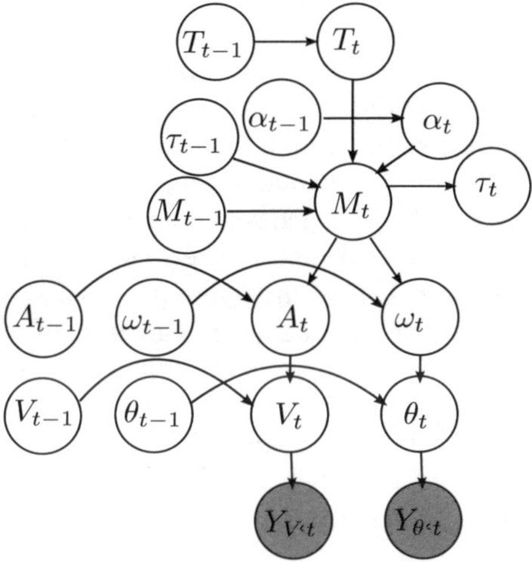

Fig. 11. Single time slice DAG showing fusion of magnitude velocity, motion direction and temporal expectancy models

models. This mapping is given by substituting the first column of Table 3 in place of the second and third columns for velocity and direction, respectively.

All quantities of interest are estimated and derived as follows.

- Mode (M_t) and articulation (α_t), since they are discrete, are estimated by maximizing the filtered posteriors $P(M_t|Y_{V,1:t}, Y_{\theta,1:t})$ and $P(\alpha_t|Y_{V,1:t}, Y_{\theta,1:t})$ respectively. Doing so gives at any instant, the minimum-error estimation given present and past feature observations [18]. Ictus locations are determined those times t where the estimated mode, $\hat{M}_t$, equals $'O1'$. Similarly, preparation onsets are determined when $\hat{M}_t = 'O2'$.
- Tempo, since it is continuous-valued, is estimated as the mean of the filtered posterior $P(T_t|Y_{V,1:t},Y_{\theta,1:t})$, which yields the minimum mean-square error estimator [18].
- The posterior temporal expectancy for the ictus, as defined in Section 1, is computed via $P(M_{t+1} = 'O1'|Y_{V,1:t}, Y_{\theta,1:t})$. Similarly the preparation expectancy is given by $P(M_{t+1} = 'O2'|Y_{V,1:t}, Y_{\theta,1:t})$.
- All posteriors are computed using a standard sequential importance resampling particle filter [2].

The overall preprocessing, feature extraction and inference steps have time complexity which is linear in the number of frames and can be easily implemented in real time.

4   Experimental Results on Real World Conducting Gestures

We have tested our method on extensive real-world data from performances by a novice conductor using a very simple marker set: left and right shoulders, right elbow, right wrist and the baton tip. The raw marker data is first normalized using the algorithm described in Section 3.1 and then magnitude velocity and motion direction features are extracted via (12). The marker data is often noisy due to missing markers and occlusions, and this noise tends to amplify when taking the approximate derivatives required to compute these features. Hence, we apply third-order Savitzky-Golay smoothing [35] to both feature sets before presenting this data to our algorithm. Fig. 12 shows results regarding the real-time estimation of tempo, articulation, and beat positions for a short segment (270 frames at 100 fps; 2.7 seconds) using a metronome running at 90 bpm. Despite the short interval, the tempo and articulation estimates clearly converge to the correct hypotheses within 1.5 seconds and 0.3 seconds respectively. The beat (ictus) segmentation given in the lower half of the figure also makes intuitive sense, as segments are closely allied with cusp minima of the magnitude velocity curve and points of rapid direction change. Fig. 13 shows similar results for the legato case.

In Figs. 14 and 15 the posterior temporal expectancies are compared for these cases. We see that there is no appreciable difference regarding the ictus expectancy; however there is a significant difference regarding the preparation expectancy. With staccato articulation, the preparation expectancy develops earlier and builds up over a longer

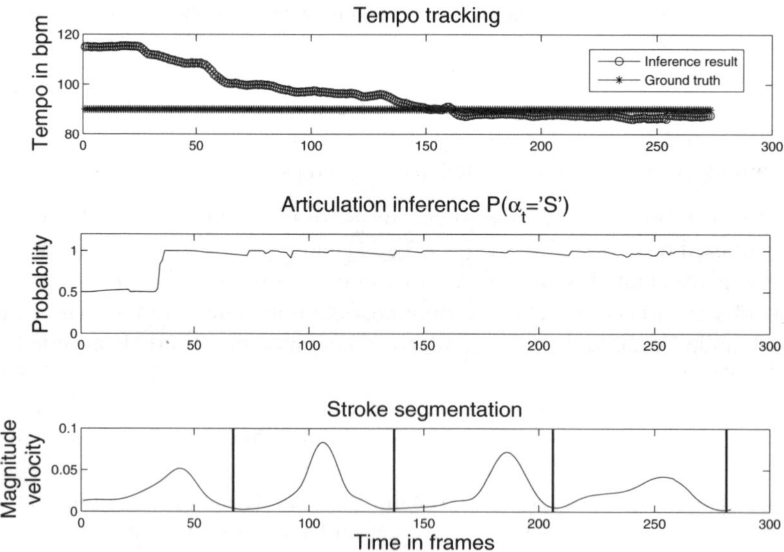

Fig. 12. Inference results on conducting data expressing staccato articulation

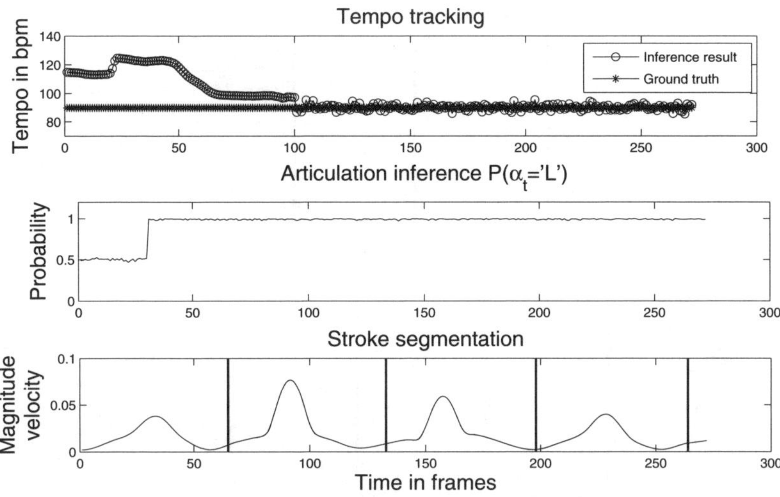

Fig. 13. Inference results on conducting data expressing legato articulation

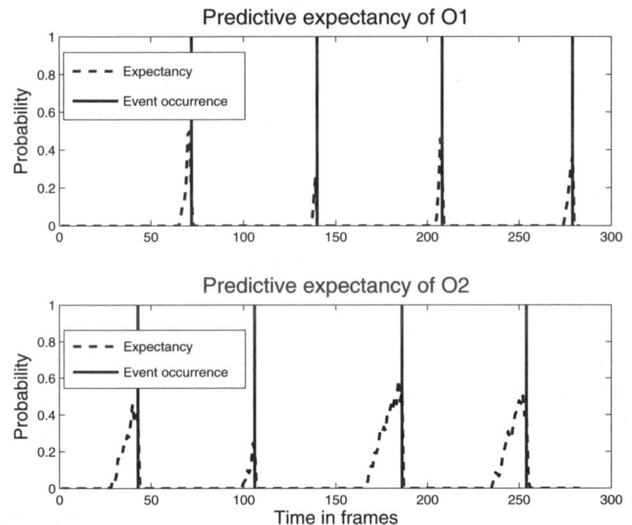

Fig. 14. Predictive posterior expectancy curves of O1,O2 segments along with event occurrences for staccato articulation

period as compared with legato. As discussed in Section 1 a prolonged increase of temporal expectancy is a key component in the build up of tension. Hence our intuitive sense is confirmed that gestures associated with staccato articulation are communicated more strongly. Furthermore, as differences in articulation exhibit such dramatic effects on expectancy variations, while exhibiting rather slight effects on the induction of indicative musical attributes such as beat and tempo, we conclude that it is primarily

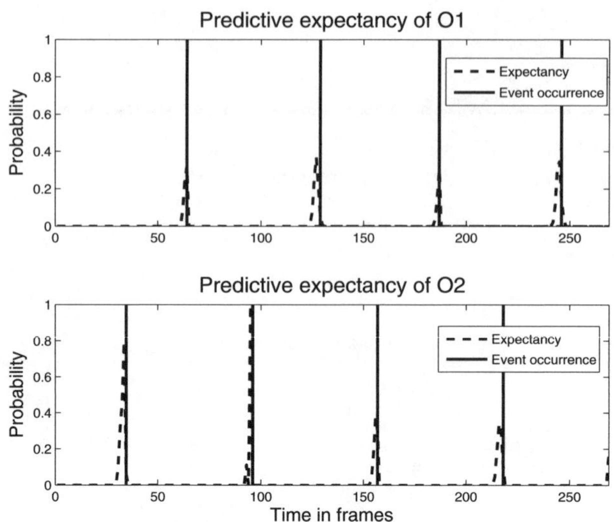

Fig. 15. Predictive posterior expectancy curves of O1,O2 segments along with event occurrences for legato articulation

through temporal expectancy that the very palpable difference in musical expressivity through different articulation styles is communicated.

5   Conclusion

In this paper we have introduced a general Bayesian framework that we call the *temporal expectancy model* and used it to develop a conducting gesture analysis tool for capturing *expressive* and *indicative* qualities based on temporal expectancies. The temporal expectancy model is a type of dynamic Bayesian network (DBN) that can be used to encode prior knowledge regarding temporal structure of event sequences and is capable of adapting this knowledge to uncertain sense-data arriving in real time. It also enables a *joint* approach for event segmentation and temporal structure inference. The conducting analysis tool is capable of jointly inferring beat, tempo (indicative) and articulation (expressive) and inducing temporal expectancies from the baton motion of a conductor. Via temporal expectancy our tool focuses on the expressive and communicative intents underlying the gestures made by a conductor. In fact, our experimental results (Section 4) do confirm an initial speculative hypothesis that musically expressive elements of the conducting gesture are communicated specifically through temporal expectancies.

While the initial realization of our paradigm is rooted in conducting gesture, virtually all of the computational tools can be generalized beyond conducting; for instance our dynamic models of motion features do not assume the standard spatial forms commonly associated with conducting (Section 3.3, Section 3.4) and the prior temporal expectancy framework discussed in Section 3.5 can be attached to entirely different types of features/controls or gestures. We have chosen to focus on "conducting-like" gesture because we believe the associations between gesture and musical expression are quite richly established through this framework.

For future work, we plan to run more extensive tests using a broader population of conductors, experienced as well as novice. Particularly from the experienced conductors we can obtain qualitative feedback on how well the musical expressivity of the gestures are captured. We also intend to generalize our framework to the induction of higher level temporal patterns (for instance meter and related accentual patterns; cf. [31]), such that a greater range of complexities and nuances of temporal expectancies associated with musical rhythm may inform the gestural control of musical expression.

Acknowledgements

We gratefully acknowledge that this material is based upon work supported by the National Science Foundation CISE Infrastructure and IGERT grants Nos. 0403428 & 0504647.

References

1. Ozyurek, S.K.A., Willems, R.M., Hagoort, P.: On-line integration of semantic information from speech and gesture: Insights from event-related brain potentials. Journal of Cognitive Neuroscience 19, 605–616 (2007)
2. Arulampalam, S., Maskell, S., Gordon, N., Clapp, T.: Tutorial on particle filters for on-line nonlinear/non-Gaussian Bayesian tracking. IEEE Transactions on Signal Processing (2001)
3. Barabasi, A.L.: The origin of bursts and heavy tails in human dynamics. Nature 435, 207 (2005)
4. Berger, J., Gang, D.: A neural network model of metric perception and cognition in the audition of functional tonal music. In: International Computer Music Conference (1997)
5. Bregler, C.: Learning and recognizing human dynamics in video sequences. In: International conference on computer vision and pattern recognition (1997)
6. Cemgil, A., Kappen, H.J., Desain, P., Honing, H.: On tempo tracking: Tempogram representation and Kalman filtering. In: Proceedings of the 2000 International Computer Music Conference, pp. 352–355 (2000)
7. Cemgil, A.T.: Bayesian Music Transcription. PhD thesis, Radboud University (2004)
8. Cover, T.M., Thomas, J.A.: Elements of Information Theory. John Wiley and Sons, Chichester (1999)
9. Desain, P.: What rhythm do I have in mind? Detection of imagined temporal patterns from single trial ERP. In: Proceedings of the International Conference on Music Perception and Cognition (ICMPC) (2004)
10. Campana, S.P.M.K.T.E., Silverman, L., Bennetto, L.: Listeners immediately integrate natural combinations of speech and iconic gesture. Language and Cognitive Processes (submitted)
11. Hackney, P.: Making Connections: Total Body Integration Through Bartenieff Fundamentals. Routledge (2000)
12. Hagendoorn, I.G.: Some speculative hypotheses about the nature and perception of dance and choreography. Journal of Consciousness Studies, 79–110 (2004)
13. Hainsworth, S.W.: Techniques for the Automated Analysis of Musical Audio. PhD thesis, University of Cambridge (2003)
14. Holle, H., Gunter, T.C.: The role of iconic gestures in speech disambiguation: ERP evidence. Journal of Cognitive Neuroscience 19, 1175–1192 (2007)

15. Huron, D.: Sweet Anticipation: Music and the Psychology of Expectation (Bradford Books). MIT Press, Cambridge (2006)
16. Jaynes, E.T.: Probability Theory: Logic of Science, Cambridge (2003)
17. Jones, M.R., McAuley, J.D.: Time judgments in global temporal contexts. Perception and Psychophysics, 398–417 (2005)
18. Kay, S.M.: Fundamentals of statistical signal processing: estimation theory. Prentice-Hall, Inc., Englewood Cliffs (1993)
19. Kolesnik, P., Wanderley, M.: Recognition, analysis and performance with expressive conducting gestures. In: International Computer Music Conference (2004)
20. Kutas, M., Federmeier, K.: Electrophysiology reveals semantic memory use in language comprehension. Trends in Cognitive Science 4, 463–470 (2000)
21. Lee, E., Grull, I., Kiel, H., Borchers, J.: conga: A framework for adaptive conducting gesture analysis. In: International Conference on New Interfaces for Musical Expression (2006)
22. Leistikow, R.: Bayesian Modeling of Musical Expectations using Maximum Entropy Stochastic Grammars. PhD thesis, Stanford University (2006)
23. McAuley, J.D.: The effect of tempo and musical experience on perceived beat. Australian Journal of Psychology, 176–187 (1999)
24. Meyer, L.B.: Emotion and Meaning in Music. University Of Chicago Press (1961)
25. Miranda, R.A., Ullman, M.T.: Double dissociation between rules and memory in music: An event-related potential study. NeuroImage 38, 331–345 (2007)
26. Moeslund, T.B., Granum, E.: A survey of computer vision-based human motion capture. Computer Vision and Image Understanding 81, 231–268 (2001)
27. Moeslund, T.B., Hilton, A., Kruger, V.: A survey of advances in vision-based human motion capture and analysis. International Journal of Computer Vision and Image Understanding (2006)
28. Murphy, D., Andersen, T., Jensen, K.: Conducting Audio Files via Computer Vision. In: Camurri, A., Volpe, G. (eds.) GW 2003. LNCS (LNAI), vol. 2915, pp. 529–540. Springer, Heidelberg (2004)
29. Murphy, K.: Dynamic Bayesian Networks:Representation, Inference and Learning. PhD thesis, University of California, Berkeley (2002)
30. Narmour, E.: The Analysis and Cognition of Basic Melodic Structures: The Implication-Realization Model. University of Chicago Press, Chicago (1990)
31. Povel, D.J., Essens, P.: Perception of temporal patterns. Music Perception, 411–440 (1985)
32. Ross, S.: Stochastic Processes. Wiley Interscience, Chichester (1995)
33. Kelly, C.K.S.D., Hopkins, M.: Neural correlates of bimodal speech and gesture comprehension. Brain and Language 89(1), 253–260 (2004)
34. Koelsch, D.S.K.S.T.G.S., Kasper, E., Friederici, A.D.: Music, language and meaning: Brain signatures of semantic processing. Nature Neuroscience 7, 302–307 (2004)
35. Savitzky, A., Golay, M.J.E.: Smoothing and differentiation of data by simplified least squares procedures. Analytical Chemistry, 1627–1639 (1964)
36. Thornburg, H.: Detection and Modeling of Transient Audio Signals with Prior Information. PhD thesis, Stanford University (2005)
37. Thornburg, H., Swaminathan, D., Ingalls, T., Leistikow, R.: Joint segmentation and temporal structure inference for partially-observed event sequences. In: International Workshop on Multimedia Signal Processing (2006)
38. Torresani, L., Hackney, P., Bregler, C.: Learning motion style synthesis from perceptual observations. In: Schölkopf, B., Platt, J., Hoffman, T. (eds.) Advances in Neural Information Processing Systems 19, pp. 1393–1400. MIT Press, Cambridge (2007)
39. Ude, A.: Robust estimation of human body kinematics from video. In: Proc. IEEE/RSJ Conf. Intelligent Robots and Systems (1999)

40. Urtasun, R., Fleet, D.J., Fua, P.: 3d people tracking with gaussian process dynamical models. In: IEEE Conference on Computer Vision and Pattern Recognition (2006)
41. Usa, S., Mochida, Y.: A multi-modal conducting simulator. In: International Computer Music Conference (1978)
42. Weisstein, E.W.: MathWorld–A Wolfram Web Resource, `http://mathworld.wolfram.com/hypotrochoid.html`
43. Wu, Y.C., Coulson, S.: Meaningful gestures: Electrophysiological indices of iconic gesture comprehension. Psychophysiology 42, 654–667 (2005)
44. Wu, Y.C., Coulson, S.: How iconic gestures enhance communication: An ERP study. Brain and Language (in press, 2007)
45. Xenakis, I.: Formalized Music. Pendragon Press, Stuyvesant (1992)
46. Zanto, T.P., Snyder, J.S., Large, E.W.: Neural correlates of rhythmic expectancy. Advances in Cognitive Psychology, 221–231 (2006)

Musicians Outperform Nonmusicians in Speech Imitation

Barbara Pastuszek-Lipińska

Adam Mickiewicz University, School of English, al. Niepodległości 4,
61-874 Poznań, Poland
energin@wp.pl

Abstract. Recently can be observed a growing interest in the effects of music on humans. Music has been called a food or a multi-sensory fitness of the brain. Many studies have already confirmed that practice and active involvement in music improve spatio-temporal functions, verbal memory, visuo-spatial abilities, reading, self-esteem, and generally cognitive processes. In the present paper, a general overview of research on the influence of music on humans has been provided. Moreover, it has been presented data on a research project, which was conducted with the aim to examine whether music education may be viewed as one of the factors, that improve second language acquisition.

Keywords: musicianship, musical abilities, foreign language acquisition, speech perception, auditory functions, cognition.

1 General Characteristics of Music Education

The faculty of music is, in a sense, unique to humans. Humans are the only creatures who have developed notation, who compose music, and who are able to learn to play and sing music as well as play instruments in a group. All activities in the music faculty – e.g. music performance, playing an instrument, singing, composing, etc. – are very demanding, requiring sophisticated abilities and skills whose attainment demands conscious and goal-directed practice.

Music education and training engages all human senses and involves all cognitive processes (sensory, perceptual and cognitive learning, memory, emotion, etc.), but it also requires motor activation (utilized while playing an instrument) and appropriate articulation (utilized while singing or playing).

1.1 Influence of Music on Humans – Musicians Versus Nonmusicians

While it is well documented that the human brain is a dynamic rather than a stable system, there are still relatively few data answering the question of whether the plasticity of neural circuits is accompanied by changes in behaviour [19].

Several factors may influence neural circuits and one of those factors seems to be music education and training, which alters the organization of the auditory and somatosensory cortices in people active in music domain. Research that conceives of music

R. Kronland-Martinet, S. Ystad, and K. Jensen (Eds.): CMMR 2007, LNCS 4969, pp. 56–73, 2008.

as an important medium for understanding the human cognitive processes and development, as well as the human brain, is relatively new.

The topic gained more attention after the study done by Bever and Chiarello in 1974 [3], in which they examined the patterns of cerebral dominance among musicians and nonmusicians and found that intensive musical training resulted in the modification of hemispheric lateralization during music processing. After the study, the traditional view of a hemispheric dichotomy in which music was processed in the right hemisphere and language in the left could not be maintained, as there was evidence that professional musicians processed music in the left hemisphere and nonmusicians processed it in the right hemisphere.

Most of the work in this field has been done in the last ten years. According to many investigators, the human brain is both functionally and structurally adaptable to environmental stimuli, as well as to different kinds of requirements and even injury-related impairments. One of the most vital topics is the question of how musicians' brains differ from the brains of nonmusicians. Several studies have reported that there is generally a high degree of plasticity in the brains of trained musicians. Several of the most recent studies reveal that the brains of musicians and nonmusicians differ in terms of function and structure/anatomy.

Some functional differences have been observed by Ohnishi and co-workers, who found that there is "a distinct cerebral activity pattern in the auditory association areas and prefrontal cortex of trained musicians" [17].

In a detailed discussion of the structural and functional brain differences between musicians and nonmusicians, Schlaug enumerated several anatomical adaptations. He reported differences in the corpus callosum that had been observed by himself and his co-workers in a study, which revealed that the anterior half of the corpus callosum was significantly larger in musicians. This difference was particularly noticeable when contrasting musicians who started training early (<7 years old) with musicians who started music lessons late (>7 years); however, the difference between the brain structures of musicians and nonmusicians was still more significant.

Schlaug also mentioned that there was greater symmetry in the intrasulcal length of the posterior bank of the precentral gyrus in musicians [25], and thus there were differences in the motor cortices of musicians and nonmusicians. Schlaug also cited studies whose results suggested "microstructural adaptations in the human cerebellum in response to early commencement and continual practice of complicated bimanual finger sequences" [25].

These results were posited to suggest that there might be differences between musicians and nonmusicians that were indeed the result of microstructural changes caused by long-term motor activity and motor skill acquisition. Schlaug also provided evidence of regional differences in gray matter volume between musicians and nonmusicians. More specifically, "professional musicians showed higher gray matter concentrations compared to nonmusicians in the perirolandic region, the premotor region, the posterior superior parietal region, the posterior mesial perisylvian region bilaterally, and the cerebellum" [25].[1]

---

[1] "The superior parietal cortex does play an important role in music performance, since it may serve to integrate of visual and auditory information with motor planning activities" [25].

Several empirical studies have also provided other evidence of functional brain differences between musicians and nonmusicians, specifically in the area of auditory processing. The main observation, that was reported by the studies and discussed by Schlaug, concerns the processing of music and the processing of several musical tasks, which seemed to be different in musicians as compared to nonmusicians; musicians apparently "process music in a different way" [25]. The results showed that music is processed by the brains of musicians by both the right and left hemispheres. It appears from the studies cited by Schlaug that the group of musicians, especially musicians with absolute pitch, demonstrated "an increased leftsided asymmetry of the planum temporale" [25].

Other structural brain changes that have resulted from musical training have been reported in a study by Gaser and Schlaug [6]. Specifically, they found that "areas with a significant positive correlation between musician status and increase in gray matter volume were found in perirolandic regions including primary motor and somatosensory areas, premotor areas, anterior superior parietal areas, and in the inferior temporal gyrus bilaterally" [6]. Also these findings suggest that intensive musical training may generate changes in the human brain.

Similarly, other studies have reported that cortical plasticity and reorganization of cortical representations have occurred due to musical training. The results of those studies revealed that increased auditory cortical representation has been observed in musicians.

Pantev and his co-workers performed a comparison of musicians who were proficient with string instrument and nonmusicians. This comparison found that cerebral representation of the cortical sources responsible for the fingers of the left hand, which are intensively used in string instruments, was increased among the musicians as compared with the controls. Therefore, Pantev and his colleagues proved that "music education and training is reflected in the organization of auditory and somatosensory representational cortex in musicians" [19]. The reported cortical response for stimulation was dependent on the age at which the musicians had started their musical training.

Similar results were observed in a study that provided auditory stimuli. On the basis of these findings, Pantev and his colleagues suggested that "intensive training can trigger a functional adaptation of the cortical organization" and induce plastic changes of the human brain [19].

It should be noted that neuroplastic adaptations in the auditory cortex and changes in auditory evoqued responses have been to date observed both in children [5] and in adults [26].

1.2 Nature or Nurture

Although the number and range of studies confirming the impact of musical training on humans is growing quickly, there is still doubt as to whether these changes are due to experience, or whether they are innate.

To answer that question, Lahav and his colleagues, among others, conducted experiments that revealed the existence of a functional linkage between actions and sounds. They taught musically naïve subjects to play a melody on the piano by ear.

The subjects were then divided into three groups – the piano-listening group[2], the "nature-listening"[3] group, and the practicing group – and over the course of one week they participated in three additional 20-minute listening/practicing sessions. After this period, the subjects' ability to play the previously learned melody was tested. The results revealed that the practicing group performed better than other groups, which is not surprising. However, the piano-listening group performed significantly better than the nature-listening group. The authors found that even passive listening to music influenced the motor performance of musically naïve subjects (the piano-listening group), and concluded that the findings may suggest that "during passive listening, neural mechanisms linking sounds and actions may implicitly facilitate musical motor performance" [12].

All of the presented studies reveal that musical practice may generate changes in both the motor and auditory areas of the brain, and that sounds and actions may interact implicitly.

The number of experiments and studies in which differences between musicians and nonmusicians were demonstrated in the results is more significant than cited above. The purpose of introducing this small sample was to provide data on the neurological evidence showing how musical training may change humans' brains. The evidence has attracted the interest of several researchers (including the present author) and has prompted the question of whether the training may also result in behavioral changes and/or affect other human abilities and disciplines, including those that use similar patterns (in this case, sounds).

According to Pantev and his collaborators "to induce plastic alterations" active practice is needed. The authors also highlighted that it was best to begin training early in life [19]. They also suggested that it is possible to adapt cortical organization even in adulthood, but added that "adults have to work harder" [19].

Research on music perception has established that "the cognition of music is underpinned by the human ability to extract, store and manipulate a range of abstract structural representations from a complex multi-dimensional stimulus stream" [14]. Moreover, musical training fosters other abilities, such as attention, motivation, concentration, and general discipline.

Thus, from the cited studies it is clear that music education may generate changes in structure and function of humans' brains. However, the question of the behavioural effects of sensory experience still requires more attention and examination [23]. Interdisciplinary approaches are needed to examine whether the observed plastic alterations are important only in music or perhaps affect also other human activities. Currently can be observed an ongoing debate on the possibility of transfer between the music and other cognitive domains. In the paper most attention is given to the influence of musical training on foreign language (speech) acquisition.

1.3   Is the Transfer Music-Language Possible?

A number of studies revealed that a range of factors affects language acquisition and various processes take place during the acquisition. Although the first component of

---

[2] The participants listened to the same melody that was played by practicing group.
[3] The participant listened to the sounds of nature.

language development, which is appropriate brain and the whole nervous system organization, seems to be crucial, however, several other factors such as e.g. environmental, emotional and motivational ones cannot be omitted.

It has been well documented that transfer effects are possible and tend to occur between the specific area of training and other areas that present similar contexts [32]. In the case of music education researchers have also found correlations between dissimilar contexts and domains. Several previous studies provided evidence of positive associations between music education and general intelligence as well as mathematical skills. Other abilities were positively associated with music education as well, such as spatio-temporal reasoning, verbal memory, visuo-spatial abilities, reading, self-esteem, and others.

Only a limited number of studies examined a possible impact of music education on language acquisition (e.g. [9], [13], [31], [32]). Moreover, there is a still ongoing discussion on the level of relationship. Namely, it is examined whether music education, music exposure or musicality improve human potential in language acquisition [24].

Jackendoff [8] mentioned the possible transfer indirectly. He claimed that "there must be levels of mental representation at which information conveyed by language is compatible with information from other peripheral systems such as vision, nonverbal audition, smell, kinaesthesia, and so forth. If there were no such levels, it would be impossible to use language to report sensory input" [8].

When looking for the possible transfer between musical training and language several approaches have been proposed. The approaches have been mainly based on the fact that training in music requires engagement and refinement of processes involved in the analysis of pitch patterns over time and then the processes may be activated during interpretation of emotions conveyed by spoken utterances. Indeed, some recent studies have provided evidence confirming the relationship (cf. [9], [31], [32]).

Some of the processes are shared by both language and music (e.g. discrimination of emotional meaning, acoustical cues), several of them are domain-specific. To date the issue has been noticed in several studies (e.g. [31], [32]). For instance, in two of their experiments Thompson, Schellenberg and Husain [31] examined the hypothesis that music lessons generate positive transfer effects that influence speech perception. The authors provided evidence that musically trained participants outperformed untrained examinees in extracting prosodic information from speech and they suggested the existence of cognitive transfer between music and speech. They have also claimed that music lessons improve the ability to extract prosodic cues as well as the ability to interpret speech prosody.

Recently, also other researchers have reported interrelations between music training and prosody processing. For instance, Palmer and Hutchins [18] highlighted the rising neurological evidence suggesting a direct connection between musical and linguistic prosody. Specifically, subjects who have impairment in musical discrimination and perception very often encounter similar impairments in the discrimination and perception of linguistic prosody [22].

Music education and training seem to stimulate mechanisms of straightening brain circuits that are involved in the performance of different tasks. Schön, Magne, and Besson compared how musicians and nonmusicians detect pitch contour violations in music and in language [27]. They found that subjects with extensive musical training were able to detect very small frequency manipulations in both music and speech, while subjects without such training could not do so.

Moreno and Besson have also conducted a set of event-related brain potential studies that examined the influence of musical training on pitch processing in children. Specifically, they provided children with eight weeks of musical training, and found that after this short period of time, changes in pitch processing in language could be noted [14].

Similar results were also reported in another study by Magne, Schön, and Besson [13], who reported in an ERP study that 3 to 4 years of extended musical training enabled children to outperform others who had not had such training in the detection of pitch violation in both music and speech. Thus, they have also provided evidence of positive transfer effects between music and language, and of a common pitch-processing mechanism in language and music perception [13].

Dodane has found some other interactions between musical and linguistic education, having focused on early second language acquisition. More specifically, Dodane conducted several experiments examining the second-language acquisition abilities of musically trained children versus those of children who had not had music lessons. She analyzed the analogies between musical and verbal forms and conducted her analyses at two levels: the global (prosody) and the local (segmental). The treatment at the global level involved pitch contour tracking, while the local treatment involved a detailed analysis of intervals in music and of the phonemic contrasts (relations between formant frequencies and phonemes) in language. Dodane compared the performance of the musically trained children with that of the non-musically trained children and found that at an early stage, music education plays an important role in learning second language, as a musically trained ear is better prepared to perceive both the intonation and the melody of a foreign language, as well as the phonetic contrasts [4].

The present author conducted a study that involved shadowing speech (i.e. stimuli repeated just after listening). She asked a pool of 106 musicians and nonmusicians (Poles) to repeat – among others – the question "May I help you?" after they had heard it three times; then she recorded their attempts. These productions were randomly presented to 7 native speakers of English, who gave their scores on them. The data revealed that musicians received better scores and were rated as being closer to native speaker production. Pastuszek-Lipińska interpreted the finding as preliminary evidence that musicians are better at perceiving and producing foreign language sounds than are nonmusicians [21]. Moreover, the finding revealed that musicians better that nonmusicians deal with foreign speech material.

Another interesting proof of the influences exerted by music education on foreign language acquisition was substantiated by Jakobson and her coworkers, who provided evidence that musical training improved auditory temporal processing skills. As a consequence, enhanced verbal memory performance was observed in musicians, and these improved skills enabled them to learn foreign languages more easily [9].

A study by Alexander, Wong, and Bradlow [2] provided evidence that musical background can influence lexical tone perception. They conducted two experiments in order to examine whether speech and music are indeed separate mental processes, as was suggested by several earlier studies. In the course of the study, they found another proof that certain aspects of music and speech may be shared between the two domains. More specifically, they provided evidence of overlapping in the processing of fundamental frequencies in both music and speech, and showed that this overlap is more visible in musicians than in nonmusicians. In a set of two perception experiments, American-English-speaking musicians proved to be more successful in identifying and discriminating lexical tones than their nonmusician counterparts. This suggests that experience with music pitch processing may facilitate the processing of lexical pitches as well.

More recently, Norton and her collaborators supported the suggestions that music and language processing may be linked, based on observed similarities in auditory and visual pattern recognition. They also suggested that language and music processing may share the neural substrates, due to innate abilities or implicit learning during early development [16].

Slevc and Miyake [28] examined whether there is a link between musical ability and second language proficiency in adults. They have demonstrated that such a relationship exists and that people "who are good at analyzing, discriminating, and remembering simple musical stimuli are better at accurately perceiving and producing L2 sounds" [28].

Moreover, a number of studies have substantiated the assertion that auditory abilities may be improved through auditory training, and that such training may be either linguistic or musical, as this kind of training affects auditory perception in general (cf. [15], [11]).

Thus, the presented data reveal that musical training may in fact exert an influence on language acquisition, and that this is possible even after a short period of training. Still, it seems that the range of existing evidence requires new approaches and analyses, and the issue of an interdomain relationship has not been sufficiently examined.

2 Research Design

A research study has been developed with the aim to investigate relationship between music education and second language acquisition. The focus was given to sounds and construct perception and production. The main goal of the study was to examine whether active involvement in music has influenced second language acquisition.

2.1 The Corpus

82 word sequences in 6 languages: American English (15), British English (14), Belgian Dutch (11), French (10), Italian (10), European Spanish European (6), South American Spanish (4), and Japanese (10) have been synthesized for the corpus. The ScanSoft® RealSpeak™ application was used for the purpose.

Languages were chosen according to the typological classification. Stimuli involved both stress-timed, syllable-timed and moraes-timed languages. Amongst the sentences were questions, statements, and orders. The corpus also contained some phonological words, names and/or other short word sequences.

Thus, the stimuli differed phonemically and phonostylistically and contained a variety of lexical items; the length of the sequences was diversified as well. All word sequences were recorded on CD, and were repeated three times each, with short gaps left between the repetitions of each sequence and a longer pause after each sequence that provided speakers with time needed to repeat the sentence. In this way, a recorded corpus was developed, which served for further data collection.

2.2 Participants

A group of 106 subjects was examined: all of the participants were native speakers of Polish, but the participants had varying levels of language competence, and some had had musical education and training while others had not. All subjects were recruited in the Lodz and Kutno areas and participated in the study they had given verbal consent on a voluntary basis. They were not paid for their participation in the study. All subjects were aged from 15 to 69 years, with a mean age of 32 (median 28). All subjects reported that they had normal hearing, although some of them filled out in questionnaires that they had some hearing-related illnesses in the past (e.g. otitis, other temporal impairments). As well, some of the subjects who were advanced in age could have had age-related hearing changes.

While planning the research, it was intended that there would be two groups, the first composed of nonmusicians and the second composed of professional musicians (who had studied music through secondary school, in Poland it is usually after 10-12 years of education).

2.3 Questionnaire

For the purpose of the study, a special questionnaire was developed. The questionnaire was designed to elicit information on each participant's sex, age, education (including the start date of their musical education and training, as well as their contact with foreign languages), music exposure, occupation, job, interests, and health (subjects were asked to give information on previous hearing problems and all illnesses that could have a negative impact on their hearing).

Although prospective participants were informed prior to the study that the main criterion of participation in the procedure was musicianship, several inconsistencies and instances of contradictory data were noticed during data analysis. After the pretest had been completed and background information had been gathered from participants in the main procedure, it was noticed that both the first classification (of musical competence) and the second one (of language competence) did not sufficiently describe the subjects, and that the earlier expectations could not be fully reached. For instance, some professional musicians who had had 10-12 years of musical education were currently not active in music, and some subjects who claimed to be nonmusicians had some musical experience in childhood. There was also a small group of subjects – nonmusicians - who, even without any formal training, had performed as non-professional amateur musicians. Some subjects could not be classified according to the current division.

The aspect of language experience was ignored, as it was almost impossible to find subjects who had no background in any language other than their native one. Instead, data on the language experience previous to the study have been collected.

2.4 Research Procedure

The current study, which was aimed at investigating the issues discussed in the previous sections, included several steps. The first step investigated participants' musical skills and memory for music sequences. The second step examined how musicians and nonmusicians tackled foreign language word sequences.

It should be noted that the successful realisation of the task, which consisted of shadowing repetitions (repeated just after listen to), has been recognised as a good indicator of phonological short-term memory. This, in turn, has been recognised as a predictor of language learning success [7]. The digitized productions of the participants were analysed and examined, using several different tests and experiments so as to obtain a view of how musicians' and nonmusicians' productions differ; some data that may be relevant in answering this question are posited in the current paper.

The procedure also aimed to evaluate which language components caused the greatest challenges to examinees; thus, the speakers' productions were analyzed both at the segmental (local) and the suprasegmental (global) levels.

2.5 Test of Musical Abilities

In order to gather data on the musical skills of the participants, a special test designed to examine their musical abilities was developed. The test was not a standardized test, but it was developed so as to examine general musical skills and memory for music stimuli in a short time. Thus, subjects without any musical background participated in a test of musical competence and abilities [20].

The test was prepared with the following tasks: participants were asked to repeat 5 tones, sing 4 words according to the model presented on a CD. They were also asked to respond to 4 sets of tones and chords: a tone, a chord of three musical tones with the middle tone to repeat, two tones with the lower tone to repeat and finally a chord of three tones with the highest tone to repeat. Participants were then asked to compare of two melodies that were slightly different in rhythm and in pitch, to compare a short melody when produced in a major key and then in a minor key, and then to reproduce 4 rhythms by clapping hands. Results of the test are provided in Figure 1.

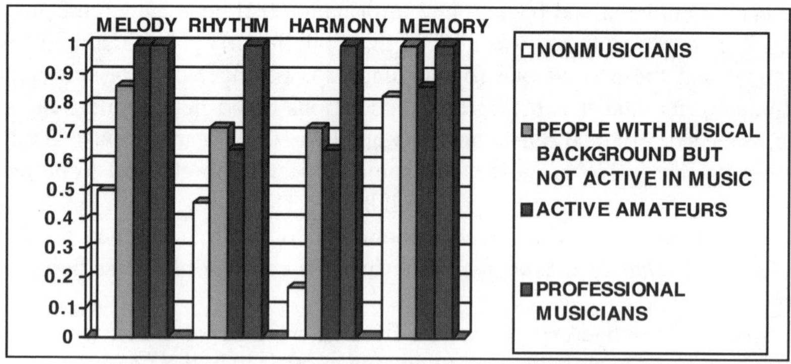

Fig. 1. Results of the test of musical abilities

All the tasks were recorded with Sharp MD-MT200 portable recorder and UNI-TRA-Tonsil Microphone MCU-53 with a linear characteristic, and then the author developed a CD with the tasks and recorded instructions. The task lasted around 5 minutes. The test of musical skills was based on the standard entrance tests to music schools in Poland; it contained similar tasks to those that are included in that standardized tests of musical skills, but the number of questions was limited. On the basis of the pre-test results, it was assumed that all musicians were able to pass the tasks without any problems. The assumption was also based on real-life cases – namely, it is not possible to start and then continue one's musical education without successful completion of the described test.

Nonmusicians' responses to musical stimuli were not recorded. The present author rated their productions auditorily[4]; she used a three-grade scale to evaluate four abilities – pitch tracking, rhythmic skills, harmonic hearing, and memory for music stimuli. Results were noted in questionnaires that had been earlier prepared separately for each participant. It can be seen that nonmusicians' performances differed significantly.

2.6 Main Procedure

Subjects' ability to imitate foreign language phrases was tested. The task was meant to examine an ability to integrate different components of linguistic information such as: phonology, syntax, and intonation. The task was meant to examine the participants' ability to integrate different components of linguistic information, such as phonology, syntax, and intonation. The task was not a pure measure of the enumerated components, but was instead aimed at finding a key to success or failure in the acquisition of language sounds and structures (perception and production).

Table 1. Example sentences used in the study

Language	Material
American English	Sorry to keep you waiting.
Belgian Dutch	Een fantastisch spektakel.
British English	Is it yours?
French	Tout le monde!
Italian	La storia si ripete.
Japanese	Konnichiwa.
Spanish	Más vale tarde que nunca.

Subjects were asked to repeat as accurately as they could some synthetic foreign language word sequences played on a CD player (Grundig) placed in a quiet area. No other information was given to the subjects. Examinees were not informed that they heard synthetic stimuli. Subjects' productions were recorded with Sharp MD-MT200 portable recorder and UNITRA-Tonsil Microphone MCU-53 with a linear characteristic. Example sentences are provided in the Table 1.

---

[4] As the present author is a professional musician and has graduated from the Academy of Music, she was able to evaluate the productions of subjects.

The data were collected in different areas, not in a laboratory, which was not available to the author. Thus, the prepared technical equipment enabled the author to move about easily and reach the subjects in different places, even at their homes.

All recordings were carefully listened to and analyzed. The main goal was to determine whether subjects with different musical expertise perform at the same, similar or different level. It was assumed that there might be differences among subjects (and statistically among groups). It was also assumed that subjects' performances might differ between languages, due to their typological differences.

2.7 Data Analysis

The study did not aim to ascertain solely whether musicians repeated word sequences better than nonmusicians, also aimed to determine which aspects or components of language caused both groups the greatest difficulties. Another aim was to observe whether accuracy at the global level accompanied with accuracy at the local level. In order to discover the exact differences in the mispronunciations, all the word sequences were analyzed.

The author rated the speech samples by auditory analysis. Recordings were examined in a randomized order and after a period of more than one year from data collection so that to ensure unbiased evaluation of all performances.

In the first round of data analysis the scoring procedure was based mainly on a general review and observation whether all speakers responded to the stimuli and were able to repeat the speech material in the given time and accurately. It was noticed that almost all subjects encountered difficulty with at least one sentence.

In order to evaluate whether the task was not too difficult the Difficulty Factor, which optimal level equals 0.5 and which is usually used to check the proportion of respondents who were able to give the right answer to a given question or task, was calculated.

The difficulty factor may be calculated using the following formula:

$$D = c / n. \tag{1}$$

D - difficulty factor,
c - number of correct answers,
n - number of respondents.

As the main purpose of the study was to discriminate between different levels of performance, thus items with difficulty values between 0.3 and 0.7 would be most effective. In the study, the factor shows that the applied procedure and its difficulty were close to optimum and the task was feasible. Namely the factor equals 0.56, in case of musicians, and 0.39, in nonmusicians which means that the task was available for both groups of speakers.

Not all subjects were able to repeat all the stimuli. The mean number of correct repetitions (i.e. these very close to the original samples) was 45.95. It should be noted that data presented in the paper refer to the stimuli taken as whole word sequences. It means that even a very slight error caused to admit a production to be incorrect.

As showed in Figure 2, musicians encountered fewer difficulties in speech repetition and produced 56.53 of correct responses to 82 provided stimuli.

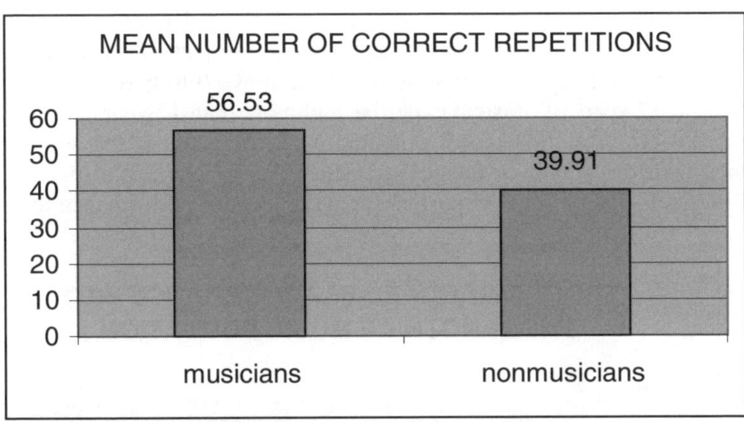

Fig. 2. Mean number of correct responses

Nonmusicians performed significantly worse than musicians and produced 39.91 of correct repetitions. It means that 65.53% of musicians' and 46.55% of nonmusicians' productions were rated as correct.

In Figure 3 below, the graph with all correct performances of all participants of the study is presented.

The presented data may suggest that musicians could have better memory, and this parameter enabled them to perform better during the whole study. They just encountered fewer difficulties with remembering speech passages thus it may be assumed that they encountered fewer boundaries with the task.

It was found that a number of correct productions differed among languages. It was reported that most musicians repeated all stimuli on time, however not all productions were fully faithful to the original.

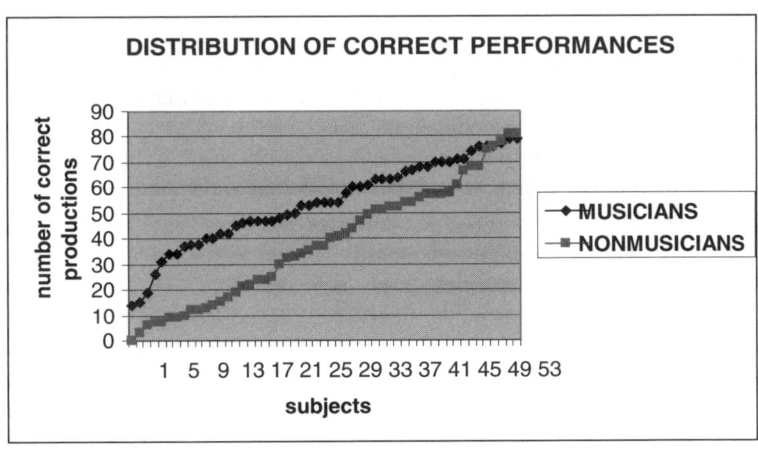

Fig. 3. Number of correct performances

Detailed analysis of all questionnaires revealed that 14 nonmusicians had had in the past some musical background. Therefore, all subjects were divided into four groups: without any musical training in the past, above 0 to 6 years of music education, from 7 to 12 years of musical expertise and more than 12 years.

In Figure 4 are presented scores obtained by participants of the study grouped in accordance with the length of musical training. The graphs reveal that even several years of musical education in the past affected the level of performance in the study.

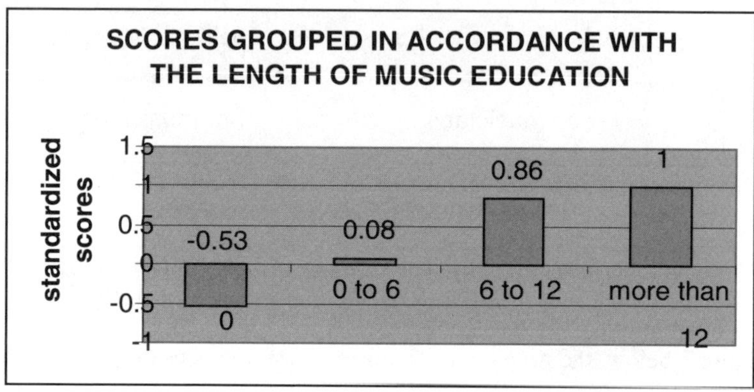

Fig. 4. Scores obtained by subjects with different musical background

This result clearly shows that music training influences humans' ability to perceive and produce foreign language speech sequences.

2.8 More Detailed Data Analysis

As one of the aims of the study was to establish what types of errors were produced by participants, the recorded data were listened to and as far as possible all inconsistencies and errors produced by the speakers were analyzed and assessed. Special attention was given to all mispronunciations that occurred systematically and in several speakers in the same words' or sounds' sequences.

Some mispronunciations and inconsistencies were observed at both segmental and suprasegmental levels, cf. [5]. It was determined that many subjects, more likely nonmusicians than musicians, changed several segments, repeated word sequences closer to Polish pronunciation, and did not follow appropriate production in foreign languages.

Moreover, it was observed that the modifications referred to vowels (e.g. their quality and length), consonants, and consonantal clusters as well. Interestingly, the least problems were encountered for intonation as both groups performed at similar level.

Several productions could be described as completely unintelligible in term of segmental level, however, with appropriate mimicry of speech melody. This may resulted of the so called phonemic restoration phenomenon observed in both music and in speech. Kashino [10], among others, claimed that "the sounds we hear are not copies of physical sounds" and "what we perceive is the result of [an] unconscious interpretation" [10]. This means that auditory perception is a subconscious process which is influenced by our experience and generally depends on the condition and sensitivity of our nervous system. In other words the previous experience can be used in supplying which phoneme or which tone is missing in a word or a music sequence, respectively. According to Aiello, "the occurrence of categorical perception and of restoration effects in speech and music demonstrates a certain level of commonality of processing across these two domains" [1].

Most commonly present mispronunciations that could be observed in almost all the word sequences were: lack of differentiation of the length of vowels occurring in a given sentence, change of vowels' quality, difficulties with repetition of longer or more complex sentences, replacement of voiced consonants into voiceless ones and vice versa, respectively. In many cases subjects were not able to repeat either whole words or their parts (e.g. syllables, segments).

Errors of segmentation were an important source of mistakes. It was observed that mispronunciation of one segment (e.g. a consonant) resulted in other mispronunciations in neighboring segments (e.g. a vowel), and vice versa. It should be also pointed out that different types of errors occurred in almost all participants' productions and almost all of them encountered some difficulties in appropriate realization of the task as a whole.

Subjects produced both errors of performance (slips of the tongue) and errors of competence (pronunciation) [30]. Moreover, in subjects' mimicry occurred some both native and foreign interferences.

The significant discrepancy between the quality of performance on segmental and suprasegmental level was observed. This may suggest that segmental and suprasegmental features are processed separately and that musicians better than nonmusicians coordinate and consolidate the independent psychoacoustic processes.

2.9 Correlations and Statistical Analysis

Pearson correlations were performed in order to establish relationship between results achieved by speakers and their musicianship, results achieved in the memory test for music stimuli, number of years of music education, number of years of learning foreign languages, and results of the whole test of music abilities.

Table 2. Recapitulation of all correlations

Variable	Variable	Correlation vs. probability level
MUS	MEAN	r=.40, p<.0001
MEM	MEAN	r=.35, p<.0002
N/Y/MUS	N/ RES	r=.38, p<.0001
START/MUS	MEAN	r=.24, p<.01
MUS	N/ RES	r=.36, p<.0001
MUS/SKILLS	N/RES	r=.43, p<.0001
ATT	N/RES	r=.50, p<.0001

Legend: *MUS* – musicianship, *MEM* - memory, *N/Y/MUS* - number of years of musical training, *START/MUS* - the age of start of musical training, *MUS/SKILLS* - musical skills, *ATT* - attitude towards learning languages, *MEAN* - mean results, *N/RES* - number of correct responses.

Pearson correlation determines the extent to which values of two variables are related. Correlation coefficients can range from -1.00 to +1.00. The value of -1.00 indicates a perfect *negative* correlation of two variables while a value of +1.00 indicates a perfect *positive* correlation. A value of 0.00 reveals a lack of correlation.

Examined variables are positively correlated, however, the correlations are small and moderate. Table 2 contains recapitulation of all correlations.

Comparison of mean results achieved by the two groups under research revealed that their performances differed significantly. Both Median and Mean values obtained by the two groups are close to each other, which means that there were not many residuals in both groups of examinees (Median 54, mean 53.74 for musicians and 37 and 38.17 for nonmusicians, respectively).

In turn, more important differences between SD in nonmusicians suggest that this group was not very coherent, and in the group were many subjects who were able to deal very well with the task but also many subjects whose performances were very poor. In addition the higher IQR[5] in nonmusicians (39) suggested less coherence of the group and more differences between subjects' performance.

Table 3. Comparative descriptive analysis of mean scores obtained by two groups of examinees

	MUSICIANS		NONMUSICIANS	
n	53		53	
mean	53.74		38.17	
SD	16.71		23.11	
SE	2.29		3.17	
95% CI of mean	49.130	to 58.341	31.801	to 44.539

	Median	**IQR**	**95% CI of Median**	
MUSICIANS	54.000	26.000	47.000	to 63.000
NONMUSICIANS	37.000	39.000	24.000	to 51.000

To check the main hypothesis, that musicians should outperform nonmusicians in the repetition of sentences in a foreign language, the t-test for independent samples was performed, and its results are provided in Table 4, below.

The t-test for independent samples, which tests whether or not two means are significantly different from each other, proved that the two groups did indeed perform their tasks with different levels of accuracy. Results of the t-test suggest that the differences between performances of musicians and nonmusicians are statistically significant.

---

[5] The Inter-Quartile Range is a measure of the spread of or dispersion within a data set. The IQR is the width of an interval which contains the middle 50% of the sample, so it is smaller than the range and its value is less affected by outliers.

Table 4. Results of t-test for independent samples

N	106			
STAND/GEN by				
MUSICIANSHIP	n	Mean	SD	SE
0	53	-0.361	1.073	0.1474
1	53	0.361	0.776	0.1066
Difference between means	-0.723			
95% CI	-1.083	To -0.362		
t statistic	-3.97			
2-tailed p	0.0001			

3   Conclusions

Production scores obtained in the general analysis evidenced that musicians performed better than nonmusicians in the whole experiment. The trained people were able to repeat more sentences and word sequences and with fewer errors.

An analysis of results achieved by subjects in the study in relation to subjects' earlier musical expertise seems to confirm that music education affects second language acquisition and that the influence is not a myth but has thorough scientifically approved basis. Therefore, it seems important to include music lessons in education programs along with other subjects and activities such as reading, writing, and mathematics in order to enhance the cognitive capacities of all students.

Acknowledgments. The author would like to thank all participants of the study for their participation in the investigation. She also thanks all collaborators for their help and encouragement.

References

[1] Aiello, R.: Music and Language: Parallels and Contrasts. In: Aiello, R., Sloboda, J.A. (eds.) Musical Perceptions, pp. 40–63. Oxford University Press, New York (1994)

[2] Alexander, J.A., Wong, P.C.M., Bradlow, A.R.: Lexical Tone Perception in Musicians and Nonmusicians. In: Proceedings of Interspeech 2005, Eurospeech, 9th European Conference on Speech Communication and Technology, Lisbon, Portugal (2005)

[3] Bever, T.G., Chiarello, R.I.: Cerebral Dominance in Musicians and Nonmusicians. Science 185, 537–540 (1974)

[4] Dodane, C.: L 'Apprentissage Précoce d'une Langue Etrangère: une Solution pour la Maîtrise de l'Intonation et de la Prononciation? [Early Foreign Language Learning: a Solu-tion for Gaining Proficiency in Intonation and Pronunciation?]. In: Guimbretière, E. (ed.) La Prosodie au Coeur du Débat: Apprendre, Enseigner, Acquérir, vol. 312, pp. 229–248. Presses Universitaires, Dyalang. Rouen (2000)

[5] Fujioka, T., Ross, B., Kakigi, R., Pantev, C., Trainor, L.J.: One Year of Musical Training Affects Development of Auditory Cortical-Evoked Fields in Young Children. Brain 129(10), 2593–2608 (2006)

[6] Gaser, C., Schlaug, G.: Brain Structures Differ Between Musicians and Nonmusicians. The Journal of Neuroscience 23(27), 9240–9245 (2003)

[7] Gilleece, L.: An Empirical Investigation of the Association Between Musical Aptitude and Foreign Language Aptitude [Unpublished Doctoral Thesis. University of Dublin, Trinity College] (2006)

[8] Jackendoff, R.: A Comparison of Rhythmic Structures in Music and Language. In: Kiparsky, P., Youmans, G. (eds.) Phonetics and Phonology. Rhythm and Meter, vol. 1, pp. 15–44. Academic Press, New York (1989)

[9] Jakobson, L.S., Cuddy, L.L., Kilgour, A.R.: Time Tagging: a Key to Musicians' Superior Memory. Music Perception 20(3), 305–313 (2003)

[10] Kashino, M.: Phonemic Restoration: The Brain Creates Missing Speech Sounds. Acoustical Science and Technology 27(6), 318–321 (2006)

[11] Kraus, N., Banai, K.: Auditory-Processing Malleability. Focus on Language and Music. Current Directions in Psychological Science 16(2), 105–111 (2007)

[12] Lahav, A., Boulanger, A., Schlaug, G., Saltzman, E.: The Power of Listening. Auditory-Motor Interactions in Musical Training. In: Avanzini, G., Lopez, L., Koelsch, S., Majno, M. (eds.) The Neurosciences and Music II: From Perception to Performance, vol. 1060, pp. 189–194. Annals of the New York Academy of Sciences, New York (2005)

[13] Magne, C., Schön, D., Besson, M.: Musician Children Detect Pitch Violations in Both Music and Language Better than Nonmusician Children: Behavioural and Electrophysiological Approaches. Journal of Cognitive Neuroscience 18(2), 199–211 (2006)

[14] Moreno, S., Besson, M.: Influence of Musical Training on Pitch Processing: Event-Related Brain Potential Studies of Adults and Children. In: Avanzini, G., Koelsch, S., Lopez, L., Majno, M. (eds.) The Neurosciences and Music II: From Perception to Performance, vol. 1060, pp. 93–97. Annals of the New York Academy of Sciences, New York (2005)

[15] Nager, W., Kohlmetz, C., Altenmüller, E., Rodriguez-Fornells, A., Münte, T.F.: The Fate of Sounds in Conductors' Brains: An ERP study. Cognitive Brain Research 17, 83–93 (2003)

[16] Norton, A., Winner, E., Cronin, K., Overy, K., Lee, D.J., Schlaug, G.: Are there Pre-existing Neural, Cognitive, or Motoric Markers for Musical Ability? Brain and Cognition 59(2), 124–134 (2005)

[17] Ohnishi, T., Matsuda, H., Asada, T., Aruga, M., Hirakata, M., Nishikawa, M., Katoh, A., Imabayashi, E.: Functional Anatomy of Musical Perception in Musicians. Cerebral Cortex 11, 754–760 (2001)

[18] Palmer, C., Hutchins, S.: What is Musical Prosody? In: Ross, B.H. (ed.) Psychology of Learning and Motivation, vol. 46, pp. 245–278. Elsevier Press, Amsterdam (2006)

[19] Pantev, C., Engelien, A., Candia, V., Elbert, T.: Representational Cortex in Musicians: Plastic Alterations in Response to Musical Practice. In: Zatorre, R.J., Peretz, I. (eds.) The Biological Foundations of Music, vol. 930, pp. 300–314. Annals of the New York Academy of Sciences, New York (2001)

[20] Pastuszek-Lipińska, B.: [Unpublished Test of Musical Abilities] (2003)

[21] Pastuszek-Lipińska, B.: An Overview of a Research Project and Preliminary Results of Two Experiments on Perception and Production of Foreign Language Sounds by Musicians and Nonmusicians. TMH-QPSR 46(1), 61–74 (2004)

[22] Patel, A.D., Peretz, I., Tramo, M., Labreque, R.: Processing Prosodic and Musical Patterns: a Neuropsychological Investigation. Brain and Language 61, 123–144 (1998)

[23] Rauschecker, J.P.: Functional Organization and Plasticity of Auditory Cortex. In: Peretz, I., Zatorre, R. (eds.) The Cognitive Neuroscience of Music, pp. 357–365. Oxford University Press, Oxford (2003)

[24] Schellenberg, E.G.: Music and Cognitive Abilities. Current Directions in Psychological Science 14, 322–325 (2005)

[25] Schlaug, G.: The Brain of Musicians. In: Peretz, I., Zatorre, R. (eds.) The Cognitive Neuroscience of Music, pp. 366–381. Oxford University Press, Oxford (2003)

[26] Schlaug, G., Norton, A., Overy, K., Winner, E.: Effects of Music Training on the Child's Brain and Cognitive Development. In: Avanzini, G., Lopez, L., Koelsch, S., Majno, M. (eds.) The Neurosciences and Music II: From Perception to Performance, vol. 1060, pp. 219–230. Annals of the New York Academy of Sciences, New York (2005)

[27] Schön, D., Magne, C., Besson, M.: The Music of Speech: Music Training Facilitates Pitch Processing in Both Music and Language. Psychophysiology 41(3), 341–349 (2004)

[28] Slevc, L.R., Miyake, A.: Individual Differences in Second Language Proficiency: Does Musical Ability Matter? Psychological Science 17, 675–681 (2006)

[29] Sloboda, J.A.: Individual Differences in Music Performance. Trends in Cognitive Sciences 4(10), 397–403 (2000)

[30] Sobkowiak, W.: English Phonetics for Poles. Poznań: Wydawnictwo Poznańskie (2001)

[31] Thompson, W.F., Schellenberg, E.G., Husain, G.: Perceiving Prosody in Speech Effects of Music Lessons. In: Avanzini, G., Faienza, C., Minciacchi, D., Lopez, L., Majno, M. (eds.) The Neurosciences of Music, vol. 999, pp. 530–532. Annals of the New York Academy of Sciences, New York (2003)

[32] Thompson, W.F., Schellenberg, E.G., Husain, G.: Decoding Speech Prosody. Do Music Lessons Help? Emotions 1, 46–64 (2004)

Cognitive Styles and Computer-Based Creativity Support Systems: Two Linked Studies of Electro-acoustic Music Composers

Barry Eaglestone[1], Nigel Ford[1], Peter Holdridge[1], Jenny Carter[2], and Catherine Upton[1]

[1] Department of Information Studies, University of Sheffield, Sheffield, UK
[2] School of Computing, De Montfort University, Leicester, UK
{B.Eaglestone, N.Ford, P.G.Holdridge}@sheffield.ac.uk,
jennyc@dmu.ac.uk

Abstract. This paper explores cognitive style as one of the factors that may explain tensions that can exist between individual electroacoustic composers and the software they use. The discussion centres on two linked studies: (a) a small scale intensive qualitative case study of 2 established composers, in which they unexpectedly revealed differences that mapped remarkably well onto one of the key dimensions of cognitive style identified in the psychological and cognitive literature, namely global and analytic; and (b) a survey, conducted using a web-based questionnaire, of composers' cognitive styles and approaches to composition. This survey was motivated by study (a). The results of the 2 studies combined suggest that there are characteristic cognitive styles traits within the electroacoustic composer community which correlate with particular approaches to composition and also to levels of satisfaction with composition software. Thus we propose a new area of research, namely, usability studies of computer music software that is sensitive to cognitive styles.

Keywords: electroacoustic composition, cognitive styles, composition software.

1 Introduction

This paper reports the results of 2 linked studies. The second follows directly from the first, and centres on a web-based questionnaire survey of electroacoustic music composers that we conducted during January and February of 2007. The questionnaire was designed to test composers' cognitive styles and their approaches to composition, with the aim of determining if correlations between composition approaches and cognitive style can explain tensions that appear to exist between the creative activities of composers and the software they currently use. This survey was motivated by an unexpected discovery which emerged when we re-examined data from the first study, which was a qualitative study of composers [23, 24]. Specifically, two established composers unexpectedly revealed differences that mapped remarkably well onto one of the key dimensions of cognitive style identified in the psychological and cognitive literature, namely global and analytic. The survey was designed to test whether cognitive styles might be useful in interpreting data from a larger sample of composers.

R. Kronland-Martinet, S. Ystad, and K. Jensen (Eds.): CMMR 2007, LNCS 4969, pp. 74–97, 2008.

Through analysis of our survey data we have drawn tentative conclusions relating to dominant cognitive style traits amongst electroacoustic composers, and their correlation with composition approaches and attitudes to software. Thus, the survey provides preliminary confirmation that cognitive style may be an important factor when assessing the efficacy of composition software. Accordingly, a new area of research is proposed, namely, usability studies of computer music software that focus on cognitive styles and the specific tensions these create, with the aim of developing interfaces that are sensitive to, and compatible with, the different styles exhibited.

The paper is organized as follows. In the subsequent sections we establish the motivation and context for this study, firstly by reviewing research into electroacoustic music composition, and secondly by examining cognitive style. The paper then presents the results of our 2 related studies of composers. Finally, implications with respect to computer music software design are discussed.

2 Motivation and Previous Work

Various studies have attempted to model the creative process by developing hypothetical and theoretical models in order to describe it. The four main theories referenced by Collins [4] are stage theory; gestalt theory; emerging-systems theory; and information-processing theory. However, most of these studies investigate the compositional processes of 'traditional' Western Art Music based on the musical grammar of tonality and notated using the traditional five line stave. In contrast, electroacoustic music is based on timbral properties of sounds.

Emmerson [7] attempts to determine a theoretical model of the creative process and some useful observations concerning the particular nature of electroacoustic composition are noted. Particularly, Emmerson [7: 136] raises the point that when working with tape or computer a composer has access to immediate feedback:

> "Working with sounds on tape (or from computer systems) one is immediately confronted with an aural result and, if following broadly the aesthetic assumptions behind this paper, a judgment to be made and a decision to be acted upon."

Vaggione [25] views the process of computer-based composition as an interaction between the composer, his tools and the musical material, rather than being algorithmic in nature. He therefore suggests that composition cannot be reduced to an algorithm, or rigid model. Rather, Vaggione views composition as a complex network of interactions, despite often being based on formal or structural devices (for example, tonality). Vaggione also highlights the 'micro-time domain' [25: 60] in computer-based music, which allows composers to manipulate the composition at a lower level of abstraction, to be able to 'get inside the sound'. This is certainly an integral part of electroacoustic composition, and adds a further dimension to the 'plurality of layers of operations of diverse kinds' [7: 56] involved in the compositional process. The compositional process can therefore be seen to be a highly complicated and intricate activity, which is difficult to model objectively.

This inherent difficulty in finding objective models of composition is exacerbated by a sparcity of insightful research into the phenomenon of creativity in electroacoustic music, particularly from a software perspective. One of the problems in conducting such research is the difficulty of determining cognitive processes of composers. As Laske (cited by Polfreman [17: 31]) oberved:

> "the kind of musical knowledge that, if implemented, would improve computer music tools is often not public or even shared among experts, but personal, idiosyncratic knowledge…the elicitation of personal knowledge and of action knowledge still awaits a methodology…."

We also note that derivation and validation of theories of the composition process require empirical studies to reveal what actually happens. However, though widely used in audio and music perception research [21], these have rarely been used to research composition. Empirical studies of conventional pitch-based music composition have used case study data [4, 18] and controlled experiment (e.g., [1,2,5]) but do not address issues relating to interaction with computer systems. Also, experimental work has largely failed to address complexities of professional composition, since subjects are typically students, sometimes children, and often musically untrained. Notably, there has been very little "time-based" analysis, or studies in naturalistic settings. Collins' [4: 56] explanation for this is that the

> "so-called scientific objectivity, claimed by researchers, has been flavoured by their background as experimental psychologists rather than musicians".

Certainly, few experiments have gone beyond observation of trivial composition exercises using crude and simple sound sources, exceptions being studies in Reitman [18], Collins [4] and Eaglestone et al. [6].

This lack of an established research base has motivated a series of studies in which research methodology used in the social sciences has been applied. These methods have included qualitative inductive analysis of data collected though naturalistic study [12], and using survey techniques, such as interviews and questionnaires. The study presented in this paper is the most recent of that series and extends past research projects by Clowes [3], Collins [4] and Tracy [22], in addition to the research done by Eaglestone et al. [6]. These have previously explored various aspects of the compositional process and the nature of the relationship between composers and the tools that they use. These projects have focused on various specific issues related to this, such as attitudes towards user interfaces [22], evaluation of software environments used in the domain [3], and user requirements [6]. This project aimed to further expand on this research, to provide new insight into electroacoustic composition and further the basis for the design of new compositional tools.

An issue that emerged from the above projects related to the skills and stances of electroacoustic music composers. Clowse [3] found that many of the composers he surveyed were skilled software engineers who valued control of, and access to, the lower levels of software architecture. This contradicted his hypotheses that composers would have limited knowledge of the technology and would have a preference for simple interfaces and high usability. Eaglestone et al [6] also identified differences with respect to the dichotomy between composing music for its own sake and the research task of exploring the artistic possibilities of digital signal processing. Three loosely classified groups of composers were identified: (i) those for whom software and hardware development and engineering is implicit in the act of electroacoustic composition; (ii) those who are more interested in timbral and aesthetic aspects of composition, but engage with software engineering 'because of "peer pressure"' [6: 21]; and (iii)those who simply see the software as a means to an ends, and are wholly concerned with the sounds themselves and their timbral and aesthetic qualities. Though such attitudes are important from a software perspective, since they will impact on the relationship between individual composers and the software they use, these are acquired skills and assumed stances, rather than intrinsic personal characteristics. Many studies, such as those reviewed below, suggest that there are also intrinsic and elementary personal traits, referred to as cognitive styles, which influence the cognitive processes of individuals when using software. Thus, a general classification based on the cognitive styles may provide a more fundamental basis from which to anticipate and thus reduce potential tensions that currently occur between composers and the software they use. However, no previous studies have analysed composition and composition software from this perspective.

3 Cognitive Styles

Cognitive styles are tendencies displayed by individuals consistently to adopt a particular type of information processing strategy. Many such differences have been identified (7, 9, 10, 12, 14, 15, 18, 19, 25].

A major focus of research into cognitive styles has been the study of what may be described as global and analytic differences, notably, work conducted and inspired by Witkin in the USA and Pask in the UK. Witkin investigated global/analytic differences in a very wide range of human activity from basic perception to career choice [26]. Pask studied global/analytic differences in relation to the learning of complex academic subject matter [15, 16]. In general terms, both Witkns and Pask develop catagorisations which determine if an individual's cognitive approaches are relatively global or analytical. The essential distinctions given in the psychological literature, between these two types are summarised in Table 1. In a series of experiments [15, 16], Pask and his colleagues monitored the routes taken by learners through a range of complex academic topics. In these experiments, people used one of two basic approaches. "Holists" tended to adopt a global approach to learning, examining interrelationships between several topics early in the learning process, and concentrating first on building a broad conceptual overview into which detail could subsequently be fitted. "Serialists" tended to use a predominantly local learning approach, examining one thing at a time, and concentrating on separate topics and the logical sequences linking them. The overall picture emerged relatively late in the learning process.

The holist is cognitively complex, and likes to have several things "on the go" in parallel at the same time. In contrast to the steady "brick by brick" approach of the serialist, the holist adopts what is a comparatively high risk, exploratory strategy, switching attention across a range of tasks before any one is securely completed and checked as a sure foundation for further progress. The holist progresses in an exploratory, relatively intuitive fashion, based on complex multi-predicate hypotheses compared to the serialist's narrow focus and step by step logical progression, making sure to build solid foundations for each next move. Using the technique of "teachback", Pask and Scott found that extreme holists were distinctive in the personalised, often idiosyncratic way in which they related new information to their existing knowledge, making sense of it in ways often not easily understood by others. They readily made use of enrichment material, as opposed to serialists who preferred to concentrate on the "pure" essential subject matter, finding enrichment material –irrelevant in a strict sense to the colonel material to be learned – distracting and unhelpful.

Pask subsequently found evidence that holist and serialist approaches were linked to more fundamental components of understanding. They represented different but equally valid routes to achieving high levels of understanding, the holist approach being particularly linked to "description-building", the serialist approach to "procedure-building". Both description-building and procedure-building are necessary to achieve full understanding. Description-building entails the construction of an overall conceptual map – a description of what may be known in a subject area. Procedure-building relates to mastering operational details – the evidence and logical arguments necessary to support the larger picture.

Pask argues that individuals may tend generally to prefer, and be better at, one or the other. People displaying a holist-like style emphasise description-building. Those displaying a serialist-like style emphasise procedure-building. Individuals who display neither pathology, succeeding in engaging in high levels of both description- and procedure-building, Pask called "versatile".

Witkin's work is of particular interest since the phenomena he identified appear to be so pervasive across a range of areas of human activity - from basic perception through academic success even to career choice. The dimensions of cognitive style identified by Witkin relate to what he termed field-dependence and field-independence. These are similar in some ways to Pask's dimensions. However, whereas holistic and serialistic styles concern an individual's overall approach to problem solving, the field dependence / independence categorisation determine their perceptions of the individual problem components and thus provide insights into "snapshots" of the overall process.

Essentially, field-independent individuals tend to experience the components of a structured field analytically, as discrete from their background, and to impose structure on a relatively unstructured field. By contrast, relatively field-dependent individuals tend to be less good at such structuring and analytic activity, and to perceive a complex stimulus globally as a gestalt. This dimension would seem to extend from perceptual through intellectual and social functioning.

Relatively field-dependent individuals operate with a relatively external frame of reference, as opposed to the greater "inner directedness" of the field-independent individual. Field-dependent people tend to be more socially oriented than more field-independent individuals, and this may even be reflected in the type of academic study and employment they choose and in which they excel.

4 Study A

4.1 Aims and Research Questions

The first study reported here consisted of an analysis of data collected for a separate more general investigation [23] of the compositional processes of electroacoustic composers. In particular this investigation sought to shed light on the working methods of composers, their use of the tools and technology, and their attitudes towards these tools. The study examined the practical aspects of the composition process, so as to gain a better empirical understanding of composers' approaches to composition and working practices.

4.2 The Sample

Composers are a heterogeneous group, who have very different aesthetic perspectives, techniques, and ways of working. Therefore, the original study [23] comprised an in-depth investigation into a small number of composers. The sample comprised four composers, all attached to UK academic institutions and therefore their composition has a Western Art music bias. All have fairly traditional musical backgrounds, having done traditional undergraduate music degrees before going on to undertake more specialised postgraduate music courses. Therefore, all four composers write, and have written, some instrumental music, although they predominantly focus on electroacoustic composition now. Two of the participants are established and experienced composers who hold teaching and research positions within their institutions; both have been composing electroacoustic music for a great number of years. The other two were PhD students in composition, specialising in electroacoustic composition and are therefore less experienced, composing in the electroacoustic genre for three to four years.

4.3 Methodology

Semi-structured interviews were used, in keeping with the qualitative paradigm, in order to allow each conversation to develop according to the specific interaction with each composer [12]. The interviews were intended to be highly flexible, and the researcher tried to allow each interviewee to have as much freedom as possible in shaping the interview process. The interview structure design began with open-ended and general questions, then honed in on more specific and in-depth queries. The interviews all followed the basic outline of three parts; questions about background information, the compositional process, and the tools and techniques used. Many planned questions were unintentionally precipitated by the participants' answers, and it was necessary for the interviewer to review the progress of the interview as it was developing to ensure that questions relevant to the conversation were asked and that answered questions were not repeated. Many of the participants' answers led down interesting and enlightening avenues which warranted further investigation and discussion. Illustrative examples of specific compositions proved to be very useful in illuminating what is a highly individual and personal process, and one of the composers even showed the interviewer live examples of his work and methods, which was particularly effective.

During the secondary analysis of the data, which constitutes the study reported here, it was striking how many comments and observations from the two most experienced and established composers (referred to henceforth as composers A and D) mapped onto the notion of the global/analytic dimensions of cognitive style. It was therefore decided in the analysis presented here to concentrate on composers A and D in order to illuminate these differences in more depth. It should be noted that similar comments also appeared in the data relating to the two less experienced music students – but not in so clear or extreme a way.

It should be noted that the notion of cognitive styles was not part of the research agenda of the original study. Upton [23, 24] was neither seeking, nor familiar with, the cognitive style differences observed. The notion of cognitive style emerged as a factor during the reading, by the first two authors of the present paper, of the original study.

4.4 Results

We now discuss the results and in particular highlight the way in which they support a categorisation of composers A and D, respectively as global and analytic individuals, as discussed in the preceding section. We first establish their backgrounds and general perspective on composition. We then explore how this translates into compositional perspectives and activities.

Notes and planning. Stylistic differences would seem to extend to note-taking. Composer A suggested that he makes extensive notes whilst working, but:

> ".. they're irrelevant, because you write them down very quickly in all sorts of mnemonics, erm codes, gestures, scribbles, colours…and really you want slightly more detail, and you want to be able to reference it well. The one thing about a notebook is it's often just sequential, and you really want something that is more, I don't know, tree-like." Composer A

This may be contrasted with Composer D, who, as well as favouring a notebook approach, also displays a characteristic of Pask's analytic individual, namely a tendency to err on the side of fragmentation.

> "I do a certain amount of handwritten diagrams and er, notes. But I wouldn't say it's fully comprehensive and certainly not collected together, usually." Composer D

> "…sometimes it'll be on pieces of paper. Occasionally, I mean every now and then, I get a notebook and I think "Right, I'm going to do them in a notebook," but then, because I tend to work on a number of computers, sometimes I work at home on the laptop, sometimes er, I'm in the studio…then I've perhaps woken up in the middle of the night and there's an envelope er, the back of an envelope to hand, so I'll jot down a few ideas on the envelope." Composer D

> "Only when I'm away from the computer, if I have an idea and I don't want to forget it." Composer B

> "Sometimes I'll write it down, like, "I want to use this with that at some point." Sometimes I'll make a little sketch of it." Composer C

> "…it's pretty much from memory. It's nearly all from memory. I just sort of, kind of know what I need from what I've got." Composer B

Software usage. Composer D mentioned that he is interested in the work of composers such as Stockhausen and Boulez, whose work stems from the German Electronische Musik. The music of Stockhausen and Boulez has often tended to be focused on using specific techniques and algorithms to achieve 'total serialism', the idea of which being that every aspect of the music is controlled sequentially. The work of Composer D is therefore of a similar aesthetic in which theories, algorithms, and techniques such as FOF and FOG synthesis, are used to create the music in a very precise way:

> "I have a technique which is central to the whole idea, to the structure, and the creative impetus of the piece, and er, that will be er, sort of be the foundation of the sound or of the processing of the sound." Composer D

The compositions of Composer D are structured very precisely, and therefore structure and technique are integral to the composition process. Specifically, the music of Composer D is centred around specific techniques, which are integral to each composition. He is highly interested in the theory, and manipulating the physical properties of the sound material. He often needs to get to the lower level of the abstraction of the sound, in order to be able to analyse the sound's properties and to implement the techniques he is using. He therefore requires a high level of control and precision, and for this reason tends to use programming languages such as Csound and MAX/MSP as his main software tools. He does a great deal of programming and software engineering, and will devise what he needs to realise a particular idea or technique. He does not consider the technical aspects of his work as being isolated from the creative process, but an integral and necessary part of it:

> "I've tended to get involved quite a lot with computer programming, er, even going into quite low levels, programming in C and that sort of thing. Er, and er, I originally did that because er, I had a specific musical idea I wanted to realise...I suppose since then, when I've come across a situation where I find that the existing software that I've got available won't do what I want, I'll sort of erm, go off into programming. It sometimes, I mean, it takes me a long time to write a piece, er, you know because it can take a long time to devise the software, but er, I see that as part of the compositional process in a way...I'm not saying everybody should do it, or it's necessary but if you want to do something it can't, you either have to wait until someone else does it for you, or find someone who will do it for you, er, or you do it yourself. So erm, so I don't see as being sort of isolated necessarily from the creative process, it feeds into it." Composer D

> "I don't sort of say, "I'm a user, and I'm going to use the technology," I say, "I'm being creative with the technology," and if that involves getting my hands dirty by getting down to the lowest level, if I'm capable of doing it I'll have a go." Composer D

Being more influenced by the research at IRCAM, Composer D tends to use some of the tools that have been created by the group, such as Audiosculpt:

> "...if I want to go into a sound and analyse its spectral components, and perhaps then er, divide them up, there's a program called Audiosculpt from IRCAM that I use. I use quite a lot of the IRCAM Forum software." Composer D

Composer D does not use plug-ins since they do not offer enough control, and are superfluous to the aesthetic of his music. They have no part to play in the realisation of a technique since they are used primarily for the development (and distortion) of timbre. He describes plug-ins, and other pieces of commercial software, as "black boxes" which can only be manipulated at a higher level:

> "I think on the whole, most plug-ins, and it's also not just plug-ins, but also quite a lot of other software, so things like Soundhack that people use and things, they tend to be what I call 'black boxes'. You can't get inside them; you simply have a few knobs you can twiddle on the outside, so to speak…You put the sound in and then you can add some extra colour or whatever to it, through doing that or transforming something. Erm, and I think I very much usually use the technology as being the way of erm, working from inside the sound, and of, so, and I want to have, erm, have therefore very precise detailed control over what's happening. That's another reason why I do the programming because it means I can, er, if I don't like the controls I've got and I've programmed it, I can go in and add another control to it to do it." Composer D

There is an interesting contrast with Composer A, who makes use of a variety of plug-ins:

> "…there's a set of plug-ins made by the Groupe de Recherche Musicales, called GRM tools, erm, and they're really quite aggressive plug-ins if you like. They really pull the sound apart in a major way. They allow you to be very hands on with the sound, erm, and they stem from, you know, decades of research at the GRM into how composers in the past have manipulated sounds."Composer A

> "…there's a variety of sound mixing programs, there's a variety of plug-ins – there's about fifty free plug-ins that you could load in here." Composer A

It is interesting that, when asked about historical aspects of their use of computers, the musical requirements of Composer A arguably required more complex computing procedures than could be provided in the early 1990s…

> "1990-'93 we really didn't have computers that were powerful enough. They were just gadgets that might squirt out the odd sound here and there. I mainly worked with analogue tape. Gradually, as the computers got more powerful, they could mirror what we were doing in the studio." Composer A

However, speaking of the same chronological period, Composer D found that computers could support his musical composition to a greater extent. This is hardly surprising since his requirements entailed the less complex – less narrowly and precisely defined – processing characteristic of the analytic as opposed to the more global individual.

Approaches to the composition process. The timbre of a sound can be regarded as more multi-faceted than its pitch when considered in terms of attention at a given point in time. Perception of timbre in this sense entails a relatively gestalt, "broad front" parallel processing type of attention to a relatively multifaceted phenomena – compared to the relatively "narrow front" approach entailing isolation and sequencing of the component parts of a more complex phenomenon. Parallel, gestalt-type processing of complex multifaceted phenomena is characteristic of the global individual. Conversely, the orientation and strength of the analytic individual relates to analytic breaking down of complex phenomena into component parts, and their relatively isolated and sequential treatment.

When refining and constructing the final composition Composer A tends to shape his compositions through intuitive connections between sound material, and uses specific techniques for a particular effect or refinement. In contrast, Composer D shapes his compositions through employment and development of a specific technique which is integral to the composition, and might use intuitive effects for colouration and refinement.

Again, the use of intuition as opposed to less "fuzzy" and more algorithmically specifiable logic is characteristic of the global individual. Typically, Pask's global individual will, when exploring new areas of knowledge, begin by constructing a complex – and relatively impressionistic and speculative – conceptual overview of how s/he "thinks it all fits together", before paying attention to procedural details to examine whether the details do in fact logically support what is a relatively intuitive overview. The pathology of Pask's global individual is in fact a conceptual picture which is not supported by such more detailed scrutiny – i.e. may be excessively intuitive and speculative. Witkin's global individual is also typically more tuned into intuitive aspects of interaction – being more socially integrated and adapted, compared to Witkin's less socially oriented highly analytic individual.

Generally, Composer A does not carefully plan the structure of his compositions, but rather they are structured intuitively according to the nature of the sound material. Composer D uses techniques which are integral to the structure of his compositions, and therefore the structures of his compositions are determined by the technique.

Interest in pitch more than timbre, lower level physical properties and techniques also resonates with the description of Pask's analytic individual, in that s/he is primarily concerned with lower level procedural detail. Indeed, Pask's analytic individuals are associated with what Pask called "procedure building" (geared to working out relatively low level procedural detail) as opposed to "description building" (geared to establishing a higher level conceptual overview).

Typically, Pask's analytic individual will be more oriented towards (i.e. will tend to concentrate early on, emphasise and be stronger in relation to) relatively low level procedural detail. Pask's global individual will be more oriented towards establishing a high level conceptual overview, only operating at this lower level after establishing this overview. Again the composers conform to these characterisations in their choice of software. Composer D uses lower level software programming languages to realise the specific techniques which are integral to the structure of his compositions. Composer A uses software with "cheap and cheerful interfaces" that provides immediate aural feedback to allow for his intuitive moulding of the sound material.

Though the process might change from composition to composition, each of the participants described some basic, fundamental stages which they often work through. Composer A indicated that he often begins work on a composition by recording fresh sounds from which to formulate musical (or sonic) ideas.

> "The first stage might be deciding upon a particular source sound to record…and the other starting point for a piece might be a title or an external influence like a poem…once you start finding sounds and you start manipulating sounds, you group them in probably in a kind of emotional content, but in a very simplistic way. The emotional content is based around things such as, probably erm, tonality – a major/minor from a basically, from a happy/sad point of view. Er, and then also speed – slow/fast, erm, distance – near/far. Or you know you start to place these sounds between these poles, erm, and that gives the sound a kind of value, if you like, as to where it might go in the piece." Composer A

As we can see, Composer A organises the sounds through making some sort of value judgement about each of them, grouping them together and considering where in the framework of the piece the sound is going to work, before processing them. Pask's global individual typically is oriented to seeking similarities in order to relate elements together to form a coherent linked framework. S/he will do this across a broad front, seeking to fit together at a relatively high conceptual overview level a diverse range of multi-predicate elements (i.e. with multiple defining parameters, as in the example above relating to tonality, major/minor, speed and distance). It is typical of Pask's global individual not to differentiate the phenomenon under consideration from the "real world", and to integrate real world and theory readily – as opposed to his more analytic individual who tends to keep them more separate.

For Composer A the construction of a composition will come through connecting and putting together sounds in a way that makes sense artistically:

> "…the act of composition is to find some kind of glue, if you like, or extend sound A and B so that they fuse together, or to hybridise A and B so that you've, you know, you've got something in between the two. And then once you've got a whole bunch of sounds, I think, you know, you'll say "Okay, I need to start putting this piece together." Composer A

> "I tend to kick off with days and days and weeks of just development. And while you're developing, you know, one or two gigabytes of sound, you play certain sounds and you think, "Oh yeah, I remember this sound from a completely different session sounding perhaps similar." Again, it's based on the composer's memory and their immersion in their own piece…you find that other sound, you compare the two to see whether your memory was right or wrong." Composer A

> "So you build the sections up from a sound, putting sounds either side, left or right, then seeing whether you can actually split up sounds and intersperse material into them, and gradually build up small sound objects, link those together in families." Composer A

In keeping with a global style, Composer A proceeded on a relatively broad front:

> "I tend to start with a large palette [of sounds]...but the problem of start-
> ing with a large palette is keeping control over it. Too much sound infor-
> mation if you like." Composer A

Composer A suggested that an audio retrieval system, in which a database could match and retrieve sounds based on similarities in spectral density of the sounds themselves, would be highly useful in helping to organise his work. Through a query-by-example facility, the composer would be able to find sounds that are similar to one another. This would be very useful in the development process when a composer, particularly a composer of acousmatic and timbre-based music, is experimenting with different sounds and connecting them together. However, although much research is being done into audio retrieval systems the current technology is not sophisticated enough to be of extensive use to this type of work as yet.

Although Composer D indicated that he felt he does not have a standard process that he works through:

> "I don't have a sort of set process...I usually have an idea in some form or
> other. It might be that someone's asked me to write a piece. That might
> be the starting point." Composer D

> "I'd say I have a, some sort of tendencies to set about things in a certain
> way with each piece, but each piece really demands its own approach."
> Composer D

he did convey quite a different approach to starting a composition. Composer D's interest in and use of formal techniques does to some extent dictate the way in which he works with his sound material. As mentioned before, he often works from a pitch basis. The general approach of Composer D is analytic rather than entailing the synthesis into a broad high level framework of disparate elements. When he does speak of synthesis, it is at a relatively low level (compared to Composer A), and interpreted specifically and narrowly in terms of synthesizing the sound of a particular instrument:

> "If I'm writing a piece for instrument and tape, or instrument and live
> processing...what I like to do is make sure that the recorded, processed
> part is closely linked to the instrumental sound...I'm quite interested in
> just subtly extending and expanding the sound that's already
> there...there's not just one approach but I might record the instrument, and
> then do some processing on it, er, and the piece might develop from there.
> Er, other times I've done it where I've synthesised a simulation of what-
> ever the instrument is." Composer D

He often takes some physical property of the sound material as a basis for his composition, as opposed to Composer A whose work seems to be more influenced by extra-musical aspects at an abstract level (i.e. emotional, conceptual characteristics of the sound).

The close linking, and subtle extension and expansion of an existing sound is characteristic of Pask's analytic individual, who progresses relatively cautiously, in small steps closely linking the next step with a previous relatively well understood concept, on a relatively narrow front – as opposed to the less cautious, more speculative and broad front approach of Pask's global individual.

For Composer D, who is more interested in the theoretical aspects of the sonic material, the refinement of a composition might come through the utilisation of specific techniques. It is interesting to note that Pask's analytic individual typically exhibits a steady sequential progression on a narrower front on basis of groundwork – as opposed to the more parallel consideration of similarities and fusions characteristic of his global individuals.

> "I'd have probably done some work already and know the techniques, and I'd have some new ideas that I'd want to explore within that range of techniques…so it would grow out of that and then…the ideas would begin to shape themselves." Composer D

Composer A exhibits a relatively gestalt approach, rather than a more sequential progression – the whole being subject to sudden global reconfiguration (rather than smaller-scale modifications).

> "Nothing appears out of nowhere. Things always tend to…something builds up energy. And then it happens, and when it does happen it often leaves shards, you know, you kind of, like…you take a bottle, an empty bottle. You give it potential energy by holding it up, at arm's length. You let it go, it has kinetic energy. Well, it's more potential energy to the kinetic energy…bangs on the floor. The energy emitting - the firm floor breaks the bottle. But after that, that energy has to disperse somewhere. So it disperses by cracking the bottle for sure, and splits these smaller bits of glass all over the place, erm, and so the same thing happens with sound. Er, it's kind of modeling nature in a, in a very hands off sort of way." Composer A

He even uses the physical size of files in very high level and impressionistic way – characterised by an intuitive approach in which a change is felt to be somehow imminent:

> "So at this point here you see three long files, mainly textual…So these textures are just interfusing kind of…some kind of metallic sounds playing off water sounds with most of the mid-range filtered out. So it's all very background, distance and twinkly…and then when you see more shorter sound files, that would tend to suggest that there's something gestural, that there's a major change coming on." Composer A

This parallel, gestalt and impressionistic processing is highly characteristic of the global individual. The narrower front, more analytic and sequential progression via small and relatively secure steps from the well understood and controlled is highly characteristic of the analytic individual. There was evidence of the use of the linear approach of the analytic individual:

> "…it usually starts out with a sound I particularly like, er, and then I don't know. It's sometimes a bit of a linear process…usually I've got some kind of idea of what I want to do with the piece as a whole but it usually quite,

> it never quite happens as I would like it to, er, and I develop sections line-arly, but sometimes I quite like to put a part in isolation that…which is a point that I want to get to." Composer C

and of the less sequential and ordered approach more typical of the global individual:

> "It's always the longer the piece goes on the harder it gets 'cause then you have to have something that fits with it. So like, the initial sounds - I just try loads of random different things and then once you've found a sound you like then get sounds that will fit with that. Then it becomes a lot more methodical later on. But the initial idea is just very random." Composer B

Background and perspectives. Composer A and D are well-established electroacoustic composers, with portfolios of many publicly performed compositions, some of which have been prize-winning. Both claimed strong backgrounds in the "electroacoustic tradition", having worked with analogue techniques before computer technology began to predominate. Also, since composers A and D are attached to UK academic institutions they compose from a Western Art music bias.

However, they defined themselves and their music in different ways, and compose for different media, highlighting their heterogeneity. The works of Composer A are very much based on timbral qualities of the sound material that he uses, whereas those of Composer D are more concerned with formal techniques and the integral physical properties of the sound material. Composer A tends to use recordings of sounds as a basis for his compositions in the initial stages of the compositional process, whereas Composer D uses the lower level physical properties of the sound material as a basis for his compositions.

Composer A described his works very definitely as "acousmatic", which has an idiosyncratic aesthetic.

> "The focus is on the spectrum morphology and the kind of change and modification of timbre, in a musical way obviously, erm, which is then diffused in a live performance over multiple loudspeakers." Composer A

The focus of Composer A's music is, therefore, on the timbral aspects of sound. Also the performance and the diffusion of the sound into a three-dimensional space is a very important and central aspect of his work.

Composer D indicated that he is interested in delving into the technical compo-nents of a sound, and manipulating its physical properties. The music of Composer D is therefore quite pitch-oriented, although not necessarily based on the tempered pitches of the chromatic scale.

> "…the techniques that I've been interested in have been techniques which…stem from the pitch basis then link into other textures." Composer D

Composer D is, therefore, still concerned with the nature of sound, but perhaps fo-cuses more on the integral structures within the sound, and the theoretical aspects of electroacoustic composition.

It is interesting that the two types of composition of the composers interviewed here map onto broad traditions which themselves exhibit characteristics strongly differentiating between global and analytic cognitive styles, i.e., the French Radiodiffusion Télévision Française (RTF) and the German Norwestdeutscher Rundfunk (NWDR) (Manning, 2004). Although similar work was being conducted elsewhere at that time, the polar extremes of these two studios continue to have an influence on the work of composers today. The French Musique Concrète, pioneered by Schaeffer and Henry, was influenced by the Italian Futurists who had been interested in the rejection of traditional instruments and the exploration of sounds and noise from the industrial environment. Schaeffer and Henry therefore used recorded everyday sounds from the environment, which were then treated by electronic processes. The German Electronische Musik, on the other hand, focused on pure electronically generated sounds and derived its influence from the Second Viennese School and the principles of serialism (the twelve notes of the chromatic tempered scale used in series):

Although the two studios started from quite extreme positions, with advances in technology and a growing interest in electronic synthesis in the 50s, the two schools of thought became less proscriptive, and a cross-pollination of techniques led to a merge in aesthetics and style. Indeed, today many composers will use a mixture of electronic synthesis and acoustic recordings in their work, and the aesthetic boundaries between composition styles is often blurred. However, distinctions still remain, highlighted for example, by the diverse research of IRCAM and GRM.

In relation to cognitive styles, relatively analytic individuals have an affinity with disembedding the discrete components of a complex phenomenon in order to isolate them and concentrate on them relatively sequentially in their "purity" – as opposed to the global individual's tendency to consider such components as a whole, embedded within a complex gestalt. Also, Pask's global individual would be oriented to "real world" aspects of phenomena as opposed to studying them in a more isolated context. Indeed, Composer A has an affinity with the first school, Composer D with the German school.

Although he refused to be categorised, Composer D indicated that he is influenced by the more technical research of IRCAM (Institute for Research and Coordination of Acoustics and Music).

> "I'm perhaps erm, not so much influenced by the Acousmatic School, and er, er, you know, places like GRM and so on. I'm more influenced by the sort of things that go on perhaps at IRCAM and that sort of thing." Composer D

5 Study B

The second study built directly on the first. It sought to investigate whether relationships between compositional activity and cognitive styles would be observed in a larger sample of composers, using a questionnaire-based approach.

5.1 Aims and Research Questions

The second study surveyed electroacoustic composers' cognitive styles and approaches to composition. The study was designed to address the research questions: Do composers display cognitive styles which conform to known classifications? If so, what are the implications with respect to software environments for composition? In particular, can knowledge of a composer's cognitive style be used to create software interfaces which are better suited to their cognitive processes and hence provide more fertile environments for their creativity in music?

The survey was conducted using a web-based semi-structured questionnaire. This was composed of three parts. The first comprised closed questions to elicit profiles of the composers. The second part, also of closed questions, comprised a test to determine the cognitive styles of the composers. This test was developed by Felder and Soloman, designed to measure Felder and Silverman's four-dimensional learning styles model [9]. The final semi-structured part elicits approaches and views on composition and related software.

This second study expanded the set of cognitive styles from the global/analytic dimension described above to include four dimensions of cognitive style. These are: global/analytic, imager/verbalizer, intuitive/sensing, active/reflector. The global/ analytic dimension was extensively described in relation to the first study. Imagers are good at working with diagrams, pictures, charts, etc., and tend to think visually, compared to verbalizers who tend to think more in words. Relatively intuitive individuals tend to be more innovative than sensing individuals, and likely to explore possibilities. They excel at taking on board new concepts and abstractions. Sensing individuals prefer more factual "real world" information, and like to make use of well established methods and approaches. Active individuals tend to be quick at trying things out, as opposed to their more reflective counterparts who prefer to think things through more before acting. Reflective individuals may often prefer to work alone, whereas more active individuals often tend to like working collaboratively.

We sought to investigate whether any of the above traits may impact on ways individuals use software, and may thus partly determine the appropriateness of the software's design. This motivates a more specific question, to what extent does cognitive styles impact on approaches adopted by composers and hence the efficacy of the software they use? Results from the previous study suggested to us this may be a fruitful line of investigation. Upton examined practical aspects of the composition process to gain a better empirical understanding of composers' approaches to composition and working practices. As previously described, her study comprised an in-depth investigation into a small number of composers using semi-structured interviews. However, the results of this secondary analysis do beg the questions, are these similarities coincidental, or are they indicative of a more fundamental influence of cognitive styles within the electroacoustic music community?

5.2 The Sample

Completed questionnaires were returned by 27 composers. This is a small sample from a small community. However, electroacoustic composers form an individualist and idiosyncratic community, characterized by creativity and originality. Therefore, in keeping with the qualitative research paradigm, our strategy was not to seeking to generalize. Instead we focused on the qualitative data relating to approaches and attitudes to composition, and the extent to which these were consistent with the profile and cognitive styles of each individual.

The respondees represent a broad slice of the international electroacoustic composer community. The two largest groups were from the UK (11) and USA (8), but there were also responses from composers with other nationalities, i.e., the Basque Country, Germany, Brazil, Australia, Canada, Greece and Israel. Respondees were mainly male (21) and in the age range, 21-30 years (11), though there were responses from all age bands, up to 71-80 years. There was a fairly even split between those who were both musically and technically qualified (6) and those without any such qualifications (5). The majority were musically qualified (10), but not technically. Only 4 respondees had technical but no music qualification. The two largest groups described themselves as amateur composers (11) and professional composers (8). Others classified themselves as either "student" (4) or "academic" (3). All professional and academic composers, and the majority of amateur composers, were qualified musically and/or technically, and only one of the professionals had only technical qualifications. Most declined to specify years of composing experience, but those who responded had composed either for 1-2 year (3), or 3-5 years (5).

5.3 Methods

The analysis proceeded in three phases. Qualitative data relating to composers' approaches to the composition process and their views on composition software were analysed in the first phase. The qualitative data was solicited by four open questions which respectively asked: how the composers classify their compositions; their five favoured composition processes; the composition approach taken for a 10 minute electroacoustic piece, either in general or in a recent significant composition; and their critique of current composition software. Our methodology was devised to avoid bias that potentially arises when interpreting data within the context of known cognitive styles scores. Accordingly, analyses were conducted independently by the authors, prior to viewing results of the cognitive styles tests. In these preliminary analyses, composition approaches were classified as (a) entailing the composer expressing explicit concern with overall structure/form, or (b) primarily a voyage of discovery (trying things out without mention of overall structure/form). In addition, composers were classified according to the issues they raised in their critiques of software. Contentious classifications were resolved through discussion. In the second phase the above analysis was compared with the results of the cognitive styles tests to establish the extent to which the cognitive and practical approaches of the composers can be explained by their cognitive styles. Finally, we analysed implications of the findings with respect to composition software requirements.

5.4 Results

Two main results emerged from the analysis, respectively concerning the link between cognitive styles and approaches to composition, and satisfaction, or lack of it, with current software.

Refinement and synthesis-based composition approaches. Two general approaches to composition emerged as dominant among the respondees, which can be characterized as *refinement* and *synthesis*. In the former, a composer establishes the structure of a composition, and then realizes and refines it. In contrast, the *synthesis* approach is more a voyage of discovery, whereby the composition inductively emerged through experimentation with audio materials.

The *refinement* approach was applied with various levels of formality by a majority (13 of the 18 composers who provided sufficient qualitative data for meaningful analysis). All of these were concerned with "form" or "structure", as is illustrated in the following quotes from the questionnaire responses, in which phrases which we feel are strongly indicative of the approach have been emboldened. (Note that here and throughout this paper we have appended each quote with a composer identification number and their dominant cognitive styles traits for reference in the subsequent discussion.). The essence of the refinement approach was encapsulated in the following quote by composer 41,

> "I would look at the brief, **map out a structure** and then compose from that as ideas developed" [41]   [Global ‖ Imager ‖ Active ‖ Sensing]

Others provided elaboration, for example, concerning interplay between seeking inspiration from audio material, and the conceptualization and elaboration of the composition as a whole. For example, the following quotes refer to collected sounds *"leading ...to new formal and sonic directions"*, the role of *"improvisation"* and discovering *"relationships between sound materials"*.

> "I would first gather sounds (either found or generated). The gathering would be shaped by some general idea I had in mind for a sound. The gathered sounds would then lead me to new formal and sonic directions. I would affect the sounds if needed or inspired to do so and continue refining the materials and general ideas. At this point I would form a more **solid conception of the piece as a whole (i.e. a formal outline).** I would set to work putting the piece together, allowing for shifts in direction but **generally sticking to the plan**. After a draft version was completed I would assess its strengths and weaknesses and begin work on a final version, or as a worst case scenario, begin anew. This is true of any piece, not just those that are to be 10 min long. After the draft is complete (no matter its length) edits and revisions can be made to adjust the piece to suit any requirements or limitations that may pertain." [56] [Global ‖ Imager ‖ Active ‖ Intuitive]

> **"I would first conceive of a structure.** Then, possibly independently, I would conceive of sound-elements and visual elements. I would then work to reconcile these elements. After creating a detailed plan controlling certain elements I would allow myself complete freedom to "improvise" the remaining elements." [64] [Global ‖ Imager ‖ Reflective ‖ Sensing]

> "choose sound materials; develop materials (processes above) to create a large palette of sounds; start to discover & develop relationships between sound materials to **develop structural components; large scale structuring** (other sounds may be sourced along the way as deemed necessary)" [47] [Global ‖ Imager ‖ Active ‖ Sensing]

The above examples also illustrate the difficulty in classifying composition approaches, since, thought all are anchored in a *"structure"* or *"formal outline"*, there are also inductive episodes in which the composer seeks inspiration from the audio material. This may be significant particularly for composers with musical qualifications, since methods may be partly determined by training and education, whereas, cognitive styles should be a factor in their application.

The above blurring of classification is also apparent for those composers whom we classified as applying a *synthesis* approach, i.e. those concerned with "trying things" out rather than having preoccupation with an overall planned structure. This approach was described by a minority (5 of the 18 composers). The essence of this approach is captured in the following quotes.

> "… **Listen for a sound** that inspires me; **experiment** with mathematical processes. Work over a long time, listening repeatedly" [46] [Analytic ‖ Verbalizer ‖ Reflective ‖ Intuitive]

> "would get some of the software tools i have been developing lately and find some sound materials (no natural, always sampled) that work fine with the processes of the tools. **Test different combinations** until once i **find something interesting** then I improvise few sets. I choose and edit/master the chosen session" [43]   [Analytic ‖ Verbalizer ‖ Active ‖ Sensing]

> "I would spend a significant length of time thinking about the approach I was going to take, then would record several hours of **improvisation before selecting the ten minutes of audio** (either a single extract, several extracts montaged, or several extracts" [50] [Analytic ‖ Verbalizer ‖ Reflective ‖ Intuitive]

> "**explore** a range of found sounds, personally sampled or collected from existing archives; **cut, arrange, merge and mutilate**; overlay with electronic sounds; mutate and develop" [63]   [Analytic ‖ Verbalizer ‖ Reflective ‖ Intuitive]

The above approaches differ in the ways the sounds are generated, experimented with, and combined to form the composition, but all essentially allow the composition as a whole to emerge through experimentation with its ingredients. However, again, there is some blurring between the approaches. For example, the following quote refers to creating a *"landscape"* which could be interpreted as the global structure or framework for the composition. Thus, our classifications are indicative of a main emphasis of the compositional approaches.

> "Collect together some interesting samples and create a landscape from them using lots of plug in automation and resampling of sections" [49] [Global ‖ Imager ‖ Active ‖ Intuitive]

Satisfaction and dissatisfaction with composition software. The second finding concerned satisfaction with current software. Again, we can make a clear binary categorisation, i.e., *satisfied* and *dissatisfied*, on the basis of the open question which solicited view on enabling and inhibiting features of current software. Of the 18 who provided substantive critiques on software, a majority (13) expressed dissatisfaction with some aspect of the software. Dissatisfaction is mainly on the grounds of lack of integration or compatibility between tools, as expressed in the following quotes.

"That they **are limited to specific platforms**. AudioSculpt - Mac, Nuendo, CDP, Audition, GRM, Native Inst - PC. If CDP were to have a VST front end, that would be extremely helpful." [41]   [Global ‖ Imager ‖ Active ‖ Sensing]

"Inhibiting: Steep learning curve and **compatibility issues** between different applications and platforms. Also many pieces of software tempt the user to make loop based music" [49]   [Analytic ‖ Imager ‖ Reflective ‖ Intuitive]

"enabling: customization, flexibility, complexity. disabling: still not enough of the above; **not enough unity between different pieces of software**" [60]   [Global ‖ Imager ‖ Reflective ‖ Intuitive]

Other related issue raised were how poor performance of the software impedes working with multiple tools or techniques, in particular on large scale compositions. Also respondees expressed a desire to have control over the processes, in preference to automatic processes, but some composers were impeded in achieving this by technical complexities and poor interfaces. One of the explanations for the latter was the continuing influence of legacy systems and standards,

"INHIBITING: **adherance to old standards or reverse compatibility** regardless of objective ease of use or usefulness in general. If a thing will work better another way, it is ok to implement that other way...." [56] [Global ‖ Imager ‖ Active ‖ Intuitive]

Thus, the main dissatisfaction with current software concerned lack of tools integration and interoperability, poor performance, too much automatic processing and over complex interfaces.

There was also a significant group (5) who were mainly satisfied with current software, as illustrated in the following quotes:

"I like SoundHack for its practical approach and csound for its universal applicability to a range of compositional approaches." [52] [Global ‖ Verbalizer ‖ Reflective ‖ Intuitive]

"The transfer of large recorded tracks and the navigation through them has become far quicker in just the few years I have been composing in this manner. As I do not use complex processes, there are no obvious inhibiting features." [50] [Analytic ‖ Verbalizer ‖ Reflective ‖ Intuitive]

"I can create algorithms the allow repetition and refinement. [I] miss provence information but am working on it" [46] [Analytic ‖ Verbalizer ‖ Reflective ‖ Intuitive]

"enabling: range of possibilities, including ability to build your own tools. That opens a huge space to explore. inhibiting: i also love to compose with an electric guitar. It is another story than using software. Less rational, i guess because of history and assumptions in the instrument give a direction to composition. Same could be said about software but the physical element gives the process a different nature." [43] [Analytic ‖ Verbalizer ‖ Active ‖ Sensing] "i have a wonderful interface to behave quite visually with, as well as the potential for electronic metamorphosis provided. inhibiting features? i think that depends on my own approach to the materials at hand." [59] [Global ‖ Imager ‖ Reflective ‖ Intuitive]

This group is not entirely uncritical, for example, composer 43 comments on the lack of a specific type of physical/tactile interfaces, but they are largely satisfied with the expressiveness and manipulative power of current software. However, inspection of the musical styles and tools they use suggests the composers in this group represent a fairly narrow thread of electoacoustic composition, mainly involving programming, for example, in algorithmic composition, rather than use of functional composition tools. Also, the final quote, by composer 59, is an endorsement of the software they use, but since this is "home made" software, there is also an implicit criticism that existing software interfaces were not sufficient for their particular composition approach.

Discussion of Cognitive Style. Subsequent to the above preliminary analysis of the qualitative data, we sought correlations between our classification and the cognitive styles traits of the composers. Cognitive styles were determined using the tests of Felder and Soloman, which quantifies four aspects of cognitive style on a scale of [-7,+7], thus positioning each respondee within a four-dimensional cognitive style space. As described in section 3, these dimensions are: global/analytic, imager/ verbalizer, intuitive/sensing, active/reflector.

Some trends are apparent in this sample. There is a small skew towards imagers (as opposed to verbalizers), and reflectors (as opposed to activists). However, there is a very pronounced skew towards global individuals (73%) (as opposed to analytics) and intuitive (77%) (as opposed to sensing). A large majority of professional and academic composer have, to some extent, possessed both global and intuitive cognitive style traits. Thus, the "typical" electroacoustic composer within our small sample is global/intuitive.

Referring back to our analysis of the qualitative data, there is an obvious interpretation in terms of cognitive style traits of the binary divide between those composers who take refinement and synthesis approaches. By initially defining a structure for the composition, it can be argued that a holistic or global approach is being taken by the former, whereas, the inductive nature of the synthesis approach is more characteristic of the analytic or serialist. Thus, one would expect composers in the two groups, respectively, to have positive and negative scores relating to the analytic/global trait. Interestingly, this proved to be true for 89% of the cases. 12 of the 13 composers who adopt the refinement approach had global traits, whereas all but one of those who described a synthesis approach had analytic traits. In addition, and more surprisingly, the refiners and synthesizers respectively mainly had imager and verbalizer traits (10 of the 13 refiners were global/imager, whereas 4 of the 5 synthesizers were analytic/verbalizers).

Our second classification in the preliminary qualitative analysis was of the composers who were respectively discontent and content with the composition software they used. We were therefore interested to see if there was any cognitive style trait which appeared to distinguish the malcontents from the contents. The characterising trait proved to be the imager/verbalizer dimension. 11 of the 13 discontents were imagers whereas 4 of the 5 contents were verbalizers. This raises the intriguing question, why are verbalizers less critical than imagers? Closer inspection of the data provides a tentative answer to this, in that all of the discontented verbalizers used programming languages as their main composition tool, e.g., for algorithmic composition, whereas the criticisms of the imagers concerned mainly the interfaces of existing tools. Also, the one imager within the contented group (composer 59) could possibly also have been classified as a malcontent, since, since rather than endorsing the quality of current software, they have created their own software interfaces, presumably to better support their particular approach to composition.

6 Implications for Composition Software Developers

The studies presented here were designed to seek evidence regarding the impact of cognitive style as a significant factor when designing composition software. After the dissemination of data from study A provided clear linkage to known cognitive style models, particularly Global and Analytic, Study B was a natural progression in order to further determine the influence of cognitive style. Though based on relatively small-scale surveys, we believe the correlations between composition approaches and attitudes and cognitive style common to both of these analyses are too strong to be dismissed as arbitrary phenomena.

We draw a number of tentative conclusions from this combined research, which in turn suggests additional research may deliver greater insight.

- Firstly, there are dominant cognitive style traits apparent in our sample of electroacoustic composers. Specifically, these are mainly global (rather than analytic) and intuitive (rather than sensing).
- This in turn explains the dominance of composition approaches based on defining and then realising a global structure, since the composers who adopted this approach are predominantly global, whereas those who adopt a more inductive approach in which the composition emerges through experimentation are mainly analytical.
- Further, satisfaction or dissatisfaction of composition software appears to be determined by the imager/verbalizer cognitive style trait, the verbalizers being largely content and the imagists being largely discontent.

A tentative conclusion could be that software is well designed for verbalizers, since these were mainly satisfied, whereas imagers are currently poorly served by composition software. Further, since the majority of the complaining imagers are also global, it is mainly the composition refinement approach that is currently ill-supported by software. However, this is clearly too simplistic since the small number of contented verbalizers in the sample are predominantly programmers, for example, for algorithmic composition, who by nature create their own functionality and are more tolerant of textual interfaces. Also, though imagers' discontents focus on the software interfaces, they identify a diversity of issues, ranging from complexity of technical interfaces through to the need for abstract notation/scoring systems and greater integration and interoperability between tools. Collectively, these are issues which are particularly important for supporting a holistic approach to composition, but it can also be argued that "voyage of discovery" composition also requires integrated use of multiple tools with "clean" interfaces.

Thus, the conclusion of this small-scale study is to add evidence that supports the hypothesis that cognitive style is an important factor when evaluating the efficacy of composition software. Therefore, we believe a more extensive survey of cognitive style and composition is required, together with usability studies to determine the efficacy of composition interfaces for specific cognitive style traits. A long term aim should then be to develop interfaces that are sensitive to, and compatible with, the different cognitive style exhibited.

References

1. Bamberger, J.: In search of a tune. In: Perkins, D., Leondar, B. (eds.) The Arts and Cognition. Johns Hopkins Press, Baltimore (1977)
2. Brumby, M.N.: Consistent differences in cognitive styles shown for qualitative biological problem-solving. British Journal of Educational Psychology 52, 244–257 (1982)
3. Clowes, M.: An investigation of compositional practices in the field of electroacoustic music, with an evaluation of the main software environments currently in use. Dissertation, Master of Science in Information Management, The University of Sheffield (2000)
4. Collins, D.: Investigating computer-based compositional processes: a case-study approach. Ph.D. Thesis. The University of Sheffield (2001)
5. Davidson, L., Welsh, P.: From collections to structure: the developmental path of tonal thinking. In: Sloboda, J.A. (ed.) Generative processes in music; the psychology of performance, improvisation & composition, Oxford Science Publications, Oxford (1988)
6. Eaglestone, B., Ford, N., Brown, G., Moore, A.J.: Information systems and creativity: an empirical study. Journal of Documentation 63(4) (August 2007)
7. Emmerson, S.: Composing strategies and pedagogy. Contemporary Music Review 3, 133–144 (1989)
8. Entwistle, N.J.: Styles of Learning and Teaching. Wiley, Chichester (1981)
9. Felder, R., Spurlin, J.: Applications, reliability and validity of the Index of Learning Styles. International Journal of Engineering Education 21(1), 103–112 (2005)
10. Ford, N.: Hypermedia and cognitive ergonomics in engineering education (1995). In: Guilford, J.P. (ed.) The nature of human intelligence. McGraw-Hill, New York (1967)
11. Jonassen, D.H., Grabowski, B.L.: Handbook of Individual Differences: Learning and Instruction. Lawrence Erlbaum, Mahwah (1993)
12. Lincoln, Y.S., Guba, E.G.: Naturalistic inquiry. Sage Publications, California (1985)
13. Miller, A.: Cognitive styles: an integrated model. Educational Psychology 7, 251–268 (1987)
14. Nuhn, R., Eaglestone, B.M., Ford, N., Moore, A.J., Brown, G.: A Qualitative Study of Composers at Work. In: Nordahl, M. (ed.) Proceedings of the International Computer Music Conference, Stockholm, International Computer Music Association, San Fransisco & School of Music and Music Education, Goteborg, pp. 572–598 (2002)
15. Pask, G.: Conversational techniques in the study and practice of education. British Journal of Educational Psychology 46, 12–25 (1976)
16. Pask, G.: Styles and strategies of learning. British Journal of Educational Psychology 46, 128–148 (1976)
17. Polfreman, R.: A task analysis of musical composition and its application to the development of Modalyser. Organised Sound 4(1) (1999)

18. Reitman, W.R.: Cognition and thought. Wiley, New York (1965)
19. Riding, R.J., Cheema, I.: Cognitive styles – an overview and integration. Educational Psychology 11, 193–215 (1991)
20. Schmeck, R.R.: Strategies and Styles of Learning: an Integration of Varied Perspectives. In: Schmeck, R.R. (ed.) Learning strategies and learning styles, pp. 317–347. Plenum, New York (1988)
21. Sloboda, J.: Do psychologists have anything useful to say about composition (Courtesy of the author). In: Third European Conference of Music Analysis, Montpellier, France, February 16-19 (1995)
22. Tracy, H.: An investigation of composers' attitudes towards the user interfaces of Electroacoustic compositional software and how to support the compositional process in a software environment, MSc Dissertation. Department of Information Studies, University of Sheffield (2002)
23. Upton, C.: An investigation into the compositional processes of Electroacoustic composers, MSc Dissertation, Department of Information Studies, University of Sheffield (2004)
24. Upton, C., Eaglestone, B., Ford, N.: The compositional processes of electroacoustic composers: four contrasting perspectives International Computer Music Conference, Barcelona (2005)
25. Vaggione, H.: Some ontological remarks about music composition processes. Computer Music Journal 25(1), 54–61 (2001)
26. Witkin, H.A., Moore, C.A., Goodenough, D.R., Cox, P.W.: Field-Dependent and Field-Independent Cognitive Styles and their Educational Research. Review of Educational Research 47(1), 1–64 (1977)

The Usability of Music Theory Software: The Analysis of Twelve-Tone Music as a Case Study

Tuukka Ilomäki

Sibelius Academy, Finland
`tuukka.ilomaki@iki.fi`

Abstract. Computer applications are an everyday tool for music analysts, composers, and music theory students. While these applications are a welcome tool to be used in the classrooms and research labs, their effectiveness could be improved by focusing on their usability.

The usability of a user interface can be evaluated and even measured with respect to the goals of its users. In order to demonstrate the evaluation of a user interface, I present an experiment in which the efficiency of user interfaces is assessed in the context of three scenarios or "use cases."

Based on the experiment, I discuss some basic principles of usability theory, such as affordances, minimization of navigation, error handling, immediate feedback, and data visibility. The evaluation of these principles suggests some new types of music theory applications.

Keywords: usability, music theory, twelve-tone rows.

1 Introduction

The popularity of personal computers has given impetus to the development of music theory software. It is now commonplace to employ computer applications for learning music theory fundamentals, generating row matrices, analyzing pitch-class sets and Klumpenhouwer networks, and so on. While many of these applications undoubtedly serve their purpose, it is worthwhile to investigate how their usability could be improved. Instead of merely examining what these applications can do, I will here explore how they do it.

Computer applications can be evaluated from a number of perspectives. In research contexts it is usually only required that the application produces the correct result in a reasonable time. If a broader audience is targeted, however, the user's experience depends not only on whether the application returns the right result, but also on the ease with which the user can interact with it.

Virtually everybody agrees on the maxim (or truism) that a user-friendly user interface makes software more usable. There is, however, significantly less agreement on what constitutes a user-friendly user interface. For example, we should not be satisfied with a popular but trivial generalization that a graphical user interface is automatically better than a command line interface. Unfortunately,

R. Kronland-Martinet, S. Ystad, and K. Jensen (Eds.): CMMR 2007, LNCS 4969, pp. 98–109, 2008.

a user-friendly user interface seems more often to be an issue for the marketing department than for the research department.

In this paper I argue, based on usability theory, against a deeply rooted myth that the quality of a user interface is a matter of opinion. In order to demonstrate the evaluation of a user interface, I will offer a hands-on experiment in which I will present two user interfaces and measure the time that it takes to finish a given task. The reading of a stopwatch is certainly not a matter of opinion. According to Nielsen [4], "Clarifying the measurable aspects of usability is much better than aiming at a warm, fuzzy feeling of user friendliness." Furthermore, the evaluation of some of the principles of a good user interface suggests some appealing directions for music theory applications.

2   Usability Theory

Usability theory (or computer-human interaction) is a relatively young branch of computer science that has its roots in cognitive psychology. Even if it does not yet belong to mainstream computer science, the awareness of its importance seems to be growing. While some of the principles of usability theory are gradually making their way to the mainstream software applications, the underlying research is less known.

In order to critically discuss usability we need to define what we mean by it. According to The International Organization for Standardization usability is "the extent to which a product can be used by specified users to achieve specified goals with effectiveness, efficiency and satisfaction in a specified context of use" (ISO 9241-11). The crux of this definition is that it does not define usability *per se*; it only defines usability with respect to the goals of the users. Hence, in order to design a good user interface and evaluate its usability, we must first discover the goals of the potential users. With respect to usability, the "features" of a computer application are insignificant. The only thing that matters is how efficiently the users can achieve their goals. (This does not mean, however, that some user interface designs would not be terrible independently of the user's goals.)

Nielsen [4] prefers the term "usability" to the vague umbrella "user friendliness." He divides usability into five categories: learnability, efficiency, memorability, error handling, and user satisfaction. The relative importance of these depends on the type of application – we can accept a steeper learning curve on software controlling a nuclear power plant than on an application that prints a row matrix. Each of these categories can be evaluated. In the following I will focus mostly on learnability, efficiency, and error handling. Learnability denotes the ease with which a first time user can interact with the user interface, and efficiency denotes the smoothness of the process when the user has mastered the application. Errors are, of course, one of the major factors behind poor learnability and efficiency.

Since usability is defined in terms of the users achieving their goals, the focus here is on the interaction between the user and the application. Even if the elements of the user interface can be improved to some degree, a good user interface for a badly designed process does not eliminate the problem that the process is badly designed. For instance, efficiently designed buttons are cold comfort if we could manage without the buttons in the first place. Hence, Cooper [1] calls for interaction design instead of interface design.

Typically, user interfaces are not designed; they simply evolve, being almost an epiphenomenon to the necessary data structures and algorithms. Giving priority to the usability means that an efficient use process is designed first – without letting the programming chores restrict the design. In particular, the user interface should not be modeled after the implementation in code.

We encounter poorly designed software frequently and are familiar with some bad designs (and might even venture to defend some of them since we are used to them). The "problem with save" is an exemplary case in point: the save function exists only because two memory types are used in computers (volatile and non-volatile). According to Cooper [2], the need to save files "is a result of the programmer inflicting the implementation model of the disk file system on the hapless user."

3   Personas, Goals, and Testing

It is not possible to predict all goals of all potential users. Hence, we need to confine ourselves to examining the goals of a few exemplary (but not average!) users. Cooper [1, 2] offers, as a tool, a set of prototypes of real people that he calls "personas." According to him, a persona "encapsulates a distinct set of usage patterns, behavior patterns regarding the use of a particular product." The personas have specified backgrounds and goals: what they want to accomplish and why.

In order to test how the personas (representing the potential users of the software) can achieve their goals, we need to design a set of "use cases." A use case is a description of a persona – with some specified background and goals – using the software to perform a task: the usability of the application can then be tested by simulating the actions of that persona.

In practice, a large number of use cases is not needed: the possible flaws of a user interface can be discovered even with a few ones. What is more important is embracing the idea that usability can be tested intersubjectively and that the issues (such as a wrong click) the users might encounter indicate problems with the application rather than with the user.

There is a distinction between how users should and how they actually use the software. Consequently, the developer of the software is a poor tester (since the developer knows how the user should use the software). If we want to evaluate the learnability and (to a degree) efficiency of the software, we need to test with people who are not involved with the development.

The aim is to streamline the process of achieving typical goals. The problem with save is a good case in point: not saving the changes is a rare exception. Nevertheless, an extra and unnecessary step is required to accomplish the usual case. Saving the changes should be the default action done automatically; the exceptional case of not saving changes can require more effort.

4 A User Interface of an Application for the Analysis of Twelve-Tone Pieces

Let us begin by considering the following use case.[1]

> Alice, a graduate music theory student, attends a course on 20th century music. She is writing her final paper on Arnold Schoenberg's *Variations for Orchestra* op. 31. She has analyzed the previous movements and is about to analyze the fifth variation (see Figure 1). She knows the row of the piece (see Figure 2) and she has discovered that in this piece rows may be split into several voices, but within the voices the pitch classes are generally in the correct order. She begins her analyses by deciphering the row forms. She has already analyzed the previous movements with pen on paper and now tries a computer application.

For the purpose of simulating usability testing, I have developed two java applets (available online at http://www.iki.fi/tuukka.ilomaki/Usability/), both of which are intended to help Alice achieve her goal. The user interfaces of these applets are shown in Figures 3 and 4. In the following, I will refer to them simply as the bad user interface and the better user interface.

Both applications have the same functionality: instead of jotting down the row matrix and finding the segments of the musical surface in it, Alice can enter the row of the piece and the segments, and the application enumerates which rows in the pertinent row class have those segments, thus helping her decipher the rows of the piece.

We can consider the following points in our evaluation of the user interfaces: What is the number of steps Alice needs to take? How does the program aid deciphering row forms in the "normal" cases? How does the program cope with incorrect input? How easy is it to spot correct but erroneous input? We should notice that one of the applications does a considerably better job.

Designing good use cases is far from trivial. The above use case was tailored to provide a starting point for comparing the two user interfaces and therefore simplified. It is a poorly designed use case, however. Is Alice's goal really to decipher the row forms? Certainly not. A mere deciphering of the row forms is seldom (if ever) the goal. Could finishing the paper be Alice's goal? In that case, an optimal user interface would be one in which pressing a big red button prints out a finished top-grade final paper. (Or, why should she even be bothered to press the button?) She rather wants to learn both twelve-tone analysis and this piece well enough to be able to finish her paper. The application, however, only helps her in deciphering the row forms.

---

[1] I borrowed the names of the three protagonists of my uses cases from cryptography in which they are used frequently.

Fig. 1. The beginning of the fifth variation of Arnold Schoenberg's *Variations for Orchestra* op. 31

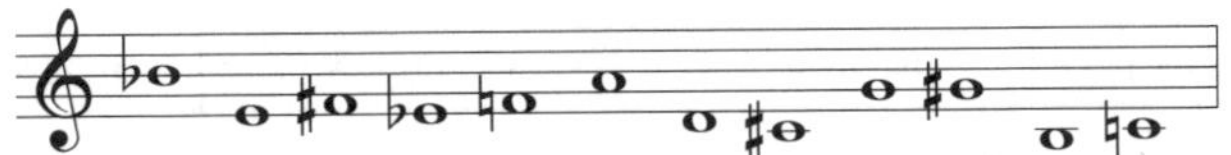

Fig. 2. The row of Schoenberg's *Variations for Orchestra* op. 31

```
┌─────────────────────────────────────────┐
│  Schoenberg Variations op. 31        ▲▼  │
└─────────────────────────────────────────┘

┌──────────┐ ┌─────────────┐ ┌────────────────┐ ┌──────────┐
│ Set row  │ │ Add segment │ │ Clear segments │ │  Find    │
└──────────┘ └─────────────┘ └────────────────┘ └──────────┘

Row: 06857B439A12              Segments: 98 AB 10 23
```

Fig. 3. The bad user interface

```
┌─────────────────────────────────────────┐
│  Schoenberg Variations op. 31        ▲▼  │
└─────────────────────────────────────────┘

Row        06857B439A12

Segments   98 AB 10 23

Found pcs:                   Missing pcs:
0 1 2 3 8 9 10 11              4 5 6 7

   T1:  17968054AB23     (24 89 05 AB)
  I10:  A4253B671098     (AB 05 89 24)
   R0:  21A934B75860     (82 95 A0 B7)
  R11:  109823A6475B     (98 50 BA 76)
  RI0:  AB2398157460     (76 BA 50 98)
 RI11:  9A128704635B     (B7 A0 95 82)
```

Fig. 4. The better user interface

The following use case depicts another real-life situation. It allows us to concretize some further usability problems in the two applications.

Bob, an established scholar on twelve-tone music, has noticed that two published analyses of Arnold Schoenberg's *Variations for Orchestra* op. 31 give different row forms for the fifth variation. He has decided to examine the grounds for such a phenomenon and to find arguments for favoring one or the other interpretation.

The two demo applications support Bob's goals poorly: they might speed up finding the potential row candidates in the non-controversial measures (such as the beginning of the variation), but not in the controversial ones (such as the second beat of measure 200, which contains the segments *F♯-G*, *B♭-C♭*, *C-D♭*, *E-F-E♭-D*, and *A-A♭*; no row form contains this particular set of segments).

Find the row of the piece	Analyze the row	Decipher the row forms	Analyze the row forms

Row: 06857B439A12

Segment sets:	Row candidates:
98 10 23 45 67 AB	I10(**AB 89 24 13 67 05**) RP11(**98 BA 76 31 42 50**)
56 12 A9 0B 87 43	P4(**AB 89 13 24 67 05**) RI3(**98 BA 31 76 42 50**)
54 98 AB 01 23 67	I6(**AB 89 24 13 67 05**) RP7(**98 BA 76 31 42 50**)
45 01 98 BA|	P3(**AB 89 13 24**) RP2(**B7 95 41 82**) RI1(**82 A0 63 B7**) RI2(**98 BA 31 76**)

Fig. 5. An improved user interface

A test run with Bob would give rise to the following questions: How does the application support deciphering row forms in measures where the pitch classes are not in the correct order? Does the application support the comparison of multiple interpretations of rows (like the opening row forms in the fifth variation) and in contradictory places (like many row forms in the fifth variation)? Does the application support making analytical observations, such as comparing various passages in the piece and finding recurring patterns or transformational relations?

The above two demo applications might have initially seemed decent little utilities. The moral of the experiment is that well-designed use cases are required in order to critically assess the usability of a computer application. Alice and Bob have different needs (pedagogical versus research-oriented), but it would certainly be possible to design a user interface that satisfies both.

In order to address the goals of a still wider audience, let us add one more use case.

> Carol, a graduate music theory student, is taking her first course on 20th century music. Her homework is to write an analysis of a brief twelve-tone composition of an undisclosed composer.

This use case adds a new need of functionality: in order to proceed with the analysis Carol needs help in discovering the row of the piece – which can sometimes be challenging – and since the composer is undisclosed she cannot do a literature search. She might also need help in discovering the basic properties of the row. Upon discovering the row and its properties, she has the same needs as Alice.

The three use cases provide a base for developing a user interface of an application for the analysis of twelve-tone music. Figure 5 sketches a portion of a user interface for an application that is designed to support the goals of Alice, Bob, and Carol. The four phases that often occur in the process of analyzing a twelve-tone composition – finding the row of the piece, analyzing the properties of the row, deciphering the row forms, and analyzing the succession of row forms – are placed in separate tabs. The first and second tabs are designed to aid Carol in discovering the row of the piece and its properties. Alice and Bob will start from the third tab. It goes without saying that data entered in one phase should be automatically transferred to the next phase.

From the usability perspective, the new user interface has some enhancements compared to those in Figures 3 and 4. The segment sets are displayed in list form and they can be edited in place. This enables the analyst to keep track of the progress, skip over problematic passages and return to them later, and compare passages. An optimal implementation of this list would allow the user to copy, move, insert, and delete segment sets directly – no buttons are needed. Naturally, the list of row candidates is updated automatically as in the user interface in Figure 4.

We must draw a limit on how far we should go to support the specifics of the use cases. In particular, with respect to the case study in this paper – the analysis of twelve-tone compositions – each composition presents its unique set of analytical challenges. Hence, the target is to develop an application that supports the most frequently occurring issues. For instance, since the pitch-class organization of the fifth variation is very peculiar, one might as well write an article that explains it instead of writing a computer application that is powerful enough to decipher it (see, for example, [3]). The target is to support the typical goals, not all possible goals.

It is difficult to design a user interface that supports even one selected goal and also scores high in all five of Nielsen's categories; designing a user interface that supports a large number of different goals is an unlikely achievement. Accordingly, it would be advisable to implement only a limited number of prominent analytical methodologies in the analysis tab, such as keeping track of the rows, analyzing the transformational relations, hexachord contents, invariant subsegments and subsets, and so on.

5   Elements of a Good User Interface

A user creates a mental model of an application based on its affordances, or "fundamental properties that determine just how the thing could possibly be used" (see [5]). The more intuitive the necessary tools are and the more readily they are available, the more easily the user is able to use them.[2]

Even if the applications in Figures 3 and 4 do not properly support the goals of Alice, Bob, and Carol, they serve to demonstrate some principles of good user interfaces.

First, both user interfaces use standard GUI elements (buttons, editable fields, and drop-down menus) and the users should have no problems in understanding how to use them. All the affordances are visible in both applications – I could

---

[2] Affordances are not limited to computer applications. For instance, a door can be pushed/pulled on the left/right side: if the affordances are hidden there is only a 25% chance that it can be opened on the first trial.

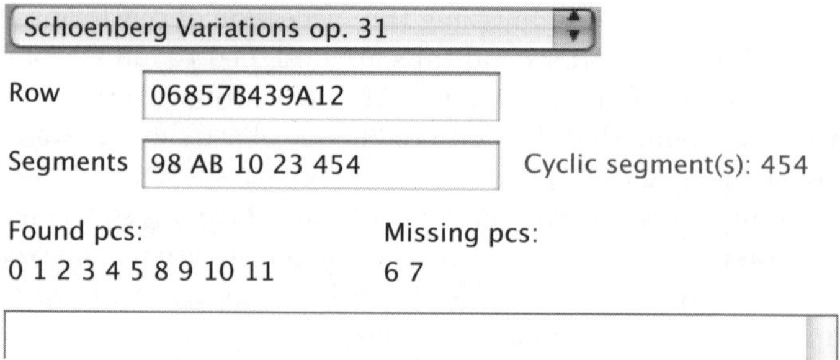

Fig. 6. Error handling in the better user interface

have made the bad interface considerably worse by hiding the affordances behind menus instead of using buttons.

Secondly, the minimization of navigation is one of the key principles of usability. The appearance of a new navigational element, such as a dialog box, always constitutes an extraneous mental effort, since the user needs to adapt to the new environment. One of the major reasons why the better of the two user interfaces performs more competently in the experiment is that all the data can be edited directly and no navigation is needed. As shown in Figure 4, this application contains no buttons, dialog boxes, or alerts. From the usability perspective, the buttons and dialog boxes in the bad user interface are unnecessary, since they force the user to navigate between different windows.

Thirdly, errors are a major hindrance to achieving specified goals effectively. The error handling strategy is divided into prevention and recovery. The former means that the user interface should guide the user to avoid errors; the latter means that catastrophic errors are not possible and recovery from minor errors should be straightforward.

The error-handling strategy in the better user interface is that, in the case of malformed input, the user is simply shown the result of such an input. Humans are used to coping with incomplete and incorrect data. Hence, rather than breaking the flow of actions, the user is notified of malformed input – the application does not come to a halt and require that the user corrects the error immediately. Figure 6 shows how cyclic segments are handled in the better user interface: no row contains cyclic segments and thus the list of row forms that contain the specified segments is empty and an error message is shown in context. The flow of actions is not broken, however. The user can continue entering the segments and fix the error at a time that is appropriate for the user (instead of forcing the user to fix it at a time that is appropriate for the computer). The application also provides a simple option for undo: editing the cyclic segment (which most likely is a typo) in the input field. In contrast, the only "undo" that the bad user interface offers is starting over from scratch. Consequently, the bad user interface does not encourage experimenting with various alternative interpretations since it does not allow the modification of the segments that have already been entered.

Fourthly, one of the key elements of a good application is that all data is visible all the time and the user can interact with the data in a straightforward manner. The better user interface supports in-place editing of data, not entering it piecemeal via a succession of dialog boxes. As the user enters the input, the immediate feedback in the form of a live update of the data makes it easy to understand the connection between the input and its effect on the data. Moreover, the user is kept informed of the progress by keeping track of those pitch classes that have already been found and those that have not, thus guiding the user to look for segments with the missing pitch classes in the score. In contrast, in the bad user interface the user needs to click a button in order to initiate a search, instead of the application performing the search automatically.

Finally, I wish to emphasize that the above considerations do not obliterate the normal accessibility principles, such as providing necessary guidance (even if the need for guidance might imply a problem in the user interface) or taking color vision deficiency into account.

6   Usability Testing

A usability test on the two user interfaces in Figures 3 and 4 was conducted. All test users were "computer literate" and were familiar with music notation, but had varied levels of knowledge on twelve-tone music. In the test the users were presented with the necessary background with regard to Alice and they were asked to play the role of Alice and try to achieve her goals. They were asked to think aloud in order to scrutinize the mental model that they had formed of the application. The interaction between the users and the applications was observed and no guidance was provided unless they came to a complete halt. The testing revealed some further usability issues in the user interfaces.

First, many of the users struggled with entering the segments. Pitch classes 10 and 11 can be notated as A and B or as T and E, respectively.[3] Both user interfaces provide only a tiny hint of the preferred syntax: when the users select the row from the drop-down menu it is written as 06857B439A12 in which pitch classes 10 and 11 are notated as A and B; most users failed to note this little detail. Ultimately, the application should support both notations (since there is no possibility of ambiguity) and the application would thus be forthcoming since it tries its best to understand the user's input. In addition, in the better user interface some users had difficulties in realizing that the segments should be separated by white space. Both of these issues could be easily solved with a hint text.

Secondly, users with only a limited experience in the analysis of twelve-tone music (or no experience at all) had substantial difficulties in discovering how the two applications should be used. Indeed, when using the first user interface they were able to accomplish practically nothing, whereas when they were using the second user interface they were at least able to recognize when a failure was due

---

[3] One of these abbreviations must be used since otherwise pitch class 10 and segment 10 could not be distinguished.

to their incorrect actions (such as typos) and when it was due to their inability to analyze the composition. This demonstrates the usefulness of immediate feedback: all test users of the second user interface could quickly link the disappearance of all rows in the row list to the idea that the segments they gave as input did not belong to the same row form, for instance. In contrast, when using the first user interface the users did realize that they were not making any progress but could not figure out the reason.

It was defined in the use case that Alice has already analyzed the previous movements. Hence, she has gained some experience on the analysis of twelve-tone music and we cannot blame the user interfaces for the fact that some users participating in the usability test did not know how to proceed with analyzing the row structure of a twelve-tone composition. In contrast, if the use case had specified that this was the very first time that Alice had analyzed a twelve-tone composition, criticism for the lack of guidance on how to proceed with the analysis would be justified.

Thirdly, the row structure of the fifth variation may be difficult to discover since the score is rather complex. One way of assessing the usability of the user interfaces is to observe how the user is able to ascertain the row structure. Throughout the variation the rows are divided into six semitone dyads. For instance, the first row form is divided into dyads A-$G\sharp$, $B\flat$-$C\flat$, $D\flat$-C, D-$E\flat$, E-F, and $F\sharp$-G. Many of the test users entered first the six pitch classes of the top voice as one segment: A-$G\sharp$-F-$G\flat$-F-E. The better user interface immediately informs the user that the segment is cyclic and the users were quickly able to figure out that those six pitch classes do not belong to the same row form. Consequently the users were also able to infer that the row is divided into short segments that are distributed among different voices, and with some trial and error some of them found the six dyads that form the first row form.

With respect to Nielsen's categories, the first and second usability issues discussed above are examples of learnability and the third is an example of efficiency. Testing the memorability of the user interfaces would require conducting a follow-up experiment with the same test users.

7   Conclusions

The above discussion suggests at least two types of music theory computer applications that could merit a place in the computer music community. The first is an application that truly supports the music analyst's goals. Such an application would support making analytical observations from multiple perspectives on both local and global levels. The above applications focused on twelve-tone music, but other compositional practices could have been used as well.

The second is data mining: the user examines the data – pitch and pitch-class sets, twelve-tone rows and shorter segments, and Klumpenhouwer networks, for instance – from different perspectives. The data could be either the entire universum or a subset derived from an analytical or a compositional context. In the above row analysis applications, for example, the data is the rows in a row class and the user examines the rows with respect to their subsegment content. The usability point here is that the actions of the user result in an immediate response, making explorations of the universum easy.

Applying the idea of data mining, I would like to explore various universums of musical entities in real time, charting relations between the entities, experimenting with diverse constraints and investigating which entities satisfy my criteria, thus revealing new, interesting and perhaps surprising facets of that universum. My hope is that this paper may give some reader the impetus to create such applications.

References

1. Cooper, A.: The Inmates Are Running the Asylum. Sams, Indianapolis (1999)
2. Cooper, A.: About Face 2.0: The Essentials of User Interface Design. Wiley, Indianapolis (2003)
3. Ilomäki, T.: Aspects of pitch organization in Schönberg's Variations for Orchestra op. 31. In: Lithuanian musicology, vol. 7 (2007)
4. Nielsen, J.: Usability engineering. AP Professional, Boston (1993)
5. Norman, D.: The psychology of everyday things. Basic Books, New York (1988)

Understanding Emotion in *Raag*: An Empirical Study of Listener Responses

Parag Chordia and Alex Rae

Georgia Institute of Technology,
Music Technology Group
840 McMillan St, Atlanta GA 30332, USA
{ppc,arae3}@gatech.edu
http://www.paragchordia.com

Abstract. A survey of emotion in North Indian classical music was undertaken to determine the type and consistency of emotional responses to *raag*. Participants listened to five one-minute *raag* excerpts and recorded their emotional responses after each. They were asked to describe the emotions each excerpt evoked and then to adjust six different sliders indicating the degree to which they felt the following: happy, sad, peaceful, tense, romantic, longing. A total of 280 responses were received. We find that both free-response and quantitative judgments of emotions are significantly different for each *raag* and quite consistent across listeners. We hypothesized that the primary predictors of emotion in these excerpts would be pitch-class distribution, pitch-class dyad entropy, overall sensory dissonance, and note density. Multiple regression analysis was used to determine the most important factors, their relative importance, and their total predictive value (R^2). The features in combination explained between 11% (peaceful) and 33% (happy) of response variance. For all models, a subset of the features were significant, with the interplay between "minor" and "major" scale degrees playing an important role. Although the explanatory power of the current models is limited, the results thus far strongly suggest that *raags* do consistently elicit specific emotions that are linked to musical properties. The responses did not differ significantly for enculturated and non-enculturated listeners, suggesting that musical rather than cultural factors are dominant.

1 Background

Raag literally means "that which colors the mind". It is a melodic abstraction around which almost all North Indian classical music (NICM) is organized. A *raag* is most easily explained as a collection of melodic gestures and a technique for developing them. The gestures are sequences of notes that are often inflected with various micro-pitch alterations and articulated with an expressive sense of timing. Longer phrases are built by joining these melodic atoms together.

NICM uses approximately one hundred *raags*, of which fifty are common. Despite micro-tonal variation, the tones in any given *raag* conform to a subset of

R. Kronland-Martinet, S. Ystad, and K. Jensen (Eds.): CMMR 2007, LNCS 4969, pp. 110–124, 2008.

the twelve chromatic pitches of a standard just-intoned scale. There are theoretically thousands of scale types; in practice, however, *raags* conform to a much smaller set of scales, and many of the most common *raags* share the same set of notes.

By building phrases as described above, a tonal hierarchy is created. Some tones appear more often in the basic phrases, or are sustained longer. Indian music theory has a rich vocabulary for describing the function of notes in this framework. The most stressed note is called the *vadi* and the second most stressed, traditionally a fifth or fourth away, is called the *samvadi*. There are also less commonly used terms for tones on which phrases begin and end. A typical summary of a *raag* includes its scale type (*that*), *vadi* and *samvadi*. A pitch-class distribution (PCD), which gives the relative frequency of each scale degree, neatly summarizes this information.

The performance context of *raag* music is essentially monophonic, although vocalists will usually be shadowed by an accompanying melody instrument. The rhythmic accompaniment of the *tabla* is also present in metered sections. There is usually an accompanying drone that sounds the tonic and fifth using a harmonically rich timbre.

2   Related Work

The emotional qualities of *raags* have been discussed extensively in NICM music theory. Traditionally, this music is said to evoke seven basic emotions: sadness, romance, peace, strength/courage, anger, dispassion, devotion [1]. In theory, each *raag* elicits a unique emotional state (*rasa*) consisting of one or more of these basic emotions.

For Western music, a variety of studies have been undertaken since the late 19th century to define what emotions music elicits, and to understand the musical factors that underly them. These studies have followed a basic experimental paradigm in which musical excerpts are presented to listeners who are then asked to respond by verbally describing their emotional states, rating emotions on a quantitative scale, or some other measurement. Musical stimuli are chosen so that certain characteristics can be systematically varied, such as timbre, tempo and tonality. Correlations between responses and musical structure are then observed, and are interpreted to account for some aspect of the listener reactions.

A common pitfall in such experiments is the fundamental difficulty of isolating the factor that is being tested. Real musical excerpts rarely vary in just one parameter, while artificial stimuli that can be systematically varied often will not generalize, lacking the "ecological validity" of real music. Most importantly, the difficulty of quantifying a person's actual emotional state, either through observation or by eliciting verbal or other responses, makes such research extremely challenging. Despite this, the field has produced a body of work that suggests consistent relationships between musical structure and emotional response [2]. In general, two broad categories of emotional responses have been found, relating to valence (happy-sad) and activity (vigorous-calm). For example, fast tempo has been shown to correlate consistently with positive valence and activity; the same has been shown for major (versus minor) tonality. A thorough overview of the field of emotion and music can be found in [3].

Although the connection between *raag* and emotion is assumed to be systematic by nearly all enculturated listeners and performers, very little empirical work relating to emotion in NICM has been published. In one study, NICM musicians were asked to play short excerpts that conveyed either joy, sadness, anger, or peace. Listeners not familiar with NICM were asked to identify the predominant emotion. The recognition of intended emotions was mostly successful except for peace [2].

3   Motivation

The current work seeks to characterize the emotional responses of listeners to different *raags* and the extent to which listeners report similar experiences; furthermore, if responses differ systematically by *raag*, it seeks to identify some of the musical factors that underly these responses. In NICM, all pitch-related activity is structured by the choice of *raag*. Each *raag* is traditionally associated with several basic emotions. For example, *Raag Yaman* is said to evoke peace, happiness, and devotion. Performers and listeners of NICM often report that the essence of *raag*-based music is the evocation of mood brought about by one or more related emotions, and that different *raags* reliably elicit different emotional states. In many cases, however, the more traditional descriptions are not accepted, or are thought of as rudimentary. Despite the central role of emotion in *raag* theory, almost no empirical work has been undertaken to systematically analyze listener response to different *raags*.

4   Survey Design

For the purpose of collecting a large number of responses, we created an online survey in which participants were asked to respond to five *raag* excerpts in terms of "how listening to each *raag* made you feel." The survey can be found at http://www.paragchordia.com/survey/raagemotion1/ and the *raag* excerpts can be heard at http://www.paragchordia.com/research.html. Some basic demographic information was collected, specifically age, sex, level of musical training (if any), and familiarity with NICM (if any). For each excerpt, there was both a free response with the directions to "describe how it makes you feel in as much detail as possible," and a series of six value sliders (ranging from zero to one hundred) corresponding to pre-chosen emotional adjectives: happy, sad, tense, peaceful, romantic, and longing. The adjectives were chosen based on preliminary research by the author suggesting that these might best capture the dominant emotional axes. Further, the first four roughly represent the valence and activity judgments discussed above.

Participants were asked to "adjust the slider to indicate how well you feel that the word applies to the *raag* excerpt you just heard." The order in which

Table 1. Summary of scale degrees used by *raags* in database. Notes are listed with C as the tonic.

	C	D♭	D	E♭	E	F	F♯	G	A♭	A	B♭	B
Yaman	•		•		•		•	•		•		•
Desh	•		•		•	•		•		•		•
Khamaj	•		•		•	•		•		•	•	•
Darbari	•		•	•	•			•	•		•	
Marwa	•	•			•		•			•		•

each of these sliders appeared was randomized for each *raag* presented. Each participant was presented with the same set of five *raags* in a random order. The specific excerpt for each *raag* was chosen at random from three possibilities, one played on *sarod* and two on *sitar*, both traditional plucked string instruments. All excerpts were approximately one minute long, unaccompanied, and from *alap*, a slower, arrhythmic introductory section of a *raag* performance. Participants had the option of replaying each segment an unlimited number of times. Without knowing in advance how much data we would be able to collect, it was impossible to determine an appropriate dimensionality for the data we sought. Therefore, an attempt was made to strike a balance, leading to the decision to limit the number of slider-values to six and include a free-response section as well. This was also the reasoning that determined on the one hand the presentation of the same five *raags* to each participant, while generalizing slightly by the inclusion of three audio files for each *raag*.

5   Survey Results

A total of 280 survey responses were collected. Participants were recruited from online NICM forums, as well as through the Georgia Institute of Technology music department. 29% of the respondents were female and 71% male, with a median age of 24. The respondents described their familiarity with NICM as "none" (11%), "a little" (24%), "somewhat" (29%), "very" (32%) and "expert" (4%).

5.1   Content Analysis of Free Responses

The descriptive language of the free responses indicated the intensity and complexity of listeners' emotions. The style ranged from lists of words and phrases describing simple emotions to lengthy and even poetic passages. A sampling is shown in Table 2.

Due to the fact that many of the free responses consisted of fragments or lists of words, highly sophisticated content analysis was not particularly relevant; instead, we focus on lower-level analysis, primarily word histograms.

Initially, simple histograms of terms appearing in each free response section were tabulated. Limiting the results to relevant descriptive terms, the most common for each *raag* were collected and are shown in Table 3. Standard variations of each word (e.g. "happy" and "happiness") were treated as examples of the same root word.

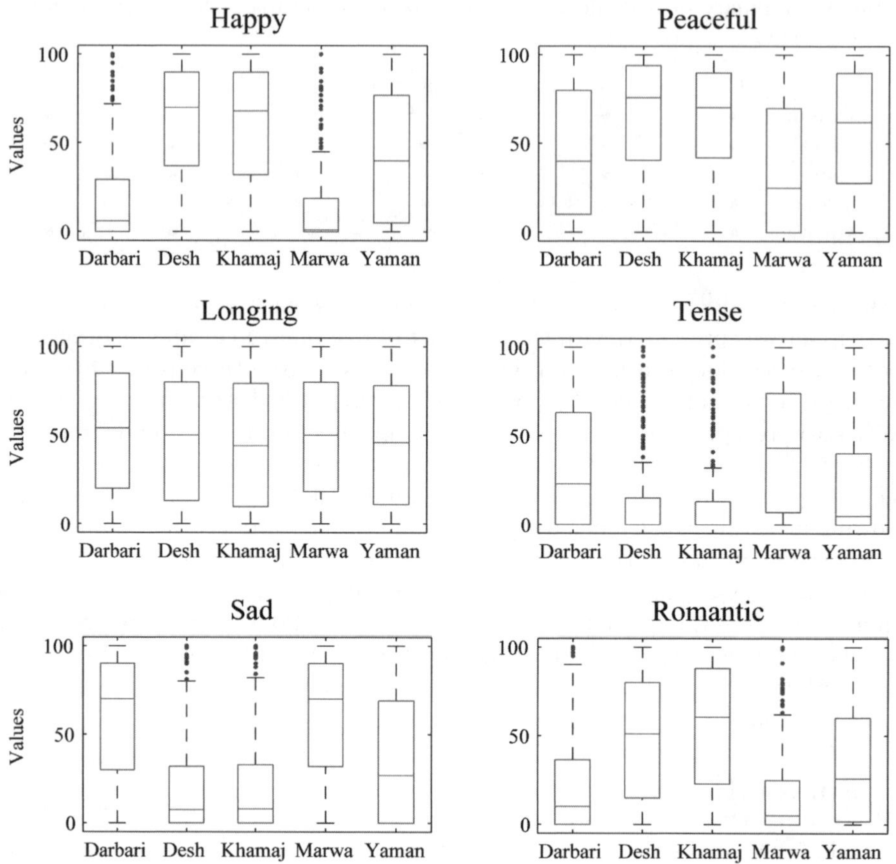

Fig. 1. Summary of quantitative survey responses. Box and whisker plots for each emotion are shown. The 25th to 75th percentile is indicated by the box, the median by the horizontal line in the middle of the box. The range of the data is shown by the whiskers with outliers notated with hatch marks. It can be seen that *Desh* and *Khamaj* form one reponse cluster, and *Marwa* and *Darbari* another.

Terms were also grouped according to various categories of meaning, in an attempt to both give a broader view of the responses and to capture information buried in the "long tail" of infrequently used but clearly related terms. For example, words such as "bliss", "exultation", "happy", "joyful", and "ecstasy" were grouped together under "Joy & Happiness". Relevant semantic groupings were based on a modified version of a standard content analysis dictionary. As before, the most common occurrences were tabulated and the results are displayed in Table 4.

The tables clearly show a common pattern of responses for certain raags. *Raags Khamaj* and *Desh* are associated with positively valenced concepts such as "joy & happiness," whereas *Darbari* and *Marwa* were consistently associated with "melancholy & sadness." Interestingly, *Yaman* was equally associated with

Table 2. A sample of free responses

Darbari: "Emptiness. I'm tumbling down a deep abyss. Weightless, then maybe. Dark and surrounding. Fall."
"It feels like pain, an agony that is long lasting and is happening at the time that the music is playing, a time of hardship."

Desh: "Absolutely fresh.... Clearing all the bad thoughts... Gives fresh meaning to life. Sounds serene. Very Peaceful i felt."
"Pure, unblemished...Something white as milk, offering to take you in, clean all your sins...Compassionate and loving, but in a distant sort of way."

Khamaj: "It so reminds me of the blossoming of flowers and prosperity... the happy chuckles of newborns... the pride of their mothers... "
"spring time. birds chirping. sun is shining. love. a mother is telling her child a story. the child is smiling. good times are upon us."

Marwa: "my reaction to this raaga was almost sexual. I felt desire. I felt the urge to look beautiful and dress up in heavy gold jewelery. felt very aware of my body. at times I felt a strange anger and the desire to control somebody else. i felt very powerful. i felt like a woman."
"very depressing...felt like crying...someone was going away... describes life in some way....the ups and downs."

Yaman: "I feel like a butterfly. The wind is streaking past me, and colors are awash in the air. Melodious colors."
"A combination of moods. It looks relaxed most of the time and ruminating about something. It seems to turn a little angry occasionally as though an unhappy event was inadvertently recollected."

Table 3. Simple word histograms for each *Raag*

Darbari		Desh		Khamaj		Marwa		Yaman	
Freq.	Term	Freq.	Term	Freq.	Term	Freq.	Term	Freq.	Term
75	sad	59	happy	53	happy	74	sad	46	sad
19	peaceful	41	peaceful	36	peaceful	16	serious	42	peaceful
14	deep	19	romantic	31	sad	14	good	38	happy
13	calm	17	sad	24	romantic	14	peaceful	13	good
10	longing	15	soothing	13	soothing	14	longing	12	calm
10	serious	11	nice	10	good	13	deep	11	longing
10	beautiful	10	pleasant	9	longing	10	tense	8	serious
9	good	10	patriotic	9	love	7	emotional	7	romantic
8	happy	9	playful	9	relax	7	happy	7	relax
5	sombre	9	remind	6	calm	6	soothe	6	devotional

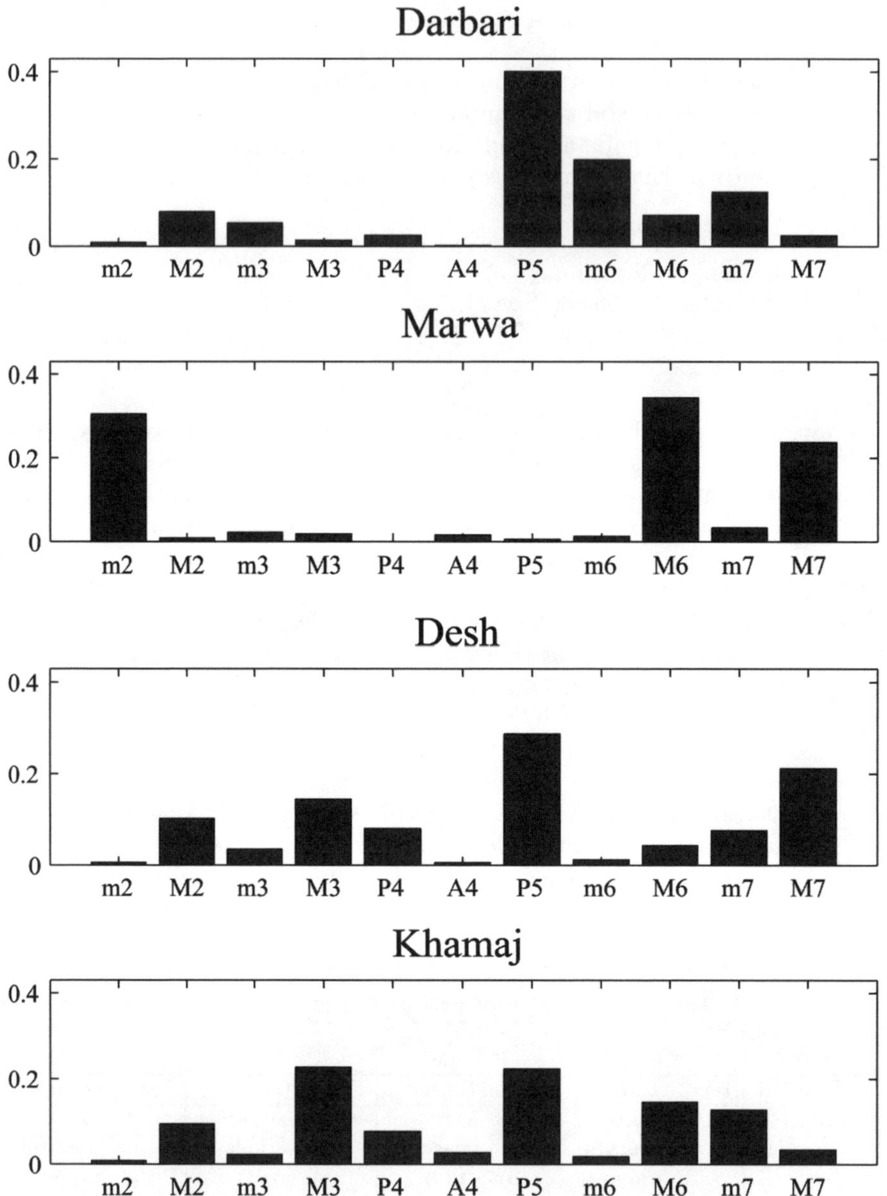

Fig. 2. Pitch-class distributions for *raags Darbari, Marwa, Desh,* and *Khamaj*

"melancholy & sadness" and "joy & happiness." The results show that, although each *raag* has a strong valence, a variety of other emotions are also present, suggesting that listeners' responses are indeed complex.

Table 4. Semantic category histograms for each *Raag*. Words with a similar meaning were assigned to a common semantic category.

Darbari		Desh		Khamaj	
Frq.	Semantic Cat.	Frq.	Semantic Cat.	Frq.	Semantic Cat.
134	melancholy & sadness	115	joy & happiness	103	joy & happiness
21	joy & happiness	41	love & affection	54	melancholy & sadness
16	pains	32	melancholy & sadness	37	love & affection
15	emotion	14	pleasures	13	emotions
12	beauty	13	composure	10	composure
11	tension	12	beauty	9	pleasures
11	love & affection	11	hope & optimism	7	passions
10	sympathy & compassion	6	emotion	7	hope & optimism
8	despair & resignation	6	desires	5	desires

Marwa		Yaman	
Frq.	Semantic Cat.	Frq.	Semantic Cat.
133	melancholy & sadness	71	melancholy & sadness
28	tension	69	joy & happiness
15	sympathy & compassion	16	emotions
12	pains	16	love & affection
12	joy & happiness	12	beauty
11	emotion	9	composure
10	love & affection	8	tension
7	anger & indignation	8	pleasures
7	emotionalities	6	passions

5.2 Quantitative Responses

Figure 2 shows the distribution of quantitative (slider) responses for each emotion and *raag*. For happy, sad, tense, and romantic, three *raag* clusters are apparent. *Desh* and *Khamaj* are strongly positively valenced (happy, romantic and not tense) and *Marwa* and *Darbari* are negatively valenced (sad, not romantic, tense) with *Yaman* falling between these poles. Multiple comparison of means confirms that differences between these three clusters for these three emotions are significant ($p < .05$) but that differences within clusters are not significant. The "longing" values show no statistically significant differences by *raag*, however all the *raags* clearly brought out this emotion. For the "peaceful" emotion there are again three clusters: *Marwa* is least peaceful followed by *Darbari* and then a cluster containing *Yaman*, *Khamaj* and *Desh*.

6 Feature Selection

In order to explore possible predictors for these emotional reactions, several features were extracted from the audio excerpts. Some of these features have previously been shown to be highly effective in *raag* classification [4], thus we sought to investigate their ability to explain emotional responses. We hypothesized that survey responses would in part be predicted by the pitches used and their relative weights, as represented by PCDs. In particular, it was expected that the relative prevalence of certain major and minor intervals would correspond to positively and negatively valenced responses.

Further, it was thought that sequential pairs of pitches, pitch class dyad distributions (PCDDs), would have a noticeable correlation. Extrapolating from Huron [5], we hypothesized that the degree of flexibility in PCDDs would correspond to a sense of tension and longing. Flexibility was calculated as the entropy of the PCDD distributions, where a low entropy would correspond to an excerpt having highly determined, or leading, note transitions, possibly leading to a greater sense of longing.

A number of other features were considered as well, notably the overall dissonance of a given excerpt, calculated as the sensory dissonance. This feature was thought likely to correspond to negative emotions, although as calculated it might give excessively large values to spectrally rich sounds. The overall note density and spectral centroids for each excerpt were also determined.

6.1   Pitch Detection and Pitch-Class Distributions

Pitch detection was done using a version of the Harmonic Product Spectrum (HPS) algorithm [6]. Each segment was divided into 40 ms frames, using a Gaussian window. The frames were overlapped by 75%, so that the pitch was estimated every 10 ms.

The PCDs were calculated by taking histograms of the pitch-tracks. The bins corresponded to each note of five octaves of a chromatic scale. Specifically, the ratios of the just-intoned scale tuned to the tonic frequency of each segment were used to calculate the bin values, and the bin boundaries were determined as the log mean. The five octaves were then folded into one, transforming pitches into pitch-classes, and the values were normalized to create a pitch-class distribution. This nulled any significance of octave errors, a common problem in the HPS algorithm.

6.2   Note Density

The average note density for each excerpt was calculated from detected note onsets. Onsets were found by thresholding a complex detection function (DF) [7]. The excerpt was divided into 128 sample regions, overlapped 50% using a rectangular window, and the DFT of each region was computed and used to construct the DF. Adaptive thresholding, proportional to the median over a sliding window, was used to choose the peaks to be labeled as onsets.

6.3   Pitch-Class Dyad Distributions

Pitch-class dyad distributions were calculated for each excerpt. The detected onsets were used to segment the pitch-tracks into notes. Each note was then assigned a pitch-class label: first the raw pitch estimates were discretized by assigning to each the center value of the bins defined for the pitch histogram, and then the mode was calculated for each note. The label of the corresponding chromatic pitch was assigned to that note. This process dealt quite effectively with variations due to micro-pitch structure, attacks, and errors by the detection algorithm. The octaves were folded into one as with the PCDs. The pitch-classes were then arranged in groups of two (bi-grams), or in musical terms, dyads. The entropy of the PCDD for each excerpt was then calculated.

6.4 Sensory Dissonance

The presence in a sound of partials which fall within the critical band for frequency resolution is the key indicator of dissonance, according to the tonotopic theory of sensory dissonance. A value for this was calculated by performing pairwise comparisons between all detected partials in each segment, and weighting the detected sub-critical-band intervals by their relative amplitudes. This calculation was performed using an algorithm developed by Kameoka and Kuriyagawa [8].

6.5 Timbral Features

The center of mass in the frequency domain (spectral centroid) was calculated for each excerpt.

7 Analysis

An initial demographic analysis showed that responses were not significantly different by age, sex, or familiarity with Indian music.

Multiple regression analysis was undertaken to determine how well the PCDs, subjective dissonance, and sensory dissonance features explained the emotion ratings. A linear model was built using these features for each of the quantitative emotional response types (with the exception of "longing", which was excluded because no statistically significant differences were found between *raags*). For example, the slider values for "happy" were modeled as

$$happy_i = \beta_1 x_1^i + \beta_2 x_2^i + \beta_3 x_3^i + + \beta_n x_n^i, \tag{1}$$

where x_k^i is the kth feature and β_k^i is the corresponding regression coefficient for the ith observation. Stepwise regression was performed to determine the subset of features to be included in the final model.

Tables 5, 6, 7, and 8 show the *beta* values, that is the standardized regression coefficients, for the each of the features, as well as the R^2 statistic for the total model. All coefficients presented have p values of less than .01. All variables in the model were normalized to have a mean of zero and a standard deviation of one, thus avoiding difficulties in comparing the scales of the independent variables. The R^2 statistic measures the total variance accounted for by the model and varies between 0 (random) and 1 (perfect fit). Of course, if measurement error is high, then the model will not be meaningful. The individual correlation between each feature and the emotion, which varies between -1 and 1, is also shown.

Additionally the variance inflation factor (VIF) for each feature is shown, giving a measure of the multicollinearity of the independent variables. This occurs when one of the variables is well approximated by a linear combination of the other variables, as is likely to be the case for PCD values. The VIF is calculated by regressing each variable using the remaining independent variables, and is computed as $\frac{1}{1-R^2}$. If the R^2 value is high, it indicates that the variable is multicollinear. In typical applications, VIF values above a threshold of 10 indicate that a variable should be removed. Interpretation of models with multicollinear variables is difficult as the relative contribution of each cannot easily be read from the beta values and the reliability of the estimate decreases (the size of the confidence interval increases for that coefficient). In some cases, multicollinearity can reverse the expected sign of the regression coefficient. For example, in Table 5 in the "happy" model, the Major 3rd coefficient is negative despite a strong positive correlation; it can be seen, however, that the variable is highly multicollinear, with a VIF of 7.74. Because scale tones in *raags* may be highly correlated, it is important to be aware of this potential confound. Stepwise regression partially avoids this problem by automatically selecting features that give the greatest incremental contribution to explaining the variance of the dependent variable. In this way, only one of a set of highly correlated features is typically included. Nevertheless, highly correlated variables may remain in the model, making VIF useful for interpretation.

Tables 5 and 6 shows that "happy" and "sad" are modeled best, with R^2 values of .34 and .28 respectively, whereas the model is only weakly predictive in the case of "peaceful" (.11) and "tense" (.16). Unsurprisingly, "happy" responses are negative correlated with the minor 2nd ($\beta = -.13$), minor 3rd ($\beta = -.16$),

Table 5. Summary of regression model for "happy". For each feature we report the standardized regression coefficients, the bivariate correlation, and the variance inflation factor measure of multicollinearity.

Total R^2 = .34

feature	β	corr	VIF
minor 2nd	-0.13	-0.29	4.23
minor 3rd	-0.16	-0.09	1.86
Major 3rd	-0.13	0.38	7.74
Perfect 4th	0.13	0.37	5.66
minor 6th	-0.43	-0.25	6.02
Major 6th	-0.35	-0.28	2.33
Major 7th	-0.37	-0.03	8.11
sensory dissonance	0.13	0.06	2.74
PCDD entropy	0.18	0.38	2.27

Table 6. Summary of regression model for "sad"

Total $R^2 = .28$

feature	β	corr	VIF
minor 2nd	0.14	0.26	2.11
Major 2nd	-0.16	-0.14	1.91
minor 3rd	0.35	0.09	2.12
Perfect 4th	-0.20	-0.29	1.66
minor 6th	0.20	0.28	1.36
Major 6th	0.20	0.25	2.29
spectral centroid	-0.18	-0.10	1.98
note density	-0.15	-0.11	1.65

Table 7. Summary of regression model for "peaceful"

Total $R^2 = .11$

scale deg	β	corr	VIF
Major 2nd	0.22	0.11	3.32
minor 3nd	-0.24	-0.05	2.76
Major 3rd	0.22	0.22	4.69
Perfect 4th	0.15	0.23	4.63
Perfect 5th	0.15	0.10	1.20
Major 7th	0.23	0.03	1.88
PCDD entropy	-0.16	0.19	3.46

Table 8. Summary of regression model for "tense"

Total $R^2 = .16$

scale deg	β	corr	VIF
minor 2nd	0.10	0.25	1.92
Major 2nd	-0.21	-0.15	1.71
minor 3rd	0.24	0.08	1.55
Major 3rd	-0.14	-0.26	1.45
Perfect 5th	-0.20	-0.18	1.74
minor 6th	0.14	0.12	1.45

minor 6th ($\beta = -.43$), and minor 7th ($\beta = -.37$). Surprisingly, the Major 3rd is also negatively correlated with a β value of -.13. As mentioned before, however, the Major 3rd has a high VIF value; examination of the correlation coefficients shows that it is strongly correlated with the Perfect 4th (.84), which is positively related to "happy" responses. "Sad" responses show an opposite

Table 9. Comparison of three regression models. The total adjusted R^2 value for each model is shown.

	Full	PCD only	Minor
Happy	0.34	0.27	0.07
Sad	0.28	0.22	0.06
Peaceful	0.10	0.10	0.02
Tense	0.16	0.13	0.05
Romantic	0.21	0.18	0.08

pattern, positively related to the minor 2nd ($\beta = .14$), minor 3rd ($\beta = .35$), and minor 6th ($\beta = .20$), and negatively to the Perfect 4th ($\beta = -.20$). Many of the other models loosely conform to the idea that *raags* with "minor" intervals are negatively valenced (sad, tense) and *raags* with "major" intervals are positively valenced (happy, peaceful).

The entropy of the PCDD distribution was a significant factor in the "happy" and "peaceful" models, positively related in the former and negatively related in the latter. We had hypothesized that low PCDD entropy values would correspond to tension and longing and higher values to a greater sense of flexibility. The effect shown here is weakly consistent with this prediction.

It is important to note that the relationship between PCDD entropy and the emotional characteristics we are testing is likely non-linear. Values outside the range represented in this study might well be expected to elicit different reactions. One might expect very low values, corresponding to predictability and repetition, to elicit "peaceful" and "sad" reactions. Very high values, on the other hand, might correspond to unpredictability and hence elicit feelings of "tension" and "stress". However, in the middle of the range, where most of the musical excerpts used here lie, low entropy corresponds to *raags* with a relatively fixed phraseology, creating a sense of tendency rather than repetition, and high entropy corresponds to *raags* with a greater degree of flexibility, conveying more variability than instability. If correlations observed in the above models are valid, this is the most likely explanation.

Two additional models were developed to see if a more parsimonious explanation of the data could be given. The first used the total strength of the minor 2nd, minor 3rd, and minor 6th in the *raag* as the independent variable, a measure of the total degree of "minorness". The adjusted R^2,

$$R_a^2 = 1 - (1 - R^2)\frac{n-1}{n-p-1}, \tag{2}$$

which allows comparison between models with a different number of independent variables, is reported in Table 9. The second model considered only the PCD features. The full model was significantly more explanatory. Although the full model suggested that a feature that combined the minor 2nd, minor 3rd and minor 6th in total measure of "minorness" might capture most of the information

in the PCD, this was not the case. The PCD features explained an additional
10-20% of variation as compared with the single "minor" feature.

8   Discussion

Survey responses have shown that different *raags* evoke a clearly differentiated
set of emotional reactions. Free responses tended to cluster strongly in particular
adjectival categories based on *raag*, and quantitative responses were significantly
different by *raag* for all emotions except "longing". Thus, a substantial step
has been taken towards empirical verification of the nature and reliability of
emotional responses to *raag*. Importantly, responses did not vary systematically
by familiarity with NICM suggesting that listeners were not simply referring
to culturally determined concepts, but responding to underlying features of the
music.

The analysis, although preliminary, suggests that responses are in part attributable to pitch-class statistics; the prevalence of certain scale degrees is
useful in predicting the valence of the emotional responses. The data suggest
that the entropy of the PCDD and the spectral centroid are also important.
These are undoubtedly just a few of the many factors that influence listener responses. As more data are collected it will be possible to more fully examine other
factors.

It is important to note that these models are currently merely suggestive.
In none of the cases were they highly predictive, with a maximum of 34%
of the variance accounted for. Because the goal here was explanatory rather
than classificatory, the models were not verified on an independent data set. As
with any task that forces respondents to verbalize primarily non-verbal mental
states, there is significant measurement error due to the inherent unnatural-
ness of the task and an imperfect ability to map the verbal space. It is also
possible that much of the true emotional feel of the music is lost in the projection onto simple emotions such as "happy" and "sad". Although it is likely
that some aspect of *raags* can be effectively captured by mapping onto these
axes, it is also likely that it is a gross simplification of the actual emotional
experience.

9   Conclusions and Future Work

We have reported the results of the first empirical survey of listeners' emotional
reactions to *raag* music. We have established that responses exhibit clear patterns and have identified several musical features which partially explain them.
Based on the current work, we are in the process of conducting a more detailed
and expansive survey. This will consider a larger set of *raags* and provide listeners with more dimensions along which to evaluate their emotional experiences.
As more data is collected, it will be possible to test a greater number of musical
features and more robustly assess their validity.

References

1. Bhatkande, V.: Hindusthani Sangeet Paddhati. Sangeet Karyalaya (1934)
2. Balkwill, L.L., Thompson, W.F.: A cross-cultural investigation of the perception of emotion in music: Psychophysical and cultural cues. Music Perception 17, 43–64 (1999)
3. Juslin, P.N., Sloboda, J.A.: Music and Emotion: Theory and Research. Oxford University Press, Oxford (2001)
4. Chordia, P., Rae, A.: Raag recognition using pitch-class and pitch-class dyad distributions. In: Proceedings of International Conference on Music Information Retrieval (2007)
5. Huron, D.: Sweet Anticipation: Music and the Psychology of Expectation. MIT Press, Cambridge (2006)
6. Sun, X.: A pitch determination algorithm based on subharmonic-to-harmonic ratio. In: Proc. of International Conference of Speech and Language Processing (2000)
7. Duxbury, C., Bello, J.P., Davies, M., Sandler, M.: A combined phase and amplitude based approach to onset detection for audio segmentation. In: Proc. of the 4th European Workshop on Image Analysis for Multimedia Interactive Services (WIAMIS 2003), London, pp. 275–280 (2003)
8. Kameoka, A., Kuriyagawa, M.: Consonance theory, part i: Consonance of dyads. Journal of the Acoustical Society of America 45(6), 1451–1459 (1969)

The Artistic Play of Spatial Organization:
Spatial Attributes, Scene Analysis and Auditory Spatial Schemata

Gary S. Kendall[1] and Mauricio Ardila[2]

[1] Northwestern University, Music Technology Program
Evanston, IL 60208 USA
g-kendall@northwestern.edu
[2] Columbia College Chicago, Audio Arts and Acoustics Department
Chicago, IL 60605 USA
mardila@colum.edu

Abstract. Electroacoustic music lacks a definitive vocabulary for describing its spatiality. Not only does it lack a vocabulary for describing the spatial attributes of individual sound sources, it lacks a vocabulary for describing how these attributes participate in artistic expression. Following work by Rumsey, the definition of spatial attributes is examined in the broader context of auditory scene analysis. A limited number of spatial attributes are found to be adequate to characterize the individual levels of organization nested within the auditory scene. These levels are then viewed in relationship to auditory spatial schemata, the recurrent patterns by which listeners understand the behavior of sound in space. In electroacoustic music the interrelationship of spatial attributes and spatial schemata is often engaged in a play of perceptual grouping that blurs and confounds distinctions like source and ensemble. Our ability to describe and categorize these complex interactions depends on having clear concepts and terminology.

1   Introduction

The expanded range of its spatial palette is one of the important features that distinguish electroacoustic music from acoustic music. In an interview with Larry Austin, Denis Smalley [2] said:

> "The spatial experience of electroacoustic music is one of the particular aspects it has to offer that no other musical art has to offer in such variety or with such vividness...so, that makes it unique. I don't mean to say that every electroacoustic piece explores or exploits this uniqueness, but the potential is there. One will quite often find that the composer has ignored many of these possibilities or maybe has not been able to harness them, for all sorts of reasons."

There are at least three reasons why the spatial potential of electroacoustic music is not always realized: 1) misconceptions about the technical capacities of spatialization

R. Kronland-Martinet, S. Ystad, and K. Jensen (Eds.): CMMR 2007, LNCS 4969, pp. 125–138, 2008.

systems, 2) misconceptions about the nature of spatial perception, especially in the context of such systems, and 3) a lack of creative engagement, possibly due to the first two issues. An area in which all three of these issues come together is that of conceptual terminology that can be out of alignment with the technical capacities of spatialization systems, out of alignment with the actual experience of spatial sound and therefore lead to under-utilization in electroacoustic composition.

David Malham [17] surveyed a wide range of spatial audio technologies and offered this critique:

> "Despite the rich possibilities inherent in current sound diffusion and spatialization systems, none of the current systems can fully mimic the spatial characteristics of natural sound systems."

Malham's standard of comparison is spatial hearing in the natural world. This would appear to be an obvious basis of comparison for spatial audio applications such as virtual reality systems. In fact, the metaphors of 'virtuality' permeate discussions of the spatial audio applications that overtly strive to replicate the experiences of the natural world (telecommunications, reproduction of concert hall music). The literature around entertainment systems is a bit more pliant, possibly because the intention is often to create an 'enhanced reality' that maximizes impact, such as in sound design for games.

Electroacoustic music though lies in the domain of art and the situation for spatiality in electroacoustic music is similar to that for sound synthesis in the sense that the experience of the natural world provides an inspiration for creativity and research, but the technology also makes possible new possibilities for artistic exploration. Why should we think of spatial audio differently? Spatial audio and especially spatial audio for electroacoustic music is a domain inspired by but not limited to experiences in the natural world. Then too, electroacoustic music's capacity to manipulate audio signals creates a context in which there can be uniquely complex interactions between spatial hearing and other domains of perception and cognition. This is especially true when electroacoustic composers play with the fundamentals of spatial organization in music by manipulating perceptual grouping and violating spatial schemata. Spatial audio, and especially spatial audio for electroacoustic music, is an artistic domain that often throws the spatial conventions of the natural world into relief by distorting or violating them. In order to appreciate the crisscrossing of boundaries and conventions in this artistic interplay, our concepts and terminology should be in good alignment with the listener's perceptual and cognitive processes.

2 Terminology

2.1 The Problem of Terminology

While the spatiality of acoustic music, even 20th century acoustic music, can be discussed in commonly understood terms [9], the spatiality of electroacoustic music still lacks a definitive vocabulary. When music is performed by acoustic instruments in an acoustic environment, the physical level of description by itself often provides a workable roadmap to both the listener's experience and the composer's intent. We have a wealth of shared experiences and traditions of acoustic performance despite the perceptual complexity and individuality of many performances. In electroacoustic music, the acoustic experience has often been a reference point, but the technology of electronic reproduction expands the scope and complexity of spatiality in a radical way. Even though the apparatus may be located within a physical space and even though our spatial hearing has developed within a physical world, electronic reproduction creates the potential for an art of spatiality. Consider how the experience of a diffuse granular cloud [30] emerges from the details of the granular synthesis or how the experience of FFT-based spectral bands distributed in space challenges [29] our notion of what constitutes a 'source.' Electroacoustic music hardly has the vocabulary to describe the scope of spatial possibilities or to explain the relationship of signal processing techniques to the listener's perceptions.

Recent perceptual research can help us begin to clarify our vocabulary. A great deal of relevant research has emerged from the study of *spatial impression* associated with subjective acoustics of concert halls [3]. Blauert [5] defines spatial impression as the perception of the type and size of an actual or simulated space. He also defines spaciousness as the extent to which auditory events are more spacious than in a free sound field under comparable conditions. Even though these definitions may seem straight forward, a multiplicity of terms has been proposed to describe the interconnected facets of spatial impression. For example, within the context of concert hall acoustics, spatial impression, spaciousness, apparent source width, envelopment, and other terms have been used to describe similar spatial percepts. Berg and Rumsey [4] consider over 30 terms that can be organized into 17 discrete categories. In the subjective acoustics of electronic reproduction, Zacharov and Koivuniemi [31] and Rumsey [25] provide in-depth discussions and classification of related spatial attributes.

It is now well established that spatial impression in concert halls consists of at least two components: *apparent source width* (ASW) and *listener envelopment* (LEV) [1] [8] that are typically related to the acoustics of early and late reflections respectively. According to Morimoto [23], apparent or auditory source width is "the width of a sound image fused temporally and spatially with the direct sound image" and listener envelopment is "the degree of fullness of sound images around the listener, excluding the precedent sound image composing ASW." These definitions presume that ASW and LEV are easily separated from one another. And while Bradley and Soulodre [6] and Morimoto [23] have conducted experiments in which subjects differentiated the two, there is disagreement as to what the threshold of separation should be, or if a clear threshold even exists. There seems to be consensus in the fact that both ASW and LEV describe aspects of spatial impression and it is also accepted that they are just two of many factors that comprise the multidimensional perception of auditory space.

While there is much that can be gleaned from this research, the difference between the contexts considered in the aforementioned research and the context for electroacoustic music is profound. For one thing, electroacoustic music is not limited to having its sound sources contained in an environment. For example, the composer can omit environmental sound or omit the source! Then too, there are profound differences in the sound material. This is especially important for two reasons: spatial

percepts are shaped in part by the content of the sound sources [18] [20] and electroacoustic composers are not limited to pre-existent acoustic sources. Not only do
electroacoustic composers have the freedom to design sounds that specifically support
spatial effects, but they can also explore ways of creating sound that have no obvious
analog in the physical world.

2.2 Spatial Attributes and Scene Analysis

In a particularly useful discussion, Rumsey [24] considers spatial sound attributes
within the framework of auditory scene analysis [7]. He states that spatial attributes
"should be unambiguous and preferably unidimensional (in other words, they should
represent a single perceptual construct)." Spatial attributes have to do with the tangi-
bly three-dimensional aspects of sound including such properties as width and distance. Most importantly Rumsey[1] separates spatial attributes from attributes of
spaces, that is, from the properties of the rooms (or other environments). The attributes of spaces have traditionally included properties such as reverberance and live-
ness. The confluence of these categories had been unexamined in the subjective
evaluation of concert halls and audio reproduction systems where sound sources are
assumed to be contained within environments, and, in fact, Rumsey's discussion is itself directed toward such typical audio reproduction settings. This confluence of
categories is essentially a misalignment of physical and perceptual acoustics. So, for
example, when we shift our orientation completely to the side of the listener's auditory organization, the early reflections that influence the perception of the auditory
source are just as much a part of the source signal as the direct sound. From this point
on we must be particularly clear about the conceptual separation between the acoustic
source signal (with all of its acoustic constituents) and the source's perceived image
(with all of its perceptual spatial attributes). The separation of the categories is particularly useful in electroacoustic music where the source-in-environment model is
only one of many possible spatial treatments.

Having achieved a clear separation of spatial attributes from other properties of
sound in space, Rumsey goes on to examine spatial attributes within the context of
auditory scene analysis. In creating an organizational framework for evaluating the
kind of sound reproduction that interests him, he proposes four levels of organization
that are common in the experience of listening to recorded music: source, ensemble,
room and scene. These labels are meant to be more general categories of nested organization than types of acoustic sources. How these four levels of organization interact with the spatial attribute of width is illustrated in Figure 1. At the lowest level
of organization an individual source has a width. At a next higher level of organization and grouping, an ensemble of sources has ensemble width. Such a grouping depends on the particulars of the scene and, for example, might variously be composed
of the violin section, the string section or the whole orchestra. At the next highest
level of organization for recorded music we can speak of room width and beyond that
the width of the entire auditory scene. This scene-based approach isolates the 'what'
from the 'where' and removes the conceptual confusion inherent in considering spatial attributes without addressing auditory grouping.

---

[1]All subsequent references to Rumsey relate to [24].

We can now propose spatial terminology to be applied to the relevant nested levels of auditory organization. Rumsey proposes that all spatial attributes be limited to five, three 'dimensional' attributes and two 'immersive' attributes. His three dimensional attributes---width, distance and depth---can be instanced by an individual sound source, an ensemble, room or scene (although it is unlikely that an individual sound source could instance depth).

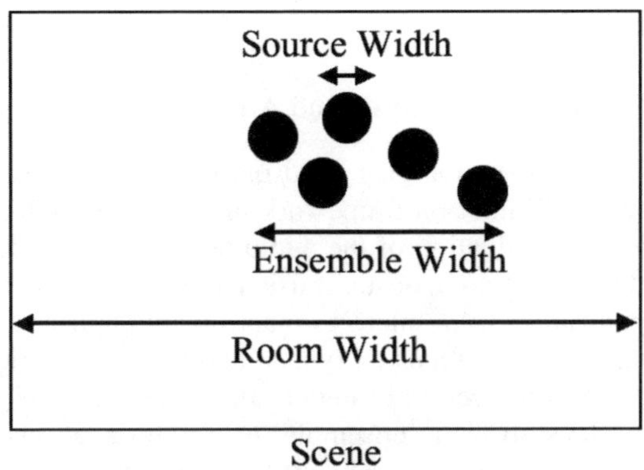

Fig. 1. Spatial attributes of nested levels within an auditory scene (after Rumsey [24])

Rumsey mentions that he is omitting the spatial attribute of height, we assume because his focus is on reproduction systems without elevation, but he also omits any other aspect of direction (even though he has contributed to its discussion in other research [19] [25]). We will add direction to our list of spatial attributes[2] Rumsey's category of immersive spatial attributes covers the domain of auditory spatial perception described by such interrelated terms as spatial impression, spaciousness and listener envelopment. Within this framework of scene analysis, Rumsey recommends the adoption of only two terms: envelopment and presence. He proposes that the term 'envelopment' be applied to the experience of being surrounded by sound either both from multiple sound sources and from a diffuse field such as reverberation. These are called 'source-related' and 'environmental' envelopment respectively. Rumsey has newly proposed that the term 'presence' be applied to the "sense of being inside of an (enclosed) space." We will adopt all of Rumsey's terminology (with our small addition) for consistency's sake and defer judgment on the use of the term 'presence' to future literature. Our resulting terminology can be summarized as follows:

dimensional attributes:

- width (individual/ensemble/room/scene)
- distance (individual/ensemble/room/scene)
- depth (individual in special cases/ensemble/room/scene)
- direction (individual/ensemble/room/scene)

---

[2] We will treat direction as a single, unambiguous perceptual attribute even though its geometrical representation requires two dimensions. The dominant role of the left-right axis in the play of perceptual grouping is considered later on.

    immersive attributes:
         - envelopment (environmental/source-related)
         - presence

Every level of organization within the scene can be characterized by the dimensional attributes, but only certain situations give rise to envelopment and presence.

3 Electroacoustic Music

3.1 Spatial Attributes, Scene Analysis and Auditory Spatial Schemata

Up to this point we have described a nested organization for scene analysis that is based in acoustic music. Rumsey's framework of source/ensemble/room/scene is intended for the subjective evaluation of the audio reproduction of acoustic recordings. And, while the content of electroacoustic music can be quite dissimilar, the notion of nested levels of organization from micro to macro would appear to be quite valid for most kinds of music. Rumsey's focus on typical audio content though complicates his framework in a way that inadvertently undermines the notion of a simple micro-to-macro organization. The shift from 'ensemble' to 'room' is not just a shift to the next higher level of nesting; it is a categorical shift that is normative only in the domain of acoustic music where instruments are indeed enclosed in rooms.

Within the context of electroacoustic music, there are two issues revealed when considering the concept of 'room'. The first issue is that the impression of 'room' can be created either through recording techniques or by the treatment of a source signal with a reverberator. And, if the contribution of the recording space or the reverberator is essentially a dense cluster of duplicated signals, we have to ask what exactly is the difference between a 'room' and an 'ensemble' as levels of nesting in the organization? Then too, in the case that the original source signal is omitted, the reverberator's output itself essentially becomes a potential source. What then is the essential difference between a source, an ensemble and a room? The answer comes in response to the second issue. A 'room' is something different from a type of acoustic signal or treatment of a signal: it is a cognitive understanding that the listener constructs in response to auditory experience. In particular, 'room' is an understanding that emerges when auditory experience matches a pattern we can describe as the auditory spatial schemata for ROOM. Depending on the circumstances, 'room' may or may not be invoked by the listener in the process of forming an understanding of the auditory scene. In most circumstances we can imagine that 'room' is automatic and akin to schema-based stream segregation [7]. For example, the ROOM schema may be invoked even with incomplete or fragmentary acoustic information. Most importantly, it is not the perceived nested relationships that determine the categories.

We have disentangled a confluence of terminology created by mixing the immediate perceptual experience with patterns of spatial understanding. The original sense of the distinctions between source, ensemble and room has faded away and they are discussed below in relation to auditory spatial schemata. So, what remains of the original concept of a nested organization of spatial relationships? Clearly, the listener's perception of spatial relationships depends on the tangible circumstances, the particulars of the auditory scene that might include nesting, overlapping or other categories of relationship. For electroacoustic music the elements in the structure are not limited *a priori* to one set of relational categories. At times, there may be no clear boundary between source and ensemble, that is, between one and many sources. A full description of spatial content and its implications within an artistic context may be very complex. Auditory spatial schemata may be stretched or even violated. Our ability to describe and categorize these complex interactions depends on having clear concepts and terminology so that we can recognize the crisscrossing of boundaries and the disruption of spatial norms in the artistic interplay.

3.2 Spatial Schemata and Audio Reproduction

Auditory spatial schemata are the recurrent patterns by which we understand the behavior of sound in space. All of our sensory capacities contribute to forming our core spatial schemata [11] and, therefore, auditory spatial schemata can be largely understood as linkages between general, multimodal spatial schemata and the auditory domain. The listener makes sense of spatial sound first and foremost in terms of the general spatial schemata that are learned and reinforced in the multimodal experience of everyday life. The general schema of OBJECT gives rise to the auditory schema of SOURCE. The general schema of COLLECTION gives rise to ENSEMBLE. Both possess spatial attributes and typical spatial behaviors.

Sound localization is generally recognized as having a weak influence on the auditory scene [7]. For that reason, spatial schemata have a particularly important role in spatial hearing because the schemata give coherence to spatial information that may otherwise be faint or incomplete. Spatial schemata are particularly important for audio reproduction when no other sensory information may collaborate the auditory spatial content. Our spatial schema for PATH gives coherence to motion effects that can otherwise be quite fragile. As the listener endeavors to *make sense* of spatial relationships, a spatial organization emerges. Then too, the disembodied sound of audio reproduction is often interpreted in a framework that is specific to this context. For example, the spatial arrangement of sources in a typical stereo pop song makes no physical sense. We accept the spatial arrangement as an idiom of audio reproduction, a musical-spatial idiom. The immaterial nature of audio reproduction enables auditory spatial art to exploit the spatial schemata of everyday life.

3.3 Artistic Play at the Level of Perceptual Grouping

In electroacoustic music there is often an artistic play of perceptual grouping that affects both the perception of spatial attributes and blurs the distinction between cognitive categories, especially SOURCE and ENSEMBLE. This play is typically driven by disruption at the level of perceptual event formation, disruption that can affect both grouping and localization mechanisms. There are numerous techniques that create such disruptions, techniques that typically can be manipulated to adjust the degree of disruption and thus enable the exploration of perceptual and cognitive boundaries. While they may be conceptually different, these techniques often create similar results. In order to adequately describe the changes in the spatial attributes associated with these techniques, we need to distinguish four different meanings associated with the word 'source.' First there is the 'source signal,' that is the acoustic signal or a representation of the acoustic signal. Second, there is the tangible 'source image,' the 'source' that has spatial attributes in the auditory scene. There is the 'conceptual source,' the object that the listener identifies with the sound independent of its spatial attributes. ('Conceptual source' is related to Smalley's concept of source bonding [28].) Lastly, there is the listener's spatial schema, 'SOURCE.' The source image, whether it is understood as one or many conceptual sources, most likely is segregated as an auditory stream, and how the artistic play reshapes the listener's perceptual organization is discussed below.

Type 1 Techniques. Let us first consider the class of techniques that disrupt the identity of the source signal by breaking it into parts. These parts might be separated on the basis of time or spectrum (or both). A primary example of a temporal technique is granular processing that disrupts the temporal order of the acoustic source signal. A primary example of a spectral technique would be phase vocoding that alters the spectral organization of the acoustic source signal. Both of these techniques involve breaking the acoustic source signal into multiple parts, manipulating those parts and then assembling a result. (Of course, there are even more ways of using these tools.) The result can range from exact reconstruction of the acoustic source signal to the construction of something essentially new. The listener's conceptual source can range from the original conceptual source to a new source to multiple new sources. Also importantly, in both cases there is the possibility of assembling the result in one or more spatial locations.

Consider the two-dimensional field of possibilities for combinations of the width of the source image and the number of conceptual sources created by play with perceptual grouping (Figure 2). In the case that the acoustic source signal is perfectly reconstructed and that it is positioned in one spatial location, there is one conceptual source and one corresponding perceptual source. This matches the characteristics of SOURCE. In the case that manipulation of the source signal gives rise to multiple conceptual sources that are positioned in one spatial location, the result is multiple conceptual sources associated as one source image. (If there is a blurring between one or more conceptual sources, it may give rise to a blurring of whether there are one or more source images with the same spatial attributes.) In another case, if there are multiple conceptual sources and the component parts are spatially dispersed, then the spatial distribution tends to support a multiplicity of source images organized as an ENSEMBLE. An example is a spatially dispersed granular cloud [30].

Most interestingly, in the case that the identity of the source signal is maintained as one conceptual source but its component parts are spatially dispersed, there is a clear competition of perceptual organizations. The degree to which the spatialized component parts segregate from the whole (and border on multiple source images) determines a wide range of combined spatial/source percepts. At one end of the continuum is the possibility of a source image with an increased spatial width. At the other end is the possibility of multiple source images associated with one conceptual source (something that cognitive organization may fight). In between are the blurred boundaries of source/ensemble and of one/many source images. One particular example is the case when the frequency bands of a single source are spread in space giving rise to the perception of a single/multiple, source/ensemble distributed in space [29] [14]. Granular synthesis and phase vocoding can be manipulated to create possibilities across the entire range of source image and conceptual source possibilities.

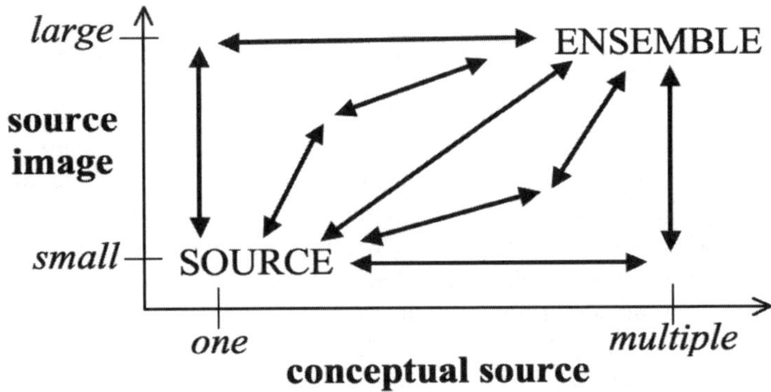

Fig. 2. Two-dimensional field of possibilities for source image and conceptual source combinations created by play with perceptual grouping

Type 2 Techniques. There is another class of techniques that often gives rise to similar boundary play. This second type of technique involves disruption of perceptual event formation by the manipulation of binaural information and is therefore a technique that primarily affects spatial attributes along the listener's left-right axis. A well-known recording technique provides a simple example. Imagine that two virtually identical vocal performances are recorded. One recording differs from the other only by micro-variations. If one recording is panned to the left loudspeaker and the other is panned to the right, the result is the perception of two instances of the same recording, one on the left and one on the right. The difference in micro-variations prevents the formation of a single spatial image. This is an extreme instance in which there is one conceptual source and two source images. More typically with type 2 techniques, the differences between the ear signals causes the source image to increase in width. (The extent of the width can be related directly to the measured similarity between the signals arriving at the ears, often expressed as the interaural cross-correlation coefficient.) There are numerous ways of creating the micro-variations that give rise to binaural differences and every one of these can be achieved either by processing a source signal to create multiple versions or by synthesizing multiple source signals directly. Creating small static frequency differences or static phase differences among source signals tends to give rise to a single conceptual source and a broadened source image [13] [12]. Dynamic frequency differences (such as jitter or vibrato) provide a particularly effective way to manipulate the relationship between conceptual sources and source images. In the case that multiple source signals with dynamic frequency differences are gathered in one location (and do not create on-going binaural differences), the magnitude of frequency differences will position the conceptual source along a continuum from one to many while maintaining a single source image. A conventional example of this is single-channel chorusing. In the case that the multiple source signals are spatially dispersed (in such a way as to create dynamic binaural differences at the listener's ears), then there will be a widened source image with one or more conceptual images. In the case that the dynamic frequency differences are of sufficient magnitude, then the broadened source image will break up into multiple images. But, of course, the power of vibrato to affect auditory grouping is well known from the demonstrations by Steve McAdams with Roger Reynolds [21] [22].

Immersive Attributes. Up to this point we have discussed the impact of these two categories of processing techniques primarily on the spatial attribute of width, although other spatial attributes such as distance and depth are also often affected. Rumsey asks the question of when source width becomes so wide as to create envelopment and thereby points out the link between dimensional and immersive spatial attributes. When creating sound images that surround the listener, techniques of the first type tend to create 'source-related envelopment' while techniques of the second type tend to create 'environmental envelopment.' Techniques of the second type are closely related to artificial reverberation and the conditions under which the listener experiences envelopment in a reverberant field [10]. In fact, we can view multi-channel reverberation as yet another processing technique of the second type that produces a narrow to wide source image with a single conceptual source. Figure 3 illustrates how the results of reverberation and chorusing can be illustrated on the two-dimensional field of possibilities.

Dynamic Changes. While dynamic changes in spatial attributes have not been directly addressed here, it should be obvious that the techniques discussed can be implemented in a dynamic fashion. The two-dimensional field of possibilities can be transversed in a dynamic way. The experience of gradual change affecting auditory grouping and spatial organization is an aspect of numerous electroacoustic works, especially works of soundscape composition.

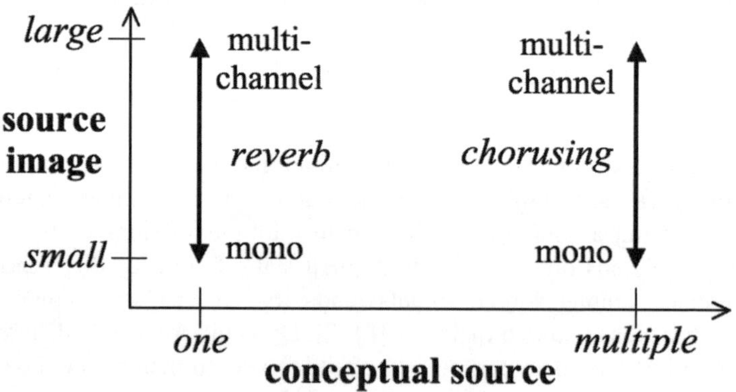

Fig. 3. The results of reverberation and chorusing are considered on the two-dimensional field of possibilities

3.4 Artistic Play with Auditory Spatial Schemata

A good example of a general spatial schema with an auditory instantiation is CONTAINMENT. We construct our understanding of *containment* through an interaction with the world that involves all of our senses. That process includes the experience of objects moving into and out of other objects with their own internal space, a space that can *contain* another object. What we learn about CONTAINMENT as an auditory schema is that an object with internal space *containing* a sounding object transforms that sounding object in a way that depends on the characteristics of the *container*. Furthermore, a *room* is a kind of *container,* a particular type of *container* that can *contain* the listener as well as sounding objects. A *room* transforms sound in a different way than other *containers*, in part, because it also produces a sense of immersion for the listener when the listener is inside the *room.* These concepts are represented graphically in Figure 4.

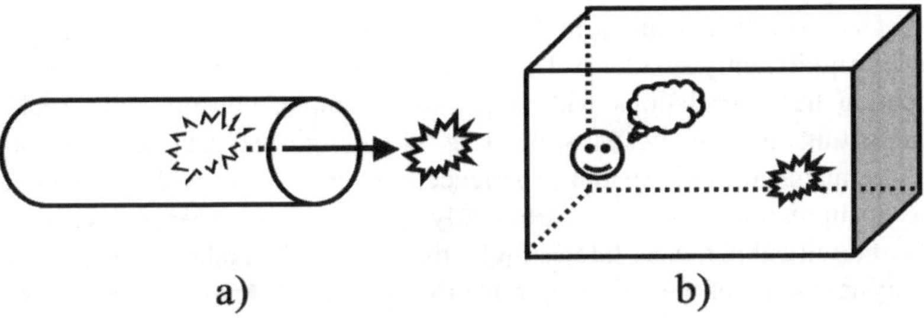

Fig. 4. Auditory spatial schemata: a) representation of containment and b) representation of room

Artistic play with auditory spatial schemata in electroacoustic music can occur in many ways. One way that is analogous to the previous examples is by manipulation of normal expectations. The violation of auditory spatial schemata has the effect of directing the listener's attention to content that is highlighted by the unusual or unexpected relationships. In this way the domain of the disruption becomes a subject for artistic expression. For example consider the possibility of the listener being inside of a container that is not a room. (The play of open space and contained space is a major element in Denis Smalley's *Empty Vessels* [26] where the listener's point of view is alternatively in an open space or inside of a large garden pot.) Consider also the possibility of the listener experiencing the sound of a source from one direction and the sound of the room containing the source coming from another. These possibilities are graphically represented in Figure 5.

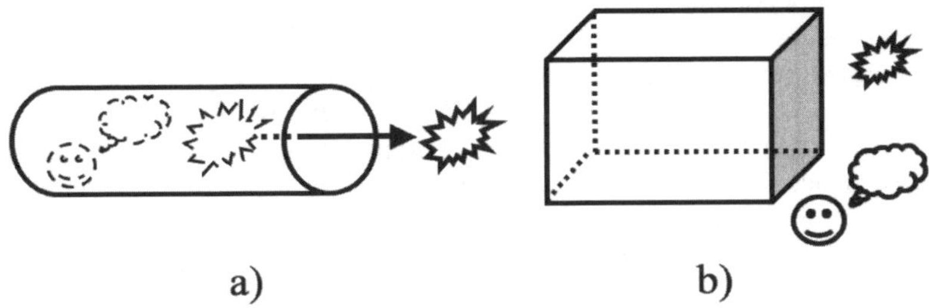

Fig. 5. Violations of auditory spatial schemata: a) violation of containment and b) violation of room

A complementary approach to the manipulation of normal expectations is found within the domain of auditory display. Lennox et al. [15] [16] describe the practice of 'cartoonification' as "a way of increasing information bandwidth without necessarily increasing the signal bandwidth." Cartoonification is essentially purposeful deviation from spatial realism in order to emphasize information that has the most 'perceptual significance.' Of course, communication incorporating such deviations depends on the foundation of spatial realism in order to be understood.

Another way in which artistic play in electroacoustic music violates spatial realism is in the manipulation of scale. Certain auditory schemata and auditory events have a normative physical scale. For example, rooms have a range of typical sizes, as do containers. There is artistic content in the manipulation of scale, say when rooms or containers are significantly smaller or larger than what is expected. The 'scene' of audio reproduction has associations with scale, for example, concert halls, rock bands, physical settings in film, etc. Most of these, like the normal scale of rooms and containers, are matched to the spatial experience of everyday life with the physical body and the manipulation of scale is particularly effective when scenes deviate from the domain of bodily experience. Interestingly, the scale of the audio scene is independent of the physical scale of the audio reproduction system. We have learned to accept the sizing of audio reproduction systems as analogous to the sizing of TV screens---we adjust our spatial frame of reference to the system. Then too, the scale of the source image may have no relationship with the scale of the conceptual source. For example, the source image of a pin dropping on a table and of a jet plane flying by can have similar spatial attributes within the audio scene. In fact, the juxtaposition of source images associated with radically different scales of conceptual source is a defining feature in the spatiality of acousmatic music.

4 Conclusion

In his review of Bregman's book, *Auditory Scene Analysis* [7], David Huron [10] says, "the act of hearing may be likened to the work of a cartographer constantly drafting maps of the *auditory scene*." Our discussion of spatiality in electroacoustic music has revealed some additional layers of complexity to that cartographer's job. More than just mapping the auditory scene, the cartographer must construct a diagram of the conceptual sources while evaluating the spatial organization of the source imagery. Auditory spatial schemata aid the cartographer in bringing order and understanding to the interrelationship of conceptual sources and spatial imagery. And, although we have not touched on it here, the cartographer's knowledge of spaces and places experienced in the past constitutes a kind of aural memoir that adds additional levels of context and meaning to auditory spatial experience. (Denis Smalley's discussion of space in relation to acousmatic music is especially meaningful when viewed from this perspective [27]). While our cartographer probably experiences a great deal of job satisfaction by managing the spatial relationships of everyday life, he/she might also enjoy the stimulating break in routine offered by the artistic play of spatial relationships in electroacoustic music.

References

1. Ando, Y.: Architectural Acoustics: Blending Sound Sources, Sound Fields, and Listeners. Springer, New York (1998)
2. Austin, L.: Sound Diffusion in Composition and Performance: An Interview with Denis Smalley. Computer Music Journal 24, 2 (2000)
3. Barron, M., Marshall, A.H.: Spatial impression due to the early reflections in concert halls: The derivation of a physical measure. Journal of Sound Vibration 77, 2 (1981)
4. Berg, J., Rumsey, F.: Systematic Evaluation of Perceived Spatial Quality. In: Proceedings of the AES 24th International Conference (2003)
5. Blauert, J.: Spatial Hearing: the psychophysics of human sound localization. MIT Press, Cambridge (1997)
6. Bradley, J.S., Soulodre, G.A.: Objective Measures of Listener Envelopment. J. Acoust. Soc. Am. 98, 1 (1995)
7. Bregman, A.S.: Auditory Scene Analysis: The Perceptual Organization of Sound. The MIT Press, Cambridge (1990)
8. Griesinger, D.: The psychoacoustics of apparent source width, spaciousness and envelopment in performance spaces. Acustica 83 (1997)
9. Harley, M.A.: Spatiality of sound and stream segregation in twentieth century instrumental music. Organised Sound 3, 2 (1999)
10. Huron, D.: Book review: Auditory Scene Analysis: The Perceptual Organization of Sound by Albert S. Bregman. Psychology of Music 19, 1 (1991)
11. Johnson, M.: The Body in the Mind: The Bodily Basis of Meaning, Imagination, and Reason. University of Chicago (1987)
12. Kaup, A., Khoury, S., Freed, A., Wessel, D.: Volumetric Modeling of Acoustic Fields in CNMATs Sound Spatialization Theatre. In: Proceedings of the International Computer Music Conference (1999)
13. Kendall, G.: The Decorrelation of Audio Signals and Its Impact on Spatial Imagery. Computer Music Journal 19, 4 (1995)
14. Kim-Boyle, D.: Spectral and Granular Spatialization with Boids. In: SEAMUS National Conference, Ames, Iowa (2007)
15. Lennox, P.P., Myatt, T., Vaughan, J.M.: 3D audio as an information-environment: manipulating perceptual significance for differentiation and pre-selection. In: Proceedings of the 2001 International Conference on Auditory Display, Espoo, Finland (2001)
16. Lennox, P.P., Myatt, T., Vaughan, J.M.: From Surround To True 3-D. In: Proceedings of the AES 16th International Conference on Spatial Sound Reproduction, Rovaniemi, Finland (1999)
17. Malham, D.G.: Toward Reality Equivalence in Spatial Sound Diffusion. Computer Music Journal 25, 4 (2001)
18. Mason, R.: Elicitation and measurement of auditory spatial attributes in reproduced sound. PhD Thesis, University of Surrey (2002)
19. Mason, R., Brookes, T., Rumsey, F.: Frequency dependency of the relationship between perceived auditory source width and the interaural cross-correlation coefficient for time-invariant stimuli. J. Acoust. Soc. Am. 117, 3 (2005)
20. Mason, R., Brookes, T., Rumsey, F.: The effect of various source signal properties on measurements of the interaural crosscorrelation coefficient. Acoust. Sci. & Tech. 26, 2 (2005)
21. McAdams, S.: Spectral Fusion, Spectral Parsing, and the Formation of Auditory Images. Unpublished doctoral dissertation, Stanford University (1984)

22. McAdams, S., Bigand, E.: Thinking in Sound: The Cognitive Psychology of Human Audition. Oxford University Press, Oxford (1993)
23. Morimoto, M.: How can Auditory Spatial Impression be Generated and Controlled? In: Proceedings of the 2001 International Workshop on Spatial Media (2001)
24. Rumsey, F.: Spatial Quality Evaluation for reproduced Sound: Terminology, Meaning, and a Scene-based Paradigm. Journal of the AES 50, 9 (2002)
25. Rumsey, F.: Subjective Evaluation of the Spatial Attributes of Reproduced Sound. In: Proceedings of the AES 15th International Conference (1999)
26. Smalley, D.: Program notes to Empty Vessels included in the compact disk About Sources/scenes. IMED 0054, empreintes DIGITALes (2000)
27. Smalley, D.: Space-form and the acousmatic image. Organised Sound 12, 1 (2007)
28. Smalley, D.: Spectromorphology and structuring processes. In: Emmerson, S. (ed.) The Language of Electroacoustic Music. Macmillan Press, Basingstoke (1986)
29. Torchia, R., Lippe, C.: Techniques for Multi-Channel Real-Time Spatial Distribution Using Frequency-Domain Processing. In: Proceedings of the 2004 Conference on New Interfaces for Musical Expression, Hamamatusu, Japan (2004)
30. Truax, B.: Composition and diffusion: space in sound in space. Organised Sound 3, 2 (1999)
31. Zacharov, N., Koivuniemi, K.: Unravelling the Perception of Spatial Sound Reproduction. In: Proceedings of the AES 19th International Conference (2001)

Semiotics of Sounds Evoking Motions: Categorization and Acoustic Features

Adrien Merer[1], Sølvi Ystad[1], Richard Kronland-Martinet[1],
and Mitsuko Aramaki[2,3]

[1]CNRS - Laboratoire de Mécanique et d'Acoustique,
31 ch. Joseph Aiguier, Marseille, France
[2]CNRS - Institut de Neurosciences Cognitives de la Méditerranée,
31 ch. Joseph Aiguier, Marseille, France
[3]Université Aix-Marseille
38 bd. Charles Livon, Marseille, France
{merer,ystad,kronland,aramaki}@lma.cnrs-mrs.fr

Abstract. The current study is part of a larger project aiming at offering intuitive mappings of control parameters piloting synthesis models by semantic descriptions of sounds, i.e. simple verbal labels related to various feelings, emotions, gestures or motions. Hence, this work is directly related to the general problem of semiotics of sounds. We here put a special interest in sounds evoking different perceived motions. In this paper, the experimental design of the listening tests is described and the results obtained from behavioural data are discussed. Then a set of signal descriptors is compared to categories using feature selection methods. A special interest is given to applications for sound synthesis.

Keywords: sound semiotics, motion, categorization, sound synthesis.

1 Introduction

In the sound design context, synthesizing sounds from verbal labels related to various sensations, emotions, gestures or motions is still an open problem. Also in a musical context, composers want to create or transform sounds by acting on parameters that are relevant from a perceptual point of view. Indeed, physical synthesis models often necessitate the manipulation of hundreds of parameters. Consequently the construction of "good" sounds is almost impossible if no mapping strategy is used. In addition, certain signal models like FM synthesis are hard to control even after a learning process since the relation between timbre and synthesis parameters is non-linear. Most approaches, consist in first building a synthesis model and then addressing the mapping between synthesis parameters and control parameters. Indeed, our approach, the so-called "semiotic"[1] approach, consists in using control parameters as a framework for the elaboration of synthesis models.

---

[1] The study of signs and symbols, what they mean and how they are used, *Cambridge Advanced Learner's Dictionary.*

R. Kronland-Martinet, S. Ystad, and K. Jensen (Eds.): CMMR 2007, LNCS 4969, pp. 139–158, 2008.
© Springer-Verlag Berlin Heidelberg 2008

This approach leads to the more general issue: understanding how listeners assign meanings to sounds and in particular, determining acoustic features that convey information.

Semiotics has been studied in several contexts such as music information retrieval [22], perception of impact sounds [1], noise annoyance [14], sound design [13], perception/cognition of romantic music [2]. In particular, in the context of product quality evaluation U. Jekosch [13] addressed a theoretical framework based on a general theory of signs and in accordance with Gestalt perception. She also explains that this approach is particularly relevant in an industrial context.

In this study, a general methodology based on 3 steps is proposed:

- Determination of sound categories;
- Determination of invariants representative of these sound categories;
- Control of synthesis processes based on these invariants (sonification).

Many aspects of sound are concerned by semiotics. Indeed, listening to the same sound, different listeners might focus on different information carried by the sound. Conversely, some information can be gathered by only a few listeners. For example listening to a voice through the telephone, you might detect different moods if you are familiar with the speaker or not. Hence, the information conveyed by sound studied through a semiotic approach should be as independent of listeners' "history" as possible. This leads to a consideration of only basic properties of sound sources (*e.g.* size, material, displacement...) experienced in everyday listening [6].

As a first attempt to identify signal parameters linked to a sound source property, we have here focused on the evocation of motion. Motion is a primordial aspect of the appreciation of music. Indeed, in [5], authors studied the association between musical parameters and images of motion, and identified important links between gesture and various parameters such as pitch, loudness and rhythm.

Following the general methodology presented above, the first step consisted in determining categories of sounds evoking motions by listening tests. For this purpose, sounds from data banks made by electroacoustic music composers were collected. Among the large number of samples, we chose sounds which sources cannot be identified, but which, however, convey a signification. This made it easier for the subjects to focus on the evocations induced by the sounds,without being influenced by the identification of sound sources. Indeed in [9], Guastavino observes that in the case of environmental sounds, listeners process sounds as semantic labels. The author also indicates that for "abstracted stimuli", obtained categories might be more correlated with acoustic features. Conversely, Schaeffer [21] (and others) assumed that when we listen to a sound, we automatically try to link this experience with a similar one, stored in our memory. In the case of electroacoustic music, we can for instance predict that listeners will make comparisons with audio effects used in science fiction movies. This comment brings us to consider the problem of context. Indeed according to the ecological approach of perception [7], [6] everyday listening is usually related to complex events. Besides, we must consider that sound perception is multi-modal.

Listening tasks through headphones or loudspeakers (corresponding to listening conditions in laboratory) have been studied by Schaeffer [21] through what he calls the "acousmatic" approach. Schaeffer explains that this approach permits to separate auditory and visual information and to make us aware of the fact that the listening changes over time when we repeatedly listen to a sound. In our daily-life a lot of information comes from loudspeakers in radio, TV, computers, alarm systems etc. These considerations lead us to the choice of stimuli from electro-acoustic music composer since they are complex and can refer to various sound source properties and are well adapted for listening tasks through headphones.

Synthesized sounds were also included in the sound material to integrate some assumptions related to the physics of moving sound sources. In practice, the following physical phenomena were simulated: Doppler effect (known to give the sensation of a passing source), air absorption (known to be important for the perceived distance of a source), reverb (known to be important for the perceived distance or for the sensation of room acoustics) and raise/decay of sound pressure level. We tested if sound transformations corresponding to each of these physical phenomena simulated independently can evoke specific motions.

To define categories from the collected set of sounds, we conducted 2 categorization tasks where participants were asked to group sounds as function of the evoked motions (or displacements). In the first experiment, participants were allowed to make as many groups as they wanted, whereas, in the second experiment, they had to group sounds in predefined categories, each of them being represented by a prototypical sound obtained from the results of the first experiment. This approach makes it possible to avoid verbal labels [2]. Free categorization has many advantages (compared to dissemblance tests for example) in the sense that a lot of stimuli can be tested. It gives simultaneously access to categories (with verbal descriptions) and corresponding sounds. In addition, no hypothesis about the existence of continuous perceptual dimensions is needed. Furthermore, we assumed that in the second task, the high variability of the results obtained in the first task will be reduced.

The categories of movements obtained from the behavioural data were further examined in order to identify signal features specific to each category. First, the analytical properties of each sound were calculated through several signal descriptors described in section 3. Then, statistical analysis lead to the most relevant descriptors (signal features) specific to each category of motion.

We finally discuss some perspectives concerning the control of these descriptors (last step of our methodology).

2   Determination of Sound Categories

2.1   Stimuli

Recorded Sounds. We preliminary collected about one thousand samples from personal data banks belonging to electroacoustic composers of the Music Conservatory of Marseille, with their agreement. Sounds were all monophonic with

16-bit 48kHz sampling rate. These samples are essentially dedicated for musical compositions and are generally used as or after some audio effect transformations. Among these samples, a selection of 62 sounds was effectuated with respect to different criteria. First, according to the acousmatic listening context, we avoided caricatured sounds (like sounds used for cartoons) and sounds for which the sources were easily identifiable. Second, we restricted our selection to sounds that present a simple morphology (single event) and that last no longer than 4 seconds. We also cared that sounds should not be dramatically cut from a longer sample. This point is of importance since it can influence the categorization task if used as a strategy of comparison between sounds. Finally, according to analysis constraints, we aimed at constituting the most heterogeneous sound panel with respect to timbre, duration and level.

Synthesized Sounds. Hypothesis about acoustic information related to a moving sound source are tested by including additional sounds obtained by transformation of 6 original recorded samples different from the 62 sounds previously selected. The original samples were first modified to freeze the evolution of signal parameters by using a phase vocoder freezing technique [19]. Then, we applied sound transformations corresponding to the following physical phenomena: air absorption, raise/decay of sound pressure level, reverb and Doppler effect. Air absorption is simulated by a first order low pass filter with varying cut-off frequency (from 13-kHz to 30-Hz). The raise/decay phenomenon is simulated by a geometric $1/r$ evolution of the sound pressure level, where r is the distance between the source and the listener. The reverb effect is effectuated by an Olaf Matthes freeverb MSP object (freeverb is a Schroeder / Moorer reverb model) without damping, max room size and varying reverb rate. Finally, the Doppler effect is reproduced with a delay line. For a monochromatic delayed sound source $s(t - D_t) = e^{i\omega_s(t - D_t)}$ with a time varying delay time D_t, the instantaneous frequency ω and the frequency measured at the listener's location (Doppler shift) ω_D are given by:

$$\omega = \omega_s\left(1 - \frac{dD_t}{dt}\right) \quad ; \quad \omega_D = \omega_s\left(\frac{1 + \frac{v_{ls}}{c}}{1 - \frac{v_{sl}}{c}}\right) \tag{1}$$

where v_{sl} and v_{ls} are the relative velocities between the source and the listener. Therefore, for a static listener ($v_{ls} = 0$) and assuming that $v_{sl} << c$, the delay time is given by: $\frac{dD_t}{dt} = -\frac{v_{sl}}{c}$. In practice, 4 sounds were constructed to simulate these 4 physical phenomena independently. In particular, reverb effect and air absorption are computed for a source approaching the listener with constant speed. The sound pressure level raise/decay and Doppler frequency shift are computed for a linear uniform movement of a sound source going past a fixed listener from -50 to 50 meters in 6 seconds. Two sounds were also constructed (with independent time dilation/compression and level variation) to simulate a rotating sound source around a listener located close to a 9 meter radius loop with an angular velocity of 18 tr/min.

2.2   Test 1: Free Classification Task

Twenty-six students (9 females, 17 males) working on the CNRS campus in Marseille participated in the experiment. They were between 19 and 30 years old (average 23,5), 19 had music experience (2 also had electroacoustic music experience).

Procedure

The listening tests were conducted in an audiometric cabin. Participants were placed in front of an imac computer screen and listened to **monophonic** sounds through a Stax 3R202 headphone set under binaural conditions with a SRM310 preamplifier (we used the internal sound card).

The 68 sound samples represented by square symbols, were initially positioned randomly on the screen. The task consisted in grouping together sounds evoking the same motion. Participants could listen to sounds and move them with the mouse as often as they wanted. We did not impose constraints about the number of categories to make and we insisted on the fact they should avoid identifying the nature of the sources that produced the sounds.

A training phase was effectuated for the participants to adopt the ecologic listening and focus their attention on the impression of motion evoked by sounds. This preliminary test allowed us to check if the participants were able or not to make abstraction from the sound source identification and if they well understood the instructions.

At the end of the task, participants were asked to describe (by sentences or a few words) the type of motion they associated with each group they formed on the screen. They finally wrote their global impression of the test (whether the task was hard or boring, the choice of sound material, etc ...).

Results

The test lasted from 21 to more than 60 min across participants. Except for one, all of them were satisfactory about the groups they made. As expected, we observed a high inter-subject variability in the number of categories. Indeed, participants formed in average 8.8 groups (standard deviation: 3.9), but the number varied from 3 to 21 groups across participants. We noted that six participants formed groups composed of only one or two sounds. One subject gave up the test, since no categories had been formed after 45 minutes and the screen was similar to its initial state.

Definition of the Most Representative Motion Categories

To highlight the most representative categories of evoked motions reflecting the participants judgement, we matched the results obtained by different (semantic and statistical) analyses of the behavioural data.

The first analysis was effectuated on the responses to the questionnaire filled by participants at the end of the listening test. In particular, words used by participants to describe the groups they formed, were compared across participants. As assumed, they used different words to describe a same evoked motion. In practice, groups which were described with similar words (synonyms) are considered together and we retained the most relevant label (following our own judgement) for each group.

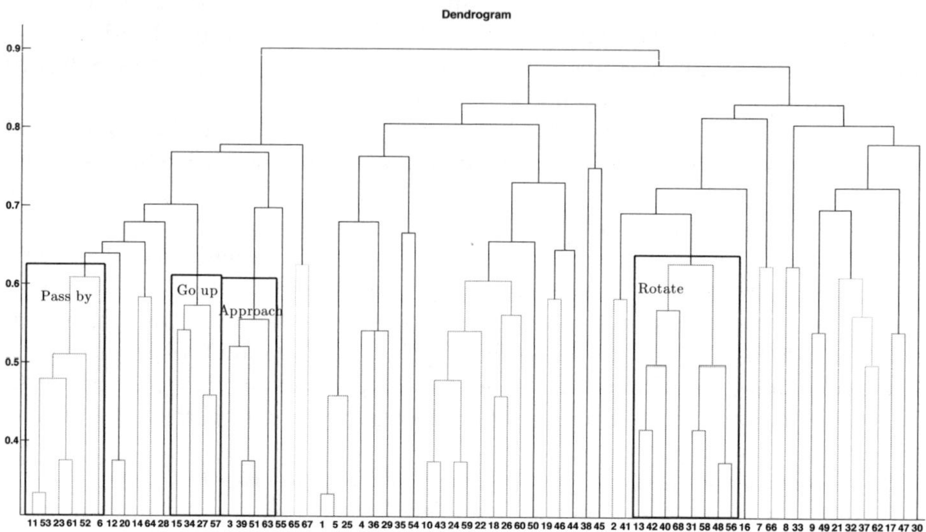

Fig. 1. Each sound (labelled with a number from 1 to 68) is linked to another according to their similarity. Each group of two sounds is linked to the closest until all sounds are linked together.

We excluded complicated expressions or metaphors, which would necessitate detailed linguistic analysis. Hence, we identified six categories corresponding to the following motions: "rotate", "fall down", "approach", "pass by", "go away" and "go up". Respectively 69%, 54%, 46%, 46%, 46% and 34% of the participants proposed these categories. We also extracted sounds corresponding to those categories according to the number of time they have been cited. Many sounds belong to different categories at a time since four of the six categories have been made by less than 50% of the subjects. Despite this, at least one sound appears more than 70% of the time for each category.

The second analysis was made on the participant' classifications. The results were represented by a 68×68 similarity matrix where each cell indicates the percentage of participants that did group together the two sounds. The hierarchical clustering analysis was conducted on the dissimilarity matrix obtained by subtracting the similarity matrix from 1. This method consists in linking together pairs of sounds with respect to their similarity, then linking these pairs with

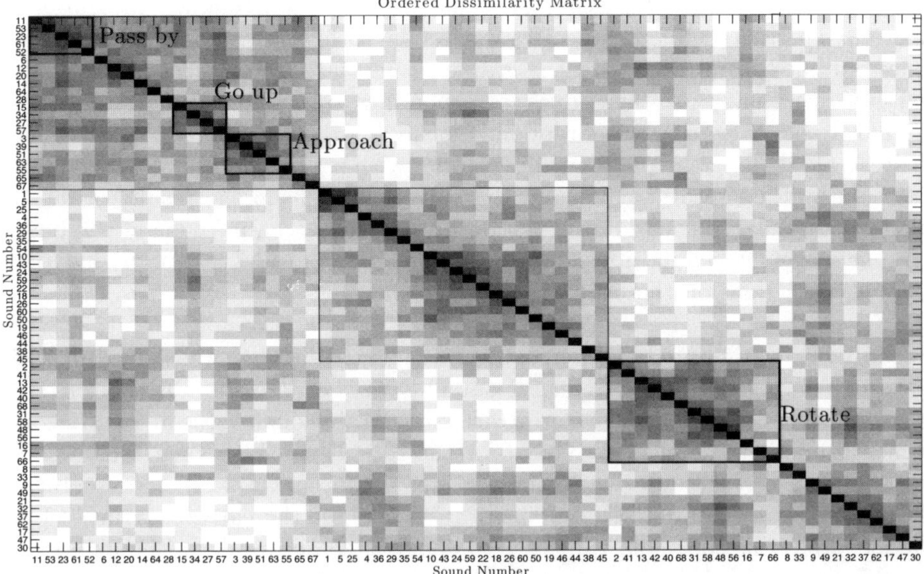

Fig. 2. Similarity matrix resorted according to the dendrogram. The grey scale corresponds to percent of time that two sounds are grouped together. Black: 100% White: 0%.

other pairs until all elements are grouped together. The obtained dendrogram is represented on Figure 1.

Finally, the results of the 2 analyses were set side by side to determine our most representative categories of motion. For that purpose, the similarity matrix was resorted according to the dendrogram (cf. fig2). It allows highlighting five groups that match five of the groups defined by semantic analysis of subjects words. For example the first six elements of the dissimilarity matrix contain the six sounds which have been cited by more than 50% of the subjects who made the category called "pass by".

Consequently, these five groups which were found both in semantic and cluster analysis, were defined as the main motion categories for our study. These groups were reported on the dendrogram of Figure 1.

Finally, for each group, we determined a "prototypical" sound representative of the category as sounds which have been cited at least by 70% of the subjects and not cited in another category. The five categories of motions are further used in test 2 as predefined categories.

2.3   Test 2: Restricted Classification Task

Sixteen subjects (6 females, 10 males) participated in this experiment and all of them participated in the first one (within a break of two weeks between the tests). Test 2 was conducted in the same experimental conditions than test 1.

The task consisted in classifying the same stimuli into predefined categories of motion. These predefined categories were deduced from the most representative ones obtained from test 1. On the graphical interface, the top half of the computer screen was split in five boxes corresponding to these predefined categories. Sounds to be categorized were randomly located in the bottom half of the screen. Instead of labelling the predefined categories with a word, we characterized each of them by the prototypical sound that was defined from the results of test 1. Participants placed sounds from the bottom of the screen into one of the boxes as function of evoked motions. They also were allowed to leave sounds that they judged ambiguous on the bottom of the screen.

Results. We computed the percentage of time each sound was sorted in each category of motion. In each category, sounds were ordered as function of their occurrence frequency. Thus, we arbitrarily fixed a threshold value at 70% beyond which sounds are defined as typical for the category[2]. With such a threshold, no sounds are representative of the category "approach", 2 are representative for "rise", 5 for "fall down" and "pass by" and 9 for the category "turn". In a further step, this threshold value has to be adjusted according to the number of sounds needed for the determination of the invariants of each category.

Most participants left some sounds at the bottom of the screen, but 62% answered "yes" to the question "Was the number of categories sufficient?". Only 2 sounds are sorted in no category more than 50% of the time.

2.4   Comparison Test 1/Test 2

Test 2 gives groups that are valid for all the participants opposite to the first test in which only two groups where valid for more than 50% of the subjects. 70% found that the second test was easier than the first one and the time to complete the task were considerably lower in the second test (average 19 min for the second 43 min for the first).

Differences between the subjects' answers to the first and to the second test are 23% (average of difference for each subject). The consistency between subjects' answers is not higher in test 2. This is most likely linked to the fact that the participants focused on different aspects of the sounds and therefore associated different motions to them. Hence, the same sound can evoke motions such as rotate, go away and rise at the same time. This shows that even if our sound selection was supposed to exclude such complex sounds, selection is indubitably subjective (i.e. depends on researcher's choice). The second test did not give the opportunity to associate more than one motion to each sound.

2.5   Physical Considerations

The two sounds simulating the Doppler effect and raise/decay phenomena for a linear movement were not categorized together. Indeed, the second was typical

---

[2] see `http://www.sensons.cnrs-mrs.fr/CMMR07_semiotique/` for sound examples.

for the category "pass by" whereas the first was not sorted in this category (same comment for rotating sound source simulation). Indeed, according to Lufti & al. [15], the most significant cues for the perception of displacement of moderate velocity (10m/s) are intensity and inter-aural time difference. For high velocity displacements, the most significant cue is related to the perception of frequency shift due to the Doppler effect. Hence, cues used to perceive a source displacement seem to differ as function of the variation range of the velocity. To go further, it is important to see that such transformations are not always efficient to give an impression of motion. There is another example in the category "pass by", where we point out a sound with increasing centroid. This variation is in opposition to low pass filtering due to air absorption (and also to pitch shift due to Doppler effects) for a going away sound source, but 72% of the subjects described this displacement to be approaching and then going away.

3   Determination of Relevant Signal Descriptors of Categories

The listening tests allowed us to determine the 5 most representative categories of motion ("approach", "rise", "fall down", "pass by" and "turn") and a set of associated typical sounds. In this section, we aim at determining the acoustic descriptors that are relevant to characterize each sound category. The problem to be solved here is quite analogous to automatic music classification in the sense that we want to find descriptors that can explain classification done by listeners. The field of music information retrieval gives lots of different answers to this problem (for example [4], [12]).

Most researches within automatic classification describe the same generic problems:

- Select the descriptors among thousand of possible
- Relevant criteria for evaluation of descriptors
- Robustness of model (which can be validated on other sound databases)

Often, the criteria are based on minimization between predictions of the model and experimental values. For example, the database is often split in two parts, the first one is used to build the model and the second for the evaluation. See [22] for a detailed analysis and complete overview of such problems.

It is important to keep in mind that we want to conduct our study while conserving as far as possible a general view of all the problems related to the semiotics of sounds in the context of synthesis. Afterwards we will be able to optimize our methodology. Indeed, as a first step, we focus on the determination of most relevant descriptors for each category instead of building a predictive model. Hence, with the results of listening tests in mind we can assert to build a model for which the validity is correlated with the number of data (between 4 and 8 among 68 sounds for each category).

3.1   Signal Descriptors

As Pachet and Roy [20] discuss, there are two different ways of selecting features: "by hand" and systematic selection. "By hand" means arbitrary selection of features according to common sense and systematic means algorithmic selection with no a priori. Our approach consists in selecting some well-known descriptors without assumption and building some others that seem to be relevant, and finally find a criterion to select the most relevant.

In most studies about timbre, the authors have developed signal descriptors to fit their perceptual dimension. Such descriptors are generally specific to musical instrument sounds, that is to say for quasi-harmonic spectra (for example in [8]). In our case, an important part of the "corpus" is composed of noisy and non-stationary sounds. Hence we cannot use traditional auditory models to take into account loudness and masking.

In this study, we focused on a dynamic problem since the evoked movement is linked to a temporal evolution of the sound. For this reason we extend our analysis to descriptors that would quantify these temporal behaviours.

To characterize our sounds from an acoustic point of view, we calculated some well-known descriptors (spectral centroid, spectral spread, spectral variation, energy envelope, temporal centroid and signal duration). Since most sounds contain stochastic contributions, the spectral descriptors are calculated from the power spectrum density (PSD). Those descriptors are calculated with a frame based method (Hanning windows of 2048 samples with 50% overlapping between two successive frames).

Since we aim at characterizing the evolutional aspect of the sounds and make these evolutions comparable across sounds, we reduce time dependent descriptors to scalars. Hence we compute average, standard deviation, monotonousness and variation rate which are described below.

Monotonousness is defined as

$$Mn = \frac{1}{N} \sum_{n=1}^{N} sign\big(va'(n)\big) \tag{2}$$

where $va'(n)$ is a derivative of a discrete variable $va(n)$ of length N. Hence $Mn \approx 1$ means an increasing curve (resp. decreasing for -1) and oscillating or horizontal if $Mn \approx 0$. Monotonousness describes both curve variation sign and curve flatness.

Variation rate is defined as :

$$Vr = \frac{1}{N-1} \sum_{n=1}^{N-1} abs\Big(sign\big(va'(n+1)\big) - sign\big(va'(n)\big)\Big) \tag{3}$$

Thus this is the zero crossing-rate of signal derivative, which is correlated with the second order moment. It makes it possible to characterize smoothness of the curve independently from global evolution (as opposed to monotonousness).

Spectral Centroid. Spectral centroid is one of the most known and used descriptors. This measure of the gravity center of the spectrum is closely related to the brightness of a sound. We used the definition proposed by Grey and Gordon [8]:

$$Sc = \sum_{k=1}^{K} \frac{kc_k}{\lambda + \sum c_k}$$

where c_k are coefficients of discrete PSD computed on frequency k and λ is a regulation parameter.

Spectral Spread is a measure of the spread of a spectrum around its mean value and can be calculated through the second order moment of the spectral centroid. From the calculation of Sc, we compute the equivalent of the second order moment (definition from Peeters [18]):

$$Ss = \sqrt{\frac{\sum_k (k - Sc)^2 c_k}{\sum_k c_k}}$$

Spectral variation (or Spectral Flux) is a measure of the time evolution of the spectrum and is defined by Peeters [18]

$$Sv(n) = 1 - \frac{\sum_k c(n-1,k) \times a(n,k)}{\sqrt{\sum_k c(n-1,k)^2}\sqrt{\sum_k c(n,k)^2}} \tag{4}$$

where $c(n,k)$ is PSD of the signal computed at the nth frame.

Amplitude Envelope. The envelope $A(n)$ is calculated by first computing the Hilbert transform $\mathcal{H}$ of the temporal signal and then by applying to its modulus, a low pass filtering (second order Butterworth filter) with cut-off frequency fc. This filter determines the time scale for the energy variation. Fluctuation strength [24] is defined for amplitude modulations under 20Hz, and we therefore use this value as cut-off frequency to get a measure of the variations in this domain.

Temporal Centroid is the energy envelope centroid from definition of [18] (but normalized by signal duration):

$$Tc = \frac{1}{N} \frac{\sum_{n=1}^{n=N} n \times A(n)}{\sum_{n=1}^{N} A(n)} \tag{5}$$

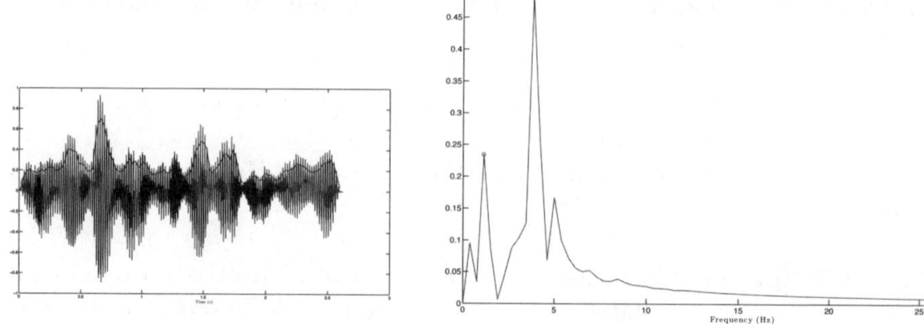

Fig. 3. <u>Left</u>: Estimation of the temporal envelope of a sound in the category "Rotate". <u>Right</u>: FFT of adjusted autocorrelation and extraction of peaks for the characterization of amplitude modulation of the temporal envelope. The selected peaks are marked by circles.

Characterization of Amplitude Modulation. The physics of moving sources states that periodicity is a fundamental characteristic of rotating sources. Thus we added to our set, descriptors that characterize amplitude modulation taking into account some specificities.

Most methods that estimate periodicity are based on the autocorrelation, which is also the case for the algorithm presented here. We compute the autocorrelation of the temporal signal. In our case, we rather consider the autocorrelation on the amplitude envelope $A(n)$ as defined previously from which some "static" components are removed. In practice, a linear or quadratic interpolation was estimated from the autocorrelation and subtracted from it. The calculation of the autocorrelation on the envelope (instead of directly on the temporal signal) allow focusing on the slowest periodicities contained in the signal. The periodicity is quantified by calculating the Fourier transform of this adjusted autocorrelation. Then we detect the most prominent peaks, taking into account the peaks' width. Thus, wide peaks are excluded (with arbitrary threshold) since they do not correspond to a detectable modulation. Actually, the threshold corresponds to a width of 5Hz from 75% of the component energy (cf. figure3). We then extract the frequencies and amplitudes of the two highest peaks.

In order to characterize variations in the amplitude modulation, we also extract the number of peaks above the energy average in the considered bandwidth (0-20Hz). Indeed, for variations of the modulation frequency, the autocorrelation "spectrum" contains more peaks and the domain containing peaks characterize the modulation boundary.

Characterization of Level Variation. Another fundamental characteristic of signals given by the physics of moving sources is the variation of loudness within a time interval corresponding to the length of the sound. For example, this is particularly important as a distance cue for low speed moving source as shown in [15].

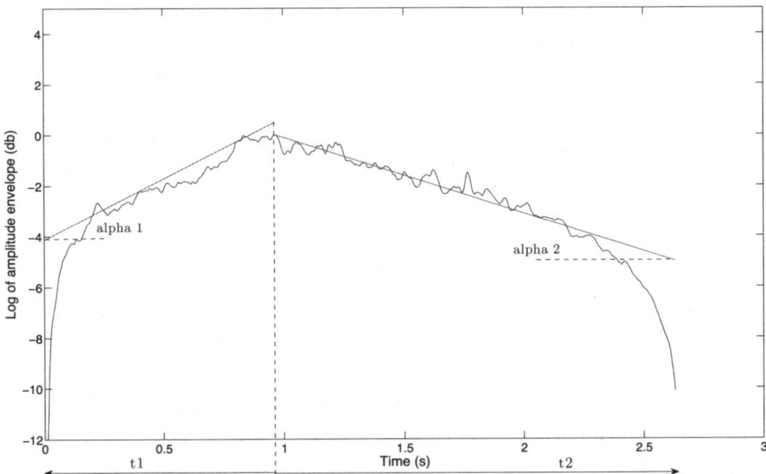

Fig. 4. Example of the Characterization of level variation for a sound from the category "go past" by the 2 slopes α_1 and α_2 of the interpolation process. The duration t_1 (from the beginning of the signal to its max value) and t_2 (from the max to the end) were also considered.

To characterize this level variation, we detect the maximum of the energy envelope and calculate a linear interpolation of the logarithm of the envelope from the beginning of the signal to its maximum value and further from the maximum value to the end. The signal descriptors characterizing the amplitude variation are defined from this interpolation process (Figure 4). They correspond to the slopes of the two curves, α_1 and α_2, and to the envelope fluctuations around these two curves, $Err1$ and $Err2$ (in practice, these fluctuations are quantified by the interpolation quadratic error). Even for highly chaotic sounds, these parameters describe a reliable evolution of the sound level and only in a few cases the interpolation was impossible to calculate.

3.2   Evaluation of Descriptors

The 32 signal descriptors defined in the previous section were computed for each sound. The abbreviations chosen for these descriptors are listed in Appendix A. Note that in some cases, the computation leads to aberrant values, which do not reflect the actual sound behaviour. For instance, the calculation of periodicity for sounds, which do not contain cyclic behaviours, would be inaccurate. In such cases, we arbitrarily fixed these meaningless values to 0.

We further aim at determining the most relevant descriptors for each sound category defined previously. This issue can be linked to the one addressed in the field of "data mining" and particularly "feature selection" research. Indeed, feature selection methods aim at optimizing prediction models based on the most explicative parameters. Consequently, they lead to reduce an initial database to its most relevant elements without reducing the performance of the prediction models. This selection is based on criteria which are different across methods and the relevance of features is highly dependent on the definition given to relevance. Hence, a general criterion is: If the exclusion of a feature from the data set involves a decrease in the learning model performance, then the excluded feature is defined as relevant. For instance, Blum and Langley [3] give five definitions for "relevant features" and we chose the more "physical" one, which can be summarized as: a relevant descriptor permits differentiation of two different observations (definition 1 in [3]: Relevant to the target).

Choice of the Method: In this study, we do not aim at defining a model which explains sound categories. Indeed, as discussed in section 3 (introduction), model validity depends on the size of the data bank and confidence in categories. Indeed, the set of typical sounds for each category are unequal in terms of number of samples and of portion of subjects that defined them as typical. Furthermore, no perceptual or physical consideration allows us to settle between linear regression and non-linear methods (like regression tree). Such consideration prevents us from building a model. Thus we will use feature selection algorithms that are not linked to a machine learning method (the so called *filter* in opposition with *wrappers*) to determine the most relevant descriptors for each sound category. In particular, the purpose is to build a subset of non-correlated descriptors (to reduce the feature set). In our case, a lot of descriptors are highly correlated, but this can be inline with our definition of relevance. Moreover, from a "physical" point of view, correlations between features can lead to interesting results.

For instance, we can consider correlation between features and classes or consider signal descriptors as statistical distributions, which can be compared with observations (categories).

Many *filter* methods are available and the results obtained with these various methods can be extremely different. For example, Herrera et al. (2002) [12] compared two different methods[3] on categories of drum sounds and showed that for each category, only one or two features coincided. This difference is due to the fact that one method considers a subset of features and compares results obtained for each subset of a given size, while the other considers each feature independently (and does not consider correlation between features). Otherwise, some methods aim at determining feature combinations (not only linear) that can be more "relevant" than independent features. As discussed in [10], "Two variables that are useless by themselves can be useful together".

For methods necessitating discrete variables, continuous variables are transformed into binary values with an optimized threshold defined from observations. This transformation is useful since different perceptual attributes correspond

---

[3] Correlation based Feature Selection (CFS) and RefiefF [11].

to different ranges of values of a same continuous physical variable. The borders (threshold values) are generally determined from discrimination tasks. For example, psychoacousticians define both fluctuation strength and roughness from the temporal variations of loudness. Fluctuation strength is defined under 20Hz and roughness between 20Hz and 200Hz. Methods that consider discrete values for a feature match this observation and particularly with Fayyad and Irani's method[4] which takes into account categorization data to perform continuous to discrete transformations. Nevertheless, such methods imply that features are considered independently.

In practice the discretization process is based on binary values and implies to split descriptor values into distinct categories. In our case, the sound categories were defined from a consensus across subjects and consequently the perception is assumed to be non categorical. Considering an intermediate domain between 2 categories would be intuitively accurate (i.e. values under threshold 1, between threshold 1 and 1, above threshold 2).

To summarize, the literature offers a large variety of statistical methods. In our case, we first consider discretization and validity according to the Fisher test[5] and the equivalent for continuous data, the so called "Fisher Filtering" method implemented in R. Rakotomalala's free software TANAGRA[6] (see [10] and [3] for more details on such methods.).

Results and Discussion. The most relevant signal descriptors highlighted by the 2 methods are presented in Tab. 1 (for discretization method) and in Tab. 2 (for the fisher filtering method). To test robustness of both methods, we also added to the feature set, a random variable between 0 and 1 attributed to each sound; The results showed that this variable has never been highlighted by the 2 methods and consequently, confirm the confidence in the one presented in this section.

Table 1. Feature discretized according to category and corresponding thresold. [+] means feature value of sound in the category is above the cut-off ([-] under). *Abbreviations are described in appendix A.*

| Category | "Rotate" | Category: | "Pass by" | Category: | "Fall down" |
Feature	Cut-off	Feature	Cut-off	Feature	Cut-off
cgs_std	224 (Hz) [-]	**Npeak**	3,5 [-]	t_2	0,875[-]
$a0/a1$	0,1 [+]	**Err$_2$**	0,26 [-]	**ls**	0,94[-]
$f1$	0,69 (Hz) [-]			α_1	6,1 (db/s) [+]
a1	0,06 [+]			t_1	0,36(s) [-]
f0/f1	0,05 [+]				

---

[4] (1993) cited by [11].

[5] Due to the small number of sounds in each category (from 12 for "rotate" to 8 for "fall"), Fisher Test is more adapted than Chi2 to compare categories and features.

[6] http://eric.univ-lyon2.fr/ ricco/tanagra/fr/tanagra.html.

As expected, results given by "Fisher Filtering" are coherent with the discretization method. Moreover, they are also coherent with our assumptions. We now discuss results obtained for the motion categories "Rotate", "Pass by" and "Fall down". In particular, we focus on the descriptors which have been highlighted by both methods in each category. For the category "Approach", no significant descriptors were found by both methods. For the category "Rise", only the discretization method highlighted the variation rate of the energy envelope (En_vr) with no statistical criterion for the validity of this descriptor regarding to the category. Note that categories "Rise" and "Approach" are the ones with the smallest amount of representative sounds (resp. 4 and 6 sounds selected by more than 50% of the subjects).

Table 2. Signal descriptors and corresponding F-value and P-value obtained by "Fisher filtering" feature selection method

"Rotate"			"Pass by"			"Fall down"		
feature	F	P-Value	feature	F	P-Value	feature	F	P-Value
a1	19,94	0,000076	**Err$_2$**	8,03	0,00748	**ls**	14,60	0,0005
$Npeak$	8,32	0,00658	**Npeak**	7,54	0,00934	Err_1	14,38	0,00055
f0/f1	8,23	0,00684	Err_1	6,31	0,01663	$a1$	9,98	0,0032
			En_mn	4	0,0531	**t$_1$**	9,67	0,0036

Category "Rotate". From a physical point of view, the parameter $a1$ (amplitude of highest peak in the adjusted autocorrelation) corresponds to the most meaningful descriptors since it quantifies the amplitude modulation rate. Note that this parameter is the most relevant (and the only significant) according to Fisher F criterion. Discretization also pointed out this feature with the information that this modulation rate must be over 0,06 (in arbitrary units). The ratio of frequency modulation ($f0/f1$) was also highlighted and indicates that 2 amplitude modulation components are necessary to completely evoke a rotating motion (with no proof according to F value).

Category "Pass by". The relevancy of the Err_2 feature can be explained from physical considerations related to the raise/decay phenomena. Indeed, the decreasing part of the amplitude envelope of the sounds should be log-linear to characterize the "pass by" motion (0.26 [-]in Table1). Err_2 also quantifies smoothness (low fluctuations) of the amplitude envelope, which can explain why it is not significant according to the F criterion (but more correlated with the category). On the contrary, the interpretation of the $Npeak$ feature is more speculative. For the moment, no physical or signal considerations made on the category can be directly related to this parameter.

Category "Fall down". By preliminary listening to the sounds representative of this category, we noticed that they mainly correspond to short impact sounds.

This observation is inline with the characteristic of the signal features highlighted by statistical analysis, i.e. short sounds (signal length ls with 0.94 [-]) with an abrupt attack (reflected by parameter t_1 with 0.36 [-]).

These results are of interest from a cognitive point of view since we can deduce that fundamental cues inducing the evocation of falling down motion are not directly contained in sounds. In particular, we can assume that participants associated this motion to sounds by imagining the motion which could have caused the resulting sounds (for instance, striking the floor at the end of its trajectory).

This particular example illustrates the necessity of taking into account some cognitive assumptions additionally to physical considerations.

4   Conclusion and Perspectives

In this paper, we aimed at proposing a global methodology for the design of synthesis tools controlled by high-level parameters, such as mental evocations induced by sounds. Through the particular case of the evocation of motions, this study addressed the general problem of semiotics of sounds for synthesis applications.

The proposed methodology addressed 3 main questions: What are the different categories of motion? What are the common acoustic features of sounds in a category? How to synthesize sounds that evoke specific motions?

First, to determine these different sound categories, we conducted a two-part listening test. The choice of the stimuli was a crucial issue since it constituted the starting point of our methodology. To help subjects to focus on "sensations" evoked by sounds and to avoid bias introduced by the identification of the sound source, we gathered "concrete" samples issued from electro-acoustic music compositions. The first part of the listening test consisted in a free categorization task in which listeners were asked to group sounds as a function of the evoked motions. Groups were quite consistent across subjects and the most representative ones were used in the second part of the listening test, as predefined categories in a constrained categorization task. The predefined categories were represented by prototypical sounds (defined by the previous free categorization test) instead of labels. In this manner, the prototypical sounds imposed an acoustic reference of a given motion category and consequently, listeners assumed to base their strategy mainly on "analytical" properties of sounds. Thus, results allowed determining a set of representative sounds for each category of motion.

Concerning the determination of acoustic features characterizing each sound category, we investigated most of well-known signal descriptors (as defined in mpeg7 standard [17] for example). In particular, according to the wide variety of our sounds (noisiness, complex temporal evolution, different durations...), we compared their evolution by calculating a scalar estimated from time dependent descriptor values (calculation based on successive frames for spectral descriptors). We determined the most relevant descriptors for each category by using the *filter* feature selection method. This method was chosen according to the validity of statistical tests and considerations on the perception of sounds, the results constitute a first step towards the determination of the so-called acoustic invariants, for which different statistical methods have to be examined among hundreds of available methods.

The third main question concerning the building of synthesis tools is still in progress. In particular, the calibration (definition of a valid range of values) of these most relevant descriptors and their control (sound manipulation from the variation of synthesis parameters) are currently being investigated.

Even if many interesting perspectives have been highlighted, we completed the first two steps of our general methodology. Now, we can address with precise questions, each concerned research field such as music, physics, data-mining and cognitive sciences.

Acknowledgments. This project has partly been supported by the French National Research Agency (ANR, JC05-41996, "senSons") to Sølvi Ystad. (http://www.sensons.cnrs-mrs.fr/)

References

1. Aramaki, M., Bailleres, H., Brancheriau, L., Kronland-Martinet, R., Ystad, S.: Sound Quality Assessment of Wood for Xylophone Bars. Journal of the Acoustical Society of America 121(4), 2407–2420 (2007)
2. Bigand, E.: Multidimensional scaling of emotional responses to music: The effect of musical expertise and of the duration of the excerpts. Cognition and emotion 19(8), 1113–1139 (2005)
3. Blum, A., Langley, P.: Selection of Relevant Features and Examples in Machine Learning. Artificial Intelligence 97(1-2), 245–271 (1997)
4. Defreville, P., Roy, B., Pachet, F.: Automatic Recognition of Urban Sound Sources. In: Proceedings of the 120th AES Conference (2006)
5. Eitan, Z., Granot, R.Y.: How music moves: Musical parameters and listeners' images of motion. Music perception 23(3), 221–247 (2006)
6. Gaver, W.W.: What in the world do we hear? An ecological approach to auditory event perception. Ecological Psychology 5(1), 1–29 (1993)
7. Gibson, J.J.: The ecological approach to visual perception. Houghton Mifflin, Boston (1979)
8. Grey, J.M., Gordon, J.W.: Perceptual effects of spectral modifications on musical timbres. The Journal of the Acoustical Society of America 63(5), 1493–1500 (1978)
9. Guastavino, C.: Categorization of environmental sounds. Canadian Journal of Experimental Psychology 61(1), 54–63 (2007)
10. Guyon, I., Elisseeff, A.: An introduction to variable and feature selection. Journal of Machine Learning Research 3, 1157–1182 (2003)
11. Hall, M.: Correlation-based feature selection of discrete and numeric class machine learning. In: Proceedings of the International Conference on Machine Learning, pp. 359–366. Morgan Kaufmann Publishers, San Francisco (2000)

12. Herrera, P., Yeterian, A., Gouyon, F.: Automatic classification of drum sounds: a comparison of feature selection methods and classification techniques. In: Proceedings of Second International Conference on Music and Artificial Intelligence, Edinburgh, Scotland (2002)
13. Jekosch, U.: Assigning Meaning to Sounds - Semiotics in the Context of Product-Sound Design. In: Blauert, J. (ed.) Communication Acoustics. Springer, Heidelberg (2005)
14. Kawai, K., Kojima, K., Hirate, K., Yasuoka, M.: Personal evaluation structure of environmental sounds: experiment of subjective evaluation using subjects own terms. Journal of sound and vibrations (2004)
15. Lufti, A., Wang, W.: Correlational analysis of acoustic cues for the discrimination of auditory motion. Journal of the Acoustical Society of America 106(2) (August 1999)
16. McAdams, S.: Recognition of sound sources and events. In: McAdams, S., Bigand, E. (eds.) Thinking in sound The cognitive psychology of human audition, pp. 146–198. Oxford University Press, Oxford (1993)
17. Kim, H.G., Moreau, N., Sikora, T.: MPEG-7 Audio and Beyond: audio content indexing and retrieval. Wiley, Chichester (2005)
18. Peeters, G.: A large set audio features for sound description (similarity and classification) in the CUIDADO project. In: IRCAM (2004)
19. Portnoff, M.R.: Implementation of the digital phase vocoder using the fast Fourier transform. IEEE Transactions on acoustics, speech and signal processing 24(3) (1976)
20. Pachet, F., Roy, P.: Exploring billions of audio features. In: Proceedings of CBMI 2007 (2007)
21. Schaeffer, P.: Traité des objets musicaux Editions du seuil (1966)
22. Widmer, G., Dixon, S., Knees, P., Pampalk, E., Pohle, E.: From Sound to "Sense" via Feature Extraction and Machine Learning: Deriving High-level Descriptors for Characterising Music. In: Polotti, P., Rocchesso, D. (eds.) Sound to Sense, Sense to Sound: A State-of-the-Art (2007)
23. Ystad, S., Kronland-Martinet, R., Schön, D., Besson, M.: Vers une approche acoustique et cognitive de la sémiotique des objets sonores, UST: Théorie et Applications (2005)
24. Zwicker, E., Fastl, H.: Psycho-acoustics, facts and models. Springer, Heidelberg (1990)

A   Appendix: Abbreviation Used for Signal Descriptors

cgs_std: Standard deviation of spectral centroid

ls: signal length

$f1$: second amplitude modulation frequency

$f0/f1$: ratio of amplitude modulation frequency

$a0$: amplitude modulation "rate" (first component)

$a1$: amplitude modulation "rate" (second component)

$a0/a1$: ratio of amplitude modulation "rates"

$Npeak$: number of peaks in Fourier transform amplitude envelope autocorrelation between 0 and 20 Hz

t_1: time from beginning to max energy point (cf. figure 4)

t_2: time from max energy point to end (cf. figure 4)

Err_1: Quadratic error for linear interpolation of logarithm of amplitude envelope from beginning to max energy point of signal.

Err_2: idem from max energy point to end of signal

α_1: slope of linear interpolation of logarithm of amplitude envelope from beginning to max energy point of signal.(cf. figure 4)

α_2: slope of linear interpolation of logarithm of amplitude envelope from max energy point to end of signal.(cf. figure 4)

En_vr: Variation rate of energy envelope

En_mn: Energy monotonousness

Exploring Perceptual Based Timbre Feature for Singer Identification

Swe Zin Kalayar Khine, Tin Lay Nwe, and Haizhou Li

Institute for Infocomm Research,
21 Heng Mui Keng Terrace, Singapore 119613
{zkkswe,tlnma,hli}@i2r.a-star.edu.sg
http://www.i2r.a-star.edu.sg

Abstract. Timbre can be defined as feature of an auditory stimulus that allows us to distinguish the sounds which have the same pitch and loudness. In this paper, we explore timbre based perceptual feature for singer identification. We start with a vocal detection process to extract the vocal segments from the sound. The cepstral coefficients, which reflect timbre characteristics, are then computed from the vocal segments. The cepstral coefficients of timbre are formulated by combining information of harmonic and the dynamic characteristics of the sound such as vibrato and the attack-decay envelope of the songs. Bandpass filters that spread according to the octave frequency scale are used to extract vibrato and harmonic information of sounds. The experiments are conducted on a database of 84 popular songs. The results show that the proposed timbre based perceptual feature is robust and effective. We achieve an average error rate of 12.2% in segment level singer identification.

Keywords: Timbre, Singing Voice Detection, Vibrato, Harmonic.

1   Introduction

The rapid evolution of the digital multimedia technologies in computer and Internet technology has enabled huge multimedia database. With these continually growing databases, automatic music information retrieval (MIR) has become increasingly important. Singer Identification (SingerID) is one of the important tasks in MIR. It is the process of identifying the singer of a song. In general, a SingerID process comprises three major steps.

The first step is detecting singing segments (vocals) in a song. Vocals can be either pure singing voice or a mixture of singing voice with background instrumentals (nonvocals). The second step is singer feature computation. Features are extracted from vocal segments. The last step is formulating singer classifier using feature parameters. In this paper, we propose new solutions for the second step of singer feature computation.

Earlier studies in SingerID use features such as Mel Frequency Cepstral Coefficients (MFCC) [6]. Recently, studies start looking into perceptually motivated features which are able to appreciate the aesthetic characteristics of singing voice

R. Kronland-Martinet, S. Ystad, and K. Jensen (Eds.): CMMR 2007, LNCS 4969, pp. 159–171, 2008.

for music content processing and analysis. For example, vibrato motivated acoustic features are used to identify singers in [1],[11]. Beside vibrato, harmonic is also a useful feature for SingerID. In fact, harmonics of soprano singer's voice are widely spaced in the spectrum in contrast to that of bass singer's voice [8]. Hence, harmonic spectrum is useful to differentiate between low and high pitch singers.

One of the basic elements of music is timbre or color. Timbre is the quality of sound which allows human ears to distinguish among different types of sounds [15]. Cleveland [3] states that an individual singer has a characteristic timbre that is a function of the laryngeal source and vocal tract resonances. Timbre is assumed to be invariant with an individual singer. On the other hand, Erickson [6] states that the traditional concept of an invariant timbre associated with a singer is inaccurate and that vocal timbre must be conceptualized in terms of transformations in perceived quality that occur across an individual singer's range and/or registers. In general, these studies suggest that timbre is invariant with an individual singer or there is a particular range of timbre quality associated to an individual singer. In this paper, we would like to study the use of timbre based features in SingerID task. Poli [9] measured the timbre quality from spectral envelope of MFCC features to identify singers. In [17], timber is characterized by the harmonic lines of the harmonic sound. In this paper, we propose determining timbre by the harmonic content of a sound and the dynamic characteristics of it such as vibrato and attack-decay envelope [15].

The rest of this paper is organized as follows. In section 2, we present the methods for vocal detection. In section 3, we study perceptually motivated acoustic features and their characteristics. In section 4, we describe the popular song database, experiment setup and results. Finally, we conclude our study in section 5.

2   Vocal Detection

We extract vocal segments from songs. Subband based Log Frequency Power Coefficient (LFPC) [10] is used as acoustic features. We train hidden Markov models (HMM) as vocal and nonvocal acoustic models to detect vocal segments. Vocal detection errors can affect SingerID performance. To reduce the vocal detection error, we formulate the vocal detection as a hypothesis test [12] based on confidence score. In this way, we only retain vocal segments, with which the acoustic models have high confidence. Vocal segments with confidence measure which are higher than a predetermined threshold are accepted for the SingerID experiment.

3   Acoustic Features

We next study several perceptually motivated features, namely harmonic, vibrato and timber features, to characterize song segments. We propose to use subband filters on octave frequency scale in formulating these acoustic features.

3.1 Harmonic

Sopranos have higher fundamental frequency than bass singers. Hence, harmonics of soprano's voice is widely spaced in contrast to that of bass singing. Upper panels of Fig. 1 (a) and (b) show the examples of harmonic spectrum of soprano and bass singing respectively. To capture this information, we implement the harmonic filters with the centre frequencies located at each of the musical notes as in middle panel of Fig. 1 (a) and (b). The list of the frequencies of the musical notes can be found in [7]. Subband filters span up to 8 octaves (16 kHz). Each octave has 12 subbands and there are 96 subbands in total. Output of subband filtering is given in lower panels of Fig. 1. For soprano, lower panel of Fig. 1 (a) shows widely spaced peaks. However, the peaks are narrowly spaced in lower panel of Fig. 1 (b) for bass singers.

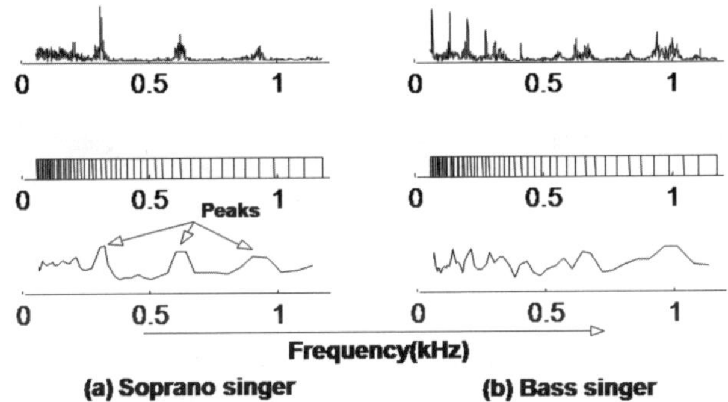

Fig. 1. Harmonics and harmonic filtering

3.2 Vibrato

Vibrato is a periodic, rather sinusoidal, modulation of pitch and amplitude of a musical tone [14]. Vocal vibrato can be seen as a function of the style of singing associated to a particular singer [11].

Vibrato is characterized by two parameters: the extent or excursion and the rate as illustrated in Fig. 2 (a). Female singers tend to have a slightly faster mean vibrato rate than male singers [4]. Vibrato excursions occurring at the tone D6 for three different singers are shown in Fig. 2 (a), (b) and (c). In Fig. 2(c), vibrato excursions to the up and down from the note is balanced. However, unbalanced vibrato excursion can be seen in Fig. 2 (a) and (b). According to [2], such irregular vibrato excursions are very common in most of the tones. In [5], vibrato extent is categorized into two different types, 'wobble' and 'bleat'. Wobble has a wider pitch fluctuation and slower rate of vibrato as in Singer-A. However, bleat has a narrower pitch fluctuation and faster rate as in Singer-C. Hence, the information such as 1) regularity or irregularity in vibrato excursion, 2) two different vibrato types of 'wobble' and 'bleat', and 3) vibrato rate is integrated into acoustic feature.

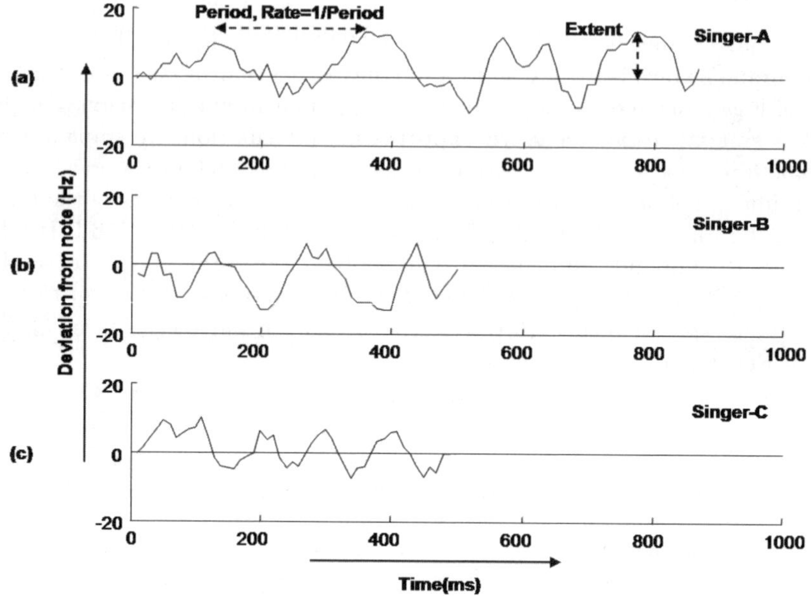

Fig. 2. Vibrato waveforms of 3 singers at note D6, 1174.6Hz

As a result of the modulation of pitch, the frequencies of all the overtones vary regularly and in sync with the pitch frequency modulation [13]. Therefore, we implement the subband filters with the center frequencies located at each of the musical notes to characterize the vibrato. The list of the frequencies of the musical notes can be found in [7]. Due to the fact that singing voice contains high frequency harmonics [16], our subband filters span up to 8 octaves (16kHz). Our subband filters are implemented with a bandwidth of ±1.5 semitone from each note since vibrato extent can increase more than ±1 semitone when a singer raises his/her vocal loudness [13]. We employ cascaded subband filters (referred to as vibrato filter) [11] to capture vibrato information from acoustic signal.

In Fig. 4, the upper panel shows spectrum partial. The middle panel presents the frequency response of the vibrato filter. The lower panel demonstrates the instantaneous amplitude output of the vibrato filter. With the output from the vibrato filter, we are able to track the local maxima to derive the vibrato extent [11]. We illustrate the vibrato filter [11] and subband outputs in Fig. 3 and Fig. 4. The filter has two cascaded layers of subbands. The first layer has overlapped trapezoidal filters. The second layer has 5 non-overlapped rectangular filters of equal bandwidths for each trapezoidal subband. Trapezoidal filters are tapered between ±0.5 semitone to ±1.5 semitone. The vibrato fluctuations are observed by tracking the local maxima in the instantaneous amplitude output of the subbands in the second layer as shown in the lower panel of Fig. 4. Local maxima indicate the position of the vibrato. The distance between the center frequency of the corresponding filter and the local maxima informs the vibrato

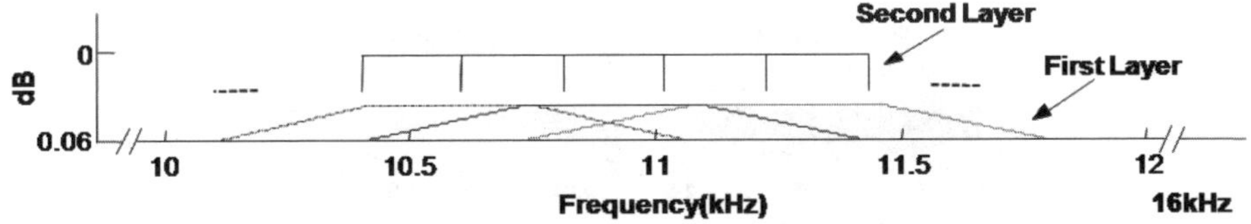

Fig. 3. A bank of cascaded subband filters

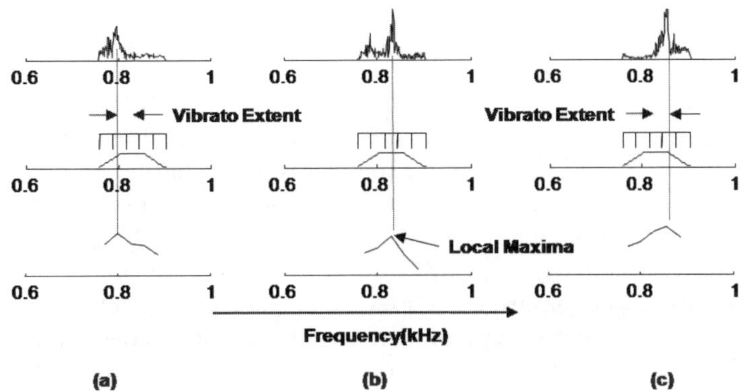

Fig. 4. Vibrato fluctuations and vibrato filtering observed at the note G#5, 830.6Hz. (a) vibrato fluctuates left (b) no fluctuation (c) vibrato fluctuates right.

extent. The tapered and overlapped trapezoidal filters in the first layer allow vibrato fluctuations of adjacent notes observed at the output of the subbands in the second layer to be 'continuous'. The vibrato filter captures irregularities or regularities in vibrato excursion and 'wobble' or 'bleat' vibrato types.

3.3   Timbre

Sounds may be generally characterized by pitch, loudness and quality. For sounds that have the same pitch and loudness, sound quality or timbre describes the characteristics which allow human ears to distinguish among them. Timbre is a general term for the distinguishable characteristics of a tone. Timbre is mainly determined by the harmonic content of a sound and the dynamic characteristics of the sound such as vibrato and attack-decay envelope of the sound [15]. Tone quality or timbre seems most strongly related to the physical phenomena of unfolding partials in the spectrum of a sound or the spectral envelope which distinguishes between two different instruments playing the same note at the same amplitude. The spectral envelop consists of the basis for our tonal judgement [18]. Attack-decay processes of two different singers are shown in Fig. 5 (a) and (b). Singer-1's voice takes more time to develop to its peak than that of Singer-2. And, the decay process of Singer-1 is more gradual than that of Singer-2.

Studies found that it takes a duration of about 60ms to recognize the timbre of a tone. If a tone is shorter than 4ms, it is perceived as an atonal click [15].

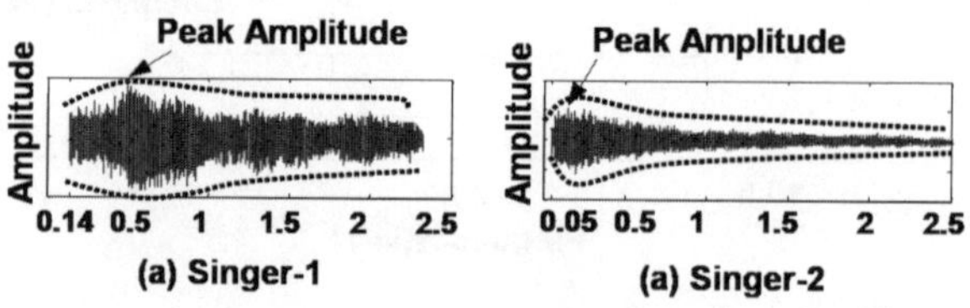

Fig. 5. Attack-decay envelopes

3.4   Cepstral Coefficient Computation

We first divide a music signal into frames of 20ms with 13ms overlapping and apply Hamming window to each frame to minimize signal discontinuities at the end of each frame. Each audio frame is passed through harmonic filters for harmonic content analysis to derive log energy of each band. Finally, we compute a total of 13 Octave Frequency Cepstral Coefficients ($OFCC_{har}$) from the log energies using Discrete Cosine Transform. We then replace the harmonic filters with vibrato filters to compute the $OFCC_{vib}$ coefficients. To account for timbre characteristics, output log energy of vibrato filter is augmented by that of harmonic and Mel-scale filters. Then, we compute 13 TimBre Cepstral Coefficients (TBCC). We augment the feature coefficients with time derivatives or delta parameters from two neighbouring frames to capture temporal information. For example, delta parameters take care of vibrato rate and attack-decay envelope in $OFCC_{vib}$ and TBCC respectively.

3.5   Formulating Singer Identification as Verification

Traditionally, singer identification system is formulated as a pattern classification problem,in which we find singer model that has the highest likelihood score. The likelihood score measures the similarity between model and test samples. However, it does not take discriminative information between singers into accounts. Here, we propose formulating the identification as a verification task [19] in which we use likelihood ratio instead of likelihood score for decision making. Let O be the sequence of input feature vectors representing a vocal segment from a song of target singer group, otherwise known as the observation. Following the statistical hypothesis test theory, we define two hypothesis. The true hypothesis H_1 is that O belongs to the target singer model λ^m. And the false hypothesis H_0 is that O belongs to non-target model λ^k. We have the following decision rule.

$$p(H_1) \begin{array}{c} \text{Accept} \\ \gtrless \\ \text{Reject} \end{array} p(H_0) \tag{1}$$

When it is applied in singer verification, equation (1) can be rewritten in the form of posterior probability:

$$p(\lambda^m|O) \quad \overset{\text{Accept}}{\underset{\text{Reject}}{\overset{\geq}{<}}} \quad p(\lambda^k|O) \tag{2}$$

where $p(\lambda^m|O)$ is the posterior probability of target singer model λ^m given the song segment O. We apply Bayesian decision rule, equation (2) can be formulated as follows.

$$p(O|\lambda^m)P(\lambda^m) \quad \overset{\text{Accept}}{\underset{\text{Reject}}{\overset{\geq}{<}}} \quad p(O|\lambda^k)P(\lambda^k) \tag{3}$$

where $P(\lambda^m)$ and $P(\lambda^k)$ are the priori probabilities of O to be target singer group or non-target singer group respectively. In our system, $P(\lambda^m)$ and , $P(\lambda^k)$ are assumed equiprobable. Equation (3) can be rewritten in terms of likelihood ratio as in equation (4).

$$\frac{p(O|\lambda^m)}{p(O|\lambda^k)} \quad \overset{\text{Accept}}{\underset{\text{Reject}}{\overset{\geq}{<}}} \quad \frac{P(\lambda^k)}{P(\lambda^m)} \tag{4}$$

In this way, we use a likelihood ratio instead of a likelihood score for decision making.

Now, let us re-examine equation (4) by considering the total cost of a singer identification system. The total cost is defined as follows [19]:

$$C = C_{\lambda^k|\lambda^m}.P(\lambda^m).p(\lambda^k|\lambda^m) + C_{\lambda^m|\lambda^k}.P(\lambda^k).p(\lambda^m|\lambda^k) \tag{5}$$

where $C_{\lambda^k|\lambda^m}$ and $C_{\lambda^m|\lambda^k}$ are the costs of a false rejection and a false acceptance respectively. $p(\lambda^k|\lambda^m)$ and $p(\lambda^m|\lambda^k)$ are the probabilities of a false rejection and a false acceptance yielded by the system. Assuming the costs of $C_{\lambda^k|\lambda^m}$ and $C_{\lambda^m|\lambda^k}$ are the same, equation (5) reflects the error rate averaged over the test database. We find that the decision strategy of equation (4) leads to minimization of this total cost in equation (5).

4   Experiments and Discussion

We compile a database of 84 popular songs from commercially available CD albums of 12 solo English and Chinese singers. The titles of the albums are shown in Table 1. A total of 7 songs are extracted from each album. Four songs of each singer are allocated to TrainDB and the remaining 3 songs to TestDB. Vocal and nonvocal segments of each song are manually annotated to provide the ground truth. The sampling frequency of the song is 44.1 kHz and 16 bit per samples. We define error rate (ER) as the number of errors divided by the total number of test trials.

We first segment a song into 1 second fixed-length segments. Then, each segment is classified as vocal or nonvocal class using the method mentioned in section 2. The average vocal/nonvocal classification error rate of vocal detection system is reported at 8.7%.

Table 1. Singers and Album Titles for 84 Popular Songs

Number	Singer	Album
1	Michael Bolton	Vintage
2	Richard Marx	My own Best Enemy
3	Adu	Tian Hei
4	Ou De Yang	Ocean
5	Jay Chou	Qi Li Xiang
6	Kathryn Williams	Relations
7	Agnetha Faltskog	My colouring book
8	Jennifer Lopez	J. Lo
9	Shania Twain	Come on over
10	Gabrielle	Play to win
11	Madonna	Like a virgin
12	Dido	Life for rent

Using the vocal segments from vocal detector, SingerID experiments are further conducted. We use the continuous density HMM with four states and two Gaussian mixtures per state for all HMM models in our experiments. Using the TrainDB, we train a singer model, λ_s, for each of 12 singers. To identify singer for a vocal segment O, we estimate the likelihood score of O being generated by each of 12 singer models. The model with the highest likelihood suggests the singer identity. We conduct experiments to compare the SingerID performance of five feature types, namely, TBCC, $OFCC_{vib}$, $OFCC_{har}$, MFCC, and LPCC. Window size is 20ms and frame shift is 7ms in all tests.

The number of misidentified singing voice errors for 12 singers are listed in Fig. 6. Each feature type is extracted from 1s segments and there are 5089

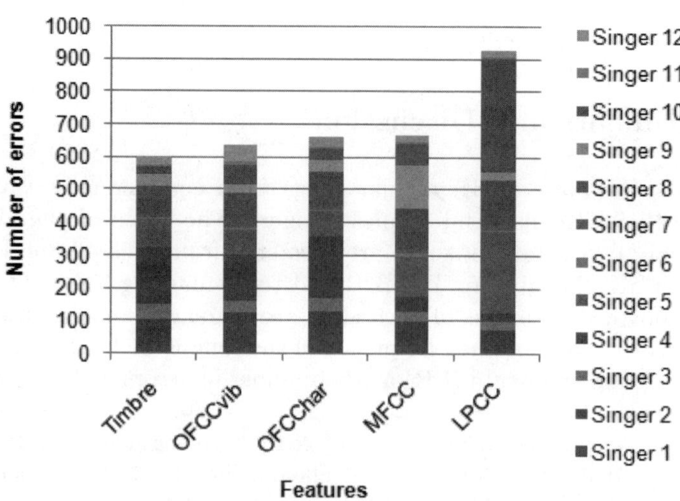

Fig. 6. Number of misidentified test samples on TestDB by 5 feature types

total segments in TestDB. From Fig. 6, we observed that the performance of the singer identification depends on the effect of song content and the singer. In general, the same gender of singers can be confused and the singers with light instrumental background achieve higher accuracy than the singers with strong instrumental background.The minimum error rate of 0.48% (Kathryn Williams) and the maximum error rate of 28.85% (Ou De Yang) are obtained based on the characteristics of the songs.

Table 2. Error rate (ER%) of SingerID on TestDB

TBCC	$OFCC_{vib}$	$OFCC_{har}$	MFCC	LPCC
12.2	12.8	13.6	12.9	21.9

Table 2 shows that the TBCC feature, with an average error rate of 12.2%, outperforms all other features. It is observed that timbre based features capture the singer characteristics well by 5% and 10.3% relative error reduction over $OFCC_{vib}$ and $OFCC_{har}$ features. Furthermore, TBCC feature perform well by 5.4% to 44.3% relative error reduction over traditional features such as MFCC and LPCC. Perceptual based acoustic features (TBCC, $OFCC_{vib}$ and $OFCC_{har}$) in general give better results than the traditional features.

A false alarm rate (FAR) is calculated to be aware of the discriminating ability of our singer models. FAR is defined as the number of false alarms to singer divided by the singer's total negative test trials. All the negative test samples for each singer are collected and so a negative sample for one singer can be a negative sample for another singer in two independent tests. From the 5089 test

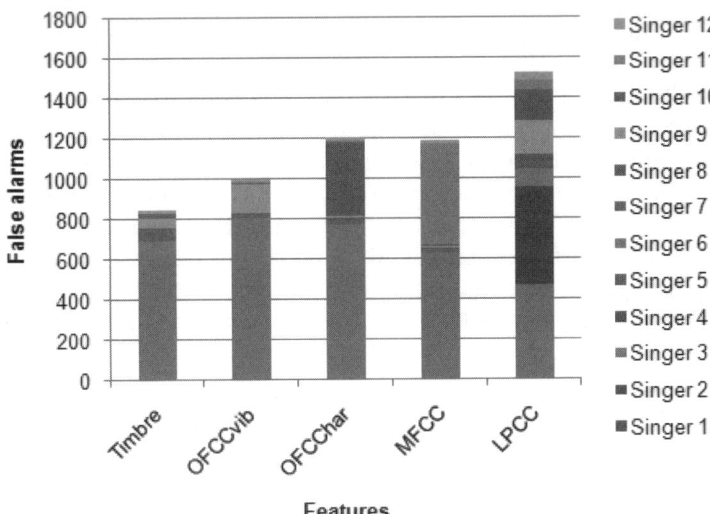

Fig. 7. Number of false alarms on TestDB by five feature types

Table 3. Average error on TestDB by five feature types

TBCC	OFCC$_{vib}$	OFCC$_{har}$	MFCC	LPCC
1.5	1.78	2.15	2.13	2.72

Table 4. Error rate (ER%) on TestDB with different window sizes of TBCC

Window size (ms)	ER (%)
59	12.1
60	15.3
61	15
63	11.9
64	15.4
65	13.6

samples, we come up with 55979 negative samples in total. The accumulated counts of false alarms are illustrated in Fig. 7.

The performance of TBCC feature consistently achieve better than the traditional spectral features in terms of both error rate and false alarm rate in Table 2 and Table 3. As mentioned in section 3.3, duration of about 60ms is necessary to recognize the timbre of tone. Hence, the error rate of 12.2% may not give the optimal performance for TBCC since window size is only 20ms. We further conduct several experiments with TBCC feature of different window sizes, with fixed frame shift of 7ms in all tests. In Table 4, the results show that performance peaks when window size is 63ms, giving the best error rate of 11.9%. It is observed that timbre based features capture the singer characteristics well by 0.9% and 1.7% (or 7% and 12.5% relative) error reduction over OFCC$_{vib}$ (reported earlier in [11]) and OFCC$_{har}$ features respectively. Furthermore, TBCC feature perform well by 5.4% to 44.3% relative error reduction over traditional features such as MFCC and LPCC. We believe that a window size of around 60ms is suitable to extract timbre characteristics from a music signal.

Both vocal and instrumental sounds have musical characteristics such as harmonic, vibrato, and timbre. This gives rise to a question as to whether the three features: TBCC, OFCC$_{vib}$ and OFCC$_{har}$, capture these musical characteristics from either vocal or instrumental sound. To look into this, we conduct SingerID experiments using manually annotated nonvocal segments. SingerID system performance using a) vocal segments, b) nonvocal segments are presented in Table 5.

Table 5. Average error rates using (a) vocal segments and (b) nonvocal segments

Features	Case (a)	Case (b)
TBCC	12.2	60.1
OFCC$_{vib}$	12.8	66.7
OFCC$_{har}$	13.6	60.6

Without surprise, in the presence of vocal timbre, vibrato and harmonic, the three features work the best as in Case (a). With absence of vocal timbre, vibrato and harmonic in Case (b), the error rate increases. This is because the singing voice usually stands out of the background musical accompaniments [13] and the three features are able to capture musical characteristics from vocal rather than from background instruments.

Inspired by speaker verification research [19], we conduct further singer verification experiments using likelihood ratio as in equation (5). We use TBCC feature with 20ms window size in this experiment. As mentioned above, we train each singer model for each of 12 singers. In addition, we train a Universal Background Model to represent non-target singer group using UBM-DB. During testing, each segment is evaluated against all the 12 models in the classifier, and is assigned to the model that gives the best match, as formulated in equation (4). Results in Table 6 show that the performance is improved by using likelihood ratio in a verification hypothesis test.

Table 6. Average Error Rate (ER) on TestDB with and without verification strategies

Method	ER(%)
without verification strategies	12.2
with verification strategies	11.4

In Fig. 8, we present the ER curve of the singer identification system after applying verification strategies. It is observed that the equal error rate (EER) is at 8.9%. It is worth noting that, with verification strategies, we have obtained average error rate of 11.4% (see Table 6) which is very close to the true optimum. With that, we believe that the proposed features and decision strategy are reliably effective.

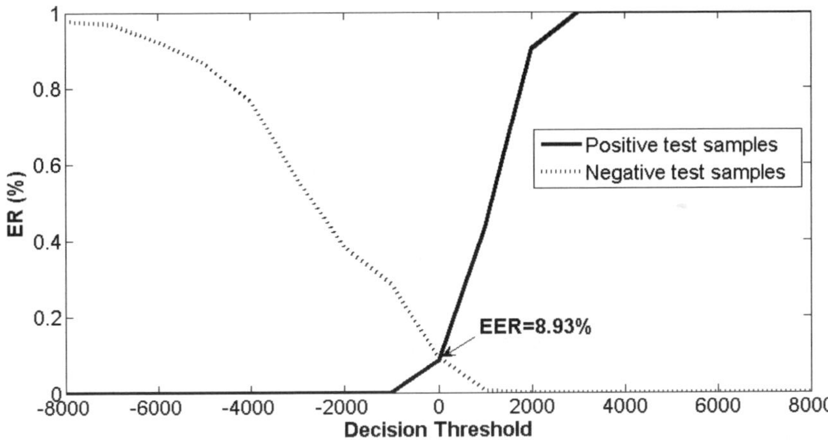

Fig. 8. Equal Error Rate (EER%) of singer identification using likelihood ratio scores

5   Conclusions

We have presented an approach for singer identification of popular songs. The proposed approach explores perceptually motivated timbre characteristics for SingerID. The main contributions of this paper are summarized as follows: 1) we propose using several perceptually motivated features using harmonic, vibrato and timbre information to represent the singer's characteristics. 2) With these features, we found that there is a strong correlation between singer characteristics and system performance. 3) We successfully apply speaker verification techniques into singer identification to achieve better system performance. We conclude that perceptually motivated features especially timbre features are effective in improving system performance.

References

1. Bartsch, M.A., Wakefield, G.H.: Singing Voice Identification Using Spectral Envelope Estimation. IEEE Transactions, Speech and Audio Processing 12, 100–109 (2004)
2. Bretos, J., Sundberg, J.: Measurements of Vibrato Parameters in Long Sustained Crescendo Notes As Sung by Ten Sopranos. Journal of Voice 17, 343–352 (2003)
3. Cleveland, T.F.: Acoustic Properties of Voice Timbre Types and Their Influence on Voice Classification. Journal of Acoustical Society of America 61, 1622–1629 (1977)
4. Dejonckere, P.H., Hirano, M., Sundberg, J.: Vibrato, ch. 2. Singular Pub., San Diego (1995)
5. Dromey, C., Carter, N., Hopkin, A.: Vibrato Rate Adjustment. Journal of Voice 17, 168–178 (2003)
6. Erickson, M., Perry, S., Handel, S.: Discrimination Functions: Can They Be Used to Classify Singing Voices? Journal of Voice 15, 492–502 (2001)
7. Everest, F.A.: Master Handbook of Acoustics. McGraw-Hill Professional, New York (2000)
8. Joliveau, E., Smith, J., Wolfe, J.: Vocal Tract Resonances in Singing: The Soprano Voice. Journal of Acoustical Society of America 116, 2434–2439 (2004)
9. Poli, G.D., Prandoni, P.: Sonological Models for Timber Characterization. Journal of New Music Research 26, 170–197
10. Nwe, T.L., Foo, S.W., De Silva, L.C.: Stress classification using subband based features. IEICE Trans. Information and Systems, Special Issue on Speech Information Processing E86-D(3), 565–573 (2003)
11. Nwe, T.L., Li, H.: Exploring Vibrato-Motivated Acoustic Features for Singer Identification. IEEE Transactions, Audio, Speech and Language Processing 15(2) (2007)
12. Sukkar, R.A., Lee, C.H.: Vocabulary independent discriminative utterance verification for nonkeyword rejection in subword based speech recognition. IEEE Trans. Speech and Audio Processing 4, 420–429 (1996)
13. Sundberg, J.: The Science of Singing Voice. Northern Illinois University Press (1987)
14. Timmers, R., Desain, P.: Vibrato: Questions and Answers from Musicians and Science. In: Proc. Int. Conf. On Music Perception And Cognition, England (2000)
15. Winckell, F.: Music, Sound and Sensation. Dover, NY (1967)

16. Zhang, T.: System and method for automatic singer identification. In: Proceedings IEEE International Conference Multimedia and Expo., Baltimore, MD (2003)
17. Zhang, T., Kuo, C.C.J.: Content-Based Audio Classification and Retrieval for Data Parsing. Kluwer Academic Publishers, USA (2001)
18. Helmholtz, H.: On the Sensation of Tone. Dover Publication, New York (1954)
19. Fredouille, C., Bonastre, J.-F., Merlin, T.: Bayesian approach based-decision in speaker verification, A Speaker Odyssey, Crete, Greece (2001)

Cognitive Implications of Musical Perception

Adam Lockhart

Center for Experimental Music and Intermedia, Division of Composition Studies,
College of Music, University of North Texas
acl0056@unt.edu

Abstract. Any musical experience is innately pertinent to cognition and psychology. This paper discusses various aspects of musical cognition, including notions of timbre in relation to spectromorphology, a term coined by Denis Smalley, a notable writer on aesthetics of electroacoustic music. Furthermore, a cognitive model will serve to explain inherent inter-relationships involving multi-modal perception.

1 Perception of Musical Motion

Motion in music is realized through perception. It is perceived as a temporally progressive event that involves three elements: 1) a continuous perceptual history of a piece of music, 2) the now constantly being organized by both the conscious and the subconscious mind, and 3) projections into the future drawn from connections made by the conscious and subconscious mind. Occurrence of perception in a musical context engages everything in our musical perceptual history, or personal environment while simultaneously redefining it [1, 2]. This is a process through which we may render expectations (while also redefining the basis for which we may render expectations in the future). Perception of motion in music is an abstraction of physical motion in a musical context.

One type of musical motion in electroacoustic music, texture motion, involves tendencies that render a sense of direction as an abstraction of change in spectral mass -- Agglomeration (an accumulation of spectral mass), and Dissipation (a dispersing or disintegrating mass) [3]. This vocabulary provides for ideas of motion that are slightly more complex than ascending or descending patterns of frequency, which are more immediately directional.

2 Cognition in the Immediate

The now is simply a notion of the present, and for the purposes of this paper it involves cognitive activities unfolding within some imperceptible temporal proximity, a transitory cache of the fleeting recent, the temporally immediate, and some alignment with the future. The subconscious mind is always organizing sensory information. Once something is generalized further abstractions are organized by making associations. While in a broad sense they represent an expansive network of meaning,

R. Kronland-Martinet, S. Ystad, and K. Jensen (Eds.): CMMR 2007, LNCS 4969, pp. 172–180, 2008.

associations that come from these cognitive activities subsequently may be regarded individually as thought entities: bundled generalizations.

2.1 Source Bonding as a Perceptual Cue

Perceptual cues are something like flags that are raised when associative connections are made subconsciously. Source bonding represents one type of perceptual cue signifying a cognitive connection made associating sound and sound source. When referring to a note or several different notes played on an instrument the idea is very clear-cut. Smalley's definition of source bonding could easily be the foundation for defining timbre in terms of "the timbre of an instrument":

> (Source bonding is) the natural tendency to relate sounds to supposed sources and causes, and to relate sounds to each other because they appear to have shared or associated origins. [4]

However, in electronic music timbre is much more complex. There are even problems with this case of an instrument having timbre. If the instrument has a timbre, then why is it that the instrumentalist can get different timbres out of the instrument? Why does it have a different timbre in a different room? Why does the recording of that instrument in a room have timbral variation when you play it on different stereo systems? The idea of source bonding coming from a perceptual cue is a better foundation for a discussion of timbre that takes a cognitive approach.

3 Timbre

A thorough definition of timbre should involve dispelling inadequate notions of timbre. I propose that timbre is not some notion of characteristic spectral qualities, but that the term more significantly defines some cognitive process. Before discussing Smalley's definition of timbre we must adopt the term spectromorphology as a description of any sound in terms of the vertical and horizontal aspects of music:

> The two parts of the term refer to the interaction between sound spectra (spectro-) and the ways they change over time (-morphology). The spectro- cannot exist without the –morphology and vice versa: something has to be shaped, and a shape must have sonic content. [3]

The term spectromorphology is well adapted for the purposes of discussing any music or sound. At the same time, the term itself describes the very nature of sound and the fundamental elements therein. Spectral profile of sound over time becomes important in the following discussion of timbre.

3.1 Definition of Timbre

Discussion of timbre involves tiptoeing through a discursive minefield. Definition of timbre (along with music itself and music technology) has evolved over centuries. The ASA (American Standards Association) defined timbre as the quality that makes sounds of equal pitch and loudness different [5]. This does not satisfy in discussion of spectrum over time. Smalley has adapted a definition for timbre in terms of spectromorphology, "a general, sonic physiognomy whose spectromorphological ensemble permits the attribution of identity." [4]. Identity is not always some result of source bonding. Any given sound object's identity comes from its spectromorphological profile -- perceived attributes that can be recognized. Also a sound object could have source bonding with some imaginary source. Therefore timbre must be a flexible notion involving cognition and recognition.

It is inadequate to think of timbre as some spectral signature, but it is identity, a perceptual cue denoting a neatly packaged bundle of abstractions that defines a sound object by its spectromorphological boundaries, that truly defines timbre. Consider now the spectromorphology of a tree falling in a forest... Does it have timbral identity? Perhaps if you imagine such a spectromorphology, in your mind it does have timbral identity -- even if it never actually happened.

3.2 Layered Identities

Any audiophile will tell you that every single component of an audio reproduction system has its own unique timbre, and any violin player will tell you that every violin has its own unique timbre. Likewise, an audio engineer will say the same of every concert hall. This is to say that one sound may result in a multitude of timbral identities.

To explain in detail, on one level, a violin is a violin is a violin. On another level, this is this violin and that is that violin. Everything is dependent on the identities of which one makes oneself aware. One may be aware of this violin in this hall on these microphones … (and so on) … this Compact Disc transport through this digital cable to this DAC - interconnects - preamp - more interconnects - amp - speaker cables - speakers and finally the room, room treatments and positioning of the speakers in the room all have their own unique timbre. This is, of course, only if one is aware; otherwise, the components do not have a multitude of layered identities. Another possible layer of timbre in electroacoustic music could be the timbre of certain processes. Comb filters, time expansions, pitch shifts, filters and granulations are just a few examples of processes that may have timbral identities to the careful ear. This explains further that timbre is a function of perception.

Identity, for the listener, is the result of consciously engaging perceptual cues: connections made unconsciously. It should be noted that in order to listen for any of these timbres one must "train the ear". This really means that one's mind must build a meaningful network of associations relative to the particular listening experience.

4 Gesture

The fundamentals of a sounding gesture are rooted in a source-cause bond whereby a human energy motion trajectory excites a sounding body and creates spectromorphological consequences [3]. Source-cause bonding allows for an inferred notion of physical gestural activity. The subconscious mind contains a wealth of psychophysical information. This information is some subsection of one's network of meaning and useful knowledge that is engaged during the musical experience. This is a tactile sense that one need not act on, but people often breathe along with swells of musical energy without even realizing that they are physically aligning themselves with the music.

From the viewpoint of both (sounding) agent and watching listener, the musical gesture-process is tactile and visual, as well as aural. Moreover, it is proprioceptive: that is, it is concerned with the tension and relaxation of muscles, with effort and resistance. In this way, sound-making is linked to more comprehensive sensorimotor and psychological experience. [3]

The experience of the watching listener is therefore multi-modal including visual and aural sensory modes as well as some tactile interpretation. Likewise, even if a listener is not watching but perhaps listening to a recording, the experience is still multi-modal. Gesture can be inferred or felt from almost any music and realized in an abstract tactile sense.

4.1 Psychophysical Re-enactment

Feeling involves a rather unusual subdivision into two distinct species of meaning: physical and emotional. This is an interesting dichotomy considering that both physical and emotional feelings relate to psychophysical information (some mental relationship with the physical qualities of any environment). For example, emotions are generally expressed in a physical manner. Be it crying, yelling, laughing, kissing, or even just a look in someone's eye, emotions engage psychophysical information for means of expression. Conversely, emotion or emotional meaning is perceived, related to psychophysical information and manifested physically or physiologically. Because emotions are communicated through physical expression and music similarly is expressive on some abstract physical level, it is reasonable that music is a medium through which humankind so persistently tries to communicate emotional meaning.

5   Perceptual Focus

Perceptual focus can be best described as a function of the conscious mind as it relates to subconscious processes. For example, one might hear music without listening to it. You step into an elevator with music playing. If the conscious effort were made to perceive the content of what was heard, then connections made by the subconscious mind could be mulled over by the conscious mind: "Gosh, that soprano sax really comes through on that 3" full-range driver." On the other hand you could be distracted and never consciously elaborate on connections being made by the subconscious mind. Later on, you might never even realize how a song you don't like very much got stuck in your head.

5.1   Reduced Listening

Reduced listening is a phenomenon that may occur upon repetition of a sound event. An example of reduced listening involves the repetition of a verbal utterance. If one were to speak a word (try a funny sounding word) over and over again, eventually the word would lose its meaning and one would start to hear how funny it sounds. The repetition causes the conscious mind to lose focus of the word's extrinsic connectedness then shift focus more towards the utterance's presence in spectral-space over time. Smalley writes:

> Reduced listening comes about through concentrated, repeated listening to a sound event, a common activity in the electroacoustic composing process. It is an investigative process whereby detailed spectro-morphological attributes and relationships are uncovered. [3]

This marks a shift in perceptual focus under which a sound event loses its extrinsic associative qualities and then even expressive qualities of its musical context. I contend that this shift in perceptual focus is similar to the mind shifting towards the first stage of hypnosis. This statement is somewhat counterintuitive. As Denis Smalley has pointed out during personal correspondence, his discussion of reduced listening was intended to describe an investigative compositional activity. It does not depend on this example of repetition. This process does seem to involve a heightened sense of awareness, however this does not necessarily indicate a higher level of conscious state. It is perhaps a shift in awareness towards the more basic elements of sound. However, states of consciousness range from conscious through different levels of trance including light trance down to the deepest level, somnambulism.

In the example of repetition of a sound event, perceptual cues are initially created as a way of relating said event to an entire perceptual history. Upon repetition, few new perceptual cues are made. When the conscious mind exhausts these cues it rests, waiting for more. Thereafter one is able to understand the sound event as a more basic element: spectral motion. In the following examples I intend to show that motion is understood unconsciously. Keep in mind that this example of repetition can be used to understand reduced listening, while it is not essential in order to engage this mode of listening. Once again, as with anything we may listen for, we must train the ear to do so.

Most everyone has experienced this first stage of hypnosis even without being aware. Highway hypnosis exemplifies the first stage of hypnosis, light trance. Anyone who has ever driven down a highway for some period of time is likely to slip into a light trance (and sometimes wonder how they missed their exit).

It is interesting to note that we know how to drive an automobile subconsciously. Another example is someone who is so deep in thought that they wonder how they even stopped properly at a red light. Even more amusing, is the motorist who stops at a green light. The reason that we are able to know how to drive subconsciously is because physical information we collect from our environment (such as motion), the mental representation of which is psychophysical information, is a function of our unconscious minds. This is the reason reduced listening, a shift towards perception of spectral motion, is a shift towards the subconscious. In other words, we don't have to think about motion: we understand it intuitively as a part of our unconscious mind. Figure 1. shows a sound event repeating over time, alongside which is a solid line indicating perceptual focus. The line indicates a shift in perceptual focus from a conscious alert state to a more subconscious hypnotic state.

Now consider the mantra. Mantra meditation, from Hinduism and Buddhism, is a form of meditation whereby words or phrases are repeatedly chanted internally or out loud as objects of contemplation. Here we find the same idea: repetition of a sound event. This paper assumes that meditation and hypnosis are both psychologically similar forms of trance. One final example of sonic phenomenon inducing trance is from riding a train. The sound a train makes in travel is constant, while it is also

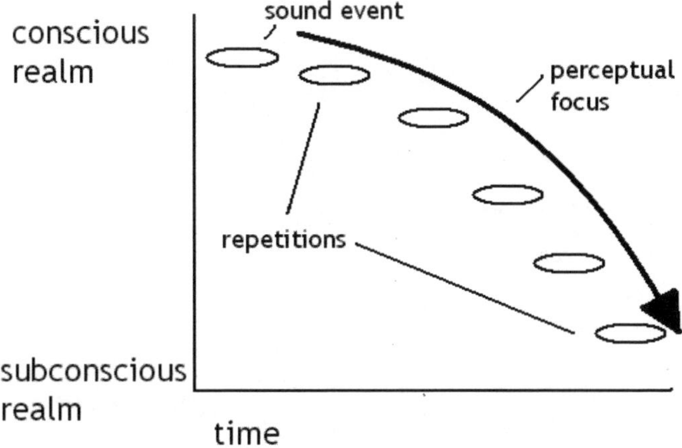

Fig. 1. Conscious state over time

repetitious. Listening to the sound of a train can make one drowsy and even help one fall asleep. These examples may aid in understanding the notion of shift in perceptual focus.

So then what is the difference between heightened consciousness and heightened awareness? It is my contention that the brain is a very powerful computer (if you will), to which our conscious mind has very little access. Therefore, whatever seems to be heightened consciousness is likely a result of being more closely in touch with the powerful subconscious mind.

6 A Cognitive Model

It is clear that a cognitive model, which allows for all of these inner workings to coexist, is necessary to further this discussion. It is important in the communication of these ideas to have some kind of representation (even if it is some kind of abstract representation that symbolizes something that doesn't physically exist). I propose a cognitive model that offers a way to explain an organized network of knowledge (other than just by those terms), a way to incorporate reduced listening and the idea of a hypnotic state into the model, and provide for the idea of perceptual cues.

6.1 Generalization Unit Theory

Every sensory modality is handled in a different part of the brain. For example, visual information is processed by the visual cortex. This example refers to modularity. A module is a set of automatic processes that occurs apart from other cognitive systems [6]. If all sensory modalities are modulated separately then they must become unified on another level of perceptual processing. Michel Chion applies the term synchresis to describe "the spontaneous and irresistible weld produced between a particular auditory phenomenon and visual phenomenon when they occur at the same time." [7] As

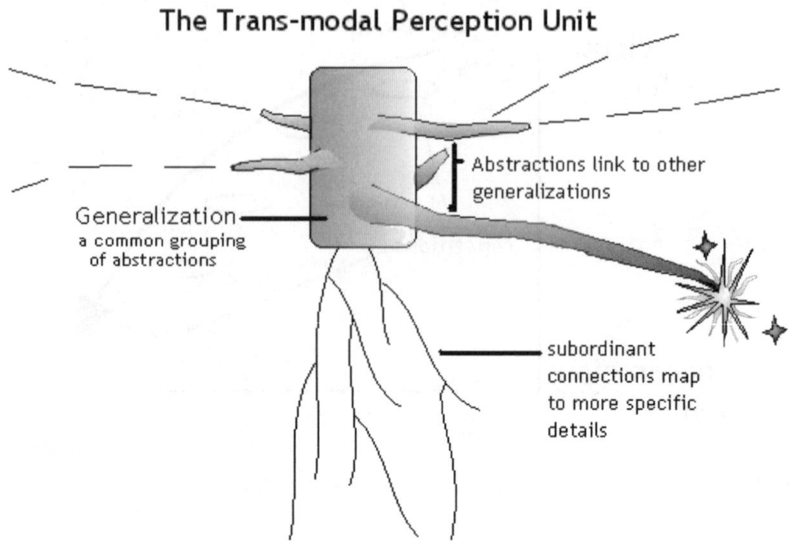

Fig. 2. A basic unit of perception

discussed, such a bond could also include inherent physical information. This paper proposes a generalization unit theory to describe any mental representation of perceived stimuli, wherein all modalities utilize the same trans-modal unit for the purpose of explaining synchresis as well as other strange audio-visual interactions.

Figure 2. is a visual representation of a thought entity. It is merely a contrivance to aid in explaining something that is difficult to imagine having a physical form at all. So it is more realistic to think of this visual representation as expressing some occurrence rather than as an object. The bulk of this unit represents a generalization. A generalization is a group of abstractions. Abstractions, similar to generalizations in essence, describe here a single basic component of a generalization that can easily form associations with other abstractions from other generalization units. A generalization here maintains a broader scope, a further level of abstractedness rendering a unified embodiment of that perception. The generalization unit can provide access to pertinent specific details. These details are by nature abstractions as well, but they exclusively belong to a specific generalization. If one were to consciously delve into those specific details and make new connections to other perceptions, they will have effectively turned some detail into a networkable abstraction to make the connection. Generalization units only connect to other generalizations through a network of abstractions. Every thought or perception embodies abstraction.

6.2 State of Consciousness Cognitive Model

The State of Consciousness Cognitive Model is contrived in order to explain the interactive process of music cognition. The network of trans-modal perception units at the bottom of Figure 3. represents one's personal environment. This diagram shows only one trans-modal perception unit being introduced into the network. When engaged in a musical experience, however, since each unit represents a generalization made of sensory information it is likely that this model would be at a constant state of accumulation.

First, new information is introduced into the working memory. Working memory attempts to make associations within the network. If an association is made then that connection creates a perceptual cue. Perceptual focus, in Figure 3, is represented as the part that breaks up the straight line from working memory to conscious elaboration. If the perceptual cue does end up in the conscious elaboration stage, then whatever connection was made to create a perceptual cue will be made evident to the conscious mind. This is to suggest that connections are made in your head before they pop up in your conscious mind. Acquirement is learning. It entails a modification of the network of knowledge.

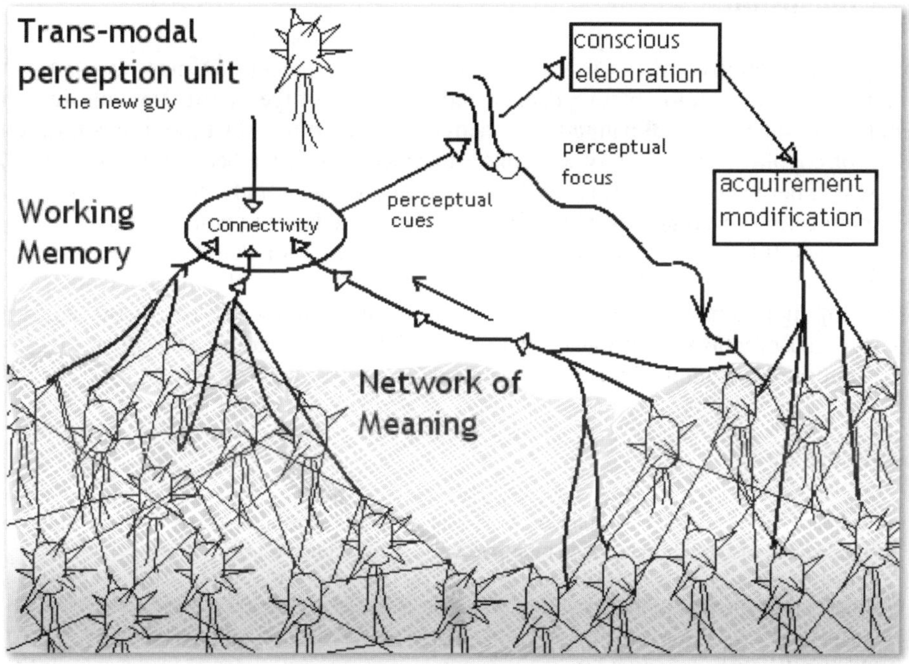

Fig. 3. A cognitive model

Perceptual focus is an aspect of the psyche. Its normal function, a conscious state of awareness, would be to actively seek out perceptual cues as they are created. Recall Figure 1. where perceptual focus is viewed within the context of conscious and subconscious states of awareness. It is important to understand that these are not fixed states, but perceptual focus will generally reside in between the two, to varying degrees. In order to achieve a subconscious state of inner awareness one must quiet the conscious mind from perceptual cues. This basically means that perceptual cues are like thoughts that pop up all the time. If one were to relax one's perceptual focus, then instead of sensory generalization units traveling normally to the conscious mind, this model has a pathway (with perceptual focus in a subconscious state) straight to the subconscious mind. In support of this model, consider the suggestibility of the subconscious mind. Suggestibility describes the working component of clinical hypnosis that acts on the subconscious. This open pathway, unfiltered by the conscious mind, could explain such a phenomenon. In music, a shift in perceptual focus towards the subconscious realm means a shift towards more fundamental elements that are less tangible as conscious thoughts. This model is appropriate for both describing musical experience (including reduced listening) and a model for the cognitive processes involved in clinical hypnosis. To date there is perhaps nothing more mysterious to mankind as the human mind. This model is intended as a crude outline describing some functions within an extremely complicated process.

7 Conclusion

Adopting a cognitive model to conceptualize musical perception may be useful for composers who wish to obtain a deeper understanding of their craft. New music such as electroacoustic music, painted on a canvas of spectrum over time, relies on these ideas of cognitive connectivity to evoke substance. When we become immersed in a musical experience, we are actually immersed in our own minds. Music is a profound communication. A composer may hypnotize, cause the heart to pound, amuse or bring one to tears. It has long been thought that musical expression could never be precisely expressed by words. While this still proves true, composers will gain an advantage by analyzing more abstract musical communications the same way basic theory helps to analyze and organize tonal music. It is important to be aware of these cognitive aspects in order to communicate abstract musical ideas most effectively.

References

1. Lockhart, A., Keller, D.: Exploring Cognitive Process Through Music Composition. In: Proceedings of the International Computer Music Conference (2006)
2. Keller, D., Capasso, A.: New Concepts and Techniques in Eco-Composition. Organ-ized Sound 11(1), 55–62 (2006)
3. Smalley, D.: Spectromorphology: Explaining sound-shapes. Organised Sound 2(2), 107–126 (1997)
4. Smalley, D.: Defining Timbre - Refining Timbre. Contemporary Music Review 2(10), 35–48 (1994)
5. ASA (American Standards Association). Acoustical Terminology. American Standards Association, New York (1960)
6. Kellogg, R.: Cognitive Psycholgy. Sage Publications, Thousand Oaks (2003)
7. Chion, M.: Audio-Vision: Sound on Screen. Columbia University Press (1994)

A Meta-analysis of Timbre Perception Using Nonlinear Extensions to CLASCAL

John Ashley Burgoyne and Stephen McAdams

Centre for Interdisciplinary Research in Music and Media Technology
Schulich School of Music of McGill University
555 Sherbrooke Street West
Montral, Qubec, Canada H3A 1E3
{ashley,smc}@music.mcgill.ca

Abstract. Seeking to identify the constituent parts of the multidimensional auditory attribute that musicians know as timbre, music psychologists have made extensive use of multidimensional scaling (MDS), a statistical technique for visualising the geometric spaces implied by perceived dissimilarity. MDS is also well known in the machine learning community, where it is used as a basic technique for dimensionality reduction. We adapt a nonlinear variant of MDS that is popular in machine learning, Isomap, for use in analysing psychological data and re-analyse three earlier experiments on human perception of timbre. Isomap is designed to eliminate undesirable nonlinearities in the input data in order to reduce the overall dimensionality; our results show that it succeeds in these goals for timbre spaces, compressing the output onto well-known dimensions of timbre and highlighting the challenges inherent in quantifying differences in spectral shape.

1 Introduction

As any computer musician knows, timbre is one of the most important compositional parameters, and yet it remains one of the most under-theorised. Part of the reason for the relative lack of theory may be due to the fact that, unlike pitch, timbre is a multidimensional auditory attribute, and it it is difficult to draw general conclusions about timbre as a whole without first identifying its constituent parts. Nonetheless, there have been a number of attempts to uncover the underlying dimensionality of timbre space over the past few decades, most based on perceptual experiments with synthesised and recorded tones. Early experiments with synthetic tones identified spectral centroid and attack time as primary components of timbre, in addition, at times, to a third dimension that was more difficult to interpret and dependent on the stimulus set (Grey 1977; Grey and Gordon 1978). Later studies with more sophisticated models came to similar conclusions, and suggested that the third component might be a measure of irregularity in the spectral envelope (Krumhansl 1989) or spectral flux (McAdams et al. 1995). A recent confirmatory study has verified that spectral centroid, attack time, and spectral irregularity are indeed recovered, whereas spectral flux is not (Caclin et al. 2005).

R. Kronland-Martinet, S. Ystad, and K. Jensen (Eds.): CMMR 2007, LNCS 4969, pp. 181–202, 2008.

All of these studies are based on a statistical technique known as multidimensional scaling (MDS) (Torgerson 1958). The basic idea of MDS is to take the set of proximities between all members of some set of data points, e.g., sample timbres, and to model them as distances in a Euclidean space of as few dimensions as possible. In the context of timbre, these proximities are usually taken from psychological experiments in which human subjects have rated their perception of the (dis)similarity between timbre pairs. The trouble with MDS in this context is that its classical form was designed to interpret a single set of dissimilarities among items, not the average over all subjects of an experiment. The first robust solution to this problem was the INDSCAL algorithm (Carroll and Chang 1970), which models a special weight on each dimension for each subject in the experiment in order to better fit model distances to the set of empirical dissimilarities. The more sophisticated CLASCAL algorithm reduces the number of parameters in INDSCAL by modelling weights not for individual subjects but for a smaller number of aggregate subject groups, called latent classes (Winsberg and De Soete 1993). CLASCAL and its variants are the standard techniques for analysing timbre spaces today.

There is another problem with these techniques, however: being linear, they consider all distances estimated by the human subjects to be equally reliable and of equal relative scale. Although some relatively straightforward extensions to MDS can treat the latter problem, e.g., CONSCAL (Winsberg and De Soete 1997), the former requires more aggressive modifications. One such modification, known as Isomap, replaces large distances in the original distance matrices with so-called geodesic distances along a hypothetical manifold (Tennenbaum et al. 2000). Previous work with Isomap has demonstrated that it and its relatives can uncover meaningful musical relationships that traditional linear MDS will always miss (Burgoyne and Saul 2005).

This paper combines the CLASCAL and Isomap models to re-analyse the data from three major studies of timbre: Grey 1977, Grey and Gordon 1978, and McAdams et al. 1995. Section 2 provides a more detailed explanation of these algorithms and best practises for interpreting their results. Section 3 presents the results of our new scaling and compares them to the original studies. Section 4 concludes with suggestions for future applications of nonlinear scaling to the study of musical timbre.

2   CLASCAL and Isomap

2.1   CLASCAL

Traditional MDS was designed to handle a single set of pairwise proximities only. A number of models have been presented to adapt MDS for multiple-subject experiments, of which the most important for studying timbre has been CLASCAL (Winsberg and De Soete 1993). The CLASCAL model seeks to minimise the approximation error in the following equation:

$$d_{ijk} \approx \left[\sum_{r=1}^{R} w_{\mathcal{C}(i),r}(x_{jr} - x_{kr})^2 \right]^{1/2} , \qquad (1)$$

where d_{ijk} is the dissimilarity rating that subject i assigned to stimulus pair (j, k), R is the number of dimensions in the output set, $w_{\mathcal{C}(i),r}$ is a special weight on dimension r for the so-called latent class $\mathcal{C}(i)$ to which CLASCAL has assigned subject i, and x_{jr} and x_{kr} are the co-ordinates along dimension r for stimuli j and k. Latent classes are meant to represent groups of subjects who pursue similar rating strategies. The number of latent classes used is a compromise between over-parametrisation, e.g., the INDSCAL model, which assigns each subject to its own class, and over-generalisation, e.g., ignoring differences between subjects by taking the average over all dissimilarity matrices. A Monte Carlo likelihood-ratio technique is used to determine the optimal number of classes (Hope 1968; Aitkin et al. 1981). The class weights can be interpreted as the rating strategies used by each class: relatively high weights for a particular dimension suggest that members of the class use that dimension more than others when distinguishing timbres.

Another potential problem with traditional MDS is that it assumes all of the variance in a data set can be explained by dimensions common to all stimuli. This assumption does not always hold for timbre: many timbres include instrument-specific components such as the sound of the returning hopper in a harpsichord. A more sophisticated version of CLASCAL separates these components, known as *specificities*, using the following model:

$$d_{ijk} \approx \left[\sum_{r=1}^{R} w_{\mathcal{C}(i),r}(x_{jr} - x_{kr})^2 + v_{\mathcal{C}(i)}(s_j + s_k) \right]^{1/2} , \qquad (2)$$

where s_j and s_k are the specificities for stimuli j and k and $v_{\mathcal{C}(i)}$ represents the weight subjects in class $\mathcal{C}(i)$ give to specificities when distinguishing timbres (Winsberg and Carroll 1989; McAdams et al. 1995).

2.2 Isomap

Isomap arose as a solution to the dimensionality reduction problem for data sets like the famous 'Swiss roll' pictured in Fig. 1 (Tennenbaum et al. 2000). Looking at the plot, it is obvious to a human that the data are arranged on a two-dimensional plane that has been coiled and presented in three dimensions. This fact is not obvious to traditional MDS, which strives to preserve every pairwise distance in the set, including those between the ends of the roll and the inner or outer loops. The ingenious solution in Isomap is to throw away all pairwise distances in the set except those at the local level, i.e., those in a small region immediately surrounding each point in the data set. These regions can be selected as a fixed number k of the nearest neighbours to each point in the data set or as those points that fall within a sphere of fixed radius ϵ around each point. The other distances are then recomputed using an all-pairs shortest-path algorithm, yielding an approximation of the so-called *geodesic distances*, or

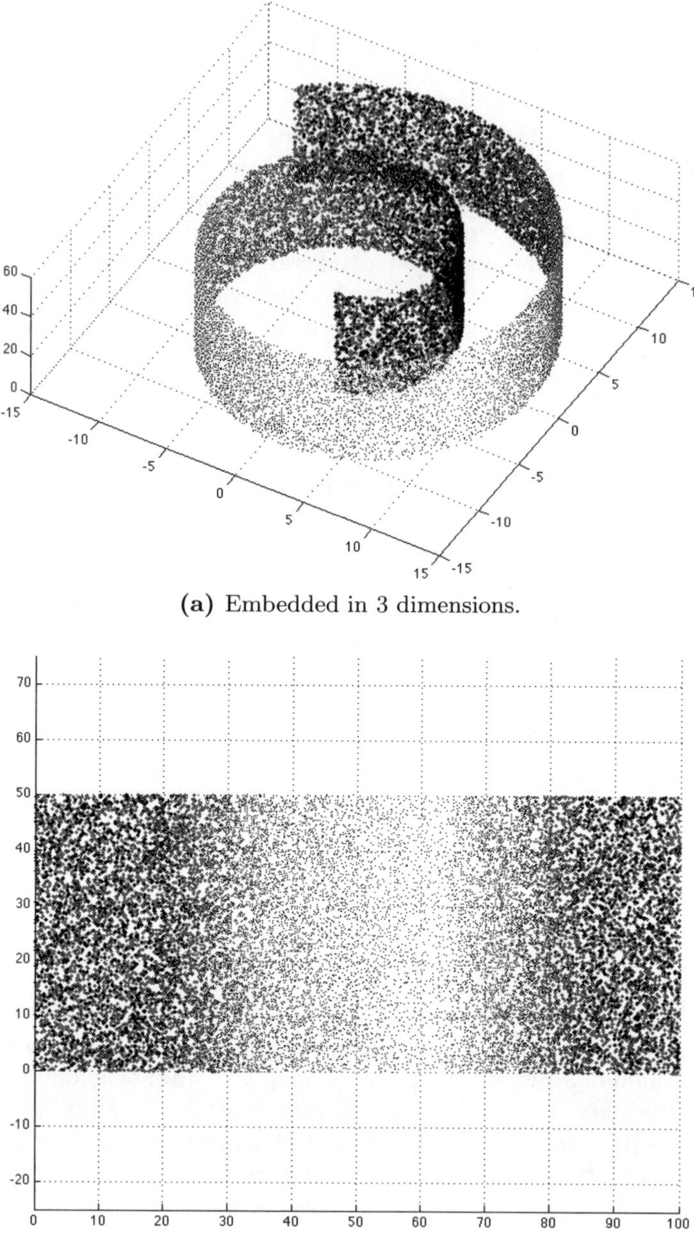

(a) Embedded in 3 dimensions.

(b) Unrolled in 2 dimensions.

Fig. 1. The 'Swiss roll' data set. On the left, the data is presented in its original form. On the right, the data is presented as it should be unrolled for human interpretation. Traditional MDS can never arrive at this solution, however, because it seeks to preserve the distances between the ends of the roll and the inner/outer loops.

distances in the lower-dimensional form. After these approximate distances are computed, traditional MDS is applied.

Like many algorithms based on nearest neighbours, Isomap can be improved by incorporating variants of the relative neighbourhood graph, e.g., the Gabriel graph (Gabriel and Sokal 1969; Jaromczyk and Toussaint 1992). The Gabriel graph retains the pairwise distance d_{ab} between points a and b if and only if there is no point c such that $d_{ac}^2 + d_{cb}^2 < d_{ab}^2$. Interpreted geometrically, the Gabriel graph retains the pairwise distance between two points if and only if the minimum-volume hypersphere connecting them, i.e, the diameter sphere, is empty. The Gabriel graph of a set of points is a superset of the minimum spanning tree, and thus, unlike the graphs based on fixed k or ϵ in traditional Isomap, is guaranteed to be connected. It is nonparametric and robust to variations in density throughout the observed space. Because of these desirable properties, all of our experiments with Isomap retained the Gabriel neighbours rather than fixed neighbourhoods specified in the original algorithm.

At first glance, the Swiss roll appears to be a fundamentally different problem than that of estimating timbre spaces. There is little reason to believe that human subjects would willfully twist their ratings of the similarities between timbre pairs into more dimensions than are already present. The larger message of Isomap, however, is that unless a space is perfectly linear, large distances in a scaling model can mask important structures in the data. It seems prudent to check for such structures in psychological data, and because Isomap is based on classical MDS, unlike a number of other nonlinear scaling techniques, it lends itself naturally to combination with CLASCAL. Each subject's dissimilarity matrix is processed according to the Isomap algorithm until the final MDS step. After this preprocessing is complete, the new dissimilarity matrices are fed to CLASCAL.

3   Experiments and Results

As stated earlier, rather than performing a new experiment, we used the data from three earlier experiments to evaluate the effects of Isomap processing. Results based on (1) are presented first, followed by a discussion of the changes to the output spaces after adding specificities to the model as per (2). In interpreting the results, we computed the acoustical features proposed in Peeters et al. 2000 for each timbre stimulus and studied the Pearson correlation coefficients of these features with the dimensions output from CLASCAL.

3.1   Grey 1977

Although the complete experimental results from the Grey 1977 are, the sound stimuli used for the experiments are still available. These stimuli comprise electronically resynthesised imitations of tape recordings of pitch E♭4 (311 Hz) played on two different oboes, an English horn, a bassoon, an E♭ clarinet, a bass clarinet, a flute, two alto saxophone sounds (one played *piano* and one played *mezzo-forte*), a soprano saxophone, a trumpet, a French horn, a muted trombone, and three cello sounds (normal bowing, muted *sul tasto*, and *sul ponticello*). These sounds were then normalised to a consistent perceived loudness, pitch, and duration based on a separate perceptual experiment. We performed a study with 22 new subjects, all professional musicians, using these stimuli, asking each subject to rate the dissimilarity between each of the 120 pairs of stimuli on a continuous scale, which was later converted to range from 0 to 1 for data analysis.

The optimal CLASCAL model prior to Isomap processing contains two latent classes and three dimensions. In descending order of prominence, the dimensions correlate with spectral centroid ($r = 0.90$), spectral slope ($r = 0.79$), and log attack time ($r = 0.71$) for the stimuli. Both latent classes weight these dimensions fairly evenly (see Fig. 2a); the primary difference between the classes appears to be that subjects in Class 1 (9 subjects) made use of a wider range of the rating scale than those in Class 2 (13 subjects). The co-ordinates of each stimulus are listed for reference in Table 1, and Fig. 3a presents a plot of the stimuli positioned in the space. In this plot and all future plots, points are connected according to their minimum spanning tree, which includes all pairs of nearest neighbours; points in the plot that appear to be close together but are not connected by a dark line are in fact farther from each other than they appear.

After Isomap processing, the optimal CLASCAL model contains three latent classes and four dimensions. Again in descending order of prominence, these dimensions correlate with a combination of spectral centroid ($r = 0.91$) and spectral flux ($r = 0.80$), spectral spread ($r = -0.74$), log attack time ($r = 0.86$), and – curiously – spectral centroid again ($r = 0.76$). Note that the first two dimensions correlate highly with the first two dimensions prior to Isomap processing ($r = 0.84$ and $r = 0.71$). Subjects in Class 1 (11 subjects) appear to have used a rating strategy emphasising spectral centroid and log attack time, whereas subjects in Class 3 (10 subjects) weighted the four dimensions more evenly. Class 2 contains a single subject who weighted the first dimension relatively less and used more of the scale overall than those in Class 3. The raw and relative weights are available in Fig. 2b. A full set of co-ordinates appears in Table 1 and a plot of the leading three dimensions of the space is presented in Fig. 3b. Despite the extra dimension and some mild changes to the minimum spanning tree with respect to the saxophones and oboes, the overall structure is similar to the space prior to Isomap processing.

The CLASCAL technique is more sophisticated than the MDS techniques that were available to Grey originally, and so some differences in the output dimensions are to be expected. The overall structure of our timbre space, however, is similar to the original published space both before and after Isomap processing.

3.2 Grey and Gordon 1978

Like Grey 1977, the complete experimental results of Grey and Gordon 1978 are no longer available, but we were able to locate the sound stimuli used. These stimuli were mostly the same as the Grey 1977 stimuli, but for four pairs of instruments – (a) oboe 1 and bass clarinet, (b) bassoon and French horn, (c) cello *sul tasto* and normal cello, and (d) muted trombone and trumpet) – the

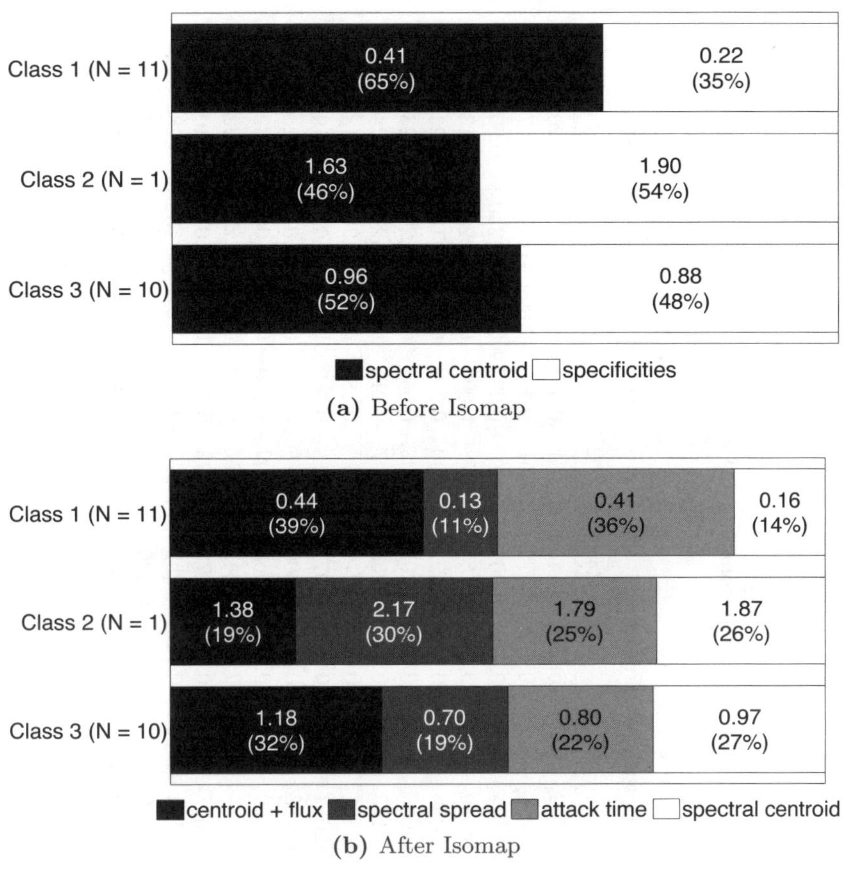

(a) Before Isomap

(b) After Isomap

Fig. 2. Raw and relative weights on dimensions for latent classes of subjects using Grey 1977 stimuli. Although the overall listening strategies (relative weights) are similar before Isomap, the raw weights reveal that subjects in Class 1 used a wider range of the rating scale than subjects in Class 2.

spectral envelopes were exchanged during synthesis. The purpose of these exchanges was to test the effect of changes in spectral envelope on timbre perception by comparing the MDS space resulting from these timbres to that of the original space. Again, we conducted a new experiment using the same 22 subjects on these stimuli, asking them to rate the dissimilarity between all 120 pairs on a continuous scale.

Before Isomap processing, the optimal CLASCAL model contains three classes and two dimensions. Like the leading two dimensions of the Grey 1977 space, the dimensions correlate with spectral centroid ($r = 0.93$) and spectral spread ($r = -0.67$). All three latent classes suggest fairly even rating strategies, although Class 1 (5 subjects) shows a slight preference for spectral spread and Class 2 (9 subjects) shows a slight preference for spectral centroid relative to Class 3 (8 subjects), which distributes the weights most evenly (see Fig. 4a). All

Table 1. Grey 1977 instruments and fitted model co-ordinates along common CLASCAL dimensions and specificities

Instrument		Before Isomap							After Isomap					
		no specificities			with specificities				no specificities				with spec.	
		1	2	3	1	2	3	$\sqrt{s}$	1	2	3	4	1	$\sqrt{s}$
BN	Bassoon	−0.288	0.111	−0.332	−0.272	0.244	−0.236	0.145	−0.181	0.351	−0.026	0.224	−0.203	0.391
C1	E♭ clarinet	0.284	−0.164	0.280	0.230	−0.270	0.179	0.179	0.051	−0.399	−0.099	−0.074	0.177	0.324
C2	Bass clarinet	−0.050	−0.344	0.144	−0.145	−0.260	0.212	0.063	−0.070	−0.295	−0.088	0.230	0.005	0.369
EH	English horn	0.203	0.097	−0.203	0.130	−0.035	−0.261	0.155	−0.078	−0.006	−0.135	−0.288	0.132	0.310
FH	French horn	−0.380	−0.055	−0.296	−0.396	0.165	−0.145	0.192	−0.290	0.160	−0.021	0.177	−0.233	0.332
FL	Flute	−0.280	0.065	0.343	−0.066	0.184	0.366	0.207	0.032	−0.050	0.359	0.205	−0.237	0.351
O1	Oboe 1	0.212	−0.005	0.165	0.195	−0.100	0.055	0.230	0.107	−0.216	−0.087	−0.218	0.280	0.000
O2	Oboe 2	0.281	0.241	0.100	0.307	0.012	−0.059	0.279	0.126	0.188	−0.158	−0.262	0.184	0.341
S1	Cello *normale*	−0.151	0.201	0.180	0.053	0.242	0.177	0.071	−0.018	0.089	0.269	−0.013	−0.194	0.219
S2	Cello *sul tasto*	−0.312	0.098	0.188	−0.120	0.249	0.259	0.000	−0.078	−0.020	0.304	0.017	−0.240	0.192
S3	Cello *sul ponticello*	−0.421	−0.177	0.019	−0.400	0.088	0.178	0.063	−0.309	−0.109	0.188	0.089	−0.320	0.243
TM	Muted trombone	0.402	0.363	−0.147	0.434	0.082	−0.269	0.241	0.377	0.142	0.085	−0.278	0.225	0.507
TP	Trumpet	−0.127	0.280	−0.180	−0.027	0.269	−0.182	0.173	−0.092	0.371	0.052	−0.071	−0.103	0.366
X1	Alto saxophone *mf*	0.422	−0.263	−0.082	0.182	−0.398	−0.127	0.251	0.326	−0.068	−0.247	0.133	0.285	0.382
X2	Alto saxophone *p*	0.051	−0.305	−0.039	−0.106	−0.270	0.004	0.126	0.103	−0.144	−0.130	0.195	0.108	0.290
X3	Soprano saxophone	0.155	−0.143	−0.141	0.000	−0.200	−0.148	0.148	−0.005	0.008	−0.268	−0.067	0.134	0.283

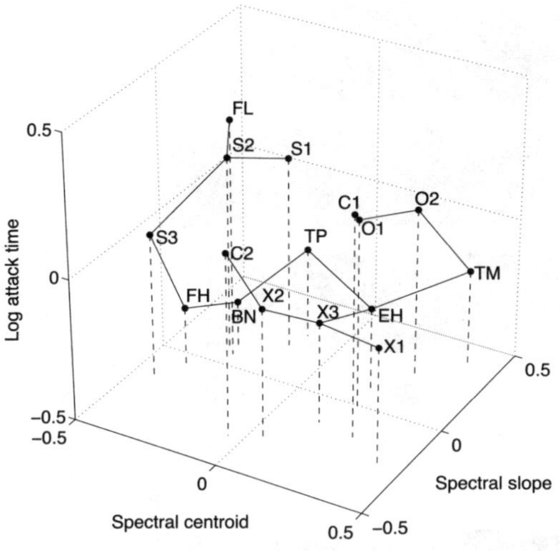

(a) Before Isomap

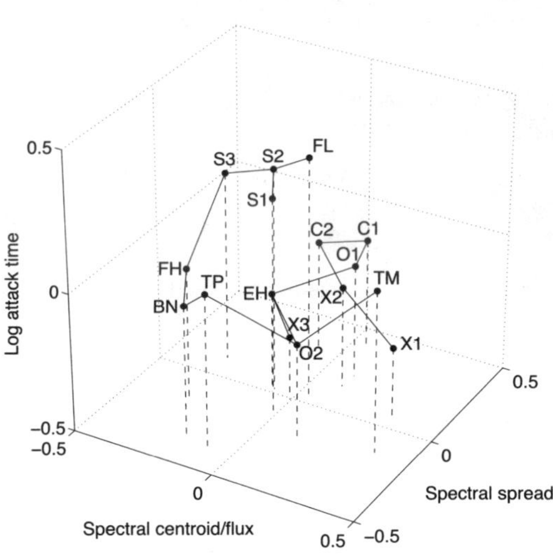

(b) After Isomap

Fig. 3. Grey 1977 timbre spaces. Axes are labelled with their acoustic correlates, and to aid visualisation, points are connected according to the minimum spanning tree in the common CLASCAL spaces. The two structures are similar, but the space groups more tightly after Isomap.

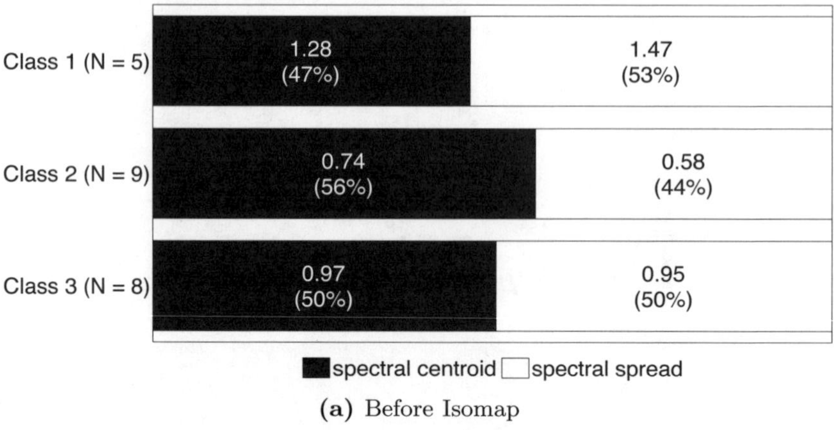

(a) Before Isomap

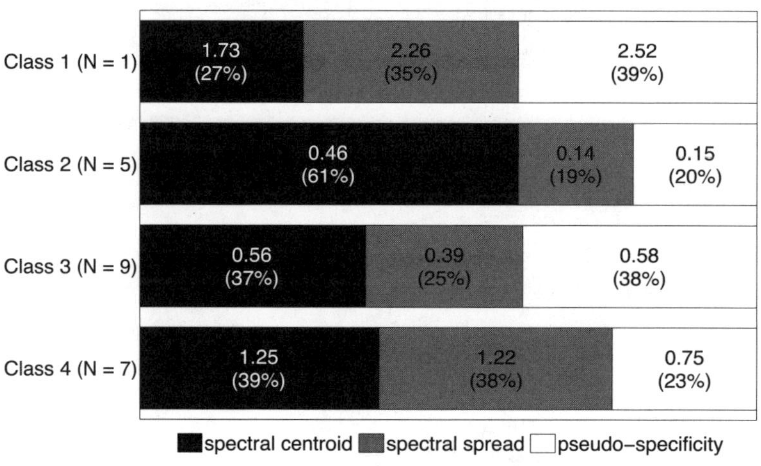

(b) After Isomap

Fig. 4. Raw and relative weights on dimensions for latent classes of subjects using Grey and Gordon 1978 stimuli

co-ordinates are listed in Table 2 for reference and a plot of the output space appears in Fig. 5a.

Before Isomap processing, CLASCAL suggests a space with 2 classes and 3 dimensions. Consistent with the dimensions recovered for the full set of 88 subjects, the first two dimensions correlate with log attack time ($r = -0.82$), spectral centroid ($r = -0.89$); the third dimension, however, correlated best with spectral spread ($r = 0.73$) rather than spectral flux ($r = 0.33$) as in the original paper. The primary difference between Class 1 (14 subjects) and Class 2 (10 subjects) is scale, Class 2 making fuller use of the scale than Class 1, although Class 1 shows a slight preference for log attack time and Class 2 shows a slight preference for

Table 2. Grey and Gordon 1978 instruments and fitted model co-ordinates along common CLASCAL dimensions and specificities

	Instrument	Before Isomap no specificities		After Isomap no specificities			After Isomap with spec.	
		1	2	1	2	3	1	$\sqrt{s}$
BN	Bassoon with French horn envelope	−0.456	0.241	−0.341	0.201	−0.041	−0.270	0.307
C1	E♭ clarinet	0.357	−0.284	0.182	−0.260	−0.013	0.168	0.241
C2	Bass clarinet with oboe 1 envelope	0.161	−0.252	0.081	−0.112	0.051	0.092	0.000
EH	English horn	−0.005	0.310	0.106	0.297	−0.023	0.060	0.346
FH	French horn with bassoon envelope	−0.408	0.306	−0.263	0.271	−0.050	−0.224	0.327
FL	Flute	−0.359	−0.322	−0.141	−0.009	0.470	−0.184	0.431
O1	Oboe 1 with bass clarinet envelope	0.044	−0.357	0.023	−0.291	−0.008	0.079	0.274
O2	Oboe 2	0.202	0.303	0.215	0.218	0.125	0.112	0.339
S1	Cello *normale* with *sul tasto* envelope	−0.291	−0.232	−0.141	−0.201	0.308	−0.136	0.362
S2	Cello *sul tasto* with *normale* envelope	0.141	−0.260	0.081	−0.115	0.057	0.091	0.045
S3	Cello *sul ponticello*	−0.502	−0.083	−0.347	−0.108	0.176	−0.364	0.032
TM	Muted trombone with trumpet envelope	0.495	0.307	0.075	0.127	−0.551	0.151	0.540
TP	Trumpet with muted trombone envelope	0.091	0.395	0.298	0.100	0.095	0.105	0.344
X1	Alto saxophone *mf*	0.478	−0.040	0.105	−0.174	−0.300	0.191	0.298
X2	Alto saxophone *p*	0.014	−0.136	−0.045	−0.127	−0.159	0.058	0.239
X3	Soprano saxophone	0.039	0.105	0.113	0.183	−0.137	0.070	0.326

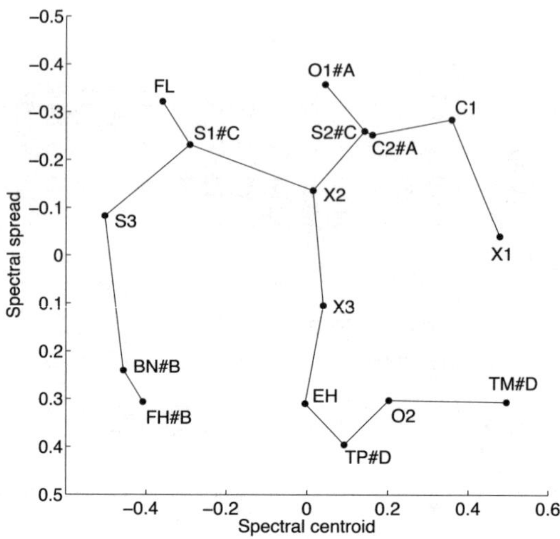

(a) Before Isomap

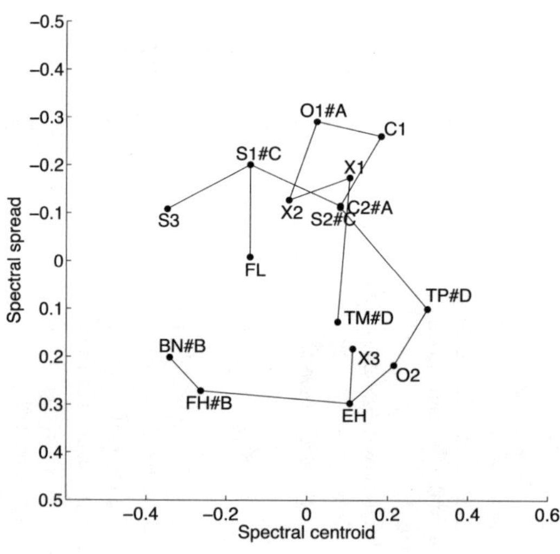

(b) After Isomap

Fig. 5. Grey and Gordon 1978 timbre spaces. Axes are labelled with their acoustic correlates, and to aid visualisation, points are connected according to the minimum spanning trees in their common CLASCAL spaces. In the post-Isomap space, the minimum spanning tree incorporates distance information from the unplotted third dimension, which is why it crosses itself.

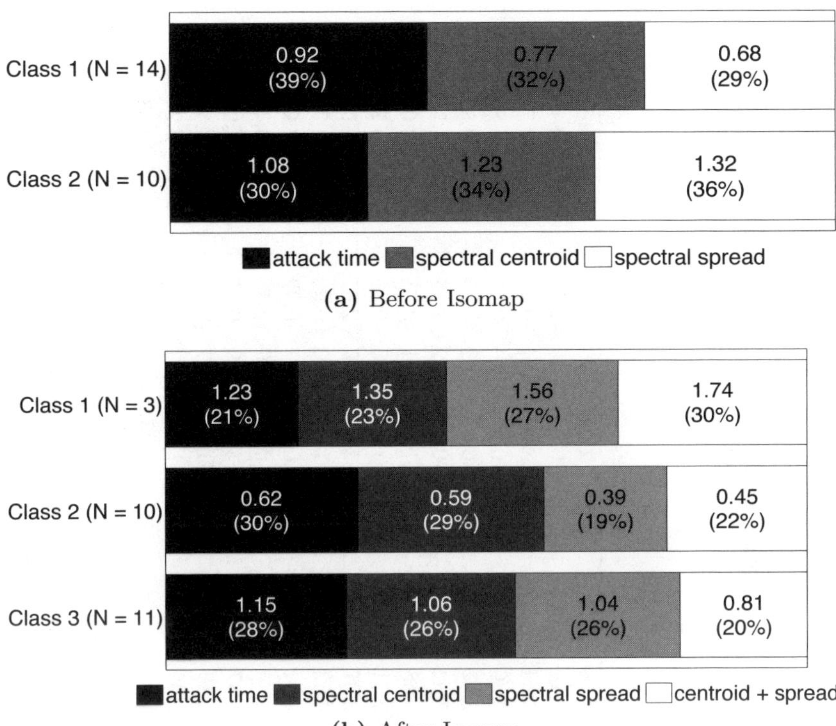

(a) Before Isomap

(b) After Isomap

Fig. 6. Raw and relative weights on dimensions for latent classes of subjects using McAdams et al. 1995 stimuli

spectral spread in their respective rating strategies (see Fig. 6a). A full set of co-ordinates appears in Table 3 and the space is plotted in three dimensions in Fig. 7a.

After Isomap processing, the optimal CLASCAL model comprises three classes and four dimensions. The first three dimensions correlate with the same acoustic features as those of the pre-Isomap space, log attack time ($r = -0.81$), spectral centroid ($r = -0.68$), and spectral spread ($r = 0.82$); the fourth dimension appears to be some combination of spectral centroid ($r = -0.69$) and spectral spread ($r = 0.78$). The first and third dimensions of the spaces correlate highly with each other ($r = 0.97$ and $r = 0.77$), but it is the fourth dimension after Isomap that correlates with the second dimension before Isomap ($r = 0.81$). Class 1 (3 subjects) shows a slight preference for Dimensions 3 and 4, Class 2 (10 subjects) shows a slight preference for Dimensions 1 and 2, and Class 3 (11 subjects) weights all four dimensions evenly (see Fig. 6b). Table 3 contains a list of the exact co-ordinates for each stimulus and Fig. 7b provides a projection of this space into three dimensions.

Table 3. McAdams et al. 1995 instruments and fitted model co-ordinates along common CLASCAL dimensions and specificities

| Instrument | | Before Isomap | | | After Isomap | | | | | |
| | | no specificities | | | no specificities | | | | with spec. | |
		1	2	3	1	2	3	4	1	$\sqrt{s}$
hrn	French horn	−3.87	0.18	−1.73	−2.96	2.21	−0.79	0.54	−2.82	2.54
tpt	Trumpet	−2.35	−2.11	1.30	−1.18	0.59	0.40	−2.50	−1.52	2.10
trn	Trombone	−2.82	0.94	−2.10	−1.86	3.00	0.14	−0.78	−2.25	2.74
hrp	Harp	3.14	0.96	−1.49	3.26	0.87	−0.56	0.53	2.84	1.85
tpr	Trumpar (trumpet/guitar hybrid)	0.31	−2.81	0.78	0.35	−0.07	−0.52	−2.63	−0.23	2.53
ols	Oboleste (oboe/celesta hybrid)	3.22	2.02	−0.27	2.79	−0.26	−0.42	2.17	3.15	1.58
vbs	Vibraphone	3.73	3.58	0.97	2.84	−1.53	0.41	3.71	3.60	3.00
sno	Striano (string/piano hybrid)	−0.70	−0.51	2.58	−1.14	−1.94	1.65	−0.86	−0.90	2.70
hcd	Harpsichord	4.22	−2.07	1.33	3.01	−2.91	0.00	−2.01	2.19	4.02
can	English horn	−1.64	−2.62	−1.35	−2.26	−1.37	−2.00	0.02	−1.91	2.76
bsn	Bassoon	−2.91	−2.34	−0.92	−2.99	−0.47	−1.67	−0.92	−2.63	2.29
cnt	Clarinet	−3.40	2.66	0.58	−3.14	0.04	1.20	2.43	−2.25	3.41
vbn	Vibrone (vibraphone/trombone hybrid)	0.37	1.37	−3.91	1.00	3.46	−1.69	0.97	0.51	4.06
obc	Obochord (oboe/harpsichord hybrid)	2.91	−2.19	−2.02	1.40	−1.24	−3.27	0.24	1.46	3.48
gtr	Guitar	3.12	1.05	2.09	2.47	−1.23	1.84	0.83	2.54	2.21
stg	Strings	−2.25	−1.13	2.41	−1.73	−0.63	1.44	−2.12	−1.65	2.33
pno	Piano	1.13	1.59	−0.27	1.80	1.38	1.23	−0.06	1.29	2.32
gtn	Guitarnet (guitar/clarinet hybrid)	−2.19	1.41	2.01	−1.64	0.10	2.60	0.42	−1.41	2.68

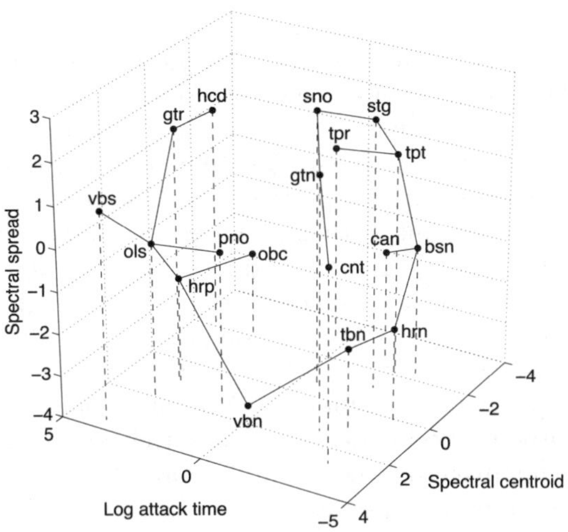

(a) Before Isomap

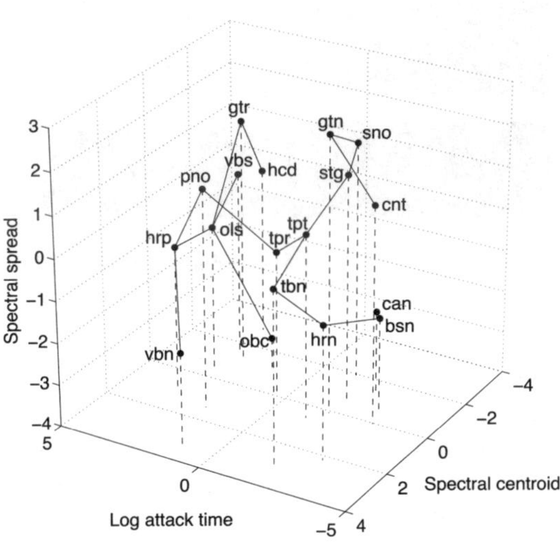

(b) After Isomap

Fig. 7. McAdams et al. 1995 timbre space before Isomap. Axes are labelled with their acoustic correlates, and to aid visualisation, points are connected according to the minimum spanning trees in their common CLASCAL spaces.

3.3   Specificities

As stated earlier, all of the above models were derived without allowing for specificities, i.e, using (1) rather than (2). Before Isomap processing, the specificities make little difference. An analogous Monte Carlo likelihood-ratio test to the one used for determining the optimal number of classes prefers models without specificities for Grey and Gordon 1978 and McAdams et al. 1995. Although a model with specificities is preferred for Grey 1977, the model structure changes very little on account of them. The optimal model including specificities still contains two classes and three dimensions. All three respective pairs of dimensions (with and without specificities) correlate highly with each other ($r = 0.89$, $r = 0.74$, and $r = 0.89$), although after including specificities, the second dimension correlates better with a psychoacoustical model for perceived roughness ($r = -0.77$; see von Bismarck 1974) than it does with spectral spread. Like the model without specificities, both latent classes weight the dimensions fairly evenly; the difference between them is that Class 1 (7 subjects) incorporates specificities into its rating strategy whereas Class 2 (15 subjects) does not (see Fig. 8). The output space, which is structurally almost identical to the space without specificities, is presented in Fig. 9, and a complete co-ordinate listing appears in Table 1.

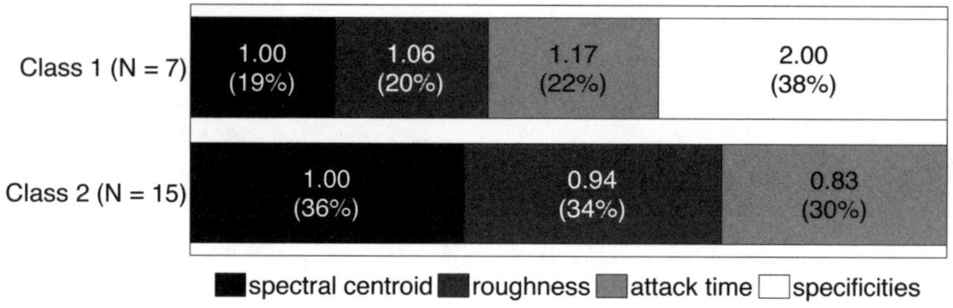

Fig. 8. Raw and relative weights for each latent class in Grey 1977 before Isomap processing and including specificities

After Isomap processing, however, the Monte Carlo test prefers models with specificities in all cases. Moreover, although the optimal number of latent classes remains unchanged, the inclusion of specificities reduces the optimal number of common dimensions to just one: spectral centroid for Grey 1977 ($r = 0.83$) and Grey and Gordon 1978 ($r = 0.91$) and log attack time for McAdams et al. 1995 ($r = -0.78$). These single dimensions correlate highly with the leading dimensions in their respective spaces before and after Isomap, with and without specificities; all other information has been pushed out into the specificity dimensions. It is impossible to visualise these models, unfortunately, although their co-ordinate values are listed in their respective tables. The latent classes within each of these models differ primarily in the relative weight they place on the specificities (see Fig. 10).

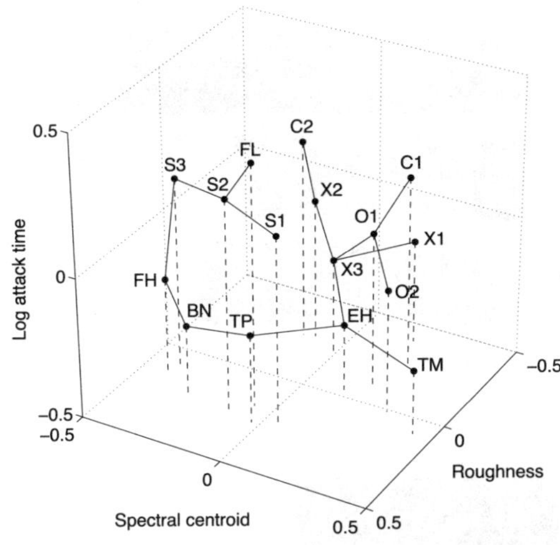

Fig. 9. Grey 1977 timbre space before Isomap and including specificities. Structurally, it is nearly identical to the analogous space without specificities.

One can see from inspecting the specificity values in the co-ordinate listings for all three spaces that it is difficult to interpret the precise meaning of specificities. Higher values denote timbres that are heard as more unique than others, but other than an informal analysis like that in McAdams, Winsberg, Donnadieu, Soete, and Krimphoof 1995, there is no scientific means to determine from our data what makes each timbre sound unique. We do find, however, that certain specificity dimensions (vectors valued at zero for all instruments but one) correlate at $p < 0.01$ with certain acoustic features, e.g., the string sound in McAdams et al. 1995 with spectral flux ($r = 0.75$). These correlations are undesirable but strictly dependent on the choice of stimulus set; confirmatory studies with artificial timbres, e.g., Caclin et al. 2005, can and should check for such correlations before conducting rating experiments.

4   Discussion and Future Work

4.1   Perceived Dimensions of Timbre

Consistent with previous studies, it is clear from all of the spaces presented above that humans use log attack time and spectral centroid when distinguishing between timbres. It is also clear that we use at least one other component, which manifests itself in the above spaces as spectral shape (spectral slope, spectral spread), perceived roughness, or specificities. Whenever specificities are included in the models above, however, the spectral shape dimensions disappear. This behaviour suggests that all of these spectral shape dimensions are poor approximations of the elusive third component of timbre, so poor that in most

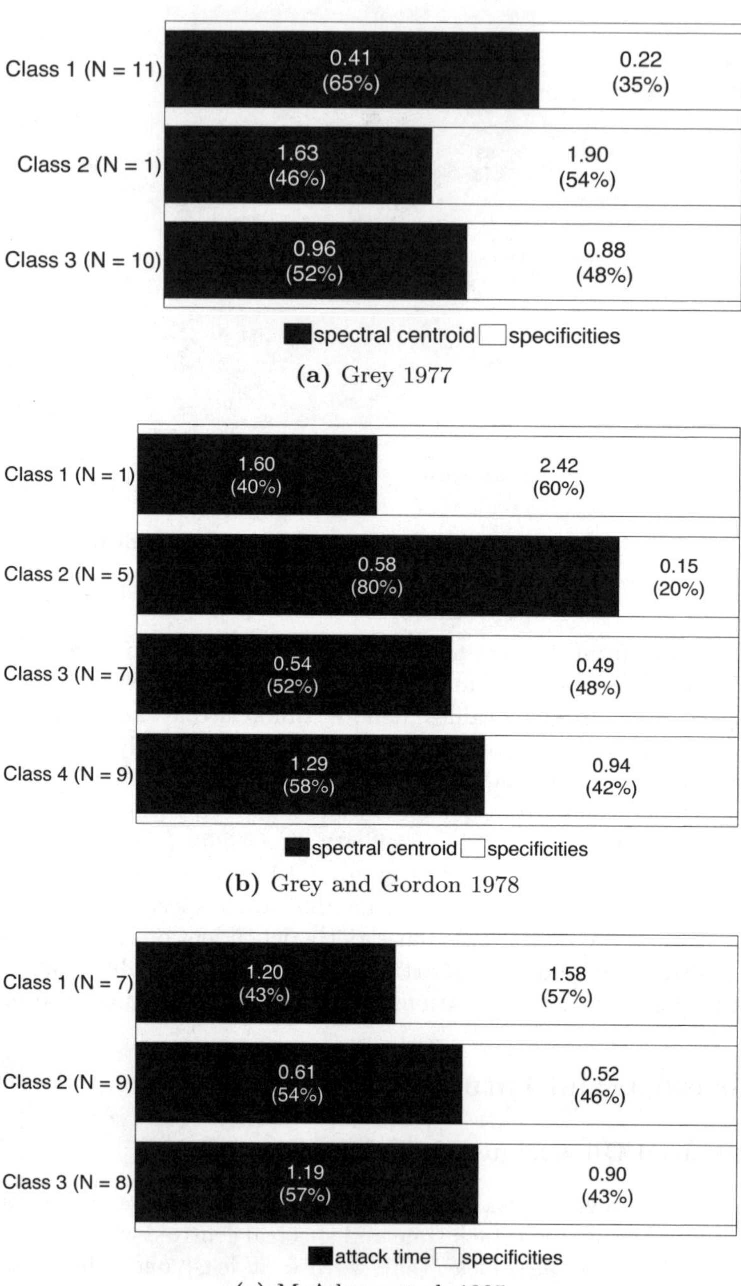

(a) Grey 1977

(b) Grey and Gordon 1978

(c) McAdams et al. 1995

Fig. 10. Raw and relative weights for each latent class after processing with Isomap and including specificities in the model

cases, it is statistically advantageous to avoid the approximation by reverting to specificities. Specificities are a sort of null model in that they take up as much unexplained variance as possible without making any assumptions about the relationships among timbres.

Ultimately, these results should not be surprising. Practitioners of sound synthesis are well aware of the trade-off between modelling a given spectral shape precisely and keeping the number of parameters manageable, e.g., basic FM synthesis produces a coarser approximation of a desired spectrum but requires many fewer parameters than an additive synthesis model; subtractive synthesis models would fall somewhere in between. In no case will a single parameter provide a meaningful approximation. Moreover, interpolating between synthesis parametrisation when replicating time-varying spectra can be quite challenging because the spaces involved are generally not Euclidean. It would be well worth investigating whether the higher dimensions of timbre perception or the specificities are ultimately correcting for problems with the assumption that it is possible to represent timbre space as a Euclidean one, which is the default assumption in CLASCAL and its relatives.

4.2   Isomap Processing

Although Isomap was ultimately successful in reducing the output dimensionality, it was not able to do so without resorting to specificities. In the models without specificities, Isomap increases the models' degrees of freedom (the total number of free parameters accounting for all dimensions and classes) in the Grey 1977 space from 50 to 71, in the Grey and Gordon 1978 space from 37 to 58, and in the McAdams et al. 1995 space from 56 to 79. Another disadvantage of Isomap, before specificities are considered, is that it can yield dimensions that are difficult to interpret. The Grey 1977 and McAdams et al. 1995 spaces include duplicate spectral-centroid dimensions and the Grey and Gordon 1978 space includes the curious pseudo-specificity in its third dimension. Furthermore, the correlation between dimensions pre- and post-Isomap can be surprising, as discussed above for the McAdams et al. 1995 space. It is impossible to know exactly what about the geometry of the timbres in this space causes these behaviours, but the geometric structures it uncovers are consistent with those of the spaces before Isomap processing.

These observations would be a blacker mark against Isomap processing for MDS studies if Monte Carlo testing did not always prefer models with specificities. Fortunately, after the introduction of specificities, the Isomap-processed spaces can reduce dimensionality greatly and become very easy to interpret. The necessary degrees of freedom for an optimal fit reduce from 67 to 38 for Grey 1977 and from 56 to 42 for McAdams et al. 1995; for Grey and Gordon 1978, the necessary degrees of freedom increase just slightly from 37 to 41. For each of the timbre sets considered, the ideal output space consists of a single dimension correlating with the leading dimensions of the pre-Isomap spaces. The trade-off for this heavy degree of compression is the dispersion of remaining variance among the specificities, which are difficult to interpret directly but, as discussed above, may be a statistical proxy for variations in spectral shape. A problem with this severe reduction, however, is that it conceptualises timbre as unidimensional with specificities, whereas many musicians feel that two to four dimensions already lose much of the subtle richness of timbral experience available in the instrument sounds tested.

In generating its geodesic distances, Isomap prefers small dissimilarities to larger ones; by construction, dissimilarities in the transformed matrix are always greater than or equal to dissimilarities in the original matrix. We chose this particular transformation because of its natural combination with the CLAS-CAL method and relative ease of computation. It is unclear exactly what such a transformation is assuming about subjects' rating strategies, however, other than a larger trust in estimations of dissimilarity between relatively similar timbres over estimations between relatively dissimilar timbres. One improvement would be to incorporate methods such as maximum variance unfolding (MVU) (Weinberger 2004; Weinberger and Saul 2006) that can emphasise particular sets of neighbouring stimulus pairs without requiring the recomputation of other dissimilarities. Such methods could be extended to allow researchers to focus not only on small dissimilarities in the matrix, but possibly on exclusively mid-range dissimilarities or exclusively large dissimilarities as well, which would allow studies to identify differing rating strategies for differing grades of dissimilarity.

Geodesic distances are a means not an end: like MVU, Isomap seeks to identify low-dimensional manifolds in high-dimensional structures. Curiously, an informal analysis suggests that Isomap has no effect on dimensionality or the interpretation of the dimensions when applied *after* CLASCAL analysis, which suggests that for our study, the primary value of Isomap was in eliminating complicated nonlinearities in individual subjects' rating strategies and reducing them to more broadly used acoustic features such as log attack time or spectral centroid. Because the dimensions that disappear on account of Isomap processing all have to do with spectral shape, it is reasonable to assume that many of these nonlinearities are connected to spectral shape in some way. Further confirmatory studies are warranted to explore exactly how Isomap (or its relatives) warp timbre dissimilarity matrices.

5   Conclusion

Designed for uncovering the true dimensionality of Euclidean manifolds, Isomap is also able to simplify the timbre spaces resulting from MDS on empirical timbre dissimilarity matrices. These simplifications are in one sense disappointing: they collapse the spaces to a single shared dimension plus a set of instrument-specific dimensions that are relatively difficult to interpret. These simplified spaces, however, confirm two known dimensional components of timbre, spectral centroid and log attack time, and highlight an important direction for future work on the perception of spectral shape. More generally, the success of Isomap in this domain should encourage all researchers using MDS models to explore how preprocessing dissimilarity matrices before MDS could be valuable and, in particular, how Isomap preprocessing could be tailored to their needs.

Acknowledgements

This research was supported in part by a Discovery Grant from the Natural Sciences and Engineering Research Council of Canada to Stephen McAdams. We would also like to thank Bruno Giordano for his insights.

References

[Aitkin, Anderson, and Hinde 1981]Aitkin, M., Anderson, D., Hinde, J.: Statistical modelling of data on teaching styles. Journal of the Royal Statistical Society, Series A (General) 144(4), 419–461 (1981)

[von Bismarck 1974]Bismarck, G., von, G.: Sharpness as an attribute of the timbre of steady sounds. Acustica 30, 159–172 (1974)

[Burgoyne and Saul 2005]Burgoyne, J.A., Saul, L.K.: Visualization of low-dimensional structure in tonal pitch space. In: Proceedings of the International Computer Music Conference, pp. 243–246 (2005)

[Caclin, McAdams, Smith, and Winsberg 2005]Caclin, A., McAdams, S., Smith, B.K., Winsberg, S.: Acoustic correlates of timbre space dimensions: A confirmatory study using synthetic tones. Journal of the Acoustical Society of America 118(1), 471–482 (2005)

[Carroll and Chang 1970]Carroll, J.D., Chang, J.-J.: Analysis of individual differences in multidimensional scaling via an n-way generalization of 'Eckart-Young' decomposition. Psychometrika 35(3), 283–319 (1970)

[Gabriel and Sokal 1969]Gabriel, K.R., Sokal, R.R.: A new statistical appraoch to geographic variation analysis. Systematic Zoology 18, 259–270 (1969)

[Grey 1977]Grey, J.M.: Multidimensional perceptual scaling of musical timbre. Journal of the Acoustical Society of America 61, 1270–1277 (1977)

[Grey and Gordon 1978]Grey, J.M., Gordon, J.W.: Perceptual effects of spectral modifications on musical timbres. Journal of the Acoustical Society of America 63(5), 1493–1500 (1978)

[Hope 1968]Hope, A.C.A.: A simplified Monte Carlo significance test procedure. Journal of the Royal Statistical Society, Series B (Methodological) 30(3), 582–598 (1968)

[Jaromczyk and Toussaint 1992]Jaromczyk, J.W., Toussaint, G.T.: Relative neighborhood graphs and their relatives. Proceedings of the IEEE 80(9), 1502–1517 (1992)

[Krumhansl 1989]Krumhansl, C.L.: Why is musical timbre so hard to understand? In: Nielzen, S., Olsson, O. (eds.) Structure and Perception of Electroacoustic Sound and Music. Excerpta Medica, vol. 846. Elsevier, Amsterdam (1989)

[McAdams, Winsberg, Donnadieu, Soete, and Krimphoof 1995]McAdams, S., Winsberg, S., Donnadieu, S., Soete, G.D., Krimphoof, J.: Perceptual scaling of synthesized musical timbres: Common dimensions, specificities, and latent subject classes. Psychological Research 58, 177–192 (1995)

[Peeters, McAdams, and Herrera 2000]Peeters, G., McAdams, S., Herrera, P.: Instrument sound description in the context of MPEG-7. In: Proceedings of the International Computer Music Conference (2000)

[Tennenbaum, de Silva, and Langford 2000]Tennenbaum, J.B., de Silva, V., Langford, J.C.: A global geometric framework for nonlinear dimensionality reduction. Science 290, 2319–2323 (2000)

[Torgerson 1958]Torgerson, W.S.: Theory and Methods of Scaling. Wiley, Chichester (1958)

[Weinberger 2004]Weinberger, K.Q.: Unsupervised learning of image manifolds by semidefinite programming. In: Proceeding of the IEEE Computer Society Conference on Computer Vision and Pattern Recognition (2004)

[Weinberger and Saul 2006]Weinberger, K.Q., Saul, L.K.: An introduction to nonlinear dimensionality reduction by maximum variance unfolding. In: Proceedings of the National Conference on Artificial Intelligence (AAAI) (2006)

[Wessel, Bristow, and Settel 1987]Wessel, D.L., Bristow, D., Settel, Z.: Control of phrasing and articulation in synthesis. In: Proceedings of the International Computer Music Conference, pp. 108–116 (1987)

[Winsberg and Carroll 1989]Winsberg, S., Carroll, J.D.: A quasi-nonmetric method for multidimensional scaling via an extended Euclidean model. Psychometrika 54(2), 217–229 (1989)

[Winsberg and De Soete 1993]Winsberg, S., De Soete, G.: A latent class approach to fitting the weighted Euclidean model, CLASCAL. Psychometrika 58(2), 315–330 (1993)

[Winsberg and De Soete 1997]Winsberg, S., De Soete, G.: Multidimensional scaling with constrained dimensions: CONSCAL. British Journal of Mathematical and Statistical Psychology 50, 55–72 (1997)

Real-Time Analysis of Sensory Dissonance

John MacCallum and Aaron Einbond

Center for New Music and Audio Technologies (CNMAT)
Department of Music
University of California, Berkeley
{johnmac,einbond}@berkeley.edu

Abstract. We describe a tool for real-time musical analysis based on a measure of roughness, the principal element of sensory dissonance. While most historical musical analysis is based on the notated score, our tool permits analysis of a recorded or live audio signal in its full complexity. We proceed from the work of Richard Parncutt and Ernst Terhardt, extending their algorithms for the psychoacoustic analysis of harmony to be used for the live analysis of spectral data. This allows for the study of a wider variety of timbrally-rich acoustic or electronic sounds which was not possible with previous algorithms. Further, the direct treatment of audio signal facilitates a wide range of analytical applications, from the comparison of multiple recordings of the same musical work to the real-time analysis of a live performance. Our algorithm is programmed in C as an external object for the program Max/MSP.

Taking musical examples by Arnold Schoenberg, Gérard Grisey and Iannis Xenakis, our algorithm yields varying roughness estimates depending on instrumental orchestration or electronic texture, confirming our intuitive understanding that timbre affects sensory dissonance. This is one of the many possibilities this tool presents for analysis and composition of music that is timbrally-dynamic and microtonally-complex.

1 Introduction

1.1 Dissonance and Perception

Since the time of Rameau and Helmholtz several psychoacoustic models have been proposed for the perception of dissonance. Ernst Terhardt observed that musical consonance is the product of sensory consonance (absence of sensory dissonance) and harmonicity (the similarity of a sound to the harmonic series) [11,12]. Sensory dissonance comprises a number of psychoacoustic factors including *roughness*, the beating sensation produced when two frequencies are within a critical bandwidth, which is approximately one third of an octave in the middle range of human hearing [6]. The partials of complex tones, in which several components are fused into a single percept, can also produce roughness when they fall within a critical bandwidth. As a result, the timbre of complex tones can effect our experience of roughness. Richard Parncutt has further extended and developed Terhardt's theory by proposing a cognition-based measure of roughness of complex tones [7,8]. Despite the availability of these tools, few current

R. Kronland-Martinet, S. Ystad, and K. Jensen (Eds.): CMMR 2007, LNCS 4969, pp. 203–211, 2008.
© Springer-Verlag Berlin Heidelberg 2008

musical theoretical techniques take advantage of them to analyze larger musical structures as they unfold in time.

1.2 Taking Timbre into Account

Previous models such as those by Richard Parncutt [7,8] and Kameoka and Kuriyagawa [3], include only a rudimentary treatment of the timbre of complex tones. They model each pitch as a generalized instrumental timbre with the first several partials of the harmonic series in decreasing amplitudes. In the case of Parncutt, these partials are further rounded to the nearest equally-tempered frequency. We can improve on this model, including timbre in a more flexible and faithful way.

Rather than using a prescribed harmonic series to model each pitch of an instrumental chord, we directly analyze audio recordings of the sound in question. We then use Fourier-transform-based analysis tools fiddle~ [10] and iana~ [13], running in the computer program Max/MSP, to retrieve frequencies and amplitudes of the partials making up the recording. We further revise Parncutt's algorithm to treat the precise frequencies of the partials available from this data, rather than rounding them to equally-tempered pitches. We do not limit our calculation to a small number of partials; instead we include all relevant partial data available from spectral analysis. By using precise frequencies rather than idealized harmonics, we make it possible to analyze sounds that contain inharmonic spectra, for example bells or electronically-generated sounds.

1.3 Benefits of Real-Time Audio

Previous dissonance measures assume that roughness is additive. However perceptual effects such as masking are not accommodated by an additive model. Dense sonorities, such as clusters, may be perceived in a non-additive way, as they do not present a single clear amplitude modulation, or "beating," frequency. While there are many cultural and contextual factors that may contribute to this "smoothing" of dense sonorities, it would be attractive to include the effect in the roughness estimate itself. By analyzing audio recordings, we make it possible to model this effect. Fiddle~ automatically mimics masking: when a loud partial is present near a quiet partial, or a large cluster of partials is present in close proximity, fiddle~ is unable to resolve the separate components, like the human ear. This therefore reduces the contributions of masked frequencies to the roughness estimate. While the precise parameters of the analyses must be fine-tuned better to match perceptual data, the results are already promising.

Another potential benefit of analyzing the audio signal is that different recordings of the same piece may be analyzed separately. This is impossible with previous measures that proceed from the printed page. However it also raises questions of experimental control, for example how to compare two performances recorded with different equipment or in different acoustic spaces.

Audio data allow for analysis to be carried out in real time, as a recording or live electronic sound is played. This suggests application to live electronic music performance, especially improvisation.

2   Implementation

To leverage real-time audio we implement our algorithm as an external object for Max/MSP.

2.1   Roughness Computation

As described in MacCallum *et al.* [4], the roughness algorithm we implement is a modified version of that of Parncutt [7,8]. The principal modifications to Parncutt's method are to work with continuous frequency rather than rounding to equal temperament and to analyze sounds directly rather than to model synthetic timbres above a given fundamental. Our object accepts a list of frequency amplitude pairs and returns a single roughness value which is the sum of the roughness of all frequency components

$$\rho = \frac{\sum_{j,k}^{n} a_j \cdot a_k \cdot g(f_{cb})}{\sum_{j}^{n} a_j^2} \tag{1}$$

where a_j and a_k are the amplitudes of the components, and $g(f_{cb})$ is a 'standard curve' developed by Parncutt that models the experimental data of Plomp and Levelt [9]

$$g(f_{cb}) = \left(e(f_{cb}/0.25) \cdot e^{(-f_{cb}/0.25)} \right)^2 . \tag{2}$$

and f_{cb} is the critical bandwidth around the mean frequency of the two components. The literature abounds with formulæ that describe the critical bandwidth; our software implements those of Hutchinson and Knopoff, and Moore and Glasberg [6] (equations 3 and 4 respectively).

$$f_{cb} = 1.72 f_m^{0.65} \tag{3}$$

$$f_{cb} = 0.108 f_m + 24.7 \tag{4}$$

2.2   Peak Extraction

Raw spectral data must be passed through a peak-extraction algorithm to remove noise. For this we use fiddle~ [10] which has consistently produced results that correspond well to our intuition, although future research plans include the implementation of a peak-extraction algorithm specifically designed for our purposes. Fiddle~ is particularly useful when analyzing noisy signals such as parts of *Mycenae-Alpha* (see below) and György Ligeti's *Atmosphères*. In the latter example, although the composition begins with a sonority made up entirely of minor seconds, the sensory experience is far from the extreme roughness that we might expect. Because there are few peaks that fiddle~ can differentiate from the rest of the spectrum, the resulting roughness calculation is low and corresponds well with our experience of a smooth sound mass.

2.3   User Interface

Critical Bandwidth Formulæ. We allow the user to choose between two of
the more commonly used critical bandwidth formulæ. The default formula (used
to produce the analyses in section 3) is that of Moore and Glasberg which is more
recent than that of Hutchinson and Knopoff, used in Parncutt's original work.

Modeling Experimental Data. In equation 1 we see that the roughness of
each pair of components is the product of their amplitudes weighted by a curve
(equation 2) that models Plomp and Levelt's experimental data. Although these
data correspond well to our experience and the curve fits the data well, the user
can instead define his or her own roughness curve by inputting a list of x-y pairs
over which the object will interpolate. The user also has access to the outer-most
exponent in equation 2 to make adjustments to the steepness of the curve.

In addition to the modified version of Richard Parncutt's algorithm, our object
also implements the algorithm of Kameoka and Kuriyagawa [3]. Although we analyze the following examples using the former method, the user has the option of
switching between the two. For a comparison of the two models see Mashinter [5].

Non-Real-Time Analysis Using SDIF data. The roughness object can be
linked to an SDIF-buffer in Max/MSP for processing an SDIF (Sound Description Interchange Format) file containing sinusoidal tracks (1TRC), harmonic
partials (1HRM) or resonance models (1RES) [14]. This allows the spectral analysis and peak extraction to be done with software outside of Max/MSP such as
AudioSculpt, AddAn, ResAn, or SPEAR.

3   Practical Examples

Three analytical examples highlight the diverse musical applications of our algorithm: Arnold Schoenberg's *Fünf Orchesterstücke* Op. 16 No. 3, "Farben,"
Gérard Grisey's *Partiels* for 16 musicians (1975) and Iannis Xenakis' *Mycenae-
Alpha* (1978). Each work highlights an analytical problem difficult to resolve
using traditional musical-theoretical tools. In "Farben," two different orchestrations of the same chord look similar on paper but produce different spectra
when excerpts of the audio recording are compared. While *Partiels* is scored
for an ensemble of orchestral instruments, the instruments are called on to play
microtones and extended techniques which are unstable and may vary from performance to performance. We analyze two recordings to show these differences.
Mycenae-Alpha is even more challenging analytically: as a purely electronic work
it does not exist as a traditional score. Furthermore, most of its sonic material is
dense and noisy and it cannot be easily abstracted to discrete notes and rhythms.
In this case the audio recording is the necessary starting point for analysis.

3.1   Farben

The first example of a musical use of the algorithms is taken from Arnold Schoenberg's *Fünf Orchesterstücke*, Op. 16 No. 3, "Farben." The opening alternates

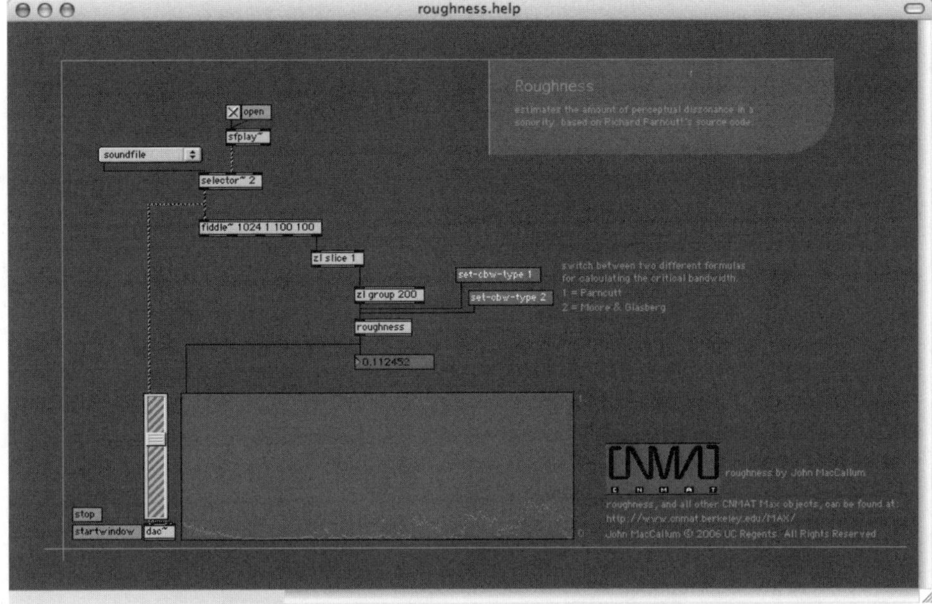

Fig. 1. Max/MSP help file for the roughness object

between two orchestrations of the same chord, creating a subtly-shifting klang-farbenmelodie (tone-color melody). The first orchestration is for Flutes, Clarinet, Bassoon, and Viola, and the second is for English Horn, Trumpet, Bassoon, Horn, and Contrabass. The first orchestration yeilds a roughness value of 0.17, while the second yeilds 0.21, on a scale of 0-1 (Figure 2). This is in contrast to pure sine tones, which give 0.02. The low value for sine tones reflects the fact that the chord contains intervals mostly greater than a critical bandwidth apart, so roughness comes mostly from the overtones of the written pitches. The fact that the second orchestration is more rough than the first corresponds to our experience of the second chord, containing bright brass instruments, as more dissonant than the first.

3.2   Partiels

Partiels is one of the seminal compostions of the "Spectral" movement and is characterized by its microtonal detail and timbral complexity. Figures 3 and 4 are plots of the roughness value of two different recordings of *Partiels*, as output by our computer patch in real time while the recordings of these pieces are played. Each roughness estimate is averaged over the previous 2.5 seconds of music, which corresponds to approximately 200 individual roughness calculations (one calculation per frame of spectral data from fiddle~).

Figures 3 and 4 plot the first three and a half minutes and four minutes respectively. The timings of the same section of the score differ due to different

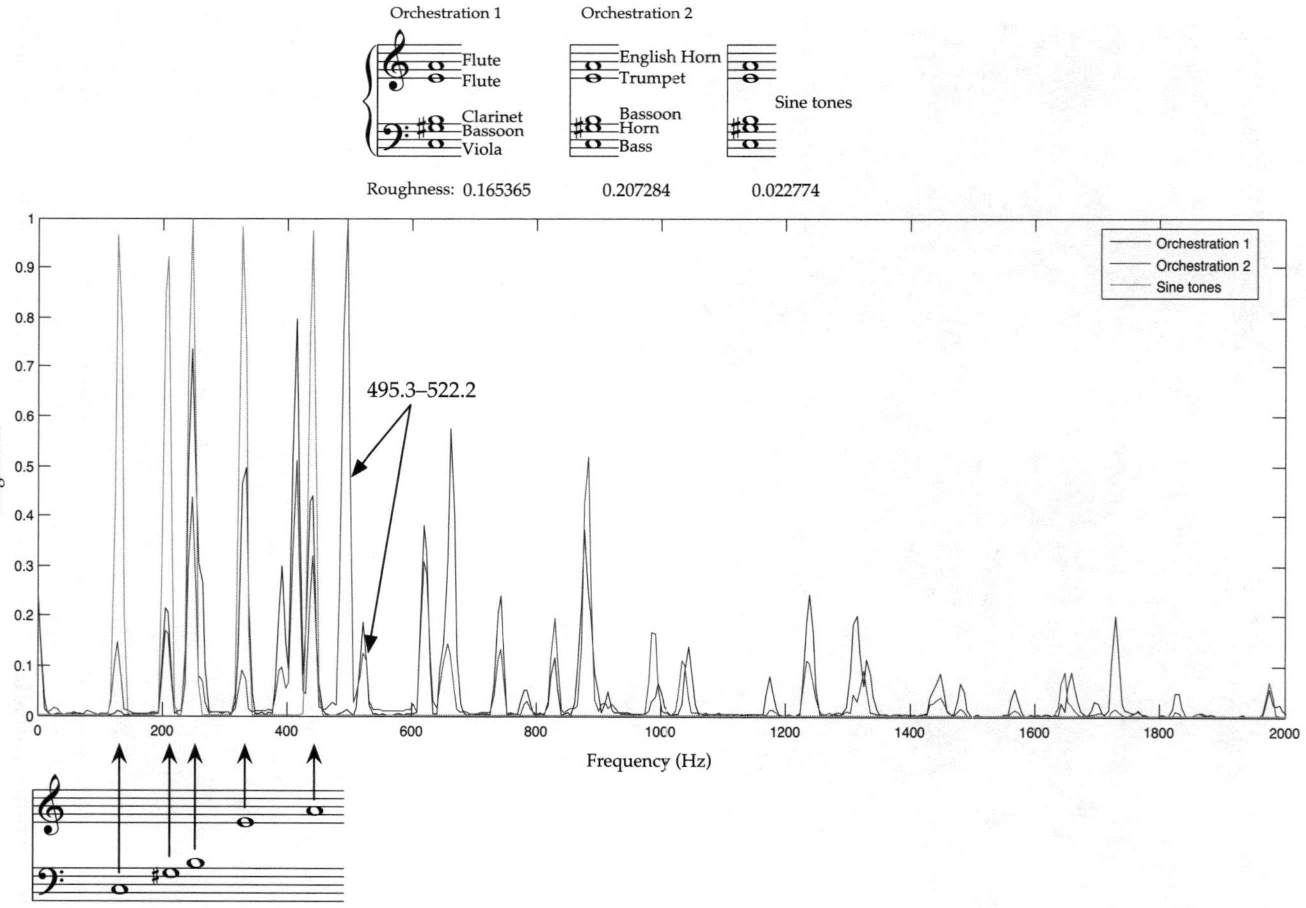

Fig. 2. The "Farben" chord from Schoenberg's Fünf Orchesterstüke, Op. 16 in its original orchestrations (blue and red) and sinusoids (green) showing differences in roughness estimates

performance tempi. The periodic attacks of contrabass and trombone are visible as troughs in both of the roughness plots. The peaks in between correspond to tutti sustained chords which gradually evolve from harmonic at the opening (less rough) to inharmonic (more rough) to flickering string sonorities in the middle register (less rough). A second excerpt from the third to the sixth minute (figure 5) follows the opposite path, as dense brass and wind clusters and multiphonics in the low register (more rough) expand out into widely-spaced wind and string chords in the upper register (less rough). The motif of inhalation and exhalation, discussed by Grisey in his own analysis of the piece, is clearly visible in the roughness plots, as is the larger trend of increase and decrease in tension governing this section.

A comparison of figures 3 and 4 reveals the value of working directly with recordings. Given the extended techniques that Grisey requires of his performers and the balance issues inherent in the composition, it is not surprising that the two plots differ substantially while retaining a similar overall shape. The gradual rise in roughness in the Valade performance as compared to Knox could reflect different interpretive decisions in performance as well as different nuances in playing technique. However the roughness plots of the two performances and recordings must be compared with caution. Although we can compare the general shapes of figures 3 and 4 we cannot infer that the peak at 120" in figure 3,

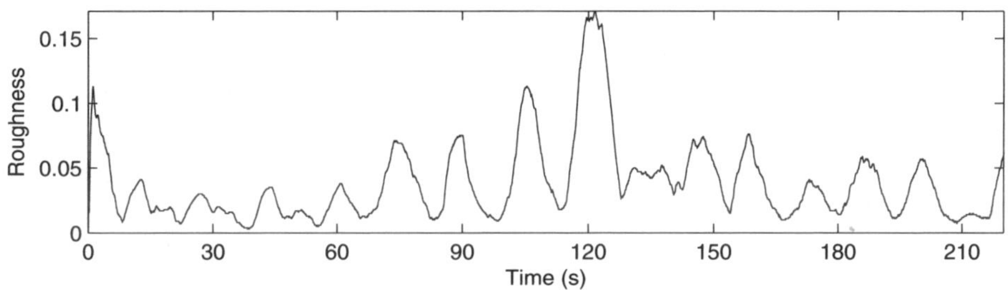

Fig. 3. Roughness in Grisey's *Partiels* (0" – 3'40") performed by Pierre-André Valade and Ensemble Court-Circuit

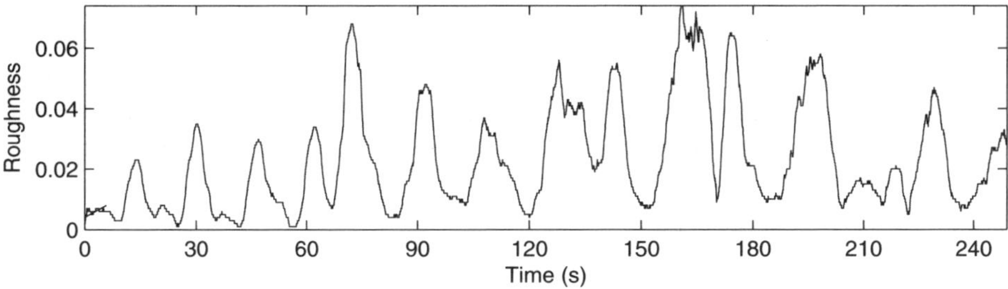

Fig. 4. Roughness in Grisey's *Partiels* (0" – 4'10") performed by Garth Knox and the Asko Ensemble

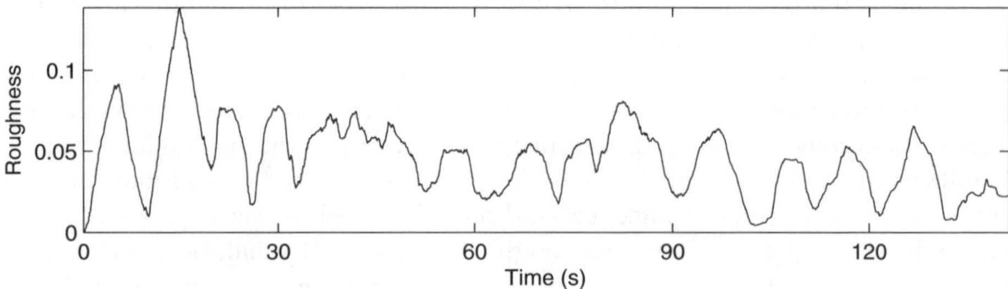

Fig. 5. Roughness in Grisey's *Partiels* (3'40" – 6'02") performed by Pierre-André Valade and Ensemble Court-Circuit

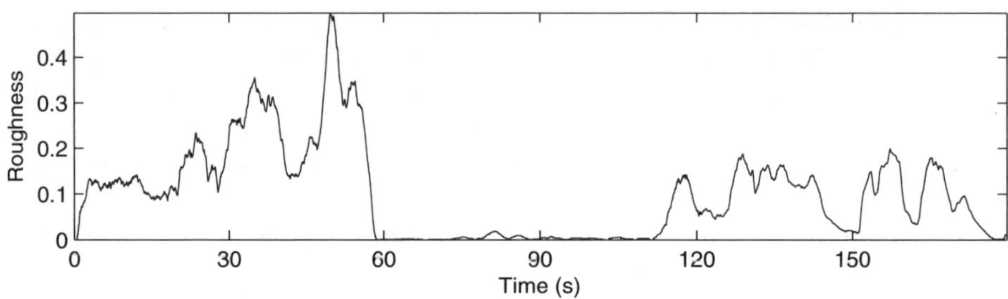

Fig. 6. Roughness plot for Iannis Xenakis' *Mycenae-Alpha* (0" – 3')

for example, is more rough than the peak at 160" in figure 4. Different recording noise levels, instrumental volume, and room acoustics are among the many factors that can account for these differences of scale.

3.3 Mycenae-Alpha

Mycenae-Alpha is the first work Xenakis realized with his UPIC graphical synthesis system. Therefore it is conceived outside the bounds of traditional music notation. The dense textures and lack of tempered or clearly-defined pitch, make traditional pitch-based analysis of this piece impossible. In our analysis of the work's first three minutes (see Figure 6), we plot roughness estimates averaged over 2.5 seconds (corresponding to 200 roughness calculations). The roughness plot recovers several prominent features of the work's profile: the sudden drop to a quiet low sound at 60 seconds and the entrance of heterophonic glissandi at 110 seconds.

4 Conclusions and Future Work

The roughness object described provides a real-time method for the analysis of sensory dissonance. This allows for the analysis of the sonic trace of an audio recording rather than the printed representation and can illuminate the extreme timbral variations found between different performances of many contemporary works. Additionally, it can be used to analyze electronic and improvised music, two genres that often defy traditional analytical tools.

While the algorithms described work well under certain conditions, we plan to improve upon their shortcomings (see Mashinter [5]) through future research to analyze amplitude modulation directly.

References

1. Bregman, A.S.: Auditory Scene Analysis: The Perceptual Organization of sound. The MIT Press, Cambridge (1990)
2. Greenwood, D.D.: Critical bandwidth and the frequency coordinates of the basilar membrane. The Journal of the Acoustical Society of America 33, 1344–1356 (1961)
3. Kameoka, A., Kuriyagawa, M.: Consonance theory, parts I and II. Journal of the Acoustical Society of America 45, 6 (1969)
4. MacCallum, J., Hunt, J., Einbond, A.: Timbre as a Psychoacoustic Parameter for Harmonic Analysis and Composition. In: Proceedings of the International Computer Music Conference (2005)
5. Mashinter, K.: Calculating Sensory Dissonance: Some Discrepancies Arising from the Models of Kameoka & Kuriyagawa, and Hutchinson & Knopoff. Empirical Musicology Review 1, 2 (2006)
6. Moore, B.C.J., Glasberg, B.R.: A revision of Zwicker's loudness model. Acustica 82 (1996)
7. Parncutt, R.: Harmony: A Psychoacoustical Approach. Springer, Berlin (1989)
8. Parncutt, R., Strasburger, H.: Applying Psychoacoustics in Composition: "Harmonic" Progressions of "Nonharmonic" Sonorities. Perspectives of New Music 32, 2 (1994)
9. Plomp, R., Levelt, W.J.M.: Tonal consonance and critical bandwidth. Journal of the Acoustical Society of America 38 (1965)
10. Puckette, M., Apel, T.: Real-time audio analysis tools for Pd and MSP. In: Proceedings of the International Computer Music Conference (1998)
11. Terhardt, E.: On the perception of periodic sound fluctuations (roughness). Acustica 30, 201–213 (1974)
12. Terhardt, E.: Ein psychoakustisch begründetes Konzept der musikalischen Konsonanz. Acustica 36 (1976)
13. Todoroff, T., Daubresse, E., Fineberg, J.: Iana~ (a real-time environment for analysis and extraction of frequency components of complex orchestral sounds and its application with a musical realization). In: Proceedings of the International Computer Music Conference (1995)
14. Wright, M., Chaudhary, A., Freed, A., Wessel, D., Rodet, X., Virolle, D., Woehrmann, R., Serra, X.: New applications of the sound description interchange format. In: Proceedings of the International Computer Music Conference (1998)

Multimodal Design for Enactive Toys

A. de Götzen, L. Mion, F. Avanzini[1], and S. Serafin[2]

[1] Department of Information Engineering, University of Padova
http://smc.dei.unipd.it/
[2] Medialogy Department, Aalborg University in Copenhagen, Denmark
http://www.imi.aau.dk/
{degotzen,luca.mion,avanzini}@dei.unipd.it, sts@imi.aau.dk

Abstract. In this paper we will investigate how non–visual senses can be used in toys to enhance and enrich the play experience of all children, while favoring accessibility and inclusion of visually-impaired children. Previous research has shown that – especially for young children developing sensory-motor skills – exploration and play are two tightly linked activities: everything is new and needs to be "investigated" and playful behaviors emerge from active exploration. We will propose a new approach in designing and creating objects that elicit this type of behavior and encourage exploration by providing real–time dynamic, haptic, tactile, auditory, and even olfactory feedback depending on children's gestures, movements, and emitted sounds. We believe that this design paradigm is highly innovative with respect to previous research and existing products – whose interaction is very often based on static feedback. Interactive and dynamic feedback is intrinsically more engaging and allows a variety of quality learning patterns.

1 Introduction

According to the traditional mainstream view, perception is a process in the brain where the perceptual system constructs an internal representation of the world, and eventually action follows as a subordinate function. Two assumptions emerge from this view. First, the causal flow between perception and action is primarily one-way: perception is input from world to mind, action is output from mind to world, and thought (cognition) is the mediating process. Second, perception and action are merely instrumentally related to each other, so that each is a tool for the other. Recent theories have questioned such a modular decomposition and have rejected both the above assumptions: the main claim of these theories is that it is not possible to disassociate perception and action schematically, and that every kind of perception is intrinsically active and thoughtful. As stated in [1], only a creature with certain kinds of bodily skills (e.g. a basic familiarity with the sensory effects of eye or hand movements, etc.) can be a perceiver. One influential contribution in this direction is [2]. The authors present an "enactive conception" of experience, which does not occur inside the animal, but is rather something that the animal *enacts* as it explores its environment. In this view, the subject of mental states is the *embodied* animal, situated in

R. Kronland-Martinet, S. Ystad, and K. Jensen (Eds.): CMMR 2007, LNCS 4969, pp. 212–222, 2008.

the environment. The animal and the environment form a pair in which the two parts are coupled and determine each other. The term "embodied" highlights two points: first, cognition depends upon the kinds of experience that are generated from specific sensorimotor capacities. Second, these individual sensorimotor capacities are themselves embedded in a biological, psychological, and cultural context. The enactive knowledge is then stored in the form of motor responses and acquired by the act of "doing" [3].

Examples of enactive knowledge are represented by the competences required by tasks such as typing, playing a musical instrument, sculpting objects, whistling, tying shoelaces etc. This type of knowledge transmission can be considered natural and intuitive, since it is based on the experience and on the perceptual responses to motor acts and it involves more than just one modality of interaction. Multimodal interaction for children however poses new specific challenges. Conceivably, the kind of support that children need is different from that of adolescents and adults. Toys for children are very often poor in term of interactivity, while multimodal interaction should be the main way of exploring the environment and learning from it. The importance of sound as a powerful medium has been largely recognized, up to the point that there are objects on the market that reproduce prerecorded sounds by pushing buttons or touching areas. However, such triggered sounds are extremely unnatural, repetitive, and ultimately annoying. The same is often true for the tactile/haptic part of the interaction. Things may vibrate (and they have basic haptic properties due to the fact that they are made of physical materials) but designing a haptic interaction that can be dynamically changed still poses several challenges. As a consequence the interaction is unrealistic and un-engaging, and the learning patterns are very stereotyped. The key for a successful exploitation of sounds in toys interfaces is to have models that respond continuously to continuous gestures, just in the same way as rattles or other physical sounding objects do when they are manipulated by children, eliciting the enactive exploration of the world through multimodal interaction and helping them to discover and recognize many different sounding gestures, each characterized by specific movement, force, velocity etc.

A third sense, which has rarely been explored in multimodal interfaces so far, is the sense of smell. Simple "scratch-and-sniff" cards are available in some toys and games, but these cannot be changed in response to the input from a child. Vision, on the other hand, has been much investigated. This is the main reason why the majority of available toys are not accessible to visually impaired children that very often have to use specially designed interfaces that are more educational instruments than amusing toys. This also implies that these instruments exclude the collaboration of sighted children in the play activity of their non sighted friends. We will focus on the non-visual senses trying, as a important side effect, to bridge the gap between educational interfaces and amusing toys, specially designed interfaces for non sighted children and toys designed for the abilities of all children.

We think that children need toys that are designed and created to be explored through all the senses: they should vibrate, they should smell, they should react to our feelings and gestures and they should respond to our actions. They should tell us where we are, what they are and what we are doing not just by looking at them but by squeezing them, smelling them, shouting to them, caressing them, letting them fall down, bouncing them one against the other etc.

2   What Do We Learn? Musical Instruments as a Compelling Example

Gesture and sound seem naturally connected in a clear and obvious way: the image of instrument players who learn to use their body in order to produce sound is indeed widespread and compelling enough. Musical gesture can be simply thought as a gesture that produces sounds in a continuous feedback loop: this is a general definition that can be used in many interactive contexts besides the musical ones. In this respect it can be useful to design interactive sounding toys that do not have to be the exact replica of original instruments, while they have to help in acquiring some basic musical skills. Children get tired soon of traditional teaching methods e.g. for bowing instruments, since they have to spend many hours before the teacher is satisfied by the sounds and modulations produced. In this case arc bowing can be taught - along with aesthetics - at a more gestural level by means of multimodal interfaces. Controllers, for instance, can be tuned in order to make children have fun during their learning, adding a visual/haptic feedback that can engage the child in exercising/playing with the instrument. Moreover very young babies could start their musical training with basic toys, learning that is not enough to kick an object to produce sound, but that it might sound in a more pleasant way by just caressing it, or finding the needed force to squeeze it.

The idea is then to teach musical gestures through simple interactions mediated by the child's body. Each object/instrument has its own way to be played: children can learn the effects of their gestures through an enactive exploration of the object, learning what are the 'musical gestures' needed to produce the sound they want. Sound and gestures are indeed very important for children in prescholar age. In fact, cognitive sciences focus on how humans interact with their environment, searching the connection between perception and action to bridge the semantic gap that humans experience in their everyday life: as sound and music are linked to their physical energy, the content of auditory information has to be linked to meaningful actions that we can use to access the encoded high-level information. This relation is crucial for non-verbal communication in general; implicit messages (e.g. expressive content) are indeed the basis of the communication process in different social situations, especially for children whose language is based on sounds and gestures, organized by semantics and constructs only at a later stage. Those sounds and gestures can be very expressive and rich of emotional content, as music can be.

Humans use recognition and expression of affect to detect meaning [4] and communication by means of vocalization, facial expression and posture, while gestures express affect (emotion) and convey information more powerfully and efficiently than spoken language. Concerning the communication between children, tactile/auditory perceptions are the major actors for emotional response and affect: the sound-making gestures of infants are the earliest attempts for separating basic emotions [5], and earlier exposure to sound patterning has profound effects on perceptual and emotional development, while deprivation can lead to future weak development of linguistic and musical skills [6]. The understanding of the emotional response related to sensory experiences and object relationships is then a crucial issue, and a novel design paradigm for expressive toys can exploit this idea of embodied-expressive knowledge; moreover, expressive paradigms based on affective and sensorial adjectives can be used to provide expressive feedback to children according to their input. Children can then associate well known feelings and basic emotions to auditory and multimodal feedback, expressed by physical metaphors which can be directly mapped to higher emotional labels [7]. Applications in this direction can be imagined for teaching/educating to musical gestures rather than to the musical language itself. Gestural skills can be developed by means of interfaces for controlling in real time the expressive information by tactile interaction and controllers to map and to transform audio data, simultaneously promoting and stimulating the communication process.

3   How Do We Learn? Touch, Movement and Sound

In light of embodied perception theories, it is clear that developing "enactive interfaces" implies developing techniques for multimodal feedback and input, including sound, touch and gesture. Sound and touch are inherently tied to movement. Without movement there would be no sound, and the sounds that we perceive are influenced by the way our ears move within the world. Most of the information received by touch is also a result of movement, this being particularly true for proprioception and kinesthesia. This is well known for children who explore the objects around them by touching, moving themselves and the objects, hearing the results of their actions etc. Therefore the study of haptic and auditory feedback is particularly interesting in this context, since we are focusing on the dynamic properties of the interaction and on the learning process that is elicited by the action.

Sound and haptic feedback in interaction are related in a number of different ways. Actions produce sounds by direct, physical manipulation of physical objects. There is a physical energetic consistency between action and produced sounds: sounds can be produced as a result of instantaneous object manipulation (the sound starts after the end of action), or as a result of continuous object manipulation (the sound continues during the manipulation). Everyday sounds are used to infer information from the environment, to know what things are, where they are, and what happens. They can be used to inform the environment about our actions or intentions, in order to show what we are doing, where and when we are doing it. Studies on the interplay between touch and audition concerning object properties have mainly focused on contact properties such as hardness, stiffness and texture. For surface roughness and stiffness it has been shown [8], that touch dominates over audition, but both of them can improve the perception or even create illusions (see [9] for an example of auditory-haptic illusion).

In light of these perceptual studies, simultaneous audio-haptic rendering is a particularly interesting problem in the development of enactive multimodal interfaces. Recent literature has proposed *physically-based models* for sound synthesis, i.e. sound synthesis algorithms based on a physical description of sound generating mechanisms. Since the resulting computational structures respond to physical input parameters, they automatically incorporate complex responsive acoustic behaviors. A second quality of physically-based approaches concerns interactivity and ease in associating motion to sound control. As an example, the parameters needed to characterize collision sounds, e.g. relative velocity at collision, can be directly used to control a physically-based model, and the sound feedback responds consequently to gestures and actions in a natural way. Various approaches have been proposed in the literature for contact sound modeling. Modal synthesis [10] was proposed in [11] as a framework for describing the acoustic properties of objects; the modal representation is naturally linked to many *ecological* dimensions of the corresponding sounds: modal frequencies depend on *shape* and geometry of the object, *materials* determine the sound decay characteristics, and so on. Physically-based models for real-time synchronous haptic-sound rendering is an approach that will ensure synchronization and perceptual similarity between haptic and audio feedback. A significant amount of recent literature deals with this problem. In [12] the modal synthesis techniques described in [11] were applied to audio-haptic rendering. A related study was recently conducted in [13]: physically-based sound models were integrated into a multimodal rendering architecture, and the setup was used to run an experiment on the relative contributions of haptic and auditory information to bimodal judgments of contact stiffness.

4   Inspiring Related Research

Pioneering works in the field of innovative toys for children are due to Seymour Papert, who developed the Logo programming language (the first children toys with built-in computation), and to Mitchel Resnick, whose research group developed the "programmable brick" technology that inspired the LEGO Mind-Storms robotics kit and the PicoCricket artistic-invention kit [14,15]. Existing applications in this area can be categorized according to broad keywords that are commonly encountered in commercial product and research: Education [16], Physical programming [17], Interactive story telling [18], Collaboration [19,20]. These general trends offer a large variety of applications that deal with the cognitive level: creating dancing creatures, animated stories, video games, and interactive/collaborative painters focus on cognitive processes based on a bottom-up communication of meanings [21]. Moreover, multimodal information provided by these toys is typically based on iconic messages, resulting in poor interaction, e.g. based on triggering some kind of recorded sample. None of the applications reviewed here is really related to enactive concepts, despite learning by doing is arguably the most efficient and effective form of exchange between e.g. the teacher and the student.

In the following section we will describe the typical interaction that will be provided by enactoys with the help of a couple of scenario examples, underlying the learning process that such toys can elicit.

5 Scenarios

The first years of a baby life are a continuous discovery: a child starts to learn which reactions he produces in the world around him, how things sound, move, smell and how they can be used. Everything can become a toy and the boundary between a tool, a toy, and a simple gadget is never clear and determined. In particular pre-scholar babies spend hours playing with very simple objects that become whatever they wish, according to their shape or properties. A large pillow can become a spaceship, while an empty box can be knocked with the hands or with a spoon and it can become a drum or the door of a little house. Any object can stimulate the imagination of babies, and the general rule is that the simpler the object is, the bigger are the transformations it can perform in the baby's mind. Children, objects and environment can be considered as the three key elements in a play scenario, as described by Garvey [22]: "They (ndr. objects) provide a means by which a child can represent or express his feelings, concerns, or preoccupying interests. (...) Further, for the child an unfamiliar object tends to set up a chain of exploration, familiarization, and eventual understanding: an often-repeated sequence that will eventually lead to more mature conceptions of the properties (shape, texture, size) of the physical world". Following these ideas, one has to create simple toy–objects that, once explored, exhibit their multimodal properties while suggesting basic and complex reactions and interactions and improving the learning process and the motor skills of children.

> **Design Paradigm N.1:** *Children impose their own meaning and mental imagery over toys and things: there is no need to explicitly suggest specific roles, functions and/or images with toys. Rather, toys should react to children actions, providing a sensible mix between redundant and unexpected information.*

The interaction with the world requires the integration of information through different senses and we should keep all the senses in mind while designing toys for children: different abilities and capacities should be stimulated and enhanced from the same tool, allowing visually impaired children and unimpaired ones to play together on equal terms. All these aspects are particularly important in building toys for visually impaired children:

> **Design Paradigm N.2:** *toys must be designed for children abilities rather than be compensating for their disabilities.*

Fig. 1. The playground: simple objects enhanced by actuators and sensors can represent different environments

For all these reasons, we are interested in creating toys which present the following characteristics: (i) focused on enactive knowledge, (ii) enhanced by haptic, auditory and olfactory feedback to provide expressive output, (iii) embedded with sensors which trigger continuous interaction, (iv) reconfigurable to stimulate children's creativity and collaboration. All these characteristics are needed to provide a learn and play context that enhances the autonomy of the child and the collaboration with other children and that focuses on the abilities of the child.

5.1   Scenario 1: Playground

The playground is designed to stimulate and motivate the child to explore the environment in order to experience cause and effect of his/her actions and to learn from physical play and manipulation of objects their characteristics and their relationships. The aim is also to engage children through more full-body play patterns. The basic idea is to let the child explore a special carpet on top of which several simple objects (cubes, spheres) of different sizes and materials will be placed, as shown in Figure 1. The set-up sketched in this figure may represents, according to the initial settings, different environments: a kitchen, a garden, a beach, the bathroom etc. The child can discover what kind of environment she/he is exploring by walking, touching and shaking and smelling the objects, talking to them. Synthetically simulated footsteps may even be produced while the children wander in the different locations of the environment.

The set-up may be realized by using a kit similar to traditional Duplo Lego kits, enhanced by low cost sensing and control (e.g. phidgets technology[1]) in order to enhance the children's awareness of everyday life's multimodal feedback. According to the environment that it is simulated, the different objects may

---

[1] http://www.phidgets.com

Table 1. The kitchen playground scenario

Objects	Metaphors	Technology
carpet	parquet, broken glasses, liquid sounds or boiling water	pressure sensors
large cylinder	the blender, if you squeeze it, it will start blending	accelerometers, pressure sensors, RFID technology, synthetic receptors
small cylinders	spoon(wood) and knife(metal)	tactile actuators, equipment for measuring static or dynamic forces or torque
large cube	the pot (hitting the pot with the small cylinder will produce a percussive sound) moving the pot some water could fall	RFID technology, accelerometers, haptic and vibrotactile sensors
small cubes	dishes: if the child make them fall on the ground they will break	accelerometers, pressure sensors
big sphere	the dish-washing machine: the child can open and close it, put inside the smaller objects: shaking it he will identify the number of objects that are inside	RFID technology, vibrotactile sensors
small spheres	spices: if you shake them they smell like coffee or spices	smell actuators, controllers for measuring the humidity and the temperature

be programmed to assume different characteristics: in the Table 5.1 a "kitchen scenario" is described as example. Some of the objects may also assume animate and/or expressive behaviors: as an example, in a garden-like environment a simple cylinder will be a dog and will bark in different ways according to the child voice or gestures, interacting with him according to some expressive features extracted from the child's voice.

5.2   Scenario 2: The Reactoy–Band

Tangible user interfaces and more precisely, table based tangible interfaces in which digital information becomes graspable with the direct manipulation of simple objects available on a table surface, can fulfil many of the special needs required in designing inclusive toys. They allow an intimate and sensitive control, with a more macro-structural and higher level control which is intermittently shared, transferred and recovered between the children and the machine. Tabletop interfaces favor multi-parametric and shared control, exploration and multi-user collaboration, while they can also allow delicate and intimate interaction (e.g. moving and turning two objects with both hands). Seamless integration of visual and tactile feedback with physical control allows for natural and direct interaction. Designing for children abilities means to design toys to be fun and enjoyable also for non visually impaired children, encouraging in this way the

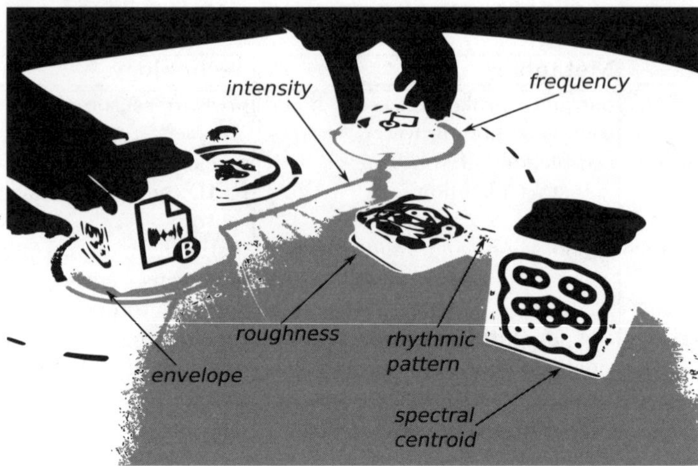

Fig. 2. Users interacting in the reactoy band scenario (the original picture of the reacTable device was taken from http://mtg.upf.es/reactable)

collaboration between children with different abilities as if they were different players in a common orchestra.

An example of a tabletop tangible musical interface is the reacTable [23]. Several musicians can share the control of the instrument by caressing, rotating and moving physical artifacts on a table, constructing different audio topologies in a kind of tangible modular synthesizer or graspable flow-controlled programming language. The objects interact with each other based on their proximity and their affinity, creating complex networks of flowing sound. Originally the resulting animated waveforms are projected from under the table, giving the performers a visual feedback which very reflects the sound flowing through the sonic network and all the inner workings of the sound generating mechanisms.

This kind of tangible musical interfaces can represent a perfect scenario for a collaborative toy that stimulates children to play a collaborative instrument that stimulates all their capabilities and collaboration by making music together around a table. The social affordances associated with tables directly encourage concepts such as "social interaction and collaboration" [24] or "ludic interaction" [25]. Tabletop interfaces should by definition include several simultaneous users, each using both hands and several objects at the same time. Visually impaired children may discover the function of each object perceiving its shape and the texture of its surface. They may understand the relationship between objects movements and effects on the music that they are hearing by simply manipulating the objects on the table. Vibro-tactile feedback, specific actuators and auditory feedback can give information about object states and table topology.

6   Conclusions

This exploratory work proposes a new way to think about toys for children, taking the particular perspective of multimodal interaction. We called these objects *enactoys* since they provide interaction based on the enactive paradigm, where multimodal feedback is intimately tied to action – i.e. the human is "in the loop". The enactoys can create new opportunities for playing and learning–through–play, as well as greatly improving accessibility and inclusion for children with special needs, who will be able to play on equal terms with sighted peers. Research in this direction has to combine state of–the–art technology on multimodal interfaces, techniques for the extraction of high-level expressive features from gestures and sound, and participatory design methodologies, in order to investigate how to design interactive objects that empower children to create their own environments and play patterns.

Acknowledgments. This research was partially supported by the EU Sixth Framework Programme – IST Information Society Technologies (Network of Excellence "Enactive Interfaces" IST-1-002114, http://www.enactivenetwork.org).

References

1. Noe, A.: Action in perception. MIT Press, Cambridge (2005)
2. Varela, F., Thompson, E., Rosch, E.: The Embodied Mind. MIT Press, Cambridge (1991)
3. Luciani, A., Florens, J., Castagne, N.: From action to sound: a challenging perspective for haptics. In: Workshop on Enactive Interfaces (Enactive 2005), Pisa, Italy (January 2005)
4. Picard, R.: Affective computing. MIT Press, Cambridge (1997)
5. Dore, J.: Feeling, form, and intention in the baby's transition to language. In: Golinkoff, R.M. (ed.) The transition from prelinguistic to linguistic communication (1983)
6. Sabbadini, A.: On sounds, children, identity and a 'quite unmusical' man. Br. J. Psychother. 14(2), 189–196 (1997)
7. De Poli, G., Avanzini, F., Rodà, A., Mion, L., D'Incà, G., Trestino, C., Pirrò, C., Luciani, A., Castagne, A.: Towards a multi-layer architecture for multi-modal rendering of expressive actions. In: Proceedings of 2nd International Conference on Enactive Interfaces (Enactive 2005), Genova, Italy (November 2005)
8. Lederman, S., Klatzky, R., Morgan, T., Hamilton, C.: Integrating multimodal information about surface texture via a probe: relative contribution of haptic and touch-produced sound sources. In: Symp. Haptic interfaces for virtual environment and Teleoperator Systems (HAPTICS 2002), Orlando, FL (2002)
9. Bresciani, J.P., Ernst, M.O., Drewing, K., Bouyer, G., Maury, V., Kheddar, A.: Feeling what you hear: auditory signals can modulate tactile tap perception. Exp. Brain Research 162(2), 172–180 (2005)
10. Adrien, J.M.: The missing link: Modal synthesis. In: De Poli, G., Piccialli, A., Roads, C. (eds.) Representations of Musical Signals, pp. 269–297. MIT Press, Cambridge (1991)

11. van den Doel, K., Pai, D.K.: The sounds of physical shapes. Presence: Teleoperators and Virtual Environment 7(4), 382–395 (1998)
12. DiFilippo, D., Pai, D.K.: The AHI: An audio and haptic interface for contact interactions. In: Proc. ACM Symp. on User Interface Software and Technology (UIST 2000), San Diego, CA (November 2000)
13. Avanzini, F., Crosato, P.: Integrating physically-based sound models in a multimodal rendering architecture. Comp. Anim. Virtual Worlds 17(3-4), 411–419 (2006)
14. Seymour, P.: The Children's Machine: Rethinking School in the Age of the Computer. Basic Books, New York (1993)
15. Wallich, P.: Mindstorms: not just a kid's toy. IEEE Spectrum 38(9), 52–57 (2001)
16. Hengeveld, B., Hummels, C., Voort, R., van Balkom, H., de Moor, J.: Designing for diversity: developing complex adaptive tangible products. In: Proceedings of the 1st International Conference on Tangible and embedded interaction, pp. 155–158 (2007)
17. Magerkurth, C., Engelke, T., Memisoglu, M.: Augmenting the virtual domain with physical and social elements. In: Proceedings of the International Conference on Advancements in Computer Entertainment Technology, pp. 163–172 (2004)
18. Montemayor, J., Druin, A., Chipman, L., Farber, A., Guha, M.: Sensing, storytelling, and children: Putting users in control. Technical report, University of Maryland, Computer Science Department (2004)
19. Konkel, M., Leong, V., Ullmer, B., Hu, C.: Tagaboo: A collaborative children's game based on wearable RFID technology. ACM Journal of Ubiquitous Computing 8(5), 382–384 (2004)
20. Itoh, Y., Akinobu, S., Ichida, H., Watanabe, R., Kitamura, Y., Kishino, F.: TSU.MI.KI: stimulating children's creativity and imagination with interactive blocks. In: Proceedings of the 2nd International Conference on Creating, Connecting and Collaborating through Computing 2004, pp. 62–70 (2004)
21. Nakamura, I., Mori, H.: Play and learning in the digital future. IEEE Micro 19(6), 36–42 (1999)
22. Garvey, C.: Play. Harvard Univ. Press, Cambridge (1990)
23. Kaltenbrunner, M., Jordà, S., Geiger, G., Alonso, M.: The reacTable*: A collaborative musical instrument. In: Proceedings of the Workshop on Tangible Interaction in Collaborative Environments (TICE), at the 15th International IEEE Workshops on Enabling Technologies (WETICE 2006), Manchester (2006)
24. Hornecker, E., Buur, J.: Getting a grip on tangible interaction: A framework on physical space and social interaction. In: Proceedings of the ACM International Conference on Computer-Human Interaction (CHI 2006), pp. 437–446 (2006)
25. Gaver, W., Bowers, J., Boucher, A., Gellerson, H., Pennington, S., Schmidt, A., Steed, A., Villars, N., Walker, B.: The drift table: designing for ludic engagement. In: Proceedings of the ACM International Conference on Computer-Human Interaction (CHI 2004), Extended abstracts on human factors in computing systems, pp. 885–900 (2004)

Psychoacoustic Manipulation of the Sound-Induced Illusory Flash

Sonia Wilkie, Catherine Stevens, and Roger Dean

MARCS Auditory Laboratories, University of Western Sydney,
Locked Bag 1797, Penrith South DC, Sydney, Australia
s.wilkie@uws.edu.au, kj.stevens@uws.edu.au,
roger.dean@uws.edu.au
http://marcs.uws.edu.au

Abstract. Psychological research on cross-modal auditory-visual perception has focused on the manipulation of sensory information predominantly by visual information. There are relatively few studies of the way auditory stimuli may affect other sensory information.

The Sound-induced Illusory Flash is one illusory paradigm that involves the auditory system biasing other senses. However, little is known about the cross-modal illusion. More research is needed into the structure of the illusion that investigates the different conditions under which the Sound-induced Illusory Flash manifests and is enhanced or reduced.

The experiment reported here investigates the effect of new auditory stimulus variables on the Sound-induced Illusory Flash. The variables to be discussed concern forming a contrast in the auditory stimulus to emphasise the illusory percept. The auditory contrasts used were single pitched beeps versus those alternating in pitch by an octave, and the presentation of sound monaurally versus binaurally.

The ultimate aim is to develop the illusory effect as a basis for new intermedia techniques and creative applications for the temporal manipulation and spatialisation of visual objects.

Keywords: Sound-induced Illusory Flash, cross-modal illusion, multisensory interaction, auditory-visual perception, temporal bias, pitch interval, spatialisation.

1 Background

Research on cross-modal interactions in auditory and visual perception has focused predominantly on conditions where visual stimuli are used to manipulate auditory perception (e.g. Alais & Burr, 2004; McGurk & Macdonald, 1976). The results of these experiments suggest that vision is the dominant sense. However, the Sound-induced Illusory Flash (Shams, Kamitani & Shimojo, 2002) exploits the capacity of the auditory system to distort visual perception.

Conditions that give rise to this cross-modal illusion involve presentation of a visual stimulus consisting of a single white dot that is flashed once in the participant's peripheral visual field. This is accompanied by an auditory stimulus of multiple beeps

R. Kronland-Martinet, S. Ystad, and K. Jensen (Eds.): CMMR 2007, LNCS 4969, pp. 223–234, 2008.

of sound. The dual presentation of temporal stimuli appearing to emanate from a single source creates confusion regarding the number of physical flashes perceived and gives rise to the percept that the dot flashes almost as many times as there are beeps. This illusory percept appears to occur because of the superior temporal resolution of the auditory system over the visual system which, in this case, overrides visual information (see comments of Sinex, 1978).

The Sound-induced Illusory Flash is a relatively recent discovery (Shams, Kamitani & Shimojo, 2000). Whilst research (Shams, Iwaki, Chawla & Bhattacharya, 2005; Shams, 2005) has focused on neural mechanisms that underpin the illusion, only the initial studies (Shams, 2002; Shimojo & Shams, 2001; Shimojo, Scheier, Nijhawan, Shams, Kamitani & Watanabe, 2001) explore basic variables of auditory structure that give rise to the illusion. It is these structural variables that are of interest for further exploration of the illusion experience. Investigation of the illusion in this way provides new opportunities for creative applications and intermedia transmission techniques where auditory stimuli might influence visual perception in novel and interesting ways.

2 The Sound-Induced Illusory Flash and Auditory Stimulus Variables – A Review

The variables manipulated in previous research consist primarily of differing combinations of the number of auditory and visual stimuli presented (Shams, Kamitani, & Shimojo, 2002), with only minor adjustments to stimuli across experiments such as pitch frequency at 1kHz or 3.5kHz, the transmission of auditory stimuli through headphones or speakers, and background screen colour of grey or black. The flashes and the beeps were each presented with a constant inter-stimulus interval. The minute alterations of the stimuli were not considered by Shams and colleagues as significant variables, hence there has been little discussion of their effects or interactions.

Brief discussion of the visual stimulus concludes that the illusory percept is stronger when the dots are placed in the periphery rather than fovea (Shimojo, Scheier, Nijhawan, Shams, Kamitani & Watanabe, 2001), but there have been no published studies on the optimal spatial position in peripheral vision. The number of dots presented has been varied. However, multiple dots or correlations with auditory spatialisation have not been investigated.

2.1 Visual and Auditory Rhythms

Shams, Kamitani and Shimojo (2000) used constant intervals between beeps of constant length. This established a constant pulse but no rhythmic or metrical structure was superimposed. For this to be achieved, either some beeps would need greater intensity, or some other novel feature arranged in a recurrent pattern. A broad examination of research into auditory perception, and more specifically, auditory scene analysis (e.g., Bregman), reveals that rhythm of stimuli and its time scale may be important variables. In the context of the Sound-induced Illusory Flash it has only been shown that if the inter-beep time exceeds 70ms the flash illusion is diminished (Shams, 2002).

Whilst this research explores the elementary formations of rhythm, research has not investigated the inter-stimulus interval that would cause perceptual fusion between the auditory and visual stimuli, nor has it investigated the combination of various durations to form rhythmic motifs, or the potential for auditory rhythm motifs to create perception of visual rhythm. Shams, Kamitani & Shimojo (2002) simply noted that "Moderate manipulation of the relative and absolute timings of the auditory and visual stimuli .... do not disrupt the illusion" (p. 152).

To have confidence in this strong conclusion, there is a need for closer and systematic examination of the spatial disparity and inter-stimulus interval for both large and short durations and the effects on fusion.

2.2 Manipulation of Fine-Grained Time Scale

Time scale is an important variable that has been employed and manipulated in many illusory paradigms. The capture of sensory information may increase with time; therefore, misperception sometimes occurs from insufficient time to process perceptual information. Employment of micro-time scales as a variable includes microsound (Roads, 1996; Roads, 2001) with stimuli generated at 600ms or less; the Octave / Scale / Chromatic Illusion (Deutsch, 1981; Deutsch, 1975) involves auditory stimuli of 250ms; The Illusory Continuity of Tones (Bregman, 1999) consists of noise at 50ms or less; and the Auditory Driving of Visual Flicker (Shipley, 1964) comprises auditory stimuli at 150ms.   For these examples, the micro time scale may limit perceptual processing resulting in an illusory percept. When the stimulus is presented on larger time scales, the provision of time allows for the acquisition of a greater amount of sensory information, that results in a more accurate representation of the physical stimulus and the illusions begin to fragment.

We have begun to explore the structural variable of auditory rhythm, a musical parameter, in the current research. We predicted that the formation of an auditory rhythmic pattern might influence the extent of illusion differently from the condition in which the auditory stimulus is merely pulsed. We next discuss other musical parameters that may influence the illusion.

2.3 Frequency and Pitch Interval

Frequency has been used only rarely as a stimulus variable for cross-modal manipulation even though Marks demonstrated clear correlations between the percepts of greyness, pitch height and loudness (Marks, 1974). Subjects, for example, stated that low pitches were greyer in colour than high. While pitch has hardly been manipulated in cross-modal illusions, it is at the core of several uni-modal auditory illusions. For example, the Octave Illusion (Deutsch, 1974; Deutsch, 1983), Scale Illusion (Deutsch, 1975) and the Chromatic illusion (Deutsch, 1988), pit the perceptual grouping principles of similarity of frequency and spatialisation against one another resulting in an illusory percept based on pitch proximity. It is possible that both of these variables – pitch relationship and spatial location – may translate to cross-modal illusions in which they influence the judgement of visual stimuli.

The variable of intervallic harmonic relationship can be used to distort perceived direction of motion of consecutive tones. This variable is most notably exploited in investigations of the Tritone Paradox (Deutsch, 1986) that employ multiple layered frequencies around the octave; and Shepard Tones (Shepard, 1964; Risset, 1972; Risset, 1986) that consist of multiple layered frequencies with partials related to the octave or augmented 5th. We argue that the main impact of pitch patterns upon the flash illusion will operate via the formation of a coherent auditory stream: conditions which accentuate such auditory streaming may facilitate the illusion. Since the octave relationship (frequencies in a 1 : 2 ratio) is the closest within tonal harmony, we chose this pitch pattern.

2.4 Stream Segregation and Spatialisation

The organisation of sound to encourage perception as coherent streams is achieved by using a contrast in the stimulus, so that similar, proximal, continuous frequencies, durations or timbres are grouped and associated as emanating from related sources (Bregman, 1999).

Stream segregation is often exemplified with the use of frequency separation, but may also be elicited by factors including a contrast of timbres, spatial proximity of sound, rhythms, amplitudes, and envelopes. These variables have been extensively researched by Bregman (1999) and van Noorden (1977). They have potential for rich creative application as a musical technique using monophonic instruments. For example, spatialisation can be manipulated by headphone presentation of a sound either monaurally (with the same signal in each channel) or binaurally (with the signal in only one or the other channel).

Our prediction was that a pitch or spatial pattern articulating the successive beeps into a metrical structure, superimposed on the basic pulse structure, would enhance the illusion.

2.5 Interim Summary

Thus, there is a need for investigation of new variables – pitch interval and spatialisation – and their effects on auditory-visual perception. In the experiment presented here, pitch interval and spatialisation were used for purposes of illusory emphasis. We anticipated that their application as variables to articulate auditory rhythm, should impact on the Sound-induced Illusory Flash and might enhance the illusion.

2.6 Aim

The aim of the experiment was to investigate the effect of pitch interval and spatialised presentation on the impact of a series of beeps of constant inter-stimulus interval on the Sound-induced Illusory Flash.

2.7 Design

The experimental design consisted of three independent variables. These were the number of auditory stimulus beeps, two, three, four and five; the pitch interval separation of the beeps with the Unison set at 261.5Hz and Octave separation of 261.5 and

523Hz; and the spatialisation of sound with monaural versus binaural presentation. Using headphones, the monaural condition transmitted the auditory stimulus through the left and right channels concurrently, whilst the binaural presentation alternated between the left and right channels. The number of beeps and pitch interval variable were presented within subjects and the spatial presentation variable between subjects.

The dependent variable concerned the visual stimulus and was the number of events perceived, that is, the perceived number of times the dot appeared.

The visual stimulus remained the same in the illusory trials, with the independent variables concerning only the aural stimuli.

2.8 Hypotheses

It was hypothesised that introducing a contrast in the auditory stimulus will cohere the series of individual beeps into a stream, drawing attention to and articulating individual beeps, thereby emphasising the illusory percept.

The contrast in the auditory stimulus is created by using a pitch separation of the octave, and spatial separation with individual beeps presented binaurally alternating between left and right channels.

It was hypothesised that the octave interval creates a greater illusory percept than the unison eliciting perception of two auditory fixation points corresponding to the high and low pitches (reflective of enhanced auditory stream coherence due to superimposition of rhythmic pattern upon pulse). The dot will be perceived to flicker accordingly and rhythmically, emphasising the illusory effect.

It was hypothesised that binaural spatial presentation creates a greater illusory percept than monaural presentation. Binaural presentation draws spatial attention to individual beeps and again articulates a rhythmic pattern that may further enhance the illusory effect.

3 Method

3.1 Participants

A sample of 40 participants naïve to the illusion were recruited. They were Psychology 1A students from the University of Western Sydney and received course credit for their participation. Participants were aged between 17 and 54 years ($M = 21.18$ years, $SD = 6.68$), with more female participants than male participants (36 female, 4 male). People reporting a hearing impairment, visual impairment (corrected to normal vision allowed), severe migraines or epilepsy were excluded from testing.

3.2 Stimuli

The visual stimulus consisted of a centrally located fixation point, and a single white dot positioned below the centre of the screen that was located in the participants' peripheral vision. The visual angle of the dot subtended 2° below the fixation point.

Fig. 1. Screen Capture of the visual stimulus. The fixation point is the centrally located cross. The dot appeared 2° below the fixation point for 17 ms.

The visual angle of the dot to fixation point, onset times, and durations of both the visual and auditory stimulus were derived from those used by Shams, Kamitani & Shimojo (2002). The auditory stimulus consisted of a sine tone generated every 50ms and lasting for a total of 7ms (attack 2ms, sustain 3ms, decay 2ms). The frequencies of the pitches used were the unison set at 261.5Hz and the Octave separation set at 261.5 and 523Hz. The visual stimulus dot was presented for 17ms, a duration that remained the same in all trials. However, the onset time of the dot presentation varied according to the number of beeps presented.

In 2-beep illusory trials the dot was presented 23ms after the auditory stimulus onset (Fig 2 illustrates this particular case); in 3-beep illusory trials the dot was presented 50ms after the auditory stimulus onset and at the same time as the second beep; in 4-beep illusory trials the dot was presented 73ms after the auditory stimulus; and in 5-beep illusory trials the dot was presented 100ms after the auditory stimulus onset and at the same time as the third beep.

Trials were also included where the dot was presented at the same time and as many times as the auditory beeps, i.e., two physical flashes with two auditory beeps; three physical flashes with three auditory beeps; etc. These trials were included as a

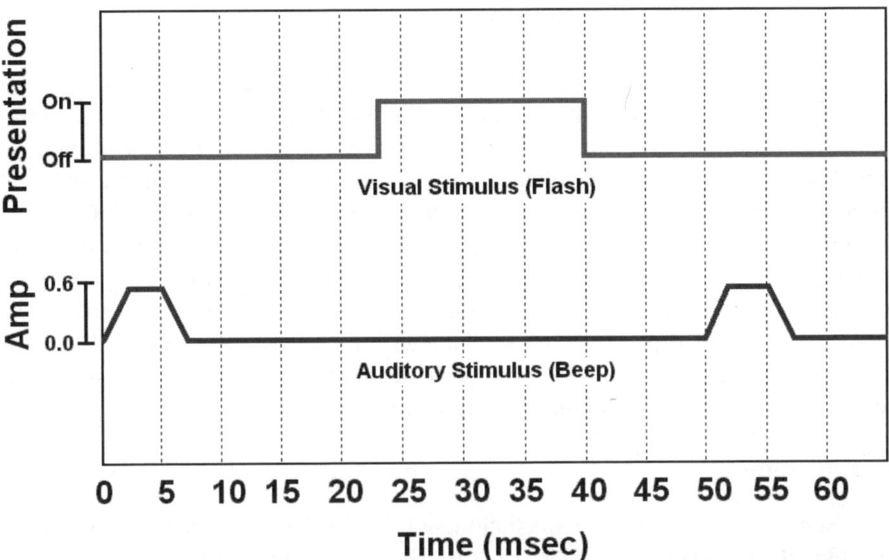

Fig. 2. Stimulus onset time for 2 beep illusory trial. The auditory stimulus is presented every 50ms and lasts for a duration of 7ms (attack 2ms, sustain 3ms, decay 2ms). The visual stimulus is presented 23ms after the auditory stimulus onset, and for a duration of 17ms.

rationale to disqualify participants with poor performance, however they may have biased the illusory percept by causing participants to expect multiple physical flashes. All trials were presented in a random order with equal chance of the stimulus being illusory or not. Our equal presentation ratio of illusory to physical flash trials is greater than that of the 15 illusory trials to 45 physical trials used by Shams, Kamitani & Shimojo (2002). Therefore, our expectation bias should be lesser than theirs.

Presented with 32 conditions in total (16 illusory flash conditions, 16 physical flash conditions), all participants were presented with trials using the variables of pitch interval (unison versus octave) and number of beeps (two, three, four and five presentations). The spatial presentation (monaural versus binaural) variable was divided into two blocks with participants receiving either monaural or binaural presentation.

3.3 Apparatus

Participants were located at computer workstations with their head positioned on a chin rest 40cm from the computer monitor and eyes level with the fixation point.

A Mac Pro G5 with a Diamond Digital cathode-ray-tube (CRT) monitor (85 Hz refresh rate) was used and sound was presented through AKG K271 headphones.

The software MAX / MSP was used to construct an application that generated the auditory and visual stimulus; presented the trials in a randomised and collected order (using the urn object); generated the questionnaire as an onscreen pop-up window; and collected the participants responses in a text file.

The presentation of the visual stimulus was recorded with a Vision Research Phantom V10 high-speed camera to determine its duration. The camera, recording with a frame rate of 1ms, showed that the presentation of the dot indeed occupied 17ms. However, the computer monitor's refresh rate presented horizontal contrasts in luminance, with complete fading of the dot at 8ms from onset, for a duration of 5ms.

This is perhaps the first high speed recording of the visual stimulus to determine the physical nature of the presentation and raises the question of the impact of the raster scan and refresh rate of the monitor on illusory percept of the illusion. However, as the stimulus is presented on such a micro time scale, the window of visibility should not impact on the temporal percept (Zele and Vingrys, 2004). It is also highly likely that our refresh rate is comparable to that used by Shams.

3.4 Procedure

Participants sat at a computer workstation and were informed of the experiment and procedure. They were given an information sheet, summarising both the experiment procedure and the ethics approval, and they signed a consent form. They were instructed to put on headphones, place their head on the chin rest, to focus on the fixation point and use their peripheral vision to count the number of times a dot was presented. Participants were assigned alternately to monaural or binaural auditory stimulus presentation.

The task required them to state on an onscreen multiple choice questionnaire the number times the dot was presented, ranging from one event to five events, within an 8 second time limit. Each trial lasted for 11 – 13 seconds. With a total of 96 trial presentations the experiment lasted for approximately 19 minutes.

4 Results

The data collected in the experiment refer to the number of flashes perceived. The experiment recovered the previously described illusion and, as hypothesised, pitch interval and binaural presentation enhanced the illusory effect. The mean perceived number of flashes, as a function of beep number, spatial presentation, and pitch separation, is shown in Figure 3.

We anticipated that the number of beeps would influence the perceived number of flashes. We performed a repeated measures analysis of variance that included two within subject variables - the number of beeps presented and the pitch interval, and one between subject variable of spatial presentation. As predicted, there was a main effect for number of beeps $F(3,36)=159.85$, $p<.001$. Our prediction that the use of pitches alternating at the octave would enhance the flash illusion was upheld : there was a main effect for pitch interval $F(1,38)=77.616$, $p<.001$, and an interaction between number of beeps x pitch interval $F(3,36)=15.09$, $p<.001$.

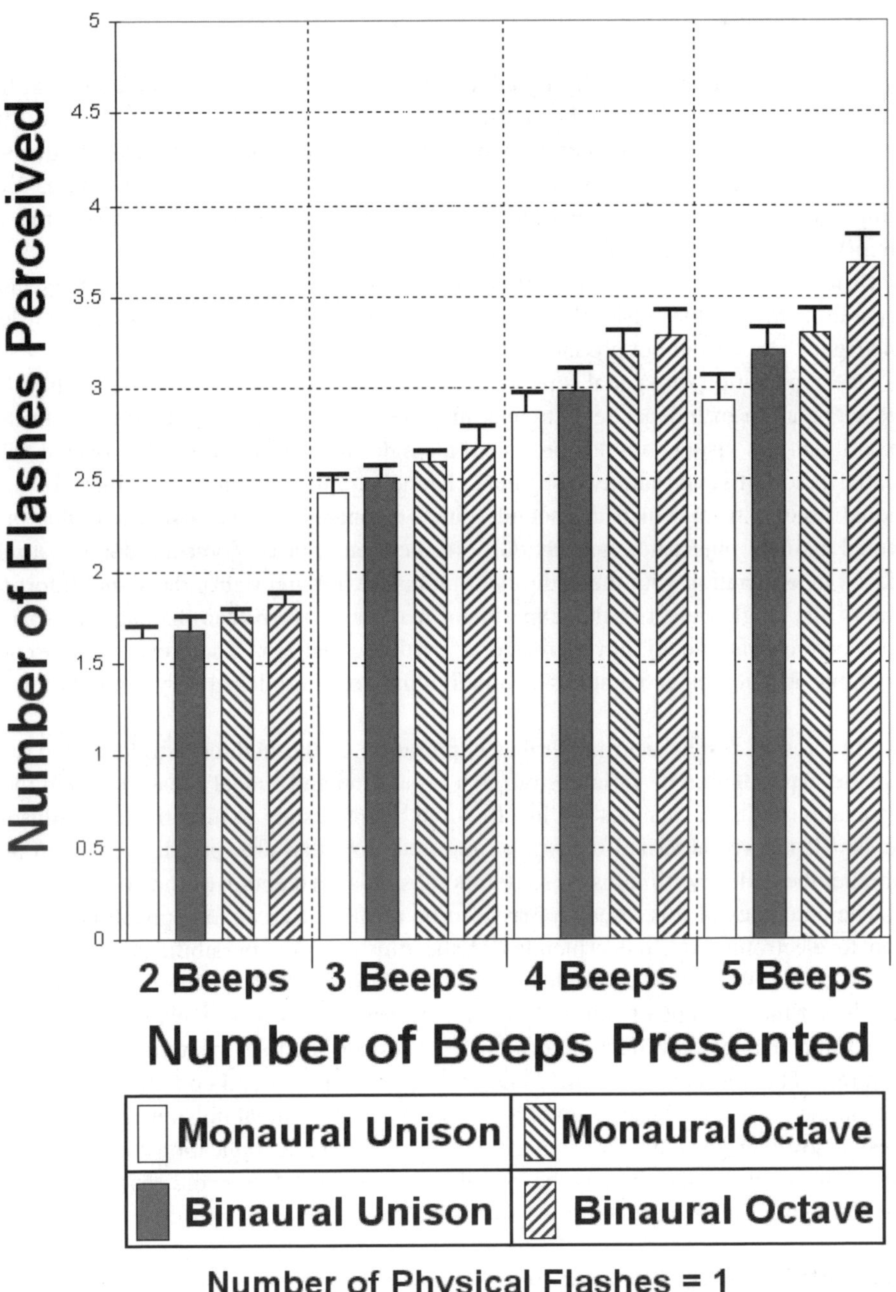

Fig. 3. The mean number of flashes perceived. Error bars refer to standard error of mean.

5 Discussion

The results indicate that modifying the auditory stimulus with the octave interval but not with binaural presentation enhanced the illusory effect of the Sound-induced Illusory Flash. That is, by creating a contrast between individual beeps with frequency separation using the octave interval segregated individual beeps which emphasised temporal information and influenced the visual event perceived. We interpret this as an influence of formation of rhythmic patterns.

However, the complementary rhythmic contrast that was created using spatial separation so that the binaural presentation alternated individual beeps between left and right channels did not produce a statistically significant effect.

One explanation for spatial separation not being as effective as pitch separation for the segregation of independent streams may be related to the visual stimulus. In this experiment the visual stimulus presented a single dot that was centrally located. The spatialisation of sound into two separate channels implies that there are multiple individual objects from which the sound source emanates. As the visual stimulus presented a single object that was centrally located, and not two objects (dots) spatially placed in association with the auditory stimulus (ie left and right), the visual information of the single object in this experiment may have overridden the auditory spatial information that would have created a rhythmic pattern. Therefore the lessened rhythmic articulation and emphasis on individual beeps produced very limited illusory effect.

The present results warrant further exploration of the auditory stimulus and systematic manipulation of variables of pitch separation and spatial separation, and their associations with the visual stimulus. It would be interesting to investigate the illusory percept if the visual stimulus involves multiple dots that are spatially separated and whether the auditory stimulus drives temporal spatial perception of the dots.

The outcomes of this research may also be useful for creative application. In relation to electronic arts, the principles of the illusion raise possibilities for use as a strobe effect. We (Dean, Whitelaw, Smith & Worrall, 2006, p317) have previously developed the concept of 'algorithmic synaesthesia' in which generated streams of sound and image share data, algorithmic processing, and segmentation, or all three features. The concept is primarily one of aesthetic and cultural cognition, and it was not claimed that it necessarily involves cross-modal perceptual illusion or true synaesthesia. However, the data here suggest that during creative applications of algorithmic synaesthetic processes, it may be possible to generate true cross-modal illusions, which might influence the cognitive and affective responses of viewers.

Acknowledgements. Thankyou to Dr. Freya Bailes for assistance with statistical analysis. The research reported here was supported by the University of Western Sydney Australian Postgraduate Award and Top-Up Award.

References

1. Alais, D., Burr, D.: The ventriloquist effect results from near-optimal bi-modal integration. Current Biology 14, 257–262 (2004)
2. Bhattacharya, J., Shams, L., Shimojo, S.: Sound-induced Illusory Flash Perception: Role of Gamma Band Responses. Cognitive Neuroscience and Neuropsychology 13, 14 (2002)
3. Bregman, A.: Auditory Scene Analysis. The MIT Press, Cambridge Massachusetts (1999)
4. Dean, R.T., Whitelaw, M., Smith, H., Worrall, D.: The mirage of real-time algorithmic synaesthesia: Some compositional mechanisms and research agendas in computer music and sonification. Contemporary Music Review 25, 311–327 (2006)
5. Deutsch, D.: An auditory illusion. Nature 251, 307–309 (1974)
6. Deutsch, D.: Two-channel listening to musical scales. Journal of the Acoustical Society of America 57, 1156–1160 (1975)
7. Deutsch, D.: The octave illusion and auditory perceptual integration. Hearing Research and Theory 1, 99–142 (1981)
8. Deutsch, D.: The octave illusion in relation to handedness and familial handedness background. Neuropsychologia 21, 289–293 (1983)
9. Deutsch, D.: A musical paradox. Music Perception 3, 27–280 (1986)
10. Deutsch, D.: The semitone paradox. Music Perception 6(2), 115–132 (1988)
11. Grove, R.: Thinking in Four Dimensions. Melbourne University Press, Melbourne (2005)
12. Marks, L.: On the associations of light and sound: the mediation of brightness, pitch, and loudness. American journal of psychology 87 (1974)
13. McGurk, H., Macdonald, J.: Hearing lips and seeing voices. Nature 264, 746–748 (1976)
14. Risset, J.-C.: Musical Acoustics. IRCAM, Paris (1972)
15. Risset, J.-C.: Pitch and rhythm paradoxes: Comments on 'Auditory paradox based on fractal waveform'. The journal of the Acoustical Society of America 80(3), 961–962 (1986)
16. Roads, C.: The Computer Music Tutorial. The MIT Press, Cambridge (1996)
17. Roads, C.: Microsound. The MIT Press, Cambridge (2001)
18. Shams, L.: Integration in the brain - the subconscious alteration of visual perception by cross-modal integration. Science and Consciousness Review 1, 1–4 (2002)
19. Shams, L., Iwaki, S., Chawla, A., Bhattacharya, J.: Early modulation of visual cortex by sound: an MEG study. Neuroscience Letters 378, 76–81 (2005)
20. Shams, L., Kamitani, Y., Shimojo, S.: What you see is what you hear. Nature 408, 788 (2000)
21. Shams, L., Kamitani, Y., Shimojo, S.: Visual illusion induced by sound. Cognitive Brain Research 14, 147–152 (2002)
22. Shams, L., Ma, W.J., Beierholm, U.: Sound-induced flash illusion as an optimal percept. Neuroreport 16, 17 (2005)
23. Shepard, R.: Circularity in judgements of relative pitch. Journal of the Acoustical Society of America 36, 2346–2353 (1964)
24. Shimojo, S., Scheier, C., Nijhawan, R., Shams, L., Kamitani, Y., Watanabe, K.: Beyond perceptual modality: auditory effects on visual perception. Acoustic Science and Technology 22(2), 61–67 (2001)
25. Shimojo, S., Shams, L.: Sensory modalities are not separate modalities: plasticity and interactions. Current opinion in neurobiology 11, 505–509 (2001)
26. Shipley, T.: Auditory flutter driving of visual flicker. Science 145, 1328–1330 (1964)

27. Sinex, D.G.: Cross-modality temporal resolution for auditory, vibrotactile and visual stimuli. Journal of the Acoustical Society of America 63(suppl. 1), 52 (1978)
28. van Noorden, L.P.A.S.: Minimum differences of level and frequency for perceptual fission of tone sequences ABAB. Journal of the Acoustical Society of America 61(4), 1041–1056 (1977)
29. Zele, A.J., Vingrys, A.J.: Cathode-ray-tube monitor artefacts in neurophysiology. Journal of Neuroscience Methods 141, 1–7 (2004)

On Cross-Modal Perception of Musical Tempo and the Speed of Human Movement

Kathleya Afanador, Ellen Campana, Todd Ingalls, Dilip Swaminathan,
Harvey Thornburg, Jodi James, Jessica Mumford, Gang Qian, and StJepan Rajko

Arts, Media and Engineering Program
Arizona State University
Tempe, AZ 85287-8709
United States

Abstract. Studies in crossmodal perception often use very simplified auditory and visual contexts. While these studies have been theoretically valuable, it is sometimes difficult to see how the findings can be ecologically valid or practically valuable. This study hypothesizes that a musical parameter (tempo) may affect the perception of a human movement quality (speed) and finds that although there are clear limitations, this may be a promising first step towards widening both the contexts in which cross-modal effects are studied and the application areas in which the findings can be used.

1 Introduction

Three intriguing occurrences—a misunderstood word, a talking puppet, and an elusive collision—have propelled the psychological research on cross-modal perception in which audition and vision are inextricably intertwined. These occurrences are now known as the McGurk Effect [16], the ventriloquist effect [1], and the bounce-inducing effect [28] respectively, and all three have proven remarkably robust. Yet the study of cross-modal perception currently relies heavily on behavioral experiments using simple sounds and simple animations. While these studies have been theoretically informative, their contexts are so simplified that it is often difficult to see how the findings can be ecologically valid or practically valuable. The present study examines possible cross-modal effects of a musical parameter (tempo) on the perception of a human movement quality (speed) in hopes that this may be a first step towards widening both the contexts in which cross-modal effects are studied and the application areas in which the findings can be used.

1.1 Cross-Modal Perception

Discussions about cross-modal perception often center around the McGurk effect or the ventriloquist effect and their variants, both of which are situations in which vision dominates the effect. This paper is primarily interested in the opposite situation—when sound affects vision—and thus draws from examples in which sound directly affects perception of spatial/temporal organization and visual movement. The way in

R. Kronland-Martinet, S. Ystad, and K. Jensen (Eds.): CMMR 2007, LNCS 4969, pp. 235–245, 2008.

which sound is combined, or not combined, with a visual display can influence perception of object organization and movement within the scene. O'Leary and Rhodes [21] for example, showed that the perceived organization of a sequence of high and low tones could influence the perceived organization of moving dots on a visual display. Auditory information alone may be perceived differently depending on tempo: at slow tempi, alternating high and low tones are perceived as a single stream of sound while at high tempi the high and low tones segregate into separate streams [4] The perception of visual information varies similarly: when dots are displayed moving from left to right in alternating high and low positions at slow rates, a viewer perceives a single dot moving up and down while at faster rates a viewer is more likely to perceive two dots moving horizontally. O'Leary and Rhodes showed that when the high and low tones were heard as two streams, viewers were more likely to see two dots even at rates which would, in a unimodal display, normally result in the perception of one dot. The perceptual organization of objects in the scene therefore also produced a change in the objects' perceived movement pathways. Examining this more directly, Sekuler, Sekuler, and Lau [28] showed that movement pathways can be interpreted differently in the absence or presence of sound through the bounce-inducing effect, where two moving targets are seen to stream through each other in silence but are seen to bounce off of each other when a sound is introduced at the moment of visual coincidence. This effect occurs because the visual stimulus is inherently ambiguous. Sound resolves the ambiguity by biasing a viewer to favor integrating sound and movement into a single event that makes sense [1].Yet Shams, Kamitani, and Shimojo [29] demonstrated that a single flash of light accompanied by multiple beeps is perceived as multiple flashes. Thus even when no ambiguity is present sound can qualitatively alter perception of a visual stimulus. These findings therefore support Vroomen and de Gelder's contention that "cross modal combinations of features not only enhance stimulus processing but can also change the percept." [31]

Perceptual judgment tasks have indicated that audition dominates vision in temporal processing. This is sometimes called auditory capture and it stems from claims that vision and audition are each more sensitive to spatial and temporal processing respectively and from evidence that one modality dominates the other when conflicting spatial and temporal information is presented. One such study by Repp and Penel [26] asked participants to tap their finger in synchrony with auditory and visual sequences containing an event onset shift, with the expectation that this would cause involuntary phase correction responses. Their auditory sequences consisted of identical high pitched piano tones and their visual sequences consisted of black X's on a screen and flashing lights. Within the unimodal conditions, audition produced the smallest variability in taps, larger phase correction responses, and better event onset shift detection. Interestingly, results from the bimodal condition were very similar to those of the unimodal auditory condition indicating that although viewers' attention was aimed at the visual sequences, they depended more upon auditory information to perform the task. If this holds true for more complex stimuli, it suggests the possibility that auditory information also dominates temporal perception when watching human movement. The bounce-inducing effect is additionally an example of congruence—the combination of two media that produces the perception of a relationship between them even when such relationships are coincidental. When two media are presented simultaneously, a viewer assumes relationships between the two media exist and thus looks for them [5][10][18]. Bolivar et al. termed this finding "visual capture" [5]; in other words, visual stimuli influence people to interpret simultaneously presented auditory stimuli as somehow related. Likewise auditory capture may occur from congruence, as when music influences people to perceive simultaneously presented visual material as somehow related. Lipscomb and Kendall [15] for example, paired an abstract film excerpt with a variety of different musical accompaniments and found that viewers perceived several musical choices as a "good fit." Similarly, Mitchell and Gallaher [18] paired three different dance sequences with three different musical sequences and found that congruence was perceived among several different combinations of dance and music (not only between the dance and its intended musical selection). Although Bolivar et al. used visual images with a strong narrative context in their experiment, the findings of Lipscomb and Kendall as well as those of Mitchell and Gallaher suggest that the simultaneous presentation of abstract sound and movement may be well suited to produce perceptions of similarity which may, in turn, facilitate crossmodal effects.

1.2 Music Perception and Human Motion

Perception of sound with human movement has been studied to some degree in the area of music perception as it relates to dance. Much of this work focuses on establishing congruence between music and dance by focusing specifically on dynamic qualities [9], general emotion or style [18], or section beginnings and endings [12] of both sound and movement. One recent study, however, examined the effects of various sound parameters on imagined motion. Eitan and Granot [8] asked participants in their experiments to visualize an animated human character (cartoon) of their choice. They were presented brief musical selections, and for each selection were asked to visualize their character moving in an imaginary animated film shot with the given melody as its soundtrack. Their purpose was to analyze the relationship between music and motion in imagined space based upon Clarke's [6] contention that "since sounds in the everyday world specify (among other things) the motional characteristics of their sources, it is inevitable that musical sounds will also specify…the fictional movements and gestures of the virtual environment which they conjure up" [8]. The experiment produced an asymmetrical model of imagined musical space—the fact that a musical stimulus seemed to suggest a particular kinetic quality did not imply that the opposite musical stimulus suggested the opposite kinetic quality. Central to the results of this experiment however, is the finding that by changing sound parameters, participants' imagined motion would change predictably. This suggests that there may be certain natural affinities between sound parameters and movement parameters, yet the asymmetries discovered suggest that the way these affinities are structured may be somewhat nuanced.

2 Experiment

Among the various sound parameters in Eitan and Granot's study, inter-onset-intervals (IOI, the interval of time between the onsets of successive sounds) were found to affect imagined motion most strongly and symmetrically. Decreasing and increasing intervals strongly influenced participants to imagine motion speeding up and slowing down respectively. In short, what we hear affects the movement we imagine. Historically and theoretically, this finding is not surprising. The association between tempo and human movement speed is arguably the most apparent sound-motion relationship. This association begins in early infancy, evident in high sensitivity towards "regular synchronization of vocal and kinesthetic patterns" [22] and this sensitivity continues to develop through childhood [19]. Humans seem to have an ingrained penchant for rhythmic synchronicity in their own movements [17], whether it is to synchronize with an auditory pulse or to synchronize with the movements of others around them. Phillips-Silver & Trainor have further established that for both infants and adults, auditory encoding of rhythmic patterns can be directly influenced by the movement of their own bodies [24][25]. In short, the movement we feel affects what we hear. Within the context of music and dance, it is also fairly common for different pieces of music to "bring out" different dynamic qualities in the same dance. Although this particular point has not been studied empirically, it may be supported somewhat by the congruence studies mentioned above and it hints at the possibility that a sonic change could cause a real change in the perception of a dynamic movement quality. In short, it may be suggested that what we hear affects the movement we see. Based on these reasons, the present study hypothesized that a decrease or increase in inter-onset-intervals would cause a change in the perception of visual movement speed. Would viewers be influenced to perceive a pairing of movement with a fast tempo as faster overall than a pairing of the same movement with a slow tempo? And if so, could it be conceptualized as a variation on auditory capture?

2.1 Method

Fourteen undergraduate students participated in this study on a voluntary basis and received one class credit for their time. They were instructed that the experiment was about the perception of human motion but beyond that, all were naïve to the purpose motivating this study. Stimuli consisted of videos showing six movements chosen from Laban Movement Analysis [14]—rising, sinking, advancing, retreating, spreading, and enclosing (Figure 1). A single dancer was recorded doing all six movements at three speeds—fast, medium, and slow—with a camcorder synchronized to a motion capture system resulting in 18 video clips and 18 corresponding motion capture data files.

The motion capture data was fed into a pattern recognition model, which analyzed the movement (100 frames/sec) based on the probability that one of these six movements was occurring (see Appendix for details). These probabilities were then put through a Max/MSP program, which generated sound from the data. The sounds produced were series of clicks, varying in IOI rate according to the speed of movement. Three base rates (550 ms, 500 ms, and 450 ms) and three maximum rates (150 ms, 100 ms, and 50 ms) were used to control the IOI and the probability ratings from the motion analysis determined the transition from base rate to maximum rate. Thus when no movement occurred, the IOI rate was simply the base rate; when fast movement occurred, the recognition model would rate the probability of one of these movements occurring very highly and consequently the IOI would decrease quickly but when slow movement occurred, the probability ratings increased more slowly causing the IOI also to decrease slowly. Each of the 18 data files was put through the Max/MSP

Fig. 1. The dancer demonstrating the shape qualities: rising, sinking, advancing, retreating, spreading, and enclosing

patch 9 times (one for each base rate/max rate pairing) and the resulting sound files were synchronized with their corresponding video clip, producing a total of 162 video clips. Participants watched the videos on a 20 inch wide screen computer and heard the sound through external speakers. They were presented each video individually followed by two statements with which they rated their agreement on a scale of 1 (strongly disagree) to 7 (strongly agree), indicated by numbered buttons. The first statement was always either "the movement was fast" or "the movement was slow." The second statement functioned primarily as a distracter. Participants saw each video exactly twice and responded to both the fast and slow statements for each video. The order in which the videos were presented was randomized and for each video, half of the participants responded to the fast statement first while half responded to the slow statement first.

2.2   Results

Changes in IOI were found to influence viewers' perception of human movement speed for one set of videos in our experiment. For the medium speed retreating movement, participants indicated significantly different levels of agreement with the statement "the movement was fast" as the minimum IOI length decreased, even though the actual movement they saw was identical across the different tempos. This difference was statistically significant ($F(2, 96) = 3.17$, $p < .05$). There were no statistically significant differences across inter-onset intervals for the other videos that we presented, although there was a main effect of actual movement speed (Figure 2), indicating that participants were attentive to movement speed and could accurately distinguish between slow, medium, and fast movements ($F(2, 1779) = 400.16$, $p < .01$).

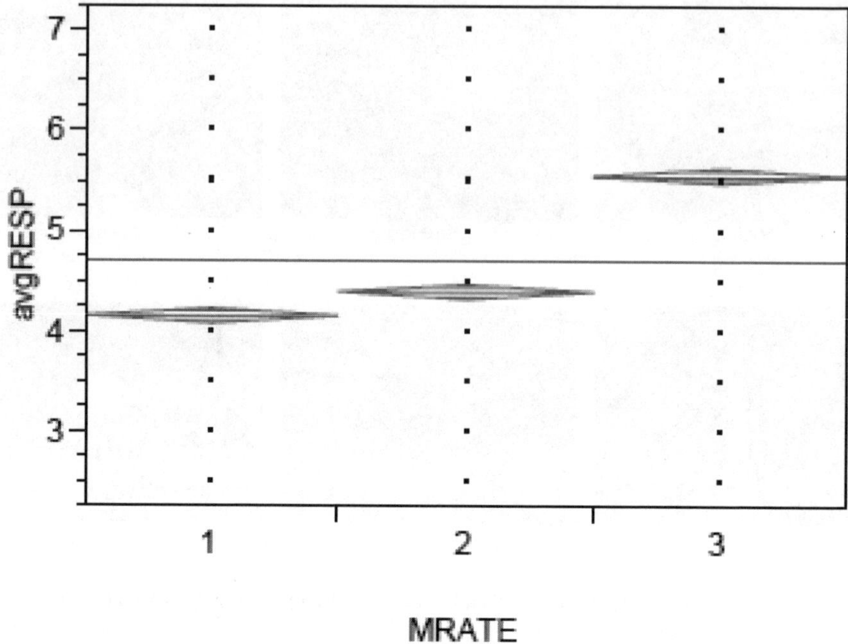

Fig. 2. This graph shows the average rating of movement speed (avgRESP) participants gave for the videos as a function of the actual speed of movement (MRATE). MRATE is defined as the actual movement rate and coded as 1 (slow), 2 (medium), and 3 (fast).

2.3 Discussion

The results provide some preliminary support for the hypothesis that differences in tempo, specifically inter-onset intervals, may be able to affect the perception of observed movement; however, the limitations of this study are clear. It is possible that the rating task used to measure perceived movement speed was either too cognitive or too coarse-grained. More precise measures achieved through a staircasing method may prove fruitful in attaining significant results. Additionally, it may be necessary to define objectively what is meant by slow, medium, and fast movement speeds. If many instances of cross-modal effects occur when there is ambiguity within one modality then it should be the case that ambiguous movement speed—the range within which it can be perceptually be interpreted as either fast or slow—would be most likely to show the effect. We are currently exploring both of these with additional tests.

3 Conclusions

Further studies will solidify the speculations prompted by this preliminary study and it remains to be seen how and where the findings of such studies can be applied. The various ways in which audition and vision have already been shown to interact make this area worth investigating further and furthermore, this area may prove interesting to artists and developers of computer interactive environments that use human movement as input. If sonic feedback is to be used as a response to movement, it will be informative to know what, if any, effects on human motion perception are caused by dynamic sound changes, how these effects may function differently within a given context, and how attention may facilitate or inhibit them.

References

[1] Alais, D., Burr, D.: The ventriloquist effect results from near-optimal bimodal integration. Current Biology 14(3), 257–262 (2004)

[2] Arulampalam, S., Maskell, S., Gordon, N., Clapp, T.: Tutorial on particle filters for on-line nonlinear/non-Gaussian Bayesian tracking. IEEE Transactions on Signal Processing (2001)

[3] Bishop, C.: Neural Networks for Pattern Recognition. Oxford University Press, Oxford (1995)

[4] Bregman, A.S.: Auditory scene analysis. MIT Press, Cambridge (1990)

[5] Bolivar, V.J., Cohen, A.J., Fentress, J.C.: Semantic and formal congruency in music and motion pictures: Effects the interpretation of visual action. Psychomusicology 2, 38–43 (1994)

[6] Clarke, E.F.: Meaning and the specification of motion in music. Musicae Scientiae 5, 213–234 (2001)

[7] Cover, T.M., Thomas, J.A.: Elements of Information Theory. John Wiley, Chichester (1999)

[8] Eitan, Z., Granot, R.: How music moves. Music Perception 23(3), 221–248 (2006)

[9] Hodgins, P.: Relationships between score and choreography in 20th century music and dance: Music and metaphor. Mellen, London (1992)

[10] Iwamiya, S.: Interactions between auditory and visual processing when listening to music in an audiovisual context. Psychomusicology 13, 133–154 (1994)

[11] Jaynes, E.T.: Probability Theory: Logic of Science. Cambridge (2003)

[12] Krumhansl, C.L., Schenck, D.L.: Can dance reflect the structural and expressive qualities of music?: A perceptual experiment on Balanchine's choreography of Mozart's Divertimento No. 5. Musicae Scientae 1(1), 63–85 (1997)

[13] Laban, R.V.: The Language of Movement: A Guidebook to Choreutics: Plays, inc. (1974)

[14] Laban, R.V.: Principles of dance and movement notation: With 114 basic movement graphs and their explanation. Macdonald & Evans, London (1956)

[15] Lipscomb, S.D., Kendall, R.A.: Perceptual judgment of the relationship between musical and visual components in film. Psychomusicology 13, 60–98 (1994)

[16] McGurk, H., MacDonald, J.W.: Hearing lips and seeing voices. Nature 264, 746–748 (1976)

[17] McNeill, W.H.: Keeping together in time: dance and drill in human history. Harvard University Press, London (1995)

[18] Mitchell, R.W., Gallaher, M.C.: Embodying music: Matching music and dance in memory. Music Perception 19(1), 65–85 (2001)

[19] Moog, H.: The development of musical experience of children in the pre-school age. Psychology of Music 4, 38–45 (1976)

[20] Murphy, K.: Dynamic Bayesian Networks:Representation, Inference and Learning. PhD thesis, University of California, Berkeley (2002)

[21] O'Leary, A., Rhodes, G.: Cross-modal effects on visual and auditory object perception. Perception & Psychophysics 35, 565–569 (1984)

[22] Papousek, M.: Intuitive parenting: A hidden source of musical stimulation in infancy. In: Deliege, I., Sloboda, J. (eds.) Musical Beginnings: Origins and Development of Musical Competence, pp. 88–112. Oxford University Press, Oxford, New York, and Tokyo (1996)

[23] Pearl, J.: Probabilistic reasoning in intelligent systems: networks of plausible inference. Morgan Kaufmann Publishers, San Mateo, Calif. (1988)

[24] Phillips-Silver, J., Trainor, L.J.: Hearing what the body feels: Auditory encoding of rhythmic movement. Cognition (in press, 2007)

[25] Phillips-Silver, J., Trainor, L.J.: Feeling the beat: movement influences infants rhythm perception. Science 308, 1430 (2005)

[26] Repp, B.H., Penel, A.: Auditory dominance in temporal processing: New evidence from synchronization with simultaneous visual and auditory sequences. Journal of Experimental Psychology: Human Perception and Performance 28(5), 1085–1099 (2002)

[27] Savitzky, A., Golay, M.J.E.: Smoothing and differentiation of data by simplified least squares procedures. Analytical Chemistry, 1627–1639 (1964)

[28] Sekuler, R., Sekuler, A.B., Lau, R.: Motion perception. Nature 385, 308 (1997)

[29] Shams, L., Kamitani, Y., Shimojo, S.: Visual illusion induced by sound. Cognitive Brain Research 14, 147–152 (2002)

[30] Thornburg, H.: Detection and Modeling of Transient Audio Signals with Prior Information, Stanford University, Department of Electrical Engineering (2005)

[31] Vroomen, J., de Gelder, B.: Sound enhances visual perception: Cross-modal effects of auditory organization on vision. Journal of experimental psychology: Human perception and performance 26(5), 1583–1590 (2000)

Appendix

Laban Movement Analysis (LMA) framework is a systematic approach to understand, analyze and notate full body human movement, originated by Rudolf Laban [13]. For the most part, LMA is divided into four categories: Body, Space, Effort and Shape. The Shape, component of LMA in general elicits the form, or forming of the body. One sub-component of Shape, Shape Qualities, concerns itself with how the body changes its shape in a particular direction. Figure3 shows a body-centered coordinate system with horizontal plane side-to-side (across the shoulders), vertical/coronal plane head-to-toe, and sagittal plane back-to-front. Rising/sinking fall on the vertical plane, retreating/advancing fall on the sagittal plane, and enclosing/spreading fall on the horizontal plane as well as reveal the general folding and unfolding of the body. All movement is comprised of one, two or three of these qualities depending on the complexity of the movement itself. Metaphorically, how one embodies Shape Qualities can reveal nuances of one's mood or character. Currently, we have focused most of our attention on Shape Quality (SQ) analysis.

While it may not seem complicated to a casual observer, doing SQ analysis computationally is quite difficult because there is no single, consistent way one can express a particular quality. One may advance, for instance, by walking towards something, by

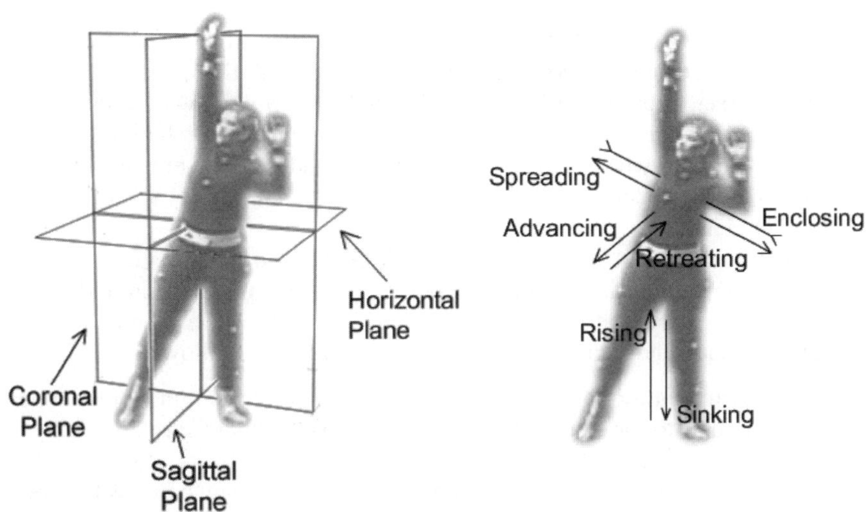

Fig. 3. Body-centric coordinate system and Shape Quality (SQ) illustrations

pointing, or simply by craning one's neck forward in a slight and subtle way. Nevertheless, SQs do imply tendencies on the movement of individual joints and limbs within the context established by a body-centric coordinate system with origin at the navel (Figure 3). For instance, if someone is rising, it is more likely that their torso will rise than sink. Similarly, SQs may imply non-local tendencies, such as an upwards shift of the body's enter of mass with respect to the horizontal plane.

We briefly present the key features of our framework "bottom-up" for inferring Shape Qualities, beginning with raw motion capture data and ending with the SQ hypothesis. First, we extract mid-level features from the raw, labeled marker position data. Second, we model movements of individual body parts and changes in global body characteristics (e.g. are the arms spreading or enclosing, the body centroid rising or sinking?) in terms of feature trajectory dynamics.

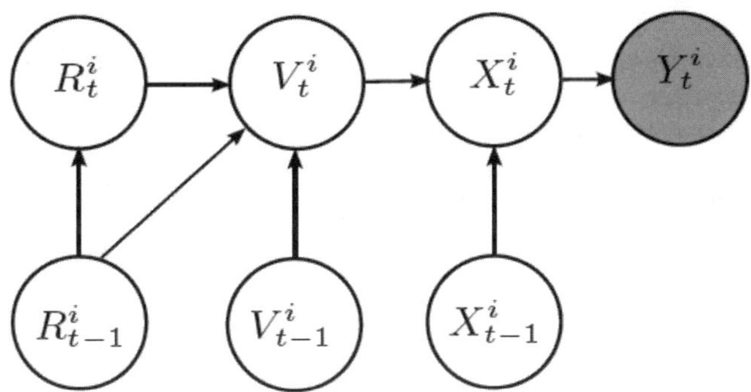

Fig. 4. Single time slice DAG of basic Shape Quality inference model

244   K. Afanador et al.

Figure 4 displays one time slice of the DAG (directed acyclic graph) or probabilistic influence diagram [20, 23, 30] underlying our model, with clear and shaded nodes representing hidden and observed variables respectively. A DAG is a graphical representation of a factorization of a joint probability distribution into conditional distributions. If a DAG consists of nodes $X_{1:N}$ the corresponding factorization of $P(X_{1:N}) = \prod_{i=1:N} P(X_i \mid Pa\{X_i\})$, where $Pa\{X_i\}$ are the parent nodes of X_i. For instance, in Figure.2 we have $P(R^i_{t-1}, R^i_t, V^i_{t-1}, V^i_t, X^i_{t-1}, X^i_t, Y^i_t) = P(R^i_t \mid R^i_{t-1}) P(V^i_t \mid V^i_{t-1}, R^i_{t-1}, R^i_t) P(X^i_t \mid X^i_{t-1}, V^i_t) P(Y^i_t \mid X^i_t)$.

In Figure 2 Y^i_t: $i \in 1{:}3$, $t \in 1{:}N$, denotes each of the mid-level feature observations calculated at the current time t (frames; 100fps) using the motion capture data. These features depend on the body-centric coordinate system shown in Figure 1, displaying horizontal, coronal, and sagittal planes. These features are as follows.

- Y^1_t -- Mean marker height describes the global body position along the vertical axis (perpendicular to the horizontal plane). Changes in this feature are highly informative of rising/sinking.
- Y^2_t -- Frontward placement is the running sum of the change in mean marker position as projected onto the front direction (perpendicular to the coronal plane). Changes in this feature are highly informative of advancing/retreating.
- Y^3_t -- Lateral marker variance is the magnitude variance of all marker positions as projected onto the coronal plane. Changes in this feature describe the folding/unfolding of the body about its navel center, and are thus highly indicative of enclosing/spreading.

To reduce the effect of noise in the marker positions, as well as marker mislabeling and occlusion, the underlying state values are partially denoised using a second order Savitsky-Golay filter [27] over 20 frames.

Each mid-level feature observation, Y^i_t, is modeled as a corresponding inherent feature X^i_t, corrupted by noise to sensor inaccuracies. We model this noise as additive zero mean Gaussian noise: $P(Y^i_t \mid X^i_t) \sim N(X^i_t, \sigma^2_{Y,i})$

Also corresponding to each Y^i_t is a discrete Shape-indicator hypothesis $R^i_t \in \{-1,0,1\}$ corresponding to different Shape Qualities depending on i and models X^i_t as *decreasing* (-1), *constant* (0), or *increasing* (1). For example, suppose the inherent mean marker height is increasing. We denote this fact by $R^1_t = 1$, which specifies that X^1_t trends upward and implies that the Shape Quality expressed on the vertical plane is rising. Similarly, $R^1_t = 0$ and $R^1_t = -1$ denote neutral and sinking qualities on the vertical plane.

We observe that the trajectory of X^1_t is smooth, and displays tendencies conditioned upon the Shape Quality expressed at time t. To model the dynamics of X^i_t, we specify V^i_t, as the time derivative of X^i_t i.e., $P(X^i_t \mid X^i_{t-1}, V^i_t)$ concentrates deterministically on $X^i_t = X^i_{t-1} + V^i_t$. The tendencies displayed by the trajectory of V^i_t given R^i_t are as follows:

    1. $V^i_t > 0$, $V^i_t \approx V^i_{t-1}$ when $R^i_t = 1$ and $R^i_{t-1} = 1$
    2. $V^i_t < 0$, $V^i_t \approx V^i_{t-1}$ when $R^i_t = -1$ and $R^i_{t-1} = -1$
    3. $V^i_t > 0$, $V^i_t \neq V^i_{t-1}$ when $R^i_t = 1$ and $R^i_{t-1} \neq 1$
    4. $V^i_t < 0$, $V^i_t \neq V^i_{t-1}$ when $R^i_t = -1$ and $R^i_{t-1} \neq -1$
    5. $V^i_t \approx 0$, when $R^i_t = 0$

$P(V^i_t \mid V^i_{t-1}, R^i_{t-1}, R^i_t)$ is developed by encoding the above tendencies using Jaynes' principle of maximum entropy, according to which maximum entropy estimate is the least biased estimate possible on the given information which is maximally noncommittal with regard to missing information. Hence to deal with situations involving uncertainty i.e., incomplete knowledge regarding the system to be modeled, the optimal solution is the model that satisfies the knowledge or constraints that we have regarding the system and the one which has the maximum entropy [11]. Let us first consider the first two cases i.e., we have $V^i_t > 0$, when $R^i_t = 1$ and $R^i_{t-1} = 1$ and $V^i_t < 0$ when $R^i_t = -1$ and $R^i_{t-1} = -1$. Furthermore, we expect some continuity of Vit; i.e., $V^i_t \approx V^i_{t-1}$, which can be controlled by $E| V^i_t - V^i_{t-1}| < \sigma^2_{V,i}$. Putting these constraints together and using the methods in [7], we can solve for the maximum entropy dependence in closed form.

$$V^i_t \sim N^{+}(V^i_{t-1}, \sigma^2_{V,i}), R^i_t = 1, R^i_{t-1} = 1 \tag{1}$$

$$V^i_t \sim N^{-}(V^i_{t-1}, \sigma^2_{V,i}), R^i_t = -1, R^i_{t-1} = -1 \tag{2}$$

where N^{+} and N^{-}, are Gaussian distributions truncated to be positive and negative respectively, sharing the mean V^i_{t-1} and variance $\sigma^2_{V,i}$.

When the Shape Quality changes from *t-1* to *t* we do not constrain $V^i_t \approx V^i_{t-1}$, we instead allow for sudden changes in dynamics, weakly constraining $V^i_t \approx V^{1,i}$ (for $R^i_t = 1$ and $R^i_{t-1} \neq 1$) and $V^i_t \approx -V^{2,i}$ (for $R^i_t = -1$ and $R^i_{t-1} \neq -1$) where $V^{1,i}, V^{2,i} > 0$ are nominal values;

$$V^i_t \sim N^{+}(V^{1,i}, \sigma^2_{V1,i}), R^i_t = 1, R^i_{t-1} \neq 1 \tag{3}$$

$$V^i_t \sim N^{-}(-V^{2,i}, \sigma^2_{V2,i}), R^i_t = -1, R^i_{t-1} \neq -1 \tag{4}$$

For $R^i_t = 0$, we have $V^i_t \approx 0$; using similar arguments as above we specify: $V^i_t \sim N (0, \sigma^2_{z,i})$. To complete the description of our model we need to specify $P(R^i_t \mid R^i_{t-1})$. We define q^{+} as the probability of transition out of state 1, meaning the probability that $R^i_t \neq 1$ given $R^i_{t-1} = 1$. The average length of 1 regions is approximately $1/ q^{+}$ and $p^{+}=1- q^{+}$. Similarly, q^{-} is the probability of transition out of state -1, with $p^{-}=1- q^{-}$. Now we can proceed to specify $P(R^i_t \mid R^i_{t-1})$ as a first order Markov, state transition distribution (Table.1).

Table 1. *Specification of* $P(R^i_t \mid R^i_{t-1})$

R^i_{t-1}	$R^i_t = 1$	$R^i_t = 0$	$R^i_t = -1$
1	p^{+}	$1- p^{+}- q^{+}p^{-}$	$q^{+}p^{-}$
0	p^{+}	$1- p^{+}- p^{-}$	p^{-}
1	$q^{-}p^{+}$	$1- q^{-}p^{+}- p^{-}$	p^{-}

The overall dynamic Bayesian network is in the form of a non-linear, non-Gaussian switching state space model. Via SIR particle filtering methods \cite{Arulampalam01}, we compute the posterior distribution of the SQ hypothesis given all feature observations up to and including the present time and choose Rit that maximizes this posterior; i.e. the filtered posterior $P(R^i_t \mid Y^i_{1:t})$, $i \in 1{:}3$. It is well known that this choice of R^i_t yields the minimum-error decision [2].

Between Mapping, Sonification and Composition: Responsive Audio Environments in Live Performance

Christopher L. Salter[1,2], Marije A.J. Baalman[1,3], and Daniel Moody-Grigsby[1]

[1] Design and Computation Arts
Concordia University
Montréal, Canada
[2] Interactive Performance and Sound
Hexagram Institute
Montréal, QC, Canada
[3] Institute for Audio Communication
Technische Universität Berlin
Berlin, Germany
csalter@gmx.net, marije@nescivi.nl, dangrigsby@gmail.com

Abstract. This paper describes recent work on a large-scale, interactive dance theater performance entitled *Schwelle* as a platform to pose critical questions around the conception, design and implementation of what is commonly labeled responsive audio environments. The authors first discuss some principal issues in the design of responsive audio environments specifically within the domain of stage performance, addressing existing human-computer interaction paradigms in three key areas: sensing, mapping and data sonification. Next, we explore larger questions of composition in relation to these key areas, suggesting that potential strategies cross three different domains: mapping within algorithmic composition, data sonification techniques, and time-based evolutionary processes emerging from dynamical systems theory. We then examine recent work on *Schwelle*, which employs real time, distributed sensor data to drive a continuous dynamical system-based composition engine. The project's conceptual and technical challenges are discussed as well as audience evaluation and feedback from the first presentation in Berlin in February 2007, and the subsequent revisions for the second presentation in Montréal in May 2007. Finally, the paper concludes with a set of issues that may act as a framework for future research focused on compositional strategies for larger scale, distributed, network-based sensor environments.

1 Introduction

This paper aims to pose some critical aesthetic and technical questions concerning the design and implementation of compositional systems in what is increasingly referred to in the literature as responsive sound environments. Responsive sound environments encompass areas ranging from urban sound installations

R. Kronland-Martinet, S. Ystad, and K. Jensen (Eds.): CMMR 2007, LNCS 4969, pp. 246–262, 2008.
© Springer-Verlag Berlin Heidelberg 2008

[1,2,3] to workaday models of auditory display [4]. We wish here, however, to focus on one small space of this potentially rich field: the design of such environments within a live performance context. The rubric of live performance not only describes familiar live performance forms such as dance, theater, instrumental or electronic music and similiar genres, but also crosses into the arena of performative installations, environments and architecture. To limit our scope, we will focus on stage performance as the central application, presenting as a case study a recent large-scale interactive dance theater performance entitled *Schwelle* which premiered in Berlin at the Transmediale Festival for Art and Digital Culture in February 2007 and was subsequently revised for presentation in Montréal at Place des Arts/Cinquième Salle in May 2007.

Fig. 1. The dancer, Michael Schumacher, during the performance of *Schwelle* in Montréal (photo by Anke Burger)

Although there is no agreed upon use of the term, interactive or responsive sound environments generally refer to a system which "regenerates a soundscape dynamically by mapping 'known' gestures to influence diffusion and spatialization of sound objects created from evolving data" [5]. Outside of a musical context, the original use of the term derives from the work of computer scientist Myron Kruger in the 1970s. Kruger more broadly defined responsive environment as a "physical space in which a computer perceives the actions of those who enter and responds intelligently through complex visual and auditory displays" [6]. Since a central component of such environments is the use of sensors or capture devices to gather data from the physical world and relay this to a computer in real time, technical and artistic research has been mainly situated within the domain of human-computer interaction (HCI) with a musical slant. Consequently, if, as Kruger stated, the intelligent response of the computer occurs at the level of *auditory* display, we would then assume that questions about compositional output would be a key focus within musical HCI circles. A review of the literature, however, finds little to support this statement, with the vast majority of work in music oriented HCI focusing on the development of either the control/sensing *device* itself (the "interface" or "instrument") or the creation of mapping strategies for synthesis algorithms that "sonify" data derived from such devices [7].

It is our contention that neither the current HCI focus nor traditional "algorithmic" computer music approaches to playback based composition sufficiently address the complexities of composing or sound designing for large scale, multi-input, sensor-based environments. This compositional challenge becomes all the more apparent when one deals with the difficult tasks of real time sonic manifestation of complex data, balancing legibility (listener perceivability of understanding what is mapped to what) with musical richness and complexity (timbral and rhythmic variation, dynamics, density, clustering) within the context of live performance where long term time evolution and duration are paramount to spectator/listener experience. Instead, our aim here is to develop a framework that exploits the tensions between mapping, sonification and composition for sensor-based responsive audio environments, suggesting that potential strategies for composition hybridize three different areas: mapping within algorithmic composition, sonification, and time-based evolutionary processes emerging from dynamical systems theory.

We first describe the areas of sensing, mapping and sonification as they are currently being explored in the HCI/New Instruments for Musical Expression (NIME) context and the tensions therein. Secondly, we describe the dance-theater project *Schwelle* as a case study for live performance-based responsive sound environments that couples compositional strategies with the use of computationally based dynamical systems fed by multiple streams of sensor data in order to generate what Roads calls *macro* and *meso* sonic structures over time [8]. Finally, we conclude with a set of questions that may act as a framework for future research focused on compositional strategies for larger scale, distributed, network-based sensing contexts.

2   Sensing and Instruments

The vast majority of literature in the area of sensor-based control and manipulation of real time audio has arisen within the NIME perspective. This is not surprising given that the New Interface for Musical Expression conference emerged in 2001 as a breakout group from the SIGCHI constituency to focus more exclusively on issues of musical import. The central focus of this approach lies specifically in the area of designing new (usually) sensor augmented devices that elicit more nuanced and expressive forms of human-computer interaction than traditional interface devices like keyboards or screens. NIME as well has explored issues as diverse as "simultaneous multiparametric control, timing and rhythm and training" [9]. This approach cuts across both areas of research and teaching. Stanford University's CCRMA HCI courses such as Human Computer Interaction Theory and Practice: Designing New Devices and HCI Performance Systems: Music Controller Design and Development primarily emphasize the chains of Gesture→ Sensor→ Sound and Human→ Sensor→ Microcontroller→ PC→ Loudspeaker [10]. Similarly, the central goal of NYU's ITP course in New Interfaces for Musical Expression is the formalization of a general set of design issues for musical expresion that were articulated in the 2001 NIME workshop [11].

Central to the NIME tenet is that the sensor-augmented device or *controller* can be seen as a new kind of instrument. While this instrument model varies depending on the context (recent controllers include everything from cell phones to giant metal stretched strings [12,13]), the general NIME orthodoxy is based on a model of musical expression that involves: (1) sensor input for the real time control of musical parameters, (2) techniques for the conditioning, analysis and feature extraction of sensor signals and (3) mapping strategies for creating relationships between input and output parameters. In many ways, these three steps directly align with the "gesture→ sensor→ sound = musical expression" model that is at the core of the standard NIME approach, most specifically through interaction with a sensor-augmented musical device by way of gestural interaction.

3   Mapping

Along with sensing-device modalities, the holy grail of HCI approaches to music is mapping. Mapping involves "the liason or correspondence between control parameters (derived from performer actions) and sound synthesis parameters" [14]. These techniques have been extensively described in the literature [15,16,17] and thus, we will not rehearse them here. What is important to note is that mapping operates in both instrumental and algorithmic contexts. While instrumental mapping focuses most specifically on the mapping of real time input data (i.e. sensor information) to sound synthesis parameters, algorithmic mapping suggests that the mapping techniques themselves are entangled within higher level structural processes (computational, mathematical, etc): "the mapping of gestures to sounds may be considered the composition itself" [14]. According to Doornbusch [18] "mapping in algorithmic composition is different from mapping in instrumental design because composition is a process of planning and instruments are for real time music production". The process of algorithmic composition thus, operates over multiple time scales, from what Curtis Roads called the *meso* scale of individual "sequences, combinations and transmutations" that are generated by sound synthesis to the *macro* scale, which involves the larger temporal-structural form and organization of musical or sonic events [8].

In relation to compositional processes, however, mapping is not without its detractors. In his 2002 NIME keynote, Joel Chadabe acknowledges a disconnect, or discrete, relationship between the various structures of an electronic musical instrument versus an acoustic instrument [19]. While he acknowledges that as "instruments become more complex to include large amounts of data, context sensitivity and music as well as sound-generating capabilities, the concept of mapping becomes more abstract and does describe the more complex realities of electronic instruments", Chadabe still focuses on an instrument model as the fundamental organizational mode for composition with electronic systems. A perhaps more germaine criticism comes from computer scientist/artist Marc Downie who claims that mapping has become a catch all phase whose meaning has become "vague almost past the point of usefulness" and whose "predictive and explanatory power has long left us" [20]. Coming from the area of synthesis character generation with AI agent-based techniques, Downie's critique stems from the argument that with the fast "binding" of "sensor" to "output", "mapping deflates the awesome power of the algorithmic before it can appear". In a sense, mapping flattens out the richness of computational complexity, confusing control parameters with the internal structure of a particular process. This mapping problematic might be summarized as follows. With little essential coincidence to preserve in the coupling of "real-world" input to digital output, correlations between the two milieus are fundamentally arbitrary and thus necessarily shaped via quasi-compositional processes. In other words, the current definition of mapping seems artificially limited in scope. A more critical approach is needed to re-invigorate the notion of mapping and move it beyond the simplistic input/output model. The task in developing richer interactive possibilities is to seek out new kinds of environments that involve unsupervised types of machine learning in order to "train" mappings and "induce them out of interactions" rather than create *a priori arbitrary relationships between input and output*. Such an approach might take into consideration an *enactive* approach to mapping, which considers the *structural coupling* of environmental data to the internal dynamics of the system [21] — in other words, its unfolding as a contextually and temporally sensitive agency whose aesthetic and/or dramatic character possesses an expressive depth. A common aesthetic criticism of current approaches is the often glaring opacity of mappings intended to provide spectators with easy access to performer/computer interactions. This overemphasis on legibility often leads to aesthetic and "interactive" facility. Although, as we discuss below in our case study, a lack of legibility (specifically, that an audience might lack sufficient perceptual access to a mapping) also poses an equally important threat. Such a threat should not, however, detract from the rich aesthetic gains that might be afforded by such a renewed approach. Chadabe and Downie's arguments suggest that we clearly need new ways of thinking about the complexities of interactive musical systems that move beyond instrumental paradigms as well as the controller-based mapping approaches that are the core of the NIME orthodoxy and instead, towards algorithmic systems that deal with real time data in a complex, time evolutionary manner at both meso and macro levels.

4   Sonification and Composition

Another avenue that seems to suggest techniques for dealing with complex, real time data in a responsive environment context is sonification. Sonification is primarily described as "the mapping of numerically represented relations in some domain under study to relations in an acoustic domain for the purpose of interpreting, understanding or communicating relations in the domain under study" [22]. Due to its scientific origins and context, sonification dispenses with an instrument model altogether, focusing instead on the auditory display of complex, real time data sets, and, in particular, providing a perceptual framework for dealing with abstract, non-representational (i.e. non-visual) data. Only recently, structural studies have started to explore which mapping techniques are suitable for certain types of data streams [23].

Although sonification uses sound as the technique and medium for representing data, the vast majority of the literature emphasizes non-musical applications in areas such as the representation of complex phenomena (chaotic or self-similar non linear systems) [24], auditory icons and audio interfaces [25] and non-speech audio representations of physiological data, in addition to other applications. What is clear is that while sonification moves away from instrument-control models, it does so at potential (or considerable) aesthetic expense. In an unpublished text, Larry Polansky makes a useful distinction between sonification for scientific versus artistic purposes. Polansky notes that the closest sonification comes to composition is when mathematical or physical processes assist in generating new musical forms that are time varying. Sonification is not the same as algorithmic composition, although both techniques might utilize similar mathematical or physical processes. Using the example of computing π through a stochastic algorithm, Polansky posits two models. The first aims at using two pitches in order to sonify the statistical procedure, revealing how close or far we are from the number based on perceived consonance or dissonance. This technique aims at illustrating or *representing* a mathematical process in order to "elucidate" or reveal information about the unfolding of that process over time. The second example, however, uses mathematical processes (in the example, probabilistic techniques) in order to inspire new kinds of time varying compositional structures; not to "hear the Gaussian distribution as much as we want to use the Gaussian distribution to allow us to hear new music". In this sense, mathematical processes become more of a manifestation or embodiment of the process. Characteristics and qualitites that are essential to reveal information used in sonification such as "clarity", "efficiency" and "economy" may be only of secondary or of no interest within an aesthetic context [26].

Despite its refreshing non instrument-oriented model of computer sound control, the sonification field maintains the same uncritical mapping approach as discussed previously. Obviously, this is perfectly understandable considering the data display underpinnings of the sonification field. What is important to note is the lesser explored terrain pointed out by Polansky. Despite its limitations, there are as yet under-explored possibilities implicit to sonification that offer a viable alternative approach to computer controlled sound for artistic purposes.

5   Composition for Responsive Sound Environments in Live Performance

Formulating compositional strategies for responsive sound environments within a live theater or dance context presents a particular thorny set of technical and perceptual challenges. First, unlike more open ended presentation contexts like walk-through sound installations or site specific environments [27], theater or dance performance (not to mention musical works) takes place over a defined and specified time duration. Furthermore, the audience/listener is present for this overall duration. Because of this, the perception of macro-structures (i.e. structural patterns, repetitions, sequences, motifs, themes and variations) becomes an essential element in the audience's understanding of how the performance evolves over time.

Second, since the seated audience is not directly involved in the manipulation of a set of controls or interfaces, the mapping model of direct gestural interaction to sound (or other forms of output) has become the default technique in establishing feedback between the human performer and the computer. Not surprisingly due to its emphasis on gestural control, the NIME model of sensing-mapping has also migrated to interactive performance contexts as many of these models also involve control of musical or visual parameters through sensor-augmented gesture and movement of performers. Due to the nature of what arts researcher Scott de La Hunta calls the "invisibility" and "transparency" of mapping various forms of input to output in a performance situation, "performer movement/action is used to trigger some sort of event (sonic, visual, robotic, etc.) in the space around or in some proximity to the performer" [28]. This kind of compositional device is used as a crutch to illustrate or render opaque a particular mapping.

Many times, this direct 1:1 feedback model results in either reducing the performer's range of bodily movements (leading to semaphore type of gestures) to activate sensors and synthesis structures, or to "visualize" the hidden mappings for the audience/listener. More importantly, as Downie described it, this mapping deflates and simplifies more potentialy interesting algorithmic compositional structures because such mappings might not be *immediately perceivable* by audience members and thus, not fulfill the feedback-based expectation that interaction seems to suggest. The consequences of focusing almost exclusively on the short term level of mapping-sound generation-feedback is that most interactive performance works fail to exploit the thing that makes musical or dramatic performance compelling and affective to the listener: the unfolding of an event over a durational time frame.

While few, there are examples of live performance events which have used multiple live feeds of sensor data for the control of both macro and meso compositional structures. Cage's *Variations V* and *Variations VII* both attempted to utilize multiple live feeds of data (in *Variations V*, capacitance and photoelectric sensing and in *Variations VII*, photoelectric and live telephone voice feeds) [29]. Other works such as Tod Machover's 1999 *Brain Opera* have also relied on simultaneous sensor based systems for the control of musical output. In the case of Cage, Machover or other similar interactive music models, however, the sensor interaction triggered already pre-composed structures that would be altered within a finite set of boundaries as determined by the composer/author rather than through a set of more unpredictable processes generated by "unsupervised machine learning". While there has been work in moving away from the arena of triggering pre-composed sequences and towards the use of live sensor data to drive longer term, time based processes [30], this work also relies principally on a controller/gesture-based model of the individual body as instrument and not the spatial and temporal complexities of an environment.

It is our contention, however, that live performance involving sensor augmented responsiveness presents a particularly robust context in which to research new techniques for computer assisted composition in that explicit attention must be paid to the organization and structuring of sound over long term time scales. Since the relationship between the structural components must be considered from both compositional and dramaturgical angles, issues of mapping must be subsumed into algorithmic processes which in turn are organized by even "higher level" narrative or dramaturgical structures. At the same time, one must explore the emerging levels of improvisation that occur between live performers, the environment (understood through sensing techniques), audience and computationally assisted structures.

The compositional challenge involves using algorithmic complexity to generate potentially interesting and compelling patterns that function both at a long term time scale while also manifesting interesting behaviors as a direct result of current inputs of sensor data at the meso scale. In this sense, Doornbusch is incorrect in stating that composition concerns preplanned structures while instruments focus on real time music production. Within a live performance context working with continuous data feeds from performers, objects, the controlled stage environment and potentially the audience's movement or behavior itself, we encounter both planned and simultaneously, real time structures.

6 *Schwelle*: A Case Study

Schwelle is an evening length theatrical event which explores the varying threshold states of consciousness that confront human beings in everyday life experience, such as the onset of sleep or the moments before physical death. The three-act project has been in development between August 2005-January 2007 in Berlin, Montréal and Amsterdam and has involved a number of cultural and academic institutions. Part II of the project had its premiere in February 2007 at the Transmediale Festival For Art and Digital Culture in Berlin followed by performances in Montréal in May 2007. Future performances will follow in Shanghai and elsewhere in Europe and North America during 2008 and 2009.

Part II of *Schwelle* consists of a theatrical performance that takes place between a solo dancer/actor and a responsive room. The exerted force of the performer's movements are captured by wireless accelerometers located on the two arms and chest. Additonally, rhythmic changes in the color temperatures and dimming curves of lighting are picked up by strips of photoelectric cells and

Fig. 2. Michael Schumacher in *Schwelle* in Berlin (photo by Thomas Spier)

wirelessly transmitted via RF to a central server. Furthermore, the room is animated by vibrating pieces of paper, and moving electro-luminescent wire which are also controlled via a wireless transmission.

The continuously generated data from both the performer and environment is then used to influence the time evolutionary behavior of a dynamically changing composition/sound design that attempts to give the impression of a living, breathing room for the spectator. The responsive sound environment that is a key element of the *Schwelle* performance consists of a multi-channel surround auditory environment whose sonic behaviour is determined continuously over different time scales, depending on the current input, past input and the internal state of the system generated by performer and environment in partnership with one another.

The conceptual and technical details for this work have already been adressed elsewhere [31] and thus, we will focus on issues of sound design and composition within the constraints of a live performance context. First, the notion of responsiveness in the context of *Schwelle* as a theatrical event signifies two things: (1) the room is responsive in that the environment provides information that is subsequently manifested (but not illustrated) through specific sonic structures having distinct timbral and rhythmic relations that behave differently depending on different "states" of the room and (2) the time evolution of this continually generating sound design has a certain set of identifiable patterns that emerge over the duration of the performance. Thus, the tension exists early on between musical structures that continuously evolve based on what is happening in the environment and, at the same time, the dramaturgical need to give those musical structures a clear sense of pattern for the audience.

The challenge of working within the aesthetic rather than informational/ display framework of data sonification involves developing a compositional infrastructure that both responds and is responsive to the behavior of the performer and room in co-production with one another. The compositional approach to *Schwelle* thus includes the division of musical relationships that were either to be associated with human influence or with the behavior of the room ambience.

6.1 *Schwelle*: Compositional System

The room composition for Part II of *Schwelle* is organized and built around 16 layers of sound structures generated within the SuperCollider3 programming environment [32] with the following qualitative characteristics (in parentheses, the parameters which can be modulated of these sounds):

- Continuous background noise (frequency, amplitude, modulation speed ('activity'))
- Clouded events (density, frequency range, amplitude range, duration, amplitude)
- Regular, discrete events (frequency, tempo, amplitude, duration)

Faced with the complexity of creating a sonic environment that was identifiable to the audience/listener as a "character" (i.e. where sound would serve a dramatic function), we arrived at the underlying sonic language by building individual instruments in SuperCollider3 and listening to each layer of sound separately in order to identify qualitivative changes. These sounds and their resulting musical parameters such as frequency, duration, rhythm and dynamics, were developed based on questions that emerged from *Schwelle*'s overarching dramatic structure: what kind of range of affective behaviors would the room environment exhibit over the course of the performance and how could such behaviors or states be manifested to the audience/listener through qualitative phenomena like density and thickness, legato-like continuous structures versus transient "events", clustered versus particulate sounds and smooth versus jittery textures, among others. Based on this principle, we utilize no external "musical" structures in the sense of background music or music that could reinforce a particular mood or heighten dramatic tension.

In choosing the types of underlying meso structures, we took into account how such qualitivative changes were coupled with psychoacoustic issues such as frequency and amplitude masking, critical bandwidth, relationships between sounds, etc. For example, one of the first steps taken was to listen to each layer of the sound in order to determine what the limits of the amplitude and the frequency occurrence should be. Other SuperCollider instruments were designed utilizing specific synthesis techniques that would consequently generate particular kinds of aesthetic effects in the audience/listener (e.g., subsonic or sounds drifting above and below perceivable frequency thresholds, higher transients that would produce interesting aliasing effects, larger, Xenakis-influenced sound masses whose pitch wavering was stochastically determined).

In search for computational models that would yield potentially interesting patterns with the existing meso sonic structures, we turned to work in the area of dynamical systems — mathematical models of dynamic processes, based on a set of differential equations that describe the dynamic behaviour of the system [33]. It is important to make this distinction, as the label "dynamical system" is often misused in other work (e.g. [2] where systems based on cellular automata and fractals are labeled as dynamical systems). The aim of the dynamical system deployed was to create a time varying model where the compositional structure would depend on the multiple feeds of real time sensor data input from the room and the performer.

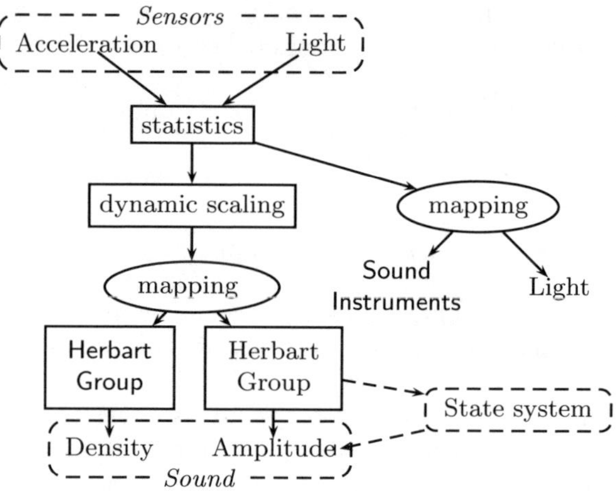

Fig. 3. *Schwelle* data flow diagram

Figure 3 depicts a schematic picture of the dataflow in the computational system (the system is described in more detail in the previously cited paper [31]). The sensor data is first gathered and analyzed statistically, so that the system reacts to changes in the environment, rather than to absolute values. The resulting data is then scaled dynamically, before being fed into a Herbartian system, on which will be elaborated below. The mapping, which is indicated between the dynamic scaling and the Herbart Groups, is a matrix which determines the degree to which each sensor influences which sound.

The dynamic scaling ensures that when there is little change in the sensor data, the system is more sensitive to it. The output of the Herbartian systems is mapped to the density, as well as amplitude of the different layers in the sounds.

The diagram also shows that there is a second data flow path, which constitutes a more classical, NIME instrumental approach of using the sensor data. Here, the mapping between a movement created within the room by the performer or objects in the room and a resulting lighting or sonic event is direct, and recognizable as an action-reaction interaction. This interaction has been carefully tuned to certain dramatic sequences within the piece, and is easily switched on and off, depending on which scene is taking place. In some scenes the strength of the interaction is changed dynamically by the artist controlling the dynamical system at suitable moments in the dance, thus creating a duet with the dancer.

These two different paths of data processing represent two very different approaches on two different time scales: the first path is concerned with using measured data on a long term, whereas the second path deals with short term use of the data, i.e. a clear action-reaction scheme.

Herbartian system. The Herbartian system is a dynamical system which is based on early ideas of J.F. Herbart [34], who developed a theory for the strength of ideas due to sensory impressions as a function of time and the strength of the impression. It is this metaphor which we also apply in *Schwelle*: the room's physical behaviour makes certain sonic ideas stronger within the room over a longer time scale. Each type of sensor input has a separate scaling factor to determine the amount of influence it has on the system. Within the multiple layers of sound, each layer consists of one single sound object (object in the sense of a sound that stands on its own), whose intensity (amplitude) and amount of occurence is dependent on how strong the "idea" within the system is at a certain moment in time. The Herbartian system functions in such a way that there is no direct one-to-one mapping, but that its output depends both on the past and present of the system. This makes sense musically, as it reflects how we perceive and understand the temporal evolution of music[1].

When an impression is fresh, a faster increase in the idea's strength results while a slower increase occurs when an impression has lingered over time. Mathematically this is described as follows:

$$S_z = \sigma(1 - e^{-it_i}) \tag{1}$$

where S_z is the strength of the idea due to an impression that is present, i is the strength of the impression, σ is the sensitivity to the impression of the idea and t_i the time the impression has been present from a certain threshold on. There has to be a threshold set above which an impulse is on, and a threshold for it to turn off.

Simultaneously, an idea decreases in strength when there is no impression, which is represented as:

$$S_{c,N} = (S_z + S_{c,N-1})e^{-d\Delta t} \tag{2}$$

where $S_{c,N}$ the strength of an idea at time point N, evaluated at each time step Δt. d is a decay factor.

These ideas are grouped. The sum of S_C of all ideas in a group produce a *Hemmungssumme H*. H is then divided over the ideas in a reverse way, that is: the weakest idea gets the strongest part of the Hemmungssumme, the strongest idea the smallest. If the current strength of an idea is below zero, it is completely pushed back to a *subconscious* level. However, if at a later time, the other ideas are weaker, the idea can come back to a *conscious* level, without the need for a new impression to excite the idea.

---

[1] In fact, Herbart applied his theory also to the understanding of "Tonlehre" [35,36].

Fig. 4. The dancer, Michael Schumacher, in front of the wall object during the performance of *Schwelle* in Berlin (photo by Thomas Spier)

6.2   *Schwelle*: Evaluation and Reception

Gathered from audience response ascertained during the initial Berlin performances of *Schwelle*, the resulting behavior of the system produced a perceivable continuously time evolving behavior with the individual sonic layers. The Herbartian system alone, however, did not suffice to achieve structures and patterns which were clearly distinguishable from each other. Audience members surveyed noted that the dynamic range of the overall sound environment sounded in fact "too static" oddly enough because of continuous change. Based on the audience feedback and our intent for the system to generate more perceivable compositional patterns at the macro scale, we have now implemented a state-based system on top of the existing Herbart model that more clearly influences the patterning of the meso sound structures over time. Specifically, we have more clearly defined five qualitative sound states that align with different emotional states that take place in the room during the performance, such as "meditation", "repressed anger", "transient anger", "sleep/dream" and "agitation". For each of these states, we have designed parameter limits within which each sound layer would shift to reflect that state. Some sound layers are more present in some layers than in others, or have different frequency ranges, durations and so on within certain layers.

The composition then moves through a statespace, which is implemented as a 3 dimensional geometrical representation. The current moment gets assigned a set of coordinates, and the output of the Herbartian system determines how it moves through the space with each output of the Herbartian system connected to a translation vector. Formally this can be written as:

$$\boldsymbol{p}_n = \boldsymbol{p}_{n-1} + \alpha \boldsymbol{h} \mathbf{V} \tag{3}$$

where $\boldsymbol{p}_n$ is the position in the statespace at moment n, α is a speed factor, $\boldsymbol{h}$ is the vector with the output from the Herbartian system, and $\mathbf{V}$ is a matrix containing the translation vectors.

In the representation a sphere is defined with a certain radius (R), and if the current state moves out of the sphere ($|\boldsymbol{p}_n| > R$), it depends on where it crosses the border, as on the sphere different regions are defined as transitions to other states in the macro composition. Consequently, we can map the Herbartian system outputs that contribute to a certain layer to vectors for moving through the space, so that on the way to a certain state, already more of that state is present within the piece; the "idea" for that sound is already getting stronger before moving into that state where the idea reaches its maximum intensity. Thus, the aim is to have two kinds of compositional systems operating in conjunction with one another: the dynamical Herbartian system which influences the time evolutionary behavior of the meso sound structures (what types of sounds are strongest and when) and the state system, which controls the larger macro clustering and repetition of the meso structures as the performance evolves. From subsequent conversations with audience members in attendance at the May 2007 Montréal performances, it was clear that the addition of the state system substantially contributed to a more perceivable sense of compositional pattern as well as a clearer experience of the room's sonic behavior. Audience members stated that they sensed that the room's behavior was not "random" but instead felt unpredictable yet "logical". The fact that audience members experienced a much more "legible" composition but could not explain exactly why points to the successful marrying of the dynamical system with the discrete state engine.

7   Conclusion and Future Work

We have described some positions on research into the development of more robust compositional models for real time, sensor driven responsive sound environments in the context of live stage performance. While the existing NIME research in gestural, controller-based mapping to sound is valuable from both technical and artistic standpoints (e.g. choosing appropriate devices, conditioning and analysis techniques for real time data) we feel it does not sufficiently address more complex compositional questions of how one designs and composes sound for sensor-driven responsive environments over longer time evolutions. This paper has attempted to articulate some of the issues and pose a concrete example of ongoing artistic work that attempts to address them. It also acts as a position statement for new research starting up between the authors and Marcelo Wanderley at McGill University's Input Devices and Musical Interaction Laboratory which will focus on the development and use of large scale, distributed wireless sensor networks for live stage performance contexts in which issues of sound design for potentially n-dimensional, ad-hoc sensor configuration will be addressed.

Acknowledgments

We gratefully acknowledge the support of the following individuals and institutions without which our research and creation work on *Schwelle* would not have taken place: Andreas Broeckmann, Carsten Seiffarth, Detlev Schneider (Tesla-Medien-Kunst-Labor, Berlin), Joel Ryan (STEIM, Amsterdam), Anke C. Burger, Concordia University, Montréal, QC, Canada, Michel Gagnon and Marie Lavigne, Place des Arts / Cinquième Salle, Montréal, QC, Canada, the Hexagram Institute for Research/Creation in Media Arts and Sciences, Montréal, QC, Canada, Alain Thibault, Elektra/ACREQ Montréal, QC, Canada, Technische Universität Berlin, Electronic Music Studio, Berlin, the Fonds de recherche sur la société et la culture, Québec, Harry Smoak (TML), Steve Bates, Joel Taylor, Mark Baehr and Paul Fournier, Hexagram, Brian Massumi and Daniel Wessolek, Brett Bergmann and Alexander Wilson, Thomas Spier, Daniel Plewe and Julia Schröder.

References

1. d'Inverno, M., Eacott, J., Lorstad, H., Oloffson, F.: The intelligent street, responsive sound environments for social interaction. In: ACM SIGCHI International Conference on Advances in Computer Entertainment Technology, ACE 2004. ACM, New York (2004)
2. Miranda, E.R., McAlpine, K., Hoggar, S.: Dynamical systems and applications to music composition: A research report. In: Proceedings of Journees d'Informatique Musicale (JIM97). French Society for Musical Informatics (SFIM), Lyon, France (1997)
3. Son-o-house (2000-2004), `http://www.noxarch.com`
4. Mynatt, E., Back, M., Want, R., Baer, M., Ellis, J.: Designing audio aura. In: ACM SIGCHI Conference on Human Factors in Computing Systems. ACM, New York (1998)
5. Livingstone, D., Miranda, E.: Composition for ubiquitous responsive environments. In: Proceedings of International Computer Music Conference (ICMC 2004). International Computer Music Association - ICMA, Miami, USA (2004)
6. Kruger, M.: Responsive environments. In: Proceedings of the American Federation of Information Processing Societies, USA. AFIPS, vol. 46, pp. 423–429 (1977)
7. NIME `http://www.nime.org`
8. Roads, C.: Microsound. MIT Press, Cambridge (2001)
9. Orio, N., Schnell, N., Wanderley, M.M.: Input devices for musical expression: Borrowing tools from hci. In: Workshop (NIME-01) during ACM CHI 2001, Seattle, USA (April 2001)
10. Gurevich, M., Verplank, B., Wilson, S.: Physical interaction design for music. In: Proceedings of International Computer Music Conference (ICMC 2003), Singapore (2003)

11. D'Arcangelo, G.: Creating a context for musical innovation: A nime curriculum. In: Proceedings of the 2002 Conference on New Instruments for Musical Expression (NIME 2002), Dublin, Ireland (2002)
12. Tanaka, A., Toeplitz, K.: Global string (1998), http://www.sensorband.com/atau/globalstring/
13. Schiemer, G., Havryliv, M.: Pocket gamelan: Tuneable trajectories for flying sources. In: Proceedings of the 2006 Conference on New Instruments for Musical Expression (NIME 2006), Paris, France (2006)
14. Miranda, E.R., Wanderley, M.M.: New Digital Musical Instruments: Control and Interaction Beyond the Keyboard. A-R Editions (2006)
15. Hunt, A., Wanderley, M.M.: Mapping performer parameters to synthesis engines. In: Organised Sound, pp. 97–108. Cambridge University Press, Cambridge (2002)
16. Hunt, A., Wanderley, M.M., Paradiso, M.: The importance of mapping in musical instrument design. Journal of New Music Research, 429–440 (2003)
17. Hunt, A., Kirk, R.: Mapping Strategies for Musical Performance. In: Trends in Gestural Control of Music. IRCAM-Centre Pompidou (2000)
18. Doornbusch, P.: Composers views on mapping in algorithmic composition. In: Organised Sound, pp. 145–156. Cambridge University Press, Cambridge (2002)
19. Chadabe, J.: The limitations of mapping as a structural descriptive in electronic musical instruments. In: Proceedings of the 2002 Conference on New Instruments for Musical Expression (NIME 2002), Dublin, Ireland (2002)
20. Downie, M.: Choreographing the Extended Agent: performance graphics for dance theater. PhD thesis, Massachusetts Institute of Technology (MIT), Media Laboratory (2005)
21. Varela, F.J., Thompson, E., Rosch, E.: The Embodied Mind: cognitive science and human experience. MIT Press, Cambridge (1991)
22. Scaletti, C.: Sound synthesis algorithms for auditory data representations. In: Kramer, G. (ed.) Auditory Display: Sonification, Audification, and Auditory Interfaces. Addison-Wesley, Reading (1994)
23. Campo, A.D.: Toward a sonification design space map. In: Proceedings of the ICAD 07-13th International Conference on Auditory Display, Montreal, Canada, June 26-29 (2007)
24. Bargar, R.: Pattern and Reference in Auditory Display. In: Kramer, G. (ed.) Auditory Display: Sonification, Audification, and Auditory Interfaces. Addison-Wesley, Reading (1994)
25. Gaver, W.: Using and Creating Auditory Icons. In: Kramer, G. (ed.) Auditory Display: Sonification, Audification, and Auditory Interfaces. Addison-Wesley, Reading (1994)
26. Polansky, L.: Manifestation and sonification (2002), http://eamusic.dartmouth.edu/~larry/sonification.html
27. Paine, G.: Reeds - a responsive sound installation. In: Proceedings of the ICAD 04-10th Meeting of the International Conference on Auditory Display, Sydney, Australia (2004)
28. de la Hunta, S.: Invisibility/corporeality (March 13, 2001), http://www.noemalab.org/sections/ideas/ideas_articles/delahunta.html/ nettime.org
29. Cage, J.: Variations VII, http://www.medienkunstnetz.de/works/variations-vii/
30. Ryan, J., Salter, C.L.: Tgarden: Wearable instruments and augmented physicality. In: Proceedings of the 2003 Conference on New Instruments for Musical Expression (NIME 2003), Montreal, CA (2003)

31. Baalman, M.A., Moody-Grigsby, D., Salter, C.L.: Schwelle: Sensor augmented, adaptive sound design for live theater performance. In: Proceedings of NIME 2007 New Interfaces for Musical Expression, New York, NY, USA (2007)
32. McCartney, J.: Supercollider http://www.audiosynth.com http://supercollider.sourceforge.net
33. Franklin, G.F., Powell, J.D., Emami-Naeini, A.: Feedback Control of Dynamic Systems, 3rd edn. Addison-Wesley Publishing Company, Reading (1994)
34. Herbart, J.F.: De Attentionis Mensura causisque primariis (orig. published 1822). In: Kleinere Abhandlungen. E.J. Bonset, Amsterdam (1969)
35. Herbart, J.F.: Psychologische Bemerkungen zur Tonlehre (orig. published 1811). In: Kleinere Abhandlungen, E.J. Bonset, Amsterdam (1969)
36. Herbart, J.F.: Psychologische Untersuchungen. Erstes Heft' (orig. published 1839). In: Kleinere Abhandlungen, E.J. Bonset, Amsterdam (1969)

Retrieving and Recreating Musical Form

Ole Kuhl and Kristoffer Jensen

Aalborg University Esbjerg, Niels Bohr Vej 8,
6700 Esbjerg, Denmark
{ok,krist}@aaue.dk

Abstract. This paper discusses musical form from a cognitive and a computational viewpoint. While several time-windows exist in the brain, we here put emphasis on the superchunks of up to more than 30 seconds lengths. We compare a strategy for auditive analysis based on human cognition with a strategy for automatic analysis based on feature extraction. The feature extraction is based on the musical features rhythm, timbre and chroma. We then consider the possible consequences of this approach for the development of music generating software.

Keywords: Music retrieval, human cognition, chunking, feature extraction, music generation.

1 Introduction

If you look through your music collection, you are bound to find that most of the music in it − perhaps 80–90 % − is structured in such a way that a formal change takes place every 30–40 seconds or so. A formal change can be a change from verse to refrain, from A-section to B-section, a repetition, a change of key, etc. Music is generally made up of sections, and the longer time span of the whole piece of music is subdivided into sections with different qualities. This is true for most of the world's musics, regardless of culture and style.

This way of structuring a piece of music is so ubiquitous that it is reasonable to assume that it reflects a built-in characteristic or constraint of the human mind/brain. Such a constraint may well be biologically determined, something that can be deduced from the fact that nursery rhymes all over the world share the same basic structure and the same temporal dimensions [1]. However, this innate tendency of human cognition to structure and group musical sound into sections of certain proportions is difficult to explain. It may be tied to the limitations of our working memory as suggested by some [2, pp 49–51]; or it could be seen as the product of an attention cycle, that would then be the result of the need of the human brain to perform an attention switch every so often in order to reorganize its content [1].

On the computational level, much interest has been put into the automatic segmentation of music into e.g. chorus/verse. The automatic segmentation can be used for many purposes, including creation of a shorter preview with no repetition of chorus, skipping of intro in live DJ situation, for live recomposition, and as an aid in music analysis. In this work, a method for automatic segmentation of music, based on

R. Kronland-Martinet, S. Ystad, and K. Jensen (Eds.): CMMR 2007, LNCS 4969, pp. 263–275, 2008.

features related to the perception of music is used as the basis for a shortest-path method to find segment boundaries. The performance of the features, *rhythmogram*, *timbregram*, and *chromagram*, are then compared to the musical analysis, and the theories from cognitive science. In all cases, the typical segment length is observed and compared. An informal analysis of the musical changes that create the segment boundaries is performed. The result of this analysis is used in a simple, stochastic-based melody generator, and simple changes to the possible notes, the dynamic level and interval between notes is inserted in order to create music and compare the structural changes of this music to that of the musical examples.

2 Temporal Cognition and Musical Form

The temporal organization and function of human cognition is full of complexity. In spite of recent advances in the technology for brain studies we still know very little about the brain's performance over time. Recently, however, the theory of chunking has gained some momentum [2 pp. 47–59, 3, 4 pp. 103–113]. According to this theory, our temporal cognition is structured in three distinct layers, serving different purposes and engaging different brain areas. At the microlevel we perceive the world pre-consciously as perceptual qualities, sometimes called qualia, which are organised in coherent structures, in order to be interpreted or conceptualized. These chunks of information are presented at the mesolevel, where we consciously consider objects and events, statements, gestures etc. In order to bring coherence into the flow of events, we organize the chunks in larger groups or super-chunks at the macrolevel, placing the individual chunk in a larger context.

Psycho-physical evidence shows that the brain has a number of distinct time-windows that can be seen as biological constraints on the cognitive processes [1]. Thus, the pre-conscious microlevel of subchunks extend from 30 ms to 300 ms; the conscious mesolevel of chunks from 300 ms to 3 sec; and the reflective macrolevel of superchunks from 3 sec to roughly 30–40 sec., where the limitation of our memory systems sets in. Naturally, we are not consciously aware of these temporal dimensions, as the brain has developed mechanisms to deal with them so that we can experience the world as a uniform flow of time.

What interests us here is the grouping of chunks into superchunks, which we see as a way of understanding the formal level in music. Individual melodic phrases or gestures are grouped together in superchunks that are limited by the brain's memory capacity. At a simple, generic level, music is organized in sections, the sizes of which fall inside certain boundaries. In fig. 1 below we see the organization of a typical popular song [5] in A-sections and B-sections, further elaborated with intro, outro and a contrasting C-section. The A-sections have a length of 32–33 seconds, while the B-sections are 30 seconds long.

Before we proceed let us note that the definitions of musical form applied here rules out certain highly developed artistic forms, repetitive forms, etc. that cannot be adequately dealt with inside these simple paradigms (see [4 pp. 20–28] for a discussion).

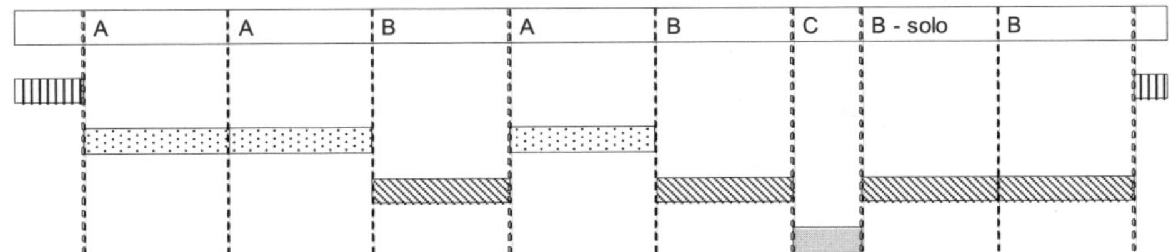

Fig. 1. Jamie Walters: *Hold On* (from [4], used with permission from Peter Lang)

2.1 Musical Form between Change and Continuity

The question we need to answer at this point is: how are the formal properties of a musical piece inscribed in the music-as-sound? Let us look at fig. 1 again. In a case like this, the form of the piece is defined by the song. The recurring refrain (B-section) and the developing verse (A-section) together determine the main aspects of the formal structure. We can imagine certain variations of the form, and indeed musicians make this kind of variations for live-versions, cover-versions etc. But the contents of the verse and the refrain cannot be changed much without jeopardizing the identity of the piece. In a song like this, the form is mainly determined by the text.

But let us set aside the question of the text for now and focus more closely on the music itself. Even without the text, for instance in an instrumental version of the same piece, the form would be clear. This is possible because the music is designed to enhance the individual qualities of the A-section and the B-section respectively, in order to emphasize the contrast between them. A number of musical parameters are shaped to this end. For instance the singer performs at an intimate medium level – more or less with a speaking voice – in the A-sections (verse), while he sings out at a higher pitch in the B-sections (refrain). Another important point is the contrast between the harmonic structure of the two sections. Also the rhythmic effect of the accompaniment and the dynamic level of the two sections differ considerably. Orchestration is yet another favourite parameter for arrangers, in this case the chorus accentuates the dynamic level of the B-section, when it joins in the *Hold On* refrain.

In other words, we have an example of musical form as established through the balance between continuity and change. Continuity is constituted by the text and its narrative; by the singer's voice and the acoustic space provided by his band (acoustic guitar, bass and drums, organ, chorus and lead-guitar is a safe and well-known frame for a narrative); and by the tempo, which makes us entrain to a certain pulse. Variation is set up in this case through the devices listed above: the level of the voice; harmonic structure; dynamic level; and orchestration. In short: some musical parameters are kept constant, while others change from section to section.

Let us look at another example (fig. 2). In the third movement of Mozart's piano sonata in A major, K. 331, also known as *Alla Turca* [6], there is no song, and consequently no text, to determine the formal division of the piece. The structure is constituted on purely musical grounds, yet we find a form comparable to the form of *Hold On*.

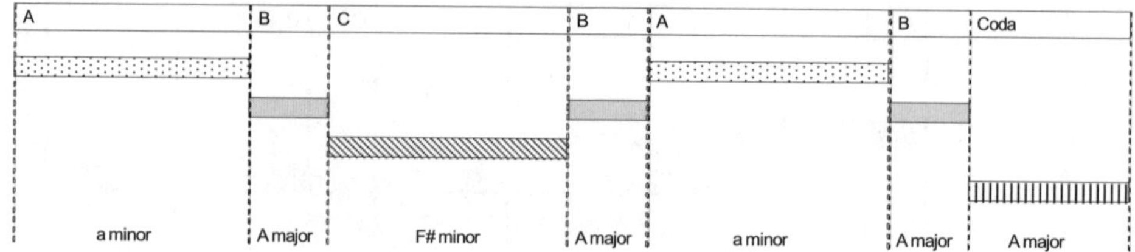

Fig. 2. Mozart's Alla Turca (from [4], used with permission from Peter Lang)

Here the A-sections last 41–42 seconds, the C-section 40 seconds, while the B-sections, that function as refrains and provide the transitions from A to C and vice versa, only last 13–14 seconds. (These timings depend of course on the tempo of the specific performance, here we have used Daniel Barenboim's recording). Continuity is established through a number of parameters: the sound of one piano playing (timbre); tempo and meter (rhythm); key and harmonic development (chroma); repetition and motivic development are some of the more obvious.

As for the parameters used in creating contrast between sections, we can take harmony and texture as evident examples. Harmonically, the A-sections are in A minor, the B-sections in A major and the C-section in F# minor. By texture we mean a combination of rhythmic and gestural qualities, timbre and density. Here the A-section presents a simple melodic gesture with an everyday 'um-da-da-da' rhythm in the left hand accompaniment. The C-section uses the same type of accompaniment, while the right hand abandons the melodic gestures and instead engages in streams of energetic 16th-notes. And the B-section, serving as a transition space between A and C, uses full chords, percussive rhythm and a high dynamic level, thus balancing out its relative brevity with more sound, so to speak.

We shall not go into more details concerning Mozart's musical architecture. The main points to be gained from these examples are, once again, that musical form is constituted through the division of the musical timespan into sections of a certain size; that the individuality of these sections is brought about through a balance between change and continuity; and that this play of variation inside a frame of overall unity is grounded on the tendency of the human mind to create coherence in event structure, which prompts us to generate expectations that can be fulfilled or disappointed.

The purpose of this study of musical form was to investigate the possibilities for a computer-based retrieval of musical form and a modelling of this form, with a subsequent regeneration of music. We will engage the question of whether the musical parameters involved in the human construal of musical form can be defined in such a way that they can be employed in a mathematical analysis of sound. In the following we shall introduce some strategies for retrieval of information pertaining to musical form from the sound stream. We will concentrate on the transition points between sections (A-B; B-C etc), as they mark the points in time, where the change of musical parameters is heard, and where fulfilment/expectation will be experienced. At this stage we have chosen to examine three parameters: timbre, chroma and rhythm.

3   Retrieving Structure in Music

It is our aim to find the same music structure through automatic segmentation as is found through music analysis. This supposedly corresponds to the temporal laws that are the result of temporal processing in human cognition.

We present methods for obtaining measurements of the music that correspond to the sound of the instruments playing (timbre), the tempo and meter (rhythm), and the key and harmonic development (chroma). In order to do this, we first identify the single musical events (notes). After this, the rhythmic feature is found by comparing the single events over time, the timbre feature is found by measuring amplitude over time and frequency, with perceptually related frequency and amplitude features. Finally the chroma is found by summing all partials into the twelve chromas. Both the timbre and chroma features are smoothed over time, to remove small irregularities that occur in addition to more consistent musical events. Finally, we present an approach to the problem of retrieving structure in music.

3.1   Feature Extraction

Notes are the fundamental events in the music considered here. A note has a starting point, a rather short attack, a sustain/decay, and a release. Because the attack generally is short it will be possible to measure the point of attack by calculating the amplitude as a function of time, and taking the time derivative of it. Here, this is done by subtracting the previous time step amplitude from the current time step amplitude. The maximum of the time derivative has been shown to be an important cue when investigating the perception of the attack [7]. By estimating all partial amplitudes, and summing the time derivative of all of them, multiplied with a frequency dependent weight in order to have perceptually normalized amplitudes, a well-performing feature, called the perceptual spectral flux (*psf*), of the note onset detection problem is obtained [8].

The rhythm feature, called *rhythmogram*, is obtained by calculating a windowed autocorrelation function on the *psf*, in which the regularity of the note onsets intervals are found in overlapping segments of the music [8]. The timbre is calculated using a front-end (acoustic pre-processor) used in speech recognition, the perceptual linear predictive (*plp*) analysis [9]. In order to remove noise and intermittent events, the *plp* is smoothed over time [10] using a Gaussian weight. The resulting feature is called the *timbregram*. Finally, the key and harmonic development is measured using the chroma that maps the partials into twelve bands, corresponding to the twelve notes of one octave. The resulting measure, smoothed in the same manner as the timbregram is called the *chromagram*. These three features are visualized in fig. 3. The *rhythmogram* has rhythm interval in seconds on the y-axis, the *timbregram* has frequency in bark [11], corresponding to the perceptual frequency scale, and the *chromagram* has note pitch names. All three have time in seconds on the x-axis.

We can read from the rhythmograms that *Hold On* has a more steady beat, while *Allaturca* varies more in tempo, and even has sections with no clearly distinguishable rhythm. The timbregram also contains the loudness, and illustrates remarkable similar structure in the two songs, with two short crescendos in the first two-thirds of each song, and a longer crescendo in the last fourth. Comparing the two *chromagrams*, the most striking difference is that of clarity. The Mozart piece presents a clear and simple tonal structure, while the Walters song seems more 'muddled'. This reflects the fact that Mozart is played on a single well-tuned piano, while the pop song combines several instruments, including drums, all with large profusions of overtones, and furthermore the style itself is defined by lots of micro pitches, melodic glides etc.

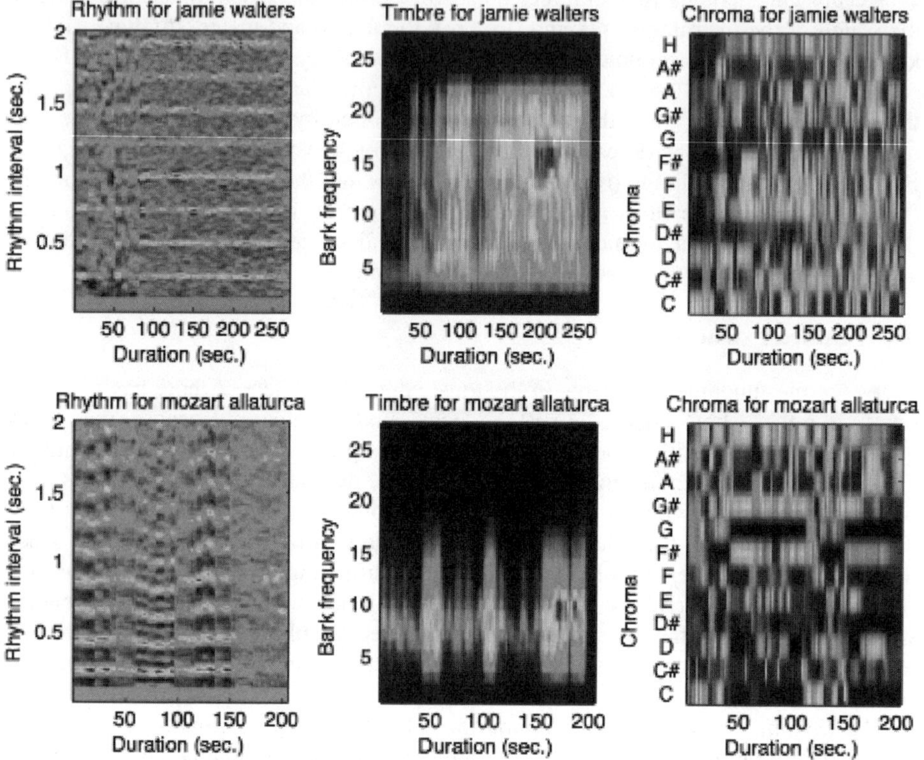

Fig. 3. Rhythmogram (left), timbregram (middle), and chromagram (right), for Jamie Walters *Hold On* and Mozart *Allaturca*. Blue corresponds to little energy and red to much energy.

3.2 Automatic Segmentation

Through a visualization of the extracted music features it is made clear that segmentation of the music should be done in time areas where the feature is homogenous (has the same shape). This is done using the self-similarity measure, originally called recurrency plots [12], which measures the similarity of all the time segments to each other. In fig. 4 the self similarity (calculated as the L_2 norm) is visualized for the same songs and features as in fig. 3.

In the self-similarity plots, the homogenous segments are easily seen climbing the diagonal, in blue/dark. Certainly, the *timbregram* has more homogenous segments than the other two features.

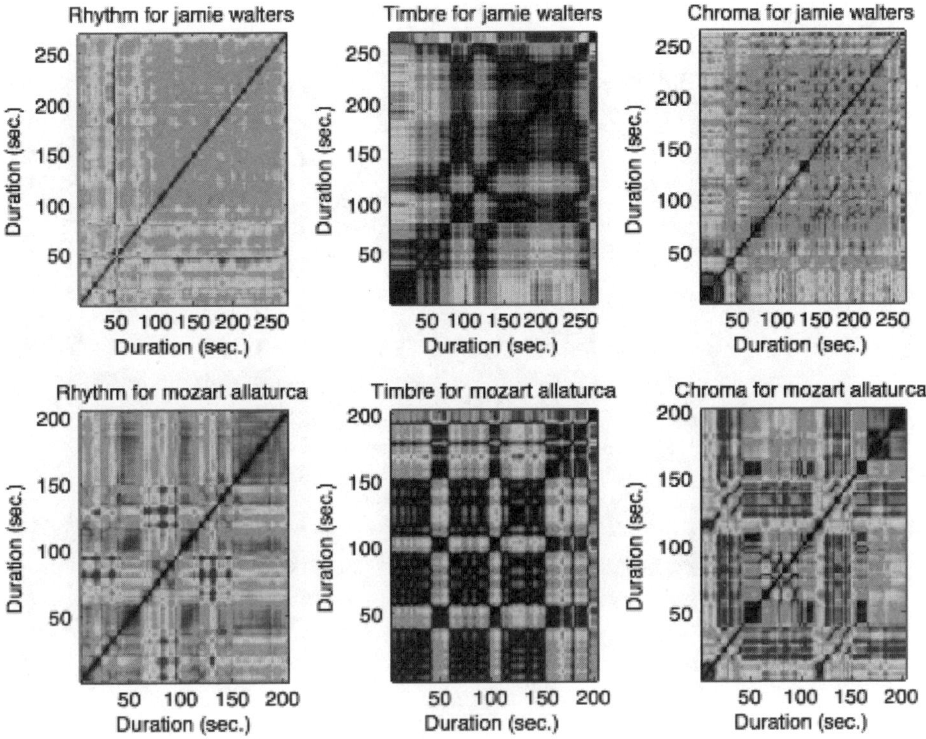

Fig. 4. Selfsimilarity for the rhythm, timbre and chroma of Jamie Walters and Mozart

Several methods exist for identifying the segment boundaries from the self-similarity features. The novelty measure [13], calculated using the checkerboard kernel, gives an indication of the degree of novelty in the audio. If larger segments are to be identified, it necessitates a larger window in the self-similarity matrix. In order to diminish the calculation demands, [8] suggested to smooth the novelty measure calculated on small windows. [14] introduced a shortest path method for finding the optimum path. This method can create segmentation boundaries in many scales, from short segments down to note level, to large segments up to chorus/verse level. This was used in [10] to show that timbre performs slightly better than rhythm or chroma when comparing manual segmentation points with automatic ones.

3.3   Retrieving Structure in Music

In the preceding sections we have introduced two distinct strategies for the analysis of musical form. One is a listening strategy, which is based on the temporal properties of human cognition. The other is a mathematical approach performed automatically by the computer. They both deal with what is almost the same thing: the first with music as sound, the other with sound files. The question we now wish to address is whether these two strategies can yield comparable results.

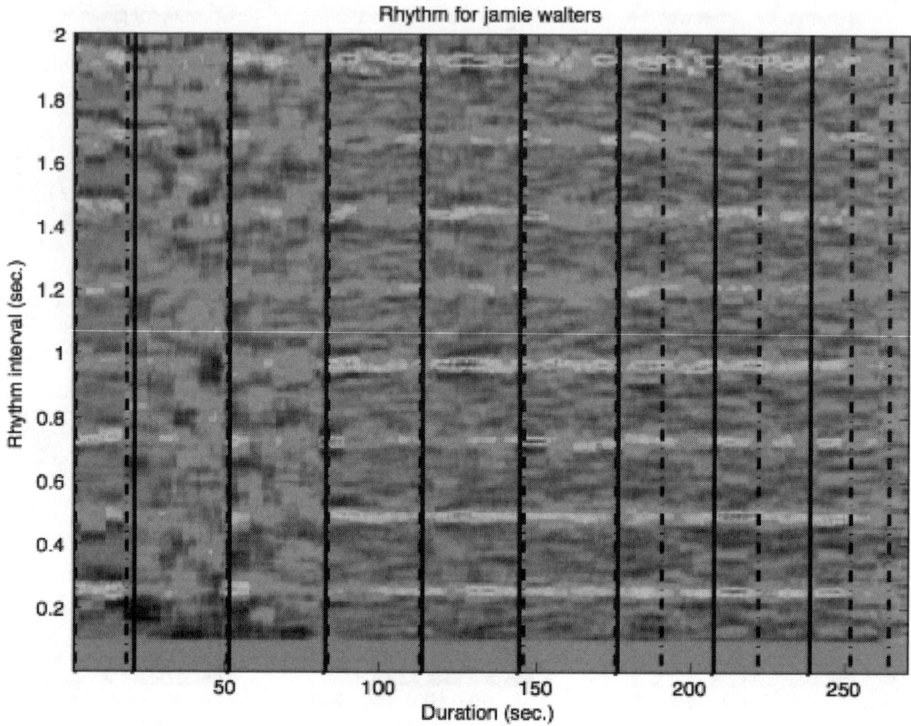

Fig. 5. Rhythmogram for Jamie Walter with automatically found boundaries (solid) and manual boundaries (stipled)

In the human listening strategy we look for changes in texture, orchestration, density, etc., while the computer establishes *rhythmograms*, *timbregrams* and *chromagrams*. Assuming that the extracted musical features, rhythm, timbre and chroma, can be interpreted as essential aspects of such musical parameters as harmony, texture, dynamics, orchestration etc, we would expect to see a correlation between the two approaches. In the following we shall be looking for the transition points between formal sections, such as A-B, B-C etc. These points mark the change from one section with a certain configuration of musical parameters to the next section with a contrasting configuration of musical parameters. They can be easily established by measuring the timing of the two pieces we have studied. The next step will be to insert these points in the *rhythmo-*, *timbre-* and *chromagrams* in order to compare them to the automatic segmentation points. Comparison between the formal and automatic segmentation using the shortest path method is shown in fig. 5 for the Walters *rhythmogram*, and in fig. 6 for the Mozart *chromagram*.

In the Walters *rhythmogram* (fig. 5) we found 11 manual boundaries and 9 automatic ones, with 7 matches between the two. In fact, there is perfect matching up to the point where the C-section, which is only half the length, is introduced. The contrast between B and C is mostly established through timbre and chroma and seems not to be discovered by the *rhythmogram*.

In the Mozart *timbregram* we found 8 manual and 11 automatic boundaries, and 8 of these (all the manual!) match. The three 'extra' boundaries calculated in the *timbregram* might be explained as the result of a barely noticeable playing strategy, in which dynamic contrasts between sections will be enhanced by the player.

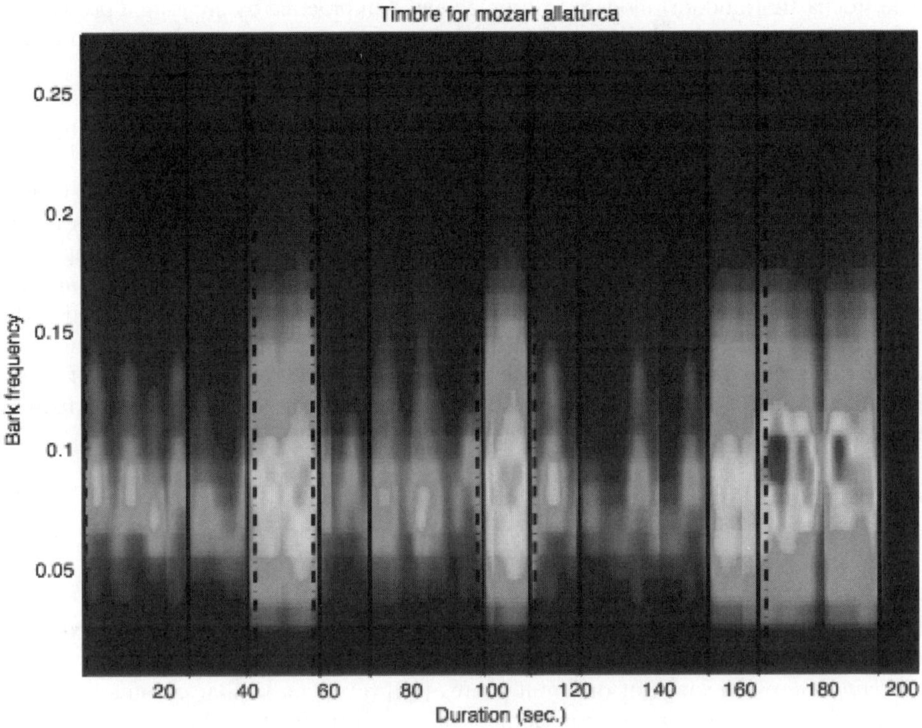

Fig. 6. Timbregram for *Mozart* with automatic (solid) and manual (stipled) segmentation

The *musigrams* visualized in fig. 5 and 6 are the best features for the two songs. The matches correspond to the standard information retrieval measures *recall* (64%, 100%) and *precision* (78%, 73%) and the combined F_1 measure of (0.7, 0.84), the best of the features, with F_1 values of (0.7, 0.54, 0.54) for *Hold On* and (0.52, 0.84, 0.7) for *Allaturca* for the *rhythmo-*, the *timbre-*, and the *chromagram*. It is interesting to observe that the rhythmogram performs better with the rhythmic song, while the timbregram performs better with the classical piece.

4   Perspectives in Music Generation

Can the findings in the previous sections be used here to improve music generation algorithms? An attempt to do so is embarked upon here, by using synthesis of melodies made from random notes, using probabilities obtained from music databases. As we wish to take into account the temporal structure of generic music, we will briefly present some methods to introduce structuring in the rhythm, timbre and chroma of synthetic music, and present some preliminary results.

4.1 Stochastic Models

The stochastic (random) models are implemented in practice by creating a probability density function (*pdf*), which states the probability of an event occurring, as a function of the variable. For instance, one *pdf* could give the probability of one note occurring as a function of the note value (pitch). In tonal music the notes of the musical scale used would typically have a larger probability. The values of the notes can then be found, in music generation, by using the inverse image formula [15].

As an example, the probability of a note being played has been estimated from a database of folk songs[1]. Music generation from simple note probability does not in itself render interesting music, but a conditional probability of the following note, when a note is played, improves the situation. This means that we add the interval probability to the note probability. The probability of an interval is assumed to be independent of the note; therefore the two probabilities can be multiplied in order to create the *pdf* used to find the next note. In this case, a rather pleasant stream of music is created, but still without enough structure to be really interesting (unless perhaps in relaxation use).

4.2 Structural Improvements

The first (*chroma*) improvement to this model is to use a subset of the notes at each structure. Indeed, from fig. 3 it is clear that only 3-5 chromas are played at the time, and from the figure and the discussion in the previous section, this set can be expected to change approximately every 30 seconds. Additional observation of the *chromagram* of 50 songs of different genres [10] reveals a similar chroma evolution for most songs, with variations in number of prominent notes and the rate of change of these notes. Nonetheless, the behavior found in the two songs analyzed here is still the most common. Therefore, this knowledge is inserted in the model, by only choosing a maximum of 5 notes initially, and replacing, adding or removing one note, or doing nothing every N seconds with equal (1/4) probability. N is a random variable with uniform probability between e.g. 30 to 40 seconds, the size of a 'super-chunk'.

The second (*timbre*) improvement is found by looking at the *timbregram* in fig 3. Indeed, both the rock and the classical music display the same structure, with respect to the timbre; a more quiet part is replaced by a louder part, this is repeated, followed by an even louder part and finally, the songs are ended by a strong segment. The strong parts seem to have relatively more energy in a higher frequency range. The quiet part is supposed to correspond to a verse, and the louder part to the chorus. Again, further observations of the *timbregram* of 50 songs [10] broadens the picture, as the number of chorus/verse repetitions, seems to vary between one and eight, the number of verses preceding the chorus vary between one and four, the dynamic difference between the chorus and the verse is also different between songs, and varying other differences are found, including more or less prominent intro/outros.

---

[1] The Spring 2002 Digital Tradition Folksong Database, http://www.mudcat.org, (1 Nov. 2007).

A simple improvement to the stochastic note generation is attempted here, by increasing or decreasing the loudness and brightness with one-third probability each every *N* seconds.

The final (*rhythm*) improvement to the stochastic music generation is found by looking at the *rhythmogram* in fig 3. Three things of importance to rhythm are observed in fig 3, and in additional observations of the rhythmograms of the 50 songs of [10]. First, the tempo may or may not drift up to perhaps 10%, secondly, there seems to be short passages of perhaps 10 seconds in which the rhythm is lost, i.e. there is no clear repetition rate in the instruments of the music. Finally, there is often inserted another rhythm of another rate.

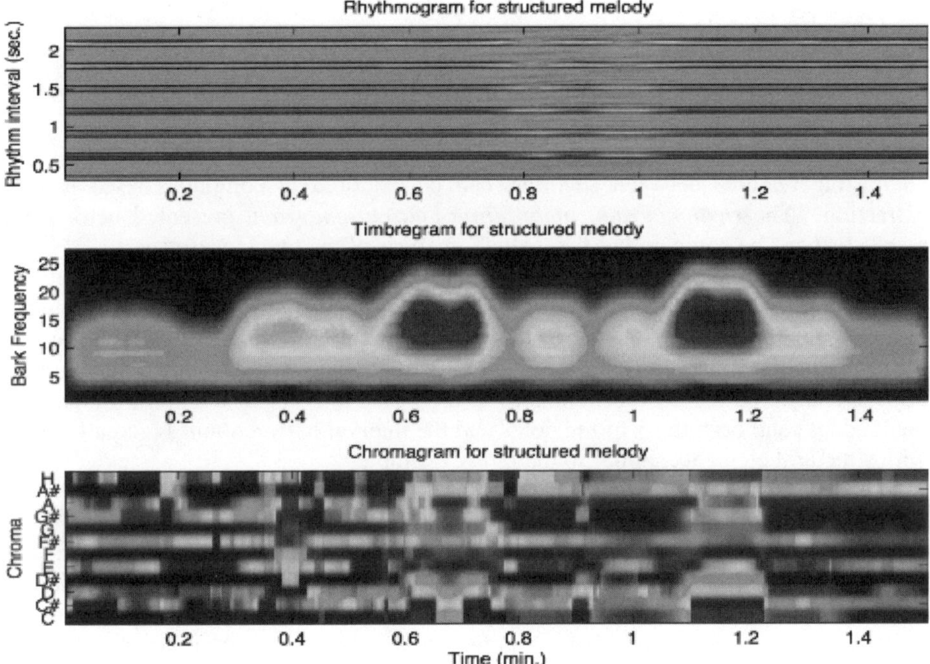

Fig. 7. Rhythmogram, timbregram and chromagram for a test signal with structural changes

The tempo drift is regenerated by inserting a pause with varying length after each note. The length of the pause is governed by a Brownian noise (integrated white noise) whose rate of change decides the tempo drift. As it does not govern the structure of the music, the tempo drift is not included here.

The short passages of arhythmic behavior can be recreated through changing the length of the notes in short passages. This is done by adding a pause of random length for short passages of approximately 10 seconds. Finally, the subtle change of rhythm is not attempted to be modeled here, as it necessitates a rhythm model. Such a rhythm model, while important, is not part of the present work.

As an example of a note-based music with the proposed structural improvement, with regards to rhythm, timbre and chroma, a short melody with these improvements has been created. The *rhythmogram, timbregram,* and *chromagram* of this sound-structure are shown in fig 7.

In an informal listening experiment performed using the authors mainly, the structural change on the chroma is the least perceptible. This is probably related to the stochastic nature of the note generation. The variation of loudness and brightness that induces structure in the timbre, seemingly renders interest and pleasure to the listening experience. The inclusion of arhythmicity that creates structure in the rhythm here dramatically breaks the listening continuity. Overall, by the simple melody and lack of rhythm by the recurrent notes of equal length, it is of course far from complex music, but we deem the structural inclusions promising.

5 Conclusion

In this paper we have compared a human listening strategy with a computational strategy. We have argued that the human tendency for organizing event structures in coherent sections or "super-chunks", with a uniform internal structure and with contrasting features between sections, can be explored in computer based feature extraction. The *rhythmogram, timbregram* and *chromagram*, presented here, yield results that can be compared to the 'actual' analysis of the two pieces used.

The two approaches seem to be reasonably compatible. It would therefore be interesting to see if we can implement some of the methods used in analyzing music into ways of improving computerbased music generation. A possible, simple, model for changing the music in order to obtain structural changes is presented here. Based on a stochastic note generator, changes to the possible notes in the current alphabet, the loudness and brightness of the notes and the interval between notes recreate music with structural elements similar to the music examples.

When comparing the two approaches we are in a way comparing human and computerbased cognition. Without entering into a philosophical discussion of the similarities and differences between human beings and computers, we would like to point out that the current study takes advantage of one obvious distinction between the two. A computational approach is basically a bottom-up approach, built on discrete events (in this case notes), while the human approach combines a bottom-up approach with a top-down approach, as seen in the organization of perceptual information is chunks and super-chunks. Further studies will not only lead to a 'naturalization' of computer generated music, but could also enhance our understanding of human cognition.

References

1. Trevarthen, C.: Musicality and the Intrinsic Motor Pulse. Musicae Scientiae, 155–211 (special issue, 2000)
2. Snyder, B.: Music and Memory. An Introduction. The MIT Press, Cambridge (2000)
3. Godøy, R.I.: Gestural-Sonorous Objects: embodied extensions of Schaeffer's conceptual apparatus. Organised Sound 11(2), 149–157 (2006)
4. Kühl, O.: Musical Semantics. Peter Lang, Bern (2007)
5. Walters, J.: Jamie Walters, Atlantic (1994)

6. Barenboim, D.: Mozart: Complete Piano Sonatas and Variations. EMI Classics (1991)
7. Gordon, J.W.: The perceptual attack time of musical tones. J. Acoust. Soc. Am. 82(2) (July 1987)
8. Jensen, K.: A Causal Rhythm Grouping. In: Wiil, U.K. (ed.) CMMR 2004. LNCS, vol. 3310, pp. 83–95. Springer, Heidelberg (2005)
9. Hermansky, H.: Perceptual linear predictive (plp) analysis of speech. J. Acoust. Soc. Am. 87(4), 131–134 (1990)
10. Jensen, K.: Multiple scale music segmentation using rhythm, timbre and harmony. EURASIP Journal on Applied Signal Processing, Special issue on Music Information Retrieval Based on Signal Processing (2006)
11. Sekey, A., Hanson, B.A.: Improved 1-bark bandwidth auditory filter. J. Acoust. Soc. Am. 75(6) (1984)
12. Eckmann, J.P., Kamphorst, S.O., Ruelle, D.: Recurrence plots of dynamical systems. Europhys. Lett. 4, 973–977 (1987)
13. Foote, J.: Automatic Audio Segmentation using a Measure of Audio Novelty. In: Foote, J. (ed.) Proceedings of IEEE International Conference on Multimedia and Expo., vol. 1, pp. 452–455 (2000)
14. Jensen, K., Xu, J., Zachariasen, M.: Rhythm-based segmentation of Popular Chinese Music. In: Proceedings of the ISMIR, London, UK, pp. 374–380 (2005)
15. Gray, R.M., Davidson, L.D.: An introduction to statistical signal processing. Cambridge University Press, Cambridge (2004)

Placement of Sound Sources in the Stereo Field Using Measured Room Impulse Responses

William D. Haines[1], Jesse R. Vernon[1], Roger B. Dannenberg[1],
and Peter F. Driessen[2]

[1] Carnegie Mellon University, Pittsburgh PA 15213, USA
[2] University of Victoria, Victoria BC, Canada

Abstract. Reverberation can be simulated by convolving dry instrument signals with physically measured impulse response data. Such reverberation effects have recently become commonplace; however, current techniques apply a single effect to an entire ensemble, and then separate individual instruments in the stereo field via panning. By measuring impulse response data from each desired instrument location, it is possible to place instruments in the stereo field using their unique early reflection and reverberation patterns without panning. A pilot study compares the perceived quality of dry signals convolved to stereo center, convolved to stereo center and panned to desired placement, and convolved with measured impulse responses to simulate placement. The results of a single blind study show a preference for location-based (as opposed to panning-based) reverberation effects.

1 Introduction

When an ensemble performs on stage before a live audience, the listening experience is undoubtedly enhanced by the physical separation of the instruments on stage. This effect does not occur by chance, as percussive instruments are often placed in the center of the stage, with bass and melodic instruments often separated to either side. The placement is formulated so as to reduce the effect of one instrument dominating the sound of another. Currently, when recording and mixing down albums, a single reverb is placed on each track, based upon either IIR filters or a convolution with a single measured impulse response. Placement is achieved using a combination of amplitude panning, pre-delays, decay times, and saturation levels in order to separate the individual instrument tracks. This method is effective, but purely artificial, providing no real psycho-acoustical clues that the instrument field is properly placed in a real acoustic space.

When an instrument is played at one location on a stage versus another, the reverberation signature is different. This effect occurs because as sound radiates from the instrument, the sound energy reflects from various walls, the floor, and ceiling, reaching one's ear at different time intervals and at differenct frequency-dependent amplitudes. The effect is subtle, but, in principle, recognizable. Consequently, there is a unique impulse response associated with each location on the stage (paired with each listening location in the room). In principle, if each

R. Kronland-Martinet, S. Ystad, and K. Jensen (Eds.): CMMR 2007, LNCS 4969, pp. 276–287, 2008.

instrument signal in an ensemble is convolved with its unique location-based impulse response, then it should enhance the psycho-acoustical illusion of the separation of the instrument field, eliminating the need for panning or other more artificial effects. We call this approach location-based reverberation. One might expect that by giving each instrument a different impulse response, the listener will find it easier to perceive each instrument individually (source separation), and this in turn might avoid the perception of one instrument overpowering the others.

However, even convolution with multiple location-based impulse responses is only an approximation of sound radiation in a room. Acoustic instruments have frequency-dependent radiation patterns. To incorporate this level of detail, one could model impulse responses as functions of source direction as well as source location. To take advantage of this more refined approach, sound sources would need to be modeled or recorded so as to capture audio signals as a function of direction. In our simplified model, we consider only multiple source locations. The impulse responses used here incorporate the directional radiation patterns of the speakers used in the impulse response measurement process, and we expect that patterns will be somewhat different from those of acoustic instruments. Another limitation is that stereo recording does not capture the complex sound field available to the listener in an acoustic space. This is a fundamental limitation of the stereo format. Our goal in this study is only to improve the listening experience within the restrictions of the stereo format, but note that extensions to other formats are at least conceptually straightforward.

The extent to which the technique of virtual instrument placement via measured room impulse responses will improve the actual perceived quality of the performance is unknown; hence, the need for an appropriate study to evaluate the qualitative difference between current methods using single impulse responses and the proposed method using location-dependent impulse responses.

2   Previous Research

Current recording techniques are the culmination of many years of research and reasoning. Numerous studies have been conducted to evaluate the utility of current techniques in addition to considering their ability to withstand the rigors of commercial practice. Formulations of the theory can be found in Pulkki among others [15]. Regarding virtual instrument placement via location-based reverberation, not much has been studied regarding the actual quality of the effect versus current methods. The theory behind the method has been outlined on several occasions, including discussions by Reller and Griesinger [16,9]. The Roland SRV-330 Dimensional Space Reverb uses 24 early reflections to create the impression of a 3-D acoustic space [17]. However, actual quality perception tests and implementation details are not available.

This method of location-based reverberation is related to the use of head-related transfer functions (HRTFs) to simulate spatial location. [4] HRTFs are often used to model changes in both sound source location and the orientation of the listeners head. Our method differs from HRTF models because our goal is to incorporate room reverberation into the impulse response, and we do not incorporate HRTF information in our impulse responses.

Many artificial reverberation models have been proposed [5,13,10]. Some of them take into account source locations, speaker locations, room geometry, and/or listener location. These systems essentially estimate the channel characteristics between each sound source and and some other room location representing the listener or a loudspeaker. As in our approach, the reverberation effect applied to each dry source depends upon the source location and the room geometry. In our approach, however, the channel characteristics from source to microphone are measured directly as impulse responses.

3   Location-Based Convolution Reverberation

The details of our reverberation system are straightforward. We will begin with an overview of current convolution-based reverberation effects and then describe the extension we have made. The principle behind convolution-based reverberation effects is that the channel from a sound source to the listener in a concert hall is linear (or at least there is a good linear approximation). Theory tells us that the channel can be modeled as the convolution of the source signal with the impulse response of the channel:

$$y(t) = x(t) * h(t) \tag{1}$$

where $y(t)$ is the signal at the listener, $x(t)$ is the source signal, and $h(t)$ is the impulse response from the source to the listener. Normally, the impulse response is estimated between a single source location on stage and a pair of microphone locations representing the left and right stereo channels. Thus, the stereo signal is computed as follows:

$$y_L(t) = x(t) * h_L(t)$$
$$y_R(t) = x(t) * h_R(t) \tag{2}$$

For a typical studio recording, multiple instruments are recorded with close microphones on separate "tracks," which can be considered to be free of reverberation and acoustically isolated. The goal is to "place" these instruments in the stereo field. Ignoring the possibility of other digital audio effects, the final mix is produced as follows:

$$y_L(t) = \left(\sum_i A_{i,L} x_i(t)\right) * h_L(t)$$
$$y_R(t) = \left(\sum_i A_{i,R} x_i(t)\right) * h_R(t) \tag{3}$$

where L and R stand for the left and right stereo channels, and $A_{i,L}$ and $A_{i,R}$ are scale factors to implement left-to-right panning on the ith instrument. Note that a single reverberation effect is applied to a mixture of the instruments. This is computationally efficient, but treats all instruments as if they were located at the same point on stage.

It should be noted that there are other panning options in commercial implementations of convolution-based artificial reverberation. For example, the Waves IR1 plug-in omits the impulse in the response corresponding to the direct sound and separates the early reflections from the reverb tail. This gives the user the option of panning each dry instrument signal to a different simulated location and then adding a global reverb to some mixture of the dry sounds.

Location-based convolution reverb modifies the computation to incorporate location-based impulse responses. The ith instrument signal is convolved with the ith impulse response $h_i(t)$ Since left and right amplitudes and delays are already incorporated into the impulse responses, no additional scaling or artificial panning is necessary:

$$y_L(t) = \sum_i (x_i(t) * h_{i,L}(t))$$
$$y_R(t) = \sum_i (x_i(t) * h_{i,R}(t))$$

$$(4)$$

Note that this approach requires more computation because there is a separate convolution-based reverberation effect on each source signal.

In practice, signals are of course discrete, and convolution is performed by converting blocks of the source signal to the frequency domain (using the FFT), multiplying by the frequency domain representation of the impulse response, and then using an inverse FFT to convert back to the time domain [14]. Convolution was implemented in the Nyquist programming language [6]. As indicated by Equation 4, a separate convolution is performed for each (mono) source signal and for each of two stereo channels.

Room (or hall) impulse responses (RIRs) were obtained from measurements of an acoustic space. Various techniques for measuring RIR have been studied [7,8,12]. The three most popular excitation signals for RIR measurement are: a Maximum Length Sequence (MLS), an impulse, and a chirp signal. For analyzing a large concert hall, however, the impulse and the MLS sequence are not good choices for a number of reasons [11]. We therefore choose the chirp signal, which contains all the frequencies required, is a linear signal so is less likely to damage the equipment and also contains a large amount of energy. Using a chirp signal longer than the RIR to be measured allows the exclusion of all harmonic distortion products, practically leaving only background noise as the limitation for the achievable SNR [7].

Our measurement system works as follows. The chirp signal is generated by a laptop computer and played to a speaker. Assuming that most RIR would not exceed 3 seconds, we use a linear chirp signal with a duration of 3 seconds and frequency sweeping from 0 to 24 kHz. At the receiver end, the output signals of a stereo microphone pair are recorded to the same laptop through a multichannel audio interface, together with the unaltered chirp to be used as the reference signal. The unaltered reference signal is important in that it eliminates the need to estimate the latency in the playback-record chain. To obtain the stereo RIR, the received signals are correlated with the reference signal. Just as in a radar processing application, this function compresses the pulse and gives rise to the room impulse response that is to be analyzed [16].

4   Methodology

Theoretically, location-based reverberation models real acoustic reverberation more faithfully than does convolution with a single stereo impulse response. However, as noted above, there are aspects of reverberation that are not modeled by either approach, including directionality and non-linearities. We wanted to evaluate location-based reverberation to determine whether it offers any subjective improvement over current techniques as judged by listeners

4.1   Experimental Design

We decided that a small pilot study would be the most appropriate initial experiment because it was unknown what, if any, differences subjects would hear. Our experimental sample, drawn from a student population, is not representative of our target demographic as a whole, but we do not believe this choice significantly altered our results.

Sample Population. We used a subject pool consisting of 25 members of the Carnegie Mellon University undergraduate population. This convenient sample allowed us to quickly gather data while maintaining a well-defined reference population. The final sample demographics reflect the Carnegie Mellon undergraduate community, with an approximately 60% male and 25% minority makeup. All participants were between the ages of 18 and 23. Subjects were not screened based on other demographics such as musical background.

Sound Samples. For our test, we generated three sound samples for our subjects to compare. All three were based on the same samples of a 30-second jazz excerpt consisting of drum set, contrabass, and saxophone, all recorded with close microphones to minimize cross-source contamination. The samples were chosen because we felt that a non-classical source would result in a more pronounced sonic differentiation between instruments, while the jazz idiom also requires a "live" enough feel that reverberation-based placement in a hall would be an appropriate effect.

To create our samples, we convolved hall-measured impulse response data with the dry jazz samples. These samples were then used to create three variations. The first, called *mono*, is a single-channel sample in which all three instruments are convolved with hall-center impulse response. The second, referred to as *panned*, is a stereo sample in which the three instruments are first panned such that the drums are center, the bass 80% right, and the saxophone 80% left. After panning the dry signals, the two mixed channels are convolved with the left and right channels of the hall-center impulse response, respectively (Equation 3). The final sample, called *placed*, convolves each instrument signal with a different impulse response: a center-based impulse response with the drum set, an audience-perspective right impulse response with the bass signal, and an audience perspective left impulse response with the saxophone signal (Equation 4).

At the highest granularity, the resulting sound samples are all reverberation-wet jazz performances, identical except for techniques regarding instrument placement in the stereo field. The samples were also normalized to peak at 0 dB so as to have matching volume levels. Upon initial listening by the investigators, the *placed* sample seemed to display a richness lacking in the other two samples. The pilot study would later corroborate this subjective observation.

The impulse responses themselves were recorded via a microphone array located in the audience at the center of the concert hall. The venue chosen was the 200 seat Recital Hall located at the School of Music, University of Victoria, Canada. The responses were measured using a swept sine wave through a microphone array and repeated at three locations on the stage [11]. This resulted in an array of 7 different impulse responses for each location on the stage. For our simple stereophonic setup for this experiment, we chose simply the left and right impulse responses (2 of the 7 measured responses) for each of the 3 locations, corresponding to stage right, stage left and stage center. Other measured stereo impulse responses are available for a variety of concert halls and other venues [2]; however, these measurements typically do not include multiple locations on stage, and thus cannot be used for the *placed* variation in this experiment.

Questionnaire. To compare the sound samples objectively, we developed a battery of comparative questions to grade the sound samples. The three categories of comparison were "realism," defined by the likeness of the sample to a live performance, "sound quality," and simple personal preference. The questionnaire asked the subject to listen to two sound samples consecutively, and then compare them on the three selected attributes. Each sample was paired with every other sample, making for a total of three individual listening tests. To reduce bias, the order of the sample pairings was randomized as well as the play order within a given sample pair.

Due to concerns about the ability of all subjects to distinguish between the samples, the realism and quality questions asked for a simple pair-wise comparison to indicate which of the two samples the subject preferred across the realism, quality, and overall preference metrics described above. The preference question also asked for a comparison, but also allowed for answers of "I have no preference" and "I could not tell a difference." In retrospect, listeners did not appear to have great difficulty in distinguishing the samples, with less than 6% of respondents selecting "no preference" or "no difference."

4.2   Experiment Administration

The experiment was administered over the course of a weekend to all 25 subjects. Administration of the study was not difficult due to the brevity and subject matter of the experiment. The study proceeded in a randomized single-blind fashion, on one of two reference systems[1]. Regarding volume, listeners were asked to initially adjust the volume to preference, and then leave it fixed for the duration of the listening test.

Process. The study involved, first, a principal investigator providing the consent form and explaining that the study intended to compare several reverberation techniques, and that the listeners would be asked to listen to several jazz excerpts, identical except for the reverberation applied. The participants were then allowed to look over the questionnaire, but the investigator provided no interpretation as to the meaning of each question or questions regarding sample specifics.

At this point, the investigator played the first sample, identified only by a number, then the second sample. After this, the subject would record their results on the questionnaire, but the sound samples would not be replayed. The process was then repeated for the other two pairs of sound samples, the end result being that each subject would listen to each sound example twice and compare each to the others. After collecting the questionnaire, the investigators provided a brief explanation of the actual experimental intent and identified the sound samples by technique applied.

Data Analysis. For a study of this size, bias due to random variation in samples is a real concern. As such, we feel that it is important to include confidence intervals along with our proportion averages so as to accurately reflect the variability of our pilot study. For this study, we considered the experimental results to be drawn from a binomial distribution, and we calculated confidence intervals based on a normal approximation of this distribution [1]. The binomial distribution assumes that each experimental trial has only two outcomes; to match this model, the preference calculations dropped "no preference" and "no difference" responses.

For example, of the 25 participants, 8 perceived *panned* as sounding more realistic than *mono*. To compute the $\alpha = .95$ confidence interval for realism, *panned* vs. *mono*, we simply used the binomial confidence interval formula for proportions:

$$CI = p \pm 1.96\sqrt{p(1-p)/N} \tag{5}$$

Here p = (8/25) = .32 and N = 25. Thus,

$$\begin{aligned} CI &= .32 \pm 1.96\sqrt{.32(1-.32)/25} \\ &= .32 \pm .182 = [.137, .503] \end{aligned} \tag{6}$$

Now we can interpret these data by saying that with 95% confidence, the true population proportion preferring *panned* to *mono* falls between 0.135 and 0.503, taking our sample size into account.

---

[1] Both systems were laptop PCs, one with Sony MDR-V500 headphones, and the other with Koss UR-40 headphones.

5   Experimental Results

Our experimental results point in favor of location-based reverberation for instrument placement based on the metrics of both sound quality and personal preference. Realism does not result in as conclusive a result, but the data yields valuable insights.

Table 1. Aggregated means and confidence intervals for proportion preferring the first listed sound clip in each cell

	Panned vs. Mono	Placed vs. Mono	Placed vs. Panned
Realism	p = .32 [.137, .503]	p = .52 [.324, .716]	p = .68 [.497, .863]
Quality	p = .72 [.497, .863]	p = .84 [.696, .984]	p = .64 [.452, .828]
Preference	p = .57 [.363, .768]	p = .70 [.508, .884]	p = .68 [.497, .863]

5.1   Realism

In this study, we defined realism as "likeness to an actual live performance." Interestingly, there does not appear to be a strong consensus that any reverberation method is most realistic. Each pair-wise comparison of realism resulted in a confidence interval that included .5, the null hypothesis that there is no perceived realism difference between the samples (see Table 1). Nevertheless, .68 rated the *mono* sample as more realistic than *panned*, and .68 rated the *placed* sample as more realistic than *panned*. This may be a reflection of a lack of realism in the *panned* sample, where the stereo spread could have been too wide to be considered realistic. Conversely, it may simply reflect a tendency of the sample population to feel that smaller stereo spreads best reflect the experience of a live performance, especially over headphones, which can exaggerate panning effects.

The other interesting observation about realism is the fact that the proportion preferring *placed* to *mono* was .52, almost exactly the null hypothesis. While the other two pairs were barely out of the 95% confidence range, it appears that our sample population could not distinguish between the two with regards to realism. We hypothesize that this indicates that the stereo spread effect is potentially a major determining factor in causing listeners to perceive a recording as realistic.

5.2   Sound Quality

In contrast to the realism judgement, our investigation found much stronger support for location-based reverberation placement with regards to "sound quality." Here, *mono* fared the worst, with .72 of the population preferring *panned*, and an extremely high .84 of the population preferring *placed*. In fact, despite the small sample size, the *placed* versus *mono* confidence interval, [.696,.984], is highly significant, and the *placed* versus *panned* interval, [.452,.828], only barely contains the .5 null hypothesis. This result suggests a larger study to determine if location-based reverberation is truly a higher-quality placement technique than panning.

One other interesting trend to note is the relationship between realism and quality for each of the three pairs. The observed relationships vary in counterintuitive ways. Quality and realism correlate positively for *placed* versus *panned*, while they correlate negatively for *panned* versus *mono*. Finally, subjects decisively find *placed* to be of higher quality than *mono*, but seem to be unable to decide which is more realistic. With our sample size, it is entirely possible that these trends are just random variation. Their further exploration on a larger sample could prove instructive.

5.3   Personal Preference

The final metric is overall personal preference of the various sound samples. This measure shows the greatest advantage for location-based reverberation. Subjects preferred *placed*, with .70 rating it over *mono* and .68 rating it over *panned*. Even with only 25 participants, the *mono* comparison is significant at the $=.95$ level, and the *panned* comparison just barely misses this level of significance (see Table 1). We feel such a consistent result in favor of convolution placement is solid evidence that the technique is a viable improvement over current postprocessing effects. More subjects and a larger variety of sample material would likely serve to add weight to this judgement.

In addition to these results, we find it interesting that preference seemed much more split when comparing *mono* and *panned*. Subjects preferred *panned*, but only .57 rated it over *mono*. If it really were true that the increased perception of realism in *mono* somehow cancelled out the increased sound quality with *panned*, this would prove to be another advantage for location-based reverberation placement, which seems to be able to combine the best qualities of both other methods. That said, this interpretation seems unlikely, and a much larger pool of subjects and samples would be necessary to give it much credence. The strongest indication of this pilot study is the overall preference for location-based placement over other techniques.

6   Discussion

Although the results of our pilot study are not overwhelmingly conclusive, we did observe a clear trend in favor of location-dependent reverberation (*placed*). For example, *placed* received a majority of positive ratings in all 6 comparisons to the other two methods. It should be noted that subjects listened with headphones, and the sample size was fairly small. Given the generally positive findings, a larger study is in order.

After listening to various sound examples, the authors agree with the experimental trend. Moreover, we feel that location-dependent reverberation is immediately recognizable as more realistic and natural, with a more spatial or three-dimensional quality reminiscent of live recordings with a stereo pair. This of course is exactly the sound one would expect and the sound this method is intended to produce. On the other hand, it should be noted that the authors prefer this sound and are likely to associate this sound with high quality and high realism.

This suggests an interesting interpretation of the experiment. Suppose that subjects hear a clear difference between different reverberation treatments, but disagree with respect to labels such as "quality." For example, some subjects might associate the sound of commercial pop music recordings with "high quality" even if they felt this sound was not realistic or preferable. Indeed, in the comparison of *placed* to *panned*, subjects gave slightly stronger ratings on realism and preference than to quality. The difference here could easily be due to chance, but it is interesting to consider that location-based reverberation could be a distinctive reverberation effect.

A future study might use a test based on analogies to see if subjects can actually identify location-based reverberation. We would predict a positive result. If this effect has a distinctive and recognizable sound, there are likely to be interesting artistic applications.

While our approach models the fact that the location of instruments has an effect on the reverberation, we ignore many acoustical details. One is the directional radiation pattern of sound sources. In our approach, it is assumed that the radiation pattern of instruments matches the radiation pattern of the loudspeaker used to excite the room when impulse responses are measured. Similarly, this approach does not consider directionality of the listener, e.g. we do not incorporate head-related transfer functions.

There are, however, some interesting and simple variations of our approach. First, impulse responses can be measured using intentionally directional sources. For example, a horn speaker might be used to estimate the impulse response for a brass instrument, or a small speaker array might be configured to mimic the radiation pattern of a violin. With a library of different impulse responses based on both location and directionality, each dry signal can be convolved with the appropriate impulse response, simulating both the location of the instrument on stage and the radiation pattern of that instrument.

Similarly, the microphones used to capture and estimate impulse responses can be selected according to the anticipated listening conditions. Microphones might be directional or omni-directional, stereo or multi-channel (for example, five microphones for a 5.1 recording), or mounted in a dummy head to incorporate a head-related transfer function, a common recording technique for headphone listening. Note that while one would normally estimate impulse responses using an ideally omni-directional, flat-response sound source and microphone, directional and even spectrally "colored" transducers can be used for various purposes.

Another important effect in a real acoustic environment is Doppler shift. As a musician moves toward the audience, the direct sound is shifted up in frequency, but reflections experience varying degrees of Doppler shift, with some of the radiated sound actually shifted downward. Furthermore, a moving sound source is constantly changing its location and thereby exciting different room modes and corresponding, different impulse responses [3]. These effects are not produced by our approach.

To incorporate moving sound sources, a direct approach would measure impulse responses from many locations and either switch between them or use some form of interpolation for intermediate locations. Note that linear interpolation between impulse responses A and B suggests that the instrument is radiating partially from both locations A and B, but not from some location between A and B. Another approach is to compute early reflections from a geometric model. If early reflection delays and amplitudes vary continuously, then Doppler shift will be produced as a by-product. Dense, diffuse reverb can be added to complete the reverberation effect.

7   Conclusion

Judging by our pilot study, location-based reverb is a very promising approach to high-quality artificial reverberation, and the potential impact of these techniques on the recording industry is large. Standard convolution reverberation plug-ins such as the Waves IR1 are already in use by industry. Location-based reverberation would use very similar software, but it will require a much larger pool of impulse response data. Since plug-ins of this sort already rely on hall-measured impulse-response data, the burden of measuring a larger number of instrument/listener location pairs should not be prohibitive. Thus, location-based reverberation offers a relatively inexpensive and effective post-processing technique that can be used in today's stereophonic applications to greatly enhance the psycho-acoustical experience for the listener.

The results of our single-blind pilot study clearly warrant further investigation. Within the bounds of our sample size and limited demographic, our results point in favor of location-based reverberation placement. The average listener preference to the location-based reverberation technique demonstrates not just a theoretical advantage but a subjective preference and thus a real viability in the commercial realm. We expect that larger studies will generate conclusively positive results and that location-based reverberation placement will replace current techniques for artificial reverberation and localization in stereophonic recordings.

References

1. Agresti, A.: An Introduction to Categorical Data Analysis. John Wiley & Sons, New York (1996)
2. Audio Ease: Impulse Responses, `http://www.audioease.com/IR/index.html`
3. Benade, A.: Fundamentals of musical acoustics, 2nd edn. Oxford Press, New York (1990)
4. Cheng, C.I., Wakefield, G.H.: Introduction to head-related transfer functions (HRTF's): Representations of HRTF's in time, frequency, and space (invited paper). In: Proceedings of the 107th Audio Engineering Society (AES) 107th Convention, New York (1999)

5. Chowning, J.M.: The simulation of moving sound sources. Computer Music Journal 1(3), 48–52 (1977)
6. Dannenberg, R.: Machine tongues XIX: Nyquist, a language for composition and sound synthesis. Comp. Music Journal 21(3), 50–60 (1997)
7. Farina, A.: Simultaneous measurement of impulse response and distortion with a swept-sine technique. In: Proc. 108th AES Convention (2000)
8. Fausti, P., Farina, A., Pompoli, R.: Measurements in opera houses: comparison between different techniques and equipment. In: Proc. of ICA 1998 - Int. Conf. on Acoustics (1998)
9. Griesinger, D.: Beyond MLS occupied hall measurement with FFT techniques. 101st Audio Eng. Society Convention, Preprint 4403 (October 1996)
10. Jot, J.: Efficient models for reverberation and distance rendering in computer music and virtual audio reality. In: Proc. 1997 International Computer Music Conference (1997)
11. Li, Y., Driessen, P.F., Tzanetakis, G., Bellamy, S.: Spatial sound rendering using measured room impulse responses. Signal Processing and Information Technology. In: IEEE International Symposium on ISSPIT 2006, August 2006, pp. 432–437 (2006)
12. Mateljan, I.: Signal selection for the room acoustics measurement. In: Proc. 1999 IEEE Workshop on Applications of Signal Processing to Audio and Acoustics (1999)
13. Moore, F.R.: A general model for spatial processing of sounds. Computer Music Journal 7(3), 6–15 (1983)
14. Oppenheim, A.V., Schafer, R.W.: Digital Signal Processing. Prentice-Hall, Englewood Cliffs (1975)
15. Pulkki, V.: Spatial sound generation and perception by amplitude panning techniques. Ph.D. Dissertation, Helsinki Univ of Technology (2001)
16. Reller, C.P.A., Jawksford, M.O.J.: Perceptually motivated processing for spatial audio microphone arrays. In: 115th Audio Engineering Society Convention, preprint 5933 (October 2003)
17. Youngblut, C., Johnston, R., Nash, S., Wienclaw, R., Will, C.: Review of Virtual Environment Interface Technology. IDA Paper P-3186. Alexandria, VA: Inst. for Defense Analysis (IDA) (March 1996),
http://www.hitl.washington.edu/scivw/scivw-ftp/publications/IDA-pdf/

Rule-Based Expressive Modifications of Tempo in Polyphonic Audio Recordings

Marco Fabiani and Anders Friberg

Dept. of Speech, Music and Hearing (TMH),
Royal Institute of Technology (KTH), Stockholm, Sweden
{himork,afriberg}@csc.kth.se

Abstract. This paper describes a few aspects of a system for expressive, rule-based modifications of audio recordings regarding tempo, dynamics and articulation. The input audio signal is first aligned with a score containing extra information on how to modify a performance. The signal is then transformed into the time-frequency domain. Each played tone is identified using partial tracking and the score information. Articulation and dynamics are changed by modifying the length and content of the partial tracks. The focus here is on the tempo modification which is done using a combination of time frequency techniques and phase reconstruction. Preliminary results indicate that the accuracy of the tempo modification is in average 8.2 *ms* when comparing Inter Onset Intervals in the resulting signal with the desired ones. Possible applications of such a system are in music pedagogy, basic perception research as well as interactive music systems.

Keywords: automatic music performance, performance rules, analysis-synthesis, time scale modification, audio signal processing.

1 Introduction

A music performance represents the interpretation that a musician (or a computer in our case) gives to a score. To obtain different performances, the musician often follows some principles related to structural features of the score (e.g. musical phrases). The KTH rules system for musical performance [1] models such principles in a quantitative way in order to reproduce a MIDI file expressively using a sequencer and a synthesizer. The quality of the synthesizer plays a major role in the naturalness of the result: a bad synthesizer will sound unnatural even if the performance itself is good. Therefore we propose an alternative approach: directly modify a recorded human performance. A similar idea is described in [2]. Other recent related works can be found in [3,4,5,6,7]. The result should contain all the subtle variations of a real instrument recording, but also comply to the performance characteristics specified by the user, which can be a musician as well as the common listener. Our aim is a system that can be used both for the analysis of a music performance, as well as a tool to modify this performance in a controlled and interactive way. An example of such a system which uses

R. Kronland-Martinet, S. Ystad, and K. Jensen (Eds.): CMMR 2007, LNCS 4969, pp. 288–302, 2008.

MIDI files can be found in [8]. Another field of application is in the study of the cognitive processes behind music listening and appreciation.

It has been shown that a musical performance is to a large degree determined by the three parameters tempo, dynamics and articulation [9]. The KTH rules system controls these three parameters and thus we will concentrate our attention on them. Their modification raises a few problems. First of all, since we aim at modifying each note independently we require the separation of each tone, or at least chord, which is a difficult task especially in the case of polyphonic recordings. In addition, if we want to use the KTH rule system, we need to compute rule values. This requires a subdivision of the musical piece in phrases. Finally, the modifications should be accurate and possibly avoid artifacts. To solve the first two problems, we propose to combine the use of score files aligned with the audio file. We approach the third problem by using analysis-synthesis techniques.

Modifications of tempo and articulation are conceptually straightforward. Modification of dynamics might a priori appear to be a simple task. However, acoustic instruments have a different timbre when played at different dynamic levels (e.g. [10]). Usually louder sounds have a brighter timbre, which means they have more energy concentrated in the higher part of the spectrum. To obtain a realistic sound level modification we need to change both the overall amplitude and the spectral characteristic of a tone. This can be done for example using an appropriate filter (e.g. shelf filter with variable slope), or by synthesizing or subtracting parts of the spectral content of the tone in the frequency domain. The filter approach is easier to implement, but the risk is to raise the noise level together with the actual tone. Modifications of the spectrum in the frequency domain are briefly described in section 3.2.

In section 2 we give a general overview of our system. Section 3 presents the methods for score alignment and analysis of the audio signal. Section 4 briefly describes a few concepts regarding the control of the modification of a performance. In section 5 we describe in detail the tempo modification and performance synthesis process, and present some test results on the accuracy of the time scale modification algorithm in section 6.

2   System Overview

The system can be divided into three main parts, as shown in Figure 1. In the analysis part (a), the audio signal is first aligned with the score using tone onset positions. It is successively analyzed in order to extract single tones and determine their acoustic parameters (length, sound level, timbre using for example the number of partials). These operations are performed once, prior to the performance generation. The analysis information can be stored for later use. In the control part (b), the performance parameters are adjusted by the user and for each note, new values of note length, sound level and tempo are computed, for example using the KTH rule system. In the modification/synthesis part (c), the new performance is generated by applying the new performance values to the

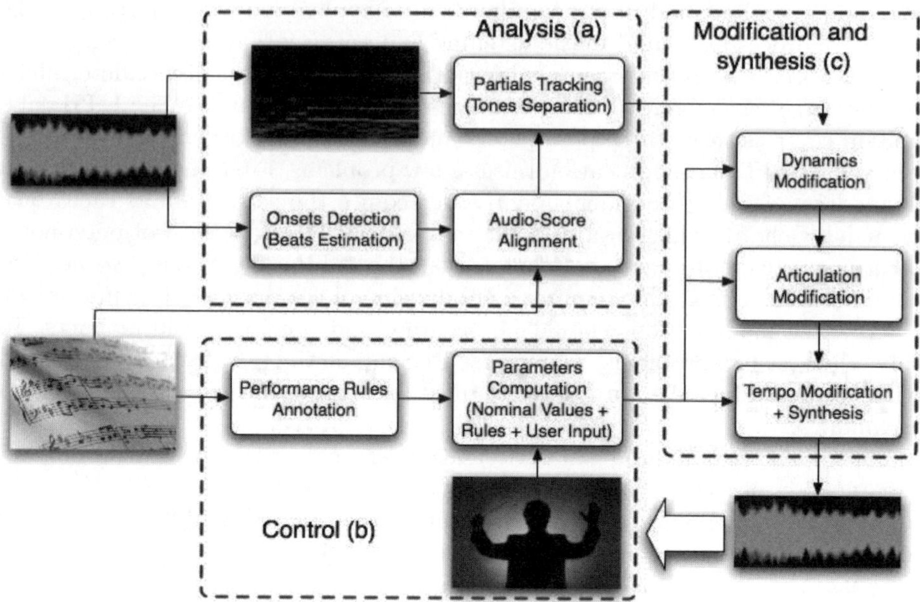

Fig. 1. Schematic representation of the system

analysis data. First sound level and articulation are changed separately. Then the tempo modifications are performed within the synthesis algorithm.

3   Analysis

3.1   Score Alignment

In order to use the information provided by the score we need to align it with the audio file. Various techniques are available to solve this task. One approach is to define a number of related points in the two file, which can be for example note onsets or beat positions. Automatic tone onset detection is an open problem which has been addressed in different ways (for an overview see [11]). None of the algorithms proposed so far are totally accurate: they tend to perform well with impulsive attacks but have problems dealing with slow attacks. Beat detection is closely connected to onset detection, as the latter is usually the first step in the beat estimation process. An overview of some recent techniques is presented in [12]. A problem that can occur with alignment based on tone onsets is the presence of non-simultaneous onsets in the audio signal which are simultaneous in the score. This can be solved using beat positions instead, or different approaches to score alignment which do not rely on onsets, like for example those based on dynamic time warping [13].

   Our system uses onset position to align the audio file with the score. One reason for this is choice is the fact that expressive modifications are performed on a note basis and thus onsets are required anyway. Onset positions are also used by the time scale modification algorithm (see section 5) to preserve transients in the signal. The system anyway can not cope with non-simultaneous onsets that are simultaneous in the score.

In the prototype system under development, onset detection is performed using a simple algorithm based on an edge detection filter[1]. It is also possible to manually correct and add wrong or missing onsets. All the tests run on the system have been performed using accurate onsets positions manually corrected.

3.2   Audio Analysis

The rule system for music performance computes a value of length and sound level for each note in the score. Too apply these changes accurately the audio file needs to be analyzed in order to detect and separate each tone which in a polyphonic recording is mixed with other tones that can also overlap. After the modifications, a new version of the audio signal must be produced. *Analysis/synthesis* systems are sets of algorithms that are designed to perform this task: a model for the signal is selected, the signal is analyzed to estimate the model's parameters and a new signal is produced from the (modified) model. An overview and comparison of some analysis/synthesis techniques can be found in [14].

Sounds produced by acoustic instruments are mostly harmonic and have a large number of partials. This suggests a model where a sound is represented by a series of harmonic, time-varying sinusoids (sinusoidal model). In the graphical representation of a time-frequency transform of the signal (most commonly the Short Time Fourier Transform, STFT) it is possible to see these *harmonic tracks* and an expert eye can point out which one corresponds to which tone. We can see the problem of separating each tone as the problem of automatically detect these tracks and associate them with the corresponding note in the score. This task is known as *partial tracking*. Normally the techniques which are used are based on heuristic rules and do not rely on a priori information. Peaks in the spectrogram are detected and grouped to form a track based on their amplitude, frequency and the surrounding peaks. This was used by McAulay and Quatieri [15], and has been successively improved and extended (see for example [16] where linear prediction is used). In polyphonic recordings, partial tracking is difficult because two simultaneous tones can have overlapping partials. One peak in the spectrogram can be the sum of the two overlapping partials, if they have roughly the same amplitude, or only one partial, if there is a large difference between the two. A possible solution to this problem is to estimate the amplitude of the two partials and assign part of the energy of the peak to one tone and part to the other, using for example the spectral smoothness principle proposed by Klapuri [17].

An audio signal is not only composed by sinusoids. The part of the signal that is not detected by the partial tracking algorithm is considered as a residual

---

[1] http://cnx.org/content/m14170/1.1/

signal. The residual can be obtained by subtracting the harmonic part from the original signal. The residual can also be modeled, for example as a stochastic component represented by a series of approximated spectral envelopes (Spectral Modeling Synthesis by Serra [18]).

For our system we decided to use an analysis/synthesis structure based on the sinusoidal model to represent the tones. Since our system has the score information already available, we decided to use it to help the heuristic partial tracking. The aligned score tells us which notes are (probably) active at any time instant, which means we are not required to perform a multiple-F0 detection to determine how many tones are simultaneously playing and their pitch. We can also estimate which partials most likely overlap and apply for example the spectral smoothness principle. We are still developing the system, and a more detailed description will be presented in the future.

To obtain a time-frequency representation, any transformation other than STFT can be used. We decided to use an analysis-synthesis technique based on the Odd-DFT as proposed by Ferreira [19], which is used in an audio coding algorithm. For a N samples frame, the value of the ODFT's kth frequency bin is

$$X(k) = \sum_{n-0}^{N-1} w_a(n)x(n)e^{-j\frac{2\pi}{N}(k+\frac{1}{2})n} \tag{1}$$

where $w_a(n)$ is the analysis window function and $x(n)$ is the discrete input signal. To test our algorithms we have been using $N = 4096$ and 75% overlap between frames.

Assuming a sinusoidal model for the signal, we have to estimate the frequency and amplitude of each sinusoid composing the signal. Suppose that we have a single sinusoid, the input signal can be written as $x(n) = A\sin(2\pi fn+\phi)$, where A, f and ϕ are the amplitude, frequency and initial phase of the sinusoid. This sinusoid will appear in the time-frequency representation as a peak in a certain bin k. The peak will also leak into the adjacent bins. f, A and ϕ are estimated from the magnitude values of the frequency bins $k-1$, k and $k+1$ [20]. We use the estimated parameters of the sinusoid to perform partial tracking and then store them in a database of notes. Each peak in the time-frequency representation is associated with a note (or several notes in case of overlapping partials) in the score.

The technique can also be inverted to compute the magnitude and phase of $X(k-1)$, $X(k)$ and $X(k+1)$ given a certain frequency and amplitude [21]. We can thus reconstruct a pre-existing peak or synthesize a new peak. This is useful in order to change articulation and sound level: we can extend the length of harmonic tracks, change their amplitude or create completely new ones to modify the tone's timbre (see section 1) as long as the analysis has been accurate. To obtain the ODFT of the residual we compute the frequency bin magnitudes for each value in the notes database and subtract them from the original ODFT.

The synthesis of the modified audio signal is performed by applying the Inverse ODFT to a new ODFT obtained as the sum of the residual's ODFT and that of the notes database modified according to the performance values. A synthesis window $w_s(n)$ is applied to the result of each frame's IODFT and the signal frames are overlap-added. $w_a(n)$ and $w_s(n)$ are chosen so to obtain perfect reconstruction if no modifications are made. Ferreira uses a sine window

$$w(n) = \sin\frac{\pi}{N}(n + \frac{1}{2})), 0 \le n \le N - 1 \tag{2}$$

which is the square root of a Hanning window. By using $w_a(n) = w_s(n)$, the window is applied twice, and the result is the Hanning window which, with 75% overlap, sums up to constant 2. To obtain perfect reconstruction we thus divide the result by 2. The synthesis integrates also the tempo modification, as explained in more detail in section 5.

4   Expressive Performance Control

The creation of a new performance is an interactive process where the user controls a number of parameters to change the output of the system. These parameters typically control high level features of the performance and are then mapped to the mentioned acoustical parameters tempo, sound level and note length. In this way it is possible to steer the performance in a more intuitive way using for example the KTH rule system for music performance [1].

pDM [8] is an example of the usage of this kind of mapping. It is a program that can play MIDI files with expressive modifications using the KTH rules system. In *pDM* 19 rules from the rules system are implemented, of which 14 rules influence tempo, 11 influence sound level, and 5 influence articulation. Each rule has a default value, which is based on the musical context such as phrase position, note relative position and length compared to adjacent notes, and expressive signs in the score. *pDM* uses a score file in which these default values are stored together with notes. The modification values for tempo, sound level and articulation are obtained by computing a weighted sum of the default values originating from each rule. Each rule weight can be controlled independently by the user. Another way to control the performance is through the so-called "activity-valence" plane, the corners of which represent basic emotions such as happiness, sadness, anger and tenderness. Each point on the plane corresponds to a set of interpolated weighting factors, representing a blend of these basic emotions.

Our system builds on the same principles as *pDM*, but uses audio recordings instead of a MIDI sequencer and a synthesizer. As explained in section 3.1, the audio file is aligned with a score file, in this case a *pDM* score which contains default rules values. The same functionalities presented in *pDM* are implemented so that in principle, using the same set of weighting factors in *pDM* and in our system should return the same performance.

5   Tempo Modification and Synthesis

As mentioned in section 1, to change a performance we modify tempo, sound level and tone duration. Examples of expressive modifications of tempo can be found in [5,6,7]. Our aim is to go beyond tempo and modify each tone in a complex mixture independently in order to change also the articulation (note length relative to the Inter Onset Interval, IOI) and the sound level. Sound level and articulation modifications have been briefly described in section 3.2. In this paper we address more specifically our solution to tempo modifications.

5.1   Time Scale Modification Background

Tempo modification is the last change performed in the system. This is due to the fact that time scale modification is an integral part of the synthesis process. There are currently many different algorithms that modify the time scale of audio files without changing the pitch. The most common are those based on the Overlap-Add method in the time domain and on the Phase Vocoder [22] in the frequency domain.

Synchronous Overlap-Add (SOLA) [23] is a simple example of a time domain technique. The signal is divided into short overlapping blocks and each block is shifted according to a time scale factor. Blocks are overlap-added synchronously correcting the new overlap step by the time lag that gives the highest cross correlation in the new overlap region.

In the Phase Vocoder, the STFT is computed over a windowed portion of the signal using an analysis window $w_a(n)$ and analysis hop factor h_a. The Inverse FFT and a synthesis window $w_s(n)$ are used to reconstruct the signal: overlap-add is performed using a synthesis hop factor h_s. To change the time scale, a synthesis factor h_s which is different from the analysis factor h_a is used. This requires an explicit correction of the phase values for each frame of the STFT, based on the underlying sinusoidal model (phase propagation). This guarantees *horizontal coherence*, which means that within each frequency channel we have coherence over time. This phase correction although does not take in consideration *vertical phase coherence*, which is the coherence across frequency channel in a given frame. Further phase corrections are needed, like for example those introduced by the Phase-locked Phase Vocoder [24], which presupposes the detection of peaks in the STFT. Notice also that with $h_a \neq h_s$, the sum of the analysis and synthesis windows does not lead to perfect reconstruction, and depending on the ratio h_a/h_s, the amplitude of the output signal will vary.

When implementing time scale modifications in our system, we had to consider a few main constraints. The first is related to the type of data that is presented to the time stretching/synthesis algorithm and that this data has already been modified to change articulation and sound level. The input to the algorithm is a time-frequency representation, which suggests the use of a frequency domain technique. The magnitude of this representation has been heavily modified by the previous blocks in the system, making the phase response inconsistent. In addition to this, frequency domain techniques present the problem known as "phasiness" or loss of presence (the audio source appears to be far away), due to loss of vertical phase coherence. This two facts led us to completely discard the phase information and to reconstruct the audio signal only from the magnitude of the time-frequency representation. This has previously been solved by using iterative methods such as the Griffin and Lim (G&L) algorithm [25]. However this algorithm is not suitable for realtime modifications since it requires the knowledge of the entire spectrogram in order to compute the time domain representation.

A realtime version of the G&L algorithm, the Real-Time Iterative Spectrum Inversion with Look-Ahead (RTISI-LA), has been proposed by Zhu et al. in [26]. This algorithm is based on the standard FFT, while we implemented this algorithm using the ODFT. To reconstruct the phase information for the analysis frame z given only the magnitude $|X(z)|$, RTISI-LA uses information provided by all the previously reconstructed frames plus m successive frames. In our system we use a 75% analysis overlap ratio (analysis hop size $h_a = N/4$). This means that frame z overlaps with frames $z-3$ to $z-1$ and $z+1$ to $z+3$ and thus $m = 3$. These frames are estimated recursively and the corresponding time domain signal $\hat{x}_{z+m}(n)$ is stored in the frame buffer (b in figure 2).

The computation of the part of the output signal for the current position, which corresponds to frame z, is as follows (see figure 2). First, the oldest frame in the frame buffer ($z-4$) is discarded and an empty space is left for frame $z+3$. At this time in the process, the first three frames in the frames buffer ($z - 3$, ..., $z - 1$) are completed and will not be changed. The following three frames (z, ..., $z + 2$) contain preliminary estimates from previous iterations and the last frame ($z + 3$) is empty.

The iterative process begins by overlap adding the time domain signals in the whole frames buffer with synthesis hop size h_s and synthesis window $w_s(n)$ (see section 3.2). The result is stored in the overlap buffer (c in figure 2). The overlap buffer is divided into overlapping frames with hop size h_s. These frames are then transformed back to the frequency domain using the analysis window $w_a(n)$ to obtain $X_p(z+m)$. The G&L magnitude constraint is then applied to $X_p(z+m)$:

$$\hat{X}(z + m) = X_p(z + m)\frac{|X(z + m)|}{|X_p(z + m)|} \quad m = 0, 1, 2, 3; \tag{3}$$

where $\hat{X}(z + m)$ is the new estimate and the $|X(z + m)|$ is the magnitude of the original transform. Note that $X(z + m)$ has the phase of $X_p(z+m)$ and the magnitude of $X(z + m)$. The whole frames buffer is finally updated with the time domain signals $\hat{x}_{z+m}(n) = IODFT(\hat{X}(z + m)), m = 0, ..., 3$. The iteration is repeated for k number of times (currently we use $k = 5$). At this point, the estimation of frame z is completed. The output of the algorithm for frame z is the part of the overlap buffer where frame z overlaps with frames $z - 3$ to $z - 1$ (dashed vertical lines in figure 2). Changing the synthesis hop size h_s allows to change time scale as it is done in the Phase Vocoder, but with the advantage that phase coherence is automatically obtained by the iterative algorithm.

As all frequency domain techniques, RTISI suffers from transient smearing: sudden changes in the signal, such as sharp tone onsets, are smeared and tend to sound less sharp. Another limitation of frequency domain techniques is that the performances deteriorate above a certain time scale ratio, since the overlapping part of two successive windows becomes too small.

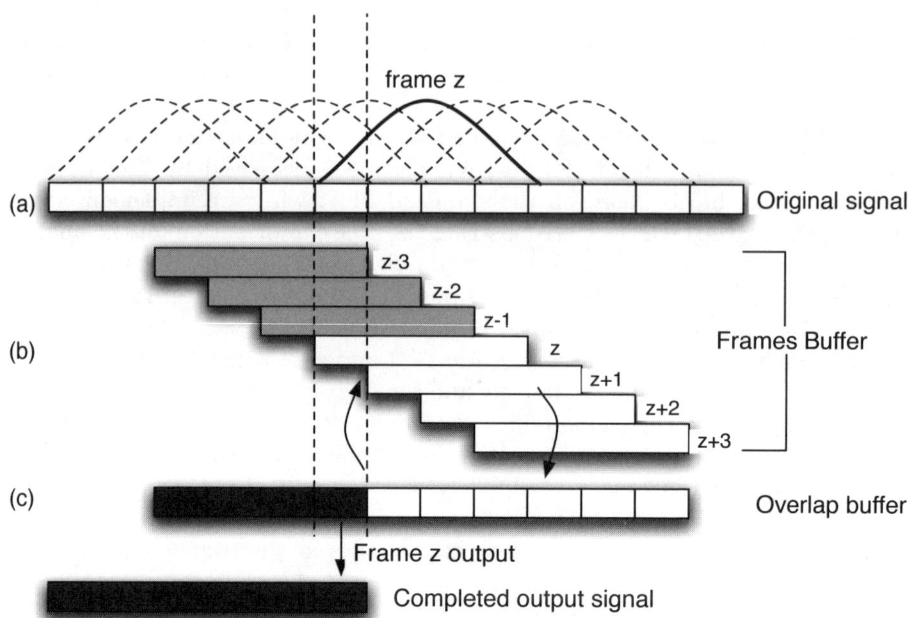

Fig. 2. RTISI-LA schematic representation (from [26]). The frames buffer (b) contains time domain signals which are iteratively updated using the magnitude constrained transform [25] and overlap-added in the overlap buffer. The contribution to the output signal (c) from frame z is the part of the overlap buffer enclosed by the two vertical dashed lines.

All the previous considerations led us to the implementation of an hybrid algorithm which combines different techniques and which is explained in details in the following section.

5.2   Tempo Modification

The rule system represents the tempo changes as a list of Inter Onset Intervals (IOI) values which can be directly applied to the original performance. This means that tempo is changed only at onset positions. The audio between two onsets is stretched or squeezed to the desired length and the tempo can not be changed again until the next onset. Since we are using overlapping windows to analyze the signal, we need to define the position of an onset in terms of windows. We decided to assign the onset to the window in which the onset appears in the first quarter of it, which is also the output from RTISI-LA for that window (see figure 2).

The basic algorithm uses the RTISI-LA method with synthesis hop size $h_s = h_a \cdot IOI_{or}/IOI_{perf}$ between two successive onsets, where IOI_{or} and IOI_{perf} are the original IOIs of the audio recording and the desired performance IOIs, respectively. In order to obtain higher scale ratios, we introduce a variant similar to that proposed by Bonada [27]. If the scale ratio is over a certain value (time expansion) and thus $h_s < h_{min}$, we duplicate (use twice) a number of windows so that the ratio can be reduced. In the opposite case, if the ratio is below a certain value (time compression), and thus $h_s > h_{max}$, we discard a few windows. The number of windows to duplicate or discard is computed so that h_s matches h_{min} or h_{max}. For $h_{min} \leq h_s \leq h_{max}$, the original number of windows is used. The output for each frame is scaled by a factor $r = 2h_a/h_s$ in order to take into account the amplitude variation in the reconstruction mentioned earlier. For $h_s = h_a$, $r = 2$ (perfect reconstruction for 75% overlap Hanning window) and for $h_s = 2h_a$, $r = 1$ (perfect reconstruction for 50% overlap Hanning window).

As previously mentioned, RTISI-LA suffers from transient smearing. Since our system has information about the position of tone onsets (which we assume to be transients), we try to solve the smearing problem by preserving the original signal in the vicinity of each onset. This principle can be easily extended to any transient in the signal, if properly detected. For the windows around an onset, the reconstruction is performed using $h_s = h_a$ and the original phase from the analysis instead of RTISI-LA, and windows are not duplicated or discarded. This has to be taken into account when computing h_s for the remaining portion of the IOI. The result is theoretically a perfect reconstruction of the original signal in the transient area. When switching from RTISI-LA to the simple inverse transform, a phase synchronization is needed. If z is the first frame reconstructed from the original data, a temporary signal is computed using the original phase, and the cross correlation with the previous window is computed, like in the SOLA algorithm. This is used to extract a correction phase $\hat{\phi}$ which is added to all the windows that will use original data, so that $\hat{X}(z) = X(z)\,e^{i\hat{\phi}}$. In this way, the synchronization as well as the phase coherence are maintained. It is worth noticing that perfect reconstruction can not be obtained for frame z if frames $z - 3$ to $z - 1$ have been computed using $h_s \neq h_a$. We thus have to update these three frames with the original data as well when switching from RTISI-LA to simple inverse transformation.

To obtain smoother transitions between the two reconstruction methods we also introduced two ad-hoc solutions. During the implementation we noticed a problem with the amplitude of the signal in the switching area caused by the fact that RTISI-LA reconstructed windows are slightly asymmetric, with the energy concentrated towards the previous window. When overlapped with a symmetric window, the amplitude of the output will fluctuate. To solve this problem we adopt a simple solution. All the frames in the frames buffer are evaluated with the technique used for frame z. This means that when the technique changes, we have to update the entire buffer using the new technique. In the switching area another problem has been encountered: the sudden change of the overlap ratio from h_a to h_s introduces a distortion caused by the sudden change in the amplitude of the overlap-add result. We attenuate this problem by linearly changing h_s from the beginning to the center of the IOI and then back to h_a. An example of the values of h_s for each window is presented in figure 3.

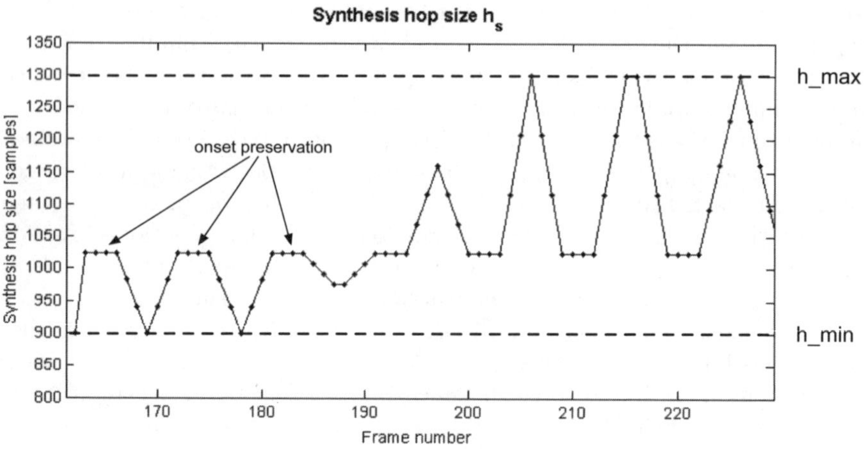

Fig. 3. h_s values for a sample performance. Notice $h_{min} \leq h_s \leq h_{max}$, with $h_{min} = 900$ and $h_{max} = 1300$ and the onset preservation parts where $h_s = h_a = 1024$.

6   Tempo Accuracy

In order to determine whether the tempo modification was successful or not, the output audio performance needs to meet two important goals: it has to correspond to the expected performance given by the rules system, and it should not contain audible artifacts. In this section we analyze only the first requirement. We performed a few informal listening test to verify that no extreme artifacts were introduced, but we leave the systematic analysis of the quality of the reconstruction algorithm to a successive evaluation which will take into account the effects of the other two expressive modification (dynamics and articulation).

To compare the output of our tempo modification algorithm with the desired values computed by the rules system, four short polyphonic musical examples have been generated from MIDI files using *pDM* (piano accompaniment with wind instrument solo). Each example has been converted into audio using a high quality sampler in 7 different variants: the nominal score plus 6 values $(-5, -3, -1, 1, 3, 5)$ for the rule Phrase Arch 5 (see [1] for details on this rule). The nominal score version has been fed to the time scale modification algorithm, and the same 6 values for the Phrase Arch rule has been used to compute the tempo variations (e.g. IOI intervals) for the output performance. The two versions (from MIDI performance and from time scaling) have been compared first in an informal listening test to check for possible artifacts. The transient preservation effect is very clear for percussive sounds (e.g. piano). In general the quality of the output audio is very good, and in certain cases the MIDI generated performance and the audio generated performance are very difficult to distinguish (for small modification values).

To measure IOIs more easily and accurately, we decided to generate another set of audio signals from the four MIDI examples. A signal was created which

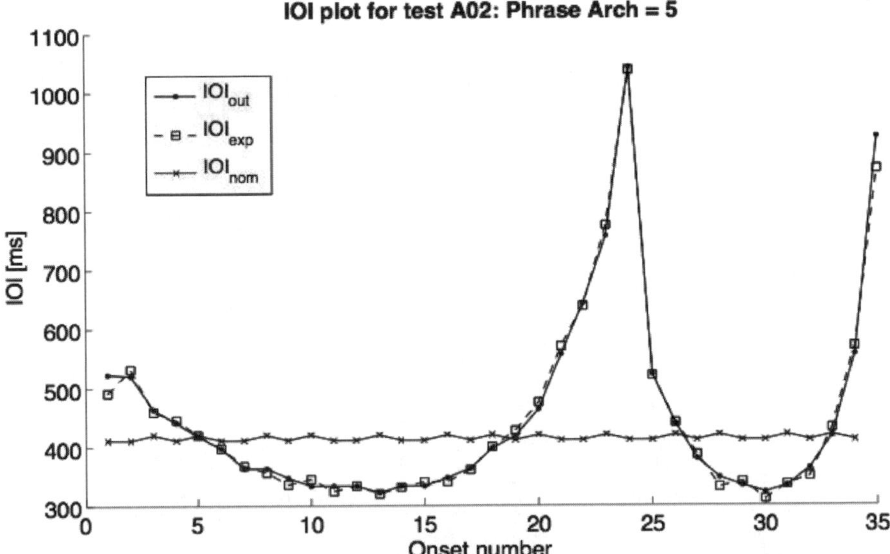

Fig. 4. Inter Onset Intervals (IOI) for test example A02 and Phrase Arch rule value $PhrArch5 = 5$. In the figure are compared the nominal score IOIs (IOI_{nom}), the expected IOIs (IOI_{exp}) computed applying the Phrase Arch rule to the nominal values and the measured IOIs from the output of the tempo modification algorithm (IOI_{out}).

was composed by short (14 ms) square wave bursts placed at each note onset (as specified in the MIDI file) plus a continuous sinusoid with 5 times smaller amplitude. The sinusoid is needed to allow RTISI to continue computing the phase between two bursts. This signal was fed to the tempo modification algorithm together with the 6 different Phrase Arch 5 values. The IOIs of the output signals (IOI_{out}) were measured by finding the beginning of each square wave burst. This was done using an onset detection algorithm followed by a more accurate hand correction. It as to be pointed out that since two of the test examples (P02 and G04) had very short IOIs, it was not possible to apply all 6 values of the Phrase Arch rule and still use transient preservation, since the expected IOI became shorter than the transient length.

The measured IOIs (IOI_{out}) were compared with the expected IOIs (IOI_{exp}) as computed applying the Phrase Arch rule to the nominal IOIs (IOI_{nom}) in pDM. An example is presented in figure 4. The Root Mean Square Error (RMSE)

$$RMSE = \frac{1}{N}\sqrt{\sum_{n=1}^{N}(IOI_{out}(n) - IOI_{exp}(n))^2} \tag{4}$$

has been also computed for each test signals, and summarized in table 1 (N is the number of IOIs for a single test signal). As seen in table 1, the error ranges from about 5 ms to 13 ms. The average over all the examples is 8.2 ms.

Table 1. Mean Square Error (RMSE) of IOI_{out} relative to IOI_{exp} for the 24 test examples

Test #	PhrArch5	RMSE (ms)	Test #	PhrArch5	RMSE (ms)
A02	5	9.3	P02	5	12.0
	3	8.5		3	9.8
	1	8.6		1	8.0
	-1	5.8		-1	8.4
	-3	6.1		-3	10.9
	-5	7.5		-5	9.1
	Average:	7.6		Average:	9.7
T01	5	7.0	G04	5	13.4
	3	5.2		3	9.3
	1	6.7		1	11.7
	-1	5.3		-1	9.6
	-3	6.7		-3	11.4
	-5	7.8		-5	13.5
	Average:	6.5		Average:	11.5

When looking at RMSE we have to take into consideration two aspects. The first is that the onset position, for as accurately as it can be detected and corrected by hand, is still an approximation that can vary by a few milliseconds. Notice how the error for the two examples where transient preservation was not applied (P02 and G04) is higher. This can be explained by the fact that pulses are smeared and thus onset positions are more difficult to uniquely identify. The second aspect to be considered is that, while onsets are measured in ms or samples, the system works with windows and the onset position has to be approximated to the center of the closest window. This does also introduce an approximation error that can be up to $\pm h_a/2$, which is typically around 10 ms. The results although show that the algorithm is quite accurate in following rules values, and from figure 4 it can be noticed how two successive IOIs usually compensate each other by fluctuating above and below the desired IOI curve.

7   Discussion and Future Work

In this paper we presented a scheme for the analysis and expressive modification of audio musical performances. After briefly describing the analysis process, we focused on the modification of tempo, presenting the algorithms used. We run a few tests in order to verify the accuracy of the time scale modification algorithm. A prototype of this performance modification system has been implemented in Matlab for test purposes (see [28] for a description). Possible applications for such a system are in the field of music cognition: highly controllable and natural sounding stimuli can be produced for listening tests where for example the effect of a certain acoustical parameter needs to be investigated. Interactive musical systems are other possible applications for this system, such as virtual conducting games. Such a system would sound more natural when compared to other performance systems based on MIDI sequencers and synthesizers [8]. It would also be more flexible than some current systems based on audio that rely on specifically made recordings [29]. Our system can in principle work with any recording as long as the score is available, although the analysis might be very difficult and the result unsatisfactory. An added feature of our system is the possibility to modify articulation.

A number of problems need to be solved to produce a modified audio signal free from audible artifacts. We must first of all improve the analysis process to obtain better tone separation. This will allow us to obtain cleaner articulation modifications and also better estimations of the timbre of each tone from the number of partials and their amplitude. Another important problem is the measurement of the sound level of a single tone, which is required in order to perform dynamics modifications. We would also like to run listening tests in order to verify the perceptual quality of the modified audio recordings.

References

1. Friberg, A., Bresin, R., Sundberg, J.: Overview of the KTH rule system for musical performance. Advances in Cognitive Psychology, Special Issue on Music Performance 2, 145–161 (2006)
2. Amatriain, X., Bonada, J., Loscos, A., Arcos, J., Verfaille, V.: Content-based transformations. Journal of New Music Research 32, 95–114 (2003)
3. Jehan, T.: Creating Music by Listening. PhD thesis, Massachusetts Institute of Technology, Media Arts and Sciences, Boston, MA (USA) (2005)
4. Maestre, E., Hazan, A., Ramirez, R., Perez, A.: Using concatenative synthesis for expressive performance in jazz saxophone. In: Proceedings of International Computer Music Conference 2006, New Orleans (2006)
5. Gouyon, F., Fabig, L., Bonada, J.: Rhytmic expressiveness transformations of audio recordings: Swing modifications. In: Proc. of the International Conference on Digital Audio Effects (DAFX 2003), London, UK (2003)
6. Janer, J., Bonada, J., Jord, S.: Groovator - an implementation of real-time rhythm transformations. In: Proceedings of 121st Convention of the Audio Engineering Society, San Francisco, USA, CA (2006)
7. Grachten, M.: Expressivity-aware Tempo Transformations of Music Performances Using Case Based Reasoning. PhD thesis, Universit Pompeu Fabra (UPF) - Music Technology Group (MTG) (2006)
8. Friberg, A.: Home conducting: Control the overall musical expression with gestures. In: Proceedings of the 2005 International Computer Music Conference (ICMC 2005), Barcelona, Spain, pp. 479–482 (September 2005)
9. Juslin, P.N.: Cue utilization in communication of emotion in music performance: Relating performance to perception. Journal of Experimental Psychology: Human Perception and Performance 26, 1797–1813 (2000)
10. Luce, D.A.: Dynamic spectrum changes of orchestral instruments. Journal of the Audio Engineering Society 23(7), 565–568 (1975)
11. Bello, J., Daudet, L., Abdallah, S., Duxbury, C., Davies, M., Sandler, M.: A tutorial on onset detection in music signals. IEEE Transactions on Speech and Audio Processing 13(5), 1035–1047 (2005)

12. Gouyon, F., Klapuri, A., Dixon, S., Alonso, M., Tzanetakis, G., Uhle, C., Cano, P.: An experimental comparison of audio tempo induction algorithms. IEEE Transactions on Audio, Speech and Language Processing 14, 1832–1844 (2006)
13. Dixon, S., Widmer, G.: Match: a music alignment tool chest. In: Proceedings of the 6th International Symposium on Music Information Retrieval (ISMIR 2005), London, UK (2005)
14. Wright, M., Beauchamp, J., Fitz, K., Rodet, X., Robel, A., Sierra, X., Wakefield, G.: Analysis/synthesis comparison. Organized Sound 5(3), 173–189 (2000)
15. McAulay, R.J., Quatieri, T.F.: Speech analysis/synthesis based on a sinusoidal representation. IEEE Transactions on Acoustics, Speech and Signal Processing 34(4), 744–754 (1986)
16. Lagrange, M., Marchand, S., Rault, J.B.: Tracking partials for the sinusoidal modeling of the polyphonic sounds. In: IEEE 2005 International Conference on Acoustics, Speech, and Signal Processing (ICASSP 2005) (2005)
17. Klapuri, A.P.: Multipitch estimation and sound separation by the spectral smoothness principle. In: Proceedings of the IEEE International Conference on Acoustics, Speech and Signal Processing (ICASSP 2001), Salt Lake City, UT, USA, pp. 3381–3384 (2001)
18. Serra, X., Smith, J.O.: Spectral modeling synthesis:a sound analysis/synthesis based on a deterministic plus stochastic decomposition. Computer Music Journal 14, 12–24 (1990)
19. Ferreira, A.J., Sinha, D.: Accurate spectral replacement. In: Proceedings of the 118th Convention of the Audio Engineering Society, Barcelona, Spain (May 2005)
20. Ferreira, A.J., Sinha, D.: Accurate and robust frequency estimation in the odft domain. In: Proceedings of the IEEE Workshop on Applications of Signal Processing to Audio and Acoustics, New Paltz, USA, NY (October 2005)
21. Ferreira, A.J.: Combined spectral envelope normalization and subtraction of sinusoidal components in the odft and mdct frequency domains. In: Proceedings of the IEEE Workshop in Application od Signal Processing to Audio and Acoustics, New Paltz, NY (USA) (2001)
22. Flanagan, J., Golden, R.: Phase vocoder. The Bell System Technical Journal, 1493–1509 (November 1966)
23. Roucos, S., Wilgus, A.: High quality time scale modification for speech. In: Proc. IEEE Int. Conf. Acoustics, Speech, Signal Processing., vol. 1, pp. 493–496 (1985)
24. Laroche, J., Dolson, M.: Improved phase vocoder time-scale modification of audio. IEEE Transaction on Speech and Audio signal processing 7(3), 323–332 (1999)
25. Griffin, D., Lim, J.: Signal estimation from modified short-time fourier transform. IEEE Transactions on Acoustics, Speech, and Signal Processing 32(2) (April 1984)
26. Zhu, X., Beauregard, G.T., Wyse, L.: Real-time iterative spectrum inversion with look-ahead. In: Proceedings of the 2006 IEEE Internationl Conference on Multimedia and Expo (ICME 2006), Toronto, Canada (2006)
27. Bonada, J.: Automatic technique in frequency domain for near-lossless time-scale modification of audio. In: Proc. of the International Computer Music Conference (ICMC 2000), Berlin (Germany) (2000)
28. Fabiani, M., Friberg, A.: Expressive modifications of musical audio recordings: preliminary results. In: Proceedings of the 2007 International Computer Music Conference (ICMC 2007), Copenhagen (DK), vol. 2, pp. 21–24 (2007)
29. Lee, E., Kiel, H., Dedenbach, S., Gruell, I., Karrer, T., Wolf, M., Borchers, J.: iSymphony: An adaptive interactive orchestral conducting system for conducting digital audio and video streams. In: Extended Abstracts of CHI 2006 Conference on Human Factors in Computing Systems, Montreal (Canada) (2006)

Exploring the Perceptual Relevance of Inherent Variability of Drum Sounds

Matthias Rath and Marcel Wältermann

Berlin University of Technology
Deutsche Telekom Laboratories
Quality and Usability Lab
matthias.rath@telekom.de, marcel.waeltermann@telekom.de
http://www.qu.t-labs.tu-berlin.de

Abstract. It is common "beat programming" practice to construct rhythmic sequences in a one-sample-per-instrument manner. Sounds of separate strokes on a drum, however, generally are not really perceptually identical, even when played with identical intention on the side of the player. Moreover, such unavoidable individual variations go beyond the effects of amplitude scaling or simple linear (e.g., low- or high-pass) filtering. One first simple approach to examine effects of this fact is to construct rhythmical patterns using several samples of each instrument. Experiences in a first pilot study with such "drum-machine-like" patterns suggest that individual note–to–note differences have a relevant influence on the overall character of the musical results.

1   Introduction

Whoever is experienced in listening to or playing traditional musical instruments will agree with the statement that their potential of emotional expression usually relies on complex variability of the sonic results in reaction to a musician's various input gestures. It has indeed often been noted that the sonic aesthetic fascination of an instrument is usually hardly captured in the quality of a single typical tone but also lies to strong degree in the dynamic behaviour of the abundance of various producible sounds. This observation is easily made in particular when dealing with electronic instruments based on playback of so-called "samples" of preexisting sound sources, as often used for the digital simulation of mechanical, electro-mechanical, or analogue-electronic instruments: sound production on the basis of sample-player simulations of mechanical instruments can easily lead to an overall result of the typical "MIDI studio sound" with its tendentially "inorganic", "static", or "cheap" character. The aspect of dynamic variation and reactiveness is therefore one of the hopes and goals connected to approaches of sound generation that are based on (physically inspired) models of processes of sound generation, and that are often denoted under the term of "physical" or "physically-based modelling". In sample-based sound generation, on the other

R. Kronland-Martinet, S. Ystad, and K. Jensen (Eds.): CMMR 2007, LNCS 4969, pp. 303–312, 2008.

hand, strategies to introduce a dynamic quality to the instrumental behaviour include the post-processing of employed signals by means of filters and amplitude envelopes with dynamically varying parameters [1]. Mechanical sound-producing processes, however, generally include much more complex dependencies between characteristics of physical actions at the beginning of the causal chain (such as an instrumentalist's gestures) and the final acoustic output. As an example, sounds of an acoustic piano played at different strengths do not simply differ in a way that may be fully described by amplitude scaling or low-pass filtering. Many sample-based digital instruments therefore use "multisamples" of instruments played at various levels of loudness. (For an example from the field dealt with here, drum programming, see, e.g., [2].)

Inherent non-repeatability of sounds of mechanical instruments? While variations of piano sound resulting from key strokes of different velocities or of the sound of a drum struck at variable velocities have received some attention (and, as just noted, have been considered by the use of multisamples), the question of a possible perceptual relevance of unavoidable, involuntary indeterminacy in such sounds has hardly been addressed so far. In more simple words: is it not possible that indeterminable differences in, e.g., piano tones or drum sounds played with identical intention on the side of the instrumentalist are an important factor for the "overall sonic characteristic" of the instrument?

To establish the potential interest of this question it is worthwhile to note that the mechanical systems of sound generation of traditional instruments in their description as dynamical systems usually include strong non-linearities (see e.g. [3]) so that even arbitrarily small variations in initial conditions or input parameters may lead to strong and perceptible differences in sonic output. The first author has been involved in the development of a sound synthesis algorithm based on a simple model of impact interaction of solid objects. As an example, for the observation just given, Figure 1 shows the vibration of a simple linear object of two vibrational modes being struck periodically with equal initial velocity by a point-mass (a sound event similar, e.g., to a mechanical door bell). Without further explanation of the model by means of which this displayed waveform has been generated (we here refer to dedicated publications [4]), it is noted that this behaviour is very different — and *sounds different* — than a simple repetition of identical copies of the signal created by one single impact. A closer look at the displayed signal reveals that the different phases between two impacts also differ more fundamentally than described simply by amplitude scaling or linear (e.g. low- or high-pass) filtering. Given this complex behaviour of even a rather simple dynamical system (derived from physical descriptions under involvement of strong simplifications), we have to assume that for "real" mechanical systems such as a drum or piano, the given observations are also, indeed even more, relevant. A played drum roll must therefore have a very different auditory quality than the periodic playback of the same drum sample (an example that has been auditorilly tested by the authors and that will later be picked up again).

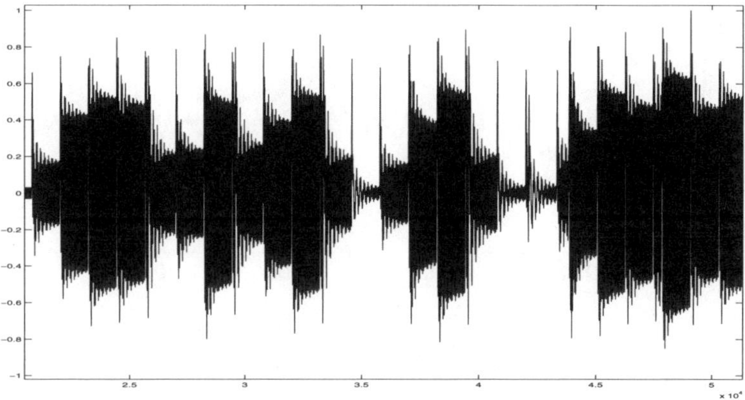

Fig. 1. Vibration (at one point) of a two-mode object struck periodically (at a frequency of approx. $20Hz$) by a point-mass

If we stick with the example of the drum, we must further consider that also many other initial conditions and parameters of the mechanical sound-emitting event beyond the initial state of movement of the membrane may be controlled by the player only up to a certain precision: examples are the velocity of the drum stick, the position at which the stick hits the membrane, the angle of the stick at the moment of contact (thus its "effective admittance"), and the force which the player exerts on the stick at the moment of contact. We must therefore take the possibility into account that even two drum strokes played at two freely chosen distinctive moments with the intention to sound the same, and with the drum being initially quiet, may actually sound clearly different. Figure 2 displays the signals of such two distinct snare drum strokes recorded under equal conditions and normalised for equal RMS power value. The two signals sound very similar, but could be distinguished auditorilly by expert listeners in a quick informal test. Their auditory difference is however not of the type achievable by amplitude scaling or linear filtering (a fact that is also reflected in the waveform displays).

From these considerations it seems convincing that the question given at the beginning of this paragraph is clearly worthwhile investigating in the case of drum instruments. Even for the piano, where variations of relevant parameters during sound generation (such as the ones listed above for the drum) are much more restricted by the mechanics of the instrument, it is imaginable that the differences between tones played with identical intention, and such that, e.g., the perceived loudness is equal, may be a perceptually (and musically) relevant factor. The work described in the following focuses on drum sounds for the reason of easier practicability and forms a first simple investigation towards the posed question.

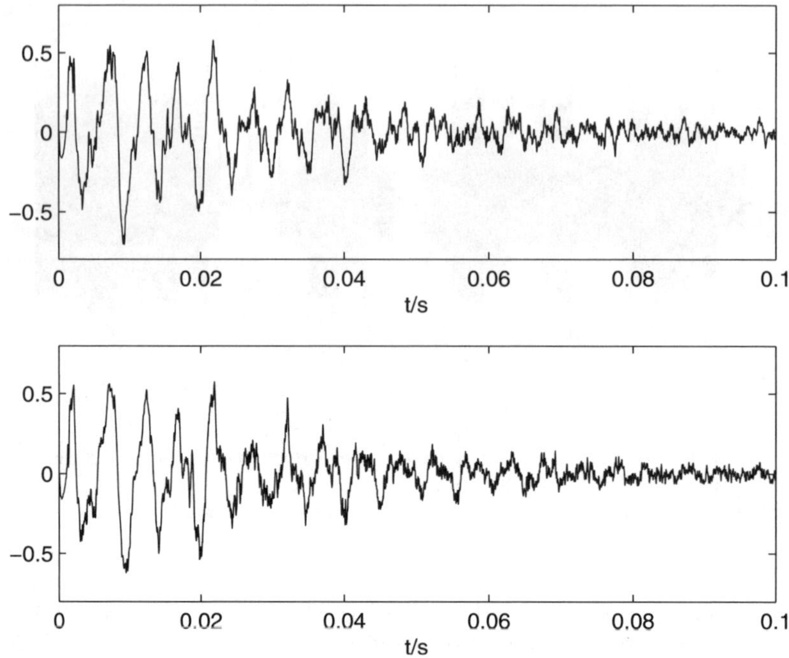

Fig. 2. Different snare drum strokes played with identical intention and normalised for identical RMS power value

2   A Simple Application of "Non-Repetitiveness" Considerations

In order to investigate the question described and motivated in the previous section we constructed drum-patterns from samples of bass drum, snare drum, and hi-hat strokes, in the way typically employed in a MIDI sequencer or drum computer. All patterns were then realised in two versions, one by using one sample of each instrument, just as in a conventional sample-based drum machine, and a second by using several samples of each drum instrument, distributed randomly among the programmed notes of the respective instrument. The different samples of each drum instrument were taken from previous recordings of the second author playing isolated notes on each instrument (bass drum, snare, and hi-hat). The single notes had been played with the same intention of loudness and playing technique to create a pool of potential drum samples for musical use. All tones of one instrument had been recorded with drum, microphone and recording room in the same constant configuration.

Individual differences beyond loudness variations? When listening to the different samples of one instrument from the recordings "in a row", or selectively comparing different such samples, differences are perceived (as already noted above) but are subtle and very hard to describe verbally. Commonly understood attributes that might be used to describe some of the perceptual differences between single drum samples are small variations in loudness, and in rare cases in the length of the decay of the snare sound. In order to minimise an influence of these consciously notable aspects on the overall impression of the drum patterns — such as for example one single extreme snare stroke dominating the appearance of one version — two measures were taken: 1. Snare samples with noticeably short or long decay were not used in the pool of samples for random selection. 2. All samples of each instrument were normalised for equal RMS power level. With these precautions, the chosen samples of one instrument appeared of equal loudness to the authors.

In order to further focus on the relevance of individual sound variations that go beyond what may be captured by a loudness attribute, all notes in all generated patterns were scaled by a random factor distributed logarithmically uniform between $1/1.15$ ($\approx -1.2dB$) and 1.15 ($\approx 1.2dB$). The motivation for the choice of this exact factor of $+/-1.2dB$, which is close to the perceptive threshold for amplitude differences (see, e.g., [5]), will become clear in the following paragraph.

Drum rolls as "most delicate scenario". It has already been noted in the introduction (Section 1) that a drum roll must be expected to sound and look different than the periodic repetition of the sound of one singular drum stroke. The authors have constructed various versions of artificial drum rolls by triggering snare drum samples out of the pool of RMS-normalised samples at constant high rate, exactly 32th notes at a tempo of 120 BPM. The different versions consisted of

1. periodic repetition of one single sample,
2. periodic repetition of 2-18 different samples *in constant order*, and
3. constant–rate triggering of 2-18 different samples — *randomly*.

Figure 3 shows waveforms of three examples. Summing up the authors' informal auditory experimentation with the different created "roll" patterns, it can be noticed that

1. the periodically repeated single sample sounds very unnatural, almost not drum-like,
2. for several samples, periodic triggering in constant order results in audible periodicity in the pattern, which gets increasingly dominant the smaller the number of used samples, and is still disturbing even for 18 samples,
3. constant–rate triggering of samples in random order generally leads to auditory results closer to a played drum roll. As expected, results improve with the number of used samples. In the authors' informal experimentation, a number of four samples was found to form a minimum below which the overall sound becomes very unnatural.

Finally we examined the effect of additional amplitude randomisation with the general findings that

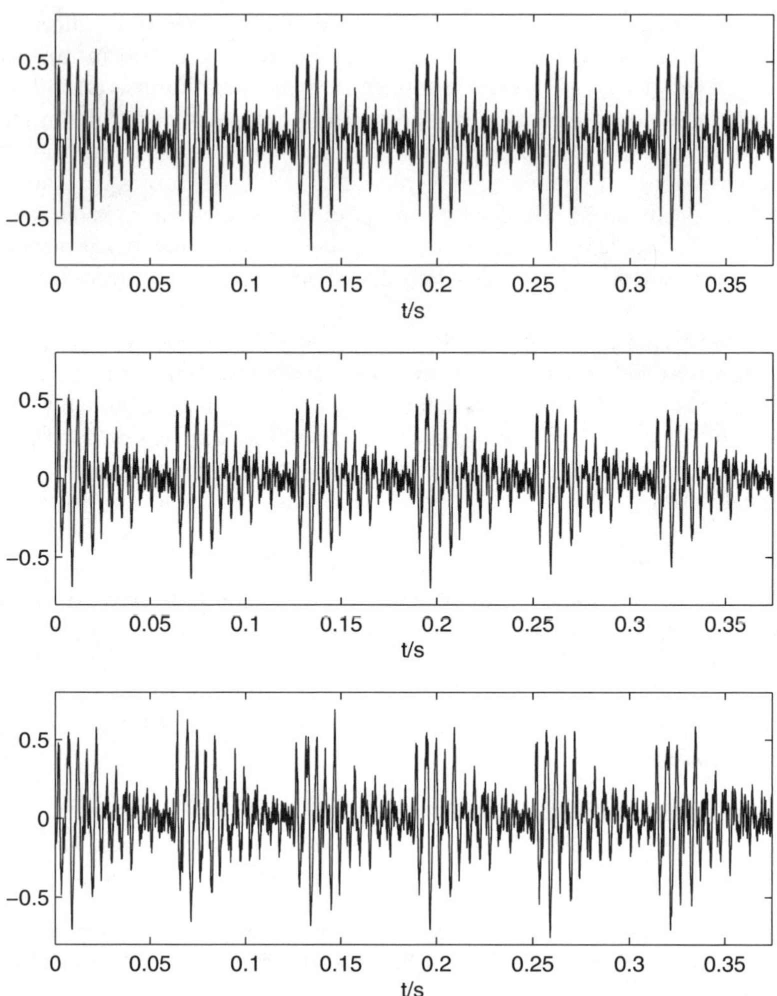

Fig. 3. "Drum rolls" created by repetition of one fixed sample (above), repetition of the same sample with random amplitude scaling of maximal $+/-1.2dB$ (middle), and constant-rate triggering of different samples of the same drum (below)

1. for periodic repetition of one sample, the sonic result gets somehow more natural up to a certain factor of randomisation above which the irregularity sounds rather awkward,
2. for the periodic repetition of several samples in fixed order, the timbral periodicities noted above remain also for "modest" amplitude randomisation, and
3. for randomly triggered samples slight amplitude randomisation has small auditory effect.

An amount of random modulation of individual amplitudes of samples between the maxima of 1.15 and 1/1.15 ($+/-1.2dB$) was chosen as leading to the most convincing sound results.

A "drum machine with sound variations". On the basis of the notions just described, a simple "sequencer" was realised that allows to program drum patterns of the three chosen instruments, bass drum, snare drum, and hi-hat in an arbitrary regular temporal grid, as with a typical "drum machine". Individual amplitudes of notes can be specified with 32-bit–float resolution and are randomised with an additional $+/-1.2dB$–factor as described above. Furthermore, each instrument (bass drum, snare drum, hi-hat) allows the specification of the number of samples in the pool out of which single notes are randomly taken. The random algorithm was enhanced such that no specific sample will appear twice in a row. The "drum machine" was realised in Matlab such that the temporal placement of drum sounds is accomplished with a precision of single time steps, i.e., precise up to approx. $0.023ms$ ($\approx 1/44100Hz$) at the used sample rate.

3   Pilot Study

In order to examine a potential auditory relevance of involuntary individual differences in drum strokes for musical character on a larger scale, a short pilot study was conducted with 12 test subjects listening to drum patterns generated by means of the experimental drum machine described in the previous section. Four drum patterns were programmed, somewhat of increasing complexity, each realised in two versions:

– one *"static"*, using only one sample per instrument and
– one *"dynamic"*, using eight samples per instrument.

The first pattern forms a rather simple, Disco-like beat at tempo 120 BPM, with a completely regular four–quarter note bass drum, and snare-strokes on beats 2 and 4. Pattern 2 is a slower, tempo 108 BPM, more complex "Funky Drummer"-like beat. Pattern 3 contains short 48th snare note rolls and is faster, tempo 130 BPM. Finally, still more complicated is pattern 4, a Drum'n Bass inspired beat with more drum rolls. All patterns are in 4/4 measure with regular 16ths as smallest rhythmical subunit (with the exception of occasional 48th note "rolls"). Figure 4 shows the first and fourth example in schematic notation.

3.1   Experiment

At the beginning of the test, each subject was asked to listen to the four drum patterns, each in the two versions. The order in which the two versions were presented was fixed for each subject but swapped in-between subjects. Each version was preceded by 4 seconds of pink noise (followed by 1 second of silence) in order to "erase" any immediate memory of preceding patterns. As an example, stimuli were presented to the first subject in the order: 1. pink noise, 2. beat 1,

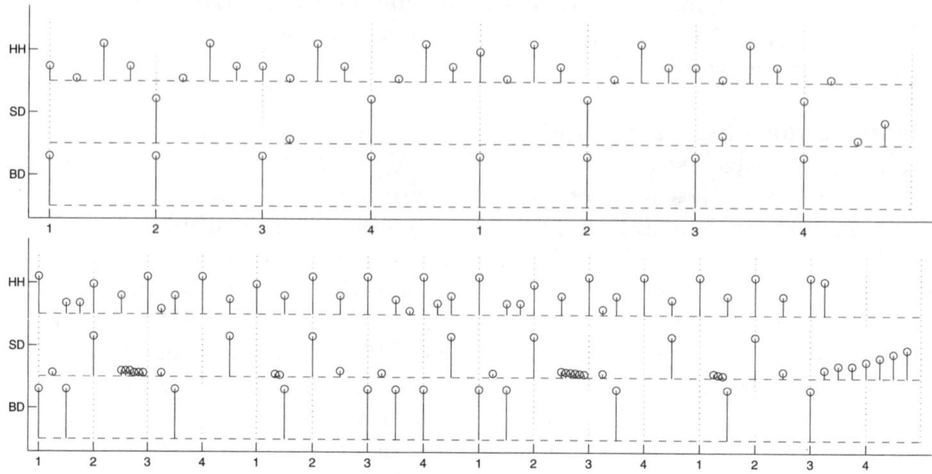

Fig. 4. The first (top) and last (bottom) of the drum patterns used in the listening experiment. The horizontal unit is given by quarter note beats.

dynamic version, 3. pink noise, 4. beat 1, *static version*, 5. pink noise, 6. beat 2, *dynamic version*, 7. pink noise, 8. beat 2...Before listening, subjects were told that they would hear four drum patterns, each in two different versions, separated by noise.

After having listened to the series of drum patterns, subjects were asked five questions, the first two of which aimed at subjects' immediate spontaneous impression: "In what respect do you feel does the first version of each beat differ from the second one?", "Which version of each beat, the first or second, did you generally like more?".

Question 3, as question 2, again aimed at the personal preference of which version the subject thought sounded better, but now the subject could (if desired) listen again to the pair of each beat before answering. The same procedure applied to the questions 4 and 5: "Which version of the beat sounds 'more natural'?" and "Which version do you feel sounds more like a human drummer rather than a machine?". All questions were read to subjects and explained in case of difficulties. In particular, subjects were told that they did not have to answer to the questions. Twelve subjects participated in the test, three female and nine male, aged between 25 and 35, with various musical experiences and interests.

3.2   Results

Spontaneously perceived difference. As a first general observation, 5 of the 12 subjects, after having listened once to the series of pairs, found it hard to spontaneously state or at least to verbalise any perceived difference. Exact answers of these 5 subjects included "no difference noticed" (one subject) and doubtful guesses without obvious relation to the real phenomenon such as "more reverb?", "more dull?, faster?" or "further away?". Of the remaining 7 subjects, one described the *dynamic version* as being "more dynamic, as if the drummer was more involved in dosing the strength of his strokes to make the beat more energetic", one labelled this version as "more natural", the other as "more artificial" and one stated the *static version* being "unnatural". One subject described the differences in the pairs as "the dynamic fluctuations in the snare drum being differently strong" without being able to give a general tendency from the *static* to the *dynamic version*. The three remaining subjects gave more generic attributes, concretely: the *static version* "sounding cleaner", "more pushing", the *dynamic version* "sounding stronger". No subject, including those with some musical and listening experience, was able to actually find out the mechanism behind the generation of the pairs of beats (namely one version being built from different samples and one containing only one sample of each instrument).

Personal aesthetic preference and "naturalness" judgements. Asked for a spontaneous preference after first listening, 5 subjects opted for the *dynamic version*, 3 for the *static* one. The remaining 4 subjects had no preference. When allowed to listen again to single pairs of beats under the aspect of preference, in few cases some subjects rendered their responses more precisely. Without going into details, the general tendency here was towards the *dynamic version* being preferred. One subject that had initially preferred the *static version* now preferred the *dynamic* one for all four beats, as well as another subject that had initially not stated any preference.

Answers to question 4 correlated strongly with those to question 3, i.e., in almost all cases subjects now labelled the version as more "natural" that was previously liked more, whereby the *dynamic version* now clearly dominated. The same overall tendency was finally seen for question 5 where 5 of the 12 subjects labelled the *dynamic version* as "sounding less machine-like" than the *static* one and only one subject said the opposite for the first pattern.

While this test and the presented results are of course preliminary, it can however generally be stated that a difference between the *static* and *dynamic* version is indeed perceived, although subjects often have difficulties describing their impression. There is at least some evidence that the *dynamic* version is preferred in average. Of course, these remarks must be considered as a first exploration and will have to be pursued deeper in extended experiments.

4   Conclusions

The presented work forms a first exploration on the question of a potential relevance of inherent variations in individual sounds of mechanical instruments. Despite the very simple approach used here to take into account possible variations in drum sound for the creation of stimuli patterns and the very simple design of the pilot study, some effects are seen. Strong hints have been found that unavoidable differences between drum sounds of essentially equal perceived volume and played with identical intent may be clearly relevant for the perceived character of a musical phrase. From these observations it appears well possible that the conventional practice of constructing rhythmic patterns from single samples of percussive instruments may be one important factor responsible for what is commonly perceived as the typical "MIDI studio sound". A closer examination of the phenomenon may form a basis for new tools for musicians with extended expressive possibilities.

References

1. Massie, D.C.: Wavetable sampling synthesis. In: Kahrs, M., Brandenburg, K. (eds.) Applications of Digital Signal Processing to Audio and Acoustics. Springer, Netherlands (2002)
2. http://www.fxpansion.com/
3. Smith III, J.O.: Physical modeling synthesis update. Computer Music Journal 20(2), 44–56 (1996)
4. Avanzini, F., Rath, M., Rocchesso, D.: Physically-based audio rendering of contact. In: ICME 2002 Proceedings. IEEE International Conference on Multimedia and Expo., vol. 2, pp. 445–448 (2002)
5. Zwicker, E., Fastl, H.: Psychoacoustics. Facts and Models, 2nd edn., Berlin (1999)

Improving Musical Expressiveness by Time-Varying Brightness Shaping

Mathieu Barthet, Richard Kronland-Martinet, and Sølvi Ystad

CNRS Laboratoire de Mécanique et d'Acoustique,
31 chemin Joseph-Aiguier,
13402 Marseille Cedex 20,
France
{barthet,kronland,ystad}@lma.cnrs-mrs.fr

Abstract. Former studies show that removing brightness temporal variations of tones in an expressive clarinet performance induces a decrease in the appreciation judgments among listeners. This study aims to investigate the reciprocal process where a time-varying brightness pattern is extracted from a clarinet performance and added to MIDI sound sequences generated by sampler-based instruments. Performances with and without brightness temporal variations have hereby been generated using samples from three sustained instruments (piccolo flute, clarinet and cello) and two non-sustained instruments (guitar and sitar). 20 listeners were asked to rate the dissimilarities between the performances in terms of interpretation, and then to select the performance they preferred. Results show that the application of the brightness temporal variations extracted from the clarinet performance increases the appreciation judgment of the performances for almost all the instruments used in the experiment.

Keywords: Musical expressiveness, timbre, analysis-synthesis, clarinet.

1 Introduction

Music Performance and Timbre. Since the beginning of the twentieth century, many experts with various backgrounds such as musicology, psychology and acoustics have worked on the characterization of expressive music performance either focusing on the control of the instrument or the produced sound [1]. The intricate process of interpretation in music is defined in [2] as "the act of performance with the implication that in this act the performer's judgment and personality necessarily have their share". As a matter of fact, the analysis of musical interpretations by measurements revealed that performers generally deviate from a regular transcription of the nominal information given by the score when playing expressively. Although studies on psychology of music and expressive music performance modeling have often dealt with timing and dynamics aspects (see for instance [3], [4], [5], [6], [7]), the influence of timbre, topic of the present work, has been much less considered. This may not be unrelated to the fact that timbre is a complex notion which does not yet have a proper definition

R. Kronland-Martinet, S. Ystad, and K. Jensen (Eds.): CMMR 2007, LNCS 4969, pp. 313–336, 2008.

and is hardly measurable. Moreover, most of the fore mentioned studies deal with traditional Western tonal music known to be governed by the structure of pitches and rhythms, hiding the importance of timbre, at least at first glance. Lerdhal explains that the secondary role of timbre in traditional music is due to the fact that, as opposed to pitches and rhythms, timbre does not possess a true hierarchical organization [8]. This lack of hierarchical organization has effectively proved to be an obstacle for memorization and musical perception [9]. Although timbre does not own specific notations in the traditional Western music system and remains an ambiguous notion, it is nonetheless a very important aspect of musical sounds; already in 1938, Seashore [10] pointed out that "timbre as a fourth attribute of tone is by far the most important aspect of tone and introduces the largest number of problems and variables".

On the Definition of Timbre. The notion of timbre strongly depends on the context. A composer willingly speaks about the timbres by reference to the instruments of the orchestra. This facet of timbre is called *timbre-identity* in [11] and expresses the link of timbre to the physical cause generating the sound. This primitive causal link with the sound source probably comes from the origin of the word timbre, initially used to design an instrument, a sort of drum composed of tensed strings which gave a specific "color" to the resulting sound [12]. On the other hand, musicians are often identified by their timbre (e.g. "the timbre of Coltrane"), which here refers to the specific sound that took them years to establish and which often allows them to be distinguished from other performers. This notion is designed by *timbre-individuality* in [11] but seems similar to the *timbre-identity* notion apart from the fact that the categories of sounds are different (in one case it identifies the instruments, in the other the musicians). Finally, psychoacousticians often refer to timbre as the character of the auditory sensation which permits the distinction of sounds having the same pitch, loudness and durations, an aspect called *timbre-quality* in [11]. The incoherences of the standard definitions (given in [13] and [14]) have often been reported in the literature (see for instance [15]). Schaeffer, one of the pioneers of timbre research raised one major paradox with timbre which states that each instrument has to possess its proper timbre while it generates sounds which all have their own timbres [16]! Such a phenomenon can be illustrated by transposing a low register piano tone into a higher pitched tone without taking care of the decrease of the harmonics energy as the pitch increases. The resulting sound no more corresponds to a piano tone showing that timbre also depends on the instrument range. A better understanding of the nature of timbre has therefore to deal with two complementary visions: one related to its morphology (study of its structure and form) and the other related to its typology (systematic classification of types that have common characteristics or invariants).

The Quest for Timbre Descriptors and Timbre Control. Some authors looked for acoustic correlates of timbre aiming at identifying different musical sounds and understanding their perceptual discrimination (see [17], [18], [19], [20], etc.). Such studies unveiled the multidimensional nature of timbre usually represented in a three dimensional space where each dimension is linked to some spectral, temporal and spectro-temporal aspects of sounds. These descriptors are often derived from the spectral envelope (its irregularity is a strong characteristic for cylindrical bore instruments) and amplitude envelopes of the harmonic components of the sound. Amongst the timbre descriptors, the brightness, which is linked to the center of gravity of the sound's spectrum (so-called Spectral Centroid [21] [22]), has often proved to be a relevant acoustic signature of the musical sounds. Other authors investigated ways to control timbre from these descriptors [23]. This process is often referred to as feature-based synthesis [24].

Timbre and Time: the Notion of Timbre Temporal Shape. As remarked in [25], most of the explorations of timbre by analysis and synthesis have focused on isolated tones. Nevertheless, when analyzing timbre in a musical context, the notion of time is of great importance as music usually involves developments and variations used to communicate the musical ideas through the course of the composition. Timbre can then no more solely be viewed as a global characteristic of a sound but also as a process that belongs to time. In music composition, Schoenberg is one of the first who used progressions of timbres instead of the traditional progressions of pitches by developing the concept of "color" melodies (*Klangfarbenmelodie*). Given these considerations, the notions of material and shape introduced by Schaeffer can be useful to describe the morphological evolutions of timbre in time. What we would capture supposing that we could hear the timbre of a musical sound at a given instant will be called the Instantaneous Timbre Quality (ITQ). If the same musical sound is heard as a whole, one may feel a trajectory that shapes the sound material in time. This trajectory will be designed by the Timbre Temporal Shape (TTS), i.e. the way the Instantaneous Timbre Quality evolves with time.

The Perceptual Effects of Timbre Temporal Shape. The focus of this study is precisely to analyze the perceptual effects of Timbre Temporal Shapes when listening to a musical interpretation. We showed in a former experiment that removing the initial brightness temporal variations of the tones of an expressive clarinet performance induced a decrease of the appreciation judgments among listeners [26]. This study investigates the influence on perception of the reciprocal process, consisting in adding brightness temporal variations issued from an expressive playing to performances played without expressivity. We namely study the consequences of applying a brightness evolution of a specific sustained instrument, the clarinet, on performances generated on other instruments either they belong to the same family or not (sustained or non-sustained instruments).

In the first part, we will explore some of the characteristics of the clarinet timbre with references to sound examples both issued from natural clarinet playing and physics-based synthesis. We will also show why the brightness is well adapted to describe the clarinet timbre and recall the main results of the former experiment. The second part will be devoted to the methodological aspects of the present study. First, the time-varying brightness shaping procedure developed to design the stimuli is exposed. Details regarding the procedure of the perceptual test based on dissimilarity and preference judgments for paired comparisons are then given, and finally, the statistical techniques used to analyze the data (multidimensional scaling and hierarchical cluster analyses) are described. In the third part, a discussion of the results is presented, as well as an analysis of the questionnaire given to the participant to explain some of their strategies. The final part exposes the conclusions and outlooks of the present work. The various sound examples to which we refer in the text can be found at `http://www.lma.cnrs-mrs.fr/~kronland/cmmr2007/cmmr2007.html`

2   Background

2.1   Links between Control, Dynamics and Timbre

Physics-based synthesis can be of great help to uncover connections between the control of the instrument and the resulting timbre. Guillemain *et al.* developed a simplified physical synthesis model of clarinet [27]. Besides the length of the bore that acts on the fundamental frequency of the tones, the main control parameters of the model are the dimensionless mouth pressure γ and the dimensionless reed aperture ζ. A hundred clarinet tones were generated with the same fundamental frequency ($f0 \approx 170Hz$) and durations ($1s$) but varying mouth pressure (10 values in the range $0.4 \leq \gamma \leq 0.5$) and reed aperture (10 values in the range $0.2 \leq \zeta \leq 0.5$). The time-varying Spectral Centroids of the clarinet tones were computed according to the formula given by [22]. Figure 1(a) shows the mean values of the time-varying Spectral Centroids calculated over the second half of the tones in order to take into account the steady-state regime for all sounds. The loudness of the tones, computed according to the algorithm defined by Zwicker and Fastl [28] is shown in figure 1(b).

As the dimensionless mouth pressure (γ) and the dimensionless reed aperture (ζ) increase, the mean Spectral Centroids increase in a quasi-monotonous way. This puts forward that a large variety of brightness values can be obtained for the same pitch (cf. Sound Example 1 [29] to hear a series of tones corresponding to increasing values of the mouth pressure and fixed reed aperture). Hence, in addition to be a recurrent acoustic correlate of timbre-space dimensions in the case of timbres generated by different instruments [20], the Spectral Centroid also seems to well explain the discrimination of timbres produced by a single instrument, here a digital clarinet. In the case of natural clarinet sounds, the Spectral Centroid has also proved to be a relevant descriptor [30].

As can be seen in figure 1(b), the loudness of the tones also increases in a monotonous way with increasing pressure and reed aperture. Hence, considering this category of synthetic clarinet tones, the correlation between mean Spectral Centroids and perceived level is strong (loud tones are brighter than soft ones). As a matter of fact, for most instruments, a natural correlation exists between dynamics and timbre. Risset [31] showed that the signature of trumpet sounds resides in the correlation between the input force (pressure) and the spectral spread.

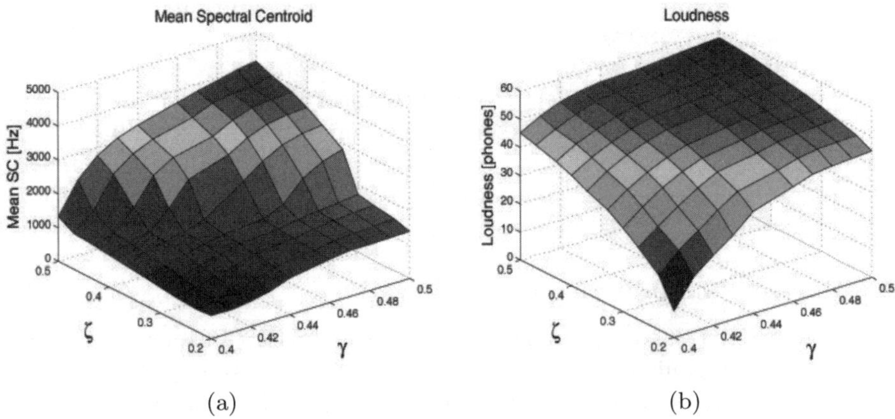

Fig. 1. Mean Spectral Centroid (a) and loudness (b) of isolated clarinet tones ($f0 \approx 170$ Hz) generated with a physics-based synthesis model for different control parameter values. The control parameters of the model are the dimensionless mouth pressure (γ) and reed aperture (ζ).

Natural instruments offer performers controls that are not yet taken into account by physical models and which can also act on the timbre of the generated sounds. In the case of woodwind instruments, performers can modify their embouchures to produce different effects. The consequences are that the vocal tract geometry and force applied by the lips to the reed change. Fritz [32] showed that different configurations of the vocal tract (e.g. "aw", "ee") induced different distributions of the harmonics energy in the sounds' spectra. Research is currently done to better understand the complex interaction between the vocal tract and the instrument bore [33]. We asked a professional clarinetist to play a same note with different timbres while trying not to alter the global sound level. Three tones with different sonorities were produced (cf. Sound Examples 2a to 2c [29]). The tones have approximately the same loudness (respectively 58, 61 and 62 phones). As mentioned by the player, the Sound Example 2a corresponds to a "normal" timbre and was obtained with a classical mouthpiece configuration. The Sound Example 2b was produced by taking much less mouthpiece, which consequently generated a "narrower", "tighter" timbre. The Sound Example 2c, which was obtained on the contrary by taking too much mouthpiece, induced the timbre to become "twisted". It hence seems possible to generate tones with different timbres but close sound levels on a natural clarinet. Reciprocally, modifications of the level without alterations of the timbre seem to be a harder task. The clarinetist performed a crescendo by trying to keep a stable timbre (cf. Sound Example 3 [29]). This effect can be sought in music but its accomplishment is only partially attainable. Although the color of the tone remains quite similar during the first portion of the sound, it then brightens up. A sudden increase of brightness occurring close to the end of the tone is clearly audible. We showed that this phenomenon was linked to the changeover to the beating reed mode (situation where the reed beats against the mouthpiece) inducing an increase of energy in a frequency range close to the resonance frequency of the reed and a global increase of energy for high-order harmonics [34].

Although physics-based models can help to uncover interesting links between the control of an instrument and the generated sound, they are generally still too simplified to reproduce the subtle possibilities offered by natural instruments. We therefore preferred to focus on natural instruments to study the influence of timbre variations on musical interpretation.

2.2   Timbre Temporal Shape

As seen, timbre can be considered as a global characteristic of a sound (helping us for instance to discriminate amongst different clarinet tones), but also as a time-varying variable. Audible timbre variations can be heard within the duration of a tone (report for instance to the crescendo of Sound Example 3). In order to point out such differences, we compared the Instantaneous Timbre Qualities at the beginning and at the end of a clarinet tone. This was done by freezing in time the signals close to the tone's onset and offset (cf. Sound Example 4a to 4c [29]). The timbre variations - to which we may not have paid attention at first glance due to the speed of the change - could then be highlighted: the signal corresponding to the end of the original tone is perceived much brighter than the one corresponding to the beginning of the original tone.

These considerations on a simple clarinet tone raise many interesting questions. From the performer's point of view: is the process of modifying timbre in time used by performers ? If it is the case, is there a link between the Timbre Temporal Shape produced by the performer and his/her musical intention ? From the listener's point of view: are the corresponding variations perceived ? What are their impacts on the musical likings ?

2.3   Consistency of Timbre Temporal Shape

In a former experiment we showed that when a performer reproduces a musical excerpt several times while keeping the same musical intention, the Timbre Temporal Shape can also be reproduced in a very faithful way [35] [26]. The results were obtained by analyzing 20 clarinet performances of the first two bars of an *Allemande* of Bach. Figure 2 presents the Spectral Centroid temporal variations corresponding to five of the recorded performances. A time warping process similar to the one used by Wanderley [36] for the analysis of gestural data was first performed in order to synchronize the Spectral Centroid variations across the repetitions.

The nature of the expressive deviations of timing (subtle changes of the tones durations compared to the values indicated by the scores) and dynamics (nuance) have shown to explain some of the commonalities and differences between performers [3] [1]. The strong correlation of the Spectral Centroid variations between the repetitions tends to indicate that the Timbre Temporal Shape (here limited to brightness aspects) could also be a signature of a performer's interpretation.

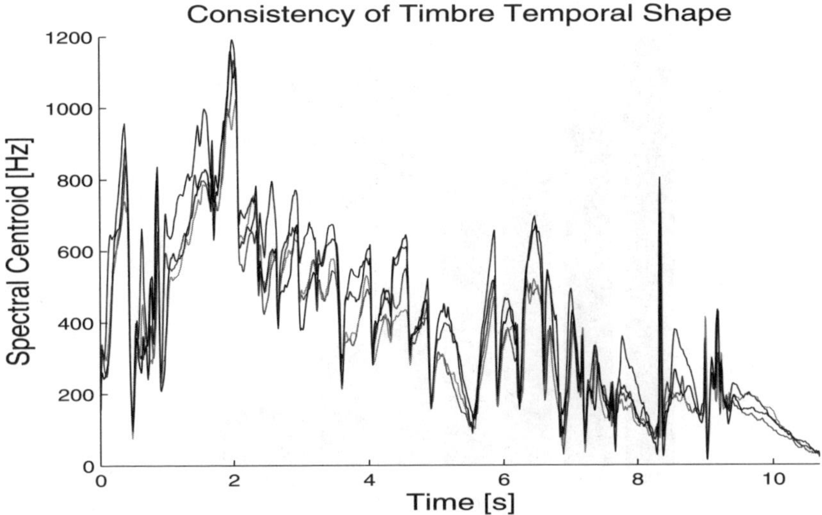

Fig. 2. Spectral Centroid temporal variations across five repetitions of the beginning of a Bach's *Allemande* played by a professional clarinetist. The Spectral Centroids were first synchronized according to the mean tones' durations thanks to a time-warping process.

2.4 Perceptual Influences of Brightness, Timing and Dynamics Variations

There is good evidence that expressive deviations have a great effect on how listeners perceive the musicality of a performance [3] [5]. So-called "neutral", "inexpressive" or "mechanical" performances are those for which the expressive deviations are less pronounced. In a former experiment [26], the effects on music perception induced by a removal of the performer's deviations of brightness, timing, and dynamics were investigated. For that purpose, three transformations acting on an original clarinet performance were designed: (1) tones' brightness temporal variations freezing, (2) expressive timing removal, (3) dynamics flattening. The combinations of these transformations allowed us to generate seven stimuli for which the various expressive deviations (timbre, timing, dynamics) were either kept or suppressed. These musical sequences and the original expressive performance were all compared in pairs by 20 skilled musicians who were asked to select which of the two performances they prefer.

The participants' answers were then derived into marks assigned to each performance by counting the number of times a performance has been preferred. The medians of these marks are shown in figure 3.

As expected, the clarinet performance with no modifications (M0) is the most expressive as it has been systematically preferred to the others. Surprisingly, the removal of the expressive deviations of timing did not induce a major loss in musical quality (see MR), but this is most likely due to the fact that Bach's music lends itself well with an interpretation with minor variations of tempo.

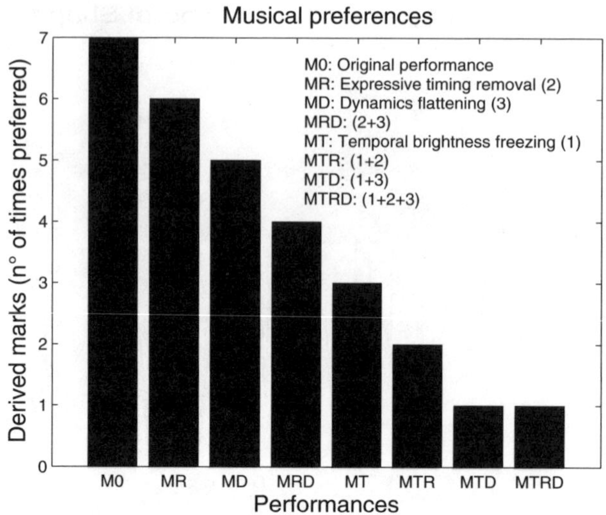

Fig. 3. Bar plot of the medians of the derived marks assigned to each performances according to the preferences of the participants. The performances are sorted according to the descending order of their marks. Given that 8 different performances were compared two by two, the marks range from 0 to 7 times preferred.

Neither did the dynamics flattening (see MD) although the appreciation of the performances decreases significantly when both expressive timing removal and dynamics flattening transformations are combined (see MRD). Conversely, all the performances for which the brightness variations were removed (see MT, MTR, MTD, MTRD) were on average the least preferred. Similar results were obtained with another musical excerpt from a Mozart piece. This tends to prove that the tones' temporal variations of brightness are an important factor of expressiveness in clarinet interpretation.

Since removing the brightness deviations decreases the quality of an expressive performance, one might reciprocally expect that adding appropriate deviations of brightness to a "neutral" performance could improve the interpretation. We therefore conducted a second experiment aiming at comparing performances presenting "neutral" brightness temporal variations and performances presenting brightness temporal variations issued from an expressive playing.

3   Method

3.1   Stimuli

An easy way to generate plausible but inexpressive performances in a reproducible way is to use samplers that control natural recorded sounds. These can be driven by MIDI (Musical Instrument Digital Interface) data which main parameters are note durations, pitch, and velocity. The velocity is closely linked to sound level and timbre. Hence, by using a constant velocity, sound level and timbre variations can be minimized. A MIDI-score was derived from the expressive clarinet performance of Bach's *Allemande* used in the previous experiment. This was done by extracting the tones' timing information from the acoustical signal and by using the pitch information given by the original score (see [35] for details on the procedure). This midi-score was then used with six different sampler-based instruments as resumed in figure 4.

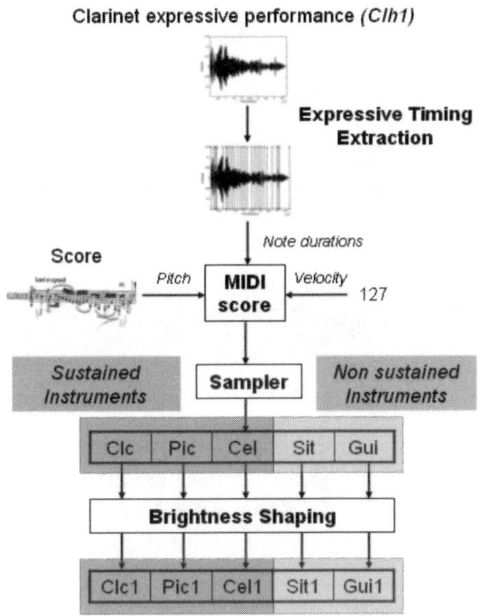

Fig. 4. Design of the stimuli

Three sustained instruments, the clarinet (*Clc*), the piccolo flute (*Pic*), the cello (*Cel*), and two non-sustained instruments, the guitar (*Gui*), and the sitar (*Sit*) were selected. These generated sequences hence present no musically meaningful intensity or timbre variations (fixed velocity) and are all time-synchronized on the expressive clarinet performance used as a reference (*Clh*1).

A feature-based synthesis technique was developed to adjust the brightness temporal variations of each input performance according to those of the reference. It relies on the use of a dynamic low-pass filter aiming at sculpting harmonically rich signals so that their brightness match the expected value. This procedure appears to be easier than adding energy to harmonically poor signals to increase their brightness (in such case a high-pass filtering would induce an amplification of the high-frequency noise which is not desired). The input signals should therefore be brighter than the reference signal. This is in practice done by setting the velocity of the sampler to the highest value (127). The adjustment method is based on the optimization of the cutoff frequency F_c of a dynamic low-pass filter. Dynamic filter optimization has for instance been used in Aramaki and Kronland-Martinet [37] to determine the parameters of an impact sounds synthesis model. Figure 5 describes the different steps of the time-varying brightness shaping transformation.

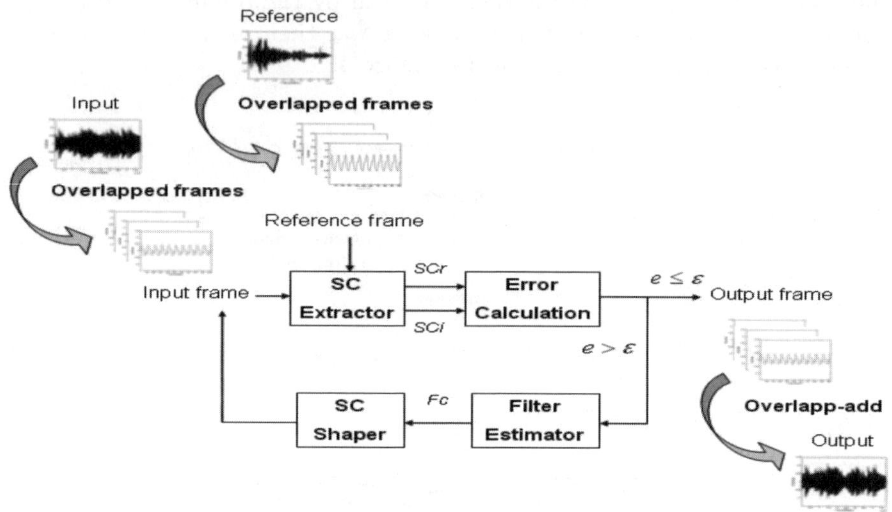

Fig. 5. Time-varying brightness shaping transformation of an input signal according to a reference signal. For each frame, the cutoff frequency F_c of a low-pass filter is optimized so as to minimize the error function e based on the distance between the Spectral Centroid values corresponding to the input SCi and reference SCr.

The reference and input signals are first segmented into overlapped frames (using 4096 samples Hann window with 50% overlap). The window size is long enough to detect the lowest fundamental frequency of the sequence (D2 - 146.83 Hz, sample frequency $f_s = 44.1$ kHz). At each time step t, the instantaneous Spectral Centroids of the reference $SC_r(t)$ and input $SC_i(t)$ signals are derived from the Discrete Fourier Transforms of the current frame. A 2nd order lowpass digital Butterworth filter is used for brightness shaping. The unknown cutoff frequency of the filter is estimated by minimizing the error criterion $e(t)$ defined by the following expression:

$$e(t) = |SC_i(t) - SC_r(t)| \tag{1}$$

A bound constraint is added in the minimization process so that the cutoff frequency F_c of the filter satisfies $0 < F_c < \frac{f_s}{2}$. As the gradient of the objective function e cannot be computed analytically, a finite-difference approximation to the Hessian matrix of the Lagrangian associated to e is used. The BFGS (Broyden, Fletcher, Goldfarb, Shanno) Quasi-Newton optimization method was chosen to update the Hessian [38]. The optimization loop ends up when the error criterion is inferior or equal to a threshold set up to $\epsilon = 1e^{-15}$. The output signal is finally obtained by performing an overlap-add on the optimized input frames.

The results of the time-varying brightness shaping transformation of the sampler-based clarinet performance (Clc) according to the reference performance ($Clh1$) are shown in figure 6. The Spectral Centroid adjustment process works well as the error between the time-varying Spectral Centroid of the output SCo and the reference SCr is almost null. The process has only a minor effect on the dynamics of the sequence as the differences between the Root Mean Square envelopes of the input and output performances are negligible.

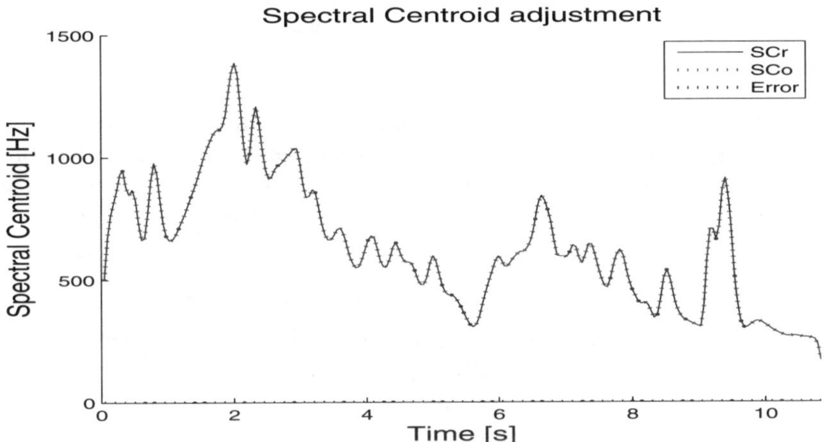

Fig. 6. Results of the optimization loop used in the time-varying brightness shaping procedure applied on the sampler-based clarinet performance (Clc). The time-varying Spectral Centroid of the output performance (SCo) matches well the one of the reference (SCr).

The generated MIDI sequences Clc, Pic, Cel, Gui, Sit are very bright since the highest velocity value is used as explained previously. Their corresponding sculpted versions $Clc1$, $Pic1$, $Cel1$, $Gui1$, $Sit1$, each of which follow the same Spectral Centroid variations extracted from the natural clarinet performance $Clh1$, have a much lower global brightness. In order to form an homogeneous group of stimuli, the mean Spectral Centroids of the input sequences (mean value of the time-varying Spectral Centroid) were adjusted on the one of the reference. This was also done by optimizing the cutoff frequency of a digital lowpass filter. The resulting sequences were all equalized in loudness. The set of stimuli used in the experiment comprise 11 sequences: the original expressive clarinet performance ($Clh1$), the five "neutral" performances ($Clc0$, $Pic0$, $Cel0$, $Gui0$, $Sit0$) and their five brightness shaped versions ($Clc1$, $Pic1$, $Cel1$, $Gui1$, $Sit1$). The index "0" hence refers to the "neutral" timbre temporal patterns whereas the index "1" refers to the expressive timbre temporal pattern. Sound Examples 5a to 5c respectively correspond to the expressive clarinet performance

($Clh1$), the "neutral" piccolo flute performance ($Pic0$) and its brightness shaped version ($Pic1$) [29].

3.2 Participants

Twenty participants (aged 23-50 years old, 6 female) took part to the experiment. Most of them came from our acoustic laboratory. 15 had received a musical training and 5 were non musicians. The musicians had received on average 12.7 years of musical practice. All had normal audition.

3.3 Apparatus

The experimental user interface was developed in the Matlab environment and was run on a Apple iMAC G4 workstation. The experiment took place in a soundproof audiometric cabin. The participants listened to the sounds with a *STAX SRM-310* headphones system including a dedicated stereo amplifier.

3.4 Procedure

As asking individuals to rank a group of performances from first to last according to their preference may not correspond to a natural "behavior", a method of paired comparisons was chosen. As a matter of fact, preferences may not be transitive (if there are three objects to be compared, A, B, and C, a participant may prefer A to B, B to C but prefers C to A).

The experiment comprised three different stages (listening, training and test). During the listening stage, the participants were asked to listen to some of the 11 stimuli (distributed randomly on the computer screen) in order to get familiarized with the range of variation occurring between the performances. After four practice trials, the listeners attended the test stage based on paired comparisons. 55 pairs resulting from the combinations of the 11 stimuli were used. All pairs of stimuli were presented in a random order. Within a pair, the first and second stimuli were also chosen randomly. This was done to further minimize possible order effects of presentation between and within the pairs. For each pair, listeners were first asked to rate the dissimilarities in terms of musical interpretations between two performances. They were then asked to select which of the two performances they preferred. The dissimilarity ratings were made by locating a cursor on a scale with the mouse. The scale boundaries which were given in french corresponded to "very similar interpretation" and "very dissimilar interpretation". The ratings were transcribed on a scale from 0 to 1. The participants were allowed to listen to the pairs as many times as they wished. Care was taken to explain that they had to judge the differences in musical interpretation and not solely the differences between the instruments. They were told that the different performances were all synchronized in time. At the end of the test, they had to fill in a questionnaire concerning the strategy(ies) they used to differentiate the interpretations and their preferences.

3.5   Statistical Analyses

Notations. In the following, the total number of participants and stimuli will respectively be noted N_p and N_s.

Analysis of the Performance Dissimilarities. A hierarchical clustering (average linkage technique) was first performed in order to detect if the ratings of the musicians and the ratings of the non musicians would systematically differ from each other. In such a case, it would be preferable to conduct further analyses in separate ways for the two groups for the sake of clarity of the results. Dissimilarity measures between the participants were based on the Pearson correlation coefficient (by complementation to 1).

The dissimilarity ratings of the selected participants were then averaged and processed with a non metric multidimensional scaling analysis (MDSCAL algorithm [39]). As the perceptual ratings do not necessary respect ratio or interval scale assumptions (the differences between any two numbers of the scale may not have a meaning), a non metric procedure was chosen. For such procedures, an ordinal scale assumption is sufficient. The algorithm is built to keep a monotonous relation between the perceptual distances and their corresponding distances in the MDS space so that the rank orders are best respected. Kruskal's stress was selected as the goodness-of-fit minimization criterion. The initial configuration of points was found using the classical multidimensional scaling CMDSCAL solution. The rate of decline of the stress as dimensionality increases and Shepard diagrams helped us define the reliable number of dimensions retained for the MDS space.

Parallel to the MDS analysis, a hierarchical clustering (complete linkage technique) was also performed on the averaged dissimilarity ratings to investigate if the performances could be separated into distinct classes according to their perceived specificities. A confrontation of the results obtained with the MDS and the cluster analysis was further done. It is important to specify at this point that the purpose of the MDS analysis is not here to verify if the dimensions of the MDS space describe a perceptive continuum. As a matter of fact, we do not expect the stimuli to be continuously distributed along the dimensions of the perceptual space since the stimuli were not designed by continuous evolutions along some predefined acoustical dimensions. Due to the design of the stimuli, the nature of the sound corpus tends to be of the categorical type: the performances present two kinds of brightness temporal variations, the "neutral" ones (indexed by 0) and the expressive ones (indexed by 1). The purpose of the MDS analysis is here to get a spatial representation of the stimuli helping to better visualize the perceptual distances between them (which appear less clearly on a dendrogram representation).

Analysis of the Musical Preferences. The preference measurements consist in binary nominal data (the preference of a performance A over another one B equals 1 if A has been preferred and 0 otherwise). For this reason and in order to have an estimation of the degree of agreement in the preferences of the participants, a nonparametric measure of association, the Kendall coefficient of agreement (u) for paired comparisons [40], has been used. It is computed from the sum of the individual preferences in the sample. It is worth noticing that, independently of the number of raters, u can attain the maximum value of 1 when there is complete agreement. Alternatively, when there are more than two raters, the minimum value of u cannot be -1 because they cannot all be in disagreement. In order to get a measure of association ranging from 0 to 1 independently from the number of raters, we also computed the Wt coefficient defined by Siegel (see [40]) and which derives from u.

The test of significance of u determines the probability that random samples presenting no association would yield a correlation as large as or larger than the one observed. The chosen level of significance was $\alpha = 0.01$. As the number of participants is large ($N_p > 6$) and the number of stimuli being ranked is large ($N_s > 8$), a large-sample approximation to the sampling distribution is used. In this case, the test statistic (X^2) derived from u, is asymptotically distributed as a chi-square distribution whose number of degrees of freedom dof is the total number of pairs of stimuli ($dof = 55$).

The step described above consists in analyzing whether or not the musical preferences of the participants are related. The way the transformations defined in section 3.1 influence the musical preferences of the participants was then investigated. For that purpose, for each participant, the performances were attributed a mark derived from their frequencies of preference when compared to the other ones. The distributions of these marks across the sample hence characterize the ranking of the performances by the participants.

4   Results and Discussion

4.1   Performance Dissimilarities

The hierarchical clustering analysis made on the dissimilarities between the participants did not reveal specific distinctions between ratings of musicians and non musicians. Although we will not infer general consequences of such results since the number of participants representing each category is disproportionate in this experiment (15 musicians versus 5 non musicians), we have chosen to pursue further statistical analyses by considering the data from all the samples (20 participants).

The MDS method yields a 3-dimensional space ($stress \approx 0.07$). The projection of the MDS solution on the first two dimensions is shown in figure 7. The figure also shows the two main levels of categorization from the cluster analysis made on the dissimilarities between the performances. The resulting dendrogram is given in the appendix (see figure 9).

The first dimension of the MDS performance space clearly opposes the performances with "neutral" brightness temporal variations (symbolized by "0") from the ones with expressive brightness temporal variations (symbolized by "1"). This distinction made by the listeners according to the type of brightness pattern is confirmed by the cluster analysis. The two main clusters (solid lines) located on both sides of the first dimension indicates that the listeners judged

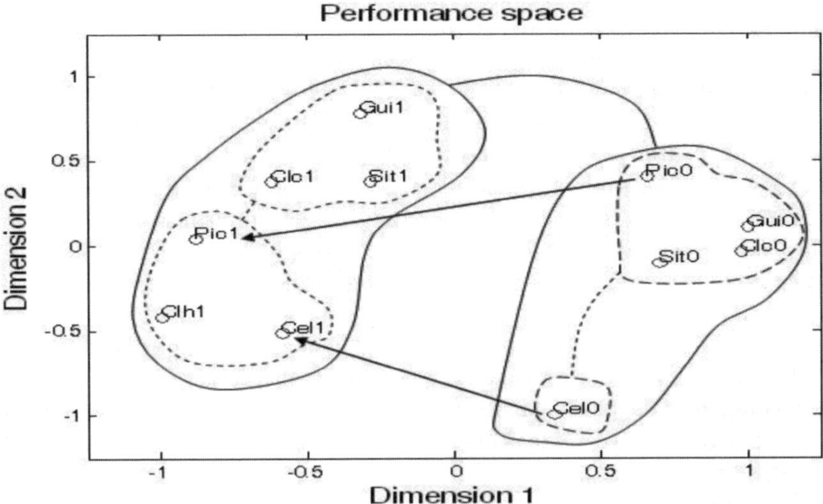

Fig. 7. Two-dimensional projection of the MDS configuration corresponding to the 11 performances' dissimilarity ratings. The first two levels of grouping resulting from the cluster analysis are superimposed on the MDS solution. The first two main clusters are represented in solid lines and the two subordinate clusters in dashed lines. The shape of the clusters has no other meaning than to represent the groups formed by the cluster analysis. The arrows put forward the change of positions of the performances played by the piccolo flute (Pic) and cello (Cel) when their brightness temporal variations are adjusted to imitate that of the expressive clarinet performance ($Clh1$).

performances possessing the same brightness temporal patterns as similar. It is worth noticing that when evaluating the similarity of two musical interpretations, the type of timbre pattern prevailed on the type of instrument that played the excerpt. Although the clarinet and the guitar belong to two different families of instruments and would be far from each other on a hierarchical structure of timbre, the performances played on these two instruments can be judged as very close as long as their brightness temporal variations are similar (see for instance the couples ($Clc1, Gui1$) and ($Clc0, Gui0$). The arrows which have been superimposed on the figure are intended to point out the perceptual effects of the time-varying brightness shaping transformation according to the reference clarinet performance $Clh1$. The reference clarinet performance $Clh1$ seems to act as a magnet on the other performances when their brightness temporal variations are adjusted: see for instance the positions of the performances played by the piccolo flute and the cello before and after the transformations ($Pic0 \rightarrow Pic1$ and $Cel0 \rightarrow Cel1$). Although this effect of perceptual closeness to the reference appears globally for all the instruments, it is less pronounced for the plucked string instruments, the sitar and the guitar. For such non-sustained instruments, transforming the brightness variations according to the ones of a sustained instrument like the clarinet, may be inappropriate.

As figure 9 reveals, the subordinate clusters seem more related to the specificities of each instrument: the plucked string instruments (guitar and sitar) having the same timbre temporal pattern remain grouped; $Gui0$ and $Sit0$ are classified in the same sub-cluster, as well as $Gui1$ and $Sit1$. The same happens for the two sustained wind instruments; the piccolo flute and the clarinet ($Clc0$ and $Pic0$ belong to a same cluster as well as $Clc1$ and $Pic1$). The fact that instruments of a same family remain grouped appears legitimate. The perception of a musical interpretation is not just a function of the expressive intentions of a performer (either they are issued from a natural playing or modeled in an artificial way), but remains linked to some global aspects of the sounds related to the acoustic properties of the source.

Hence, the modification of the brightness variations of a sequence according to those of an expressive performance has an effect on the resulting musicality of the performance. The following study of the musical preferences of the raters will help to uncover how this effect affects the listeners' musical likings.

4.2   Musical Preferences

The value of the Kendall coefficient of agreement based on the preferences of the 20 participants is $u = 0.21$. The corresponding coefficient of concordance value is $Wt = 0.25$. The derived statistic $X^2 = 277$ ($p < 0.0005$) distributed as a chi-square distribution with 55 degrees of freedom indicates that the hypothesis of no association among the participants may be rejected with the $\alpha = 0.0005$

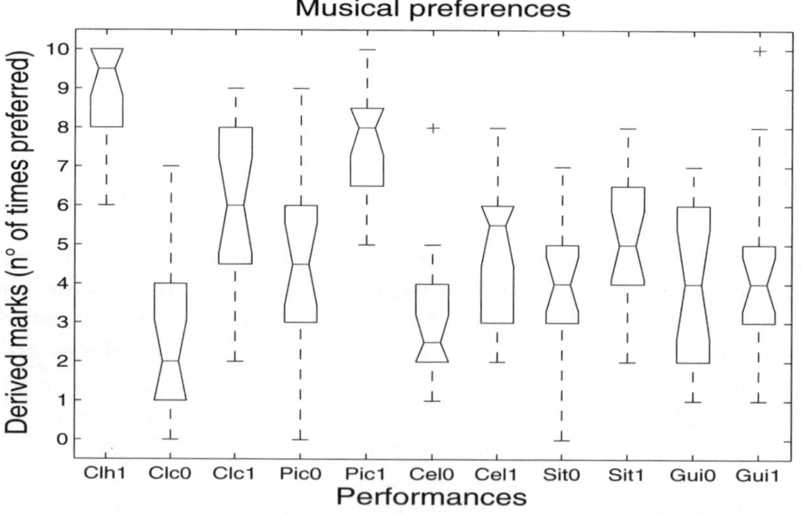

Fig. 8. Box and whisker plots of the marks assigned to each performance across the participants. The marks range from 0 to 10. The box has lines at the lower quartile, median, and upper quartile values. The length of the whiskers is 1.5 the interquartile range. Outliers are represented by crosses. The box notches represent an estimate of the uncertainty about the medians.

level. We conclude that there is a strong agreement among the participants in their preferences. The transformations on the brightness hence seem to produce a common effect on the likings of the listeners. The distributions of the marks assigned to each performance across the participants are described by figure 8.

Given that there are 11 stimuli which have been compared in a pairwise way, the marks corresponding to the frequencies of preference of a performance to the others range from 0 to 10. The brightness transformation has a striking influence on the preferences of the participants. The performances which went through the time-varying brightness shaping according to the reference $Clh1$ tend to be preferred to their corresponding "neutral" versions. However, this seems to depend on the type of instrument. In order to compare the different rates of preference increase between the instruments, we computed the rate of change of the performance marks before and after the brightness transformations (cf. respectively to the sequences indexed by 0 and by 1). The rates were calculated from the medians of the performance marks and expressed as a deviation percentage from the initial mark. They are presented in table 1.

Table 1. Rate of increase of the preferences due to the time-varying brightness shaping. The rates are given for each instrument as a deviation percentage between the median marks of the performances before and after the transformation.

Instruments	Clc	Pic	Cel	Sit	Gui
Rate of preference increase (%)	200	78	120	25	0

The increase of preferences after transformation is strong for all the sustained instruments (clarinet, piccolo flute, and cello). The change of brightness temporal variations is most efficient for the clarinet Clc (200% of increase). This is most likely linked to the fact that reference brightness temporal variations were extracted from the same type of instrument, a clarinet ($Clh1$), and that the listeners judged the effect as consistent. The increase of preferences is much less pronouced or even null for the non-sustained instruments (25% for the sitar and 0% for the guitar). Although the participants did judge the interpretations of $Sit1$ and $Gui1$ closer to the reference than their "neutral" versions, they may have found the consequence of the transformation incoherent with the acoustic behavior of the instruments. Effectively for plucked instruments, the coupling between the excitor and the resonator appears just at the beginning of the sound and this prevents the performer from acting on the timbre of the sound during its production.

4.3   Analysis of the Questionnaire

Several points that arise from the analysis of the questionnaire of the participants are worth to be mentioned. When questioned on the stimuli, the participants often referred to a specific performance which was often preferred to the others as it appeared more expressive and more natural (notably due to the "breath noise" and the "key noise"). These distinctions clearly refer to the reference performance played by the clarinet player $Clh1$. The fact that it was recorded in an anechoic chamber here explains the very precise rendering of the natural clarinet playing (there is no reverberation that could diminish the presence of accessory noises). These remarks coincide with the statistical analysis: this sequence is the one that is the leftmost along the first dimension of the MDS performance space (see figure 7) and which obtained the highest mark (the mark's median is 9.5/10 as seen in figure 8). Even after application of the brightness transformation the other performances were judged as less expressive than this one. It is worth noticing that the accessory noises of the clarinet playing appear in this context as a positive attribute of the sound and contribute to its pleasantness. Conversely, the cello performance $Cel0$ was often described as sounding unnatural. This sequence effectively appears in a distinctive subordinate cluster within the cluster of "neutral" performances (see figure 9) and has been poorly marked (see figure 8). These considerations may be linked to the low-pass filtering performed during the design stage of the stimuli applied to adjust the global brightness of the different performances and making the timbre of the cello too dull. Nevertheless, the interesting point is that the brightness transformation brings the cello performance closer to the reference and that the modified version is considered as a much better performance (average increase of the preferences of 120%).

Three main factors explaining how the participants rated the performances emerged from their remarks. The first one is linked to the dynamics aspects of the performances (definition of dynamics from the Freedictionary [41]: "variation in force or intensity, especially in musical sound"), the second one is related to the articulation, and the third one refers to timbre (the order of importance is linked to the frequencies of verbalizations associated to each factor). The following examples have been translated from French.

Dynamics Factor. Some interesting examples of verbalizations linked with the dynamics factor are: "nuance", "amplitude variations", "sound intensity", "accents, location in time", "force fluctuation of the tone", "shape of the tone (development in time, round, flat, etc.)". It is worth noticing that some analyses come from the musical domain ("nuance", "accents", "shape"), whereas others come from the acoustical domain ("amplitude", "intensity", "force") which might be linked to the fact that most participants work in the acoustic field. It is striking to see the strong presence of words expressing the notions of variation or shape of the acoustical signal with time. Nevertheless, although the transformations of the brightness temporal variations only slightly affected the acoustical level (characterized by the Root Mean Square envelopes) of the performances, they undeniably seem to alter their perceived level. Experiments made by Zwicker showed that the annoyance produced by sounds of equivalent loudness increases when the acuity (auditive equivalent of the physical Spectral Centroid) of the sounds increases [28]. What prevail for the perception when modifying the Spectral Centroid variations of a musical performance hence seems to be mainly related to loudness variations. As no accurate models of loudness yet exist for non-stationary sounds (as are the sounds of a musical performance), we did not have means to verify by measurements the considerations evoked above. It is however interesting to see that the correlations observed between force, dynamics and timbre in the production process of the sounds seem to have a counterpart in the perception process.

Articulation Factor. The use of expressions such as "fluidity", "flow", "legato", "attack" lead to think that modifying the brightness temporal variations has an effect on the articulation of the performance. Adding brightness variations issued from an expressive clarinet performance to the sequences generated by the sampler hence seems to enhance the coherence or the links between the tones. Effectively, sampler-based performances provide poor connections between the tones since they constitute a patchwork of isolated tones recorded separately.

Timbre Factor. References to the third timbre factor were "brightness of certain tones", "sound quality", "heat of the sound", "attack". Faure [42] showed that the verbal descriptions of timbre by the use of a vocabulary coming from other sensorial modalities ("brightness", "heat") are common. Note that the term "attack" has been placed in the articulation and timbre factors, as it appears to be connected to both factors. The fact that few participants directly referred to timbre may be linked to the fact that it is still a misunderstood notion and that most people only consider the typological facet of timbre by associating the timbre to the instrument, the notion of timbre variation then having no meaning.

The free verbalizations of the participants hence give interesting cues to understand the strategies they used to judge the stimuli. It brings complementary elements to the cluster and the MDS analysis that the latter cannot reveal. The modification of the brightness variations seems to affect the perception of dynamics, articulation and timbre aspects in a combined manner. It (indirectly) induced the listeners to divide the performances into two different categories: a category gathering the expressive and preferred performances with variations providing them coherence and liveliness (cluster on the left along the first MDS dimension), and a category of performances which are less preferred relatively to the performances of the first category, since they are less homogeneous and present less variations (cluster on the right along the first MDS dimension).

Independently of their musical experience, several participants reported that they found the test difficult. The evaluation of an intricate process such as music performance has already been reported as problematic; regarding the criteria used by raters in such tasks, the author of [43] states that "the measures employed are typically subjective judgments based on irregular and uncontrolled observations" even when the raters are professional music teachers. For that matter, research on the design of specific music performance rating scales based on the use of a common set of evaluative dimensions was conduced in [44]. In our case, at the expense of the difficulty of the task, we did not use such common sets of music descriptors or semantic differential scales not to bias the evaluation process by an a priori knowledge. Difficulties in rating the dissimilarities between the interpretations may also have been due to difficulties in using the rating scale to its whole extent: the two main groups obtained by the cluster analysis tend to show that the interpretations were judged either very close, either very different. The complexity of the task may also be correlated to the relatively long duration of the musical excerpt (approximatively *10 s*). However, long sequences have already been employed successfully in paired-comparison tasks. For example, in [45], the authors used sequences of *15 s* duration in a study on the perceived quality of sound-reproducing systems (after having judged that 30 s long sequences were inappropriate for paired comparisons). The comparison or assignment of rates to sounds of long durations may be hard tasks for the perceptive and cognitive systems. Supposing that we would know how the ear integrates the information it gets across time, the final judgment still can be biased by a preponderant influence of the last heard events due to a memorization process [46]. A so-called recency effect has been reported by one of the participant who was more sensible to the three last tones of the performances. We hope this effect was minimized across the sample thanks to the possibility the participants had to hear the stimuli as many times as they wished.

5   Conclusions and Outlooks

The exploration of the role of timbre in music performance is a large problem. We decided to focus our study on one aspect of timbre, the brightness, which is quantified by the Spectral Centroid derived from the Fourier analysis of the spectrum. Brightness has caught our attention for several reasons. In the case of the clarinet as for most instruments, a variation of the input force induces a variation of brightness of the resulting sound. The control of the instrument hence generally offers performers sufficient degrees of freedom to act on this dimension of timbre. From the perceptual point of view, brightness changes seem to well explain how the auditory system discriminates different musical sounds [20]. Regarding music perception, Wessel demonstrated that brightness could control stream segregation in a similar way as pitches: when a same ascending triplet of tones of different brightness is repeated in time, the ear tends to follow tones with the same brightness [47].

Even at a tone level, audible brightness variations can occur. We highlighted such variations by time-stretching small portions of sounds close to the onset and the offset of a clarinet tone (cf. Sound Examples 4a to 4c [29]). The study of various repetitions of an excerpt from a Bach piece by a professional clarinet player have shown that Spectral Centroid variations are highly consistent across the repetitions [26]. There hence seems to be a link between the expressive intention of the performer and the way he manipulates timbre. A first perceptual experiment showed that clarinet performances generated with tones having no brightness variations were judged as inexpressive [26]. Conversely, in this study we investigated the effect of applying the brightness temporal variations issued from an expressive clarinet performance to sequences generated by samplers set up with a fixed velocity. The performances appear to be discriminated by listeners according to their temporal brightness pattern. This shows that modifications carried out on brightness temporal variations while keeping other musical modalities constant (timing, dynamics) change the perception of the musical interpretation. A performer might then change the significance of the musical message he conveys to the listener by solely acting on the timbre dimension. Secondly, the performances that were considered as the most expressive are those with brightness temporal variations issued from an expressive clarinet playing. Improvements of listeners' musical preferences occurred especially for sustained instruments (clarinet, piccolo flute, cello) for which timbre variations are known to be possible during the course of the tones. For non sustained instruments (guitar, sitar), the much less pronounced benefits of the transformation on the affect judgments of the participants tend to show its incoherence for this type of instruments. This might be related to the impossibility for listeners to recognize familiar sounds which could have been produced with these instruments. As mentioned in [8], sounds that are identifiable tend to be more appreciated than sounds that we are not accustomed to. The incapacity to alter the brightness during the course of the tones in a standard guitar playing may not be extraneous to the success met by the famous "wah-wah" effect pedal which acts on the sound spectrum by means of a sweeping bandpass filter.

Being inspired by the demonstration of Sundberg which shows that reversing the tones' subtle timing deviations from the score occurring in an expressive performance (a lengthening becoming a shortening and vice versa) induced absurd musical performances, we generated excerpts for which the brightness temporal variations were reversed during the course of the tones (an increase of brightness becoming a decrease and vice versa). The result clearly sounds unmusical and seems to go against a natural playing (cf. Sound Example 6a and 6b, respectively generated with normal and reversed tones' brightness variations [29]). Deviations of timing and dynamics participating to the musicality of a performance are designed by "expressive deviations" in the literature (see for instance [1]). It appears legitimate to use the qualification "expressive deviations of timbre" when referring to timbre temporal variations that procur the sensation of expressiveness.

The notions of timbre variations and shape, emerged from the various statistical and semantic considerations, have shown to be preponderant for the listeners' affect judgments. The prospects of these results are interesting regarding the modeling of expressive performances. Models aiming at efficiently reproduce an expressive play on instruments allowing temporal modifications of timbre should then take into account the temporal variations of brightness in addition to timing, dynamics, intonation, etc. A more systematic description of the different timbre temporal variation profiles (shapes, role of the range of variation, derivative of the brightness profile, etc.) could improve the understanding of musical expressiveness perception. The importance of timbre in music has already been sensed by contemporary composers. When analyzing the temporal structure of the piece *Chronochromie* from Olivier Messiaen, Lerdhal [8] fairly remarks that: "Timbre is no more a simple "color", it becomes an essential element holding shape." (translation). In his preface to the score of *Chronochromie* Messiaen effectively remarks that one of the functions of timbre is to bring out the framework of durations (which is no more handled in by the structure of pitches).

We introduced the concept of Timbre Temporal Shape to include that aspect of timbre in music analysis and perception which refers to timbre temporal variations and which may be put in the shade by the classical psychoacoustic definition of timbre, the latter tending to exclude timbre from time. We do not however pretend to have defined the notion of Timbre Temporal Shape in a rigorous way yet and hope, on the contrary, that it will give rise to further investigations.

Acknowledgments. The authors would like to thank the clarinetist Claude Crousier for his participation and the rich discussions that we had. This project has partly been supported by the French National Research Agency (ANR, JC05-41996, "senSons", http://www.sensons.cnrs-mrs.fr/).

References

1. Gabrielsson, A.: The Performance of Music. In: Psychology of Music, 2nd edn., Academic Press, London (1999)
2. Scholes, P.A.: The Oxford Companion to Music, 2nd edn., p. 521. Oxford University Press, Oxford (1960)
3. Repp, B.H.: Diversity and Commonality in Music Performance: an Analysis of Timing Microstructure in Schumann's Träumerei. J. Acoust. Soc. Am. 92(5), 2546–2568 (1992)
4. Palmer, C.: Music Performance. Annu. Rev. Psychol. 48, 115–138 (1997)
5. Sundberg, J., Friberg, A., Frydén, L.: Rules for Automated Performance of Ensemble Music. Contemporary Music Review 3, 89–109 (1989)
6. Widmer, G., Goebl, W.: Computational Models of Expressive Music Performance. J. New Music Research 33(3), 203–216 (2004)
7. De Poli, G.: Expressiveness in Music Performance. In: Algorithms for Sound and Music Computing, Creative Commons (2006)
8. Lerdahl, F.: Les Hiérarchies de Timbre. In: Le Timbre, Métaphore pour la Composition, pp. 182–203. I.R.C.A.M. (1991)
9. Deutsch, D.: Grouping Mechanisms in Music. In: Psychology of Music, Cognition and Perception, pp. 299–348. Academic Press, New York (1999)
10. Seashore, C.E.: Psychology of Music. McGraw-Hill - Reprinted 1967 by Dover Publications, New York (1938)
11. Marozeau, J.: L'Effet de la Fréquence Fondamentale sur le Timbre. PhD thesis, Université Pierre et Marie Curie, Paris VI (2004)
12. Cadoz, C.: Timbre et Causalité. In: Le Timbre, Métaphore pour la Composition, pp. 17–46. I.R.C.A.M (1991)
13. ANSI: USA Standard Acoustical Terminology (1960)
14. AFNOR: Recueil des Normes Françaises de l'Acoustique, Tome 1 (Vocabulaire), NF S 30-107 (1977)
15. Bregman, A.: Sequential Integration. In: Auditory Scene Analysis, p.97 (1990)
16. Schaeffer, P.: Traité des Objets Musicaux. Editions du Seuil ed. (1966)
17. Grey, J.M.: Multidimensional Perceptual Scaling of Musical Timbres. J. Acoust. Soc. Am. 61, 1270–1277 (1977)
18. Krumhansl, C.L.: Why Is Musical Timbre so Hard to Understand? In: Nielzén, S., Olsson, O. (eds.) Structure and Perception of Electroacoustic Sound and Music: Proc. of the Marcus Wallenberg Symposium Held in Lund, Sweden, pp. 43–53. Excerpta Medica, Amsterdam (1988)

19. McAdams, S., Winsberg, S., Donnadieu, S., De Soete, G., Krimphoff, J.: Perceptual Scaling of Synthesized Musical Timbres: Common Dimensions Specificities, and Latent Subject Classes. Psychological Research 58, 177–192 (1995)
20. Caclin, A., McAdams, S., Smith, B.K., Winsberg, S.: Acoustic Correlates of Timbre Space Dimensions: A Confirmatory Study Using Synthetic Tones. J. Acoust. Soc. Am. 118(1), 471–482 (2005)
21. Grey, J.W., Gordon, J.W.: Perception of Spectral Modifications on Orchestral Instrument Tones. Computer Music Journal 11(1), 24–31 (1978)
22. Beauchamp, J.W.: Synthesis by Spectral Amplitude and Brightness Matching of Analyzed Musical Instrument Tones. J. Audio Eng. Soc. 30(6), 396–406 (1982)
23. Jensen, K.: The Timbre Model - Discrimination and Expression. In: Proceedings of the Mosart Midterm Meeting, Esbjerg, Denmark (2002)
24. Hoffman, M., Cook, P.: The Featsynth Framework for Feature-Based Synthesis: Design and Applications. In: Proc. Int. Comp. Music Conf (ICMC 2007), Copenhaguen, Denmark, vol. 2, pp. 184–187 (2007)
25. Risset, J.-C., Wessel, D.L.: Exploration of Timbre by Analysis and Synthesis. In: Psychology of Music, 2nd edn., Academic Press, London (1999)
26. Barthet, M., Depalle, P., Kronland-Martinet, R., Ystad, S.: From Performer to Listener: an Analysis of Timbre Variations. J. Acoust. Soc. Am. (under revision)
27. Guillemain, P.: A Digital Synthesis Model of Double-reed Wind Instruments. Eurasip Journal on Applied Signal Processing, Special Issue on Model-based Sound Synthesis 7, 990–1000 (2004)
28. Zwicker, E., Fastl, H.: Psychoacoustics, Facts and Models. Springer, Heidelberg (1990)
29. Barthet, M., Kronland-Martinet, R., Ystad, S.: Improving Musical Expressiveness by Time-Varying Brightness Shaping,
http://www.lma.cnrs-mrs.fr/~kronland/cmmr2007/cmmr2007.html
30. Loureiro, M.A., de Paula, H.B., Yehia, H.C.: Timbre Classification of a Single Instrument. In: ISMIR 2004 5th International Conference on Music Information Retrieval (Barcelona, Spain), Audiovisual Institute, Universitat Pompeu Fabra (2004)
31. Risset, J.-C.: Computer Study of Trumpet Tones. J. Acoust. Soc. Am. 38(912) (1965)
32. Fritz, C., Wolfe, J.: Acoustic Impedance Measurement of the Clarinet Players Airway. In: CFA/DAGA 2004, Strasbourg, pp. 101–102 (2004)
33. Guillemain, P.: Some Roles of the Vocal Tract in Clarinet Breath Attacks: Natural Sounds Analysis and Model-Based Synthesis. J. Acoust. Soc. Am. 121(4), 2396–2406 (2007)
34. Barthet, M., Guillemain, P., Kronland-Martinet, R., Ystad, S.: On the Relative Influence of Even and Odd Harmonics in Clarinet Timbre. In: Proc. Int. Comp. Music Conf (ICMC 2005), Barcelona, Spain, pp. 351–354 (2005)
35. Barthet, M., Kronland-Martinet, R., Ystad, S.: Consistency of Timbre Patterns in Expressive Music Performance. In: Proc. 9th Int. Conf. on Digital Audio Effects (DAFx 2006), Montreal, Quebec, Canada, pp. 19–24 (2006)
36. Wanderley, M.: Quantitative Analysis of Non-Obvious Performer Gestures. In: Gesture and Sign Language in Human-Computer Interaction: International Gesture Workshop, p. 241. Springer, Berlin (2002)
37. Aramaki, M., Kronland-Martinet, R.: Analysis-Synthesis of Impact Sounds by Real-Time Dynamic Filtering. IEEE Trans. on Acoust., Speech, and Sig. Proc. 14(2), 695–705 (2006)
38. Goldfarb, D.: A Family of Variable Metric Updates Derived by Variational Means. Mathematics of Computing 24, 23–26 (1970)

39. Dillon, W.R., Goldstein, M.: Multivariate Analysis. Wiley series in probability and mathematical statistics. John Wiley & Sons, New York (1984)
40. Siegel, S., John Castellan Jr., N.: Non Parametric Statistics for the Behavioral Sciences. In: Measures of Association and their Tests of Significance, 2nd edn., p. 272. McGraw-Hill International Editions (1988)
41. Farlex: The free dictionary, http://www.thefreedictionary.com
42. Faure, A.: Des sons aux mots, comment parle-t-on du timbre musical ? PhD thesis, École des Hautes Etudes en Sciences Sociales (2000)
43. Whybrew, W.K.: Measurement and Evaluation in Music, p. 63. William C. Brown Company Publishers, Dubuque (1962)
44. Abeles, H.F.: Development and Validation of a Clarinet Performance Adjudication Scale. Journal of Research in Music Education 21(3), 246–255 (1973)
45. Gabrielsson, A., Lindstrom, B.: Perceived Sound Quality of High-Fidelity Loudspeakers. J. Audio Eng. Soc. 33(1), 33–53 (1985)
46. Susini, P., McAdams, S.: Effet de Récence dans une Tâche de Jugement de la Sonie. In: 5ème Congrès français d'acoustique, Lausanne, Suisse (2000)
47. Wessel, D.L.: Timbre Space as a Musical Control Structure. Computer Music Journal 3(2), 45–52 (1979)

Appendix

The results of the hierarchical cluster analysis made on the performance dissimilarities are presented in figure 9.

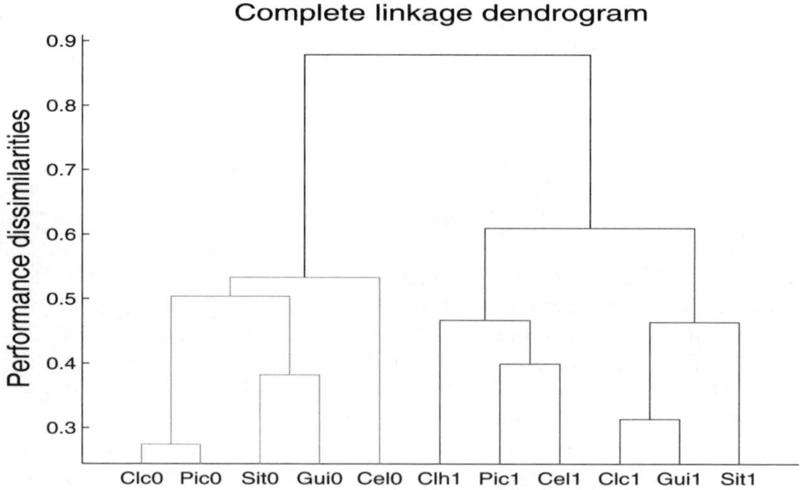

Fig. 9. Complete linkage dendrogram from the hierarchical cluster analysis made on the performance dissimilarities

NN Music: Improvising with a 'Living' Computer

Michael Young

Music Department, Goldsmiths, University of London
New Cross, London, SE14 6NW. UK
m.young@gold.ac.uk

Abstract. A live algorithm describes an ideal autonomous performance system able to engage in performance with abilities analogous, if not identical, to a human musician. This paper proposes five attributes of a live algorithm: adaptability, empowerment, intimacy, opacity and unimagined music. These attributes are explored in NN Music, a performer-machine system for Max/MSP that fosters listening and learning. Live improvisation is encoded statistically to train a feed-forward neural network, mapped to stochastic processes for musical output. Through adaptation, mappings are learnt and covertly assigned, to be revisited by both player and machine as a performance develops.

Keywords: Live algorithms, improvisation, performance systems, artificial neural networks.

1 Introduction

Advances in our understanding of machine intelligence, in areas such as music informatics, evolutionary computation and self-organising maps, open new avenues for creative performance systems in music. Such systems might collaborate in many musical contexts, not merely follow pre-programmed scores or depend on direct stimuli, but engage with performers at a commensurate level. This is the vision of the UK Live Algorithms for Music network, founded in 2004 by the author and Tim Blackwell[1]. A live algorithm is the function of an ideal autonomous system able to engage in performance with abilities analogous, if not identical, to a human musician [1]. Such an approach differs radically from the established paradigms of 'live electronics'; the computer-as-instrument (a tool that relies on human agency), or the computer-as-proxy, (a substitute for the 'composer' that implements pre-designed functions laid out in a musical score or rule set). A true live algorithm would offer a high degree of autonomy: capacities to invent, provoke and respond.

Live algorithms are most germane when there are opportunities for such behaviours, i.e. when there is creative, group interaction. In this scenario there is no 'top-down' control, no hierarchical human-to-human management analogous to user-to-computer control. In truly 'free' improvised music, structure and character – in so far as they are evident – are emergent properties, products of heterarchical group

---

[1] A collaboration between the Departments of Music and Computing at Goldsmiths, with the support of the Engineering and Physical Sciences Research Council.

R. Kronland-Martinet, S. Ystad, and K. Jensen (Eds.): CMMR 2007, LNCS 4969, pp. 337–350, 2008.

interaction, and not the product of pre-defined rules. Musical languages are formulated pragmatically, self-referentially and on-the-fly. Free improvised music offers a model for aspiring live algorithms and a challenging context in which one could be tested to the full.

Section 2 below discusses potential attributes of live algorithms that are far-reaching and intended only as a framework for discussion and future investigation. There are five attributes; adaptability, empowerment, intimacy, opacity, and (summatively) the unimagined, as proposed by the author [2], [3]. These concepts are explored practically in the performance system NN Music, which has been developed in a number of compositional guises, with instrument-, timbre- and concept-specific titles: *piano_prosthesis, cello_prosthesis,* and *au(or)a.* There is a technical explanation of this system in section 3.

2   Attributes of 'Living' Computer Music

Adaptability. This is the ability to acclimatise to a shared environment, demonstrable in changes of behaviour. A musical environment capable of change – and therefore to demand adaptation – is unlikely to be pre-determined by fixed rules, stylistic assumptions or other formal constraints. Adaptation is not necessarily conscious or intentional, even though performers may wish to communicate with a machine. Lewis's term emotional transduction, defined as a *"bi-directional transfer of intentionality through sound"* [4] establishes by implication that adaptations should occur in and of the medium itself, not via controllers, irrelevant gestural information or control data. However, Lewis's assertion that a performer's original intention – *"emotional and mental"* – can be preserved and then co-represented in the machine's response is open to question.

It can be argued that performers adapt to their shared sonic environment, not personally to one another. Stigmergy avoids the problem of personal intention and emphasises adaptation; this provides a model that is potentially valid for both human-human performance and human-machine collaboration. Stigmergy is the process in which an insect population self-organises through the adaptation of individuals to their environment, and initially described termites interacting with their environment. Individuals do not commune directly, even though the resultant phenomena – nests – can be extraordinarily complex and seemingly designed. Computer simulations of this have been and other self-organising behaviours are well established and they are evidenced in the application of evolutionary computing to music [5]. Stigmergy as a model avoids the problem of intentionality and machine cognition; consequently, it avoids the potential pitfalls of anthropomorphism. It proposes a flexible, dynamic and adaptable system capable of novel problem-solving: An effective model of human creativity and more specifically, of improvised computer music [6].

Musical performance, whether between humans or machines, might be regarded as a complex and dynamic self-organising system if individuals commune with the shared audio environment rather than directly with one another. This assumption ignores visual or other physical cueing, and emphasises listening.

Musical collaboration in a human/social context involves a continuous process of adaptation based on mutual listening. Goals are identified by group members – who actively assume and cast roles – in order to adapt to the changing audio environment.

Goals might be attributable to 'supra-personal' social facts (such as norms of acceptable behaviour, actions consistent with expectations or requirements). Even so, an entirely new, shared history evolves as the cooperative experience develops. Players become aware of the appropriateness of their response to others' contributions and appraise their own ability to initiate behaviour from others. Such processes have been observed in jazz groups [7]. Arguably, all such social behaviours occur by proxy in the shared environment: they are adaptive and essentially indirect. Whether or not it might ever be possible for computers to have an intentional response is an open question. However, optimisation methods, available in evolutionary computation and machine learning, might present the affect of intention. If interaction occurs only between performer and the environment, and between machine and its environment, the products of adaptation might be regarded as equivalent, and equally significant. It is then, arguably, inconsequential whether the interactions depend on machine algorithms or human cognition.

Empowerment. This entails control over decisions that impact upon future experience. Decisions have a context: the properties and consequences of options, the strategies that might inform choices and the criteria for their evaluation. In creative practice, such as improvised performance, decisions do not have easily definable strategies or evaluative criteria, but a framework must be at least implicit. Established AI systems that are effective in adapting to environments and delivering pre-defined outcomes are not necessarily useful. For example, BDI (belief, desire, intention) systems implement a rule-base, respond only to knowable environmental measures and have clear pre-determined aims, even though they actively respond to input and output while running [8]. Such behaviours are potentially antithetical to the exigencies of creative performance.

Algorithms do not cognate – so they cannot make creative decisions – but they can produce non-arbitrary changes in state. Such changes can be instigated by non-linear dynamical systems; cellular automata, particle swarms, genetic algorithms and neural networks. The potential self-organising properties of these algorithms offer potential for novel problem-solving, invention and surprise. They do not necessarily achieve intended goals, but might find new ones. In musical performance, a non-arbitrary change of state is manifest as a 'decision' when it modifies the audio environment, even if this is the product of an adaptation. Consequently, the change is 'empowered' to demand a response from both human and machine participants alike; it has the affect of intention.

There is mapping problem. What structural and temporal features of music should be determined by a change of state manifest as 'a decision'? It is easy to find examples of generative music where state changes are applied to the very surface of music. For instance in evolutionary computer music, genotype (genetic code) and phenotype (characteristics) have been mapped schematically and literally. Such approaches are, in effect, simple sonifications of a data space exploration, which may be of potential use for scientific enquiry [9] but have limited interest as a means of creative production.

Creative decisions might reference the structural properties, and implicit methodologies of music-making, and offer new possibilities at these levels. Computer 'decision-making' cannot define context, but could engage with it. A common problem is time; algorithms function independently of time, so for music, a real-time clock must be imposed as a function of data sonification. It is unavoidable that contexts such as this – however fundamental and transparent – are established by the designer, in order to provide relations for creative behaviour. Eco's term, the *"field of relations"*, emphasises the finite nature of an open work's discontinuities and its field of possibilities [10]. These relations provide a framework for decisions. So, even though a single point of view is absent and there is some devolution of creative responsibility, this does not entail an *"amorphous invitation to indiscriminate participation"*. Neither, by extrapolation, does the absence of a point of view (algorithms do not cognate) necessitate a wholesale and literal transfer of state changes to the surface of the music, or to the framework and context for creative acts. Relations are underpinned by the capabilities of the machine system, the technical approaches and aesthetic attitudes of the designer and live player. It is through an interplay of all these relations that empowerment might be perceived.

Intimacy. This is experienced – or apparent – if there is a binding understanding shared by performers through informed listening and observation. This is a social process, but can be experienced in and through sound itself. A machine emulation of closeness and intimacy should attend to sonic experience, both in nuance and wider characteristics.

Technological devices that produce control data from a user's actions can only be receptive, not intimate. In music technology, the discourse around intimacy is really about responsiveness, i.e. emulation of a performer's physical interaction with his/her instrument [11]. A truly intimate relationship – as occurs between musicians – is learned, rather than provided, and is an experiential phenomenon within the sound environment. (At least during a performance, before or after is another matter). It is, though, genuinely interactive.

Intimacy suggests the psychological process of *"optimal flow"*; a goal-orientated, mental state that explores the limits of experience and expectation, obtaining pleasure in meeting challenges with appropriate skills [12]. It has been conjectured that the effectiveness of group collaborations can be evaluated with this measure [13]. A machine's contribution cannot be evaluated, of course, but a human performer, in his/her musical experience and interaction with the shared sonic environment, might infer that flow is occurring for all participants. This is particularly relevant when, for example by using neural networks, a machine can evidence prior learning and experience.

Opacity. This is a prerequisite for this flow, an avoidance of the naïve processes of cause and effect (and their frequent boredoms for players and audiences alike). Interactivity is a well-discussed term in computer music but its currency has become a little devalued. It is often equated with a one-directional transfer of information from user to machine; reaction, not interaction. A lack of opacity and uncertainty distances the performer from the machine. The relationship is then that of a familiar 'subject-to-object', which by implication denies the possibility of intimacy: *"...interactivity has gradually become a metonym for information retrieval rather than dialogue, posing the danger of . . . reifying the encounter with technology"* [4]. George Lewis offers Voyager's capacity for *"variation and difference"* as an alternative that avoids transparent and consistent input-output mapping, but still provides against the appearance of randomness.

A truly interactive system ought to offer an ambiguous and shifting balance between the reactive and proactive, and across the threshold of the apparently chaotic and the readily comprehensible.

Unimagined. The result of these attributes might be a 'living' computer music, an unimagined music, its unresolved and unknown characteristics offering a genuine reason for machine-human collaboration. If computers might extend, not parody, human creative behaviour, machine music should not emulate established styles or practices, or be measured according to any associated, alleged aesthetic. In living computer music the contributions of all performers involved – human and machine –have equal significance, but may not necessarily be equivalent. Such music cannot be imagined or reproduced.

Unimagined music, free from pre-defined rules or overt control, moves *"... toward a permanent discovery – comparable to a 'permanent revolution'."* [14]. Boulez refers to compositional method, the exigencies of musical form given a *"fluidity of vocabulary"*, and the consequent need to de-linearise temporal structure. However, a 'living' computer music might be even more apposite, permanently exploring all elements of its emergent language, and in real-time, not just in concept.

Freedoms, whether open to the player or to computer (e.g. by stochastic methods) might be better described as 'informalities'. Unimagined music is a technological *"musique informelle"*, emergent and idiosyncratic; its coherence neither derived nor dictated. It *"discards all forms which are external or abstract or which confront it in an inflexible way, free of anything irreducibly alien to itself or superimposed on it"* [15]. Adorno's term is not synonymous with the informal and intuitive; it does not deny the potential for objective and measurable structural complexity. This approach is arguably apposite to free improvisation and the claims of its practitioners. In 'living' computer music, unpredicted acts of a performer, and implicit (i.e. virtual) acts of the machine should exemplify this objective complexity, but not through the simple sonfication of rules or sheer randomness. There should be a critical engagement between intended behaviours, an appraisal of potential behaviours and response to actual sonic realisations and their unfolding history. Ideally, there should be an integration of subject (performer) and organism (the musical system regarded as a whole).

3 NN Music: A Performance System

These five properties are addressed in the NN Music (Neural Network Music) performance system, which brings together a solo player with a computer to mutually interact by proxy in the sonic environment. Implementation is in Max/MSP, including the neural net external object op.fann.mlp by Olivier Pasquet[2]. NN Music has been deployed with a number of instrumental combinations under the titles *au(or)a*, *piano_prosthesis* and *cello_prosthesis*, the titles indicating a particular musical/compositional ethos. *Au(or)a* is intended for any solo instrument with Disklavier piano; the system produces MIDI data intended to emulate a virtual pianist (with the veracity of real-life instrumental sound offered by the Disklavier). The two *_prosthesis* works begin a projected series of pieces that bring together a specific

---

[2] Available at www.maxobjects.com

instrument with a related (and transformed) library of samples and real-time manipulations. There is therefore an added dimension of digital synthesis. The common creative concerns in these works are **distance** (conceptual and physical distances, human-machine aesthetic differences) and **embodiment** (to explore the notion of 'prosthesis' an alternative to the user-interface paradigm for HCI [16]).

3.1 PQf

NN Music system is best described according to the modular PQf architecture proposed for improvising performance systems [6]. This simple modular structure offers an empirical algorithmic model of the process of listening and comprehension (P), rendering of performance (Q) and creative thinking (f) experienced by human performers. It offers a direct analogy for machine musicians, although there is no attempt at symbolic representation. For a machine, P is an audio analysis function, Q is a synthesis function and f(h) is some form of hidden, organising algorithm. P and Q interpret, and interface with, the sonic environment, and also communicate with the hidden algorithm: P obtains an analysis parameter set $\{p_0, p_1, ...p_n\}$ from an audio stream X, relaying these to the algorithm. Q generates a synthesis set $\{q_0, q_1, ...q_n\}$ from the output of the algorithm, which creates a new audio stream Y. This supposes that changes in state evidenced in f(h) are scheduled in real-time, subject to the contingencies of the inputs and outputs from and to the environment. X and Y may be considered either as distinct audio streams that contribute to the total sonic environment, or as two temporally spaced points on one continuous stream, depending on the musical application and hidden functions.

$$P(fX) \qquad\qquad Q(fY)$$
$$X \rightarrow \{p_0, p_1, ...p_n\} \rightarrow \boldsymbol{f(h)} \rightarrow \{q_0, q_1, ...q_n\} \rightarrow Y \ . \tag{1}$$

There is a vast array techniques deployed for all three modules in this schema. Creative computing applications have explored many approaches to 'hidden' generative algorithms f(h); often, non-linear dynamical processes that display complexity, capacity for self-organisation, and/or patterns perceived to have some artistic value. Cellular automata, genetic algorithms, particle swarm and flocking algorithms and self-organising maps might be classed as such. Although differing widely in approach, these sub-symbolic techniques can be distinguished from those that have recourse to a pre-defined, 'expert' rule-base. The latter approach constitutes a direct mapping from P to Q, i.e. an interface between performer and machine via a set of contingent rules in which all circumstances may be predicted in advance. Such approaches cannot be classed as 'live algorithms'.

Real-time Neural Networks. The feed-forward neural network allows unsupervised sub-symbolic learning and classification; the potential for self-organising, learning behaviours effective as an f(h) patterning algorithm. The multilayer perceptron neural network is trained using a back-propagation error algorithm that minimises the error between required and actual outputs by gradient descent, given a set of pre-defined input and output conditions. As noted by Toivianen, this type of network benefits from a capacity for generalisation and tolerance to apparently unpredictable or contradictory data; consequently it is well suited to classifying analysis of improvised music, the input state comprising attributes of the improvisation [17].

In NN Music, audio analysis P and synthesis Q are mapped via a feed-forward neural network in real-time. The network adapts to attributes of the performance, and outputs synthesis parameters accordingly. This is an original application for feed-forward networks in that the training phase occurs during the musical performance, not prior to it. Training repeatedly recurs during performance, depending on the variance in musical behaviour measured from the human-produced sound. It compares the current behaviour to the history of classified behaviours in that performance, rather than simply to a set of previously defined classifications. This enables the system to adapt to the contingencies of a specific performance, and also, through the writing/reading of network weight files, to previous performances. There is capacity for immediate short-term learning and long-term memory, represented in the simple form of neural network mapping.

The knowledge of the trained network is opaque, embedded in its re-formulation of internal weights, and can only be ascertained through experimental enquiry. This affords opportunity for creative investigation, but only in the intimate moment of performance itself.

3.2 Analysis and Learning: $P \rightarrow f$

There are two analysis functions, P_{pitch} and P_{audio}. The first focuses on pitch; the implied harmonic characteristics of the improvisation (rather than just step-by-step note progression) and executes a harmonic function to extend the characteristics logically, providing a related, wider pitch resource. The second analysis, P_{audio}, is independent of this, and measures characteristics of the performance based on various audio descriptors to be used as inputs to the neural network.

Pitch analysis and generation. Figure 1 shows the pitch analysis function, P_{pitch}. Audio to pitch conversion produces a stream of data, accurate to the nearest quarter-tone, which is filtered by an *attentiveness* function; the probability that a pitch will be allowed to update the dynamic set S_{chord}, a list of most recently admitted pitches $\{x_0, x_1, ...x_n\}$. In current versions, $n = 6$. The filter is deployed dynamically, mapped from the mean onset density detected over an adjustable time Δt, so relative inactivity on the performer's part fosters more attentive machine listening. When the primary set S_{chord} is updated with a new pitch, a generative function, f_{gen}, recalculates ten other hexachords by cross-multiplying each pitch within the primary set. The resultant chords are identical, other than in their transposition, and each member of $S_{chord\text{-}set}$ contains at least one of the pitches from the original hexachord S_{chord}.

$$f_{gen}: S_{chord} \quad \rightarrow \quad S_{chord\_set}$$
$$\{x_0, x_1, ...x_n\} \; X \; \{x_0, x_1, ...x_n\}. \tag{2}$$

This method emulates the post-serial technique of chord multiplication, devised by Boulez (as, for example, identified in the 'L'artisanat Furieux' cycle of *Le Marteau sans Maitre* [18]). The difference in this instance is that this function continuously updates $S_{chord\text{-}set}$ in real time as new pitches are admitted. $S_{chord\text{-}set}$ is a dynamic pitch corpus, deployed as a resource for the synthesis function Q (explained below). The system adapts to the pitch content of the player (who may to decide to opt for a particular musical approach – e.g. freely atonal, modal etc.), providing a cohesive harmonic framework that is neutral and apposite to *"non-idiomatic"* free improvisation, as advocated by Bailey [19]. It also creates opacity, due both to the detailed statistical filtering of note admission and the complexity of f_{gen} itself, offering a challenging but comprehensible environment to which the performer in turn may adapt.

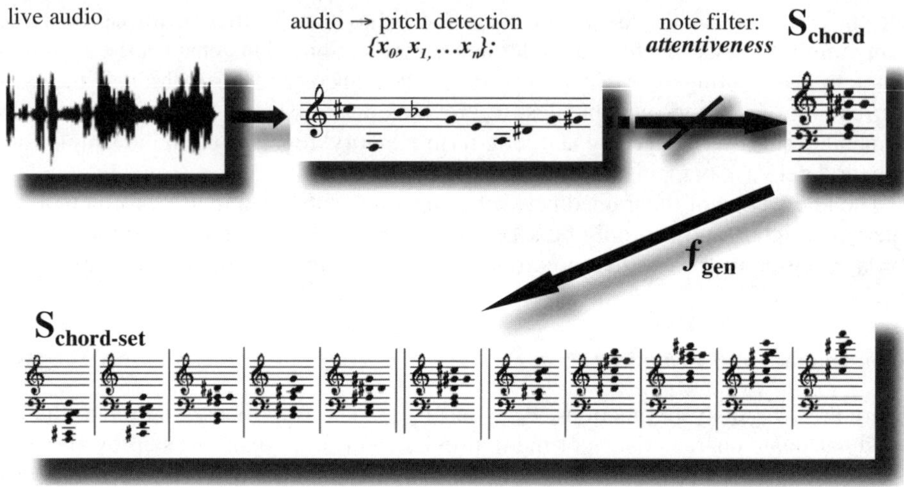

Fig. 1. Pitch analysis and f_{gen} function

Audio analysis and training. The second analysis function, shown in figure 2 below, applies audio descriptors to the live performance (loudness, brightness, duration between events, sustained-ness, frequency etc.) with an analysis window of 50ms. It creates a dynamic performance state, S_{audio}, which is a statistical representation of the performance behaviour, measured over time, Δt, comprising the normalised mean ($\bar{x}$) and normalised standard deviation (σ) of all the descriptors, where $5s < \Delta t > 30s$. The state S_{audio} might indicate a musical behaviour as follows:

- very loud dynamic: $\bar{x} \approx 1., \sigma \approx 0.$
- intermittent bursts of rhythmic activity: $\bar{x} \approx 0.5, \sigma \approx 1.$
- low pitch: $\bar{x} \approx 0., \sigma \approx 0.$

Rather than observing a simple stream of events, the analysis attempts to represent a musical behaviour in such broad terms: this is relevant to the exigencies of freely improvised music, although the analysis is, in itself, only indicative. It is adaptable however, as the individual descriptors in themselves are of less significance than the composite representation offered by S_{audio}.

The purpose of network A is to classify novel performance behaviours, as represented by S_{audio}, in order to acquire a library of learned states for future reference $\{S_0, S_1, ...S_n\}$. This learning is applied – while the improvisation continues and the network runs – to assess incoming states in comparison to those already known: the aim being to identify musical behaviours that are well defined and contrasting, so the network can respond effectively to a broad range of subsequent musical activity. To achieve this, the dynamic state S_{audio} is considered for retraining only if it satisfies the fitness function f_{fit}, a measure of the similarity of the current S_{audio} to all those previously learned. The function, found through experimentation, is represented as co-efficient a, the sum of the mean and standard deviation of the absolute difference between the new state under consideration and a previously admitted state. This produces a list of values, $\{a_0, a_1, \ldots a_n\}$, where n is the number of already admitted states. If any value of a is greater than a predetermined threshold z, the new state is allowed to update the network, which is retrained on the fly; otherwise it is discarded.

$$f_{fit} : S_{audio} \rightarrow \{a_1, a_2, \ldots a_n\} > z . \tag{3}$$

In the current implementation, the threshold is set by the user; to be effective it must adjust to characteristic behaviours of both instrument and performer. The number of output nodes increases every time a new state is classified, $\{O_0, O_1, \ldots O_n\}$ representing an addition to the network's accumulated learning.

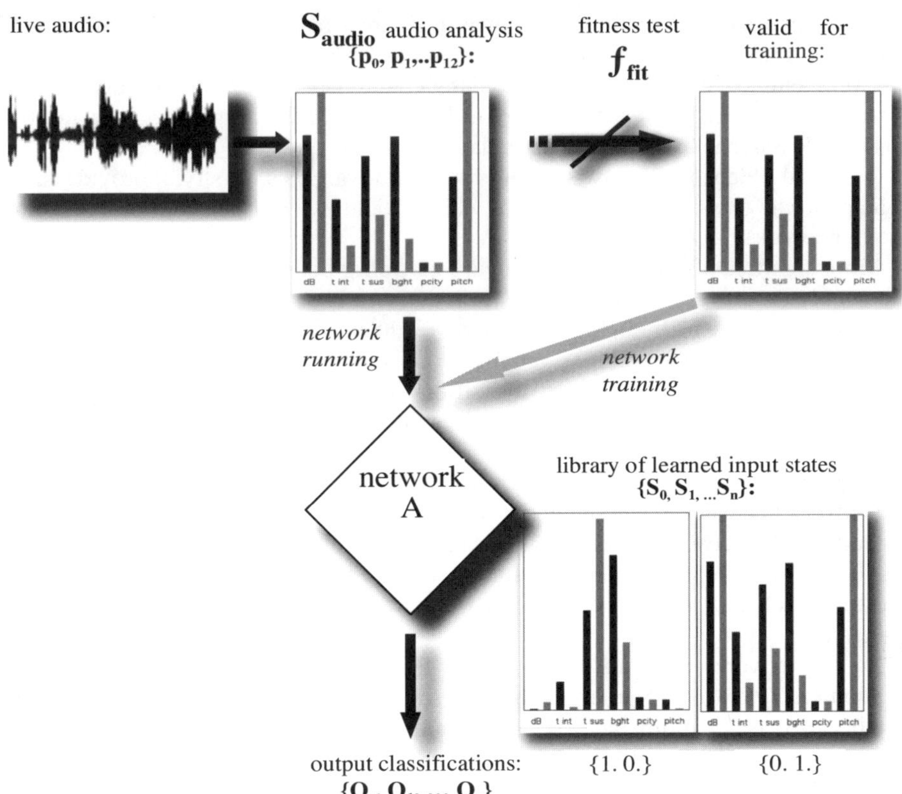

Fig. 2. Audio analysis and training of network A for classification

When the music begins, the network trains several new states, usually within the first few seconds. The time interval between retraining then tends to increase, depending upon the character of the improvisation and the consequent variance of S_{audio} over time. Retraining might be thought of as adaptation, sensitive to the conditions of the sonic environment. As the performance develops, new analysis states will approximate one or, more often, several of those previously obtained. The network is continually queried to evaluate how far the current state S_{audio} approximates any of those previously learned. For example, if four states have been previously learned, an output response of {0. 1. 0. 0.} would indicate certain recognition of state 2; {0.3 0.7. 0. 0.} would indicate that relative characteristics of states 1 and 2 are evidenced.

One limitation of real-time use of the network is that it is "off-line" for this recognition when training is underway. It cannot report on current behaviour and map this assessment onwards. The time-period necessary to obtain an acceptable error during training increases dramatically as the number of output notes increases. This imposes a practical limit of c. 20 output nodes, which results in a maximum of c. 45 seconds for real-time training.

3.3 Maps and Synthesis: $f(h) \rightarrow Q$

Network mapping and synthesis is shown in figure 3 below. A second network (B) is deployed, trained in advance to generate synthesis functions Q, in response to 'ideal' (i.e. very simple) input conditions. The number and meaning of the resultant synthesis parameters is specific to each instance of the system: MIDI data for *au(or)a* and various sample playback and modification data for *piano_* and *cello_prosthesis*.

A second independent network offers several advantages. Firstly, it provides transparency in the classification processes (which would otherwise be embedded within a single network).

More significantly, it allows for **covert mapping** between networks. The expanding list of outputs (i.e. classifications) from network A , {O_0, O_1, ...O_n} is mapped via the function f_{map}, which randomly re-sorts the indices of the data. This jumbling up of output and input nodes provides genuine opacity; it is covert, challenging the player to adapt as the system's behaviour diversifies. The player is invited to attempt to learn which performance actions elicit a given response, and even if this is not a simple or attainable task, the process itself is closely related to the experience of human-only group improvisations.

Network B creates new input nodes as the list {M_0, M_1, ... M_n} increases, which in turn allows the network to access more data from its previously learned set of outputs; this library of potential outputs constitutes the 'knowledge-base' of the system. It is decisive in characterising the music; a framework, a field of relations for aesthetic judgement.

Lastly, network A outputs are mapped with a power function to expand the classification set, i.e. to converge on the highest result. This becomes more apposite as the number of classifications increases. Consequently, network B is more likely to produce an output with a well-defined profile (as opposed to a more equally-weighted, and, amorphous, composite) even if this represents more than one original defined state.

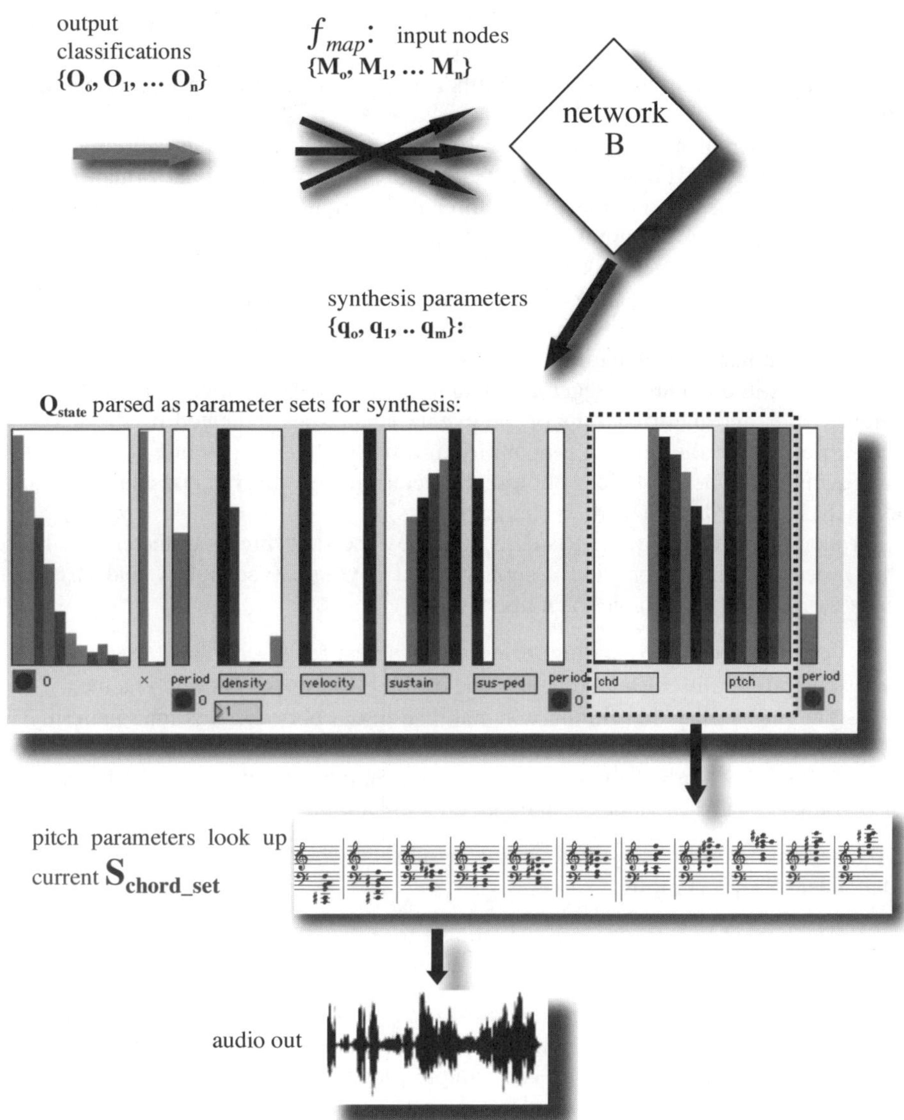

Fig. 3. Mapping to Network B to create parameters for stochastic synthesis

Sound synthesis. Sound events are generated stochastically, in a method tolerant to the contingencies of the neural network output and complementary to the statistical method used for analysis. Stochastic techniques are well established in notated music and synthesis [21]; for NN Music, highly complex, mutable musical behaviours can be generated from an evolving probability distribution (or 'parameter profile') that is a composite of well-defined, theoretical, network outputs. As a consequence of this approach, and depending on the rate of iteration, the sonic environment can develop a "laminal" (textural) character or be more definitively "atomized" (event-based); codifications of sound established in free improvisation [20]. In the case of *_prosthesis*, sounds may be similar or timbrally distinct to the live instrument due to electronic transformation.

The behaviour of network B is entirely dependent on the classifications made by network A as it runs. If a player suggests three previously learned performance states, this will be reflected in a composite of three output synthesis states, summed in proportion to the network A output classification.

The final output of network B is Q_{state}; a list parsed into subsets according to parameter type. In figure 3, values for Q_{state} are shown at a given moment, each subset shown as a separate table. (Normally, due to the varying outputs of network B as it runs, Q_{state} is constantly changing). Q_{state} is then accessed as a probability distribution; each time a sound event is triggered, all subsets are invoked to determine the various characteristics and modifications of the event. The values indicated by the y axis in each subset denote the relative probability of a particular x axis value to be selected. Consequently, the network does not directly determine events, but constantly reshapes the stochastic distribution of their characteristics.

For example, musical timing is determined by the first three parameter sets These three processes aim to provide a sophisticated rhythmic vocabulary and structural syntax akin to those available to an improviser:

- A geometrically expanding series of 11 values: $53ms - 53^{11}ms$
- The probability of selecting any one of three values for i (stretch factor).
- The probability that timing will stabilise into a periodic rhythmic pattern. The most recent 11 durations are recorded; for every new iteration there is a probability that these values – or a selected number of them – will be recalled rather than fresh values generated, creating a looped rhythm.

Pitches are determined by two parameter subsets, which are cross-referenced to the independent $S_{chord-set}$ corpus:

- The hexachords from $S_{chord-set}$ available for use.
- The note position allowed within each hexachord (1 to 6).

The outcome of the hexachord/note position is then referred to the current $S_{chord-set}$, from which the actual pitch is obtained. These techniques are extended to include a range of MIDI data for *aur(or)a,* and sample playback/transformation data, such as filtering, ring modulation and granular synthesis in *piano_prosthesis* and *cello_ prosthesis.* The Q_{state} function can easily be generalized for any desired synthesis technique appropriate to the iterative method used.

4 Conclusion

The NN Music system comprises a web of analysis and synthesis functions, linked by a number of functional mapping and hidden algorithms, including the principle methods of unsupervised learning and classification on-the-fly, and covert parameter mapping. The modular approach follows the proposed PQf model for improvisation systems, which indicates how individual components may be replaced, generalised or enhanced without undermining the structure of the whole. The system evidences, to some extent, attributes of a 'live algorithm': adaptability, empowerment, intimacy and opacity – aspiring to unimagined outcomes.

Future developments will need to address the time-delay problem incurred by on-the-fly training, and the consequent practical limit on the number of output nodes (analysis classifications). Other algorithms, such as k-means clustering, may offer more efficient methods for classification. The fitness function, which intercedes in network training should ideally be adaptive or unsupervised if the system is autonomous and entirely 'empowered'. Recurrent neural networks may offer new possibilities in bringing together adaptive and creative generative processes. In addition, greater insights into the improviser's performance, at appropriate structural levels would provide better material for network training, and impact on the responses of the system as a whole

The ultimate aim is to provide a stimulating and challenging environment for improvisers, which examines the liminal space between composition (intentional designs) and improvisation (collaborative or intuitive actions) in a musically convincing way. Artificial intelligence and learning offer great potential for further creative exploration of this.

Acknowledgements. The performers who have worked enthusiastically with the system and helped its development: Kate Ryder, Roger Redgate, Neil Heyde, to Goldsmiths Electronic Music Studios, and to Olivier Pasquet for *op.fann.mlp*.

References

1. Blackwell, T., Young, M.: Live Algorithms. Artificial Intelligence and Simulation of Behaviour Quarterly 122, 7–9 (2005)
2. Young, M.: NN Music: Improvising with a 'Living' Computer. In: Proc.of the International Computer Music Conference, ICMA, San Francisco (2007)
3. Young, M.: Au(or)a: Exploring Attributes of a Live Algorithm. Electroacoustic Music Stud-ies Network Conference (2007),
   `http://www.ems-network.org/spip.php?rubrique49`
4. Lewis, G.E.: Too Many Notes: Computers, Complexity and Culture in Voyager. Leonardo Music Journal 10, 33–39 (2000)
5. Miranda, E.R., Biles, J.A. (Eds.): Evolutionary Computer Music. Springer, London (2007)
6. Blackwell, T., Young, M.: Self-Organised Music. Organised Sound 9(2), 123–136 (2004)
7. Bastien, B.T., Hostager, T.: Cooperative as communicative accomplishment: a symbolic interaction analysis of an improvised jazz concert. Communication Studies 43, 92–104 (1992)
8. Rao, A.S., Georgeff, M.P.: Modeling rational agents within a BDI-architecture. In: 2nd Internationl Conference on the Principles of Knowledge Representation and Reasoning, pp. 473–484. Morgan Kaufmann, San Francisco (1991)
9. Hermann, T., Ritter, H.: Sound and Meaning in Auditory Data Display. IEEE Special Issue on Engineering and Music - Supervisory Control and Auditory Communication 92(4), 730–741 (2004)
10. Eco, U.: The Open Work. In: Trans. Anna Cancogni. Harvard University Press, Cambridge (1989)

11. Wessel, D., Wright, M.: Problems and Prospects for Intimate Musical Control of Computers. Computer Music Journal 26(3), 11–22 (2002)
12. Csikszentmihalyi, M.: Flow: The Psychology of Optimal Experience. Harper Collins (1991)
13. Sawyer, R.K.: Group creativity: Music, Theater, Collaboration. Lawrence Erlbaum Associates, Mahwah (2003)
14. Boulez, P.: Sonate, que me veuxtu? In: Orientations: Collected Writings, Faber and Faber, London (1986)
15. Adorno, T.: Vers une Musique Informelle. In: Quasi une Fantasia, trans. Rodney Livingstone. Verso, London (1963)
16. Stojanov, G., Stojanoski, K.: Computer Interfaces: From Communication to Mind-Prosthesis Metaphor. In: Beynon, M., Nehaniv, C.L., Dautenhahn, K. (eds.) CT 2001. LNCS (LNAI), vol. 2117, pp. 301–311. Springer, Heidelberg (2001)
17. Toivianen, P.: Symbolic AI versus Connectionism in Music Research. In: Miranda, E. (ed.) Readings in Music and Artificial Intelligence. Harwood Academic (2000)
18. Koblyakov, L.: Pierre Boulez: A World of Harmony. Harwood Academic (1990)
19. Bailey, D.: Improvisation: Its Nature and Practice in Music. Da Capo Press (1992)
20. Xenakis, I.: Formalized Music: Thought and Mathematics in Composition. Rev. Ed. Pendragon Press (2001)
21. Prevost, E.: No Sound Is Innocent: AMM and the Practice of Self-invention. Copula (1995)

A Real-Time Genetic Algorithm in Human-Robot Musical Improvisation

Gil Weinberg, Mark Godfrey, Alex Rae, and John Rhoads

Georgia Institute of Technology,
Music Technology Group
840 McMillan St, Atlanta GA 30332, USA
{gilw,mark.godfrey,arae3}@gatech.edu,
jfrhoads@gmail.com
http://music.gatech.edu/mtg/

Abstract. The paper describes an interactive musical system that utilizes a genetic algorithm in an effort to create inspiring collaborations between human musicians and an improvisatory robotic xylophone player. The robot is designed to respond to human input in an acoustic and visual manner, evolving a human-generated phrase population based on a similarity driven fitness function in real time. The robot listens to MIDI and audio input from human players and generates melodic responses that are informed by the analyzed input as well as by internalized knowledge of contextually relevant material. The paper describes the motivation for the project, the hardware and software design, two performances that were conducted with the system, and a number of directions for future work.

Keywords: genetic algorithm, human-robot interaction, robotic musicianship, real-time interactive music systems.

1 Introduction and Related Work

Real-time collaboration between human and robotic musicians can capitalize on the combination of their unique strengths to produce new and compelling music. In order to create intuitive and inspiring human-robot collaborations, we have developed a robot that can analyze music based on computational models of human percepts and use genetic algorithms to create musical responses that are not likely to be generated by humans. The two-armed xylophone playing robot is designed to listen like a human and improvise like a machine, bringing together machine musicianship with the capacity to produce musical responses on a traditional acoustic instrument.

Current research directions in musical robotics focus on sound production and rarely address perceptual aspects of musicianship, such as listening, analysis, improvisation, or group interaction. Such automated musical devices include both Robotic Musical Instruments — mechanical constructions that can be played by live musicians or triggered by pre-recorded sequences — and Anthropomorphic Musical Robots — humanoid robots that attempt to imitate the action of human

R. Kronland-Martinet, S. Ystad, and K. Jensen (Eds.): CMMR 2007, LNCS 4969, pp. 351–359, 2008.

musicians (see a historical review of the field in [4]). Only a few attempts have been made to develop perceptual robots that are controlled by neural networks or other autonomous methods . Some successful examples for such interactive musical systems are Cypher [9], Voyager [6], and the Continuator [8]. These systems analyze musical input and provide algorithmic responses by generating and controlling a variety of parameters such as melody, harmony, rhythm, timbre, and orchestration. These interactive systems, however, remain in the software domain and are not designed to generate acoustic sound.

As part of our effort to develop a musically discerning robot, we have explored models of melodic similarity using dynamic time warping. Notable related work in this field is the work by Smith at al. [11], which utilized a dynamic-programming approach to retrieve similar tunes from a folk song database. The design of the software controlling our robot includes a novel approach to the use of improvisatory genetic algorithms. Related work in this area includes GenJam [2], an interactive computer system that improvises over a set of jazz tunes using genetic algorithms. GenJam's initial phrase population is generated stochastically, with some musical constraints. Its fitness function is based on human aesthetics, where for each generation the user determines which phrases remain in the population. Other musical systems that utilize human-based fitness functions have been developed by Moroni [7], who uses a real-time fitness criterion, and Tokui [12], who uses human feedback to train a neural network-based fitness function. The Talking Drum project [3], on the other hand, uses a computational fitness function based on the difference between a given member of the population and a target pattern. In an effort to create more musically relevant responses, our system is based on a human-generated initial population of phrases and a similarity-based fitness function, as described in detail below.

2   The Robotic Percussionist

In previous work, we developed an interactive robotic percussionist named Haile [13]. The robot was designed to respond to human drummers by recognizing low-level musical features such as note onset, pitch, and amplitude as well as higher-level percepts such as rhythmic stability and similarity. Mechanically, Haile controls two robotic arms; the right arm is designed to play fast notes, while the left arm is designed to produce larger and more visible motions, which can create louder sounds in comparison to the right arm. Unlike robotic drumming systems that allow hits at only a few discrete locations, Haile's arms can move continuously across the striking surface, which can allow for pitch generation using a mallet instrument instead of a drum. For the current project, Haile was adapted to play a one-octave xylophone. The different mechanisms in each arm, driven either by a solenoid or a linear-motor, led to a unique timbral outcome. Since the range of the arms covers only one octave, Haile's responses are filtered by pitch class.

Fig. 1. Haile's two robotic arms cover a range of one octave (middle G to treble G.) The left arm is capable of playing five notes, the right arm seven.

3   Genetic Algorithm

Our goal in designing the interactive genetic algorithm (GA) was to allow the robot to respond to human input in a manner that is both relevant and novel. The algorithmic response is based on the observed input as well as on internalized knowledge of contextually relevant material. The algorithm fragments MIDI and audio input into short phrases. It then attempts to find a "fit" response by evolving a pre-stored, human-generated population of phrases using a variety of mutation and crossover functions over a variable number of generations. At each generation, the evolved phrases are evaluated by a fitness function that measures similarity to the input phrase, and the least fit phrases in the database are replaced by members of the next generation. A unique aspect in this design is the use of a pre-recorded population of phrases that evolves over a limited number of generations. This allows musical elements from the original phrases to mix with elements of the real-time input to create unique, hybrid, and at times unpredictable, responses for each given input melody. By running the algorithm in real-time, the responses are generated in a musically appropriate time-frame.

3.1   Base Population

Approximately forty melodic excerpts of variable lengths and styles were used as an initial population for the genetic algorithm. They were recorded by a jazz pianist improvising in a similar musical context to that in which the robot was intended to perform. Having a distinctly "human" flavor, these phrases provided the GA with a rich pool of rhythmic and melodic "genes" from which to build its own melodies. This is notably different from most standard approaches, in which the starting population is generated stochastically.

3.2 Fitness Function

A similarity measure between the observed input and the melodic content of each generation of the GA was used as a fitness function. The goal was not to converge to an "ideal" response by maximizing the fitness metric (which could have led to an exact imitation of the input melody), but rather to use it as a guide for the algorithmic creation of melodies. By varying the number of generations and the type and frequency of mutations, certain characteristics of both the observed melody and some subset of the base population could be preserved in the output.

Dynamic Time Warping (DTW) was used to calculate the similarity measure between the observed and generated melodies. A well-known technique originally used in speech recognition applications, DTW provides a method for analyzing similarity, either through time shifting or stretching, of two given segments whose internal timing may vary. While its use in pattern recognition and classification has largely been supplanted by newer techniques such as Hidden Markov Models, DTW was particularly well suited to the needs of this project, specifically the task of comparing two given melodies of potentially unequal lengths without referencing an underlying model. We used a method similar to the one proposed by Smith [11], deviating from the time-frame-based model to represent melodies as a sequence of feature vectors corresponding to the notes. Our dissimilarity measure, much like Smith's "edit distance", assigns a cost to deletion and insertion of notes, as well as to the local distance between the features of corresponding pairs. The smallest distance over all possible temporal alignments is then chosen, and the inverse (the "similarity" of the melodies) is used as the fitness value. The local distances are computed using a weighted sum of four differences: absolute pitch, pitch class, log-duration, and melodic attraction. The individual weights are configurable, each with a distinctive effect upon the musical quality of the output. For example, higher weights on the log-duration difference lead to more precise rhythmic matching, while weighting the pitch-based differences lead to outputs that more closely mirror the melodic contour of the input. Melodic attraction between pitches is calculated based on the Generative Theory of Tonal Music model [5]. The relative balance between the local distances and the temporal deviation cost has a pronounced effect — a lower cost for note insertion/deletion leads to a highly variant output. A handful of effective configurations were derived through manual optimization.

The computational demands of a real-time context required significant optimization of the DTW, despite the relatively small length of the melodies (typically between two and thirty notes). We implemented a standard path constraint on the search through possible time alignments in which consecutive insertions or deletions are not allowed. This cut computation time by approximately one half but prohibited comparison of melodies whose lengths differ by more than a factor of two. These situations were treated as special cases and were assigned an appropriately low fitness value. Additionally, since the computation time is proportional to the length of the melody squared, a decision was made to break longer input melodies into smaller segments to increase the efficiency and remove the possibility of an audible time lag.

3.3   Mutation and Crossover

With each generation, a configurable percentage of the phrase population is chosen for mating. This "parent" selection is made stochastically according to a probability distribution calculated from each phrase's fitness value, so that more fit phrases are more likely to breed. The mating functions range from simple mathematical operations to more sophisticated musical functions. For instance, a single crossover function is implemented by randomly defining a common dividing point on two parent phrases and concatenating the first section from one parent with the second section from the other to create the child phrase. This mating function, while common in genetic algorithms, does not use structural information of the data and often leads to non-musical intermediate populations of phrases. We also implemented musical mating functions that were designed to lead to musically relevant outcomes without requiring that the population converge to a maximized fitness value. An example of such a function is the pitch-rhythm crossover, in which the pitches of one parent are imposed on the rhythm of the other parent. Because the parent phrases are often of different lengths, the new melody follows the pitch contour of the first parent, and its pitches are linearly interpolated to fit the rhythm of the second parent.

(a) Parent A   (b) Parent B

(c) Child 1   (d) Child 2

Fig. 2. Mating of two prototypical phrases using the pitch-rhythm crossover function. Child 1 has the pitch contour of Parent A and rhythm pattern of Parent B while Child 2 has the rhythm of Parent A and the pitch contour of Parent B.

Additionally, an adjustable percentage of each generation is mutated according to a set of functions that range in musical complexity. For instance, a simple random mutation function adds or subtracts random numbers of semitones to the pitches within a phrase and random lengths of time to the durations of the notes. While this mutation seems to add a necessary amount of randomness that allows a population to converge toward the reference melody over many generations, it degrades the musicality of the intermediate populations. Other functions were implemented that would stochastically mutate a melodic phrase in a musical fashion, so that the outcome is recognizably derivative of the original. The density mutation function, for example, alters the density of a phrase by adding or removing notes, so that the resulting phrase follows the original pitch contour with a different number of notes. Other simple musical mutations include inversion, retrograde, and transposition operations. In total, seven mutation functions and two crossover functions were available for use with the algorithm, any combination of which could be manually or algorithmically applied in real-time.

4   Interaction Design

In order for Haile to improvise in a live setting, we developed a number of human-machine interaction schemes. Much like a human musician, Haile must decide when and for how long to play, to which other player(s) to listen, and what notes and phrases to play in a given musical context. This creates the need for a set of routines to handle the capture, analysis, transformation, and generation of musical material in response to the actions of one or more musical partners. While much of the interaction we implemented centers on a call-and-response format, we have attempted to dramatically expand this paradigm by allowing the robot to interrupt, ignore, or introduce new material. It is our hope that this creates an improvisatory musical dynamic which can be surprising and exciting.

4.1   Input

The system receives and analyzes both MIDI and audio information. Input from a digital piano is collected using MIDI while the Max/MSP object pitch~ (http://web.media.mit.edu/~tristan/maxmsp.html) is used for pitch detection of melodic audio from acoustic instruments. The incoming audio is filtered and compressed slightly in order to improve results.

4.2   Simple Interactions

In an effort to establish Haile's listening abilities in live performance settings, simple interaction schemes were developed that do not use the genetic algorithm. One such scheme is direct repetition of human input, in which Haile duplicates any note that is received from MIDI input, creating a kind of roll which follows the human player. In another interaction scheme, the robot records and plays back complete phrases of musical material. A predefined chord sequence causes Haile to start listening to the human performer, and a similar cue causes it to play back the recorded melody. A simple but rather effective extension of this approach utilizes a mechanism that stochastically adds notes to the melody while preserving the melodic contour, similarly to the density mutation function described in Sect. 3.3.

4.3   Genetic Algorithm Driven Improvisation

The interaction scheme used in conjunction with the genetic algorithm requires more flexibility than those described above, in order to allow for free-form improvisation. The primary tool used to achieve this goal is an adaptive call-and-response mechanism which tracks the mean and variance of inter-onset times in the input. It uses these to distinguish between pauses that should be considered part of a phrase and those that denote its end. The system quickly learns the typical inter-onset times expected at any given moment. Then the likelihood that a given pause is part of a phrase can be estimated; if the pause continues long enough, the system interprets that silence as the termination of the phrase.

If the player to whom Haile is listening pauses sufficiently long, the phrase detection algorithm triggers the genetic algorithm. With the optimizations described in Sect. 3.2, the genetic algorithm's output can be generated in a fraction of a second (typically about 0.1 sec.) and thus be played back almost immediately, creating a lively and responsive dynamic. We have attempted to break the regularity of this pattern of interaction by introducing some unpredictability. Specifically, we allow for the robot to occasionally interrupt or ignore the other musicians, reintroduce material from a database of genetically modified phrases generated earlier in the same performance, and imitate a melody verbatim to create a canon of sorts.

In the initial phase of the project, a human operator was responsible for controlling a number of higher-level decisions and parameters during performance. For example, switching between various interaction modes, the choice of whether to listen to the audio or MIDI input, and the selection of mutation functions were all accomplished manually from within a Max/MSP patch. In order to facilitate autonomous interaction, we developed an algorithm that would make these decisions based on the evolving context of the music, thus allowing Haile to react to musicians in a performance setting without the need for any explicit human control. Haile's autonomous module thus involves switching between four different playback modes. "Call-and-response" is described above and is the core. "Independent playback" mode is briefly mentioned above; in it, Haile introduces a previously generated melody, possibly interrupting the other players. In "Canon" mode, instead of playing its own material, the robot echoes back the other player's phrase at some delay. Finally, "Solo" mode is triggered by a lack of input from the other musicians, and causes Haile to continue playing back previously generated phrases from its database until both other players resume playing and interrupt the robotic solo.

Independently of these playback modes, the robot periodically changes the source to which it listens, and changes the various parameters of the genetic algorithm (mutation and crossover types, number of generations, amount of mutation, etc.) over time. In the end, the human performers do not know a priori which of them is driving Haile's improvisation or exactly how Haile will respond. We feel this represents a workable model of the structure and dynamic of interactions that can be seen in human-to-human musical improvisation.

5   Performances

Two compositions were written for the system and performed in three concerts. In the first piece, titled "Svobod," a piano and a saxophone player freely improvised with the robot. The first version of "Svobod" used a semi-autonomous system and a human operator (see video excerpts — http://www.coa.gatech.

edu/~gil/Svobod.mov). In its second version, performed at ICMC 2007, the full complement of autonomous behaviors described in Sect. 4.3 was implemented. The other piece, titled "iltur for Haile," also utilized the fully autonomous system, and involved a more defined and tonal musical structure utilizing genetically driven as well as non-genetically driven interaction schemes, as the robot performed with a full jazz quartet (see video excerpts http://www.coa.gatech. edu/~gil/iltur4Haile.mov).

Fig. 3. Human players interact with Haile as it improvises based on input from saxophone and piano in "Svobod" (performed August 31, 2007, at ICMC in Copenhagen, Denmark)

6 Summary and Future Work

We have developed an interactive musical system that utilizes a genetic algorithm in an effort to create unique musical collaborations between humans and machines. Novel elements in the implementation of the project include using a human-generated phrase population, running the genetic algorithm in real-time, and utilizing a limited number of evolutionary generations in an effort to create hybrid musical results, all realized by a musical robot that responds in an acoustic and visual manner. Informed by these performances, we are currently exploring a number of future development directions such as extending the musical register and acoustic richness of the robot, experimenting with different genetic algorithm designs to improve the quality of musical responses, and conducting user studies to evaluate humans' response to the algorithmic output and the interaction schemes.

References

1. Baginsky, N.A.: The Three Sirens: A Self-Learning Robotic Rock Band (Accessed May 2007), http://www.the-three-sirens.info
2. Biles, J.A.: GenJam: a genetic algorithm for generation of jazz solos. In: Proceedings of the International Computer Music Conference, Aarhus, Denmark (1994)
3. Brown, C.: Talking Drum: A Local Area Network Music Installation. Leonardo Music Journal 9, 23–28 (1999)
4. Kapur, A.: A History of Robotic Musical Instruments. In: Proceedings of the International Computer Music Conference, Barcelona, Spain, pp. 21–28 (2005)
5. Lerdahl, F., Jackendoff, R.: A Generative Theory of Tonal Music. MIT Press, Cambridge (1983)
6. Lewis, G.: Too Many Notes: Computers, Complexity and Culture in Voyager. Leonardo Music Journal 10, 33–39 (2000)
7. Moroni, A., Manzolli, J., Zuben, F., Gudwin, R.: An Interactive Evolutionary System for Algorithmic Music Composition. Leonardo Music Journal 10, 49–55 (2000)
8. Pachet, F.: The Continuator: Musical Interaction With Style. Journal of New Music Research 32(3), 333–341 (2003)
9. Rowe, R.: Interactive Music Systems. MIT Press, Cambridge (1992)
10. Rowe, R.: Machine Musicianship. MIT Press, Cambridge (2004)
11. Smith, L., McNab, R., Witten, I.: Sequence-based melodic comparison: A dynamic-programming approach. Melodic Comparison: Concepts, Procedures, and Applications. Computing in Musicology 11, 101–128 (1998)
12. Tokui, N., Iba, H.: Music Composition with Interactive Evolutionary Computation. In: Proceedings of the 3rd International Conference on Generative Art, Milan, Italy (2000)
13. Weinberg, G., Driscoll, D.: Toward Robotic Musicianship. Computer Music Journal 30(4), 28–45 (2007)

A Musical Framework with Swarming Robots

Yuta Uozumi, Masato Takahashi, and Ryoho Kobayashi

Graduate School of Media and Governace, Keio University, Japan
{isana137, masatooo, ryoho}@sfc.keio.ac.jp
http://www.csp.sfc.keio.ac.jp

Abstract. In this paper, we describe an approach to a musical framework with interactions among numerous physical autonomous devices. The devices behave as metaphors of life and self-organize sounds and rhythm. Users can manipulate the system by affecting the interactions of the devices. We implemented the system as two different installations.

Keywords: Swarming Robotics, Multi Agent System, Self-organize, Swarming Instruments, Musical Controller.

1 Introduction

This system is implemented as a sound-installation, which generates sounds through interactions among swarm robots. Various models for swarm robots have already been proposed [1]. Almost all of them have been focused on how to play musical instruments using robots. However, the model proposed here is unique in that it is focused on the generation of musical structures through the interactions of autonomous, swarming robots [2]. The robots are called "agent-robots". The agent-robots behave as metaphors of actual lives. They were developed in the image of insects. They have insect-like shapes and, like insects, they swarm to seek food. Therefore each agent has a microcontroller and sensors mounted on it. The agents are programmed to seek, chase and eat food. Their food is light, which they seek with their sensors. If they find light, they move to eat it. An LED flashes on the agent's body when it is eating. The LED's color and position are tracked by a CCD-camera that is mounted on the overhead. The sound generator on an external PC generates sounds based on the information.

Users can give the agents light as food. When users place red paste or red LEGO blocks on a scan-board, these shapes of those items are displayed as LCD light below the agents. The agents eat the light when they find it. They also interact with each other. In response, the agents self-organize [3] rhythm and pitch. Six agent-robots are employed in this system.[1]

2 System

The system consists of four sections as follows (Figure 1)

    A: Insect type agent robot
    B: Human interface

---

[1] Please refer the demo movie online. http://www.mag.keio.ac.jp/~isana137/bd/Demo.htm

R. Kronland-Martinet, S. Ystad, and K. Jensen (Eds.): CMMR 2007, LNCS 4969, pp. 360–367, 2008.
© Springer-Verlag Berlin Heidelberg 2008

C: Tracking system with overhead camera
D: Sound generator

2.1 Insect Type Agent Robot

The agent robot is mounted a microcontroller and sensors. It is programmed to seek light. Light is food for the agents. Agents react to light on LCD (See Fig.1-B1) and in the environment. If an agent finds a light, it chases the light to eat. When the agent chases a light, an LED on its body flashes its predefined color. The LED color and position are utilized in the tracking system (See Fig.1-C). The tracking system is described later. Six agents are employed in this installation.

2.2 Human Interface

A scan-board[2] is set in front of the user (See Fig.1-B3). The board is captured by a USB camera (See Fig.1-B2). A user places red paste or red LEGO blocks on the board, and then the shapes are expressed below the agents as LCD[3] light (See Fig.1-B1). If the agents locate the light, they chase it to eat it. During this process, these insect type robots repeat flashing their LEDs. The flashes are utilized for generation of rhythm and pitch.

2.3 Tracking System with an Overhead Camera

The overhead camera tracks the movements of the agents. It detects the color and position of the LEDs flashed by the agents. The tracking system sends the detected information to a sound generator (See Fig.1-D).

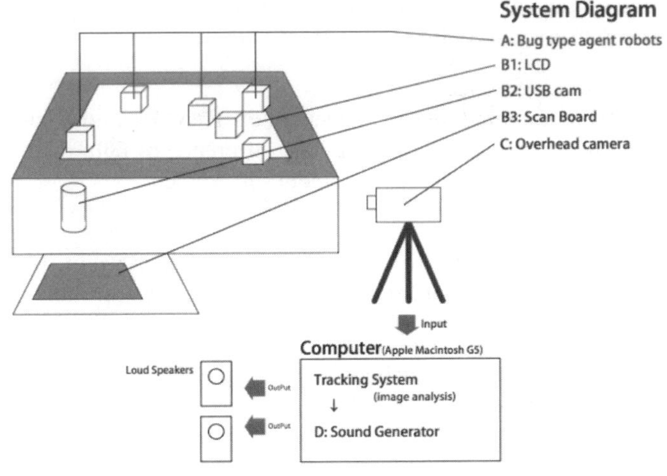

Fig. 1. System Overview

---

[2] The scan-board size: Width: 300mm Depth: 210mm.
[3] The LCD size: Width: 930mm Depth: 520mm.

2.4 Sound Generator

The sound generator plays sounds in accordance with signals from the tracking system (see above section 2.3).

The agents have sexuality. Male agents emit LEDs with blue color when they are eating light. On the contrary, female agents emit LEDs with red color when eating. The blue lights are utilized for rhythm. The sight, which is viewed through an overhead camera, is separated to multiple grids by the system. The sound generator plays predefined sounds based on the grid where the blue flash is detected. If the system detects a red flash, it plays low-frequency sounds depending on x-axis value of the position. An agent has a built-in contact microphone. It plays physical noises of motor and scratch. These sounds are processed as effect source by the sound generator.

3 Agent-Robot

The agent-robot is the most important component of the system. Commonly, most devices for sound control run individually and statically. However in the proposed system, the physical components swarm and interact with each other as agents. In this section, we see the implementation of the agent-robots.

3.1 Architecture of an Agent-Robot

An agent-robot consists of the following components (see Fig.2).

A. Micro Controller
Each agent-robot has a micro controller for autonomous control. The controller can process multiple outputs and inputs, which are digital or analog signals. It is made by AVR Inc. Plural sensors and motors are connected to it.

B. Cadmium Sulfide (CDS) sensor
Two CDS sensors are mounted on each agent-robot. They detect the intensity of lights on the left and right in front of each agent. The difference of light intensities between left and right decides the direction of each agent's movement.

C. Infrared (IR) sensor
An IR sensor is employed to detect barriers in front of each agent. If the sensor detects barriers 2 or 3 centimeters ahead, it notifies the Micro Controller.

D. Motor
Two motors are incorporated into each agent-robot for its moving. The drive power of each motor is decided based on the difference between the values of the two CDS sensors.

E. LED
Each agent-robot has a LED. It can emit three colors simultaneously. According to the combination of the three colors, it generates multiple colors. An agent flashes the LED with red or green or blue color based on the agent's condition for generating sounds. It normally flashes an LED with green color.

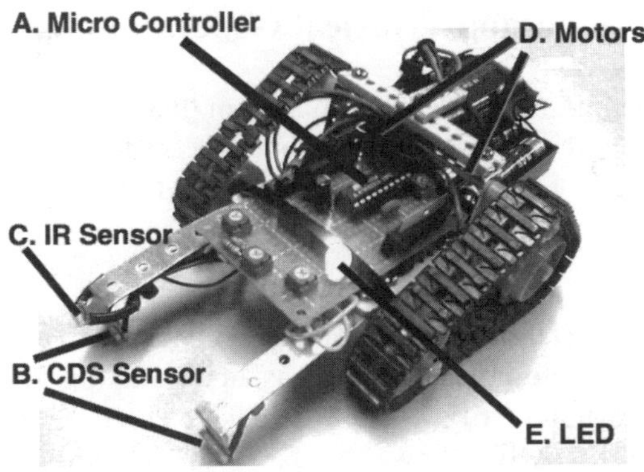

Fig. 2. Architecture of an agent-robot

3.2 Algorithm of the Agent-Robots

The algorithm of the agent robots is as follows.

1. An agent sets the light intensity of the environment as initial value when the power is on.
2. At first, the agent moves slowly to seek light. The direction of movement changes at random.
3. If the agent detects light intensity larger than the initial light value, it moves in that direction.
4. When the agent loses track of the light intensity, it goes back slightly because it has passed over the light below. Through the repetition of this process, eating behavior emerges.
5. If an agent detects a barrier, it changes direction of movement to the left or right at random.

The algorithm is simple, however, complex interactions emerge from it. They are behaviors like scrambling for foods or yielding them according to the user's feed.

4 Results of the First Implementation

A lot of physical interfaces, which correspond to user's input directly, already exist. These linear interfaces often run statically. However, this project approached an interface model by which the user affects interactions between plural physical autonomous devices. This interface is dynamic. If we adopt a new specification for a model like this, anyone can put in a newly designed agent based on the specification. Then the interface's behavior might change dramatically.

The project has many future works such as how to balance between control and out of control, how to stimulate meaningful self-organization and how to develop more optimized models for musical purposes.

5 Attempt of Autonomous Musical Generation for an Installation

In addition, we attempt to implement a system that generates musical patterns autonomously based on the proposed framework. The system was updated for it.

It was implemented as a next step of our installation-project, named "musicalBox".[4]

5.1 Concepts

The idea of the implementation was inspired by a concept of autopoiesis (Maturana, Varela, 1980) [4]. It was designed to exhibit as an installation. An autopoietic system continues to behave evolutionarily, even if there is no external signal. This is because it can generate signals by itself.

In the proposed system, the input was changed from feed by users to environmental sound. This generates new musical-evolutions through agent-robots' interactions according to their own self-organized and/or environmental sounds. The generated sounds brew up the next interactions of agent-robots. In such a system which includes feedback, nonlinear components are needed to obtain interesting behaviors. Therefore, the sound component of a system is changed from digital sound-synthesis to playing the physical piano. This can enhance the dynamic behavior of the system because such feedbacks from physical-components take in errors and environmental noises or reverberation of the space.

In addition, agent-robots are mounted a communication system to aid of interactions among agent-robots.

5.2 System Overview

In this section, we see embodiment of the system.

5.2.1 Feedback System

Interaction source for agents is changed from feed via users to feedback of environmental sounds (see Fig.3). The feedback system is implemented to always analyze the pitch and amplitude of the environmental sounds. If the system detects a sound which has certain amplitude, the system displays lights below the agent-robots, based on the frequency and amplitude of the detected sound. An agent-robot flashes a LED on its body when eating the lights (Section 3.1E). The flashes are detected by the system. The system drives piano-actuators according to the detection with predefined rules. Consequently, the flashes are transformed to piano playing. The lights below the agent-robots and piano playing form recursive-loops via the interactions of the agents.

5.2.2 Implementation of Playing the Piano

Eight notes are utilized to play the piano. These notes are selected carefully to accord with the atmosphere of installation by the author (see Fig.4). Therefore, when the notes are played asynchronously by the agent-robots, the sounds can keep the image

---

[4] Please refer to the demo to observe agents' behavior of this implementation.
http://www.mag.keio.ac.jp/~isana137/dock/icmc07/

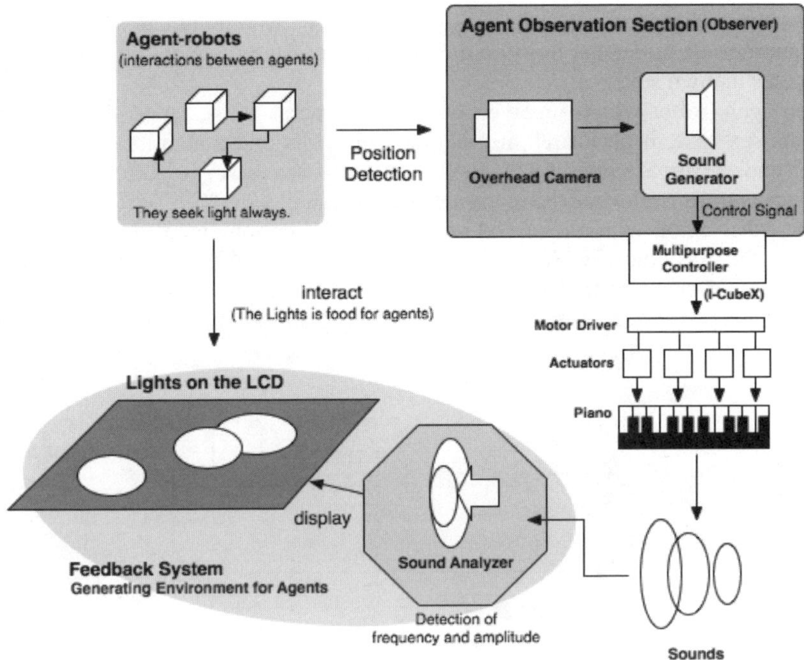

Fig. 3. Diagram of secnd implementation

of the installation. The keyboards corresponding to each note are assigned actuators (Section 5.3.2), and are pressed by the system with the actuators. Two types agent-robots, male and female, exist. They flash LEDs based on their sex and predefined algorithm (Section 2.4). If the male agent-robot flashes a blue light, from its LED, a note is selected according to the position, and is played. When the female agent-robot flashes a red light from its LED, a simple motif consisting of the eight notes is played according to the detected position.

In consequence, the system generates music which has a fluctuation structure.

5.3 Added Components of the System

Added components for the autonomous system are as follows:

5.3.1 Communication System of Agent-Robots

Agent-robots are modified to communicate with each other. The communication system was implemented with infrared radiation (IR). Agent-robots are programmed to chase away neighbor agent-robots of the same sex when detected. On the contrary, when the neighbor agent-robot encounters one of the opposite sex, it performs court-ship dance. If other agents come to the pair of agents, they perform the dance too. Consequently, the courtship dance has contagiousness.

The communication algorithm is as follows:

1. An agent-robot always transmits signal code-"A", which indicates its existence.
2. If another agent detects the signal code-A, it transmits signal code-"B", which indicates its own sex.
3. The agent-robot which received code-B, compares its sex with the other. In the same sex case, it performs intimidation behaviors and transmits intimidation signal codes (signal code-"C1"). In the opposite sex case, it performs a courtship dance and transmits courtship-signal codes (signal code-"C2").
4. The other agent which received code-C1 (intimidation-signal) backs away to escape. On the contrary, if it receives code-C2 (courtship-signal), it performs a courtship dance and transmits signal code-C2 again. The courtship dance will be continued until each courtship-signal is obstructed by other agent-robots.

Fig. 4. Selected notes

5.3.2 Piano Actuator

A physical instrument (piano) was utilized to generate sounds in this system. It builds up non-linear attributes and impact for the installation. Eight actuators are utilized to play the piano (see Fig.5). To control them, an I-CubeX[5] was utilized.

Fig. 5. Piano actuators

---

[5] The I-CubeX is a universal interface to control actuators and sensors with MIDI, Bluetooth or USB connection. *http://infusionsystems.com*

All actuators are designed to push each specific keyboard with its arm according to the control signal. The system sends the control signal to the actuators based on LEDs flashing on the agent-robots. In consequence, the piano is played. The system generates melody and rhythm.

6 Conclusions

We have presented a musical framework with interactions among plural physical autonomous devices via two different installations.

The results of the second implementation attempting to generate music autonomously is as follows:

Firstly, the implementation could obtain more impact through the utilization of a traditional and physical instrument. Secondly, the agent-robots generated and evolved music through their interactions and the feedback system. Thirdly, dynamic attributes existed, in which sounds were sometimes very few and sometimes plentiful. Finally, the attribute occasionally caused out of control as a sound installation. However, it can generate fluctuation which is very musical, according to circumstances. We will develop a method of control via each agents behavior.

In addition, there are many future works. First, We have to search for a battery which has a longer operating life. In the present version, the duration of activity for agent-robots is only 30 minutes. Second, there is the possibility of behavior evolution for agent-robots with GA or GP. It can realize advanced self-organizing of music in this framework. Finally, it is third implementation task with the framework for more practical purposes such as musical-controller or self-organizing instruments with swarming components.

References

[1] Kapur, A.: A History Of Robotic Musical Instruments. In: Proc. ICMC 2007, September 2005, pp. 21–28 (2005)
[2] Sahin, E.: Swarm Robotics: From Sources of Inspiration to Domains of Application. In: Swarm Robotics SAB 2004 International Workshop, July 17, pp. 10–20 (2004)
[3] Kauffman, S.: At Home in the Universe: The Search for Laws of Self-Organization and Complexity. Oxford University Press, New York (1997)
[4] Maturana, H.R., Varela, F.J.: Autopoiesis and Cognition: the Ralization of the Living. D. Reidel Publishing Co., Dordrecht (1980)

Emergent Rhythms through Multi-agency in Max/MSP

Arne Eigenfeldt

School for the Contemporary Arts
Simon Fraser University
Burnaby, BC
Canada
arne_e@sfu.ca

Abstract. This paper presents a multi-agents architecture created in Max/MSP that generates polyphonic rhythmic patterns which continuously evolve and develop in a musically intelligent manner. Agent-based software offers a new method for real-time composition that allows for complex interactions between individual voices while requiring very little user interaction or supervision. The system described, *Kinetic Engine* is an environment in which networked computers, using individual software agents, emulate drummers improvising within a percussion ensemble. Player agents assume roles and personalities within the ensemble, and communicate with one another to create complex rhythmic interactions. The software has been premiered in a recent work, *Drum Circle*, which is briefly described.

Keywords: Multi-agents, evolutionary rhythm, interactive systems.

1 Introduction

The promise of agent-based composition in musical real-time interactive systems has already been suggested [13], [17], specifically in their potential for emulating human-performer interaction. Agents have been defined as autonomous, social, reactive, and proactive [16], similar attributes required of performers in improvisation ensembles.

Kinetic Engine [6], created in Max/MSP, arose out of a desire to move away from constrained random choices within real-time interactive software, and utilize more musically intelligent decision-making processes. Agents are used to create complex, polyphonic rhythms that evolve over time, similar to how actual drummers might improvise in response to one another. A conductor agent loosely co-ordinates the player agents, and manages the high-level performance parameters, specifically *density*: the number of notes played by all agents.

The software is written by a composer with compositional, rather than research, objectives, and is the first stage in a long-term investigation of encoding musical knowledge in software. As such, the encoded knowledge is my own; my experience as a composer suggests that I have some knowledge as to what determines interesting music, so I am relying upon that knowledge. No attempt has been made to create a

R. Kronland-Martinet, S. Ystad, and K. Jensen (Eds.): CMMR 2007, LNCS 4969, pp. 368–379, 2008.

comprehensive compositional system that can reproduce specific styles or genres; the system is rule-based, rather than data-driven, and the rules and logic within *Kinetic Engine* are derived from auto-ethnographic examination.

This paper will describe the implementation of multi-agents in *Kinetic Engine*. Section 2 gives an overview of existing research into multi-agent systems and rhythm generation. Section 3 describes the specific implementation of agents. Section 4 describes how agents activate themselves. Section 5 discusses how rhythms are generated and checked. Section 6 describes the social behaviour of agents. Section 5 describes how messaging between agents operates. Section 8 describes how agents learn and evolve. Section 9 offers conclusions and future directions.

2 Overview of Existing Research

2.1 Multi-agent systems

Multi-agent architectures have been used to track beats within acoustic signals [5], [9] in which agents operate in parallel to explore alternative solutions. Agents have also been used in real-time composition: Burtner [3] created a multi-agent, multi-performer system; Dahlstedt and McBurney [4] developed a multi-agent model based upon Dahlstedt's reflections on his own compositional processes; Wulfhurst et.al. created a multi-agent system where software agents employ beat-tracking algorithms to match their pulse to that of human performers.

Many of these systems incorporate improvisatory elements. As already noted, agents seem to suggest the same sorts of specifications required of human improvisers. Benson suggests that there are many shades of improvisation in music, ranging from standard performance – in which musicians fill in certain details which are not specified by the score – to complete melodic and harmonic freedom; as such, the role agents could play in such works is widely varying.

Murray-Rust and Smaill [13] create a theory of Musical Acts, an expansion of Speech Act Theory, to describe the actions of musicians (represented as agents) engaged in improvisatory ensemble playing. However, the authors are interested in creating a system that will "enable a wider range of people to create music," provide a "new approach to musical composition," and facilitate "the interaction of geographically diverse musicians," none of which are motivating forces behind *Kinetic Engine*.

2.2 Rhythm Generation

The generation of rhythm through software processes has been explored through a variety of methods, including genetic algorithms [10], cellular automata [2], neural networks [11] and multi-agents [8]. Brown suggests that CA provides "a great deal of complexity and interest from quite a simple initial setup"; while this may be the case, he also comments that his generated rhythms "often result in a lack of pulse or metre. While this might be intellectually fascinating, it is only occasionally successful from the perspective of a common aesthetic." He concludes that musical knowledge is required within the rule representation system in order for the system to be *musically* successful.

Gimenes explores a memetic approach that creates stylistic learning methods for rhythm generation. *RGeme* "generates rhythm streams and serves as a tool to observe how different rhythm styles can originate and evolve in an artificial society of software agents." Using an algorithm devised by Martins et.al. for comparing similar rhythms, agents choose rhythmic memes from existing compositions and generate new streams. The highest scoring memes, however, proved to be of questionable rhythmic interest.[1]

Pachet [14] proposes an evolutionary approach for modelling musical rhythm. Agents are given an initial rhythm and a set of transformation rules from a shared rule library; the resulting rhythm is "the result of ongoing play between these co-evolving agents." The agents do not actually communicate, and the rules are extremely simple: i.e. add a random note, remove a random note, move a random note. The system is more of a proof of concept than a performance tool; seemingly, it developed into the much more powerful *Continuator* [15], which is a real-time stylistic analyzer and variation generator.

Finally, Miranda [12] describes an unnamed rhythm generator in which agents produce rhythms that are played back and forth between agents. Successful rhythms (those that are played back correctly) are stored, and unsuccessful ones are eventually deleted, while rhythms that are too close to each other are merged by means of a quantiser mechanism. A repertoire of rhythms eventually emerges, which Miranda suggests is a cultural agreement between agents. This suggests an interesting possibility for evaluating rhythms outside of a database.

3 Agents in Kinetic Engine

Agent-based systems allow for limited user interaction or supervision. While this may seem like a limitation, this allows for more higher-level decisions to be made within software. This models interactions between intelligent improvising musicians, with a conductor shaping and influencing the music, rather than specifying what each musician/agent plays.

Kinetic Engine can run as a distributed network, in which each computer operates as a separate agent, or internally within a single computer. *Drum Circle*, an installation/performance using *Kinetic Engine*, was premiered with one central computer operating as a conductor agent, and nine networked computers operating as player agents.

In *Kinetic Engine* v.2, there are two agent classes: a conductor and an indefinite number of players.

3.1 The Conductor Agent

The conductor agent (hereafter simply referred to as "the conductor") has three main functions: firstly, to handle user interaction; secondly, to manage (some) high-level organization; thirdly, to send a global pulse.

---

[1] The two highest scoring memes were [11111111] and [01111111], where 1 is a note, and 0 a rest, in a constant rhythm (i.e. one measure of eighth notes).

Kinetic Engine is essentially a generative system, with user interaction being limited to controlling *density* – the relative number of notes played by all agents. This value can be set directly via a graphic slider or an external controller. The user can also influence the system by scaling agent parameters (see section 3.2).

Metre, tempo, and subdivision are set prior to performance by the conductor; these values remain constant for the duration of a *composition*. The user can force a new composition, which involves new choices for these values. Each of these values is dependent upon previous choices using methods of fuzzy logic; for example, if the first tempo was 120 BPM, the next cannot be 116, 120, or 126 (which would be deemed to be "too close" to be considered new). If a subsequent tempo is considered "close" to the previous (i.e. 108/112 or 132/138), then the *next* tempo would have to be significantly different.

The conductor also manages the initialization routine, in which agents register and are assigned unique IDs. A more truly evolutionary model eventually could be used, in which agents are created and destroyed during the performance, modeling the notion of musicians entering and leaving the ensemble.

The conductor also sends a global pulse, to which all player agents synchronize.

3.2 The Player Agents

Player agents are instances of a single Max patcher running on separate machines. Upon initialization, agents "report in" to the conductor with their instance number, and are assigned a unique ID, which is stored in the agent as a local value (see figure 1).

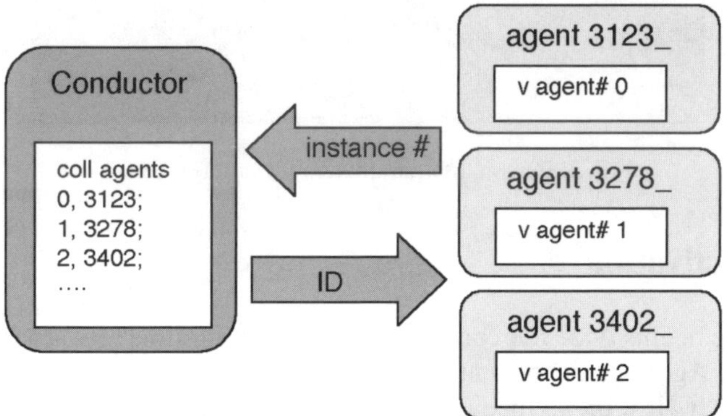

Fig. 1. Initialization of agents

The conductor also counts the number of agents online, and sends this information out: agents adjust their internal data arrays accordingly.

Upon initialization, player agents (hereafter referred to simply as "agents") also read a file from disk that determines several important aspects about their behaviour; namely their *type* and their *personality*.

Type can be loosely associated with the instrument an agent plays, and the role such an instrument would have within the ensemble. See Table 1 for a description of how type influences behavior.

Table 1. Agent *types* and their influence upon agent behaviour

	Type *Low*	Type *Mid*	Type *High*
Timbre	low frequency: • bass drums	midrange frequency: • most drums	high frequency: • rattles, • shakers, • cymbals
Density	lower than average	average	higher than average
Variation	less often	average	more often

The stored personality traits include *Downbeat* (preference given to notes on the first beat), *Offbeat* (propensity for playing off the beat), *Syncopation* (at the subdivision level), *Confidence* (number of notes with which to enter), *Responsiveness* (how responsive an agent is to global parameter changes), *Social* (how willing an agent is to interact with other agents), *Commitment* (how long an agent will engage in a social interaction), and *Mischievous* (how willing an agent is to upset a stable system). A further personality trait is *Type-scaling*, which allows for agents to be less restricted to their specific types [2]. See figure 2 for a display of all personality parameters.

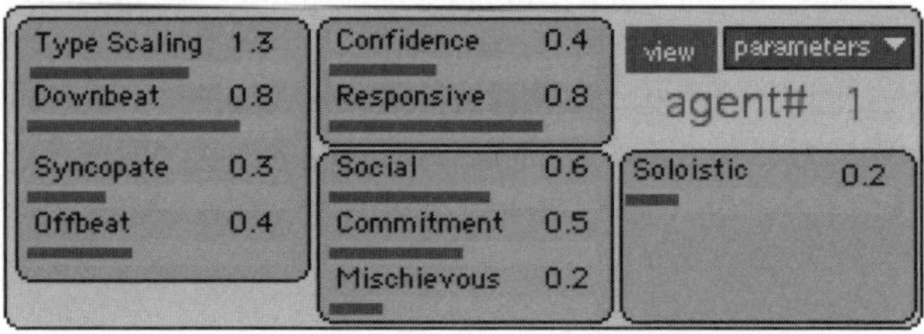

Fig. 2. Personality parameters for a player agent

4   Agent Activation

A performance begins once the conductor starts "beating time" by sending out pulses on each beat. Agents independently decide when to activate themselves by using fuzzy logic to "wait a bit". Once these pulses begin, agents do not respond immediately, nor synchronously; instead, agents react every few beats – a *checkbeat* - using such a fuzzy counter. Each beat is tested[3], and agents wait on average between 3 and 6 beats before passing a checkbeat. This amount is scaled by the agent's responsiveness parameter, as well as the overall system responsiveness; less responsive agents will take longer to react to the conductor's demands (see Figure 3 to see how probabilities increase with each test).

---

[2] For example, low agents will tend to have lower densities than other types, but a low agent with a high type-scaling will have higher than usual densities for its type.

[3] A random value between 0.0 ad 1.0 is generated, and compared to an increasing "chance of success" parameter in a Boolean test.

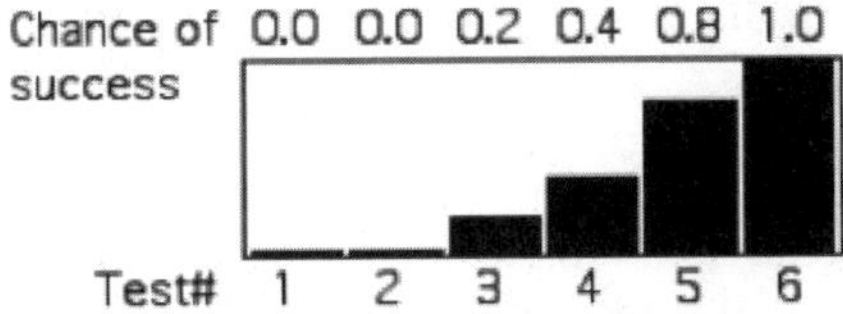

Fig. 3. Using fuzzy logic to "wait a bit" by controlling chance of success for each test

The system responsiveness parameter scales the test number, whereas the agent responsiveness parameter scales the chance of success. The former thus controls how quickly success is possible - allowing for all agents to react immediately - whereas the latter controls how soon success is reached after the initial wait of three beats.

When an agent becomes active, it determines its density.

4.1 Fuzzy Logic Ratings

Kinetic Engine attempts to model human approximation through the use of fuzzy logic to judge success. In the case of density, agents are unaware of the exact global density required. Instead, the conductor rates the global density as "very low", "low", "medium", or "high" and broadcasts this rating.

Agents know the average number of notes in a pattern based upon this rating, which is scaled by the agent's type and type-scaling parameter. Agents generate individual densities after applying a Gaussian-type curve to this number (see Figure 4 for the Gaussian curve in Max's **table** object), and broadcast their density.

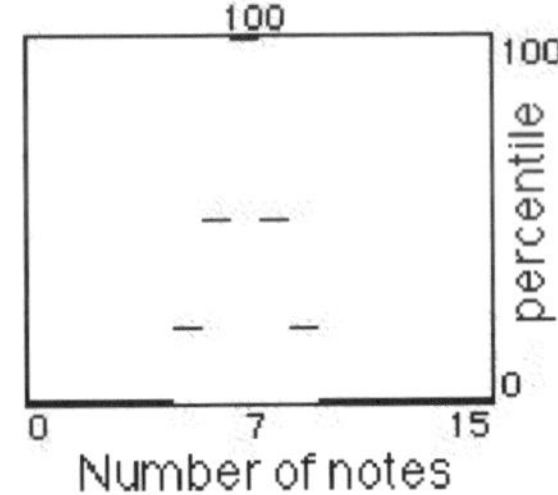

Fig. 4. A Gaussian curve in Max's **table** object

The conductor collects all agent densities, and determines whether the accumulated densities are "way too low/high", "too low/high", or "close enough" in comparison to the global density, and broadcasts this success rating.

- if the accumulated density is "way too low", non-active agents can activate themselves and generate new densities (or conversely, active agents can deactivate if the density is "way to high").
- if the accumulated density is "too low", active agents can add notes (or subtract them if the density is "too high").
- if the accumulated density is judged to be "close enough", agent densities are considered stable.

5 Generating Rhythms

5.1 Density Spread

An agent's density is spread across the available beats using fuzzy logic to determine probabilities, influenced by the agent's downbeat and offbeat parameters (see Figure 5 for an example of probability weightings spread across four beats).

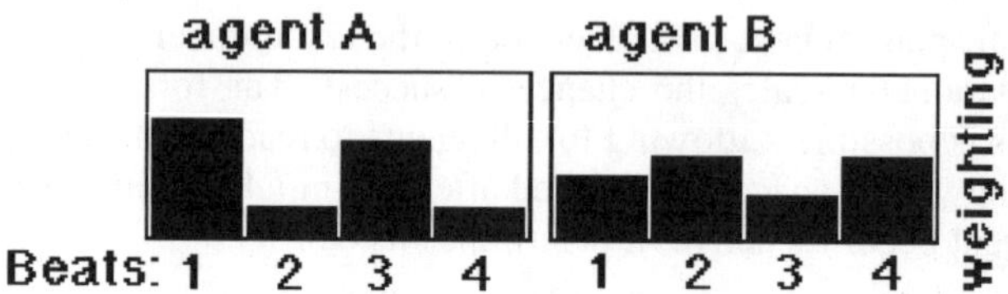

Fig. 5. Example density spread weightings for two agents, 4/4 time with different downbeat and offbeat parameter values

Agents determine the placement of the notes within the beat using a similar technique, but influenced by the agent's syncopation parameter.

Notes are represented using simple binary values over a grid of potential notes within a measure, given the time signature and subdivision. Thus, in 2/4 metre with a subdivision of 4, (0 0 0 0 0 0 0 0) represents an empty measure, whereas (1 0 0 0 1 0 0 0) represents a quarter note on each beat (durations are not represented).

5.2 Pattern Checking

After an initial placement of notes within a pattern has been accomplished, *pattern checking* commences. Each beat is evaluated against its predecessor and compared to a set of rules in order to avoid certain patterns and encourage others.

Previous beat	Pattern A	Pattern B

	30%	90%

Fig. 6. Example pattern check: given a previous beat's rhythm, with one note required for the current beat, two "preferred" patterns for the current beat

In the above example, pattern A is tested first, and there is a .3 percentile chance that this pattern will result. Failing that, pattern B is tested, and there is then a .9 percentile chance that this pattern will result. If this last test fails, the original rhythm is allowed to remain.

6 Social Behaviour

Once all agents have achieved a stable density and have generated rhythmic patterns based upon this density, agents can begin social interactions. These interactions involve potentially endless alterations of agent patterns in relation to other agents; these interactions continue as long as the agents have a *social bond*, which is broken when testing an agent's social commitment parameter fails[4].

Social interaction emulates how musicians within an improvising ensemble listen to one another, make eye contact, then interact by adjusting and altering their own rhythmic pattern in various ways. In order to determine which agent to interact with, agents evaluate[5] other agent's *density spreads* - an agent's density distributed over the number of beats available, given the composition's metre.

Table 2. Example density spreads in 4/4: comparing agent 1 with agents 2 and 3

Agent #	1	2	3
Density Spread	3 1 2 2	1 2 2 1	2 3 3 3
Similarity rating		0.53	0.48
Dissimilarity rating		0.42	0.33

An agent generates a *similarity* and *dissimilarity* rating between its density spread and that of every other active agent. The highest overall rating will determine the type of interaction[6] : a dissimilarity rating results in rhythmic polyphony (interlocking), while a similarity rating results in rhythmic heterophony (expansion).

Once another agent has been selected for social interaction, the agent attempts to "make eye contact" by messaging that agent. If the other agent does not acknowledge the message (its own social parameter may not be very high), the social bond fails, and the agent will look for other agents with which to interact.

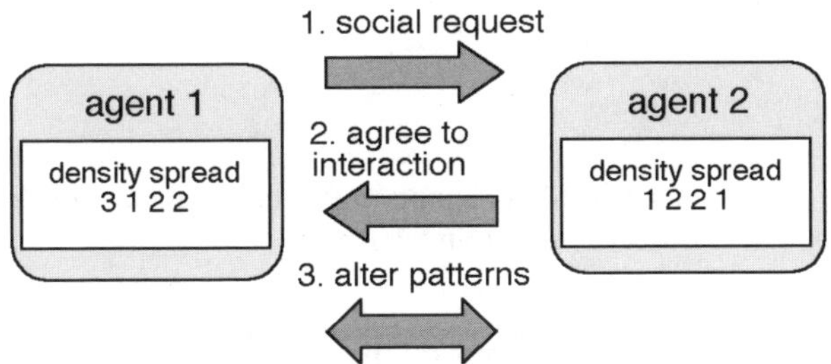

Fig. 7. Social messaging between agents

---

[4] This test is done every "once in a while", another fuzzy counter.
[5] Evaluation methods include comparing density spread averages and weighted means, both of which are fuzzy tests.
[6] Interlocking interactions (dissimilarities) are actually encouraged through weightings.

6.1 Interaction Types: Polyphonic

In polyphonic interaction, agents attempt to "avoid" partner notes, both at the beat and pattern level. For example, given a density spread of (3 1 2 2) and a partner spread of (1 2 2 1), both agents would attempt to move their notes to where their partner's rests occur[7] (see Figure 8).

Fig. 8. Example polyphonic interaction between agents A and B, with density spreads of (3 1 2 2) and (1 2 2 1). Note that not all notes need to successfully avoid one another (beats 3 and 4).

6.2 Interaction Types: Heterophonic

In heterophonic interaction, agents alter their own density spread to more closely resemble that of their partner, but no attempt is made to match the actual note patterns (see Figure 9).

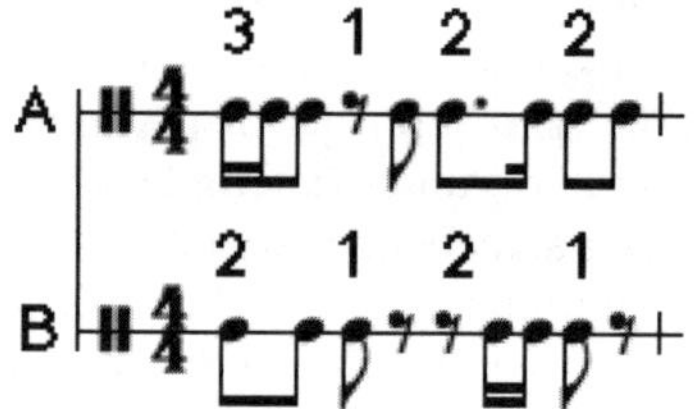

Fig. 9. Example heterophonic interaction between agents A and B, with density spreads of (3 1 2 2) and (2 1 2 1). Agent B had an initial spread of (1 2 2 1).

7 Messaging

Through the use of instances in Max, agents hide their data within local values and colls, two of Max's data objects (see Figure 10).

Fig. 10. The value object as a local variable

---

[7] Because both agents are continually adjusting their patterns, stability is actually difficult to achieve.

Certain variables are required to be global: they can be accessed by any agent, but are only altered by the conductor agent (see Figure 11). When the conductor alters a global variable, it broadcasts this to the network, and agents update their internal values.

Fig. 11. A global variable

Data that is shared between agents – i.e. an agent's note density – is stored as an array within every agent. Each time an agent alters its internal value, it broadcasts it to the network (see Figure 12).

Fig. 12. Broadcasting new values to the network

Agents receive the new value(s), and store them in their own arrays, using the agent number as an index.

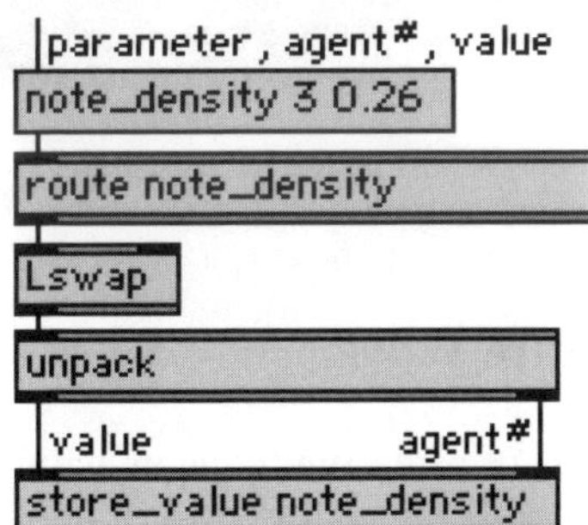

Fig. 13. Storing data from other agents

Example data-handling abstractions, such as "store_value" in Figure 13, are given in [Eigenfeldt 2007].

8 Evolution of Agents

Agents adapt and evolve their personalities over several performances, and within the performance itself. After each composition (within the performance), agents evaluate their operation in comparison to their personality parameters. For example, an agent that was particularly active (which relates to both the responsiveness and confidence parameters) during one composition, might decide to "take a rest" for the next composition by temporarily lowering these parameters.

Agents also judge their accumulated behaviours over all compositions in a performance in relation to their preferred behaviour (as initially read from disk), and make adjustments in an attempt to "average out" to the latter. At the end of the performance (of several compositions), the user can decide whether to evolve from that performance. Comparing the original parameter with the final accumulated history, an exponential probability curve is generated between the two values, and a new personality parameter – close to the original, but influenced by the past performance – is chosen and written to disk, to be used next performance.

Fig. 14. The premiere of *Drum Circle* in Vancouver, April 2007, with the author controlling the system using a P5 Dataglove (photo R. Bader)

9 Conclusion and Future Work

This paper presented methods of using multi-agents within Max/MSP to create complex polyphonic rhythmic interactions that evolve in unpredictable, yet musically intelligent ways.

The software has already been premiered in the performance piece *Drum Circle*, demonstrating the potential for Max/MSP to create music that explores "groove-based" rhythm through such complex methods, music that can be described as displaying emergent properties.

There are several planned strategies for improving the machine musicianship of *Kinetic Engine*, including the use of a dynamic rule base to avoid a homogeneity of rhythms, the ability to incorporate predefined (scored) ideas, and the ability to interact with human performers.

Example music created by *Kinetic Engine* is available at www.sfu.ca/~eigenfel/research.html. The software is also available at this URL as applications (Max OSX only).

References

1. Benson, B.E.: The Improvisation of Musical Dialogue. Cambridge University Press, Cambridge (2003)
2. Brown, A.: Exploring Rhythmic Automata. In: Rothlauf, F., Branke, J., Cagnoni, S., Corne, D.W., Drechsler, R., Jin, Y., Machado, P., Marchiori, E., Romero, J., Smith, G.D., Squillero, G. (eds.) EvoWorkshops 2005. LNCS, vol. 3449, pp. 551–556. Springer, Heidelberg (2005)
3. Burtner, M.: Perturbation Techniques for Multi-Agent and Multi-Performer Interactive Musical Interfaces. In: NIME 2006, Paris, France (2006)
4. Dahlstedt, P., McBurney, P.: Musical agents. Leonardo 39(5), 469–470 (2006)
5. Dixon, S.: A lightweight multi-agent musical beat tracking system. In: Pacific Rim International Conference on Artificial Intelligence, pp. 778–788 (2000)
6. Eigenfeldt, A.: Kinetic Engine: Toward an Intelligent Improvising Instrument. In: Proceedings of the 2006 Sound and Music Computing Conference, Marseilles, France (2006)
7. Eigenfeldt, A.: Managing Complex Patches in Max (2007),
   http://www.cycling74.com/story/2007/2/5/142639/8843
8. Gimenes, M., Miranda, E.R., Johnson, C.: Towards an intelligent rhythmic generator based on given examples: a memetic approach. In: Digital Music Research Network Summer Conference (2005)
9. Goto, M., Muraoka, Y.: Beat Tracking based on Multiple-agent Architecture - A Real-time Beat Tracking System for Audio Signals. In: Proceedings of The Second International Conference on Multi-agent Systems, pp. 103–110 (1996)
10. Horowitz, D.: Generating rhythms with genetic algorithms. In: Proceedings of the International Computer Music Conference, Aarhus, Denmark (1994)
11. Martins, J., Miranda, E.R.: A Connectionist Architecture for the Evolution of Rhythms. In: Rothlauf, F., Branke, J., Cagnoni, S., Costa, E., Cotta, C., Drechsler, R., Lutton, E., Machado, P., Moore, J.H., Romero, J., Smith, G.D., Squillero, G., Takagi, H. (eds.) EvoWorkshops 2006. LNCS, vol. 3907, pp. 696–706. Springer, Berlin (2006)
12. Miranda, E.R.: On the Music of Emergent Behaviour. What can Evolutionary Computation bring to the Musician? Leonardo 6(1) (2003)
13. Murray-Rust, D., Smaill, A.: MAMA: An architecture for interactive musical agents. In: Frontiers in Artificial Intelligence and Applications. ECAI 2006, 17th European Conference on Artificial Intelligence, vol. 141 (2006)
14. Pachet, F.: Rhythms as emerging structures. In: Proceedings of the 2000 International Computer Music Conference, ICMA, Berlin (2000)
15. Pachet, F.: The Continuator: Musical Interaction With Style. Journal of New Music Research 32(3), 333–341 (2003)
16. Woolridge, M., Jennings, N.R.: Intelligent agents: theory and practice. Knowledge Engineering Review 10(2), 115–152 (1995)
17. Wulfhorst, R.D., Flores, L.V., Flores, L.N., Alvares, L.O., Vicari, R.M.: A multi-agent approach for musical interactive systems. In: Proceedings of the second international joint conference on Autonomous agents and multiagent systems, pp. 584–591 (2003)

Experiencing Audio and Music in a Fully Immersive Environment

Xavier Amatriain, Jorge Castellanos, Tobias Höllerer, JoAnn Kuchera-Morin,
Stephen T. Pope, Graham Wakefield, and Will Wolcott

UC Santa Barbara

Abstract. The UCSB Allosphere is a 3-story-high spherical instrument in which
virtual environments and performances can be experienced in full immersion. The
space is now being equipped with high-resolution active stereo projectors, a 3D
sound system with several hundred speakers, and with tracking and interaction
mechanisms.

The Allosphere is at the same time *multimodal, multimedia, multi-user,
immersive*, and *interactive*. This novel and unique instrument will be used for
research into scientific visualization/auralization and data exploration, and as a
research environment for behavioral and cognitive scientists. It will also serve as
a research and performance space for artists exploring new forms of art. In particular, the Allosphere has been carefully designed to allow for immersive music
and aural applications.

In this paper, we give an overview of the instrument, focusing on the audio
subsystem. We give the rationale behind some of the design decisions and explain the different techniques employed in making the Allosphere a truly general-
purpose immersive audiovisual lab and stage. Finally, we present first results
and our experiences in developing and using the Allosphere in several prototype
projects.

1 Introduction

The Allosphere is a novel environment that will allow for synthesis, manipulation, exploration and analysis of large-scale data sets providing multi-user immersive interactive interfaces for research into immersive audio, scientific visualization, numerical
simulations, visual and aural data mining, knowledge discovery, systems integration,
human perception, and last but not least, artistic expression.

The space enables research in which art and science contribute equally. It serves
as an advanced research instrument in two overlapping senses. Scientifically, it is an
instrument for gaining insight and developing bodily intuition about environments into
which the body cannot venture: abstract, higher-dimensional information spaces, the
worlds of the very small or very large, the very fast or very slow, from nanotechnology
to theoretical physics, from proteomics to cosmology, from new materials to new media.
Artistically, the Allosphere is an instrument for the creation and performance of new
avant-garde works and the development of new modes and genres of expression and
forms of immersion-based entertainment, fusing future art, architecture, science, music,
media, games, and cinema.

R. Kronland-Martinet, S. Ystad, and K. Jensen (Eds.): CMMR 2007, LNCS 4969, pp. 380–400, 2008.

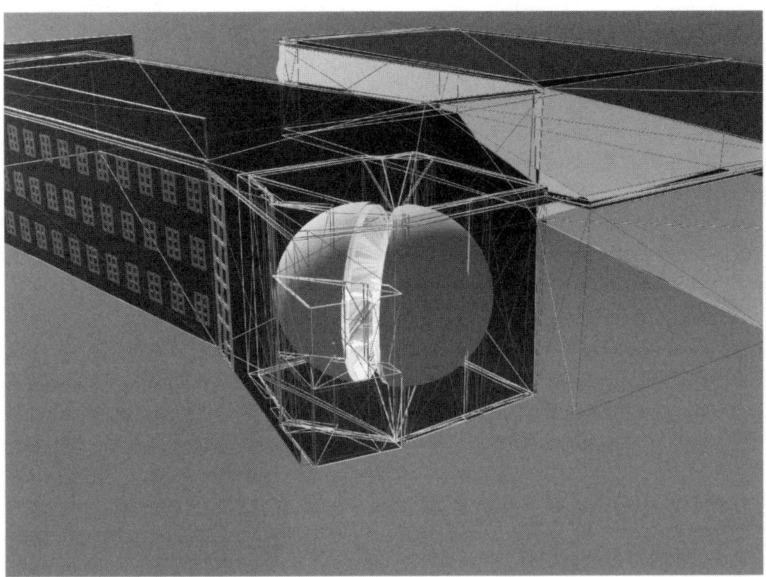

Fig. 1. A virtual rendering of the Allosphere

The Allosphere is situated at one corner of the California Nanosystems Institute building at the University of California Santa Barbara (see virtual model in Figure 1), surrounded by a number of associated labs for visual/audio computing, robotics and distributed systems, interactive visualization, world modeling, and media post-production. The main presentation space consists of a three-story near-to-anechoic room containing a custom-built close-to-spherical screen, ten meters in diameter (see Figure 3). The sphere environment integrates visual, sonic, sensory, and interactive components. Once fully equipped, the Allosphere will be one of the largest immersive instruments in the world. It provides a truly 3D 4 π steradians surround-projection space for visual and aural data and accommodates up to 30 people on a bridge suspended in the middle of the instrument.

The space surrounding the spherical screen is close to cubical, with an extra control/machine room in the outside corner, pointed to by the bridge structure. The whole outer space is treated with sound absorption material (4-foot wedges on almost all inner surfaces), forming a quasi-anechoic chamber of large proportions. Mounted inside this chamber are two 5-meter-radius hemispheres, constructed of perforated aluminum that are designed to be optically opaque (with low optical scatter) and acoustically transparent. Figure 4 is a detailed drawing showing a horizontal slice through the Allosphere at bridge height. The two hemispheres are connected above the bridge, forming a completely surround-view screen.

We are equipping the instrument with 14 high-resolution video projectors mounted around the seam between the two hemispheres, projecting onto the entire inner surface. A loudspeaker array is placed behind the aluminum screen, suspended from the steel infrastructure in rings of varying density (See speaker in the bottom left corner in Figure 2).

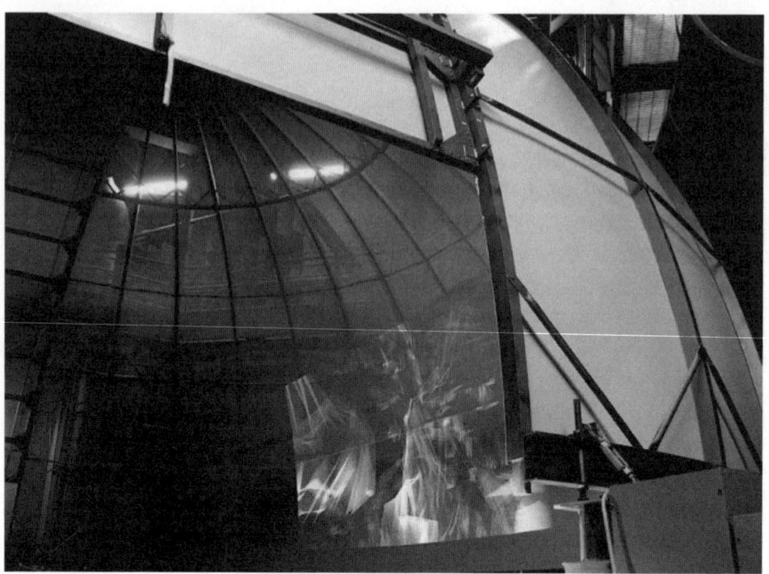

Fig. 2. Looking into the Allosphere from just outside the entrance

The Allosphere represents in many senses a step beyond already existing virtual environments such as the CAVE [9], even in their more recent "fully immersive" reincarnations [15], especially regarding its size, shape, the number of people it can accommodate, and its potential for multimedia immersion. In this paper, we focus on a particular aspect of the multimedia infrastructure, the audio subsystem.

Although the space is not fully equipped at this point, we have been experimenting and prototyping with a range of equipment, system configurations, and applications that pose varying requirements. We envision the instrument as an open framework that is in constant evolution, with major releases signaling major increments in functionality.

2   A Truly Multimedia/Multimodal System

An important aspect of the Allosphere is its focus on multimedia processing, as it combines state-of-the-art techniques both on virtual audio and visual data spatialization. There is extensive evidence of how combined audio-visual information can influence and support information understanding [19]. Nevertheless, most existing immersive environments focus on presenting visual data. The Allosphere is a completely interactive multimodal data mining environment with state-of-the-art audio and music capabilities [28].

Figure 5 illustrates the main subsystems and components in the Allosphere, as well as their interactions. The diagram is a simplified view of the integrated multi-modal/media system design. The exact interactions among the various media data (visual, aural, and interactive) are dependent on the particular individual applications to be hosted.

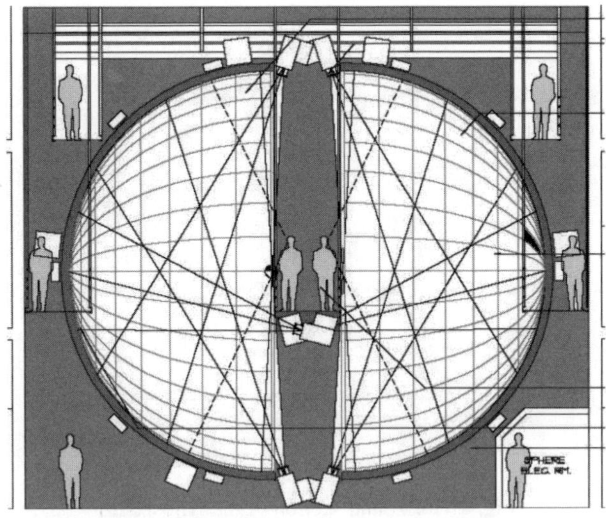

Fig. 3. The Allosphere

The remainder of this section will briefly introduce each of those components and subsystems, as well as the way they interact. In Section 3 we will then discuss the audio subsystem (*Allo.A*) in detail.

The main requirements for the Allosphere visual subsystem (*Allo.V*) are fixed both by the building and screen characteristics and the final image quality targeted [12]. The sphere screen area is 320.0 m^2 and its reflective gain, FOV averaged, is 0.12. The Allosphere projection system (*Allo.V.D.P*) requires image warping and blending to create the illusion of a seamless image from multiple projectors. We have designed a projection system consisting of 14 3-chip DLP active stereo projectors with 3000 lumens output and SXGA+ resolution (1400x1050) each. The projectors are being installed with an effective projector overlap/blending loss coefficient of 1.7.

A typical multi-modal application in the Allosphere will integrate several distributed components, sharing a LAN:

- back-end processing (data/content accessing)
- output media mapping (visualization and/or sonification)
- A/V rendering and projection management.
- input sensing, including real-time vision and camera tracking (related to *Allo.V.V*), real-time audio capture and tracking (related to *Allo.A.C*), a sensor network including different kind of regular wireless sensors as well as other presence and activity detectors (related to *Allo.SN*).
- gesture recognition/control mapping
- interface to a remote (scientific, numerical, simulation, data mining) application

It follows from our specification requirements – and our experiments have confirmed this view – that off-the-shelf computing and interface solutions are insufficient to power the sphere. Allosphere applications not only require a server cluster dedicated to video

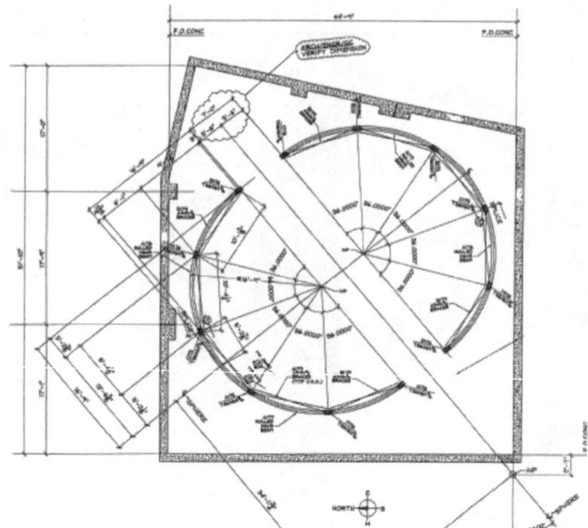

Fig. 4. Horizontal section of the Allosphere

and audio rendering and processing, but also a low-latency interconnection fabric so that data can be processed on multiple computers (in a variety of topologies) in real time, an integration middleware, and an application server that can control the system in a flexible and efficient way.

The computation infrastructure will consist of a network of distributed computational nodes. Communication between processes will be accomplished using standards such as MPI. The Allosphere Network (*Allo.NW*) will have to host not only this kind of standard/low-bandwidth message passing but also multichannel multimedia streaming. The suitability of Gigabit Ethernet or Myrinet regarding bandwidth and latency is still under discussion. In our first prototypes, Gigabit has proved sufficient, but our projections show that it will become a bottleneck for the complete system, especially when using a distributed rendering solution to stream highly dynamic visual applications. We are considering custom hardware technologies as a possible necessity in the future.

3   The Audio Subsystem

The Allosphere is designed to provide "sense-limited" resolution in both the audio and visual domains. This means that the spatial resolution for the audio output must allow us to place virtual sound sources at arbitrary points in space with convincing synthesis of the spatial audio cues used in psychoacoustical localization. Complementary to this, the system must allow us to simulate the acoustics of measured or simulated spaces with a high degree of accuracy.

In a later stage we also plan to complement the audio subsystem with a microphone array in order to arrive at fully immersive audio [25]. However, this component is still at the very early stages of design and will therefore not be discussed in this section.

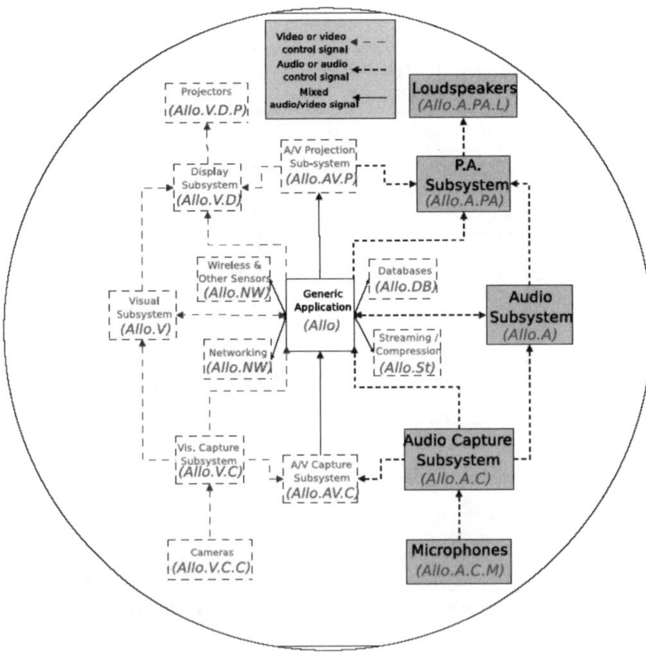

Fig. 5. The Allosphere Components with a highlighted Audio Subsystem

3.1 Acoustical Requirements

In order to provide "ear-limited" dynamic, frequency, and spatial extent and resolution, we require the system to be able to reproduce in excess of 100 dB sound pressure level near the center of the sphere, to have acceptable low- and high-frequency extension (-3 dB points below 80 Hz and above 15 kHz). We designed the spatial resolution to be on the order of 3 degrees in the horizontal plane (i.e., 120 channels), and 10 degrees in elevation. To provide high-fidelity playback, we require audiophile-grade audio distribution formats and amplification, so that the effective signal-to-noise ratio exceeds 80 dB, with a useful dynamic range of more than 90 dB.

To be useful for data sonification [4] and as a music performance space, the decay time (the "T60 time") of the Allosphere was specified to be less than 0.75 seconds from 100 Hz to 10 kHz [6]. This is primarily an architectural feature related to the properties of the sound absorbing treatment in the quasi-anechoic chamber, which was designed to minimize the effect of the aluminum projection screen. The perforations on the screen have also been designed to minimize its effect across most of the audible spectrum. Initial experiments confirm that the absorption requirements have indeed been met.

3.2 Speaker System

It has been a major project to derive the optimal speaker placements and speaker density function for use with mixed-technology many-channel spatialization software

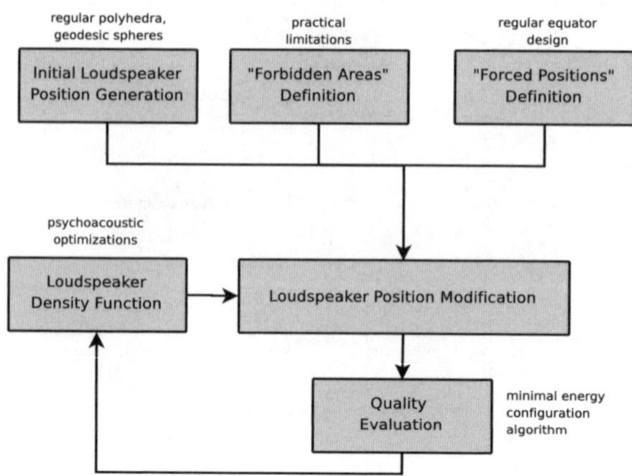

Fig. 6. Allosphere speaker placement iterative design method and variables

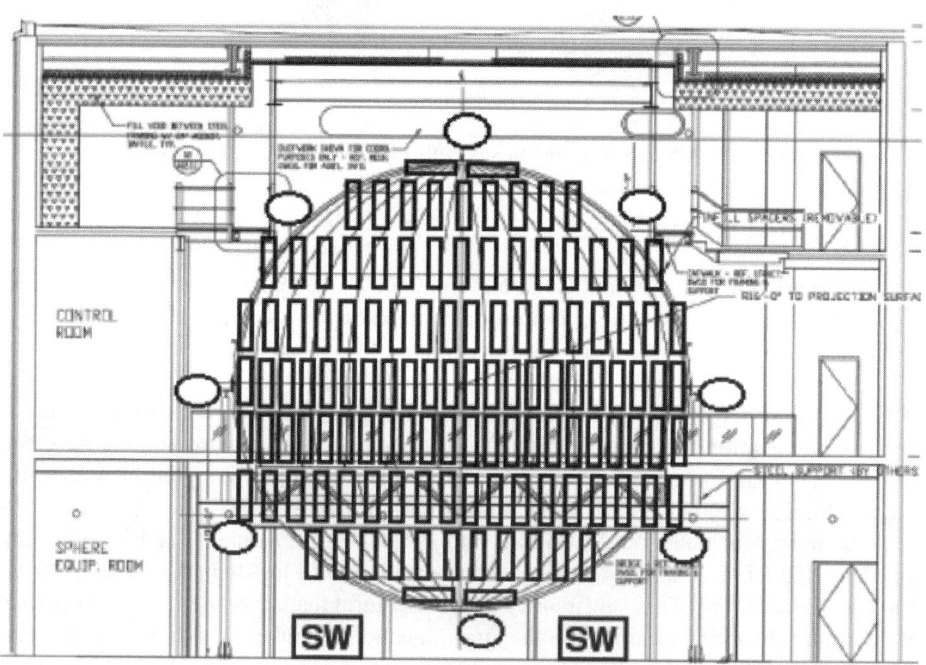

Fig. 7. Allosphere speaker placement design, initial results after first iterations taking into account VBAP requirements

(see discussion and calculations in [13], summarized in figure 6). Our driver placement design comprises between 425 and 500 speakers arranged in several rings around the upper and lower hemispheres, with accommodations at the "seams" between the desired equal and symmetrical spacing and the requirements of the support structure. The loudspeakers will be mounted behind the screen.

We have projected densely packed circular rings of speaker drivers running just above and below the equator (on the order of 100-150 channels side-by-side), and 2-3 smaller and lower-density rings concentrically above and below the equator. The main loudspeakers have limited low-frequency extension, in the range of (down to) 200-300 Hz. To project frequencies below this, four large sub-woofer(s) are mounted on the underside of the bridge.

At this moment, because of timing and construction constraints, we have installed a prototype system with only 16 full range speakers installed along the three different rings mentioned above and two subwoofers under the bridge. Those speakers are connected to the computer via Firewire audio interfaces that support 32 channels.

For the imminent growth of the prototype into the full system, we plan to switch to passive speaker elements wired to a set of 8-16 networked digital-to-analog converter (DAC) amplifier boxes, each of which supports in the range of 32-128 channels and has a Firewire interface. As an alternative, we are also considering building custom interface boxes consisting of a Gigabit Ethernet interface, digital/analog converter, power amplifier, and step-up transformer (this would be based on a design developed at CN-MAT for their 120-channel loudspeaker array [10]).

4   Spatial Sound System

Since the Allosphere is to foster the development of integrated software for scientific data sonification and auditory display, as well as artistic applications, it is essential that the software and hardware used for audio synthesis, processing, control, and spatial projection be as flexible and scalable as possible. We require that the audio software libraries support all popular synthesis and processing techniques, that they be easily combined with off-the-shelf audio software written using third-party platforms such as Csound, Max/MSP, and SuperCollider, and that they support flexible control via (at least) the MIDI and Open Sound Control (OSC) protocols. Due to the sophistication of the audio synthesis and processing techniques used in Allosphere applications, and the expected very large number of final output channels, we require that the core audio libraries support easy inter-host streaming of large numbers of channels of high-resolution (24- bit, 96 kHz) audio, probably using both the CSL/RFS and SDIF networked audio protocols.

This section discusses the design of the spatial audio software library developed for the Allosphere. The CREATE Signal Library (CSL) [20] is intended to function as the core library, handling all audio needs of the Allosphere. We have developed a flexible software framework based on the CSL, in which different techniques, sets of psychoacoustical cues, and speaker layouts can be combined and swapped at run time (see Castellanos thesis [7]).

The first step towards this goal was to design a spatial audio library that integrated seamlessly with CSL. To this end, the spatial audio software developed for the Allosphere consists of the implementation of a library written in C++ as part of CSL. By designing this framework, we provided an immediate solution for spatial sound reproduction in the Allosphere, but also, most importantly, opened the path towards the development of a universal spatial-sound reproduction system. The system aims to be intuitive and easy to operate by those that need a ready-to-use surround sound system, but at the same time sufficiently complex and flexible for the initiated user who may desire to fine-tune the system and or add new configurations and techniques. Such system would ideally include, in one package, all major currently existing spatialization techniques. The next paragraphs give an overview of the framework that was designed to that effect.

4.1 Spatial Audio Framework

The design of the spatial audio framework was driven by the goal of using the Allosphere as a multipurpose environment, equally suitable for scientists and artists for a variety of applications. This goal required flexibility in the systems configuration and interfaces manipulation. Its most current version [7] was designed using the "Metamodel for Multimedia Processing Systems" (also known as 4mps) proposed by Xavier Amatriain [1]. This metamodel provides a solid ground for a flexible, dynamic and extensible library.

The flexibility vs. simplicity trade-off was solved by using a layered interface, where each layer provides different levels of flexibility, with the trade-off of complexity. Essentially, the system provides different interface layers, where higher-hierarchy layers conceal the complexity of lower (and more flexible layers), while providing more default / standardized options. Thus, a higher degree of complexity and flexibility is available on to those who need it.

The simplest interface conceals from the user all spatialization mechanisms, not offering the option of choosing any distance cues or the spatialization technique for sound reproduction. The user is responsible only with determining the desired location of the sound source in a 3D coordinate space, and providing the audio material. The framework will handle everything else, including the encoding/decoding technique and the loudspeaker configuration. At the other end, by using the lowest layer, the user can determine the distance cues, filters and spatialization algorithm. It is also possible to perform changes dynamically at run-time.

The most complex configuration of the framework is created around the concept of a Spatializer. A spatializer constitutes a processor capable of manipulating a stream of audio with its output appearing to originate at a particular location in a virtual/simulated space. A spatializer is composed of various processing units, such as distance filters, panners and a layout of the loudspeaker setup. Ideally, the Spatializer would simplify the spatial audio reproduction by loading the most appropriate "panner" (vbap, ambisonic, etc.) based on the audio setup description (loudspeaker layout). This technique would eventually appear to the user as a single spatialization engine that performs satisfactorily under any circumstances. When more flexibility is needed, the various components of a spatializer can be used individually creating custom or more complex audio graphs.

The current design does not place any restrictions on the number of loudspeakers to be used and their placement. The limit to the number of loudspeakers to be used in a particular configuration is primarily imposed by the computing resources available.

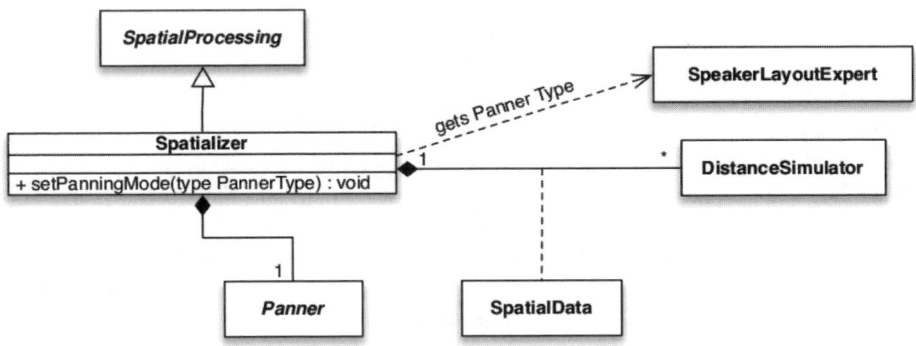

Fig. 8. Spatializer Class Diagram

The loudspeaker layout has to be specified as needed for audio spatialization processing. The framework is designed to load the loudspeaker layout from a text file containing the position of each individual component (loudspeaker). For the more user-friendly configurations, there are several default loudspeaker layouts that can be chosen without the need of manually entering the coordinates of the loudspeakers For instance, a Stereo setup will automatically add two loudspeakers -30 and 30 degrees.

5   Spatial Audio Techniques

There are three main techniques for spatial sound reproduction used in current state-of-the-art systems: (1) vector-base amplitude panning [21], (2) ambisonic representations and processing [17], and (3) wave field synthesis (see [23] and [5]). Each of these techniques provides a different set of advantages and presents unique challenges when scaling up to a large number of speakers and of virtual sources.

In the following paragraphs we outline how we have approached the challenges and opportunities of each of these techniques in the context of the Allosphere project.

5.1   Vector-Base Amplitude Panning

With the Vector base Amplitude Panning technique, a sound can be located in a virtual space by manipulating the balance of the audio signal sent to each speaker. It is assumed that the speakers are equidistant from the listener, and that panning only allows moving the source position along the arc between speakers (i.e., source distance must be simulated independently). The first step is to determine which three speakers define the smallest triangle that includes p (the desired position), and what the contribution of energy from each of these will be to simulate a source at position p. Given a desired source position, one can apply an arbitrary weighting function to derive the factors for the output channels given the position of the vector for the loudspeaker triplet L (see equation 1).

$$gains = p^T L_{mnk}^{-1} = [\,p_1\ p_2\ p_3\,] \begin{bmatrix} l_{k1} & l_{k2} & l_{k3} \\ l_{m1} & l_{m2} & l_{m3} \\ l_{n1} & l_{n2} & l_{n3} \end{bmatrix}^{-1} \tag{1}$$

Practical VBAP systems allow interactive performance with multiple moving sound sources, which are mapped and played back over medium-scale projection systems. VBAP has been mainly promulgated by groups in Finland and France and is used effectively in 8-32-channel CAVE virtual environments.

The drawbacks of VBAP are that it does not directly answer the question of how to handle distance cues (relatively easy to solve for distant sources and low Doppler shift), and that it provides no spatialization model for simulating sound sources inside the sphere of loudspeakers. This is a grave problem for our applications, but also a worthy topic for our research. The question boils down to how to spread a source over more than 3 speakers without limiting the source position to the edges of the surface described by the chosen set of speakers.

The VBAP algorithm involves a search among the geometrical representations of the speakers defining the playback configuration, and then some simple matrix math to calculate the relative gains of each of the three chosen speakers. There are several open-source implementations of VBAP that support multiple sources (with some interactive control over their positions), and flexible speaker configurations involving up to 32 channels.

Members of our research group implemented a system in which the user can move and direct a number of independent sound sources using a data glove input device, and play back sound files or streaming sound sources through VBAP, using a variable number of loudspeakers specified in a dynamic configuration file (see McCoy thesis [18]). VBAP can be integrated with a spatial reverberator, allowing early reflections from a reverberator to be individually panned, though this gets computationally expensive with many sources, complex room simulations, or rapid source (or listener) motion.

Because VBAP is so simple, most implementations are monolithic, 1-piece packages. This is obviously unacceptable for our purposes, so we needed to consider both (1) how the VBAP system scales to large numbers of sources, rapid source motion, and many output channels, and (2) how such a scaled-up application can best be distributed to a peer-to-peer server topology streaming data over a high-speed LAN. The scalability of VBAP encoding software is excellent, since the block-by-block processing is very simple, and the computation of new output weights for new or moving sources can be accelerated using well-understood geometrical search techniques. For the case of many sources or rapid source or listener motion, VBAP scales linearly, because each source is encoded into 3 channels, meaning that many mappers each write 3 channels into a many-channel output buffer. Alternatively, if the servers are distributed, each mapper sends 3 channels over the LAN to its output server. If the output servers are themselves distributed (each taking over a subset of the sphere's surface), then most encoding servers will stream to a single output server.

Computational distribution of a VBAP-based spatial reverberator is more difficult, since by definition the individual reflections are not localized to a small number of channels; indeed, if you calculate a reasonable number of reflections (e.g., 64 or more) for a complex room model, you can assume that the reflections will approximate an even distribution among all channels, leading us back to a monolithic output server topology. We look forward to attacking this scalability and partitioning issue in the full system. For the time being, we run the reverberator on a single server.

The assumptions of the speaker elements and system configuration for playing VBAP are that elements be identical full-range speakers, and that they be placed in triangles of more-or-less equal size in all directions. The speaker density can be made a function of height, however, leading to somewhat poorer spatialization accuracy above (and possibly below) the listener. All that being said, since VBAP makes so few assumptions about the constructed wave, it supports non-uniform speaker distributions quite well. Directional weighting functions to compensate for an uneven distribution of speakers can be built into the VBAP amplitude matrix calculations, and the fidelity of spatial impression is a directional function of both the speaker density and regularity of spacing. In our earliest designs for the sphere, we ran a set of programs to tessellate spherical surfaces, leading to the 80-channel configuration shown in Figure 7. Note the two regular rings above and below the equator; one can rotate the upper hemisphere by 1/2 the side length to form a zigzag pattern here (which handles VBAP better) Continuing this process, we can design and evaluate further regular subdivisions of a sphere.

5.2   Ambisonics

Ambisonics [11] is a technique to re-create the impression of (or synthesize) a spatial sound-field via a two-part process of encoding recorded or virtual spatial sources into an Ambisonic domain representation, and then decoding this representation onto an array of spatially located loudspeakers. The Ambisonic domain is a multi-channel representation of spatial sound fields based upon cylindrical (2-D spatialization) or spherical (3-D spatialization) harmonics. First-order Ambisonics, also known as the B-Format, encode sound-fields as an omni-directional signal (named W) plus three additional difference signals for each of the axes X, Y and Z. Higher Order Ambisonics (HOA) increases the detail of directional information and expanding the acceptable listening area of the decoded spatial sound field by using higher ordered cylindrical/spherical harmonic orders, and thus increasing the number of encoded signals [17]. The number of Ambisonic domain channels depends only on the order and dimensionality of the representation chosen, and is somewhat independent of the number of sources and of the number of loudspeakers (it is required that the speakers outnumber the domain channels).

To implement an Ambisonic encoder, one generates an encoding matrix based upon the virtual source orientation (azimuth, elevation) relative to the center-spot and uses this matrix to mix a scaled copy of the input signal into each of the Ambisonic domain channels. An Ambisonic encoder does not need any information about the speaker layout. The encoding matrix must be recalculated whenever the center to source orientation changes. A decoder pre-calculates a decoding matrix of weights per Ambisonic domain channel for each of the loudspeakers in the array, again using cylindrical or spherical coordinates and harmonics. The decoder uses these weights to mix each received Ambisonic domain channel to each speaker, and thus is essentially a static NxM matrix mixer.

One of the main benefits of the Ambisonic representation is that it scales very well for large numbers of moving sources. Since the encoding and decoding operations are linear and time-invariant, as many sources as needed can be encoded into the same Ambisonic domain channels, and encoder matrix recalculation can occur at less than sample-rate resolution (and be interpolated).

Ambisonic encoders and decoders can also therefore be decoupled from one another. For a simple scaled-up system, multiple 3rd-order encoders would run on machines in our server farm, each of them streaming a 16-channel signal to the output driver(s). These signal buses can be summed and then distributed to one or more output decoders. The decoding scales well to large numbers of speakers because decoders are independent of one another, each receiving the same set of inputs. CPU limits can therefore be circumvented by adding more encoding and/or decoding nodes. The scalability to higher orders is well understood, and scales with the number of channels required by the representation, bounded by LAN bandwidth.

Ambisonic decoders work best with a regular and symmetrical loudspeaker configuration. There is no way in the standard algorithms to compensate for irregular speaker placement, though this is an area for future research, along with spatial radiation patterns and near-field encoding. What is interesting is the fact that very large speaker arrays can especially benefit from higher-order ambisonic processing, using ever-higher orders of spherical harmonics to encode the sound field, and then decoding it using these factors to play out over a (regular and symmetrical) many-channel speaker array with a very large acceptable listening area.

As with VBAP, graduate researchers from our group (see [13])) have implemented higher- (up to 11th-) order ambisonic processing and decoding in C++ using the CSL framework. The encoder and decoder are separate classes, and utility classes exist for processing (e.g., rotating the axes of) Ambisonic-encoded sound. We also implemented the algorithm for Max/MSP [27], and there are also open-source implementations in both SuperCollider and PD.

Using Ambisonics for Navigable Immersive Environments. Adapting Ambisonics for navigable virtual environments presents a number of challenges. Ambisonics models spatial orientation well [17], but does not inherently model distance. We have extended our implementation to incorporate multiple distance cues for point sources using standard techniques (amplitude attenuation, medium absorption/near-field filtering, Doppler shift and global reverberation mix [8]). Additionally, we implemented a rudimentary radiation pattern simulation by filtering spatial sources according to the orientation of the source relative to the listener. A more realistic approach to radiation pattern simulation can be found in [16]. This system was used in the AlloBrain project described in section 6.

Though an Ambisonic sound-field in its entirety can be efficiently rotated around three axes using equations based upon spherical harmonics [17], this efficient feature is unfortunately inapplicable to navigable virtual worlds, since any navigation movement changes the spatial orientations on a per-source basis rather than as a group.

Sound source direction in Ambisonics is expressed in terms not immediately appropriate to virtual environments. C++ code was written to efficiently translate absolute positions and quaternion orientations of sound sources and the mobile viewpoint into the appropriate Euler angles of azimuth and elevation for Ambisonic encoding, and the relative distance and angle needed for distance/radiation simulation.

5.3   Wave Field Synthesis

Wave field synthesis (WFS) is an acoustic spatialization technique for creating virtual environments. Taking advantage of the Huygens' principle, wave fronts are simulated with a large array of speakers. Inside a defined listening space, the WFS speaker array reproduces incoming wave fronts emanating from an audio source at a virtual location. Current WFS implementations require off line computation which limits the real-time capabilities for spatialization. Further, no allowances for speaker configurations extending into the third dimension are given in traditional wave field synthesis.

A wave field synthesis system suitable for real-time applications and capable of placing sources at the time of rendering is presented. The rendering process is broken into logical components for a fast and extensible spatializer. Additionally, the WFS renderer conforms to the spatial audio framework designed by Jorge Castellanos [7] and thus fits well in CSL. A broad range of users and setup configurations are considered in the design. The result is a model-based wave field synthesis engine for real-time immersion applications.

WFS Theory and Supporting Work. Wave field synthesis is derived from the Kichroff-Helmholtz integral,

$$P(w,z) = \iint_{dA} G(w,z|z')\frac{\partial}{\partial n}P(w,z') - P(w,z')\frac{\partial}{\partial n}G(w,z|z')dz' \qquad (2)$$

which states that the pressure $P(w,z)$ inside an arbitrary volume and due to an incoming wave can be determined if the pressure at the surface of the volume $P(w,z')$ and wave transmission properties $G(w,z|z')$ (free field Green's function) are known. Applying this, the wave field synthesis principle states if the volume surface is lined with speakers, exact acoustic scene reproduction is possible for listeners inside the volume. It should be noted from the integral the volume shape is not defined and the speaker configuration can be irregular. However, there is a disconnect between the outlining theory and practical WFS system.

Berkhout [5] describes three of the assumptions needed for a WFS driving signal at each speaker source. First, the two terms inside the integral of the Kirchoff-Helmholtz integral represent both monopole and dipole sound reproduction sources along the volume surface. Dipoles are an unrealistic expectation in a numerous channel environment. Fortunately, dipole sources can be omitted at the expense of an incorrect sound field outside the speaker-enclosed volume. Given the reproduction room in anechoic, this is a reasonable assumption. In place of the dipoles, a windowing function is applied to the speaker signal allowing sound only when a virtual source is behind the speaker.

Next, the Kirchoff-Helmholtz integral requires a continuous sound reproduction surface which must be discretized for practical speakers. Discretization to monopole point sources results in a 3dB per octave boost to the original signal. The WFS driving signal corrects for this effect with a high-pass filter. Additionally, the spatial sampling of speakers creates spatial aliasing. Unlike the more familiar temporal aliasing, spatial aliasing does not produce as pronounced artifacts, but instead confuses spatialization above the aliasing frequency. The aliasing frequency is proportional to the distance between sources in linear arrays. Aliasing for circular speaker arrays are described by Rabenstein et al. in [24].

Finally, Due to hardware and computational limitations, most WFS designs range contain less than 200 speakers, not enough to surround a listening space. Instead, the dimensionality is reduced from three to two. Ideally, a speaker array is in the plane of the listener's ear.

Based on assumptions and limitations listed above, a driving signal is derived from the Kirchoff-Helmholtz integral by Rabenstein [22]. The driving signal defines the filter computed per each virtual source at each speaker in the array.

$$D_\theta(w,x|x') = 2w(x',\theta)A(|x-x'|)K(w)e^{j\frac{w}{c}|x',n_\theta|}F(x,\theta) \tag{3}$$

$w(x',\theta)$ is a window function as a result of eliminated dipole speakers and the normal dot product of the incoming wave. $A(|x-x'|)$ is the amplitude attenuation due to distance and the reduction to 2 dimensions. $K(w)$ is a square root of the wave number spectral shaping also due to the dimension reduction. $e^{j\frac{w}{c}|x',n_\theta|}$ applies the appropriate delay to the incoming wave. Finally, $F(x,\theta)$ is the signal emitted from the source.

Model-based wave field synthesis simulates acoustic sources by modeling the properties of its incoming wave to the WFS speaker array. Any arbitrary acoustic shape or radiation pattern is viable for wave field synthesis. However, due to computational complexity, point and plane wave sources are used as audio emitters. Baalman [3] has demonstrated how an arbitrarily shaped WFS system can work.

Interactive Environments. Additional requirements are placed on a wave filed synthesis renderer for use in an interactive environment. Most importantly, rendering must happen at as close to real time as possible. Psyco-accoustical experiments from Wenzel [29], find that audio latency of 250ms presents a perceivable lag when paired with visual or user feedback. Existing WFS implementations such as WONDER [2] or CARROUSO [26] offer real-time processing, but restrict virtual sources to pre-computed positions, panning between points to simulate source movement. Using this method, not only is WFS rendering incorrect between points, but the perceptual cue of Doppler effect inherent in WFS is omitted.

A different method is presented in which WFS filters are calculated in real time per each sample with a small computational overhead. For each buffer, audio is processed by a filter calculated from the sources current position. Stationary virtual source cost no additional cycles and are treated in the traditional way from [22]. For moving sources, an arbitrary source position determines the new filter for the current audio buffer and corresponding source metadata. The source's relative speed is then used to find the Doppler rate corresponding to the buffer's sample rate due to its speed. The result is a sample accurate WFS rendering with buffer rate position updates.

Outer and Focused Point Sources. Another necessity for effective immersion is continuity of the audio scene. WFS allows for virtual sources outside the speaker array and inside (often called 'focused sources'). Rendering virtual sources inside the speaker array is non-causal and different filters must be used. Special consideration is given to the transition from outside to inside filters in order to prevent dead spots or discontinuous audio. The windowing function $w(x',\theta)$, which determines if the source is in front or behind the speaker, is reversed for focused sources. For this reason, knowing a speaker's and source's positions alone is not sufficient to determine the source's location in the speaker array and which filter should be applied. To overcome this confusion, an expert container class is implemented which models the speaker array shape and informs the rendering chain the correct filter for the virtual source. A third state for virtual sources is near field. When a source is placed at a speaker, the 3db per octave approximation from discretized speakers no longer applies. To accommodate the near-field effect, The spectral filtered audio is mixed with unfiltered audio proportional to is distance to the speaker at small distances.

Separation of Processing. For large scale systems, the WFS rendering process may need to be distributed to keep up with real-time computational requirements. Separating the WFS rendering chain into smaller components allows the distribution of work to multiple machines. Calculation of the auditory scene using the driving signal can be split into two groups, source and speaker calculations. Separation of these processes removes the need for an m (virtual sources) times n (speakers) number of applied filters as suggested in [22]. Additionally, splitting the rendering in this way allows the entire process to be distributed in a way that suits the particular WFS system. If a large number of virtual sources are given, all source-related DSP could take place on multiple machines. Likewise, for a large speaker array, multiple machines could each be synced to handle their own smaller number of speakers.

Finally, an WFS interface is designed to accommodate a range of audio applications and operating systems. The interface must not only allow for the connection of block-rate source audio, but also asynchronous control messages describing the virtual audio source.

CSL and Spatial Audio Interface. The WFS rendering engine is integrated as a spatial audio technique in the spatial audio framework outlined above. Virtual audio sources and positions serve as input to a scene rendered for a certain number of speaker outputs. However, wave field synthesis, while similar, requires additional information compared to VBAP, Ambisonics and other spatial audio techniques.

Due to the physical model of WFS, virtual sources can be easily represented as point or plane sources, a concept unique to WFS. This source attribute would normally accompany its position data. Secondly, a wave field scene rendering requires not only each speaker's position but its normal vector. As a result, the WFS module extends the spatial audio framework to allow for source shapes and extra speaker data. When other spatialization modules, such as VBAP or ambisonic, are used inside CSL, the additional components brought on by WFS are ignored allowing integration between all spatial audio techniques.

6   Testbed Applications

In parallel to the development of the core libraries described above, several tests, prototypes and demonstrations of the Allosphere capabilities have been performed. This section describes the approaches adopted for some of these prototypes.

In the first iteration over the prototype we have set up an environment consisting of the following elements:

* 4 active stereo projectors (Christie Digital Mirage S+2K), 3000 ANSI lumens, DLP

  2 rendering workstations (HP 9400), AMD Opteron 64@2.8Ghz, NVidia Quadro FX-5500
* 1 application manager + Audio Renderer (Mac Pro), Intel Xeon Quad Core @3Ghz
* 2 10-channel firewire audio cards.
* 16 full-range speakers + 2 subwoofers
* Several custom-developed wireless interfaces.

The research projects described below make use of this prototype system to test the functionality and prove the validity of the instrument design.

In the first project, we are developing an immersive and interactive software simulation of nano-scaled devices and structures, with atom-level visualization of those structures implemented on the projection dome of the Allosphere (see Figure 9). When completed, this will allow the user to stand in the middle of a simulation of a nano-scaled device and interact with the atoms and physical variables of that device.

Fig. 9. Rendering of a 1M atom silicon nanostructure in real-time on a single CPU/GPU (Allosphere rendering occurs in stereo projection)

Our science partners are implementing algorithms for nano-material simulations involving molecular dynamics and density functional theory using GPUs, transforming a single PC workstation into a 4 Teraflop supercomputer. This allows us to run nanoscale simulations that are 2-3 orders of magnitude faster than current implementations. We will also be able to use this extra computational power to solve for the physical properties of much larger structures and devices than were previously possible, allowing nano-system engineers to design and simulate devices composed of millions of atoms. Sound design will play an important role in such simulations and visualizations. The sound system will be used to bring important temporal phenomena to user's attention and to pinpoint it precisely with 3D sound. For instance, to alleviate the difficulty of finding specific molecules in the vast visual space of the Allosphere, subtle auditory clues can alert the user to the emergence or presence of a specific molecular event in a particular direction (which is especially relevant when the object is behind the user's back!).

In another project, we focus on molecular dynamics. We are extending the VMD [14] package through the use of Chromium in order to have seamless visualization of complex protein molecules and their interactions, immersively supported with direct manipulation and spatial sonification by the Allosphere.

6.1   AlloBrain

The last ongoing research project, called AlloBrain, explores brain imaging data as an immersive environment, following a desire to meld data from the sciences with the artistic pursuits of new media art. Our goal is not to interpret the data in a scientific way, but rather to indicate and provoke inspiration regarding immersive three-dimensional media offers in terms of new insights and interaction with data sets from other disciplines. Digital artist and transvergent architect Marcos Novak undertook the fMRI brain scanning and even before the Allosphere building was completed. The AlloBrain project became our driving prototype and experimentation platform.

While the brain data provides an intricate architecture for navigation (see figures 6.1 and 6.1), it does not by itself create a compelling interactive experience. Dynamic elements are added to the world through mobile, agents that indicate their presence spatially, visually, and sonically 11. Their distinct behaviors within the system provide a narrative for the installation based around exploration for features in data-space, and clustering activities around features of interest. The immersant can navigate the space and call specific agents to report the status of their findings using two wireless (Bluetooth) input devices that feature custom electronics, integrating several MEMs sensor technologies.

Several synthesis techniques were used to inform the immersant about the agents' current actions in the environment. Short noise bursts were used as spatial cues since wideband signals provide more precise elevation cues. In addition, we created a bed of ambient sound serving to draw the immersant into the environment. We found that in this sonic atmosphere immersants felt more inclined to spend longer stretches of time within the world.

Rather than building a software solution specific to the AlloBrain project, graduate students at MAT designed a generalized system, the Cosm toolkit, to support the rapid development of many different kinds of projects within the Allosphere and similar spaces, incorporating audio spatialization, stereographic distributed rendering within a real-time fully navigable scene graph. The toolkit is currently implemented as a C/C++ library, and has been embedded within the Max/MSP/Jitter environment [30] to support real-time project design and testing. To make the best use of the Allosphere's current audio capabilities, the Cosm toolkit currently employs third-order 3D Ambisonics and distance-coding software developed at MAT (described earlier in this document), coupled with 3D motion and navigation algorithms for virtual environments.

398   X. Amatriain et al.

Fig. 10. Screen capture of the AlloBrain interactive recreation of the human brain from fMRI data. External frontal view in which even facial expressions are visible.

Fig. 11. Screen capture of the AlloBrain offering a side view with only some active layers. Users are able to navigate through the different layers of tissues and analyze the data in a collaborative immersive environment.

7 Conclusions

Once fully equipped and operational, the Allosphere will be one of the largest immersive instruments in existence. But aside from its size, it also offers a number of features that make it unique in many respects. In particular, it features immersive spherical projection, multimodal processing including stereoscopic vision, 3D audio, and interaction control, and multi-user support for up to 30 people. In this paper, we have focused on the audio infrastructure in the Allosphere, discussing the requirements, approaches, and initial results.

We envision the Allosphere as a vital instrument in the future advancement of fields such as nanotechnology or bio-imaging and it will stress the importance of multimedia in the support of science, engineering, and the arts. We have demonstrated first results in the form of projects of highly diverse requirements. These initial results feed back into the prototyping process but also clearly support the validity of our approach.

Although the Allosphere is clearly still in its infancy, we believe that the presented results are already meaningful and important, and will inform other integrative endeavors in the computer music research communities. The development of our prototype test-bed applications is geared towards an open generic software infrastructure capable of handling multi-disciplinary multi-modal applications.

References

1. Amatriain, X.: A domain-specific metamodel for multimedia processing systems. IEEE Transactions on Multimedia 9(6), 1284–1298 (2007)
2. Baalman, M.A.J.: Updates of the WONDER software interface for using Wave Field Synthesis. In: Proc. of the 3rd International Linux Audio Conference, Karlsruhe, Germany (2005)
3. Baalman, M.A.J.: Reproduction of arbitrarily shaped sound sources with wave field synthesis - physical and perceptual effects. In: Proc. of the 122nd AES Conference, Vienna, Austria (2007)
4. Ballas, J.: Delivery of information through sound. In: Kramer, G. (ed.) Auditory Display: Sonification, Audification and Auditory Interfaces, vol. XVIII, pp. 79–94. Addison Wesley, Reading (1994)
5. Berkhout, A.J.: A holographic approach to acoustic control. Journal of the Audio Engineering Society 36, 977–995 (1988)
6. Blauert, J.: Spatial Hearing. MIT Press, Cambridge (2001)
7. Castellanos, J.: Design of a framework for adaptive spatial audio rendering. Master's thesis, University of California, Santa Barbara (2006)
8. Chowning, J.: The simulation of moving sound sources. Journal of the Audio Engineering Society 19(11) (1971)
9. Cruz-Neira, C., Sandin, D.J., DeFanti, T.A., Kenyon, R.A., Hart, J.C.: The CAVE: Audio visual experience automatic virtual environment. Communications of the ACM (35), 64–72 (1992)
10. Freed, A.: Design of a 120-channel loudspeaker array. Technical report, CNMAT, University of California Berkeley (2005)
11. Gerzon, M.A.: Periphony: With-height sound reproduction. Journal of the Audio Engineering Society 21(1), 2–10 (1973)

12. Höllerer, T., Kuchera-Morin, J., Amatriain, X.: The allosphere: a large-scale immersive surround-view instrument. In: EDT 2007: Proceedings of the 2007 workshop on Emerging displays technologies, p. 3. ACM Press, New York (2007)
13. Hollerweger, F.: Periphonic sound spatialization in multi-user virtual environments. Master's thesis, Austrian Institute of Electronic Music and Acoustics (IEM) (2006)
14. Humphrey, W., Dalke, A., Schulten, K.: Vmd - visual molecular dynamics. Journal of Molecular Graphics (14), 33–38 (1996)
15. Ihren, J., Frisch, K.J.: The fully immersive CAVE. In: Proc. 3 rd International Immersive Projection Technology Workshop, pp. 59–63 (1999)
16. Malham, D.G.: Spherical harmonic coding of sound objects - the ambisonic 'o' format. In: Proceedings of the AES 19th International Conference, pp. 54–57 (2001)
17. Malham, D.G., Myatt, A.: 3-d sound spatialization using ambisonic techniques. Computer Music Journal (CMJ) 19(4), 58–70 (1995)
18. McCoy, D.: Ventriloquist: A performance interface for real-time gesture-controlled music spatialization. Master's thesis, University of California Santa Barbara (2005)
19. McGurk, H., McDonald, T.: Hearing lips and seeing voices. Nature (264), 746–748 (1976)
20. Pope, S.T., Ramakrishnan, C.: The Create Signal Library ("Sizzle"): Design, Issues and Applications. In: Proceedings of the 2003 International Computer Music Conference (ICMC 2003) (2003)
21. Pulkki, V., Hirvonen, T.: Localization of virtual sources in multi-channel audio reproduction. IEEE Transactions on Speech and Audio Processing 13(1), 105–119 (2005)
22. Rabenstein, R., Spors, S., Steffen, P.: Wave Field Synthesis Techniques for Spatial Sound Reproduction. In: Selected methods of Acoustic Echo and Noise Control, Springer, Heidelberg (2005)
23. Spors, S., Teutsch, H., Rabenstein, R.: High-quality acoustic rendering with wave field synthesis. In: Proc. Vision, Modeling, and Visualization Workshop, pp. 101–108 (2002)
24. Spors, R., Rabenstein, S.: Spatial aliasing artifacts produced by linear and circular loudspeaker arrays used for wave field synthesis. In: Proc. of The AES 120th Convention (2006)
25. Teutsch, H., Spors, S., Herbordt, W., Kellermann, W., Rabenstein, R.: An integrated real-time system for immersive audio applications. In: Proc. 2003 IEEE Workshop on Applications of Signal Processing to Audio and Acoustics, New Paltz, NY (2003)
26. Theile, G.: Wave field synthesis - a promising spatial audio rendering concept. In: Proc. of the 7th Int. Conference on Digial Audio Effects (DAFx 2004) (2004)
27. Wakefield, G.: Third-order ambisonic extensions for max/msp with musical applications. In: Proceedings of the 2006 ICMC (2006)
28. Wegman, E.J., Symanzik, J.: Immersive projection technology for visual data mining. Journal of Computational and Graphical Statistics (March 2002)
29. Wenzel, E.M.: Effect of increasing system latency on localization of virtual sounds. In: Proc. of the AES 16th International Conference: Spatial Sound Reproduction (1999)
30. Zicarelli, D.: How I Learned to Love a Program that Does Nothing. Computer Music Journal 26(4), 44–51 (2002)

A Network-Based Framework for Collaborative Development and Performance of Digital Musical Instruments

Joseph Malloch, Stephen Sinclair, and Marcelo M. Wanderley

Input Devices and Music Interaction Laboratory
Centre for Interdisciplinary Research in Music Media and Technology
McGill University – Montreal, QC, Canada
`joseph.malloch@mcgill.ca`, `sinclair@music.mcgill.ca`,
`marcelo.wanderley@mcgill.ca`

Abstract. This paper describes the design and implementation of a framework designed to aid collaborative development of a digital musical instrument mapping layer[1]. The goal was to create a system that allows mapping between controller and sound parameters without requiring a high level of technical knowledge, and which needs minimal manual intervention for tasks such as configuring the network and assigning identifiers to devices. Ease of implementation was also considered, to encourage future developers of devices to adopt a compatible protocol.

System development included the design of a decentralized network for the management of peer-to-peer data connections using OpenSound Control. Example implementations were constructed using several different programming languages and environments. A graphical user interface for dynamically creating, modifying, and destroying mappings between control data streams and synthesis parameters is also presented.

Keywords: Mapping, Digital Musical Instrument, DMI, OpenSound Control, Network.

1 Introduction

Although designers of Digital Musical Instruments (DMI) are interested in creating useful, flexible, and inspiring interfaces and sounds, this process often depends on the vision and insight of a single individual. The McGill Digital Orchestra project instead brings together research-creators and researchers in performance, composition and music technology to work collaboratively in creating tools for live performance with digital technology [1]. A large part of this research focuses on developing new musical interfaces.[2]

---

[1] This paper is a revised and substantially expanded version of a preliminary report on this project presented at ICMC 2007[16].

[2] The McGill Digital Orchestra is a research/creation project supported by the *Appui à la recherche-création* program of the *Fonds de recherche sur la société et la culture* (FQRSC) of the Quebec government, and will culminate with concert performances of new works during the 2008 MusiMars/MusiMarch Festival in Montréal.

R. Kronland-Martinet, S. Ystad, and K. Jensen (Eds.): CMMR 2007, LNCS 4969, pp. 401–425, 2008.
© Springer-Verlag Berlin Heidelberg 2008

In the process of creating instruments for this project, we have found ourselves faced with the unique challenge of mapping new instruments in collaboration with experienced performers, as well as with composers tasked with writing pieces for these instruments. Because this ambitious project has taken on these three main challenges of the digital performance medium simultaneously, we have found ourselves in need of tools to help optimize the process. Specifically, mapping the various streams of controller output to the input parameters of synthesis engines has presented us with situations where both ease of use and flexibility were both of the utmost importance. We needed to be able to modify connections between data streams during precious engineer-composer-performer meeting time, while minimizing wasted minutes "reprogramming" our signal processing routines. Although arguably both powerful and intuitive, even graphical environments like Cycling 74's Max/MSP did not seem appropriate for these purposes, because non-programmers who had limited familiarity with such tools were expected to help in experimentation and design.

In consideration of several ongoing projects, including GDIF [13], Jamoma [18], Integra [2], and OpenSound Control (OSC) [24], we have created a "plug and play" network-based protocol for designing and using digital musical instruments. Controllers and synthesizers are able to announce their presence and make their input and output parameters available for arbitrary connections. Any controller is able to connect to any synthesizer "on the fly," while performing data scaling, clipping, and other operations.

In the course of developing an adequate working environment for this project, we have made developments in three main areas: the design of a network architecture which lends itself to a distributed "orchestral neighbourhood", in which controllers and synthesizers can interface with each other over a UDP/IP bus by means of an OSC-controlled arbitrator; the creation of a "toolbox" containing many useful functions which we found ourselves using repeatedly, coded as Max/MSP abstractions; and lastly a graphical mapping tool with which gestural data streams can be dynamically connected and modified.

We have tried to create a GUI that is intuitive and transparent: relationships between parameters are visible at a glance, and changing mappings and scaling requires only a few mouse clicks. We have used all of these tools in a real collaborative context, allowing us to present not only implementations, but also observations of their effect on our group dynamic and workflow. We have tried to create an interface that is useful not only for technical users, but also as a creative tool for composers and performers.

The remainder of this paper is organized as follows: section 2 provides background information and explains the motivations behind our approach to mapping for this project. Section 3 describes the design and implementation of the networked mapping system. Section 4 gives some details of how users might experience the mapping system through the provided graphical interface, and also provides information for developers on how to make compatible software. Section 5 briefly outlines some of the functions and tools we have created to help speed such development, available as a software package entitled the *Digital*

Orchestra Toolbox. Finally, sections 6 and 7 provide discussion, insights, and plans for future development.

2   Gesture Mapping

The digital instrument builder is faced with several tasks: after considering what sensors should be used, how the musician will likely interface with them, and what sounds the instrument will make, there is still the decision of which sensors should control which aspects of the sound. This task, known as *mapping*, is an integral part of the process of creating a new musical instrument [10].

2.1   Mapping Methods

Several past projects have developed tools for mapping between sound and control. However, "mapping" is a term with a wide scope, and these projects do not necessarily agree on methods or terminology. One way to categorize mapping methods is by whether the connections are known explicitly, or are the result of some process which builds implicit relationships [8].

An example of the latter is [14], in which it is seen that neural networks can be used to adapt mapping to a performer's gestures rather than the inverse. In contrast, toolboxes such as LoM [22] or MnM [6] are in the former category. They are intended to aid in developing strategies for using low-dimensional control spaces to control higher-dimensional timbral spaces through the use of several interpolation techniques. [21] also created a tool box of mapping functions for PureData (Pd) [19]. This work is similar to the set of Max/MSP abstractions that we present in Section 5, and, as we'll see in the next section, can be a useful resource for performing signal conditioning in the context of our system.

In the current work, we focus on easing the design of mapping by representing the individual connections between parameters in a very direct and explicit way, rather than worrying about signal conditioning or transformation strategies. Additionally, we feel that the choice of algorithm, or even programming language, used to communicate with physical devices and perform signal processing should have limited impact on inter-device interaction if they are connected on the same network. Thus, while tools such as LoM and MnM are useful for Max/MSP programmers, or the Pd mapping toolbox can be a useful resource for PureData programmers, we decided that approaching the problem of interoperation from a networking and protocol point of view would yield greater long-term results, and provide useful functionality for development of mapping techniques in a collaborative environment, while not necessarily precluding the use of other mapping approaches within its framework.

2.2   The Semantic Layer

An important result of previous discussions on mapping has been the acknowledgement of the need for a multi-layered topology. Specifically, Hunt and Wanderley [9] suggested the need for 3 layers of mapping, in which the first and last

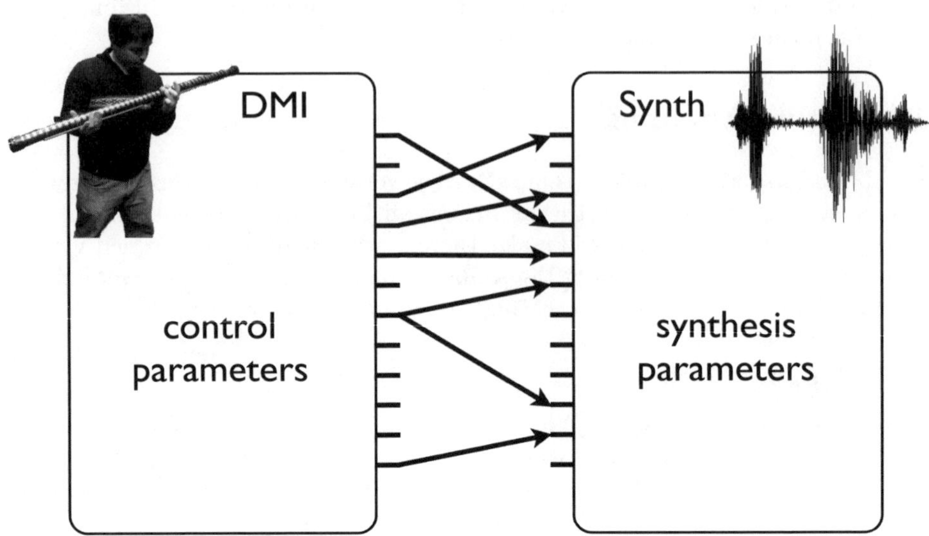

Fig. 1. An example single-layer mapping. One-to-many and many-to-one mappings are defined explicitly.

layers are device-specific mappings between technical control parameters and gestures (in the case of the first) or aesthetically meaningful "sound parameters", such as *brightness* or *position* (in the case of the third). This leaves the middle layer for mapping between parameter names that carry proper gesture and sound semantics. We shall refer to this layer as the "semantic layer", as described in Figure 2.

The tools presented here adhere to this idea. However, since the first and last mapping layers are device-specific, the mapping between technical and semantic parameters (layers 1 and 3) are considered to be part of the controller and synthesizer interfaces. Using an appropriate OSC addressing namespace, controllers present all available parameters (gestural and technical) to the mapping tool. The tool is used to create and modify the semantic layer, with the option of using technical parameters if needed.

As a simple example, the T-Stick interface [15] presents the controller's accelerometer data for mapping, but also offers an event-based "jabbing" gesture which is extracted from the accelerometers. The former is an example of layer 1 data which can be mapped directly to a synthesizer parameter. The latter is a gestural parameter presented by layer 2, which can be mapped, for example, to a sound envelope trigger. The mapping between layers 1 and 2 for the "jabbing" gesture, (what we call *gesture extraction*), occurs in the T-Stick's interface patch (see Figure 3).

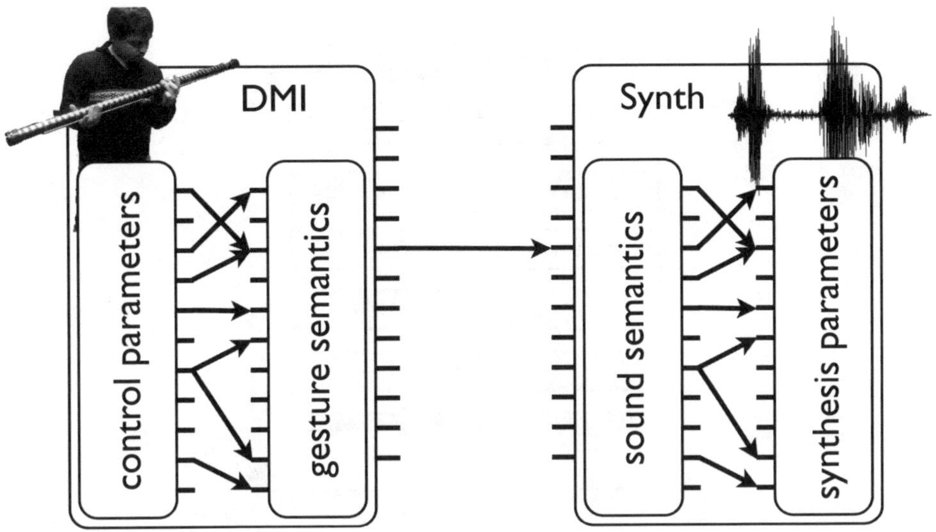

Fig. 2. A diagram of the 3-layer framework used for Digital Orchestra development, adapted from [9]. Note that the simple "one-to-one" connection shown in the center semantic mapping layer may in fact describe a much more complex relationship between technical parameters.

We have also used this system in another project[3] for mapping gesture control to sound spatialization parameters [17]. In this case a technical mapping layer exposes abstract spatialization parameters (such as sound source trajectories) to the semantic layer, rather than synthesis parameters.

2.3   Connection Processing

Gestural data and sound parameters will necessarily carry different units of measurement. On the gestural side, we have tried, whenever possible, to use units related to physical measurements: distance in meters, angles in degrees. In sound synthesis, units can sometimes be more arbitrary, but some standard ones such as Hertz and MIDI note number are obvious. In any case, data ranges will differ significantly between controller outputs and synthesis inputs. The mapping tool attempts to handle this by providing several features for scaling and clipping data streams.

One useful data processing tool that is available is a filter system for performing integration and differentiation. We have often found during sessions that a particular gesture might be more interesting if we could map its energy or its rate of change instead of the value directly [7]. Currently the data processing is

---

[3] Compositional Applications of Auditory Scene Synthesis in Concert Spaces via Gestural Control is a project supported by the NSERC/Canada Council for the Arts New Media Initiative.

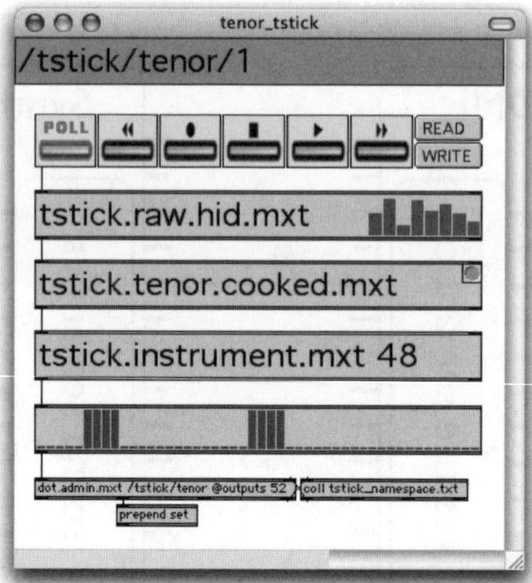

Fig. 3. A screenshot of the Max/MSP patch used for the T-Stick DMI, showing two layers of control data abstraction. The "cooked" sub-patch contains smoothing routines for sensor data, while the "instrument" sub-patch computes instrument-related gesture information such as "jabbing".

limited to first-order FIR and IIR filtering operations, and anything more complex must be added as needed to the "gesture" mapping layer and included in the mappable namespace.

2.4 Divergent and Convergent Mapping

It has been found in previous research that for expert interaction, complex mappings are more satisfying than simple mappings. In other words, connecting a single sensor or gestural parameter to a single sound parameter will result in a less interesting feel for the performer [10, 20].

Of course, since our goal is to use abstracted gesture-level parameters in mapping as much as possible, simple mappings in the semantic layer are in fact already complex and multi-dimensional [11]. Still, we found it would be useful to be able to create one-to-many mappings, and so the mapping tool we present here supports this. Each connection may have different scaling or clipping applied.

We also considered the use of allowing the tool to create many-to-one mappings. The implication is that there must be some *combining* function which is able to arbitrate between the various inputs. Should they be summed, or perhaps multiplied, or should some sort of comparison be made between each of the inputs?

A combining function implies some relationship between gestural parameters; in some cases, the combination of gestural data may itself imply the extraction of a distinct gesture, and should be calculated on the first mapping layer and presented to the mapping tool as a single parameter. In other cases the

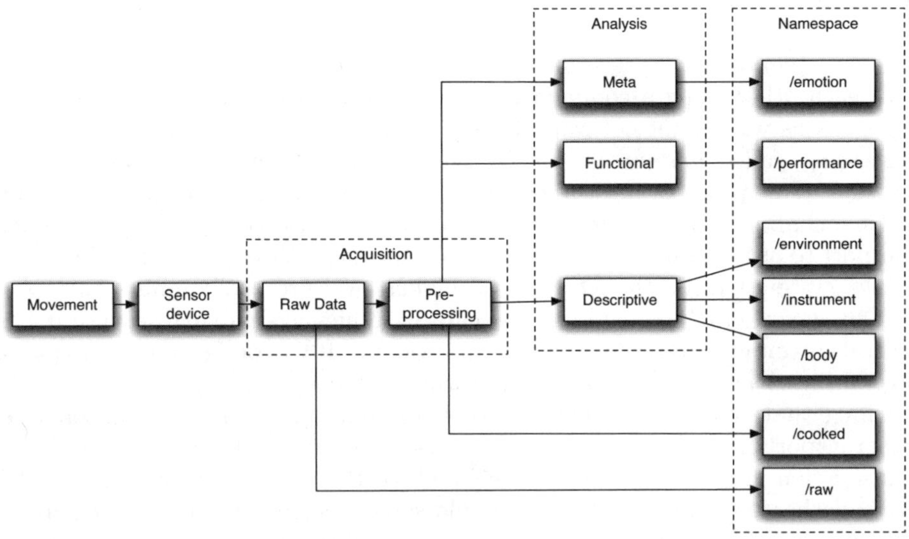

Fig. 4. A diagram from [12] showing the namespace hierarchy proposed for GDIF and used for the mapping system

combination may imply a complex relationship between synthesis parameters that could be better coded as part of the abstracted synthesis layer. In yet other cases the picture is ambiguous, but the prospect of needing to create on-the-fly many-to-one mappings during a working session seems to be unlikely. We did not implement any methods for selecting combining functions, and for the moment we have left many-to-one mappings for future work.

2.5   Portability of Mapping Sets

An important goal of the GDIF project is to pursue portability of mapping sets between similar devices. Control devices and DMIs using OSC namespaces structured using the hierarchy proposed for GDIF (Figure 4) will likely share subsets of their namespaces, especially at the higher levels, which are focused on interaction or environment rather than specific interfaces. Likewise, synthesizers receiving mapped parameters also often have named parameters in common, provided they have been constructed according to GDIF guidelines. The motivations for and structure of this hierarchy is described in detail in [12].

We designed the loading functionality of our system to permit portability of mapping sets between different classes of device, as described in Section 4.4. An important result of this pursuit is that different controllers and synthesizers may be swapped without the bulk of the mapping being redefined. This provides another motivation for encouraging users of a mapping system to make use of high-level abstracted parameters whenever possible.

3   The Orchestral Network Neighbourhood

In our system, there are several entities on the network that must communicate with each other using a common language. These include controllers and synthesizers, as well as the software devices used for address translation and data processing, called *routers*, and finally the GUI used to create and destroy connections. This protocol must allow them to perform some basic administration tasks, including: announcing their presence on the network; deciding what name and port to use; and finally describing what messages they can send and receive.

The system can be thought of as a higher-level protocol running on top of an OSC layer. OSC was chosen to encapsulate message passing because it has several advantages in the domain of audio systems. It was designed to take care of several drawbacks typically associated with MIDI: it is transport-independent, meaning that it defines a sequence of bytes but makes the assumption that the transport layer will take care of accurately carrying these bytes over some transmission medium. This lends itself well to IP networks, but is equally valid over another transport, such as a simple serial transmission line for example. OSC can specify data in several formats such as floating point values, strings, or integers, instead of being restricted to a specific range as in MIDI. Data type is specified in the message header. It is clear that OSC can be a flexible and useful messaging system, but its main advantage for us is that it is already supported by a large number of audio software packages, (although some support it better than others.) This means that while we were able to efficiently design the system described here using Max/MSP, the protocol we describe can be supported by several other audio-oriented programming languages. This topic will be covered more completely in Section 4.7.

In any case, while OSC can be a powerful tool, it suffers the disadvantage in comparison to MIDI in that it dictates nothing about what lower-level transport protocols and ports to use, nor what kinds of messages should be exchanged. We needed to devise a common set of OSC messages to allow the use of a standard interface to control all devices in question. The approach we have taken—that of translating arbitrary messages from a controller into inputs for a synthesizer— was chosen because we did not wish to impose a particular restriction on the device namespaces themselves: we do not assume to be able to enumerate a set of control messages as was done for General MIDI (GM). GM was designed primarily for keyboard controllers, and this is apparent in its semantics, which has been found limiting when exploring the use of alternative controllers for electronic sound. Instead, we propose a set of messages for *discovering* and *describing* controller outputs and synthesizers inputs, as well as messages for describing the connections and signal conditioning that might occur between them.

3.1   Topology and Protocol

Because OSC addressing is designed to uniquely identify any particular value, it is possible to broadcast messages on a common bus and have them be correctly targeted to the intended recipient. This makes it mostly trivial to switch between

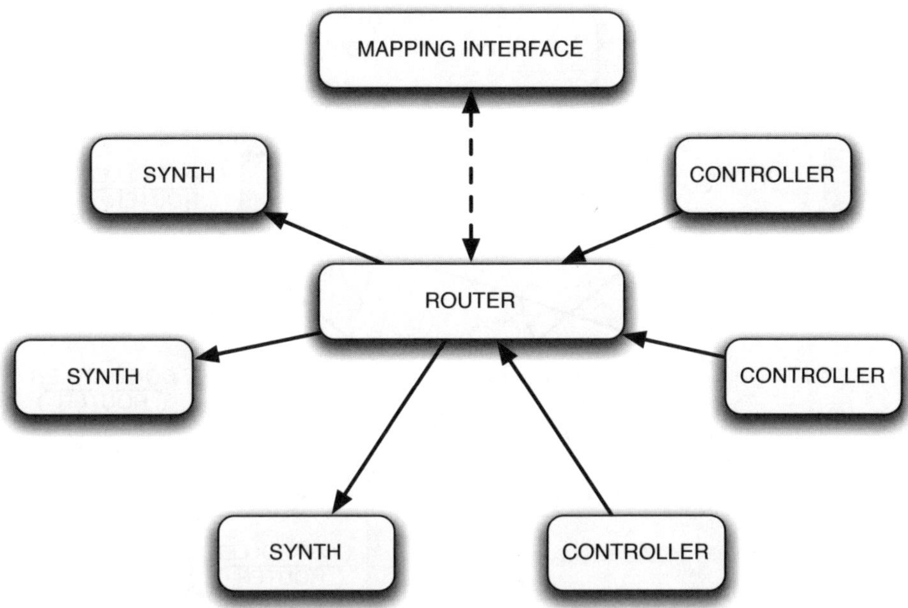

Fig. 5. A centralized topology in which all traffic is routed through a central router service

various network topologies. While a common bus is necessary for locating devices, it is not necessary nor is it optimal to have gestural data streams sharing the same bus.

We have decided to use a multicast UDP/IP port for administrative tasks such as device announcement and resource allocation. This common port is needed to resolve conflicting device identifiers and to allow new devices to negotiate for a unique private port on which to receive messages. We shall refer to it as the "admin bus".

For routing mapped data streams, several topologies can be used. Though it simplifies programming, sharing a bus for high-traffic gestural streams wastes communication as well as processing resources. Messages must be received and addresses must be parsed before being rejected. If several devices are present on the network, a high percentage of traffic may be rejected, making a common bus inefficient. In our system, each device reserves a UDP/IP port for receiving data streams. Thus the OSC traffic is quickly routed and filtered on the transport layer and address parsing is only necessary for properly targeted messages.

Another factor affecting the network topology is the role of the router in mapping. In a previous revision of our system, controllers sent their data streams to a router which performed address mapping and scaling before re-transmitting the transformed messages to a synthesizer. This implies a centralized topology as seen in Figure 5. However, with the protocols described in this section, it is perfectly feasible to have multiple router instances on the network. This can help

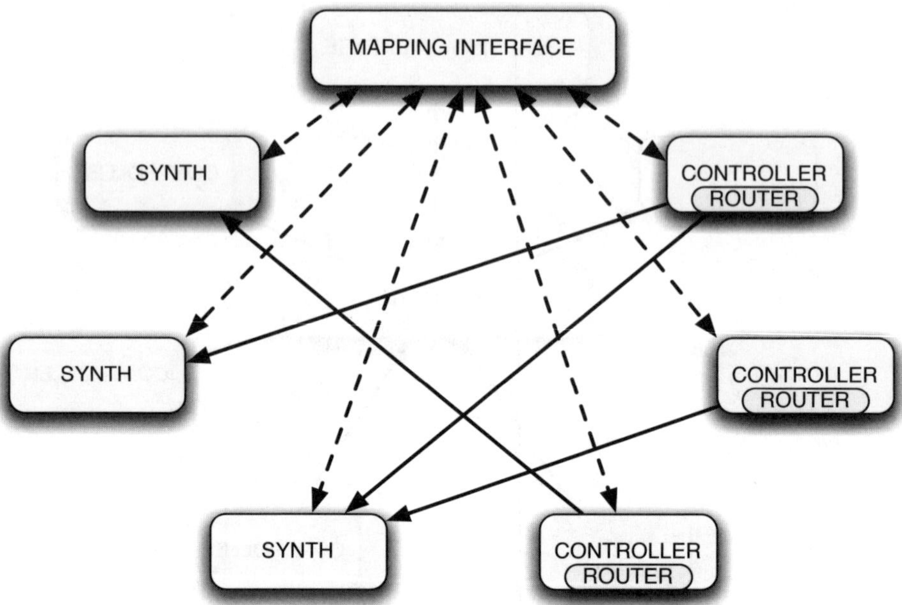

Fig. 6. Equivalently, a router can be embedded in each controller to create a true peer-to-peer network

reduce traffic loads and distribute processing. Extending this idea to the extreme, we embedded the routers inside each controller, in order to create a truly peer-to-peer topology, as described by Figure 6. The signal conditioning and message transformation then takes place on the controller itself, and messages are sent through the network already formatted for the target synthesizer. However, for clarity we consider the embedded router devices to be distinct entities on the network.

3.2   Name and Port Allocation

When an entity first appears on the network, it must choose a port to be used for listening to incoming data streams. It must also give itself a unique name by which it can be addressed. A simple solution would be to assign each device a static name and port. However, we are not interested in maintaining a public database of "claimed" ports, and, (being a digital "orchestra"), we expect multiple instances of a particular device to be available for use.

In an attempt to be more dynamic and decentralized, we have developed a collision handling algorithm for port and name allocation: when a new entity announces itself, it posts to the admin bus a message stating which port it tentatively intends to use. If this port is reserved or is also being asked for by another device, a random number is added and the device tries again. If multiple devices are attempting to reserve the same numbers, several iterations may occur, but

Input: p_t (tentative port number)
Output: p_f (final port number)
$T = 0$;
$c = -1$;
announce(p_t);
while $T < 2000$ **do**
    update time T;
    update collision count c;
    if $T > 500$ *and* $c > 0$ **then**
        $p_t = p_t + \mathrm{random}(0..c)$;
        $T = 0$;
        $c = -1$;
        announce(p_t);
    end
end
$p_f = p_t$;
...
repeat
    if *collision* **then** announce(p_f);
until *forever* ;

Fig. 7. Port allocation scheme, also used for device identifier ordinals

eventually each device ends with a unique port number to use. (Strictly speaking, this is only necessary for devices hosted on the same computer, though we currently run the collision algorithm on the shared admin bus over the network.) The same algorithm is used for determining a device name composed of the device class and a unique ordinal. This unique name is prepended to all messages from that device. Some pseudo-code of this algorithm can be found in Figure 7.

3.3   Discovery

Device discovery is an important step toward a truly "plug and play" environment. Previously, a method has been proposed for device discovery making use of the ZeroConf protocol, which is a decentralized network configuration and announcement protocol available in all major operating systems. A Max/MSP implementation of the idea, called *OSCBonjour*, has been created by Rémy Müller, which we have explored[4]. While the idea is promising, it currently only handles device discovery, leaving us still to deal with port and name allocation for the devices. We decided that, since we are already using a common multicast UDP bus for the allocation scheme, it would be sufficient and more consistent to use it also for device discovery. A pure OSC solution is adequate for our purposes, but this does not preclude the possibility of using *OSCBonjour* in the future, perhaps in parallel with our current scheme.

When a device appears on the network, and after it successfully receives a unique name and port number, it queries the network for other compatible devices by submitting a simple request on the multicast admin bus:

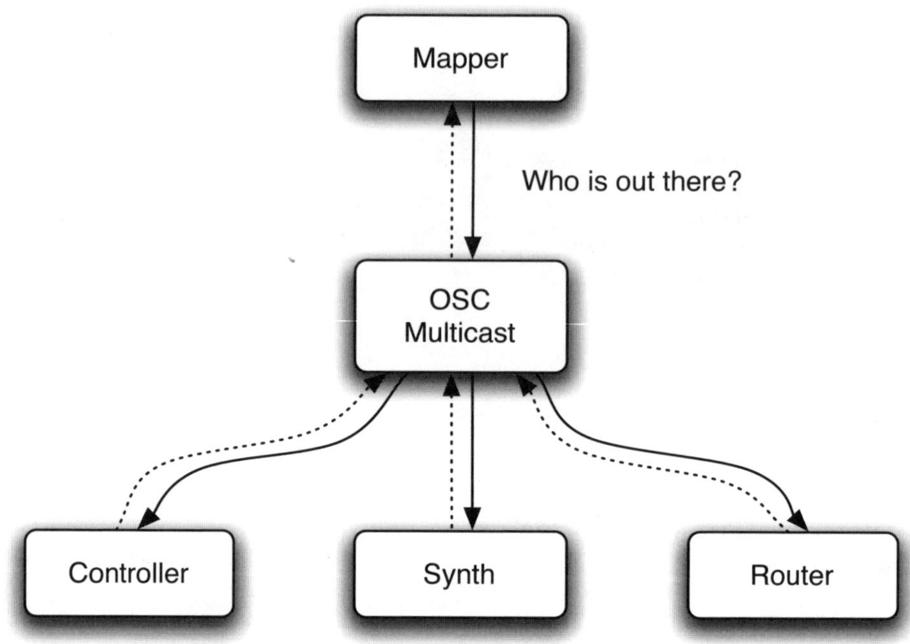

Fig. 8. The mapper GUI requests that devices on the network identify themselves

```
/device/who
```

All compatible devices, including the device just launched, respond to this message with a simple message stating their unique name, device class, I/O, IP address and port:

```
/device/registered /tstick/1 @inputs 1 @outputs 52 @class /tstick
    @IP 192.168.0.3 @port 8001
/device/registered /granul8/1 @inputs 80 @outputs 0 @class
    /granul8 @IP 192.168.0.4 @port 8000
```

3.4   Making Connections

Each device records the names, IP addresses and UDP ports of the other instances on the network. Mapping interfaces (Section 4) also listen on the admin bus and display the available devices as sources (controllers), destinations (synths), or both. In this way, a user can refer to a device by name rather than being required to know the address and port of a particular device. To create a direct network connection between two devices, a message must be sent on the admin bus specifying the devices to connect:

```
/link /tstick/1 /granul8/1
```

The source device dynamically creates a router data structure for each linked destination device. It then responds on the admin bus to acknowledge that it has successfully initialized the connection:

```
/linked /tstick/1 /granul8/1
```

Similarly, devices can be disconnected,

```
/unlink /tstick/1 /granul8/1
```

resulting in the destruction of the corresponding router in the source device, and a response on the admin bus:

```
/unlinked /tstick/1 /granul8/1
```

Once two devices have been connected with the /link message, individual OSC datastreams can be connected to their desired destination:

```
/connect /tstick/1/raw/pressure/1 /granul8/1/gain
/connect /tstick/1/raw/pressure/1 /granul8/1/gain @scaling
    expression @expression x*10 @clipping minimum 0
```

The appropriate router instance records the mapping connection, and sets up address translation, scaling, and clipping. Once complete, the response is sent on the admin bus:

```
/connected /tstick/1/raw/pressure/1 /granul8/1/gain
/properties /tstick/1/raw/pressure/1 /granul8/1/gain @scaling
    expression
/properties /tstick/1/raw/pressure/1 /granul8/1/gain @expression
    x*10
/properties /tstick/1/raw/pressure/1 /granul8/1/gain @clipping
    minimum 0
```

Note the optional connection properties (scaling, clipping) which can be specified as part of the /connect message. If no properties are given, the connection will be created using the defined default properties. (At this time, no scaling or clipping is performed by default.) It is notable that scaling may not be appropriate for certain types of OSC message arguments, such as character strings, and applied to these messages it will cause undefined behaviour. In the case of gain-related destination parameters, use of the "@clipping both" property at connection creation might be advisable to avoid damage to ears and audio equipment. However, this is not done automatically.

Also notable is the two-stage process described for connecting parameters: the first to define a network connection, and the second to define the connection between parameter addresses. Although it is useful to separate device-level and address-level connections, the "admin" Max/MSP abstraction described in Section 5 automatically creates necessary device-level links if a simple "/connect" message is sent.

Similar to the "/unlink" message at the device-connection level, individual addresses can also be disconnected:

```
/disconnect /tstick/1/raw/pressure/1 /granul8/1/gain
/disconnected /tstick/1/raw/pressure/1 /granul8/1/gain
```

To query the properties of a connection,

```
/connection/properties/get /tstick/1/raw/pressure/1
  /granul8/1/gain
```

To modify the properties,

```
/connection/modify /tstick/1/raw/pressure/1 /granul8/1/gain
  <desired properties, @scaling...>
```

Both the "/connection/properties/get" and the "/connection/modify" messages elicit a response specifying the current mapping properties:

```
/connection/properties /tstick/1/raw/pressure/1 /granul8/1/gain
  <@scaling...>
```

3.5 Namespace Queries

Lastly, each orchestra member must be able to tell others what it can do. In other words, it must be able to say what messages it can receive and what messages it can send. Wright et al. [24] proposed the use of the /namespace message for causing a device to enumerate its available namespace. We have implemented this for each transmitter and receiver on the network. In addition to listing the namespace itself, each available parameter optionally can include information about data type, data range and units used. These come into play when the mapper is to set up automatic scaling between data streams, as described below.

In order to make this metadata optional, we have used a tagged argument scheme, similar to the syntax used in Jitter for object "attributes." In the example below, the mapper interface communicates with a controller named "/tstick/1" and a granular synthesizer named "/granul8/1". (These ordinals were previously established by the allocation scheme, so as not to be confused with other devices of the same type.) The exchange is described in the sequence diagram seen in Figure 9.

4   The Mapping Interface

A graphical interface has been developed to aid in mapping tasks. It forms a separate program from the other devices, but transmits and receives OSC messages on the same multicast admin bus. In addition to allowing the negotiation of mapping connections from another location on the network, this approach has allowed us to simultaneously use multiple mapping interfaces on the network, with multiple users collaborating to map the parameters of a common set of controllers and synths. The mapping interface has several main functions.

4.1   Browsing the Network Neighbourhood

The first use of the mapping interface is naturally choosing the devices that you wish to work with, both for gesture and for sound synthesis or processing. The interface queries devices on the network, to discover mappable inputs and outputs, and displays this information in an easily understandable format. New devices appearing on the network are automatically added to the display as seen in figure 12.

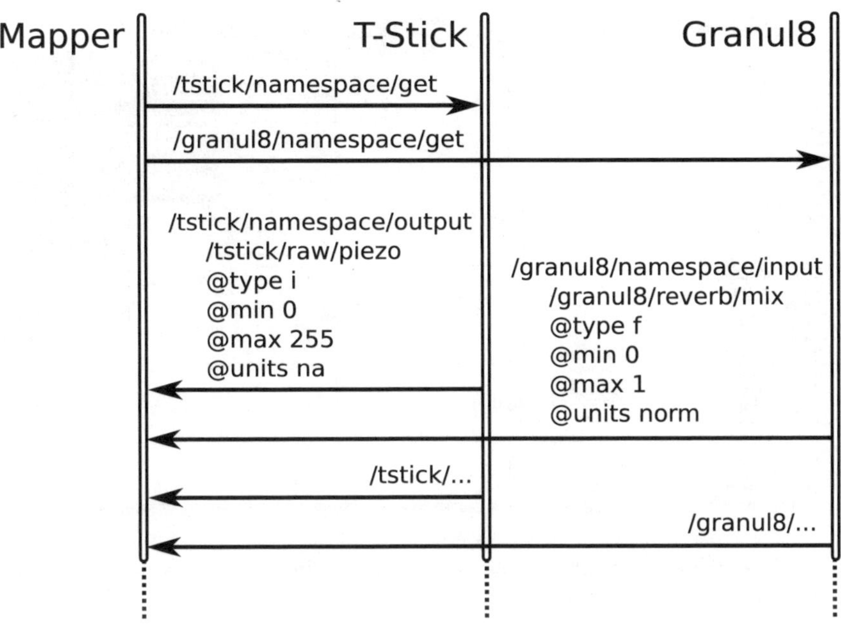

Fig. 9. On receipt of a namespace request, devices return a message for each input or output parameter they support, with information about data range and units

4.2   Browsing and Searching Namespaces

When devices are selected in the mapping interface, a message is sent on the admin bus requesting them to report their full OSC address-space. The interface displays the parameters by OSC address, which is especially informative to the user when strong semantics are used in the namespace. In addition, some other information about each parameter is requested, including whether it is an *input* or an *output*, the data type (i, f, s, etc.), the unit type associated with the parameter (Hz, cm, etc.), and the minimum and maximum possible values. OSC address patterns for controller outputs are displayed on the left side of the mapping interface, and synthesizer inputs are displayed on the right.

In order to manage the browsing and mapping of very large or deep namespaces, the mapping interface also allows for filtering and searching using pattern-matching. Two stages of namespace filtering are available, which may be used together. One stage allows filtering by OSC address-pattern prefix, chosen from an automatically-populated drop-down menu, so that the user may view the set of parameters which are children of a particular node in the address hierarchy. The other stage allows filtering by regular expression, so that only parameters matching a particular pattern are displayed.

On occasions where the namespace can change, such as for entities that have a configurable interface, addition or removal of addresses is announced on the

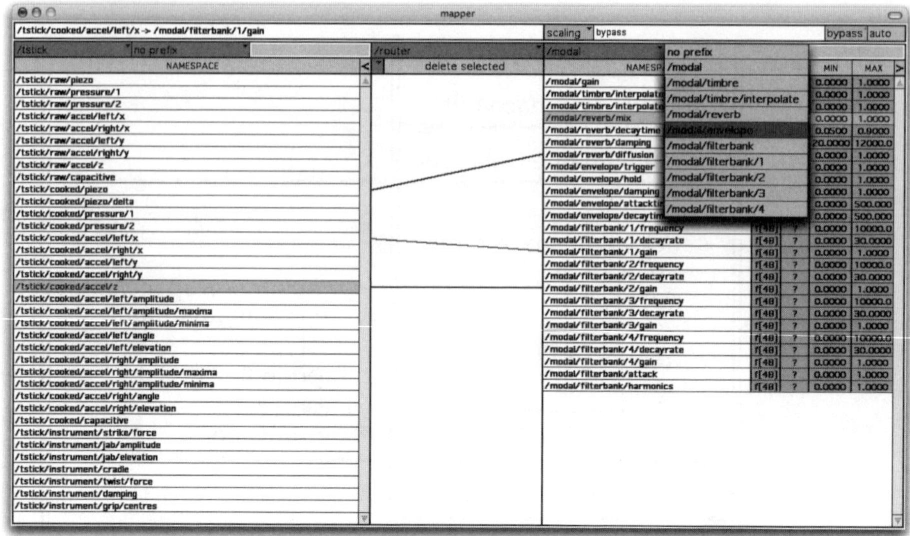

Fig. 10. The mapping graphical user interface can be used to explore the available namespace, make connections, and specify scaling and other data processing

multicast bus so that routers can destroy any connections appropriately, and mappers can add or remove entries.

4.3   Negotiating Mapping Connections and Properties

The mapping interface is essentially memoryless, merely reflecting the state of devices and connections present on the network. Simple methods are provided for creating and destroying mapping connections, and for editing the properties of existing connections (i.e.: scaling, clipping). Connections are created by selecting displayed namespaces on each side of the interface (inputs and outputs), and lines are drawn connecting mapped parameters. Mapping connections can be selected (in which case they are highlighted) for editing or deletion. By selecting multiple namespaces or connections, many mappings can be created, edited, or destroyed together.

When a connection is made, by default the router does not perform any operation on the data ("bypass"). A button is provided to instruct the appropriate router to perform basic linear scaling between the provided data ranges. Another button instructs the router to commence calibration of the scaling using the detected minima and maxima of the input data stream. The user can also manually type "linear" in an expression textbox with arguments defining a specific input and output ranges. Options are also available for defining a clipping range.

The expression box is quite versatile. For more advanced users, it accepts any string which can be understood by Max/MSP's "expr" object, and evaluates the mapped data according to the entered expression. Additionally, expressions can refer to the current value, or a single previous input or output sample. This

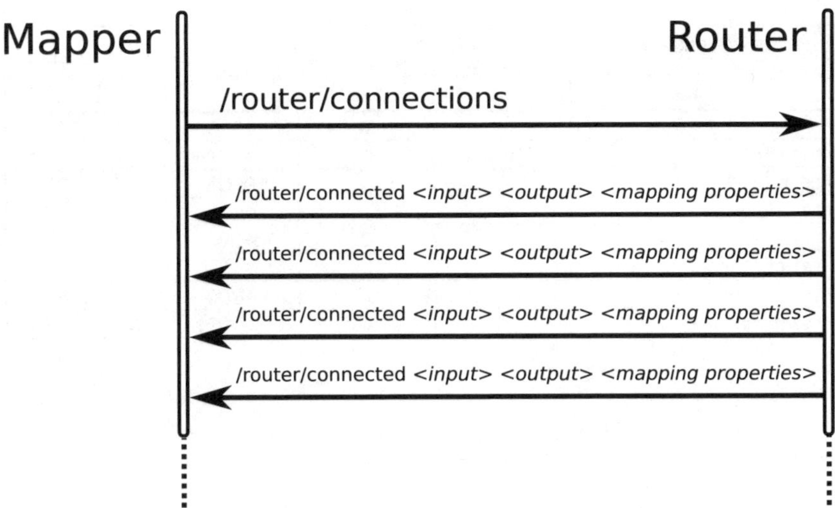

Fig. 11. A router device can report its current set of connections. The mapper GUI requests it when the router is first selected.

control may be used to specify single-order filters, or non-linear, logarithmic mappings, for example. There is currently no support for table-based transfer functions.

4.4   Saving and Loading Mapping Sets

The mapping interface also provides buttons for saving defined mapping sets locally as a text file. This file stores the properties of each connection between the viewed devices, along with the unique names of the devices involved. This information is formatted according to Max/MSP's `coll` object storage, although we have considered that it may be more useful in some XML-based standard as a language-agnostic data format to be easily imported into other implementations. We intend to define such a format in collaboration with the GDIF project at some point in the future.

When using the mapping interface to load a stored mapping file, devices must first be chosen between which the connections will be made, since it is possible that instance numbers and thus unique device names will differ between sessions. The loading function strips each defined connection of its original device identifier and replaces it with the name of the currently selected device. An advantage of loading mapping sets in this way is the possibility of loading the mapping with a different device class, as discussed in Section 2.5. Connections involving parts of the namespace shared by the original and replacement devices will be created normally, otherwise they will simply be discarded.

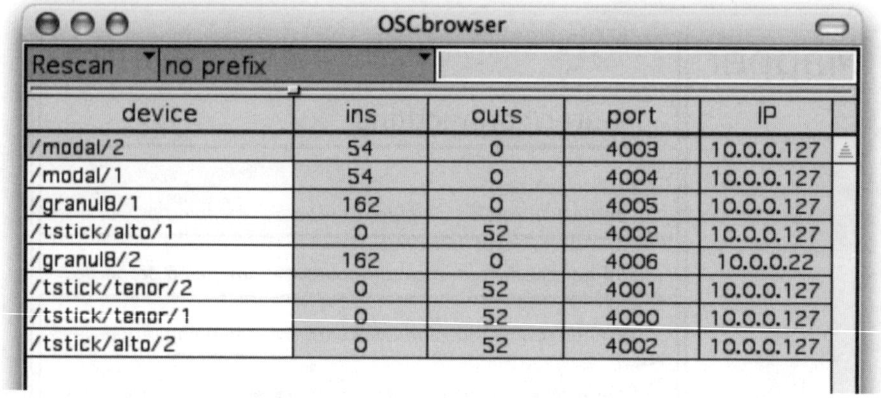

device	ins	outs	port	IP
/modal/2	54	0	4003	10.0.0.127
/modal/1	54	0	4004	10.0.0.127
/granul8/1	162	0	4005	10.0.0.127
/tstick/alto/1	0	52	4002	10.0.0.127
/granul8/2	162	0	4006	10.0.0.22
/tstick/tenor/2	0	52	4001	10.0.0.127
/tstick/tenor/1	0	52	4000	10.0.0.127
/tstick/alto/2	0	52	4002	10.0.0.127

Fig. 12. The device browser used in the mapping GUI can also be launched as a stand-alone application. It displays all compatible devices along with their inputs, outputs, ports and IP addresses.

4.5   Message Examples

Using the mapping interface, the user selects the controller namespace `/tstick/instrument/damping`, and the synth namespace `/granul8/1/grain/1/filter/frequency`:

Mapper `/connect <controller parameter> <synth parameter>`
Example `/connect /tstick/1/instrument/damping`
  `/granul8/1/grain/1/filter/frequency`

The T-Stick receives the message and creates mapping with default parameters:

Device `/connected <controller parameter> <synth parameter>`
  `<properties>`
Example `/connected /tstick/1/instrument/damping`
  `/granul8/1/grain/1/filter/frequency @scaling bypass @clipping`
  `none`

The user begins calibration:

Mapper `/connection/modify <controller parameter> <synth`
  `parameter> <properties>`
Example `/connection/modify /tstick/1/instrument/damping`
  `/granul8/1/grain/1/filter/frequency @scaling calibrate 20 1000`
T-Stick `/connection/properties <controller parameter> <synth`
  `parameter> <properties>`
Example `/connection/properties /tstick/1/instrument/damping`
  `/granul8/1/grain/1/filter/frequency @scaling calibrate 20 1000`

Example `/connection/properties /tstick/1/instrument/damping`
`/granul8/1/grain/1/filter/frequency @scaling calibrate 20 1000`
`@expression (x-32)*0.00345+100`

The user ends calibration:

Mapper `/connection/modify <controller parameter> <synth`
`parameter> @scaling expression`
Example `/connection/modify /tstick/1/instrument/damping`
`/granul8/1/grain/1/filter/frequency @scaling expression`

The user deletes the mapping:

Mapper `/disconnect <controller parameter> <synth parameter>`
Example `/disconnect /tstick/1/instrument/damping`
`/granul8/1/grain/1/filter/frequency`
T-Stick `/disconnected <controller parameter> <synth parameter>`
Example `/disconnected /tstick/1/instrument/damping`
`/granul8/1/grain/1/filter/frequency`

4.6 Adapting Existing Max/MSP Patches for Compatibility

The Max/MSP implementation of the tools presented here has been carefully designed for easily adapting existing device patches (both controllers and synthesizers) for compatibility with the system. If the pre-existing patch already uses OSC for input and/or output, there is in fact very little left to do: the messages simply need to be connected to a copy of the `dot.admin` abstraction described in section 5. The last step is simply to create a text file containing a list of OSC parameters the patch can send and/or receive, and load it into a `coll` object connected to `dot.admin`. More detailed documentation accompanies the distribution when downloaded, but essentially after this the adaptation is functional. Optionally, the properties can be defined for each parameter, specifying its data type, associated unit, and range; these properties, while not required, make scaling and calibration easier when in use.

We recommend that anyone adapting an existing patch—or creating a new patch—for use in this context use strong semantics in their choice of parameter names and avoid obscure abbreviations. This allows users to immediately understand the functions of each parameter without referring to external documentation. While we also advocate the use of hierarchical parameter naming as proposed for GDIF, this is not required;the system itself does not depend on a particular approach.

4.7 Other Implementations

While the main body of work for this project has been developed using Max/MSP, our choice of using OpenSound Control, a well-defined communication protocol

420   J. Malloch, S. Sinclair, and M.M. Wanderley

```c
#include <mapper.h>

mapper_admin_init();
my_admin = mapper_admin_new("tester", MAPPER_DEVICE_SYNTH, 8000);
mapper_admin_input_add(my_admin, "/test/input","i"))
mapper_admin_input_add(my_admin, "/test/another_input","f"))

// Loop until port and identifier ordinal are allocated.
while (    !my_admin->port.locked
        || !my_admin->ordinal.locked )
{
  usleep(10000); // wait 10 ms
  mapper_admin_poll(my_admin);
}

for (;;)
{
  usleep(10000);
  mapper_admin_poll(my_admin);
}
```

Fig. 13. Framework for a synth-side C program using libmapper. This is the minimal code needed for a synth-side device to announce itself and communicate with other devices on the network.

with growing support, has allowed us to ensure that the system remains independent of specific software and hardware (provided it has IP networking capabilities). To demonstrate this point, and to encourage the use of our protocol, we are developing patches and libraries in several languages that make it easy to create compliant software interfaces. For instance, we have shown that a synthesizer written in PureData can be made to communicate with the system by adding a similar `dot.admin` object to a patch and filling in namespace details. Similarly, we have created a library in C that will enable a wide variety of C and C++ programs to easily support this platform. This has been tested using several synthesizers developed with the help of the Synthesis Toolkit in C++[5] and the LibLo OSC library[3]. An example of the use of this library is given in Figure 13.

5   The Digital Orchestra Toolbox

In the process of creating controller, synthesizer, and mapping patches, we have made an effort to modularize any commonly used subroutines. These have been organized, with help patches, into a toolbox that we find ourselves re-using quite often. Like the rest of the software presented in this paper, this toolbox is freely available on the Input Devices and Music Interaction Laboratory website [4]. It currently contains over 40 abstractions, some of which we will briefly describe.

---

[4] http://www.idmil.org

5.1   OSC and Mapping Helpers

dot.admin Handles communication on the admin bus. It is used by the synthesizer and controller patches to allow them to communicate with the mapping system. It uses instances of `dot.alloc` to negotiate for a unique port and identifier, and it responds to namespace requests. When required to do so, dot.admin dynamically creates instances of `dot.router` corresponding to each peer-to-peer device link on the network.

dot.alloc The abstracted algorithm used by `dot.admin` for allocating a unique port and device name. On its own, it may be useful for negotiating any unique resource on a shared bus.

dot.prependaddr Prepends the given symbol onto the first symbol of a list, without affecting the remaining list members. This is intended for constructing OSC addresses.

dot.autoexpr Given a destination maximum and minimum, `dot.autoexpr` will automatically adjust the linear scaling coefficients for a stream of incoming data. Calibration can be turned on and off. It can also handle arbitrary mathematical expressions (through the use of an internal `expr` object), and dynamically instantiates objects necessary for performing specified transformations, including first-order FIR and IIR filters.

dot.router The Max/MSP version of our "router" data-structure; performs namespace translation of mapped parameters, and scaling and clipping of data streams.

5.2   Gesture Extraction Helpers

dot.play/dot.record These objects can be used to record up to 254 incoming data channels into a `coll` object using delta timing, and later played back. It is useful for gesture capture and off-line mapping experimentation. The objects `dot.recordabsolute` and `dot.playabsolute` perform the same function with absolute time-stamping.

dot.extrema Automatically outputs local maxima and minima as peaks and troughs are detected in the incoming data. Helps in extraction of gestural events from sensor data.

dot.leakyintegrator A configurable integrator which leaks over time. The integration can either be linear, exponential, or use an arbitrary transfer function specified as a table.

dot.timedsmooth An averaging filter for asynchronous control data that makes use of DSP objects for reliably timed smoothing.

dot.transfer Performs table-based waveshaping on control data streams with customizable transfer function. (This is used in controller patches for signal processing, but not yet accessible through the mapping GUI.)

5.3   Case Example

Sally is a composer of electro-acoustics who has written a piece requiring soundfile triggers. Bob is a percussionist interested in exploring the use of ballistic body movements for electronic performance. Sally creates a Max/MSP patch using `dot.timedsmooth` and `dot.extrema` from the *Digital Orchestra Toolbox* to extract arm movements from 3-axis accelerometers held by Bob in each hand. She exposes the smoothed accelerometer data as well as the trigger velocity information through OSC.

Sally loads the mapping interface. She then loads her accelerometer patch as well as a sampler patch which has been configured for OSC messaging. After loading, these devices are listed in the mapping interface, where she selects them, making the accelerometer and extrema data visible on the left-hand side, and the sample triggers visible on the right-hand side. To begin, she guesses that it would be good to trigger sample 1 using the right-hand forwards movement, scaling the volume according to the movement's speed. She clicks on `/body/hand/right/forward_trigger`, selecting it, and then clicks on `/sample/1/play_at_volume`, connecting them. Since she had originally determined an estimated range of values for the accelerometer data, it automatically scales to the volume information, and the scaling coefficients are visible in the upper right-hand corner of the screen.

Bob tries the configuration for a few minutes, but decides there is not enough control, and it requires too much energy to achieve even modest volume on the sound. They decide to re-calibrate. Sally clicks on "calibrate", and Bob makes several triggering gestures with his right hand, until the volume range seems consistent. He makes some extreme gestures to maximize the range, so that he is able to achieve better control with a moderate amount of effort. Sally then toggles "calibrate" and saves the mapping. Bob plays for a while, and decides some small adjustments to the range are needed, so Sally manually changes the scaling coefficient instead of re-calibrating again.

Next they decide to map a low-pass filter, which is available through the sampler, to the motion of Bob's left hand. Sally chooses `/body/left/hand/accel/x` and then clicks on `/sample/1/filter/frequency`. Instantly the sound drops to a bass tone, much too low. Sally chooses clipping options from the drop-down menu and sets the minimum to 100 Hz, and the maximum to 5000 Hz. They re-calibrate the left-hand accelerometer range while triggering samples with the right hand. Bob begins to understand how to control the sound more accurately as they practice, and eventually they start looking at the score together.

6   Discussion

From their earliest use, the solutions we have developed have allowed us to streamline the process of mapping in collaboration with performers and composers. The ability to quickly experiment with a variety of mapping connections democratizes the mapping process, since it is easier to try everyone's ideas during a mapping session. Showing the performers that the connections are malleable allows them to contribute to the development of a comfortable gestural vocabulary for the instrument, rather than accepting the mappings provided. Composers are able to explore control of sounds that interest them without supervision or assistance of a technical member. Using common tools for the group means that the work of others is easily viewed and understood.

Controllers and synths that are still in development are also easily supported: as the supported parameter-space increases, the device simply presents more namespaces to the GUI.

Naturally this system does not solve all of the problems encountered in a collaborative effort of this type. The technical knowledge of the group members varies widely, and some technical knowledge of the individual controllers and synths is still necessary, not least because they are still in development and may not always respond predictably. As much as possible, however, we have made the connection, processing, and communication of data between devices easy to both comprehend and perform.

One area of frustration in our work has been dealing with devices (specifically commercial software synths) which communicate solely using MIDI. Since the norm in this case is to use MIDI control-change messages, many software environments allow flexible mapping between MIDI input values and their internal semantically labeled synth parameters. This means that although the synth parameters are easily understood from within a sequencing environment for adjustment or automation, external access to these parameters is provided only through an arbitrary set of MIDI control change identifiers. Our solution is to create a static set of MIDI mappings for our use, and provide a translation layer outside the environment to expose semantic parameters identical to those used internally. It is hoped that as users become familiar with see the advantages of semantic mapping, they will move away from a dependence on the traditional MIDI workflow.

In namespace design we have tried throughout to conform to the hierarchy proposed for GDIF [13], since we are also involved in its development, and this also raises some implementation questions. An important part of the GDIF hierarchy concerns representing gesture information in terms of the body of the performer, using the /body OSC prefix, and indeed several of our controllers already use this namespace. However, distinguishing performers using OSC address patterns proves much more complex when considering the various possible permutations of multiple performers and controllers.

7   Future Work

In addition to incremental improvements in function and usability, we have planned the addition of several new features:

Many-to-one mapping: As discussed above, we would like to implement the ability to negotiate many-to-one mapping relationships explicitly within the mapping interface, with simple GUI control over the desired combining function.

Vectors: Many OSC devices currently send or receive data in vectors or lists. The ability to split, combine, individually scale, and reorder vector elements will be added.

OSC pattern-matching: Pattern-matching and wild-card functionality is defined in the OSC specification [23] but generally has not been fully implemented in OSC systems. It is easy to imagine scenarios in which using wild-cards in mapped OSC address patterns would be a powerful addition to our system.

Data rates: Rather than sending controller information as quickly as possible, we would like to make the data rate a property of the mapping connection. A data stream might be used to control very slowly-evolving synthesis parameters, in which case very high data rates may be unnecessary and wasteful.

Remote collaboration: The implementations described above currently work over a local area network, however we would like to explore their use between remote locations communicating over the internet. In addition to collaborative mapping sessions between remote locations, this scenario could permit low-bandwidth communication of performance data for remote collaborative performance, in which control data is sent to instances of a software synthesizer at each location.

Acknowledgements

The authors would like to thank Alexander Refsum Jensenius for important discussion related to this effort, as well as the members of the Digital Orchestra Project group, especially Heather Hindman, Xenia Pestova, Chloé Dominguez, Fernando Rocha, D. Andrew Stewart, and Sean Ferguson. This project was supported by funds from the *Fonds de recherche sur la société et la culture* (FQRSC) of the Quebec government, the Natural Sciences and Engineering Research Council of Canada (NSERC), and the NSERC/Canada Council for the Arts New Media Initiative.

References

[1] The McGill Digital Orchestra (2007),
    `http://www.music.mcgill.ca/musictech/DigitalOrchestra`
[2] Integra: A composition and performance environment for sharing live music technologies (2007), `http://integralive.org`
[3] liblo: Lightweight OSC implementation (2007),
    `http://liblo.sourceforge.net`
[4] OSCTools (2006), `http://sourceforge.net/projects/osctools`
[5] The Synthesis ToolKit in C++ (STK) (2007),
    `http://ccrma.stanford.edu/software/stk`
[6] Bevilacqua, F., Müller, R., Schnell, N.: Mnm: a max/msp mapping toolbox. In: Proceedings of the conference on New Interfaces for Musical Expression, Vancouver, Canada, pp. 85–88. National University of Singapore (2005)
[7] Hunt, A.: Radical User Interfaces for Real-time Musical Control. PhD thesis, University of York, UK (1999)
[8] Hunt, A., Kirk, R.: Mapping strategies for musical performance. In: Wanderley, M., Battier, M. (eds.) Trends in Gestural Control of Music, IRCAM - Centre Pompidou, Paris (2000)
[9] Hunt, A., Wanderley, M.M.: Mapping performance parameters to synthesis engines. Organised Sound 7(2), 97–108 (2002)

[10] Hunt, A., Wanderley, M., Paradis, M.: The importance of parameter mapping in electronic instrument design. In: Proceedings of the 2002 Conference on New Interfaces for Musical Expression, pp. 149–154 (2002)

[11] Hunt, A., Wanderley, M.M., Paradis, M.: The importance of parameter mapping in electronic instrument design. Journal of New Music Research 32(4), 429–440 (2003)

[12] Jensenius, A.R.: Action - Sound: Developing Methods and Tools to Study Music-related Body Movement. PhD thesis, University of Oslo, Norway (submitted, 2007)

[13] Kvifte, T., Jensenius, A.R.: Towards a coherent terminology and model of instrument description and design. In: Proceedings of the conference on New interfaces for musical expression, Paris, France, pp. 220–225. IRCAM – Centre Pompidou (2006)

[14] Lee, M., Wessel, D.: Connectionist models for real-time control of synthesis and compositional algorithms. In: Proceedings of the International Computer Music Conference, pp. 277–280 (1992)

[15] Malloch, J., Wanderley, M.M.: The T-Stick: From musical interface to musical instrument. In: Proceedings of the 2007 International Conference on New Interfaces for Musical Expression (NIME 2007), New York City, USA, pp. 66–69 (2007)

[16] Malloch, J., Sinclair, S., Wanderley, M.M.: From controller to sound: tools for collaborative development of digital musical instruments. In: Proceedings of the International Computer Music Conference, Copenhagen, Denmark, pp. 65–72 (2007)

[17] Marshall, M., Malloch, J., Wanderley, M.M.: A framework for gesture control of spatialization. In: Proceedings of the 2007 International Gesture Workshop, Lisbon, Portugal (2007)

[18] Place, T., Lossius, T.: Jamoma: A modular standard for structuring patches in max. In: Proceedings of the International Computer Music Conference, New Orleans, USA (2006)

[19] Puckette, M.: Pure Data: another integrated computer music environment. In: Proceedings, Second Intercollege Computer Music Concerts, Tachikawa, Japan, pp. 37–41 (1996)

[20] Rovan, J.B., Wanderley, M., Dubnov, S., Depalle, P.: Instrumental gestural mapping strategies as expressivity determinants in computer music performance. In: Proceedings of Kansei- The Technology of Emotion Workshop, Genova (1997)

[21] Steiner, H.-C., Henry, C.: Progress report on the mapping library for pd. In: Proceedings of the PureData Convention, Montreal, Canada (2007)

[22] Van Nort, D., Wanderley, M.M.: The LoM mapping toolbox for Max/MSP/Jitter. In: Proceedings of the International Computer Music Conference, New Orleans, USA (2006)

[23] Wright, M.: OpenSound Control specification (2002),
http://www.cnmat.berkeley.edu/OSSC/OSC-spec.html

[24] Wright, M., Freed, A., Momeni, A.: OpenSound Control: State of the art. In: Proceedings of the Conference on New Interfaces for Musical Expression (2003)

The ImmApp: A Digital Application for Immersive Interaction with Sound Art Archives

J. Milo Taylor

CRiSAP Research Unit [1]
(Creative Research into Sound Art Practice)
London College of Communication,
University of the Arts, London
j.taylor23@lcc.arts.ac.uk

Abstract. This paper introduces a doctoral research project which is developing an innovative digital research methodology based around a MySql [2] database. The project's aim is to deliver an innovative re-presentation of sound art discourse from a digitized, post-modern, post-Cageian perspective.

Keywords: Sound Art, Immersive Digital Environments, Database, MySql, XML, X3D, OSC.

1 Introduction

The late twentieth century saw an upsurge in the exposure and circulation of what is variously called 'sound art', 'audio art' or 'sonic art'. In such work, the auditory is given a rare foregrounding over the unquestionable dominance of the visual in western art practice. Closely associated with the emergence of affordable technologies, considerations of the contextual contingences of presentation, network art, telematic art and the continued development of intermedial practice, the rather sudden proliferation of sound art within galleries and museums highlighted a serious absence of theory or significant literature contexualising a rather liminal and apparently new form of artwork.

Since this time however, a retrospective on artists working with sound has taken place, and whilst practice 'resembles a poorly mapped geography' [2] a number of publications have appeared addressing this art of sound. The various examples of this ([3], [4], [5], [6], [7], [8]) have approached their theorizing and mapping of practice from within natural language, or through an impoverished engagement with digital strategies, as typified by the unreconstructed adoption of inherited print-based page layouts of such online resources as UbuWeb [9] , The Australian Sound Design Project [10] and The Sonic Arts Research Archive [11]. While search engines on such sites present an alternative semantic entryway into creative practice, subverting the linearity and sequentiality evident in written texts, these resources remain structured along more or less modernist lines with material organized around specific artists, geographical locations, and temporal events.

R. Kronland-Martinet, S. Ystad, and K. Jensen (Eds.): CMMR 2007, LNCS 4969, pp. 426–440, 2008.

As I shall show later on, the ImmApp offers a new reading of sound art based upon a more contemporary discourse, a deeper exploration of today's technology, and assesses the contribution this may make to a reinvigorated conceptualization of a marginalized art history, when further enriched by contemporary critical theory

2 The ImmApp

"A synthesizer places all of the parameters in continuous variation, gradually making 'fundamentally heterogeneous elements end up turning into each other in some way."([12]. pp 121)

The above quotation from Deleuze and Guattari provides some insight into the overall aim of the research process; the development of a unique means of interacting with a historical practice. While the ImmApp will involve significant aspects of sound synthesis, the above quotation should be understood as metaphorical and an application of post-structural cultural philosophy to an example of embodied digital sound practice. The ImmApp can be understood as a conceptual or cultural synthesizer; using the flattening of difference typical of digital technology to create spaces and tensions between divergent practice in order to investigate broader historical (dis)continuities.

2.1 Data Gathering and MySql Database

Following work reviewing contemporary and historical sound art practice in terms of a traditionally-styled context review, an initial sample of 20 sound artists was taken, and an in-depth search for relevant material undertaken.

There were two main strategies in selecting artists; firstly, a 'control group' of core sound artists, those artists reported as being such, who individually claim that for themselves, (Christina Kubisch, Christian Marclay, Ros Bandt for example), and secondly, more liminal artists, working on the edge of sound art practice. It soon became clear that a larger sample of artists and works was required, and the number of case studies increased over a period of three months from September to December 2006 from the original 20 to 160. This increase was decided necessary, if not to provide a comprehensive coverage of sound art practice, then at least to open up a space inclusive of as much diverse activity as possible in these early stages.

Alongside this data-gathering was the urgent need for establishing a robust research method for storing and managing this information. The vision informing decisions at this point were based upon contemporary web design, with particular interest in the possible vectors suggested by Web 2.0 discourse and open source software. Through a creative and subverting use of available technologies, a unique application may be developed.

The first stage in this was to install a database and server technology. The rationale behind this activity suggested that the combined use of a server and relational database bundle, conventionally used to deliver dynamic web sites from geographically remote sites, could be usefully deployed on a single, non-networked computer, facilitating rapid and scalable data retrieval and manipulation functions.

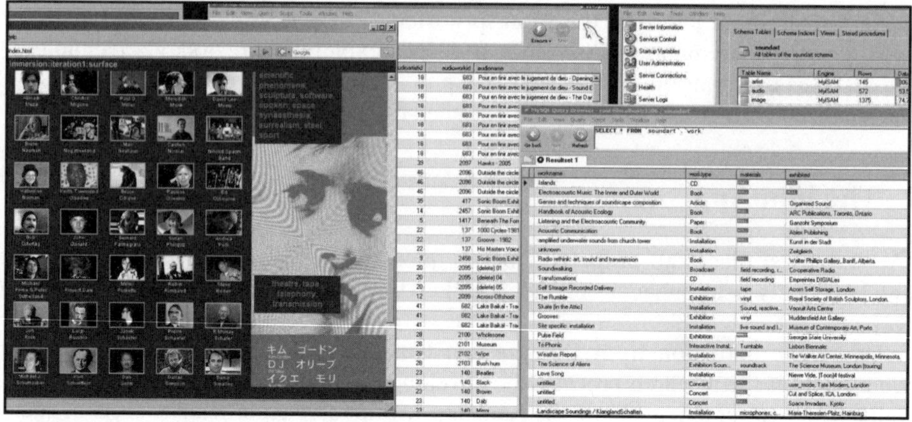

Fig. 1. Early example of the database interface (left) and an underlying MySql table (right)

The MySql **[13]** relational database is ubiquitous in contemporary database design. Open source, scalable and free, it is used from the smallest of dynamic data applications to the most demanding of situations. It has a light footprint, is fast and runs easily on the open source Apache server technology **[14]** which was simultaneously adopted for similar reasons.

2.2   Search Mechanism and Conventional Taxonomy

The next step in the development of the application was the means by which the data could be semantically manipulated, and this was achieved through a sophisticated search engine acting to shape and morph a dynamic immersive datascape. We can explore this by discussing two different aspects of this step; first by a review of the nature of the data to be accessed, and secondly by a discussion of database search techniques.

The nature of the data has been shaped in a way comparable to the strategy of selecting artists to be included in the database; a balance of the conventional and established, with the unconventional and exploratory.

The former can be applied to the inclusion of such staples of modernism as 'artist', 'location' and 'year'; self-explanatory discrete units that run through discourse. It is seemingly quite apparent how these inter-connected elements relate within sound art and how a digital application may spatialise returned queries based upon historical and geographical co-ordinates. First efforts were directed towards grouping data from proximate years and locations closely together, and data separated by greater spatio-temporal distance further apart; it is noted that these conventions are open to questioning and dependant upon progress in the development of the application; they may be challenged as structuring forces, and it is hoped that through the second category of association that this will be made apparent.

2.3 Artist Nodes [1] : An Alternative Ontology

In 'Noise, Water, Meat' Douglas Kahn [15] provides some precedence for a radically different approach to an art history of sound. While the book is admittedly problematic, uneven and idiosyncratic and has been critiqued for its many shortcomings ([16], [17], [18], [19]) in its contextualization of an art of sound within wider creative modernist practice it offers a perspective that until its appearance was sorely lacking. While the results of his approach reinforce a culturally entrenched view of sound art based in high modernism, his method is worthy of closer scrutiny.

The book is divided into three sections, noise, water, and meat, which for the purposes of this paper I will call *nodes*, defined as attractors around which practice can be seen to converge. Kahn uses these nodes not only to demarcate areas of sound art practice, but also to connect these, in unexpected ways, to contemporaneous cultural changes. In the section 'Water' for example the node is used in a complex discussion of a shift in creative practice occurring in the early 1950s. A node, water, is then used to articulate a disciplinary dissolution that "would come to signal a greater saturated and fluid state within the late modernist arts" [15] (pp 244).

The second method of organizing data within the ImmApp reflects this approach as instigated by Kahn. Each artist and work has been cross-referenced with a number of 102 nodes. While some nodes are used reflectively within discourse (installation, music, laptop etc) other terms have not been directly addressed or are strangely absent as a focus of discourse. These, as yet, silenced nodes appear as potential sites of significance within the dataset. For example, the ImmApp has already picked up on the presence of 'queer', 'gender', 'race', as significant aspects of practice. That these aspects of sound art have received very little discussion in conventional coverage of sound art was made quickly apparent by the methodology embodied by the ImmApp project.

So for each entry in the database, there is an associated array of key terms. Statistical treatment of these arrays (i.e. which specific nodes are likely to appear together, or which are less likely to appear together) will provide the numerical basis for associating data in real space.

By this time, I hope to have demonstrated my intention to present sound art as a number of dynamic and interrelated elements, described in part by geographical and historical placement and further modified through a shifting array of nodes. Practice is to be mapped based on a direct investigation of materials, techniques, and the more slippery entities and relationships found within sound art that seem well suited to this method.

2.4 Dynamic Generation of Spatialised Datascapes from MySql Queries

In the current research I am interested in run-time generation of 3 dimensional spaces in response to a performative interaction with a database. The emergent properties of an environment generated in this way are of great creative interest, especially when

---

[1] Within the ImmApp project there is an unfortunate convergence of terminology. 'Node' is used in this discussion of artistic practice to refer what could alternatively be called a 'keyword' or 'tag'. 'Node' also has a specific, and different meaning in regards to X3D code where it is the equivalent of an XML 'element' i.e. a fundamental block from which X3D environments are written.

coupled with an 'open' dataset able to be updated and modified at any time. These run-time possibilities offer an approach very different from pre-rendered scenes that share much with the closed texts of the printed page.

While an immersant in a pre-rendered virtual world may have choices in the way that he/she may interact with the virtual world, the world itself is static, in a comparable way that architecture in the real world is static. A run-time environment is generated 'on the fly' and constructed according to the semantic search string. Due to this, the virtual architecture is fluid and dynamic, modeled on nothing found in the physical world.

A number of different technologies were considered to deliver upon this vision, some of the candidates included:

- Max/MSP [20]
- Macromedia Director [21]
- Pure Data [22]
- Processing [23]

These have been rejected for various reasons; at the time of writing, the technologies being explored are:

$$\text{MySql [13] ->XML [24] -> X3D [25] -> audio engine}^2 \text{ [26]}$$

I will briefly discuss each of these in turn to provide an overview of the 'signal flow' within the ImmApp and I will describe how information inputted to the MySql database will create a generative sound field within a real world environment.

3 Technical Context: MySql, XML and X3D

"A machinic assemblage, through its diverse components, extracts its consistency by crossing ontological thresholds, non-linear thresholds of irreversibility, [...] phylogenetic thresholds [and] creative thresholds of heterogenesis and autopoiesis." Felix Guattari in [27].

3.1 MySql vs. XML

In contradistinction to the linearity of language used in natural language, the structure of MySql operates 'relationally' as an array of interlinked and reconfigurable tables of information, each of which can be reorganized according to on the one hand processes and search mechanisms designed by the developer, and on the other hand, criteria provided by the user of the application. While hierarchies and linearities are sublimated in MySql structures, what is paramount is its support of relationships *between* entities (i.e. one-to-one, one-to-many, many-to-one and many-to-many).

This represents a drastically altered dynamic between *author*, *reader* and *text*, if indeed we can use these terms within the context of the ImmApp. The focus of the current research should not be understood as an unpicking of the semantics of these

---

2 At the time of writing, a number of different options are being explored e.g. PureData, Max/MSP, Supercollider, LISP.

terms, but rather upon the specificities of sound art practice, the discourse surrounding this, and the potential of a dynamic immersive application to provide an alternative understanding of what such practice and discourse involves.

The search engine described above will allow the performer some choices in his/her search criteria in a manner modeled from advanced search engines as found on the web. For example:

```
SELECT * from work
    WHERE Materials = 'metal'
            EXCLUDE 'steel'
    AND year >= '1985'
    AND location = 'Europe'
```

or,

```
SELECT * from work
    WHERE node = 'acoustic ecology'
    AND YEAR > '1984'
    AND materials = 'multichannel'
            EXCLUDE 'tape'
    AND location = 'Canada'
```

It is also useful to compare the relational characteristics of MySql with the strict hierarchical structure of XML, the language into which the ImmApp queries results are transformed. It is too early to speculate upon the significance of this, but the comparison of MySql and XML being shaped by quasi-mathematical algorithmic processing with the strict linearity of natural language, used so far in analyses of sound art, is quite compelling.

3.2 XML and the Semantic Web

Web 2.0 is synonymous with what Tim-Berners-Lee has called *The Semantic Web* ([28], [29], [30]) a concept that outlines a vision of information becoming machine-readable. As HTML, the first language of the web, marks up text for *layout* upon web-pages, so XML, the language of Web 2.0 marks up the *meaning* of the elements laid out in electronic documents. For example, a simple piece of HTML:

```
<!DOCTYPE html PUBLIC "-//W3C//DTD XHTML 1.0 //EN"
"http://www.w3.org/TR/xhtml1/DTD/xhtml1-frameset.dtd">
<html xmlns="http://www.w3.org/1999/xhtml">
  <head>
  <meta http-equiv="Content-Type" content="text/html;
  charset=iso-8859-1" />
  <title>Soundart01 - Surface</title>
  </head>
  <body><b>Luigi Russolo</b></body>
</html>
```

The HTML tags (generally in pairs and always contained within < >) in this example simply tell a web browser that the document is HTML and that it is of a particular specification of HTML. The <meta> tags provide information about the document to such machine agents as search engines, and provide an early indication of the direction of Web 2.0. The <b> opening and </b> closing tags simply tell the browser to make the text *Luigi Russolo* appear in bold.

This simple example illustrates HTML as a code hidden to general users that defines the appearance of web-pages, as well as providing limited information about the document to machines (typically the <meta> section of a html document contains a description of the page's content as well as a list of indexed keywords). The example above, all HTML, and all content held within its tag pairs, remains meaningless to a machine; it is from this starting point that Berners-Lee proposed the concept of the Semantic Web, where machines are given a limited means to interpret meaning within documents through an e**X**tensible **M**arkup **L**anguage (XML).

While HTML is used to 'mark up' the *appearance* of text, XML is used to describe its *meaning*. In this way, XML is a form of metadata (data about data), something that existed in a limited form in HTML <meta> tags. To illustrate this difference between HTML and XML, the example below extends the previous code fragment, and demonstrates the clear hierarchy of elements central to well-formed XML syntax[3].

```
<?xml version="1.0" encoding="UTF"?>
<Early_Originators>
        <Artist>
                <1stName>Luigi</1stName><2ndName>Russolo</2ndName>

        <Workname> L'arte dei Rumori </Workname>
                                        <Workdate> 1916 </Workdate>
        <Workname> Intonarumori</Workname>
                                        <Workdate> 1916 </Workdate>
        <Workname> Gran Concerto Futuristico </Workname>
                                        <Workdate> 1917 </Workdate>
            <Workname> Risveglio di una Cita </Workname>
                                        <Workdate> 1921 </Workdate>
        </Artist>
        <Artist> content </Artist>
        <Artist> content </Artist>
        <Artist> content </Artist>
        etc.
</Early_Originators>
```

XML is only the first level of the Semantic Web however. For meaning to be constructed it is clearly not enough to simply tag elements with metadata, it is also necessary to define these concepts and the relationships between them. In this way, this process within the current research can be viewed as the creation of a unique ontology of sound art. While based in natural language, contemporary philosophical concerns and the specific practices of sound artists, the project is equally informed by a practice-based approach located in the field of computer science. It is from this basis in Web 2.0 discourse about knowledge representation in artificial intelligence, that the ImmApp will present a model of sound art distinct from previous print-based approaches.

3.3 X3D

Since the first wave of internet hyperbole in the 1990s, visions of the web as an immersive space rather than a collection of 2 dimensional pages have occupied a

---

[3] HTML tags are specific and defined. In XML, the equivalent is called the 'element'. XML elements are e**X**tensible, which means they are open, and can be defined by the programmer.

peripheral fringe of popular consciousness. The technology that facilitated the early 'worlds', VRML (Virtual Reality Modeling Language) has been superseded by the XML-based X3D protocol [31].

That X3D is based upon XML is demonstrated below where the underlying code forms a very simple X3D scene, and shows a clear relation to the XML code shown earlier. While the X3D is more complex, the similarities in structure and syntax are obvious.

```
<?xml version="1.0" encoding="UTF-8"?>
<!DOCTYPE X3D PUBLIC "ISO//Web3D//DTD X3D 3.0//EN"
"http://www.web3d.org/specifications/x3d-3.0.dtd">
<X3D profile='Immersive' >
<Scene>
        <Transform DEF='dad_Luigi_Russolo' translation='-0 0 0'>
                <Shape DEF='Luigi_Russolo' containerField='children'>
                        <Text DEF='GeoText1' containerField='geometry'
                        string='"Luigi Russolo"'>
                        </Text>
                </Shape>
        </Transform>
</Scene>
</X3D>
```

When viewed in an X3D compatible browser, (of which there are several including BS-Contact VRML/X3D [32], Flux Player [33], Octaga Player [34], the Java-based Xj3D [35], FreeWRL [36], Blaxxun [37], and Cortona [38]) we would experience something like the image shown in Figure 2.

Fig. 2. Screen Grab from FluxPlayer

This simple scene can be interacted with in virtual space. It is generated at run time by the simple example of X3D code shown above.

3.4 Audio in X3D

"It's an interesting field, and one where major advances are now possible. X3D has progressed quite well in terms of graphics, but the interfacing, especially audio, has left something to be desired. " [4]

John A. Stewart. Team Leader of the FreeWRL browser project

---

[4] From email correspondence 25th May 2007.

Before addressing the specific issues around audio in X3D we need to have a brief look at X3D nodes in a little more detail. The equivalent of XML *elements* (for example `<Artist>` `</Artist>` and `<1stname>` `</1stname>`) are, in X3D terminology, called *nodes*[5]. In XML, elements can be modified through the inclusion of *attributes*, and in a comparable way, the nodes contained in X3D documents can be modified by *fields*. In the X3D fragment above we see how the `<Transform>` node is modified by two fields `DEF` , and `translation`, containing the values `'dad_Luigi_Russolo'`, and `translation='-0 0 0'` respectively.

More detailed coverage of the X3D specifications can be found online [25], and in a growing body of literature [39], [40]. Here all that needs stating is that an incrementally increasing number of X3D nodes are supported through a number of profile specifications which have been put in place to allow browser developers to target particular implementations.

In the X3D example above, the 'Immersive' profile is specified, which is aimed at multimedia content, other specifications include the 'Core Profile', 'Interchange Profile', 'CADInterchange Profile' (aimed at computer-aided design applications) and others. Each particular browser supports different levels of nodal functionality as defined by each specification. We should also note the eXtensibility of X3D; which, in practice, means the particular developers associated with particular browsers have extended their flavour of X3D in certain directions. Additionally, it is possible, and usual, for scripts to be run within X3D (with ECMAscript) and so X3D's functionalities can also be eXtended in this way.

Audio within X3D is dealt with by two nodes `<Sound>` and `<AudioClip>`, as specified in the Immersive X3D Profile. The `<Sound>` node deals with sound spatialisation whilst `<AudioClip>` deals with streaming and file playback.[6] In the words of Brutzman and Daly, "The Sound node enables sound-spatialisation capabilities by providing fields that define sound location, direction and relative intensity". ([40] pp 342).

However, the claims for sound spatialisation in X3D are based in a very primitive understanding of spatial audio, and it is, to me vital, to link the practices of real time 3D environments, such as X3D, with the much more developed explorations of sound in space as suggested by acousmatic music, and the explorations of the ambisonic, wavefield synthesis, and soundscape communities. It is also of great interest to expand the X3D community's understanding of sound through the application of the recent ideas of such important audio theorists and practitioners as Bregman [42], Blesser [43] and Smalley [44] who not only have extensive technical capabilities, but also profound understanding of the use, or indeed, misuse, of spatialised audio.

In theory, X3D supports spatialisation, yet it remains dependant upon the specific browser chosen as to whether anything more than stereo attenuation is supported. Before providing a short overview of the browsers that are available, it must be noted

---

[5] This is the area of potential confusion I touched on earlier in the paper, due to an unfortunate convergence of terminology.

[6] A more in-depth discussion of audio in X3D/VRML , although over 5 years old, can be found at 41.   Pohja, M. *X3D and VRML Sound Components*. [cited 09.07.2007]; mikko.pohja@hut.fi:[Available from: http://www.tml.tkk.fi/Opinnot/Tik-111.590/2002s/Paperit/pohja_x3d_sound_OK.pdf.

that immersive audio within X3D is notoriously buggy, and has remained problematic throughout the current research. It is in the hope of improving this situation that I continue to explore this area.

There are a number of X3D browsers available, all with slightly different emphases; significant effort has gone into the exploration of these different technologies. Table 1 below summarises some relevant aspects of the most prevalent X3D browsers available today.

Table 1. X3D Browsers

	License	OS	Audio	Notes
Flux Player	Open-source	Win	Stereo	Direct X
Octaga	Commercial	Win / Linux / OS X	?	Supports panoramic video projection
BS Contact VRML/X3D	Commercial	Win	Up to 8 channel (Configured in SDK package)	Direct X OpenGL (industry standard browser)
FreeWRL	Open-source	Linux / OS X	Stereo	Rewire/ MIDI enabled
XJ3D	Open-source	Win /Linux /OS X /Solaris	?	Java Based (Java3d audio handling very buggy)
Cortona	Commercial	Win	Configured in SDK	Direct X OpenGL. VRML specifications, only a few X3D nodes supported
Blaxxun Contact	Commercial	Win	?	DirectX OpenGL Focus on multi-user collaboration. Java based. RealAudio.

As can be seen from Table 1, the attitude of the X3D development community towards audio is rather obscured. While the protocols of visual 3-dimensionality (DirectX, OpenGL) are made explicit by many of the groups and companies concerned, audio standards are clearly not a priority for (m)any of these groups. Information regarding auditory 3-dimensionality is hardly forthcoming, and development of sophisticated immersive audio with X3D is restricted to complex develop activity within the software development kits (SDKs) of the major commercial X3D applications.

3.5 The Helian Browser

The sole exception to this is the Helian browser [45] developed by Niall Moody as part of a recent PhD project at the Centre for Music Technology, University of Glasgow. The Helian X3D browser is cross-platform and designed specifically with audio in mind. This project is the only example approaching the requirements necessary for the ImmApp. Particular aspects of Helian that distinguish it from the technologies discussed above are:

- Support for low latency audio   (MME, ASIO, DirectX on Windows)
                                        (Jack, ALSA, OSS on Linux)
                                        (CoreAudio on OS X)
- B-format Ambisonic audio engine supporting sophisticated multi-channel speaker arrays.
- Open Sound Control support for all nodes.
- Multi-threaded audio engine allows processing of audio to be split into discrete threads and potentially processed by separate processors.

There would however be problems with using Helian as the browser of choice for the ImmApp.

- No http/ftp support (required for interaction with the MySql database).
- Helian is unable to dynamically load objects (required as response to MySql queries).
- OSC control is unidirectional (Helian receives OSC, and does not send it. This is the inverse of what is required for the ImmApp, where the location of spatialised nodes will be sent to the spatialisation engine).
- The Ambisonics implementation docs not support camera movement (i.e. Soundfield rotation).

While it is clear that at the current time the Helian browser is unsuitable for the ImmApp project, the problems highlighted above are only problems from my own research perspective. Moody's work is a significant contribution to knowledge, on many levels, most explicitly through the innovative development of an X3D browser with a focus upon audio. An auditory focus, that is absolutely lacking in broader X3D discourse, as is illustrated in Table 1 above. The Helian browser has been developed for his particular research goals, and the limitations I have highlighted are simply not relevant to his aims.[7]

3.6 Technical Context: Summary and Conclusions

In this discussion of the technical context for the project I began by articulating the kind of discursive modality enabled by the relational dynamics of MySql, modulated by quasi-mathematical manipulation as facilitated by raw SQL coding.

I then moved on to an overview of the type of machine semantics envisaged by Berners-Lee in his conception of Web 2.0 and introduced XML, the primary language associated with this type of discourse, and the starting point for the development of machine ontologies in the context of the Semantic Web.

The next stage was to explain the relation between XML and X3D in order to clarify the modulation of cultural flows from dematerialized digital artifacts, through the shifting grids of a relational database, transformed and translated into a real world audio-visual-spatial synthetic environment.

---

[7] I would like to extend my thanks to Niall for taking the time to correspond with me, and to answer the questions I had regarding his work.

The technical discussion ended highlighting the real research opportunity for developing an immersive, audio-aware, and audio-enabled X3D environment by demonstrating the current lack of such systems. I would like to end this paper by returning to the writing of Douglas Kahn and to give a simple example of how the ImmApp may provide an alternative narrative of sound art to a traditional text-based presentation.

4   The Water Face-Off: The ImmApp vs. Kahn InfoClash

For the sake of this discussion, I will focus upon the node 'water' selected by Kahn in his text 'Noise, Water, Meat'. I will give a short précis of his version of 'water' in relation to an art of sound, and open up a short discussion of water from an admittedly primitive early iteration of the ImmApp, which while in its current state has none of the sensory richness anticipated in more developed later versions, proves a certain value in this methodology.

4.1   Water from Kahn's Printed Page

The second section of Kahn's book attempts 'a short art history of water sound' and situates this with a retrospective view on the use of worldly water sounds in the earlier art musics of Eric Satie, Richard Wagner, and Henry Cowell, tape compositions by Hugh Le Caine and Toru Takemitsu and a more general watery inspiration found in works by Kurt Schwitters, André Breton, Raymond Roussel, Aldous Huxley, Marcel Duchamp and Salvador Dali. He then dedicates the majority of the section to a discussion of John Cage and Jackson Pollock and relates this to broader tendencies within the Fluxus movement and the work of Allan Kaprow and George Brecht.

In essence, this is the total extent of Kahn's exploration; a few passing remarks on Yoko Ono, Andy Warhol, Carolee Schneemann and Meiko Shiomi, ends his analysis. The last reference to a water based art-work being Annea Lockwood's 'A Sound Map of the Hudson River' (1982).

4.2   A Narrative of Water from the ImmApp

The ImmApp returns 18 works, only one of which, Brecht's Water Yam, is mentioned by Kahn. This in some ways is due to the semantic weakness of the existing search mechanism and once full-text indexing is implemented, a much richer response will occur.

However, even in its current primitive state it provides proof of several things. Firstly that the database has been populated with significant evidence of sound art. Of the 18 records returned, 15 different artists are represented from America, Australia, Austria, Canada, Germany and New Zealand.

An alternative reading focuses on the institutions associated with sound art, ranging from the important Austrian festival Kunst in der Stadt, the Otis Art Institute, Los Angeles, the Hirshhorn Museum and Sculpture Garden, Smithsonian Institute, Washington DC and The Centro Brasileiro Britânico, São Paulo amongst others. It also provides an insight into the diversity of practice with tape compositions, field recordings, instrument design, sound sculpture and site-specific installation all returned.

Finally, acknowledging Kahn's work, this exercise provides some vindication of his rather idiosyncratic method in approaching a history of sound in the arts. While his work connects creative practice to deeper cultural and philosophical debates occurring in modernity and pre-modernity, the ImmApp connects elements historically and geographically dispersed that conventional analysis has not related, fixated as they are upon a small number of possible variables.

5 Conclusion

This paper has attempted to introduce the ImmApp project, to provide some background to the area of study, to give a review of recent practice and to give a summary of my methodology within the context of contemporary technologies relevant to my research goals. I moved on to a discussion of the Semantic Web and the place of X3D within this discourse before summarizing the capabilities of the major X3D browsers before highlighting the poor support for audio functionality within such technologies. I ended the paper with a comparison of results obtained from a modernist, print-based methodology, as typified by Douglas Kahn's discussion of water, with an alternative reading of the same theme provided by the ImmApp. I hope to have proven by this the evident contribution that such a digital strategy can contribute.

In the brief comparative study presented above (The Water Face-Off: The ImmApp vs. Kahn InfoClash) Kahn's presentation of 'water' seems remarkably thin, and leaves the last 20 years of work wholly unaddressed. The stark difference in the material covered by him, and the artists and works returned by the ImmApp is highly pertinent. It not my intention in any way to belittle Kahn's work, but the demonstration above clearly highlights his fixation upon modernist art, and more specifically modernist art music. While Kahn explicitly acknowledges his agenda and his casting of modernism as a static, object-based practice compared to the fluidity and flow of a nascent post-modernism provides an essential background to sound art, his approach delimits and defines the diversity of sound art practice inappropriately.

Much contemporary sound art is produced by artists with little or no formal musical training, and music, or musicality is of reduced importance. In addition to this, critics and gallery presentation of sound work connect more closely to a discourse based in fine art than one of music. The works of such artists as Dan Senn, Steve Roden, Max Neuhaus and Janet Cardiff relate to a visual discourse and immersed listening practices within locational specificities that are intrinsic elements of the ImmApp, and these sensory resonances knit tightly with the design and development of a technical solution to a conceptual problematic.

The level of detail provided by the ImmApp, and the primary nature of the information, allows an understanding of practice to develop based in the specifics of practice of individual artists. Through this, and the diversity it represents, we may avoid totalizing overcodings of narrative as typified by Kahn.

The ImmApp project is then a practice-based project and one that attempts an articulation of sound art practice through the use of contemporary technologies. Such mappings of art practice are usually found within arts and humanities discourse; while I am aware of such discourse, the ImmApp project is essentially interdisciplinary, and alongside the exploration of sound art, is a detailed and in-depth investigation of an area concretely within the domain of computer science. Research findings so far support claims that this is a fertile ground for continued investigation.

The particular strength of the project comes about through the ongoing shift in perspective and emphasis between the areas of art history, computer science and the goals of a practice-based creative project. The digital methodology opens an alternative interpretation of sound art history through the application of algorithm which is distributed throughout the ImmApp, and operates on many levels (ontologically, semantically, sensorially and spatially). Moving along the opposite vector, the critical theory associated with the study of an art history provides a critical philosophical framework with which to problematicise the creation of a sophisticated immersive digital application.

Finally, the ImmApp will involve sustained and focused interactions and manipulations of audio visual artifacts, facilitated by the later development of a robust audio engine. The choices made in performance, aimed at articulating one or more aspects of sound art, are of a very different order to those made by an author writing text for print media. While I refuse to speculate upon the final experience of this for performer and audience, I remain convinced that this performative presentation of sound art based upon a dynamic database will open a valuable space for a reinvigorated debate on sound art and the potentials of digital immersion.

References

1. CRiSAP (Creative Research into Sound Art Practice) (2006),
   `http://www.crisap.org`
2. W3C. OWL Web Ontology Language Guide (2004) [cited 2007 2.10.2007],
   `http://w3.org/TR/owl-guide`
3. Kahn, D.W.G.: Wireless Imagination, Sound, Radio and the Avant-Garde. MIT Press, Cambridge (1992)
4. Lander, D.: Sound by Artists. Art Metropole & Walter Philips Gallery, Toronto (1990)
5. Bull, M.: The Auditory Culture Reader. Berg (2004)
6. Cox, C.: Audio Culture - Readings in Modern Music. Continuum International Publishing Group Ltd (2004)
7. Toop, D.: Haunted Weather. Serpent's Tail (2004)
8. Toop, D.: Ocean of Sound: Aether Talk, Ambient Sound and Imaginary Worlds. Serpent's Tail (1996)
9. UbuWeb, `http://www.ubu.com/`
10. The Australian Sound Design Project,
    `http://www.sounddesign.unimelb.edu.au/site/about.html`
11. Sonic Arts Research Archive, `http://www.sara.uea.ac.uk/`
12. Deleuze, G., Guattari, F.: A Thousand Plateaus: Capitalism and Schizophrenia. University of Minnesota Press (1987)
13. MySQL, `http://www.mysql.com/why-mysql/`
14. Apache, `http://www.apache.org/`
15. Kahn, D.: Noise Water Meat. MIT Press, Cambridge (2001)
16. Shaw-Miller, S.R.: Analysing musical multimedia (Book Review); Noise, water, meat (Book Review). Art History 24(1), 139–146 (2001)
17. Sobaskie, J.W.: Noise, Water, Meat: A History of Sound in the Arts (review)(2001)

18. Hunter, A.: Stuttering Screams and Beastly Poetry (2001) [cited 19th March 2007],
    `http://www.electronicbookreview.com/thread/musicsoundnoise/undigitized`
19. Clark, You're Twisting My Melon, in Variant, pp. 8–9 (2000)
20. Max/Msp, `http://www.cycling74.com/products/maxmsp.html`
21. Macromedia Director, `http://www.adobe.com/products/director/`
22. Pure Data (PD), `http://puredata.info/`
23. Processing, `http://www.processing.org/`
24. XML, `http://www.xml.com/`
25. X3D, `http://www.web3d.org/`
26. SuperCollider, `http://www.audiosynth.com/`
27. Guattari, F.B.: Paul, Chaosmosis: An Ethico-Aesthetic Paradigm (1995)
28. Berners-Lee, T.: Semantic Web Road Map (1998),
    `http://www.w3.org/DesignIssues/Semantic.html`
29. Berners-Lee, T.: Sematic Web - XML (2000),
    `http://www.w3.org/2000/Talks/1206-xml2k-tbl`
30. Berners-Lee, T., Hendler, J., Lassila, O.: The Semantic Web. Scientific American, 05(01)
    (2001)
31. Web 3D Consortium, `http://www.web3d.org/`
32. BS Contact VRML/X3D, `http://www.bitmanagement.com/`
33. Flux Player, `http://www.mediamachines.com/`
34. Octaga Player, `http://www.octaga.com/`
35. Xj3D, `http://www.xj3d.org/`
36. FreeWRL, `http://freewrl.sourceforge.net/`
37. Blaxxun, `http://www.blaxxun.com`
38. Cortona, `http://www.parallelgraphics.com/products/cortona`
39. Geroimenko, V., Chaomei, C. (eds.): Visualising Information Using SVG and X3D.
    Springer, London (2005)
40. Brutzman, D., Leonard, D.: X3D Extensible 3D Graphics for Web Authors. Morgan Kaufman, San Francisco (2007)
41. Pohja, M.: X3D and VRML Sound Components. [cited 09.07.2007]; mikko.pohja@hut.fi:
    `http://www.tml.tkk.fi/Opinnot/Tik-111.590/2002s/Paperit/pohja_x3d_sound_OK.pdf`
42. Bregman, A.S.: Auditory Scene Analysis: The Perceptual Organization of Sound.
43. Blesser, B., Linda-Ruth, S.: Spaces Speak, are you listening? MIT Press, Cambridge (2007)
44. Smalley, D.: Space-Form and the acousmatic image. Organised Sound 12(1), 35–58 (2006)
45. Moody, N.: Helian X3D Browser

BioTools: A Biosignal Toolbox for Composers and Performers

Miguel Angel Ortiz Pérez and R. Benjamin Knapp

Queen's University Belfast, Sonic Arts Research Centre,
Cloreen Park Belfast, BT7 1NN, Northern Ireland
{mortizperez01,b.knapp}@qub.ac.uk
http://www.sarc.qub.ac.uk
http://www.miguel-ortiz.com/biotools.php

Abstract. In this paper, we present the current state of BioTools, an ongoing project to implement a modular hardware and software toolbox for composers and performers, which allows fast deployment of biosignal monitoring and measuring systems for musical applications. We discuss the motivations for this work and additionally three examples are shown of how this set of tools and the compositional strategies were used in the pieces *Díamair* for choir and physiological sensors, *Out of Time*, a project in which BioTools was used to record and analyse biosignals for their later use to inspire and aid in composition, and *Carne*, an improvisational piece that uses BioTools modules as the control interface.

Keywords: Composition, Biosignals, Integral music controller, performance.

1 Introduction

Currently, there is an extensive and constantly growing body of research and artistic exploration in the use of biosignals for musical applications [16], [21], et al. (See [17] for a description of what physiological signals are and their relationship to human-computer interaction.) However, as of yet, there is no universally available set of hardware and software tools that enable easy access to a wider community of practitioners to start composing and performing using physiologically controlled interfaces. Usually, the hardware tools have to be adapted from the medical field, often requiring custom electronics, expensive or electrically unsafe equipment, and specialised analysis algorithms. Thus, using biosignals to control music generally requires a case-by-case methodology, and often involves either a long development process/period of time by the composer or the participation of a specialised engineer (or group of engineers) in the creative process. With the development of BioTools, we attempt to limit this time/effort in order to enable the composer to focus on designing the interaction model i.e. the actual physical positioning and implementation of the diverse sensors from their desired piece and not the low level electronics required. In providing such a toolkit, we believe other researchers and artists can benefit from our efforts, and the field of

R. Kronland-Martinet, S. Ystad, and K. Jensen (Eds.): CMMR 2007, LNCS 4969, pp. 441–452, 2008.

biosignal interfaces for music can go past implementation issues and work can be done in the aesthetic, idiomatic, and stylistic aspects of musical practice as they relate to these specific technologies.

2   Motivation

As early as the turn of the 16th century, western music production started turning its focus of attention from the singing voice to *"new machines"* which we currently know as musical instruments. The importance of this shift wasn't immediately noticeable, since the first instrumental pieces were still based on choral compositional practice, and could as well have been composed for voices. It wasn't until the 17th century, with the works of composers like Johann Sebastian Bach, Claudio Monteverdi, Antonio Vivaldi and others, that instruments started to develop their own *voice* - their idiomatic language. Soon music which was not be suitable to human voices started to emerge.

Ever since, advances on musical instrument design have had a major role in the development of musical language, to name a few we could consider the following cases:

- The development of the well tempered tuning system, due to constraints in keyboard instruments and it's influence on baroque music.
- The invention of the piano and the establishment of the string quartet as a fixed ensemble in the classical period
- The establishment of the symphony orchestra of the classic period, the advances on solo instrument techniques for the romantic period
- The rediscovery of percussion instruments at the end of the XIX century as solo concert instruments and their leading to pitch-less conception of musical discourse.

In the 20th century the constant developments in electrical engineering and computer science have spawned a wide range of changes in musical composition. To detail the work of such important figures such as Lev Sergeyevitch Termen, Max Mathews, John Chowning. *et al* is outside the reach of this paper, but it is within the tradition of music technology (understood as the current state of instrument design development) that the present research is relevant, specifically on the use of biosignal interfaces for composition; in the hope to find something inherent to the use of physiological data for musical applications that might suggest deeper changes in musical thinking.

In 1965 Alvin Lucier first used brain waves as the main generative source for the composition and performance of his piece *Music for solo performer* [10]. Since then the use of biosignals for musical applications has been of great interest to composers and researchers. In the following years great advances have been made both in the artistic expression related to this medium and the underlying technologies involved. Several composers ranging from pioneers Richard Teitelbaum, David Rosenboom and Jacques Vidal to more recent sound artists as Robert Hamilton, Ken Furudachi and Atau Tanaka have made great advances in this field. The work of these artists is highly personal and appears to be more characteristic of their individual artistic expression rather than a more generalised practice that we could define as biomusic in a broader sense. By developing an accessible toolkit for fast implementation of biointerfaces we intend to enable a wider community of musicians to work at a higher level towards finding or suggesting a style of idiomatic music written for biosignal interfaces.

3   BioTools

There are two main tasks we have focused on in the development of BioTools. The first task is recording, assessing, analysing and plotting physiological data obtained from naturally experienced and induced emotional states for its later use on composition. (See [5] for information on this process). This allows for the use of physiological data not only as a control layer at performance time for triggering and controlling sound events or processes, but using this data for biosignal-informed composition, which can be even for acoustic instruments only. Measurements of biosignals through set experiences (performing a particular piece, responding to a questionnaire, watching a succession of images, listening to music, news, etc.) can be used to inform compositional decisions such as: musical structure, polyphony (if we take measurements of different biosensors or different users), rhythm, pitch class sets and others. This approach is very important, as the core characteristics of each type of signal is kept regardless of the diverse stimuli or conditions being measured. Thus, we can start thinking of *biomusic* where certain characteristics are always kept while composers are still free to explore their individual artistic expression.

The other purpose of our toolkit is to allow easy implementation of the required algorithms to use biosignals as part of an Integral Music Controller for musical performances [14] [15].

We attempt to address these two distinct tasks with a set of standardised hardware and software modules which allow for a more widespread use of biosignals for both aims.

Our initial software implementation for BioTools is built upon the Max/MSP platform, due to its widespread use amongst composers and performers. However, we have also begun implementing the data collection and analysis modules in the EyesWeb platform [9] because, as has been pointed out previously [13], Max/MSP still has problems with scheduling and time-stamping synchronised multiple streams of data. EyesWeb is far superior for this precise timing of real-time events and its built-in strengths for image emotive analysis and synthesis capabilities will be beneficial to the composer as well. Different approaches exist for mapping gestures to sound and choosing the appropriate mapping strategy is one of the main artistic decisions composers make on their pieces. We will not attempt to discuss the extensive field of gesture mapping in this paper (please see [4], [19] and [24] for more details). Instead, we focus on the behaviour of biosignals when responding to diverse stimuli to try to create music which is idiomatic to this type of controller. In doing so, we examine two elements:

1. The type of gestures possible for triggering and controlling individual music events on the course of any given composition.
2. The technical, philosophical and aesthetic connotations related to the use of this type of signals for composition, in a similar manner as additive synthesis and FFT analysis techniques have informed the French *musique spectrale* school [23].

4   Hardware Toolkit (The Next BioMuse)

The BioMuse system has evolved over the past 15 years from a high-end research system to a wireless mobile monitoring system [15] [16] [20]. The BioMuse has been redesigned once more to now be a simple toolkit of bands that can be worn on the limbs, chest, or head to measure any of the underlying physiological signals. Fig 1. shows the basic bands which have self-contained dry electrodes with the amplification, adaptation, and protection electronics imbedded within the band.

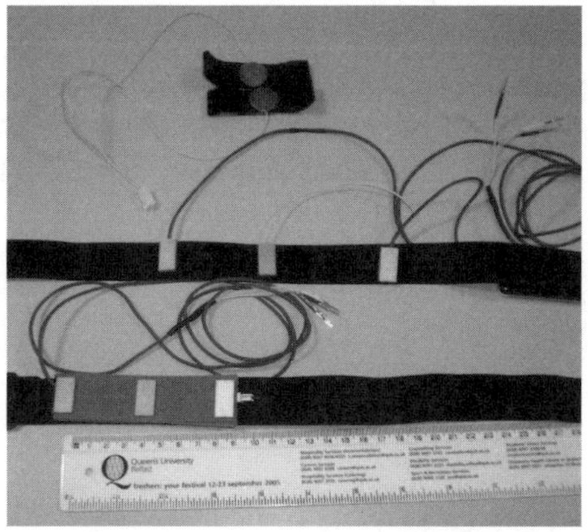

Fig. 1. Headband, Armband, Chest-band and GSR electrodes

Each band has the appropriate signal conditioning and protection circuitry necessary for the type of signal being measured. For example, the headband is specifically designed for measuring EEG and EOG signals. The limb band is designed to measure EMG and GSR signals. The chest band is designed to measure EKG. The output of these bands can then be plugged to any of the standard wireless transmitter systems such as the ICubeX [11] or the Arduino Bluetooth [6]. Fig. 2 shows the diverse bands being used during a rehearsal.

5   Software Modules

The software layer we are currently working on consists of a series of Max/MSP abstractions, GUIs (for fast analysis and visualisation of data) and their related

Fig. 2. Hardware modules during rehearsal

help files. The modules are implemented as a collection of patches instead of external objects to allow for easy modification and improving of these implementations by ourselves as well as others. Upon being captured, all the incoming data from the sensors is converted to the signal domain using the *sig~* object, this allows using Max's built in objects for signal processing and analysis, as well as the numerous third party external objects created for this purposes. Fig 3. shows a simple patch to monitor EMG, EKG and GSR from a performer.

5.1 Electromyogram (EMG)

The EMG hardware module measures underlying muscular activity generated by motor neurons. This signal is the most versatile for musical applications because

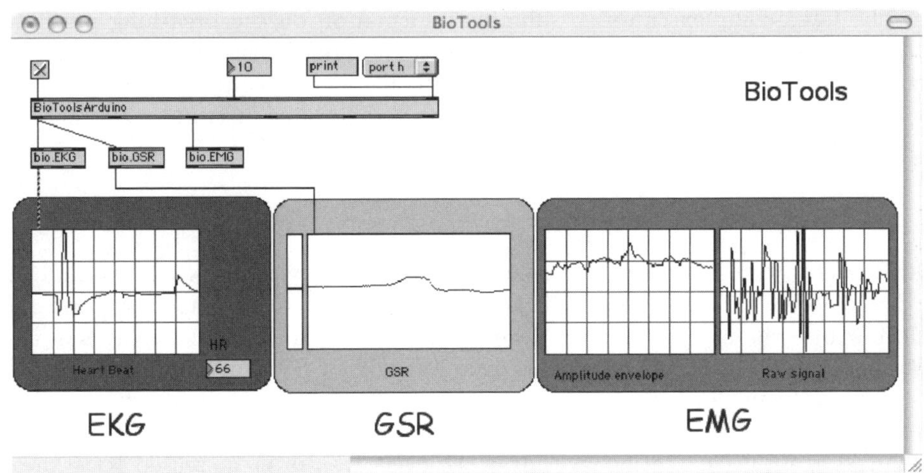

Fig. 3. BioTools' Max/MSP modules

it can be measured above any muscle, including arm (using armband) and face (using headband or glasses) and can be used both for continuous control and state recognition. Thus, it can track not only emotional information, but can be used in conjunction with more traditional non-physiological sensors to measure any of the physical gestures related to playing musical instruments and other performing arts.

As demonstrated by Atau Tanaka [7] and others, the most common placement of EMG sensors for musical practice is in the forearms of the performer. This is a convenient place for the sensors because it allows finger activity to be tracked without an intrusive device such as gloves which can directly affect the performance. The current implementation of the EMG module of BioTools has been developed for this purpose. The abstraction provides simple envelope following of the overall muscular activity tracked by the sensor and incorporates dynamic low-pass/high-pass filters and an adaptive smoothing algorithm to address the trade-off between stability of the signal and accurate response to fast gestures.

As a sub-group of the EMG module, we are currently working on gesture recognition of specific sets of muscles in order to assess information related to the specific performance practice of different musical instruments.

5.2   Electrocardiogram (ECG, EKG)

Created by the electrical impulses of the heart as it progresses through the stages of contraction, the EKG is one of the largest bioelectric signals. **Fig. 4** shows the components of a typical EKG signal. Our abstraction reads this signal and currently measures two key components: the RR and the QRS complex segments. The heart rate is computed directly from the length of the RR interval, The change in the duration of the RR interval measures the overall heart rate variability (HRV) which has been found to be strongly correlated with emotional stress [18].

The QRS complex can give valuable information on the breathing patterns of the performer without requiring an additional breath sensor, thus it makes it possible to voluntary use breath as a direct controller for sound manipulation as well as to use ancillary breath patterns related to specific instrumental practices (wind instruments and voice).

5.3   Galvanic Skin Response

GSR refers to the change in skin conductance caused by changes in stress and/or other emotional states. The GSR is extremely sensitive to emotional changes. Both subtle changes in the tonic level of the GSR and dramatic changes in the phasic level can be tracked with this technique. The GSR signal in its raw format is often confusing for musicians who are not familiar with the way it works, higher arousal levels (stress, increased involvement) cause the skin resistance to drop; reduced arousal (relaxation, withdrawal) levels results in increased resistance. To address this non-intuitive behaviour, our abstraction extracts both tonic and phasic behaviour and inverts the resultant control signals.

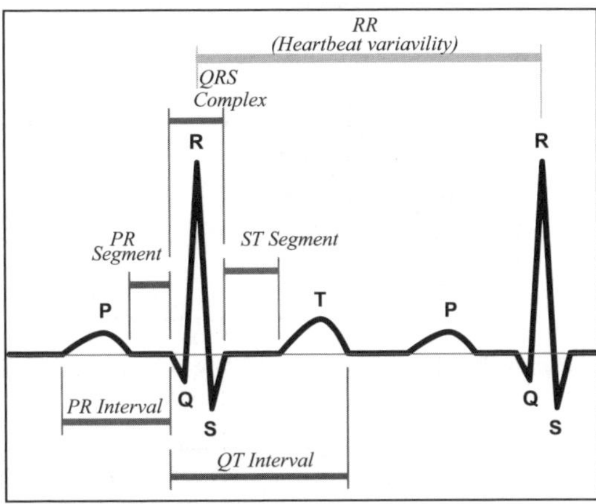

Fig. 4. Ideal EKG signal

6   Examples, Pieces Composed Using BioTools

The presented toolbox has been employed recently for the composition of the pieces *Díamair, Out of Time* and *Carne*. For these compositions, BioTools has proved to be extremely helpful - we were able to focus on the physical implementation and the musical contents of the pieces.

6.1   Díamair: A Piece for Choir and IMC

Díamair [22]is a piece for choir and Integral Music Controller inspired by the poem of the same name, often translated as *A Mystery* or *The Song of Amergin* (after the author to whom it is attributed), this text is contained in the *Lebor Gabála Érenn* (The Book of Invasions) [1]. For this composition we used the GSR and EMG modules of the IMC in addition to real-time face tracking. The conductor is equipped with EMG sensors on each forearm and the modules are used to gather basic information on his/her muscular tension. We use this data to identify staccato and legato articulations (as well as interpolation between them) on his/her conducting gestures. This information is then used to control spatial spread of the electronic sound sources and to apply amplitude and frequency envelopes. A group of eight soloists are equipped with GSR sensors. These sensors are placed in custom choir folders that the singers hold in their hands as shown in Fig. 5. This implementation succeeds in being non-intrusive for the singers.

The GSR signals from the choir where mapped to a granular synthesis engine to control transposition (specifically levels of dissonance), number of grains (polyphony) and grain size in order to shape the materials through involuntary autonomic physiological reactions, creating a direct interface between emotion and sound manipulation. The choir is laid out in two concentric circles with the conductor at the centre as showed in Fig. 6. The inner circle is formed by the

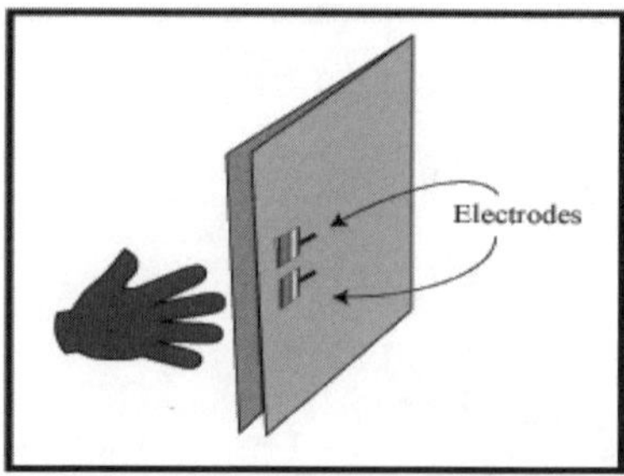

Fig. 5. Hardware implementation of GSR sensors for choir soloists

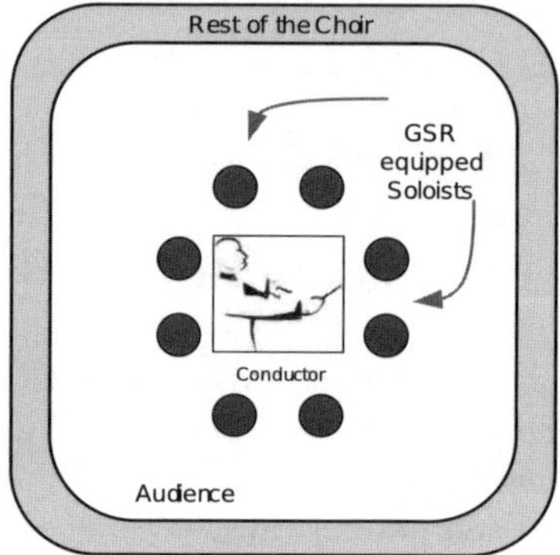

Fig. 6. Spatial choir configuration

eight soloists. The rest of the choir who are not equipped with sensors are placed surrounding the audience.

An imposed challenge for this project was to keep the hierarchical conductor-soloists-choir relationships in their interaction with the electronic sounds. Using the distributed IMC [14] concept to allow all the possible levels of interaction, we distributed the interface (GSR and EMG sensors) between the conductor and choir. The conductor has the capability of controlling the choir through his physical gestures. His control is augmented by the GSR module so that his gestures also remotely control the live electronics. The soloists do not have direct control over their sound manipulations but rather interact with them through ancillary and induced involuntary autonomic physiological reactions. The remaining choir members who are below the soloists in the hierarchical tree (conductor-soloists-choir), have no direct interaction with the live electronics, but close a feedback loop by their singing which affects the conductors gestures and soloists emotional states. The use of the interface had a major role in the final compositional result. The GSR signals evolve slowly over time which in initial tests proved to lack more dynamic changes. To address these limitations specific fragments of the piece were written to induce different stress levels to the soloists.

6.2 Out of Time: Physiologically Informed Soundtrack to the Film Out of Tune

Out of Tune is a short film by director and writer Fran Apprich. This work depicts women's exploitation in a world in which girls want to be women. The story is set in a strip club in reference to Jean-Luke Goddard's *Vivre sa vie*. The collusion of a girl backstage with a stripper triggers an unexpected clash of personalities and generations. The music for this film explores further this idea of exploitation by measuring the emotional responses of the actress during the main stripping scene and analysing such measurements for their later use as a compositional framework for the whole soundtrack. The EKG and GSR modules of BioTools were used to measure, record and plot the actress' stress levels during rehearsals and shooting. The recorded data from the different takes was averaged to find consistent curves in her emotional state changes during acting. As well as the overall plotted curve, we found spikes at different points actions in her stress levels (i.e. the increase in stress seconds before stripping and slow relaxation afterwards as she managed this stress). As she played the role of the stripper, subtle changes on her emotional states where identified relating to the different elements of the performance (i.e. dancing dressed, stripping, dancing naked afterwards). The soundtrack is composed almost exclusively for an out of tune piano; the overall emotional curve measured by the GSR module is used to dictate the form and structure of the piece. Changes in the heart rate variability were found to be associated to more specific actions and were used to organise dynamics, articulations and harmony. This project was (in a sense) more restricted, as the outcome couldn't be just a personal musical expression or aesthetic statement, but it had to work within the film's context. Another restriction imposed by this fixed medium was the impossibility to use biosignals as a real-time performance tool. The physiological information on this project was used to layout more traditional musical parameters. For the final result, there is no direct sound generation or manipulation by the biosignals, but rather the recorded data serves as a structural framework for the compositional process. This data was averaged between the different takes and then rendered into form, harmony and rhythmic structures for the composition of the piece, some other elements of the composition as melodic outline and style references are not related to the physiological information recorded from the actress, but rather from the specific requirements of the film's narrative.

6.3 Carne

Carne is an interactive piece for two EMG sensors. It was composed as part of the activities carried on by group 8 [2] on the eNTERFACE summer workshops '07. It was premiered at the Boğaziçi University Music Club on August 8 2007. The piece is an audiovisual collaboration between Miguel Angel Ortiz Pérez (interface and sounds) and Hanna Drayson (visuals). Fig. 7. shows the performer at the premiere.

Carne is loosely inspired by Terry Bison's 1991 short story *They're made out of meat*[12]. The concept behind Carne is based on a very simplistic view of

Fig. 7. Premiere performance of *Carne*

muscle activity as the friction between slices of meat. Taking this idea further, we could say that all types of arms movement from minimal arm gestures up to the highly complex synchronised movements of fingers during musical instrument performance, are simple variations of this meat grinding activity.

The sounds in this piece, evolve inside a continuum from imaginary muscle sounds to pre-recorded sounds of western bowed string instruments, while always keeping focus on friction as a unifying metaphor.

The hardware implementation of *Carne* consists of 2 EMG sensor bands from Biocontrol Systems[3] connected to an Arduino BT board. These hardware components interact with a computer running EyesWeb software and a custom built patch for data acquisition. Analysed data is then transferred in real-time through OSC protocol to a second computer running a slightly hacked version of the CataRT[8] application by Diemo Schwartz. Within this patch, a large database of samples are loaded, analysed and organised using psychoacoustic descriptors. The resulting sound units are laid on a two dimensional descriptor space where the X axis represents noissines and the Y axis represents pitch. The EMG signals from each arm controls movement on one of these axes. The values from the EMG are dynamically scaled throughout the duration of the piece, allowing the performer to explore cluster areas of the sound corpus and giving a sense of structure and evolution to the piece.

7   Conclusions

We have described a new set of tools, BioTools, which are currently being created for rapid development of musical applications using physiological sensors. The new hardware sensors enable flexible placement of the sensors anywhere on the body and measurement of any type of physiological signal. The initial software tools are working on the Max/MSP platform because of its widespread use by composers and performers. However, as pointed out previously, time coding different data streams in Max/MSP for analysis purposes is a complex and time consuming process and due to this we have also begun to implement BioTools on the EyesWeb platform, Additionally, we are looking at implementing the modules on other programs such as PD, Anvil, and Chuck to offer more flexibility. The use of BioTools has made the process of creating a piece, Díamair, for Integral Music Control as well as a piece, Out of Time using pre-recorded physiological signals an exercise in composition not electrical engineering.

Our current work is increasingly moving towards musical creation and performance and promoting the use of BioTools amongst other artists. We believe the toolkit provides a stable foundation for incorporating biosignals to musical practice for a wider community than previously available.

References

1. Anonymous.: Book of Leinster, Section 1 Folio 12b 40, `http://www.ucc.ie/celt/published/G800011A/index.html`
2. Benovoy, M., Brouse, A., Corcoran, T., Drayson, H., Erkut, C., Filatriau, J.-J., Frisson, C., Gundogdu, U., Knapp, B., Lehembre, R., Muhl, C., Perez, M., Sayin, A., Soleymani, M., Tahiroglu, K.: Audiovisual content generation controlled by physiological signals for clinical and artistic applications. In: Proc. of the 3rd summer workshop on Multimodal Interfaces (eNTERFACE 2007), Istanbul, Turkey (2007)
3. `http://www.biocontrol.com/`
4. Bowler, I., Purvis, A., Manning, P., Bailey, N.: On mapping N articulation onto M synthesiser-control parameters. In: Proc. Int. Computer Music Conf. (ICMC 1990), Glasgow, Scotland (1990)
5. Camurri, A., et al.: The Premio Paganini project: a multimodal gesture-based approach for explaining emotional processes in music performance. In: Proceedings of The 7th International Workshop on Gesture in Human-Computer Interaction and Simulation 2007, Lisbon, Portugal, May 23-25 (2007)
6. `http://www.arduino.cc/`
7. `http://www.gyoza.com/ate/atau/html/index.html?305,185`
8. `http://imtr.ircam.fr/index.php/CataRT`
9. `http://www.infomus.dist.unige.it/eywindex.html`
10. `http://www.lovely.com/titles/lp1014.html`
11. `http://infusionsystems.com/catalog/index.php/`
12. `http://www.terrybisson.com/meat.html`
13. Jensenius, A.R., Gody, R., Wanderley, M.M.: Developing Tools for Studying Musical Gestures within the MAX/MSP/JITTER Environment. In: Proc. of the 2005 International Computer Music Conference (ICMC 2005), Barcelona, Spain (2005)
14. Knapp, R.B., Cook, P.R.: Creating a Network of Integral Music Controllers. In: Proceedings of the New Interfaces for Musical Expression (NIME) Conference, IRCAM, Paris, France, June 5-7 (2006)
15. Knapp, R.B., Cook, P.R.: The Integral Music Controller: Introducing a Direct Emotional Interface to Gestural Control of Sound Synthesis. In: Proceedings of the International Computer Music Conference (ICMC), Barcelona, Spain, September 4-9 (2005)

16. Knapp, R.B., Lusted, H.S.: A Bioelectric Controller for Computer Music Applications. Computer Music Journal 14(1), 42–47 (1990)
17. Knapp, R.B., Lusted, H.S.: Designing a Biocontrol Interface for Commercial and Consumer Mobile Applications: Effective Control within Ergonomic and Usability Constraints. In: Proceedings of the 11th International Conference on Human Computer Interaction, Las Vegas, NV, July 22-27 (2005)
18. Lee, C.K., Yoo, S.K., Park, Y.J., Kim, N.H., Jeong, K.S., Lee, B.C.: Using Neural Network to Recognize Human Emotions from Heart Rate Variability and Skin Resistance. In: Proceedings of the 2005 IEEE Engineering in Medicine and Biology 27th Annual Conference, Shanghai, China, September 1-4 (2005)
19. Lee, M., Wessel, D.: Connectionist models for real-time control of synthesis and compositional algorithms. In: Proceedings of the International Computer Music Conference, San Jose, USA (1992)
20. Lusted, H.S., Knapp, R.B.: Controlling Computers with Neural Signals. Scientific American (October 1996)
21. Nagashima, Y.: Interactive multi-media performance with bio-sensing and bio-feedback. In: Proceedings of the New Interfaces for Musical Expression Conference, Montreal, QC, Canada, May 22-24 (2003)
22. Ortiz Pérez, M.A., Knapp, R.B., Alcorn, M.: Díamair: Composing for Choir and Integral Music Controller. In: Proceedings of the New Interfaces for Musical Expression 2007 Conference, New York, NY, June 7-9 (2007)
23. Rose, F.: Introduction to the Pitch Organization of French Spectral Music. Perspectives of New Music 34(2), 6–39 (1996)
24. Wanderley, M.M.: Mapping Strategies in Real-time Computer Music. Organised Sound 7(2) (August 2002)
25. Warner, D.: Notes from the timbre space. Perspectives of New Music 21(1/2), 15–22, (Autumn, 1982 - Summer, 1983)

Focus-Plus-Context Audio Interaction Design

David Gerhard*, Brett Park, and Jarrod Ellis

Department of Computer Science
*Associate, Department of Music
University of Regina
Regina, SK CANADA S4S 0A2
{gerhard,park111b,ellisjja}@cs.uregina.ca
http://armadilo.cs.uregina.ca

Abstract. We present an audio browsing and editing paradigm that incorporates the "focus plus context" visual interaction metaphor. A traditional waveform is displayed in full, and an area of focus is dynamically re-calculated to provide maximum detail in-focus and minimum detail in-context. The interaction metaphor also simultaneously re-scales a frequency-domain display, with increased detail available in both time and frequency domains by means of sub-sampling and window overlap. Various methods for selecting focus, identifying focus, and transitioning between the focus and context display areas are presented, and advantages for typical audio interaction applications are discussed. A collection of these ideas has been implemented within an open-source audio editing environment, and a discussion of this implementation and the related issues is presented.

Keywords: Human Centered Computing, Audio Interaction, Interface Design, Focus-Plus-Context.

1   Introduction

The standard interaction metaphor for editing digital audio presents a waveform which can be resized to any scale, from a single sample or sample-per-pixel representation to a display of the full waveform. Users interacting with such an interface may find that, depending on the work being performed on the waveform, a number of different scales are appropriate. For example, when correcting localized recording errors such as clicks and pops from a vinyl recording, the user may need to zoom in to the sample level; however, when mixing multiple parts, duplicating, or re-recording sections, a larger scale may be required. Regardless of the working scale, for anything longer than a single note or acoustic event, the user loses the *context* of the work being done when zooming in to a reasonably workable resolution. This is closely related to the problem of interactively navigating large information spaces in a limited context.

Subsequently, most audio interaction software separates the global view of the raw waveform from its local view or focused portion. This involves multiple separate windows or "panes" to represent a single track of audio data, one for

R. Kronland-Martinet, S. Ystad, and K. Jensen (Eds.): CMMR 2007, LNCS 4969, pp. 453–477, 2008.
© Springer-Verlag Berlin Heidelberg 2008

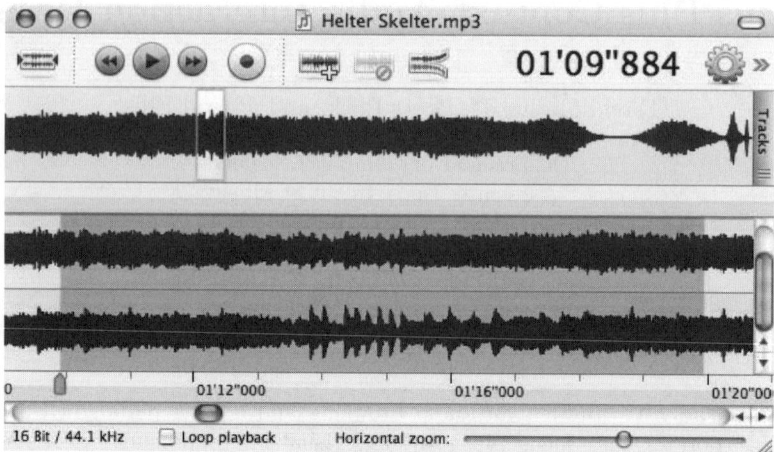

Fig. 1. Audio interaction window in *Amadeus*. A context pane is available, but it is outside of the user's locus of attention, and presented at a different scale with no scale markings.

the local work site and one for the context or overview. This multiple-window metaphor is used in many other applications, and has been critiqued [2], [5]. Perhaps more problematic in the audio interaction realm is the loss of context when working with multiple tracks of audio simultaneously. Most current audio interface programs require the view to be focused at a consistent point across all tracks, effectively locking all tracks together and forcing a user to zoom out to a wider context to jump from one point to another in the project. Several improvements have been made to facilitate this process, including bookmarks, labels, hot-key zooming and complex navigation controls. Some programs even allow a user to be localized at a different point in multiple tracks, but these adaptations are primarily attempts to mitigate the difficulties of working in multiple focus levels in the same document. The user has to mentally assimilate these time-based domains, creating and maintaining a large *mental model* of the entire project at high cognitive expense. This can be particularly difficult when a project contains several portions that are acoustically similar, as is the case when mastering music with a repeating verse-plus-chorus structure. A user may think she is working on chorus 1 when she is in fact working on chorus 3, since the waveform visualization of both choruses look similar. There is no indication in the user's *Locus of attention*[6] of the overall location of the work-point in the wider piece.

Figure 1 shows an audio interface window from the program *Amadeus*[1], typical of such interfaces. There are two panes showing audio information. The top pane shows the complete context of the audio clip, while the bottom pane shows the focused work area. There is a rectangular selection box in the context pane

---

[1] `http://www.hairersoft.com/Amadeus.html`

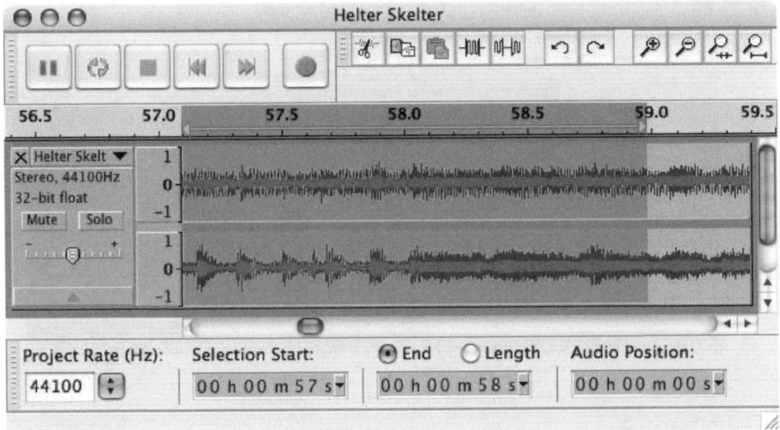

Fig. 2. Audio interaction window in *Audacity*. No context window is available, and the user must create a complete mental model based only on the relative time and duration shown on the display.

that both selects and indicates the area of the focus pane. The scroll bar at the bottom of the window indicates, in a minimal way, the overall location and context of the focus window. The "Horizontal zoom" slider is a second way to change the amount of audio data in the focus window. Complete information about the context of the focused area is not presented, and a user must look at three separate interface elements to get a complete picture. Although the context is presented, it is not in the user's locus of attention and the user must either consult the context pane (thus leaving the focus pane) or maintain a mental model (at cognitive cost).

Figure 2 shows an audio interface window from the program *Audacity*[2], a popular open source cross platform audio editor which presents similar problems. Audacity presents only one audio window to the user, offering no visual context. The location of the focus window in the larger sound file is displayed numerically both in a ruler-bar at the top of the window and in a series of text boxes at the bottom of the window. The user must maintain a mental model of the local context of the part they are working on.

Figure 3 shows a spectrum window from *Amadeus*. In this case, any familiarity the user might have acquired interacting with the time-window is lost since the frequency window is significantly different. The contextual information is gone, replaced with a localized and aligned version of the time waveform.

Context is critical in audio editing and manipulation. While most of the existing audio editing software attempts to inform the user of the overall context using cues such as numerical ranges or context windows, it remains cognitively expensive to maintain a mental model of the piece being viewed.

---

[2] http://audacity.sourceforge.net/

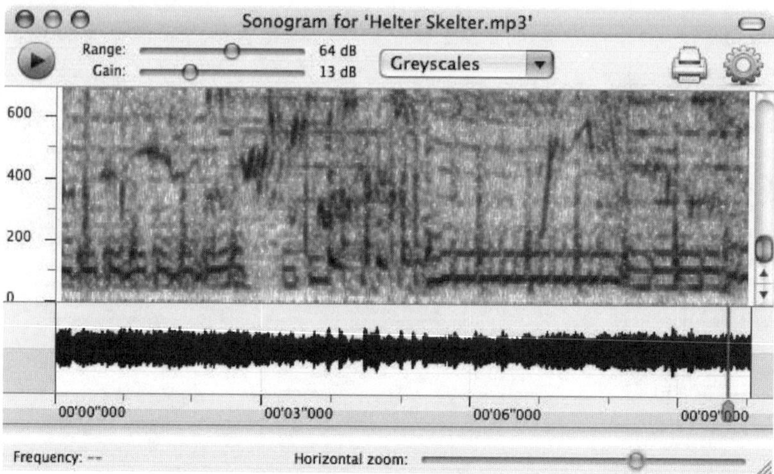

Fig. 3. Spectrogram display in *Amadeus*. There is no context pane, as the waveform displayed is aligned with the spectrogram.

1.1   The Detail-In-Context Problem

Alan Keahey[3] describes the detail-in-context problem thus:

> "How can we effectively utilize the additional space made available by any nonlinear magnification transformation to enhance the visualization of the data or objects located within that space?"

Physical high-resolution presentations of information, such as printed photographs or line drawings, allow the user to examine an area of interest in more detail by looking closely or even magnifying the area with a lens. Traditional film photographers have decried a lack of low-level detail in digital print images, since film resolution theoretically goes to the level of granularity in the film itself. There is an inherent multiresolution aspect to these physical presentations, but when information is presented digitally, the ability to zoom in to an area of interest is affected. On-screen, view magnification is performed digitally and the limitations of magnification are shifted to the limits of the information contained within the displayed data itself. The drawback of this is that the *context* of the magnification is also removed.

When a viewer uses a magnifying lens to look at an area of a photograph, the entire photograph is still within the viewer's perception. When a user zooms in to a digital image, the context is immediately lost. The user does not know which portion of an image is being considered, unless they were present when the zoom took place, and even then the user must maintain, at cognitive expense, a mental model of the entire data space and the context of the area being considered. Most data interfaces that support zooming also present a "context" or overview as a second display, but since this information is not presented in the user's locus of attention, the user may not incorporate this information into their mental model. Further, an additional window for context adds to "palette clutter," taking screen-space away from the primary data.

A solution to this problem is the non-liner magnification transform, which places a digital "lens" over the data, allowing the user to zoom in on one area while maintaining the overall context. "Focus plus context" (FPC) is one of many terms used to describe such zoomable display systems employing continuous non-linear magnification transformations [4], [8], [9]. Terms such as detail-in-context, polyfocal projection, fisheye [7] and distortion-oriented presentation have also been used.

FPC displays present both a focus area and the wider context in the same window. The user does not have to switch between looking at different panes, nor does she need to maintain a mental model of the context. In FPC displays, the metaphor of the magnifying glass is taken several steps beyond the isolated bounds of the focal lens. Nonlinear transformations provide varying levels of detail in the surrounding context, providing more focused detail for visually perceptive purposes. Using the multi-window approach in audio display analysis, the user must judge the relative position of the focal region using limited visual cues in the global context. Using an FPC display would eliminate the need for this difficult perceptive judgment.

FPC versus magnification overlays. There are three ways to display FPC information. The first way is to create a focal area and contract the contextual area in order to make room for the focal area. This method makes sure that all of the context information is displayed. As a side effect, it is often harder to code and slower to display as the context information needs to be altered whenever the focal point is moved.

The second way to create a focal area is to have the focal area cover up some of the context area. This allows for quicker and more efficient code to be written as the context area does not have to be recalculated. A good example of this method is the magnifying glass option in Apple's Aperture[3] program.

The third way to create a focal area is to split the context area and shift each side away from the focus area, leaving sufficient room between the two context areas. The dock on the Mac OSX[4] (see Figure 4) is a good example of this. As a focal point is selected, the context information is moved outward in order to compensate for the larger focal point.

1.2   Current Focus-Plus-Context Applications

Aside from dock magnification in Mac OS X, there are very few mainstream examples of FPC applications. Zoomable user interfaces (ZUIs) are an attempt to provide a context-specific view of larger data spaces by allowing the user to zoom in on a subspace of a display. The most common example of a ZUI is the Virtual Desktop metaphor, where each desktop is a subset of a larger set of

---

[3] `www.apple.com/aperture`
[4] `http://www.apple.com`

Fig. 4. Dock magnification in Macintosh OS X

desktops, shown in a contextualized window. While this does constitute an FPC display, it shares the same problem of other systems, in that the context for the focus is not within the user's locus of attention and instead is presented as a second, separate view of the full context, often requiring a command to make the virtual desktop set visible. This means that the user must maintain a mental model of the complete virtual desktop context in order to know which desktop to use at what time.

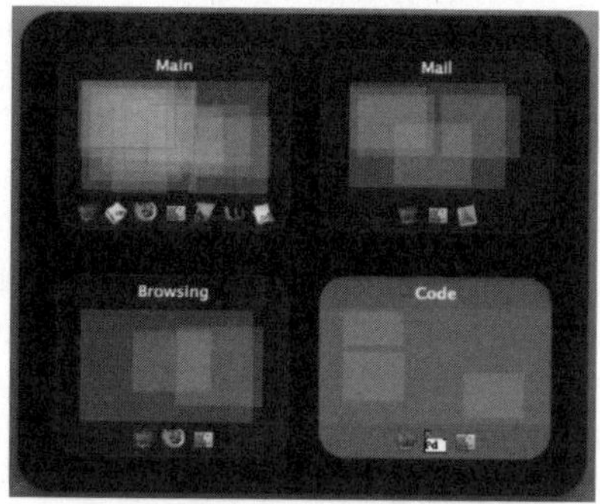

Fig. 5. An example of the virtual desktop metaphor overlayed on top of a normal desktop display. The context is brought into view with a hotkey combination.

A classic example of a "stronger" version of a zoomable user interface is the *Pad++* interface[1] developed by the University of Maryland Computer Science department, but no longer actively being worked upon. Pad++ is like a virtual desktop environment, but it allows for multiple views and varying scales. The idea behind Pad++ is to provide the user with the ability to navigate large amounts of data using an FPC transformation method for semantic magnification. Some issues with Pad++, mentioned by the authors, are a lack of customization for sizes of objects (or nodes) with no location constraints and no animation between magnified transitions. Transitions are immediate and abrupt, giving no visual cues to the user as to what object has been magnified. One benefit of Pad++ is its ability to use multiple foci on the same data.

Persons with visual disabilities have varying specific needs when it comes to presenting data at readable resolutions. Many current operating systems provide an accessibility feature which allows the user's display to be zoomed in to varying levels of magnification. The focus window is centered on the mouse, and moves around the (virtual) user interface with the mouse movements. The advantage is that the entire display is enlarged by the same amount (rather that only increasing font size, for example), however, there is no context presented, and the user must maintain a mental model of the underlying environment.

More and more, web browsers and other traditional applications are being offered on mobile devices with very small screens. Previous attempts at rendering web content on small screens has been most successful with so-called "mobile content," alternative versions of websites designed for smaller screens. There are two main difficulties with this implementation: First, the familiarity that a user develops with the normal version of a website is defeated by these smaller versions, making them difficult to navigate; and second, websites without these minimalist versions are rendered poorly by the mobile browsers. New browsers are being developed, including Apple's mobile Safari and Microsoft's Deepfish, which render a website as if it were on a large screen and allow the user to scroll around within a zoomed sub-view of the full rendered page. Once again, a lack of context requires the user to maintain a mental model of the page as they are maneuvering around within it. New interface paradigms such as multi-touch may reduce the cognitive load associated with non-contextualized focus applications, but this remains to be studied.

1.3   Pseudo-non-linear and Multi-level Mappings

The computational cost of nonlinear transformations has been prohibitive to implementing true FPC displays in the past, and while modern systems provide sufficient computational overhead, The need to dedicate significant processing power to implementing such transforms continues to be a barrier to mainstream usage. The transitions from focus to context do not have to be non-linear, however. With piece-wise discrete interfaces such as menus and icon displays, each element can be linearly scaled to a degree relating to the distance from the center of the focus, making an apparent non-linear zoom. This is the technique employed by dock magnification in Mac OS X described above, and it has been used in other contexts as well. Figure 6 shows an example of "text zooming," where a large textual hierarchy, for example a menu or a document, can be navigated with the use of FPC magnification. Each menu item or word is a discrete object in the contextual space, and can be zoomed using the font size to indicate distance from the focus.

While discrete elements can be zoomed with little computational cost, continuous information such as linear time audio data must be handled differently. Each pixel in the context image can be expanded into many pixels in the focus area, up to the maximal data resolution. Further, continuous data that does not have a natural analog must have overt indicators to describe the amount of focus and the type of transition between the focus window and the context. Because of this, a simple zoom of the data point is not possible—instead, a re-interpolation must be used to draw the data at higher resolutions in the focus window. Three methods of this re-interpolation are: multiple zoomed layers; linear interpolation; and non-linear transformation.

Fig. 6. Text zooming for large lists

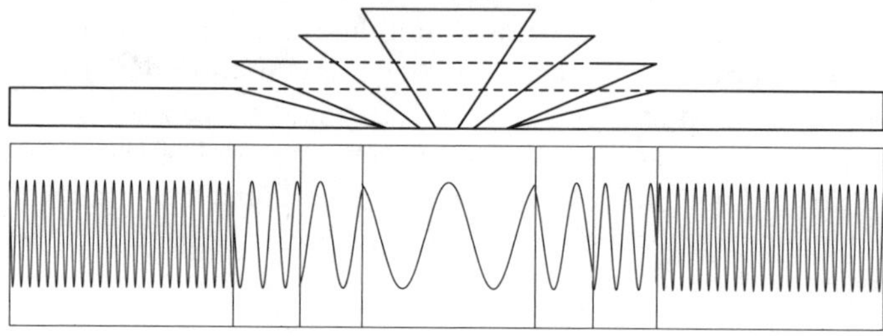

Fig. 7. One-dimensional FPC display using multiple zoomed layers

Multiple zoomed layers. Because the metaphor of discrete elements is prevalent in modern FPC implementations, it makes sense to begin with a translation of discrete elements into the continuous arena. The "multiple zoomed layers" approach consists of defining a focus region and constructing a set of concentric levels between the focus region and the underlying context (Figure 7). Each level is at a resolution between that of the focus and the context.

Linear transformation. The next obvious transition is to draw a straight line from the focus area to the context area, and linearly transform the scale function across this line (Figure 8). This implementation is more complex, requiring a linear interpolation across a significant amount of data, but computationally this will add only minimal additional burden. The result is a smooth transition and a more natural localized structure for the focus window.

Non-linear transformation. The most flexible but also most complex transform is to present a generalized nonlinear transition between the focus and the context area. In general, this means a single continuous function across the entire context space, but since the focus window display will need to be re-calculated at each shift of its location, it makes more sense to re-calculate only on the portion that is different from the initially calculated contextual backdrop. An example of a spherical transition is presented in Figure 9.

As noted earlier, in an FPC display, the context can either be hidden, contracted, or spread out to make room for the data in the focus window. The

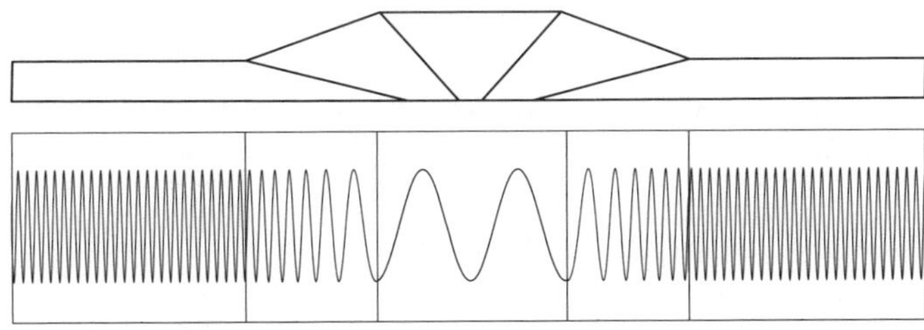

Fig. 8. One-dimensional FPC display using linear transformation

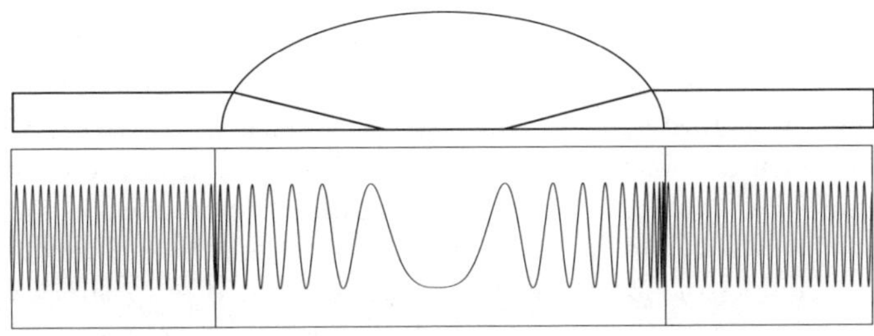

Fig. 9. One-dimensional FPC display using a spherical non-linear transformation

contraction method can be seen in the above diagrams. In each case, when the focus area is enlarged, the context area is reduced by a proportional amount to make room for the focus area.

1.4   Compressed Context Display

One of the fundamental issues inherent in the use of an FPC audio editing application is that the waveform in the context area for long tracks is compresses and lacks detail. When displaying an audio track longer than a few minutes, the detail of the waveform in the context area becomes difficult to see as each pixel represents a increasingly large time interval. This causes the waveform to look uniform in most places and only audio events that happen over several pixels (a large period of time) can be seen. This issue is caused for two reasons; the whole track must be shown for context, and the width of the computer screen is finite. There are two possible solutions to this problem, which involve modifications to the way the context is displayed.

More and more, display devices are becoming available with higher resolutions than the standard 72 dpi of a workstation monitor. A first solution to the compressed context problem would be the use of such higher resolution displays. With higher resolution displays, the context area will contain more detail even if it is compressed, and the user will be more able to discern events of interest. A second solution would be to display the context area in such a way that it is less compressed. There are several alternatives for this method, including multi-line displays and multiple monitors. We propose a solution which involves drawing the context in a second dimension orthogonal to the focus area. This method, which we call "Horizontal Focus plus Vertical Context" is presented as future work in Section 5.1.

2   Focus and Context in Audio

There are a number of standard interaction paradigms for working with audio, many of which would benefit from an FPC interface of some form. We present a discussion of some of the inherent difficulties in such implementations, as well as some resolutions to these difficulties.

2.1   Audio Interfaces and Typical Tasks

As seen earlier in Figure 1, the typical audio interface displays a waveform at a single scale, with a vertical bar indicating the "play head" corresponding to the next sound that would be heard if the "play" button were clicked. Other standard interface elements include playback and selection controls. Users are able to select chunks of audio by indicating start and stop times or samples, or by dragging in the audio display window. Global track information is often presented in the form of muting, stereo panning and local sound characteristics. It is important to recognize that these indicators and track-level features are a holdover from the days of solid-state mixing boards, where each channel in the board corresponds to an audio input, with muting, soloing, trim, pan and other controls in a vertical stripe up the board for each channel.

The audio interaction interfaces are designed to facilitate common tasks relating to recorded audio. Some of these tasks will be discussed here, along with how these tasks could be made easier with FPC displays.

Splitting a large file. One of the more common audio tasks performed by the average user is transferring audio media from one format to another, usually from a physical audio format such as tape or vinyl to a digital format. The typical sequence for such a transfer is to attach the physical media player to the computer, start the media playing at normal speed and start recording, then walk away for half an hour. The nature of this task means that the transfer is real-time, and no time saving is available. Vinyl and Tape albums are often divided into tracks, and if these tracks are separated with silence, then some automated track segmentation can be done. This process can be easily frustrated by recording noise and live or continuous albums with no silence between tracks.

The standard metaphor for splitting a large file into smaller tracks is to look at the full file, try to see where natural track splits might have occurred (by finding small low-energy areas in the waveform), zooming in to these areas, splitting the track, and zooming out to find the next one. The difficulties in this method are numerous:

- not every low-energy area is a track break;
- not every track break is low-energy;

- track breaks are best made at the sample level;
- track breaks should incorporate fading out of the new track ending and fading into the new track beginning.

Further, once a track break is made, the user must zoom out to the complete context and start to search for the next track break.

FPC displays can help this process in many ways. When a user focuses on an area that they suspect is a track break, they can see immediately if it is a candidate or not, without having to zoom in. A medium-level context can be selected to more easily show the potential track breaks, and false positives can be more easily discarded without having to zoom in to verify. The user can manipulate the focus window until it corresponds with the desired fade in and fade out, and then execute a single command instead of selecting a break point and creating a fade-out and a fade-in.

Soundtrack composition. When creating a soundtrack for a movie, television show or video, there are three components that are typically employed: ambience, foley and effects. Ambience is the underlying noise of the surroundings, such as street noise, office noise, or nature noise, depending on the surroundings in the video. Foley is the addition of sound samples which correspond to actions by actors or other objects in the scene. A classic example of foley is footsteps added to a scene after it has been shot. Foley is used because it is often very difficult to record sound events live, especially in wide shots. Foley is typically recorded in a studio as the video is played. Effects are similar to foley, but are not recorded live and are often taken from existing effects libraries, such as honking horns and telephone rings.

Composing a soundtrack usually consists of interacting with multiple tracks simultaneously. FPC displays would allow a user to accurately manipulate the location of a foley sound within the context of the entire soundtrack without having to zoom in and out. Manipulating the location of a series of footsteps would be considerably easier. Further, a more natural correspondence between the audio and video representations can be maintained if the user does not have to continually zoom in and out to alter the location of an effect.

Filtering and processing. Filtering and effects processing are common sound manipulation activities. Here, manipulations are applied to the entire file or to larger chunks of the piece being considered. Reverb, compression and equalization are examples of this type of task. In existing systems, the typical procedure is to apply the filter to a small subset of the sound file (often called a preview) to verify that the filter parameters are appropriate, then apply the filter to the entire piece. Application of a filter to a large sound file can take time, and normally the only feedback is a progress bar. Once the filtering is done, information is sometimes presented to the user to indicate whether there were any problems with the filtering, but the user usually must listen to the entire work to verify that the desired acoustic effect was achieved.

An FPC display can help in this instance as well, to give an indication of the progress of the application of a filter. The full context of the file is displayed, and as the filter is applied to each local section, a focus window is traced across the file showing the application of the filter and the result, and the user can identify problems as they arise, or stop the filter if there is a problem. Traditional displays can follow along with the progress of the filter, but it is difficult and cognitively expensive to integrate the progress of the filter into a the context of the full file.

Simple playback. Every sound editor is also a sound player, and in traditional interfaces the user has the option of watching the playhead slowly traverse the entire file or watching the zoomed-in waveform pass under a stationary playhead. FPC displays can enhance this process in much the same way as the following of filter progress described above. By following a focus window as it traverses an overall context, the user can see both what is happing at a low level and where the sounds are occurring at a higher level. This combines the two interface options for playback: the playhead remains in the center of the focus window, and the audio moves past it, while at the same time the focus window itself moves along the audio track, following the playback and displaying the audio which is about to be played and which has just been played.

Breathers and other vocal editing. One of the classic vocal editing problems is the removal of "breathers," or audible inhalations just before a sung or played musical phrase. Although the presence of breathers can be stylistically desirable (for example, in the piano recordings of Glen Gould, where Gould can be heard quietly humming along as he plays), many professional studios do what they can to remove breathers. The typical procedure is to examine the onset of each phrase in the vocal (or instrumental) line, detect breathers by observation of the waveform, or more typically the spectrogram, and then delete or filter out the breath noise using a fade in, noise removal or other technique depending on the surrounding noise.

FPC techniques can make this process easier and more accurate by enhancing the spectral context of the breather, thereby confirming that the sound to be removed is the desired target. As before, finding events of interest within the timeline can be facilitated with the incorporation of FPC methods, which allow a user to examine the low level details of the editing without losing the context.

Regardless of the task, there are two classic forms of information that are used to analyze and interact with audio: the time waveform and the spectrum. Several methods exist for converting from the time domain to the frequency domain, the most popular of which continues to be the Fourier transform. In the following sections, we will discuss FPC display issues surrounding both time-domain and frequency-domain displays.

3   Zooming Issues

In the early days of focus-plus-context research, investigators employed tricks to make a two-dimensional visual area appear to be warped in 3-D space. Computing power was at a premium, so simple graphical transformations were employed to simulate the expansion of an area of focus. It might be tempting to look back on these methods and expect that with the rise of dedicated 3-D graphics processing units (GPUs), all one needs to do is map the visual area onto a 3-D surface and stretch the surface to provide a closer view of one area. The problem with this is that in order to provide sufficient focus detail, the surface would have to be stretched by a large proportion, leading to distorted contextual information. Orthogonal 3-D graphics views are typically optimized for a high degree of detail in the foreground with a less-detailed background, or in some cases a static image as a background. Rarely are the background and foreground connected in the way that an FPC display would require.

In audio applications, there are two primary displays: the time waveform and the spectrogram. Both displays can benefit from FPC integration, and the following sections will describe the theoretical basis for zooming in time and in frequency.

3.1   Time Zooming

The time display of the waveform is perhaps the most prevalent audio display, being found in oscilloscopes and used in many movies and TV shows when it is required to show that someone is interacting with audio. There are typically two classical implementations of time waveform presentation, depending on the viewing range. When viewing large sections of audio, each pixel on the screen represents a range of time and the average energy in the waveform at that time. For smaller ranges, each pixel represents the waveform value at that time, either interpolated or sub-sampled to fill the range.

The difficulty with perceiving a time waveform in isolation is that there are no perceptual cues to indicate the current scale. When viewing information that has familiar visual characteristics, such as a photograph, humans achieve a sense of scale by making use of perspective and falling back on familiar metaphors. We are familiar with, for example, the average size of a person, so when a visual field is ambiguous (as in an architectural model, for example) person-shaped objects are often added to give a sense of scale. If a person is very familiar with audio processing and has looked at many waveforms, they may be able to pick up cues as to the scale of the waveform, for example, if they know they are looking at music and they know the approximate tempo, they can infer the scale from the distance between prominent peaks. This method and other "landmark finding" methods are not reliable, however, because landmarks in audio waveforms are typically ambiguous and can be very difficult to interpret. Tempo doubling errors are common, for example, because music often has sub-beats between the primary peaks. Speech is another interaction area where landmarks can be used to give a sense of scale, since humans tend to speak at a rate of around 4 syllables per second. Again, this method proves useful only when a user has considerable experience on which to draw.

Applying FPC to a time waveform can give a sense of scale, since the entire waveform is present and can be viewed at once. The user must still be aware of the time duration of the sample in order to disambiguate the display, but this is easier than maintaining a complete mental model of the waveform itself. The amount of zoom utilized in such an application must also be indicated, since the user may make scale errors if the amount of zoom is unknown. There are a number of ways to indicate the amount of scale, including the size and slope of the transition from context to focus, the thickness of the waveform trace itself, or an external iconic or numeric scale display. Regardless, the difficulties with scale perception in audio must be considered when designing such interfaces.

3.2   Frequency Zooming

The frequency display of an audio file normally corresponds to the short-time Fourier transform (STFT) of the waveform, although other techniques are employed for specific purposes. The STFT is calculated by breaking the waveform into overlapping fixed-size windows and calculating the spectrum of each window. The display is typically collocated in time with the waveform itself, to make corresponding analysis easier. STFTs and other spectral transforms suffer from an uncertainty principle: the more accurately you measure the frequency of a signal, the less accurately you can know the time at which that frequency occurred. This is evident in two extremes: If the STFT window is taken to be the entire length of the waveform, the complete frequency information can be calculated but it corresponds only to the entire waveform and not to any specific part within it. Similarly, the smallest unit of time in a waveform is the sample, corresponding to a single measure of air pressure. In itself, a sample has no frequency information but is located as accurately as possible in time.

As a consequence of this spectral uncertainty, audio interfaces typically allow a number of parameters to be manipulated when displaying the spectrogram. If the user is more interested in time-accuracy of the spectrogram, a compactly-supported window is employed. If frequency-accuracy is demanded, a larger window is used. Wavelets and other multi-resolution techniques have been employed to allow better time-resolution at higher frequencies, but low frequencies cannot be extracted using a compactly-supported window. Despite the problems, the STFT remains the frequency analysis method of choice because it represents frequency information visually in a way that people can learn to interpret.

The spectrogram representation is fundamentally an image, and as such, it is reasonable to expect that focus-plus-context zooming paradigms designed for images would also be appropriate for spectrograms. This is not the case for two reasons. The first is that image zooming metaphors assume that the image is available at full resolution, and the context area is created by down-sampling the image. Spectrogram data is fundamentally different at different frequency and time resolutions, so it is not sufficient to simply calculate the best possible spectrogram and zoom in. As has been stated, there is no "full resolution" spectrogram, and zooming must incorporate re-calculation. The second reason is related to the difficulty of zooming in the time waveform. General images often have landmarks or contextual information that provide a hint of the scale at which it is being viewed. Spectrograms have no such cues, and two different spectra can look the same when viewed at different resolutions if they are harmonically related. For these reasons, a re-calculating metaphor is required.

3.3   Spectrogram Re-calculation

It is worthwhile to re-visit the classic formulation of the short-time Fourier transform to see where our modifications take place. Equation 1 shows the discrete STFT.

$$X(m,\omega) = \sum_{n=-\infty}^{\infty} x[n]w[n-m]e^{-j\omega n} \tag{1}$$

The windowing function $w[\cdot]$ is a function which establishes a finite range for the window, and tapers to zero at both ends of the range to reduce discontinuities. Typical windowing functions include the Hanning, Parzen, and Triangular windows. The windowing function provides time-localization to the STFT, and windows are overlapped to compensate for the discarded information in the tapering of the windowing function. The *length* (*support*) of the window dictates the minimum frequency that can be represented; the *sampling frequency* f_s dictates the maximum frequency, and the relationship between the amount of *overlap* and the window size determines the time-resolution of the resulting spectrogram image. It should be noted that no additional information is presented when the overlap is greater than what is required to compensate for the tapering.

There are three inter-related parameters, then, in the construction of a spectrogram based on the STFT: The window length, the sampling frequency, and the overlap. If an audio waveform is sampled at 44,100 Hz (the standard CD sampling rate), and a 1024-sample window is used in the STFT, the longest sinusoid that can be detected is 1024 samples which is equivalent to 0.023 seconds or 43 Hz. The shortest sinusoid that can be detected is half the sampling frequency, in this case 22,050 Hz.

The key to frequency zooming is in adjusting the time and frequency bounds of the spectrogram. A full spectrogram can be calculated with a reasonable balance between time and frequency to create the background context. A zoomed window over top of the spectrum provides detail. The three parameters over which we have control can manipulated to alter the frequency and time bounds of the resulting spectrogram.

Time bounds. The upper and lower time bounds can be manipulated by adjusting the beginning and ending of the waveform to be analyzed. In order to fill the pixel range, the window size and the window overlap can both be manipulated. As we will see, the window size has an effect on the frequency bounds, so it cannot be considered an independent variable in this case.

Upper frequency bound. Since the maximum frequency that can be displayed is dependent on the sampling frequency of the signal, we can reduce the sampling frequency in order to bring down the upper frequency bound. Down-sampling can be achieved by interpolating between the waveform samples and re-sampling at a lower sampling frequency. Initially, it might seem like this would reduce the amount of information available to the viewer, and while this is strictly the case, it is necessary to keep in mind that the goal of this transformation is only to increase the viewing resolution for a small portion of the frequency display, and contextualizing this focused portion with the complete spectrum.

Lower frequency bound. Since the minimum frequency that can be displayed is dependent on the window size, we would like to re-sample *within* the window in order to modify the displayed frequency. A window size could be selected which corresponds directly to the minimum frequency desired, and this window would then be up-sampled (through the same interpolation and re-sampling procedure discussed above) to make a window of standard size (for example 1024 samples). The difficulty with this method is that in modifying the window size, the calculation of the entire spectrum is altered, rather than just the low frequency bound. In this case, the easiest and least intrusive method to assign the lower frequency bound is simply to discard the information below that frequency.

The complete focus-generation sequence is then:

1. Select the upper frequency limit f_l desired for the window.
2. Select the time range for the focus window, and copy $\frac{1}{2}f_s/f_l$ times that number of samples from the original waveform.
3. Re-sample using a sampling ratio defined by $f_l/\frac{1}{2}f_s$.
4. Calculate the STFT on this new waveform, using a window overlap appropriate for the number of pixels required in the image
5. Discard the result below the lower frequency limit.

If a signal is discretized at a sampling frequency of f_s, the maximum frequency that can be represented is $\frac{1}{2}f_s$.

Parametrization. Because one of the goals of such a system would be usability, a user should not be required to interface with the algorithm-level parameters if they are not familiar to her. A "zoom amount" parameter could equally well define the maximal frequency, resample factor and overlap, given the appropriate mathematical mapping.

If a user wanted to double the scale of the spectrogram, the maximal frequency would correspond to the location and size of the focus area. Imagine the focus area was at the center of the display, and was one-third the size of the full spectrum display. The maximal frequency of the focus area would then be two-thirds of the maximal frequency of the overall spectrogram, or $f_s/3$.

Limitations. Re-sampling and window overlapping will work best when using whole-number ratios of the original values. This has the potential to impart an undue restriction on the usability of the system. The spectrogram zooming will also have limits imposed by time-frequency tradeoffs.

In a linear FPC display, the context can be shifted, scaled or overlapped to make room for the focus window. In a two-dimensional FPC display such as the one proposed for the spectrogram, these context manipulations are less direct— splitting the context in one dimension means that the entire display will be split

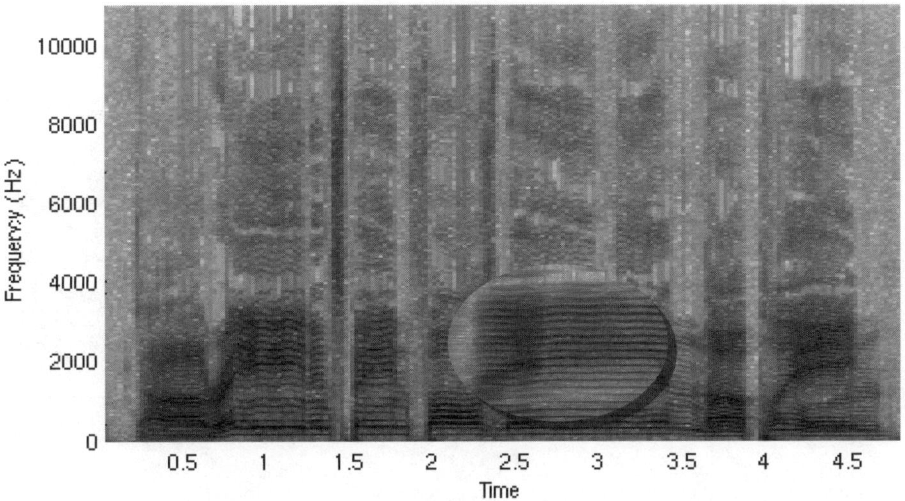

Fig. 10. Two-dimensional FPC display using a single layer of focus on top of a cohesive context

and a gap would be present where the focus in the other dimension is not present. Alternatively, the contextual area can be scaled to incorporate one dimension of scaling, but this removes familiarity with the standard appearance of an STFT, and further obfuscates the interaction. Nonlinear zooming is more likely to be useful here, with the metaphor of the "bubble," magnifying part of the STFT and smoothly transitioning to the context.

4   Implementation

As a proof-of-concept, we have implemented a Focus-Plus-Context display as part of the *Audacity* audio editor described earlier. We have implemented the focus window as an overlay in the main editing environment. Additional transition areas have not been implemented at this point. The primary purpose of the implementation was to explore the technical issues inherent in implementing an FPC display in an existing application. Our results were encouraging, showing that although significant modifications to several underlying structures were required, implementation overall is possible including some of the more complicated transition techniques discussed above. Figures 11 and 12 show examples of the FPC display in Audacity.

4.1   Deciding Where to Focus

One issue to consider with an FPC audio editing system is how the focus area is moved around through the audio track. Three approaches were considered. The first is to have the center of the focus area follow the location of the cursor when

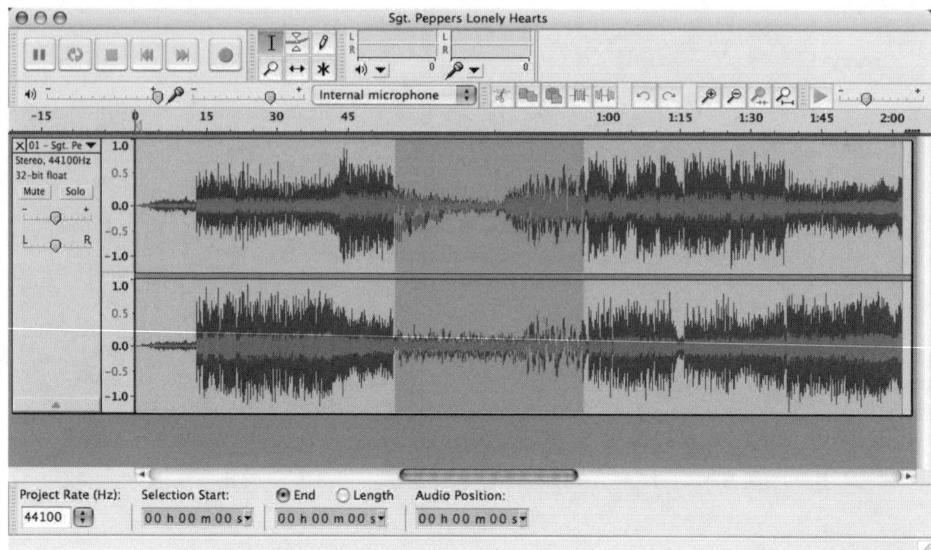

Fig. 11. A Screenshot of the FPC display as implemented within the framework of the Audacity audio editor

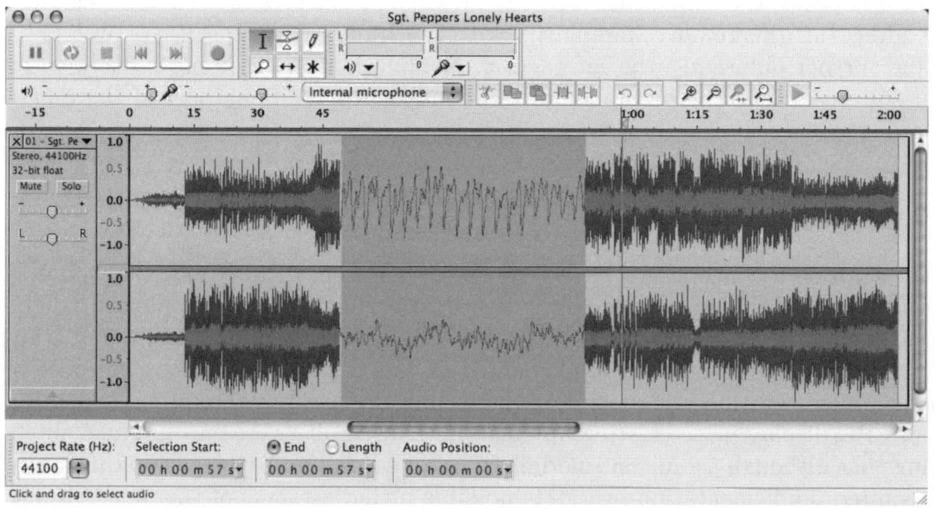

Fig. 12. FPC display at a higher focus-zoom level

the cursor is over the audio track. This method allows the user to scan through the audio track and quickly and accurately focus in on an event or target of interest. A problem with this approach is that it makes selecting audio difficult because as you are moving the mouse to do a selection, the focus area is also moving. This causes a side effect such that for each pixel the mouse moves in one direction, the waveform underneath the cursor moves in the opposite direction at a rate proportional to the focus window magnification. If the focus window is magnified to a great extend, each pixel of mouse movement will result in many samples of focus window movement.

The granularity of selection by the mouse could be partially offset by altering the size and magnitude of the transition between the focus area and the context area. For example, if a user is selecting an area from left to right, the right transition area can be expanded both in zoom and width in order to compensate for the mouse movement. The transition area on the left would be contracted in zoom and width. By changing the transition area on both sides, we can then move the audio displayed in the focus area at a slower rate, which should produce a better user experience as well as finer control.

The second method to move the focus area within the audio track is by using mouse and keyboard queues. There are many ways in which this can be implemented. For example, the user may just have to click on any point in the track, and the focal area will surround the selected point. This conflicts with many programs as clicking on a track usually results in moving the play head to that location. Another queue could be by clicking on the track (which positions the play head) then pressing a keyboard button to signify that we want to move the focal area to this point. Yet another option could be to hover the mouse over the position and press a key in order to select the focal point and in addition, this would allow a user to change the focal point without changing slide location.

The third method is to use the horizontal selection bar. This method is appealing since we are showing the whole context of the audio. The track is always the width of the screen so the there is never an occasion when it would be used in its conventional manner. The highlighted part of the bar could be the same width and in the same location as that of the focal point. Scrolling is an intuitive user interface technique, although horizontal scrolling typically requires the user to move the cursor away from the focus area. Devices are becoming available which allow both horizontal and vertical scrolling, and a common interface device for audio interaction is the "jog wheel" which often implements horizontal scrolling. WIth dedicated input devices such as these, using the scroll bar becomes less necessary. By using the scroll bar as the focus selection control, we create a relation between the two objects, however, we are also removing the user from the normal paradigm of using the bar to "scroll" the whole window.

Focus To Selection. While editing audio, quite frequently a user wants to get more detail on a section of audio. In order to do so, the user usually selects the area that they want to view, and focus on the selection. However, in the FPC environment, there are two parameters to the focus area: width and zoom. It may not always be possible to display the selected area with the present zoom. Therefore, focusing on the selection may not have the desired outcome for the user. There are two ways in which this problem can be solved.

The first option is to adjust the width of the focal area so that the zoomed selection can fit into the new focal width. Depending on the level of zoom, the focus window may not be able to expand far enough to fit the whole selection into the focal area. It is suggested that a threshold be created (for example 75% of the track window) such that, if the width of the focal area were to extend beyond this threshold (due to a large selection and high zoom level) then the zoom level of the focal area would be scaled down to the point that the selection can fit in the focal area while retaining a minimal focal zoom level of two (twice the context area). It would also be possible to discard part of the selection rather than changing the zoom level. However, changing the selection or the zoom level of the focal area will not provide the user with the expected result. The user expects to see the full selection in the focal area with the original focal zoom level which may not always be possible. Therefore, a compromise must be made in these cases. Since the user has explicitly selected an area on which they wish to focus on, changing the zoom level should provide the closest result to the users expectations.

The second option is to only adjust the zoom level of the focal area so that the selection can fit into the focal area without adjusting the focal width. This option may work well if the user is consistently making selections with approximately the same width as the focal area. This will result in the zoom level being more or less constant. However, if the user is making large changes in selection width, the corresponding large change in zoom level could confuse the user. A good example is if the user has a small focal width with a high level of zoom, and the user makes a very large selection and wants to zoom in on the selection. This would result in the zoom level being dramatically decreased, possibly to the point where the focal area would have a smaller zoom level then the context area (essentially swapping the focal and context areas). Since the focal area should never have a smaller zoom than the context area, the program would be forced to not widen the focal area beyond a large portion of the track width, and as a result not enclose all of the selection in the focal area.

4.2   Moving the Focal Area During Playback

As discussed earlier, when playing back audio, a playhead is drawn on the track in the location of the audio that is currently playing. As the track plays, the playhead is slid along the track. It is possible for the focal area to follow the playhead such that the playhead is always in the middle of the focal area. This allows the user to see in greater detail the waveform of the audio as its being played. This has two negative effects. The first being that the focal area moves from the previous point that it was set to. The second effect is that the waveform moves very quickly past the playhead. This can make it harder to predict what the waveform will look like next and confuse the user as to where they are in the track. It may be recommended to move the focal area but only at a moderately low zoom level such that the waveform does not move overly fast. An issue with our particular implementation is that the focal area moves at a consistent rate but the playhead jumps back and forth within the focal area at different rates because of the change in pixels per second from the context to the focal areas. The real-time continuous changing of the focal point also results in high demand of the processor.

4.3   Rendering a Waveform in FPC

The implementation method chosen was to alter the open source audio editing program Audacity to use FPC. The major issue with modifying an existing application to use FPC is that the basic assumption of almost all editing applications is that a direct relation exists between audio track time and pixel location. For example, Audacity uses a variable called zoom which represents how many pixels are displayed per second of audio. Therefore, if a pixel location is given in a function, the corresponding time of that pixel can be calculated by dividing the number of pixels by the zoom. Also, if a time is given, the number of pixels needed to represent that quantity of audio can be calculated by multiplying the time by the zoom. Being that the conversion from time to pixels and pixels to time is a primary calculation that is done during audio selection, editing, and display, it is heavily entrenched into the program. When creating an FPC editor, the basic assumption that a direct relation exists between pixels and time is false. This difference causes many issues when trying to modify an existing audio editing application.

Even after all of the time/pixel relations are modified to use the new FPC mappings, several problems still exist due to caching and file reading issues which are used to speed up Audacity. For example, when displaying the audio waveform, Audacity checks to see how many file blocks are used to calculate the pixel to be displayed. It then reads in the audio data in large chunks (256B or 64KB) if possible in order to speed up file reading and calculation of the minimum, maximum, and root mean square points. When using FPC the number of blocks per pixel varies depending on pixel location. This results in the inability to read data in large chunks using Audacity's existing functions and structures because they do not allow for different chunk sizes concurrently. In addition to file reading issues, caching also creates many problems with FPC.

Caching. During normal use, Audacity caches the information it needs to display the audio waveform. The end result is that the waveform only needs be calculated a single time unless the zoom factor, start time, or window width changes. The existing caching methods are not compatible with an FPC application because of the lack of constant time/pixel relation and the ability to move the focal window. A caching scheme similar to Audacity's could be implemented. In order to do this, two caching arrays could be used; one for the context area and one for the focal area. The context area cache would have to be the same size as the number of pixels being displayed for the waveform minus the number of pixels being displayed in the focal area. The focal area cache would be approximately the size of the focal window times the focal zoom factor. This caching scheme would be ineffective in several situations. The whole cache would have to recalculated when the focal window zoom or width was changed. The transition area between the focal window and context area would have to be recalculated on the fly as caching this information would be inefficient and the transition area would have to remain a constant size to avoid cache recalculation. Also, the cache size of the focal window could become very large at large zoom factors.

Therefore, caching at a level closer to the sample level would be more useful. The cache resolution should be of a rate equal to the number of samples per pixel of the focal area. This will result in a large cache if the resolution is small or the track length is long. As a compromise, if the cache size grew too large the resolution could be increased to be equal to the number of samples per pixel of the context area. This would speed up the rendering of the context area but would not be useful for the focal or transition areas. Due to these caching issues, it is recommended that different caching schemes be utilized.

One way to speed up waveform display calculation is by pre-computing some of the commonly used conversion variables. For example, when using FPC with Audacity if we compute the pixel per second value for each pixel once and then store it in an array, we can speed up many function as this value is used very often. A mapping between pixel location and track time could also be stored in an array. The values stored in the array are only valid if the display width, focal zoom, focal start point, and focal width do not change. The end result is that calculations for the current waveform display can be sped up. By using some change information we can reduce the number of calculations that are needed when re-computing the cache arrays.

As an example of efficient re-computation of the cache array, the pixel per second (PPS) cache will be used. If the focal window is moved 50 pixels to the left, only 100 values of the cache array have to be re-calculated (50 pixels at the start of the focal window and 50 pixels past the end of the focal window). Similarly, if the focal window is 20 pixels wide and is moved 100 pixels to the right, only 40 values need to be recalculated (the 20 pixels at the new location and the 20 pixels at the old location). These informed changes to the caching arrays can reduce the number of new values that are being computed and stored. However, they may not yield an overly large performance benefit when compared to the existing caching methods of Audacity.

Performance. Another speed issue caused by FPC results from the fact that we have to show the entire track on the screen. Normally, Audacity only has to calculate display values for the portion of the track that is displayed on the screen. Because Audacity only displays a subset of the whole track, the number of samples that need to be read for calculating the waveform does not correlate to the length of the track. With FPC, we need to read all of the samples for the entire track in order to display the waveform. This creates a large performance hit when drawing the waveform of long tracks. A one minute track could take almost twice as long as a half minute track to display.

An additional way of speeding up the rendering of the waveform in both tradiational Audacity and Audacity with FPC is to speed up the rate of performing calculations. This could be done quite practically through the use of the graphics processing unit (GPU). The GPU's in modern machines are much faster at floating point calculation than CPU's. By moving the root mean squared calculations as well as other common expensive calculations off of the CPU and onto the GPU a very large performance increase can be gained.

5   Future Work

5.1   Horizontal Focus Plus Vertical Context (HFPVC)

One improvement on the standard horizontal editing bar is to utilize more screen real estate by expanding the waveform in a vertical direction at both edges which can be referred to as Horizontal Focus Plus Vertical Context, seen in Figure 13.

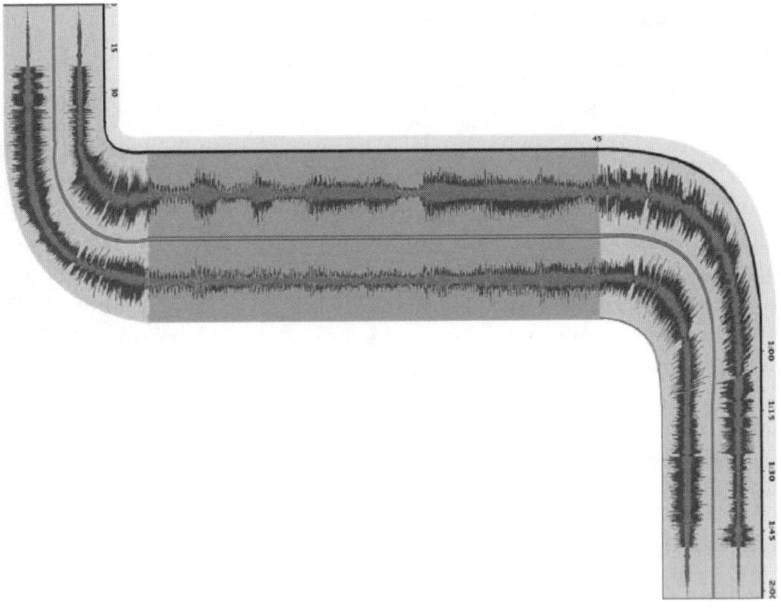

Fig. 13. Horizontal Focus Plus Vertical Context (HFPVC) display mock-up

The waveform begins in the upper left corner of the screen and is drawn in a downward direction. Just before the focal area is encountered, the waveform is warped into a horizontal direction. The entire horizontal run of the waveform is the focal area. As the waveform reaches the right side of the screen the context area is again displayed and warped in a downward direction until it hits the bottom of the screen. The HFPVC interface has several benefits over standard FPC and conventional user interfaces.

One of the most important aspects of the HFPVC user interface is the additional screen space that the waveform can be displayed in. By using more space, the context area can be larger which helps to mediate the issue of losing context detail when viewing long tracks. The curved corners between the context area and focal area provide a natural transition between the two which may make it easier for a user to understand the boundaries and degree of zoom change between the areas. By having the context area and focal area drawn in different directions, a very clear difference is made between the two areas so they will not likely be confused.

In order for a user to change the focal point most of the same methods from the normal FPC environment can be used. The main focal selection method that needs to be changed is the scroll bar. The scroll bar should now be in the vertical direction at the right side of the screen and positioned at the location of the horizontal focus. As the scroll bar is moved up or down, the focal area will move accordingly. The context area warps itself to the focal area as the focal area moves. When the focal area is at the top of the screen it is focusing on the start of the track and the majority of the context area is shown along the right side of the screen. Also, when the focal area is at the bottom of the screen it is focusing on the end of the track and the majority of the context area is shown along the left side of the screen.

Several issues also exist with an HFPVC environment. Selecting an area of track other than the focal area may cause some difficulties. To start with, the cursor would have to change to a horizontal bar in the context area in order for the user to select a point with greater accuracy. Also, it may be beneficial to manipulate the cursor so it follows the curve between the context and focal areas. Having the context waveform being displayed vertically may cause initial discord for the user as audio editing is always done in a horizontal fashion. This could probably be overcome in a short period of time. Another issue with the HFPVC interface is drawing speed. The focal area and context area would not create more overhead than the original FPC interface. However, the transitional curve between the two would be quite a bit more complex and slower to draw.

6   Conclusions

We have presented a discussion of the issues involved in focus-plus-context displays for audio interaction. While it may be true that these displays will add a computational burden to what has traditionally been a relatively simple task, it is perhaps more appropriate to think of this as a *shift* in cognitive burden from the human to the computer. In traditional audio editing displays, users are forced to maintain and update a mental model of the entire file being considered, and difficulties can arise when there are repeated segments in a file. FPC interfaces can alleviate many of the current task-related difficulties of audio interaction. We have presented theoretical aspects of generating FPC displays of waveform and spectral information. Additionally, we have presented an implementation of some of these ideas in the context of an open-source audio editor (Audacity), and we have discussed the issues and difficulties inherent in this implementation.

While it may be tempting to suggest that audio interaction programs have been successfully used for many years and that, although learning is required, the current systems are capable of performing the tasks, it is worthwhile to recall that most of the people who work with these programs have extensive experience and strong familiarity with the paradigm, the result of which can be overestimating the ease of use of the familiar interface. FPC audio displays have the potential to remove considerable cognitive burden for people who work with audio, regardless of whether they consider themselves burdened.

References

1. Bederson, B.B., Hollan, J.D.: Pad++: a zooming graphical interface for exploring alternate interface physics. In: UIST 1994: Proceedings of the 7th annual ACM symposium on User interface software and technology, pp. 17–26. ACM Press, New York (1994)
2. Hornbæk, K., Bederson, B.B., Plaisant, C.: Navigation patterns and usability of zoomable user interfaces with and without an overview. ACM Trans. Comput.-Hum. Interact. 9(4), 362–389 (2002)
3. Keahey, A.: The generalized detail-in-context problem. In: INFOVIS 1998: Proceedings of the 1998 IEEE Symposium on Information Visualization, Washington, DC, USA, pp. 44–51. IEEE Computer Society, Los Alamitos (1998)
4. Keahey, A.: Nonlinear magnification infocenter [accessed November 13, 2007], http://alan.keahey.org/research/nlm/nlm.html
5. Plumlee, M.D., Ware, C.: Zooming versus multiple window interfaces: Cognitive costs of visual comparisons. ACM Trans. Comput.-Hum. Interact. 13(2), 179–209 (2006)
6. Raskin, J.: The Humane Interface: New Directions for Designing Interactive Systems. Addison-Wesley Professional, Reading (2000)
7. Rauschenbach, U.: The rectangular fish eye view as an efficient method for the transmission and display of images. In: ICIP 1999: Proceedings of the 1999 IEEE conference on Image Processing, Washington, DC, USA. IEEE Computer Society, Los Alamitos (1999)
8. Rauschenbach, U., Weinkauf, T., Schumann, H.: Interactive focus and context display of large raster images. In: WSCG 2000: The 8-th International Conference in Central Europe on Computer Graphics, Visualization and Interactive Digital Media (2000)
9. Woodruff, A., Landay, J., Stonebraker, M.: Constant information density in zoomable interfaces. In: AVI 1998: Proceedings of the working conference on Advanced visual interfaces, pp. 57–65. ACM Press, New York (1998)

Maps and Legends: Designing FPS-Based Interfaces for Multi-user Composition, Improvisation and Immersive Performance

Robert Hamilton

Center for Computer Research in Music and Acoustics (CCRMA),
Stanford University,
660 Lomita Drive,
Stanford CA, 94305, USA
`rob@ccrma.stanford.edu`
`http://ccrma.stanford.edu/~rob`

Abstract. This paper describes an interactive multi-channel multi-user networked system for real-time composition and immersive performance built using a modified version of the Quake III gaming engine. By tracking users' positional and action data within a virtual space, and by streaming that data over a network using OSC messages formatted as UDP packets to a multi-channel Pure Data patch, actions in virtual space are correlated to sonic output in a physical space. Virtual environments designed as abstract compositional maps or representative models of the users' actual physical space are investigated as means to guide and shape compositional and performance choices. This paper analyzes both the technological concerns for building and realizing the system as well as the compositional and perceptual issues inherent in the project itself.

1   Introduction

In the context of highly realistic 3-dimensional video games, sound is commonly utilized as a critical element in the communication of virtual spatial cues as well as in the enhancement and definition of actions by gamer-controlled avatars and other game entities alike. By presenting a user-centric sound field to the gamer - where the intended listening audience is one player alone within a front-focused stereo, 5.1 or other commercially standard sound field - designers create insular sound-worlds, reinforcing the immersive experience through their use of realistic 3D models and environments with auditory cues and behaviors based in the reality of the virtual world.

As platforms for creating, interacting with and acting within virtual environments, "First-Person Shooter" or FPS-style video game engines such as the open-source Quake III engine offer artists a powerful new paradigm to explore novel methodologies for the control of sound and music with a low cost to entry and a flexible and extensible development environment. Used in conjunction with a data-transmission protocol like Open Sound Control (OSC) over UDP,

R. Kronland-Martinet, S. Ystad, and K. Jensen (Eds.): CMMR 2007, LNCS 4969, pp. 478–486, 2008.

in-game parameters controlled by multiple game users can be passed to any number of music and sound generation software environments, creating a seamless network-based transmission of data from the virtual realm to physical auditory space. In this manner, composers and performers alike can explore new relationships with composed and improvised musical materials by subverting traditional models of performer/composer/audience relationships and by distributing them in new contexts across networked physical and virtual space.

Towards this goal, from the standpoint of the composer, it becomes necessary to explore novel forms of compositional structure based in the virtual environment which are designed to fully exploit the dynamic nature of both control and sound-generation systems alike. At the same time, for composers wishing to retain a level of control or influence over the musical work as a whole, it is necessary to design a system capable of imparting a level of intention and logical structure upon what could easily become a fully improvisatory musical form. One solution - referred to henceforth as the "compositional map" - draws inspiration and structure from the topography of the virtual environment itself and aims to build upon this visual and musical structure by leveraging the inherently flexible and indeterminate system of player motions and actions. Within this composer-defined visual and musical space, in-game performers reacting with their virtual environment as well as with one another via their avatars, collectively move the musical work forwards from inception to completion in a quasi-improvisatory fashion.

2   System Overview

Maps and Legends is a dynamic software system making use of the immersive environment of the Quake III engine as the user-interface for a flexible composition and performance system. Pre-composed computer-generated musical cells are assigned to each in-game performer and are triggered, processed and controlled through performers' interactions with and paths through the environment. By tracking multiple performers' coordinate locations within virtual space and by subsequently spatializing those locations across a multi-channel performance space, an auditory correlation can be formed between the physical and virtual environments, engaging the attentions of both performers and audience members alike within the musical soundscape.

Maps and Legends was designed as a fully-rendered 3-dimensional virtual compositional map built using the GtkRadiant game-level editing software [5] (see Figure 1). While clearly-visible pathways, directional arrows, and active directional jump-pads are built into the map to encourage or force performer motion in certain predefined or composed directions, each performer retains a high-level of independence and improvisatory flexibility, allowing for spontaneous new interpretations of the pre-composed materials.

Users running the game-client software and connected over a standard high-speed network control their avatars and through them the musical work using standard Quake III game control methodologies - typically a combination of computer-keyboard controls for motion and a mouse for view-angle. Game-clients

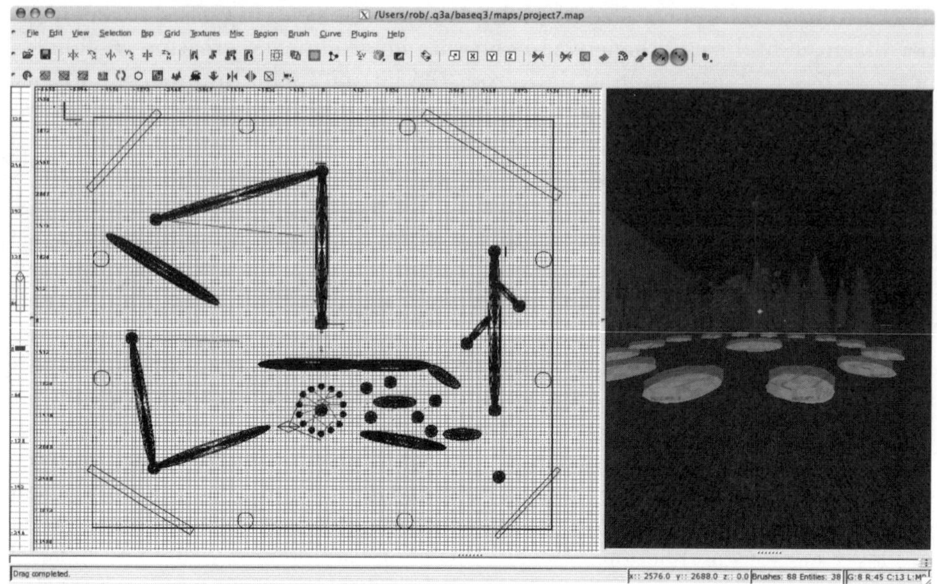

Fig. 1. *Maps and Legends* compositional map shown from both a top-down structural view (left) and a rendered "ground-level" view (right) in the GtkRadiant editor

connect to a host game-server which in-turn streams OSC-formatted data reflecting their players' actions and coordinates to a sound-server in the performance venue running Pure Data (PD). Sound generation and processing for each independent performer are handled by and spatialized within an 8-channel PD patch, circumventing the sound-system of the game itself and substituting the composer's musical environment for Quake III's stock in-game sounds and music.

At the heart of *Maps and Legends* is a set of software modules, currently Linux-only, created by multimedia artists Julian Oliver and Stephen Pickles entitled *q3apd* [6] which modify the open-source network code of the Quake III game engine to stream a variety of ingame data - including global XYZ player positioning coordinates, directional velocity and view-angle - formatted as OSC messages over a network as UDP packets. As users connect to the host game server, data from their characters' movements and actions are sent to a PD patch which parses incoming OSC messages and extracts multiple player-specific data points. In this manner, the global position of individual game players within the virtual game-space, and certain subsequent actions performed by each user, are mapped to a number of sound-generation and spatialization control parameters creating a rich interactive-system for musical control.

3   Prior Work

The use of networked/multi-user video game paradigms for music and sound generation has become increasingly common as generations of musicians who have

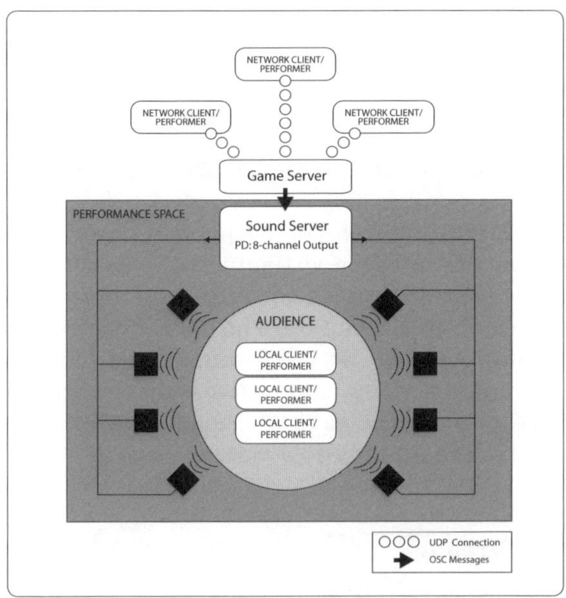

Fig. 2. System diagram of Client/Server interactions

grown up with readily accessible home video game systems, internet access and personal computers seek to bring together visually immersive graphical game-worlds, wide-spanning networks and interactive control systems with musical systems. Though its graphical display is rendered in 2-dimensions, *Small_Fish* by Kiyoshi Furukawa, Masaki Fujihata and Wolfgang Muench [4] is a game-like musical interface which allows performers/players to create rich musical tapestries using a variety of control methods. *Auracle* [3], by Max Neuhaus, Phil Burk and their team from Akademie Schloss Solitude allows networked users to collaborate and improvise using vocal gesture. Oliver and Pickles' own works, including *q3apd* and *Fijuu2* [7], a fully-rendered three-dimensional audio/visual installation controlled with a game-pad, tightly marry the videogame and musical worlds through the use of immersive graphics and familiar game control systems. And work on the *Co-Audicle* by Ge Wang, Perry Cook and the Princeton Soundlabs team is actively seeking to build a user-community of collaborative performers through networked extension of the ChucK language and its *Audicle* front-end [11].

Compositional precedents for modular composed forms allowing for performer control over a work's structure can be found in the polyvalent form of Karlheinz Stockhausen's *Zyklus* [9] for one percussionist, as well as in the variable form of his *Klavierstück XI* [10] for solo piano. In *Zyklus*, Stockhausen's strictly composed sectional materials are designed to be interpreted in a performer-chosen direction, reading through the score either forwards or backwards, starting performance on any given page. Similarly, in *Klavierstück XI*, nineteen composed and precisely notated musical fragments are ordered by the performer. These flexible structural concepts are also prevalent in John Cage's body of chance-based musical works including his *Music of Changes* [1] or *String Quartet in Four Parts* [2], where pre-composed musical cells were selected through chance operations and formed into a definitive compositional structure.

4   Mappings and Sound-Generation

By mapping OSC data-streams from the q3apd mod to various sound processing and spatialization controls in PD, a virtually-enactive control system is created allowing for musically expressive and flexible gestural control through the virtual physicality of performers' avatar motion. The linking of virtual gesture to sound and spatialized auditory motion sets the stage for an exploration of musical control through a manner of virtual interactive choreography. Towards this end, sound-generating subsystems making use of sample-playback, active filters, delay and reverb parameters are all linked to various possible performer motions or actions.

4.1   *q3apd* Data Streams

Making use of the Quake III engine's native ability to run user-created software library modifications or "mods," q3apd's customized code streams a number of game-state and positioning parameters for each connected user from the game server to a specified IP and Port address as OSC messages. The q3apd libraries export player-specific data, including XYZ positioning and view-angle, directional velocity, selected weapon, and player states such as jumping, crouching or falling. q3apd also formats each message with a prepended user-id tag ensuring that multiple user data-streams can easily be separated in PD and tracked independently.

4.2   PD Mappings

Basic control values supplied by q3apd such as player-motion and XYZ position, (Figure 3: section A) are used to calculate constantly changing horizontal-plane distance vectors from a performer's current position to pre-defined virtual speaker locations within the compositional map (Figure 3: section B). Similarly, distance between multiple performers is calculated and mapped to sound events - complementary or disruptive depending on composer-defined performance states - in an effort to support or discourage performers from moving too close or too far from one another.

At key points in the compositional map, circular trigger regions lie in the suggested path of motion. Precomposed musical materials are triggered when performers move over these coordinate spaces, viewed in-game as bright yellow circles on the virtual ground. In this manner, separate sets of mono sound files, all complementary parts of the composition, are assigned to individual performers and triggered in PD based on each performers' position (Figure 3: section C).

These sets of sound files, a mixture of synthesized and sampled sound, generated using custom software systems built in Max/MSP and PD, make up the

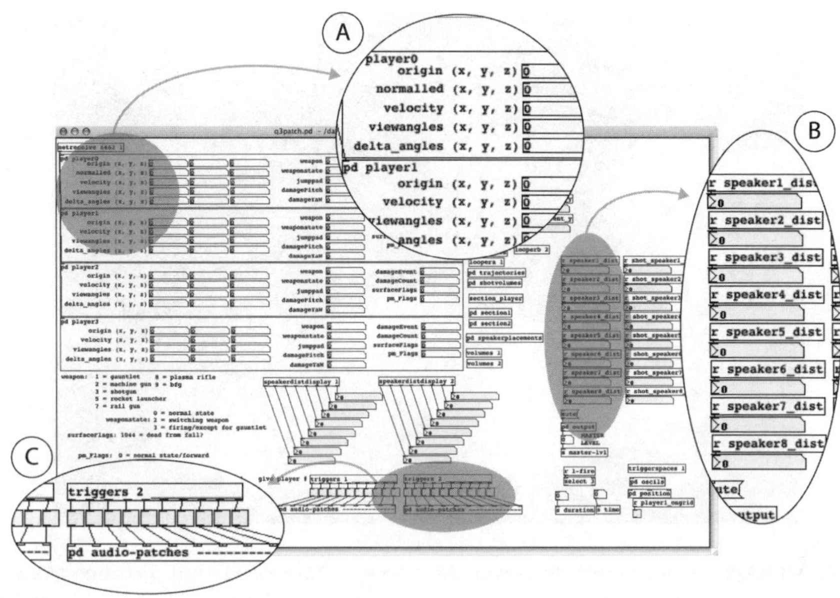

Fig. 3. Pure-Data patch with highlighted sections for A) player coordinates, directional velocity and viewangle tracking, B) player-to-speaker distance values, and C) player-specific map triggers

bulk of pre-composed materials for maps and legends. Other basic mappings include a light chorus and reverb processing applied to a performer's current sound when moving over a highlighted pathway - a bonus of sorts for moving in pre-composed patterns - as well as a longer reverb and longer delay applied when the user's Z coordinate indicates that they are fairly "high" in the map's vertical dimension - a state that can be triggered more often by lowering game-server-side parameters like virtual gravity.

By coordinating the speed of various "weapon" projectiles in the game, it has also been possible to create a satisfactory illusion of a "shooting-sound" which travels independently across the map, tracking the trajectory and speed of a visible fired projectile. One particularly effective mapping matches the speed of a large glowing orb moving relatively slowly across the map with the panning for a particular sound event.

4.3   Multi-channel Output and Spatialization

To clarify the relationship between individual performers and their respective sound sets, triggered sound files are spatialized based on a performer's distance from each of eight defined speaker locations. In short, sounds follow the performers' motions through space, spatialized between multiple speakers at any given time (see Figure 4).

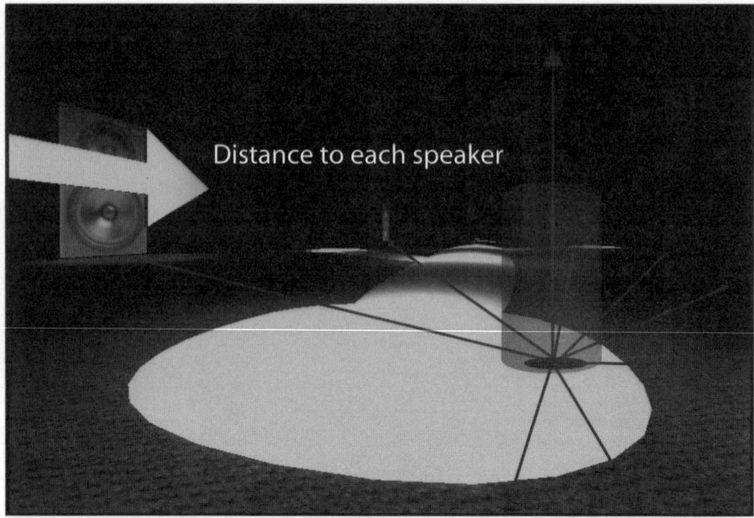

Fig. 4. Multi-channel amplitude is calculated as a factor of virtual distance from performer to each speaker. Shown also are yellow circular trigger-locations, speaker locations, directional guide-arrows and suggested pre-composed pathways.

Speaker locations are defined in PD as XY coordinate pairs, with independent gain levels for each performer for each speaker determined by a simple distance function. In this manner, multiple speaker configurations for multi-channel output can be easily configured without any changes to the compositional map itself. While at this time additional reverb or delay-based panning cues, or more accurate multi-planar spatialization methods like vector based amplitude panning (VBAP) [8] or Ambisonic encoding are not used to either simulate the acoustics of the virtual space or to provide more realistic panning effects, such approaches are being investigated.

5   Discussion and Conclusions

As an immersive environment for interactive networked performance and modular composition, the system designed for *Maps and Legends* affords composers and performers alike an extremely powerful and novel musical experience. As the tools for generating virtual environments are flexible and robust, and through the use of q3apd and OSC can interface with a variety of software-based musical environments, there exist many compositional and performance methodologies which can be explored using such a system.

One important goal in building *Maps and Legends* was the development of a system capable of immersing an audience in a virtual sound world, creating a perceptual super-imposition of virtual and physical environments (see Figure 5).

And during the early stages of system development it became clear that this relationship between virtual environment and physical listening space played

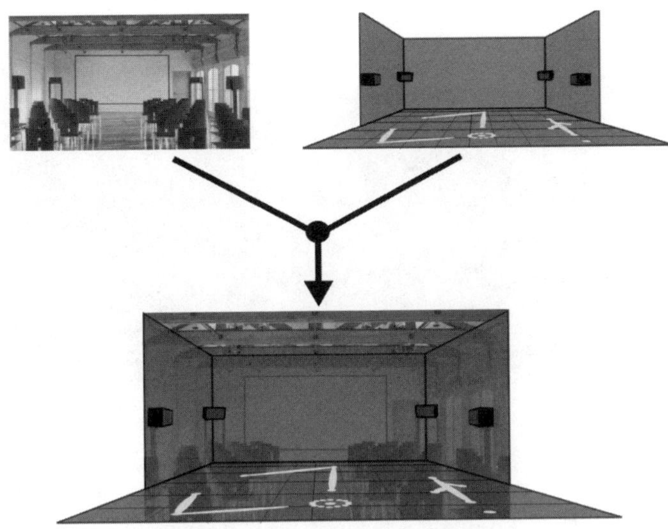

Fig. 5. Perceptual super-imposition of a virtual game-space on top of a physical performance space

a key role in an audience's ability to become immersed in the projected audio-visual landscape. After presenting different visual displays to an audience during performance - either an in-game global vantage point or a performer's standard first-person view - early usage indicates that perhaps the perceptual illusion of super-imposed spaces succeeds or breaks down based at least in part on the perceived alignment of the virtual viewpoint with the audience's physical viewpoint. When no visual environment is projected to an audience, the resulting musical experience changes dramatically, offering less sensory confusion and a seemingly greater ability for audience members to focus on the musical work at hand. However, without visual cues to help define the virtual environment, the musical soundscape lacks the clear indications of performers' deterministic vs. improvised gestures.

While working to better understand this idea of perceptual super-imposition, a realistic slightly larger-than-scale virtual model of CCRMA's new heptagonal 16-channel Listening Room was created, complete with representative virtual speaker placements (see Figure 6). Game players sitting in the actual Listening Room could enter the model and move their avatars through the virtual room, controlling sound across an 8-channel sound field mirroring corresponding real-world physical speaker locations. For individuals controlling the system as well as individual watching on a projected video screen, effects ranging from sensory confusion to mild discomfort were reported. Though not intended as a full-blown perceptual study, the immediate reactions of those involved hint at deeper issues with users' cognitive abilities to separate virtual environments from physical environments.

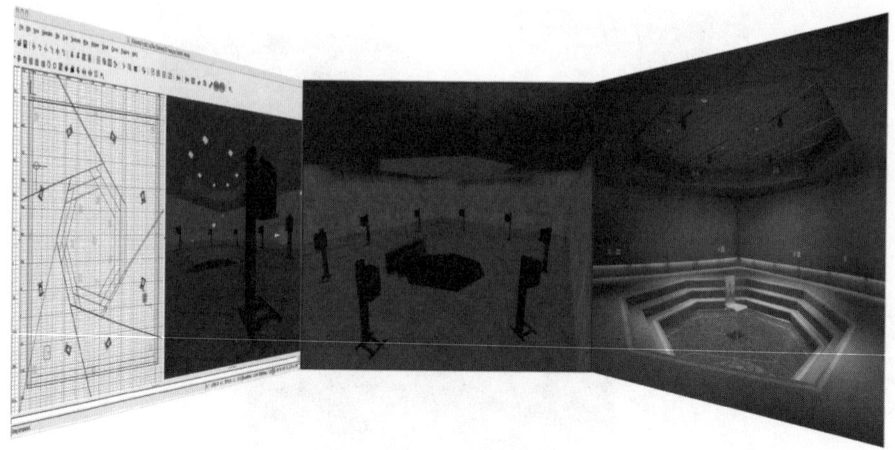

Fig. 6. Three representations of CCRMA's heptagonal 16-channel Listening Room (from Left to Right): GtkRadiant schematic view, in-game Quake III capture and real-world photograph

References

1. Cage, J.: Music of Changes (Score). Henmar Press, C.F. Peters, New York (1951)
2. Cage, J.: String Quartet in Four Parts (Score). Henmar Press, C.F. Peters, New York (1950)
3. Freeman, J., et al.: The Architecture of Auracle: A Voice-Controlled, Networked Sound Instrument. In: Proceedings of the International Computer Music Conference, Barcelona, Spain (2005)
4. Furukawa, K., Fujihata, M., Muench, W.:
   `http://hosting.zkm.de/wmuench/small_fish`
5. GtkRadiant, `http://www.q3radiant.com`
6. Oliver, J., Pickles, S.: q3apd (2007) (as viewed 4/2007),
   `http://www.selectparks.et/archive/q3apd.htm`
7. Pickles, S.: fijuu2. Henmar Press, C.F. Peters, New York (1950) (as viewed 4/2007),
   `http://www.fijuu.com`
8. Pulkki, V.: Virtual sound source positioning using vector base amplitude panning. Journal of the Audio Engineering Society 45(6), 456–466 (1997)
9. Stockhausen, K.: Zyklus. Universal Edition, London (1960)
10. Stockhausen, K.: Klavierstück XI, Universal Edition, London (1957)
11. Wang, G., Misra, A., Davidson, P., Cook, P.: Co-Audicle: A Collaborative Audio Programming Space. In: Proceedings of the International Computer Music Conference, Barcelona, Spain (2005)

DECONcert: Making Waves with Water, EEG, and Music

Steve Mann[1], James Fung[1], and Ariel Garten[2]

[1] University of Toronto
Dept. of Electrical and Computer Engineering
Toronto, Ontario, Canada
[2] Neuroconsulting
Toronto, Ontario, Canada

Abstract. We describe events in which music, water and the brain form an immersive environment for human-computer and human-computer-human collective engagement. The theme of sound wave production, regeneration and audition from water waves and brain waves is our central exploration, beginning with our DECONcerts in which participants, immersed in water and connected to EEG equipment, regeneratively create or affect live music by varying their alpha wave output. We explored the five states-of-matter (Classical Elements) of solid ("Earth"), liquid ("Water"), gas ("Air"), plasma ("Fire"), and quintessence ("Idea"), in the context of immersive media (e.g. when the surrounding state-of-matter was liquid). Some of these immersive environments spanned multiple countries, by way of networked connectivity. We also expanded from philosophical to therapeutic contexts by including Parkinson's patients in our immersed environments.

1 Introduction

This paper presents a series of performances, art exhibits, and concerts, that explored the relationships between water waves, sound waves, and brainwaves (see figure 1). These events merged a custom built EEG (Electroencephelograph or "brainwave") computational system with music generation, immersive aquatic spaces, and groups of immersively engaged performers and participatory audiences. Participatory performances explored collective consciousness by creating both physically shared spaces (connecting various groups of participants across distant geographical boundaries) and shared human-computational networks.

The resulting collective immersive experiences were created using the media of a shared immersive audio environment, and an aquatic environment where, in some events, groups of participants and performers were actually immersed, in whole, or in part, in water. These media are explorations of waves: in one medium, acoustic waves; in another, aqueous waves (various performances studied caustics and wavefronts, as well as water-induced sounds); and, of course, brainwaves.

R. Kronland-Martinet, S. Ystad, and K. Jensen (Eds.): CMMR 2007, LNCS 4969, pp. 487–505, 2008.
© Springer-Verlag Berlin Heidelberg 2008

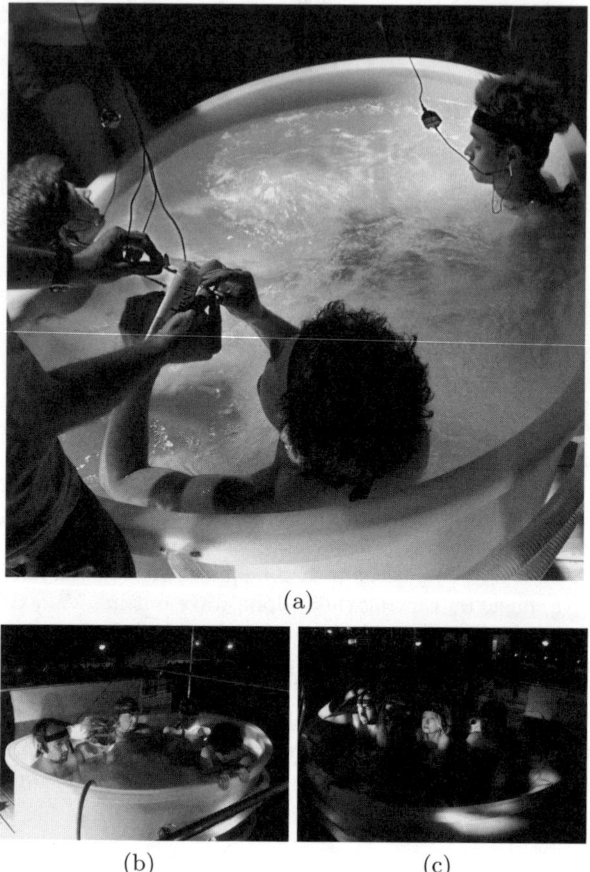

(a)

(b)   (c)

Fig. 1. DECONcert events allowed participants to explore issues of DECONtamination, music, water, and brainwave. (a) Participants being prepared with electrode paste for EEG readings. (b,c) A separate spotlight on each participant responds to their individual level of visual arousal, thus turning participants into performers who are on stage in the bath.

This theme of waves not only occurred at the observational (output) side of the performance, but also at the input: both the ambient and acoustic environments were generated by directly measuring and interpreting the brainwaves of the participants. This paper discusses various performance art events together with the philosophical implications and artistic narratives developed in the various events.

2   Creating Immersive Experiences with Humanistic Intelligence

Humanistic intelligence (HI) is defined [7] as a signal processing framework in which the processing apparatus is inextricably intertwined with the natural capabilities of our human body and mind. Within the processing framework of HI, the computational apparatus and user, in being intertwined as such, are considered as a signal processing block, interacting as one with the outside world. Within this block, the human and computer work together in a tight feedback loop, with each accepting information and outputs from, and providing information and inputs to, each other. In contrast to AI, which seeks to recreate human intelligence on the machine, HI seeks to utilize the abilities of both the human and machine to their fullest.

HI forms the structural framework in our explorations. In each of our exploratory performances, exhibits, and concerts, water, music and brainwaves, and states-of-matter become the media to express Humanistic Intelligence. Though at first inspection the HI framework may appear to express an individual's relationship to computational apparatus, our events demonstrate the collective nature of HI, where groups of participants are *all* connected to the computational system and thus to each other: a collective consciousness.

We use music and water and brainwaves as mediums to create group immersion to allow participants to experience and become a collective consciousness. We explore collective consciousness through: (1) collective consciousness (i.e. using multiple participant brainwave inputs to drive an artistic process), (2) representing these brainwave signals in a shared multimedia environment where audiovisual experiences, such as sound and visuals, are collectively experienced; and (3) using water as a physical agent to bring participants into a shared space that is truly, and literally immersive (in the sense of a communal bathing experience). These media explore issues of privacy and personal space.

3   The Events

Starting in July 2001[1] we had a series of events addressing issues of contamination and biological warfare. The authors created a number of events, performances, and concerts that dealt with issues surrounding **decon**tamination. These events were named DECONference, DECONversation, DECONsortium, DECONtrol, DECONcert, and the like, making reference to DECONtamination. For example, a series of DECONcerts were presented as DECONtamination concerts in which participants were washed down with water prior to being connected to EEG (brainwave) instrumentation.

Our DECONcert series explored a regenerative feedback loop between brainwaves and music, as the collective consciousness of a large audience either generated music or modified music generated by other performers.

In our Powerplant [2] DEConcert, individuals contributed directly by playing their brain as an instrument in an improvising live band, directing and taking direction from more traditional musical interactions.

---

[1] Our first event took place prior to the anthrax scare that came shortly after the September 11th 2001 terrorist attacks.

[2] The "Powerplant" is a Canadian contemporary art gallery.

In many of our DECONcerts, groups of people from around the world were connected, over the Internet, from various different communal baths or aquatic spaces. For example, in one DECONcert, we had groups of six bathers, at a time, in one rooftop tub, each outfitted with EEG electrodes, connected to bathers, three-at-a-time, in another distant tub that was located on the sidewalk of a busy downtown street. Situating the bath on a busy sidewalk established a juxtaposition of public and private, while inviting passers-by to stop, "doff their duds", put on the EEG electrodes, and join in. The different group baths were connected audiovisually, as well as electroencephalically (using EEG sensors), across the World Wide Web, also by way of web cameras, microphones, and various physiological signals such as EEG and ECG (Electrocardiogram).

In another concert, we invited a number of Parkinson's patients to participate remotely from their hospital beds using equipment we sent out on loan. What was remarkable about this form of participation, was the fact that the DECONcerts were inclusive for people of any physical ability. In this form of cyborg space, a person of lesser physical ability is still a full participant, since the primary experimental control modality is brainwaves. All that is needed to be a full participant is a sufficiently engageable brain.

An important artistic narrative was the juxtaposition of this corporeal transcendence, combined with the physicality of passers-by in their disrobed and electrified bodies, situated in a bath on a busy street.

One set of mini-concerts within the DECONcert series was called "Telematic Tubs Against Terror". This was a series of events in which groups of individuals were immersed in tubs of water and connected by way of EEG to form a collective consciousness. This emerged as participants projected a sub-collective from each tub (each "wash node"). These events explored a collective and distributed consciousness as people's brainwaves were made public, in concert with the collectively shared experience of water and music.

Water and music also formed the backbone of our concert at the International Computer Music Conference (ICMC). The creation of a novel instrument called the hydraulophone, whose sound production is created using water as a medium, invited the examination of other mediums in which sound could be produced. Thus we created a physics-based orgonology in which musical instruments are classified based on the state-of-matter (solid, liquid, gas, plasma, or quintessence) of the intial sound-producing mechanism. We already created instruments from non-matter, i.e. quintessence (bio)informatics, e.g. brainwaves.

3.1 DECONcert: Collaborative Music in the Key of EEG

DECONcerts were a form of audience-participatory concert in which the participants' brainwaves determined the music they were experiencing.

The first DECONcert was, to the authors' knowledge, the first exploration of music generated by collective consciousness (i.e. more than one person generating music with their brainwaves together).

Our first collectively created concert, DECONcert 1, attracted enough interest to require three separate sessions in the same evening, each for a different group

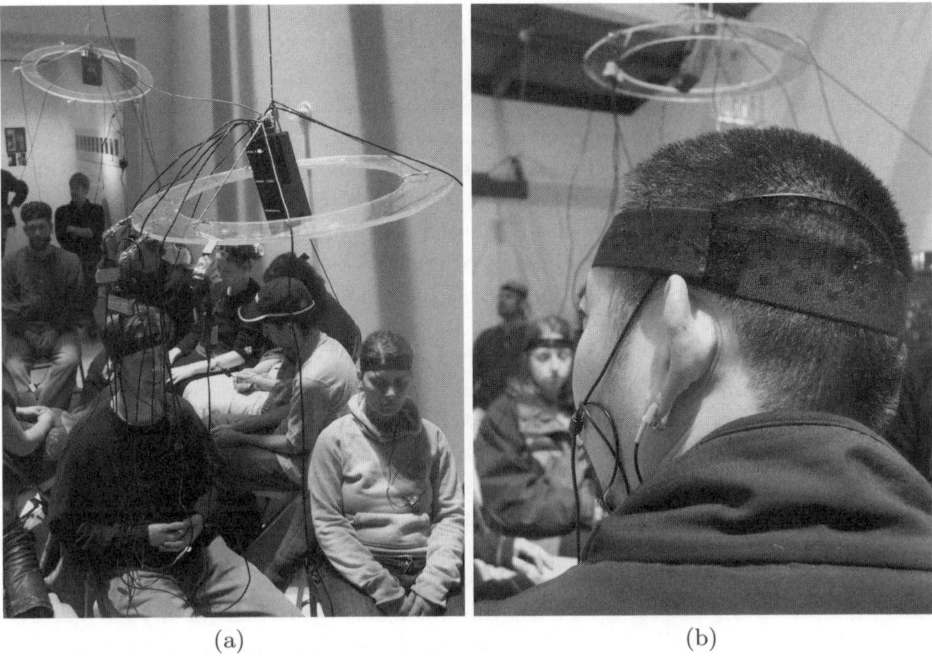

(a)   (b)

Fig. 2. DECONcert Performance: This group of 48 participants simultaneously and collectively adjusted the musical environment with their brainwaves while remotely connected to groups in other countries

of participants. For each session, we connected 48 people by way of their EEG signals, which were collectively used to affect the audiovisual environment.

Using six 8-person EEG machines, donated by manufacturer Thought Technologies Limited, we were able to obtain connections from 48 people at the same time.

In order to have the greatest flexibility we wrote our own GNU/Linux device drivers for these machines, and we developed and implemented our own signal processing algorithms. We developed a system to utilize multiple EEG signals to clean the signal and look for collective alpha synchronization (which occurs, for instance, when people close their eyes). Figure 2 shows images taken of the first DECONcert performance.

DECONcert utilized electroencephalogram (EEG) sensors which sensed electrical activity produced in the brains of the participants. The signals from the brainwaves of the 48 participants were used as input to dynamically alter a computationally controlled soundscape. DECONcert allowed the participants to form a feedback loop with the computational process of musical composition. The soundscape being generated was in response to the participants: the collective response from the group of participants is sensed by the computer, which then alters the music based upon this response. Again, the participants hear the music, and again respond, and again the computer senses and further alters the sound. In this way, collaborative biofeedback is being used in conjunction with an intelligent signal processing system to continually re-generate the music on the fly.

A total of 3 DECONcerts were held with different configurations exploring different methods of audience interaction. In each of the 3 DECONcerts that were held, up to 48 audience members sat in front of the stage in 6 groups. On stage, jazz musicians improvised on some combination of electric keyboard, electric clarinet, trumpet, saxophone, drums, and/ or base. As audience members listened to the concert, each member's brainstate determined the modulation of the output of the musician's synthesized instruments. Some acoustic qualities that the audience was able to modulate included pitch, volume, FM oscillation, chorus, and distortion. Figure 3 shows images from DECONcerts 2 and 3.

The participant's raw EEG signal, and frequency distribution, were plotted and projected onto a screen, so the participant could determine if he or she was in an alpha brain state or a beta state. When all of the participants in a single group reached alpha frequency (as determined by an averaging process), the acoustic quality controlled by that group was modulated accordingly.

In this way, the participants' brainwaves collectively and continuously affect music that was being heard. This process was both fluid and regenerative, in that participants' brain states influenced the musical output, which in turn was received (heard) by the participant's brain, which then influenced the participant's brainstate which influenced the music output.

3.2   Powerplant Performance

In 2007, we undertook a new iteration of the brainwave musical interface system. Rather than creating a feedback interaction between performer and audience, we allowed participants to "jam along" with a renowned live improvising band in a concert setting. We assigned each participant a note or chord. By reaching a certain threshold of alpha activity (20% of total brainwave output measured from occipital lobe) participants were able to increase the volume of that tone. The increase was cumulative (temporally integrated) whereby the longer the participant remained over threshold, the higher the volume went. This cumulative (integrated) response mimics the response of aquatic instruments like the hydraulophone, which responds to absement or presement (time time-integral of displacement or reciprocal displacement) rather than to displacement or to velocity (many other polyphonic instruments like the piano respond to velocity rather than displacement or absement). This kind of response simulates the effect of a water reservoir that fills up or empties out over time, giving the instrument's user-interface an aquatic feel.

Once participants learned, through usage, how to gain control over the system, they could play and mute, warp and vibrate their note, in time with the band. Not only did the participants play along, but they also gave musical cues to the other players. This is a direct example of a humanistic intelligence signaling block, where human and machine work together directly affecting and responding to one another's output as it becomes reified in the external physical world. See Fig 4.

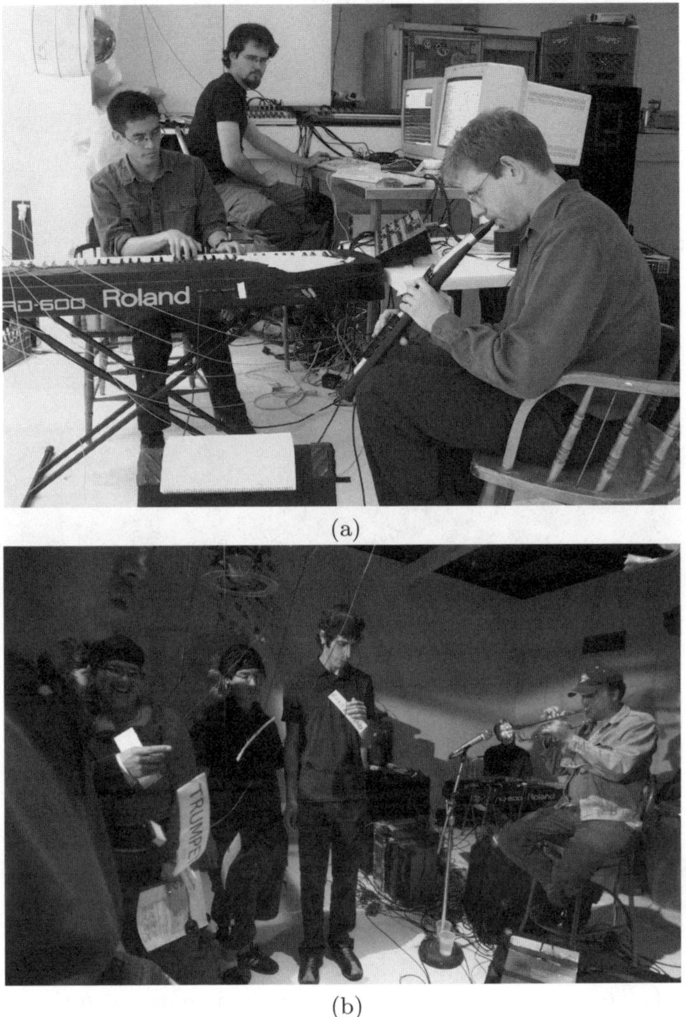

(a)

(b)

Fig. 3. Regenerative Jazz Performance (a) DECONcert 2: Audience brainwaves modulate the sounds of a trio of performers. (b) DECONcet 3: A Jazz ensemble is affected by audience brainwaves, with acoustic instruments modulated via sound filter.

3.3   Telematic Tubs Against Terror

Telematic Tubs Against Terror, also explored the creation of a collective and communal consconsious, this time using the mediums of water and brainwaves, rather than music and brainwaves. Figure 5 shows images taken from these events. Two tubs of water were set up in different locations, one on a main street, and one indoors 1.5 miles away. Eight EEG leads and several ECG leads were suspended over the tubs.Two screens abutted the tubs. Each location received the EEG and ECG information of the sister tub and projected it on one screen,

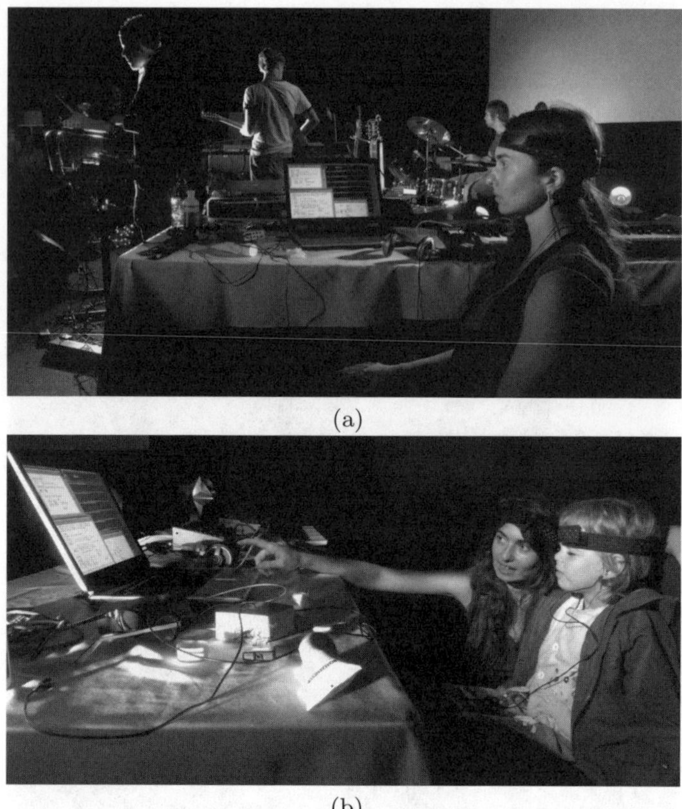

Fig. 4. Brainwave Performance at the Powerplant Art Gallery in Toronto: (a) Quintist Ariel Garten performing; (b) A young audience member performs in the concert, after a brief 5 minute training session

as well as receiving live video feed from the sister location projected onto the second screen. Up to 8 (and sometimes more) participants at a time entered the tub together, and connected themselves to the EEG and ECG leads. In this way the participants were sharing not only physical space, but mental space as well.

3.4   Differentiating Brainstates to Create Control Interfaces

In DECONcert 1, we hooked up 48 people's EEG signals, which were collectively used to affect the audio environment. Each audience member had a single EEG lead held against the back of his or her head with comfortable headband, at the location of the occipital lobe. As well, a wire was clipped to each ear for grounding. The collective signals from groups of eight participants were cleaned, and collective alpha synchronization (which occurs, for instance, when people close their eyes) was detected.

The alpha-wave intensity increases when a person approaches a calm meditative state of concentration and it is inversely proportional to the amount of

(a)   (b)

Fig. 5. Telematic Tubs Performance. (a) and (b) show two different "wash nodes" where participants' EEGs and ECGs were read and shared between sites. A video link connected each wash node with the others as well, and brainwave data was displayed and re-presented remotely.

visual stimulant the person receives [3]. Experiments have shown that there exists a correlation between the mental activity of a person and their respective EEG spectrum [2]. Lusted and Knapp explored brainwave interfaces [6]. An early musical brainwave implementation was conducted by Lucier [4,5], also employing alpha waves as a sonic device. Rosenboom [8] worked with alpha waves for music production. The music of this work extends the group dynamic of brain wave music to 48 simultaneous participants, and explores both light and water as additional mediums for immersive experiences.

Humans are generally described as being in one of 5 brain states, Alpha, a calm creative state that is described by brainwave activity of 8-12 Hz, Delta, slow brainwave less thank 2 Hz, is associated with deep sleep. Theta, a state achieved by those in deep meditation or earlier stages of sleep, are classed as 4-8 Hz. Most individuals spend most of their day in beta waves, classified as any wave activity over 12 Hz. [1] For our purposes, we tracked whether participants were in Alpha state (8-12 Hz) or another state.

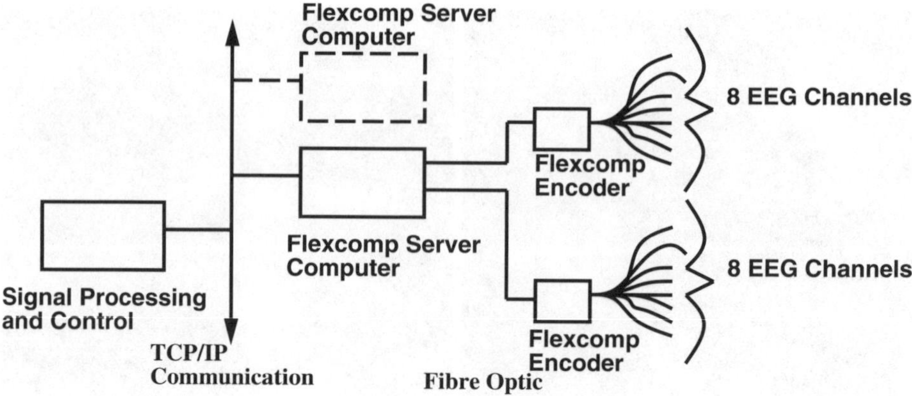

Fig. 6. EEG Multimedia Control System. The system is expandable to accommodate a number of EEG channels, which may be connected to multiple participants. Additionally, the TCP/IP connection allows the possibility of remote and wireless data analysis and storage.

System Configuration. The basic configuration of the system is shown in Figure 6. To digitize brainwave activity for analysis, a Thought Technology FlexComp A/D encoder and ISA DSP2 Data Acquisition Card (DAC) are used. These devices can provide up to a 2KHz brainwave sampling rate, and measure brainwave activity down to a maximum of 5% error and 1V accuracy.

A set of custom programs were written to utilize the hardware for music generation. Additionally a Linux device driver was written to interface with the ISA data acquisition card. A server program communicates with the DAC, placed on the ISA bus of a Linux system, and optically connected to the FlexComp encoder hardware thereby making raw EEG data available over TCP/IP. A client system connects to the server via TCP/IP and receives the EEG data, upon which it performs the filtering and processing of brainwave data. Both programs can run on a single Linux PC using the loopback address (127.0.0.1), if the PC is sufficiently fast. Similarly the TCP/IP interface can be exploited to allow communication between remote locations, as in the implementation of the Telematic Tubs exhibit, and the remote Parkinson's patients event.

Additionally control of standard AC room lighting was achieved using a DMX-512 dimmer system is used. DMX-512 is a simple packet-based digital protocol for controlling stage lighting and other devices using an RS-485 serial interface at 250kbaud connecting to a LanBox LCX DMX-512 Controller over a TCP/IP socket.which sends a single text command to change room lighting levels. This change is transmitted via the DMX protocol to a set of DMX dimmers, which change the light intensities in the room as required. Figure 7 shows the EEG controlled lighting environments used in the exhibits.

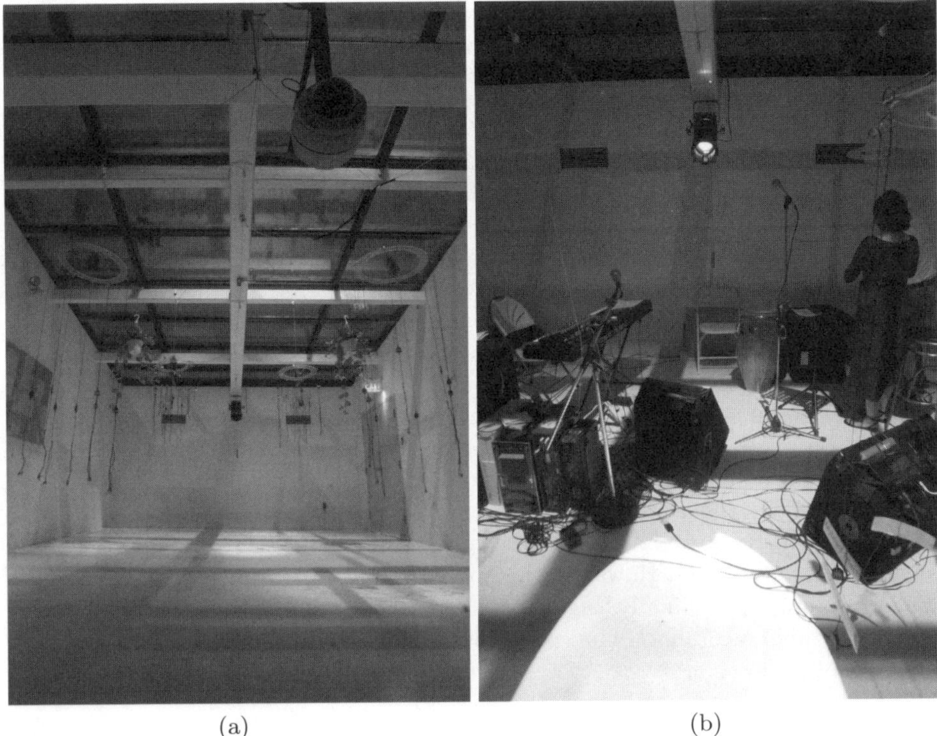

(a)   (b)

Fig. 7. Brainwave Controlled Immersive Lighting and System Sculpture. (a) The DECONcert theatre. Six stations of EEG Electrodes hang from the ceiling. Gelled lighting systems shining from above the skylights of the space use light to create a collective immersive environment. The custom designed circular discs form EEG nodes for eight participants, reflecting the "neuron" like design of the system where multiple branches of input flow to a signal processing machine. (b) In turning the audience into a participant, DECONcerts invert the relationship between audience and performer, bringing the two together. A brainwave controlled spotlight shines on the participants with the intensity controlled by their concentration state.

3.5 Screening Out Unusable Signals

EEG signals are typically orders of magnitude weaker than muscular signals. Consequently, if the participant is moving their head, or their muscles are not sufficiently relaxed, the EEG signal signal strength is weak in comparison to the muscular electrical activity, which we consider noise. In this situation, we cannot rely upon the analyzed EEG bands to produce a usable signal. In order to detect these cases, we calculated the power of the received signal, and rejected the signal above a certain threshold, which could be calibrated as the system was used.

3.6   Real-Time Control of Live Musical Input

Because the system is used for real-time control, latency between the onset of a desired EEG trend, and response of the system was found to be of interest. We implemented several approaches to control. The first approach was to use a variable counter which incremented so long as the participant's alpha waveband strength was above a threshold. The counter decremented when the alpha waveband strength was below a threshold. Sound effects were triggered when the counter was above a certain threshold. The advantage of this method was that only sustained period of high alpha activity triggered a sound response from the system, and made it quite robust with respect to a "false positive" alpha strength detections. Additionally, this method allowed us to verify the efficacy of our system at detecting alpha activity. However, the requirement for sustained periods of alpha activity meant that the sound effects would only occur at typically longer than 10–15 seconds after the onset of the alpha activity state. This latency made it difficult for a casual participant to perceive their effect on the sound. Similarly the window sized used for the frequency analysis is related to the latency in the system. Longer windows allow for more reliable detection of sustained mental state. However, this increased overall latency of the produced control signal. Additionally, high, but short lived alpha activity is not well detected in this case. Short windows allow for faster system response, but were affected by noise.

3.7   EEG Based Music Composition

Our approach to EEG based musical composition was that of creating a general programming framework, whose variables were continuously controlled by the EEG signals of the participants.

There was a simple sequenced bassline (randomly choosing from 4 note progressions), a simple sequenced drum track (the complexity of the track altered by the persons alpha), which utilized a sequencer. We used the counter method described above. However, instead of only a single event above a preset threshold, different ranges of the current value was used to determine the complexity of the tracks.

For the bassline, several sets of notes' on and off toggles were under control of the EEG. Thus, for higher activity, more notes were turned on and this made the sound of the baseline appear more busy and complex. For the sequenced drum track, the EEG was used to toggle different rhythm tracks on and off. When more instruments were triggered on, the rhythm appeared more complex. Again, these were turned on and off with respect to current alpha counter range. Additionally pad and background sounds were randomly triggered by the amount of alpha activity of the participant.

To maintain a musical consistency the tones (notes) were chosen from a predetermined scale (aeolian mode) so as minimize the disonnance which would occur if completely random notes were used. For these effects, however, the primary contribution of EEG control was to affect the filter frequencies of the tones, which dramatically affected their quality. The control was achieved via sending MIDI control signals to synthesizers.

Typically observed minimum and maximum alpha waveband strengths were mapped to the range $[0, 127]$ used by MIDI. This method represented a continuous form of mapping alpha strength to control variables as no thresholding was used. Additionally, however, we found that the most effective sound effects were those which changed dramatically over their MIDI controlled range. In some instances, we restricted the MIDI controller value into a range which produced dramatic changes instead of the full $[0, 127]$.

We found that this approach allowed the system to emulate the pseudo-randomness of sweeps and pads which tend to occur, for instance, in electronic music, and create those events under the control of the alpha. Similarly, the kick drum or delay effects on a drum track are additionally triggered on and of under the control of alpha waves.

Overall, we found that these approaches allowed for different parts to fade in and out. For instance, the kick sometimes provided a beat, and would then fell out, giving way to a more open segments and so on. The participants were able to learn and control the system well by listening to the music feedback, over the 30 minutes they had to use it. At the end of the performance, the participants understood their control of the music well.

3.8 Affecting Live Performance with EEG Signals

DECONcerts 2 & 3 used participant brainwaves to alter the sound qualities of instruments being played by live musicians. Both acoustic and electronic instruments were affected. Electronic instrument sound qualities were affected by varying MIDI parameters using the system of DECONcert 1. An electronic keyboard, electronic wind instrument and electronic drum pad were used.

To achieve variation on acoustic instruments, a digital mixer was used. For acoustic instruments such as an amplified bass [3], two audio channels were fed into the mixer. One channel was the unaltered audio channel, and the second was the same input run through a filter. The filter was either a pedal filter, or a digital filter applied internally: a feature of the mixer equipment. Brain wave signals drove the system to, via MIDI, crossfade between the unfiltered and filtered channels. In this way the brainwaves altered the sound quality of the acoustic instruments used at the event.

This created a challenging playing environment for the musician. The sound quality of the musician's instrument changed in ways that were not under the conscious, direct control of the musician. As the sound quality changed, the musician needed to adapt their playing style to match. For instance, the decay of the note would change. With a short decay, the musician could perform quick, stacatto phrases, while longer decays, phrases incorporating sustained notes were more appropriate. In this way, participants affected the overall qualities of the music despite the fact that the musicians were playing the instruments themselves.

---

[3] For the moment, we consider the analog nature of the amplification of the vibration of the strings of an electric bass guitar as "acoustic".

4   Aquatic Context: Waves in Water and Mind

The connection between brainwaves, water waves, and sound waves (in both air and in water) was made all the more apparent in a recent performance at the International Computer Music Conference (ICMC 2007) in Copenhagen. The theme of the 2007 conference was "Immersed Music".

In keeping with this theme, we developed various forms of "Immersive Media" for public performance in Copenhagen's Vandkulturhuset. The name "Vand kultur huset" means "water culture house" in Danish.

4.1   The States-of-Matter Quintet

This Immsersed Music concert at ICMC 2007 consisted of a performance by the States-of-Matter Quintet, involving musical instruments we created that produced sound from each of the five states-of-matter:

- Solid ("Earth");
- Liquid ("Water");
- Gas ("Air");
- Plasma ("Fire");
- Quintessence ("Idea").

These correspond to the Greek Classical Elements, the fifth element being Idea (non-matter).

See Fig 8.

4.2   Surrounding Medium

Vandkulturhuset (Fig. 9),

The existence of **immersive media** raises the question of **media** itself. Thus we may ask:

- in what medium is the sound initially produced;
- what is the surrounding medium;
- in what medium is the listener immersed?

For example, the fact that a listener may be immersed in air, or in water, suggests also that the sound need not be produced in the same medium in which it is experienced.

5   Philosophical Implications/ Discussion

5.1   Human/Computer Feedback Interaction (HI)

Both Telematic Tubs Against Terror and DECONcert create a Humanistic Intelligence feed-back loop using the elements of music, water and brain. As discussed, Humanistic Intelligence is defined as intelligence that arises from the human being in the feedback loop of a computational process in which the human and computer are inextricably intertwined, in otherwords, it is a regenerative feedback loop. In DECONcert, regenerative music is the expression of HI in music. In regenerative music the computer, instead of taking only active cues from the musician, reads physiological signals from the musician/performer. The music which the regenerative algorithm then creates will be heard by the musician/performer. It is hoped that the music will in turn generate an emotional response on the part of the musician/performer, and that that emotional response will be detectable by the computer, which can then alter the music in some way in response. Continuing in this fashion, it is clear that there is a well defined feedback loop occurring between the human and the computer.

5.2 Regenerative Music

Jazz, the musical genre of the DECONcert performances, is a natural non-computation example of regenerative music. Jazz is a free flowing style of musical improvisation in which the performers intuitively read one another's states, mood and musical intention based on both the performer's sonic output as well as conscious and subconscious communication between players. The players in a sense create an immersive, responsive environment. Immersed in the music that surrounds them, in the musical and collective 'zone', they respond to one another's output. The response of the audience, also encourages or discourages the musicians' particular output. DECONcert takes this intuitive process and turns it inside out.

Regenerative Music looks not only at the audience-musician interaction, but also the musician-instrument response. It brings in the problem of how a musician can learn to respond to this new physiologically driven instrument, as well as how the instrument can learn to infer the wishes of the musician through their physiological signals, in addition to the normal playing of the instrument. In a sense, the musician and instrument each play off of each other, and together, both can be viewed as an "instrument". The choice of how to map from physiological signals into instrument behavior would be an artistic one, under the control of the musician.

5.3 Collective Unconsciousness

Creating regenerative music then becomes a distributed process, where no one individual has conscious control over the sound. In a sense, all individuals enter a collective state in which no single individual is aware of or has conscious control over the outcome. Collectively and communally, the audience determines what will be heard musically, using the interface of their brains. The audience has no determination over what the final outcome of the music will be, nor do the musicians. Thus, with brains physically connected to one another though EEG leads, the audience enters both physically and metaphorically into a collective unconsciousness.

In Telematic Tubs Against Terror, collective unconsciousness was explored not through music as its medium of expression, but through water. Sitting together

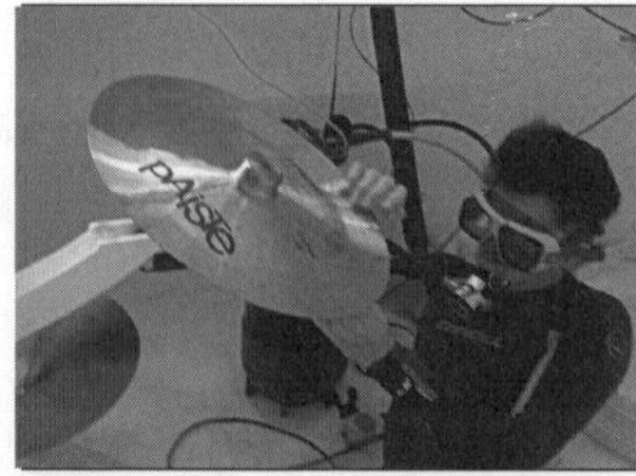

Solid ("Earth")

Instruments such as the guitar (chordophone) or cymbal (idiophone), pictured at left, produce sound by matter in its solid state. Most idiophones such as the cymbal, or Franklin's glass harmonica, will operate immersed in air or in water.

Liquid ("Water")

A new category of instruments called hydraulophones produce sound by matter in its liquid state. These instruments work well immersed in air or in water.

Gas ("Air")

Instruments such as the flute, work only in air. To get them to sound underwater requires a surrounding of air around the fipple mechanism and at least some air in the resonant cavity. The organflute ("florgan"), a newly invented musical instrument (invented, designed, built, and played by by S. Mann), combines the user-interface of the flute (played by blocking finger holes) with the sound of the pipe organ.

Plasma ("Fire")

The plasmaphones, another newly invented category of musical instruments, produce sound by matter in its fourth state, namely plasma.

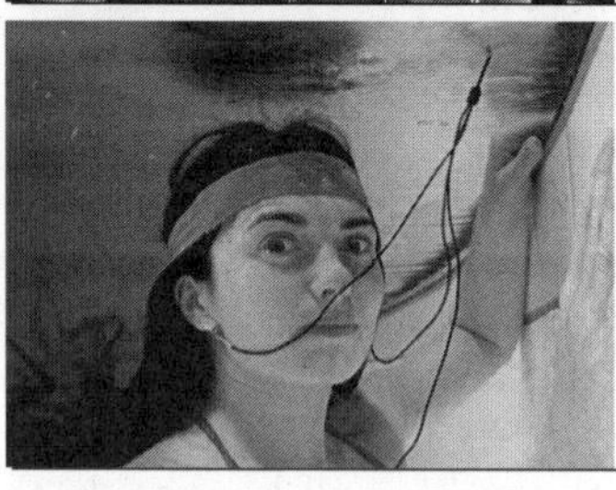

Informatics ("Idea")

Plato and Aristotle postulated a fifth state-of-matter, which they called "Idea" or "Quintessence" (from "quint" which means "fifth"). This covers thoughts, mathematics, algorithms, and the like. A direct brain-machine interface was used in the performance by the States-of-Matter Quintet to represent the fifth state-of-matter.

Fig. 8. Five States of Matter in Immersive Music. These five states-of-matter correspond to the five Classical Greek Elements. Earth, Water, Air, Fire, and Idea ("Quintessence" meaning "fifth" element). Immersed Music concerts explored the immersion of these five elements in both water and air. Immersed Music was the theme of ICMC 2007, which included concerts at the DGI-byen "Vandkulturhuset" swim center.

(a)   (b)

Fig. 9. "Vandkulturhuset" is Danish for "Water Culture House". This cultural venue in Copenhagen was the site of our "Immersed Music" concert.

in a pool of water collecting and sharing brainwave information, participants were brought into the same collective DECONsciousness, as DECONcert. In also known as the DGI Swim Centre, consists of six pools in the main DGI-byen aquatics area, which provide a variety of different kinds of bathing experiences at a variety of different temperatures. One of these pools is a 100 metre (320 foot) round pool called "the ocean". The ocean pool allows for "endless" (no need to stop and change direction) swims. This round pool also has a hydraulic stage in the center for concerts or banquets, in which the round pool forms a moat around the musicians or diners. Our performance actually brought a variety of musical instruments right into the pool itself, creating truly immersive music! See Fig. 10.

5.4   Sousveillance

Surveillance pervades our society, ostensibly to mitigate danger. As a collective of individuals whose information is being shared amongst one another, we are engaging in a "sousveillance" [9] of sorts. Whereas traditional surveillance is a top-down affair, where some hierarchically superior "Big Brother" is watching the movements of the general populace, in Telematic Tubs Against Terror and DECONcert, the distributed sharing of private information creates a sousveillance, a situation in which the subjects themselves are recording and sharing their own information with one another. In an interesting twist, this sousveillance creates a feedback loop between the audience and the recording device, particularly the complex feedback loop in Telematic Tubs Against Terror between the video cameras and 2 separate wash nodes. In being recorded, particularly while in the vulnerable situation of bathing, one's behavior changes. In Telematic Tubs, one realizes one is being recorded, and ones actions are affected as such. Those different reactions are broadcast to the sister tub, who in seeing the actions of their fellow bathers at a separate location, act differently. These

Fig. 10. Instruments that make sound from solid matter (left), liquid matter (middle) and gaseous matter (right). Here instruments making sound from all three states-of-matter (solid, liquid, and gas) are immersed in a surrounding medium of liquid. Only the hydraulophone is designed to work properly when immersed in liquid.

reactions of the participants in the second tub are then recorded on video projected on a screen by the first tub, to further effect the behavior of the participants there, who cannot directly view on a screen their own behavior, only that of the second tub. Thus a self-conscious distributed self-surveillance feedback loop is created.

6   Conclusion

DECONcert and Telematic Tubs Against Terror speak of the interconnected relationships between water, music and the brain. Using an intelligent signal processing system to control musical output we created a collective consciousness by highlighting both the humanistic intelligence human-computational feedback loop as well as a physical shared immersive environment. In creating what we refer to as a collective DECONsciousness, issues of privacy, contamination, and control become significant. Participants become performers who are on stage in the bath, self powering a distributed immersive experience with the pooling of their brainwaves.

Acknowledgements

The authors would like to acknowledge the contributions from Corey Manders, Chris Aimone, and Ryan Janzen. We also thank Thought Technologies Limited, www.thoughttechnology.com, for donation of equipment that made much of this work possible.

References

1. Brankack, J., Stewart, S.F.M.: Current source density analysis of the hippocampal theta rhythm: Associated sustained potentials and candidate synaptic generators. Brain Research 615(2), 310–327 (1993)
2. Cromwell, L., Weibell, F.J., Pfeiffer, E.A., Usselman, L.B.: Biomedical Instrumentation and Measurements. Prentice Hall, Inc., Englewood Cliffs (1973)
3. Legewie, H., Simonova, O., Crutzfeldt, O.D.: EEG Changes During Performance of Various Tasks Under Open- and Closed-eyed Conditions. Elsevier Publishing Company, Amsterdam (1969)
4. Lucier, A.: Music for Solo Performer (1965), for enormously amplified brain waves and percussion. Lovely Music, Ltd., (1982)
5. Lucier, A.: Music for alpha waves, assorted percussion, and automated coded relays, on "imaginary landscapes". Elektra/Nonesuch 79235-2 (1989)
6. Lusted, H.S., Knapp, R.B.: Controlling computers with neural signals. Scientific American Magazine, 82–88 (October 1996)
7. Mann, S.: Humanistic intelligence/humanistic computing: 'wearcomp' as a new framework for intelligent signal processing. Proceedings of the IEEE 86(11), 2123–2151 (1998), `http://wearcam.org/procieee.htm`
8. Rosenboom, D.: Method of producing sounds or light flashes with alpha brain waves for artistic purposes. Leonardo 5(1) (1972)
9. Steve Mann, M.F., Fung, J., Baccanico, G.: Panopdecon: deconstructing, decontaminating, and decontextualizing panopticism in the postcyborg era. Surveillance & Society 1(3), 375–398 (2003)

Author Index

Afanador, Kathleya   34, 235
Amatriain, Xavier   380
Aramaki, Mitsuko   139
Ardila, Mauricio   125
Avanzini, Federico   212

Baalman, Marije A.J.   246
Barthet, Mathieu   313
Burgoyne, John Ashley   181

Campana, Ellen   34, 235
Carter, Jenny   74
Castellanos, Jorge   380
Chordia, Parag   110
Chowning, John   1

Dannenberg, Roger B.   276
Dean, Roger   223
de Götzen, Amalia   212
Driessen, Peter F.   276

Eaglestone, Barry   74
Eigenfeldt, Arne   368
Einbond, Aaron   203
Ellis, Jarrod   453

Fabiani, Marco   288
Ford, Nigel   74
Friberg, Anders   288
Fung, James   487

Garten, Ariel   487
Gerhard, David   453
Godfrey, Mark   351

Haines, William D.   276
Hamilton, Robert   478
Holdridge, Peter   74
Höllerer, Tobias   380

Ilomäki, Tuukka   98
Ingalls, Todd   34, 235

James, Jodi   34, 235
Jensen, Kristoffer   263

Kalayar Khine, Swe Zin   159
Kendall, Gary S.   125
Knapp, R. Benjamin   441
Kobayashi, Ryoho   360
Kronland-Martinet, Richard   139, 313
Kuchera-Morin, JoAnn   380
Kühl, Ole   263

Leistikow, Randal   34
Li, Haizhou   159
Lockhart, Adam   172

MacCallum, John   203
Malloch, Joseph   401
Mann, Steve   487
McAdams, Stephen   181
Merer, Adrien   139
Mion, Luca   212
Moody-Grigsby, Daniel   246
Mumford, Jessica   235

Nwe, Tin Lay   159

Park, Brett   453
Pastuszek-Lipińska, Barbara   56
Pérez, Miguel Angel Ortiz   441
Pope, Stephen T.   380

Qian, Gang   235

Rae, Alex   110, 351
Rajko, StJepan   34, 235
Rath, Matthias   303
Rhoads, John   351

Salter, Christopher L.   246
Serafin, Stefania   212
Sinclair, Stephen   401
Stevens, Catherine   223
Swaminathan, Dilip   34, 235

Takahashi, Masato   360
Taylor, J. Milo   426
Thornburg, Harvey   34, 235
Tillmann, Barbara   11

Uozumi, Yuta   360
Upton, Catherine   74

Vernon, Jesse R.   276

Wakefield, Graham   380
Wältermann, Marcel   303

Wanderley, Marcelo M.   401
Weinberg, Gil   351
Wilkie, Sonia   223
Wolcott, Will   380

Young, Michael   337
Ystad, Sølvi   139, 313

Printing: Mercedes-Druck, Berlin
Binding: Stein+Lehmann, Berlin

Lecture Notes in Computer Science

Sublibrary 3: Information Systems and Application, incl. Internet/Web and HCI

For information about Vols. 1– 4721
please contact your bookseller or Springer

Vol. 5120: S. Helal, S. Mitra, J. Wong, C.K. Chang, M. Mokhtari (Eds.), Smart Homes and Health Telematics. XV, 220 pages. 2008.

Vol. 5105: K. Miesenberger, J. Klaus, W. Zagler, A. Karshmer (Eds.), Computers Helping People with Special Needs. XXVIII, 1350 pages. 2008.

Vol. 5094: V. Atluri (Ed.), Data and Applications Security XXII. IX, 347 pages. 2008.

Vol. 5093: Z. Pan, X. Zhang, A. El Rhalibi, W. Woo, Y. Li (Eds.), Technologies for E-Learning and Digital Entertainment. XVII, 791 pages. 2008.

Vol. 5080: Z. Pan, A.D. Cheok, W. Müller, A. El Rhalibi (Eds.), Transactions on Edutainment I. X, 305 pages. 2008.

Vol. 5075: C.C. Yang, H. Chen, M. Chau, K. Chang, S.-D. Lang, P.S. Chen, R. Hsieh, D. Zeng, F.-Y. Wang, K.M. Carley, W. Mao, J. Zhan (Eds.), Intelligence and Security Informatics. XXII, 522 pages. 2008.

Vol. 5074: Z. Bellahsène, M. Léonard (Eds.), Advanced Information Systems Engineering. XVII, 588 pages. 2008.

Vol. 5071: A. Gray, K. Jeffery, J. Shao (Eds.), Sharing Data, Information and Knowledge. XI, 293 pages. 2008.

Vol. 5069: B. Ludäscher, N. Mamoulis (Eds.), Scientific and Statistical Database Management. XIII, 620 pages. 2008.

Vol. 5068: S. Lee, H. Choo, S. Ha, I.C. Shin (Eds.), Computer Human Interaction. XVII, 458 pages. 2008.

Vol. 5066: M. Tscheligi, M. Obrist, A. Lugmayr (Eds.), Changing Television Environments. XV, 324 pages. 2008.

Vol. 5061: F.E. Sandnes, Y. Zhang, C. Rong, L.T. Yang, J. Ma (Eds.), Ubiquitous Intelligence and Computing. XVI, 763 pages. 2008.

Vol. 5053: R. Meier, S. Terzis (Eds.), Distributed Applications and Interoperable Systems. XI, 303 pages. 2008.

Vol. 5039: E. Kapetanios, V. Sugumaran, M. Spiliopoulou (Eds.), Natural Language and Information Systems. XIX, 386 pages. 2008.

Vol. 5034: R. Fleischer, J. Xu (Eds.), Algorithmic Aspects in Information and Management. XI, 350 pages. 2008.

Vol. 5033: H. Oinas-Kukkonen, P. Hasle, M. Harjumaa, K. Segerståhl, P. Øhrstrøm (Eds.), Persuasive Technology. XIV, 287 pages. 2008.

Vol. 5024: M. Ferre (Ed.), Haptics: Perception, Devices and Scenarios. XXIII, 950 pages. 2008.

Vol. 5021: S. Bechhofer, M. Hauswirth, J. Hoffmann, M. Koubarakis (Eds.), The Semantic Web: Research and Applications. XIX, 897 pages. 2008.

Vol. 5017: T. Nanya, F. Maruyama, A. Pataricza, M. Malek (Eds.), Service Availability. XII, 225 pages. 2008.

Vol. 5013: J. Indulska, D.J. Patterson, T. Rodden, M. Ott (Eds.), Pervasive Computing. XIV, 315 pages. 2008.

Vol. 5006: R. Kowalczyk, M. Huhns, M. Klusch, Z. Maamar, Q.B. Vo (Eds.), Service-Oriented Computing: Agents, Semantics, and Engineering. X, 154 pages. 2008.

Vol. 5005: V. Christophides, M. Collard, C. Guttierez (Eds.), Semantic Web, Ontologies and Databases. VII, 153 pages. 2008.

Vol. 4997: B. Monien, U.-P. Schroeder (Eds.), Algorithmic Game Theory. XI, 363 pages. 2008.

Vol. 4993: H. Li, T. Liu, W.-Y. Ma, T. Sakai, K.-F. Wong, G. Zhou (Eds.), Information Retrieval Technology. XIII, 685 pages. 2008.

Vol. 4976: Y. Zhang, G. Yu, E. Bertino, G. Xu (Eds.), Progress in WWW Research and Development. XVIII, 699 pages. 2008.

Vol. 4969: R. Kronland-Martinet, S. Ystad, K. Jensen (Eds.), Computer Music Modeling and Retrieval. XII, 508 pages. 2008.

Vol. 4956: C. Macdonald, I. Ounis, V. Plachouras, I. Ruthven, R.W. White (Eds.), Advances in Information Retrieval. XXI, 719 pages. 2008.

Vol. 4952: C. Floerkemeier, M. Langheinrich, E. Fleisch, F. Mattern, S.E. Sarma (Eds.), The Internet of Things. XIII, 378 pages. 2008.

Vol. 4947: J.R. Haritsa, R. Kotagiri, V. Pudi (Eds.), Database Systems for Advanced Applications. XXII, 713 pages. 2008.

Vol. 4936: W. Aiello, A. Broder, J. Janssen, E.E. Milios (Eds.), Algorithms and Models for the Web-Graph. X, 167 pages. 2008.

Vol. 4932: S. Hartmann, G. Kern-Isberner (Eds.), Foundations of Information and Knowledge Systems. XII, 397 pages. 2008.

Vol. 4928: A.H.M. ter Hofstede, B. Benatallah, H.-Y. Paik (Eds.), Business Process Management Workshops. XIII, 518 pages. 2008.

Vol. 4918: N. Boujemaa, M. Detyniecki, A. Nürnberger (Eds.), Adaptive Multimedial Retrieval: Retrieval, User, and Semantics. XI, 265 pages. 2008.

Vol. 4903: S. Satoh, F. Nack, M. Etoh (Eds.), Advances in Multimedia Modeling. XIX, 510 pages. 2008.

Vol. 4900: S. Spaccapietra (Ed.), Journal on Data Semantics X. XIII, 265 pages. 2008.

Vol. 4892: A. Popescu-Belis, S. Renals, H. Bourlard (Eds.), Machine Learning for Multimodal Interaction. XI, 308 pages. 2008.

Vol. 4882: T. Janowski, H. Mohanty (Eds.), Distributed Computing and Internet Technology. XIII, 346 pages. 2007.

Vol. 4881: H. Yin, P. Tino, E. Corchado, W. Byrne, X. Yao (Eds.), Intelligent Data Engineering and Automated Learning - IDEAL 2007. XX, 1174 pages. 2007.

Vol. 4877: C. Thanos, F. Borri, L. Candela (Eds.), Digital Libraries: Research and Development. XII, 350 pages. 2007.

Vol. 4872: D. Mery, L. Rueda (Eds.), Advances in Image and Video Technology. XXI, 961 pages. 2007.

Vol. 4871: M. Cavazza, S. Donikian (Eds.), Virtual Storytelling. XIII, 219 pages. 2007.

Vol. 4858: X. Deng, F.C. Graham (Eds.), Internet and Network Economics. XVI, 598 pages. 2007.

Vol. 4857: J.M. Ware, G.E. Taylor (Eds.), Web and Wireless Geographical Information Systems. XI, 293 pages. 2007.

Vol. 4853: F. Fonseca, M.A. Rodríguez, S. Levashkin (Eds.), GeoSpatial Semantics. X, 289 pages. 2007.

Vol. 4836: H. Ichikawa, W.-D. Cho, I. Satoh, H.Y. Youn (Eds.), Ubiquitous Computing Systems. XIII, 307 pages. 2007.

Vol. 4832: M. Weske, M.-S. Hacid, C. Godart (Eds.), Web Information Systems Engineering – WISE 2007 Workshops. XV, 518 pages. 2007.

Vol. 4831: B. Benatallah, F. Casati, D. Georgakopoulos, C. Bartolini, W. Sadiq, C. Godart (Eds.), Web Information Systems Engineering – WISE 2007. XVI, 675 pages. 2007.

Vol. 4825: K. Aberer, K.-S. Choi, N. Noy, D. Allemang, K.-I. Lee, L. Nixon, J. Golbeck, P. Mika, D. Maynard, R. Mizoguchi, G. Schreiber, P. Cudré-Mauroux (Eds.), The Semantic Web. XXVII, 973 pages. 2007.

Vol. 4823: H. Leung, F. Li, R. Lau, Q. Li (Eds.), Advances in Web Based Learning – ICWL 2007. XIV, 654 pages. 2008.

Vol. 4822: D.H.-L. Goh, T.H. Cao, I.T. Sølvberg, E. Rasmussen (Eds.), Asian Digital Libraries. XVII, 519 pages. 2007.

Vol. 4820: T.G. Wyeld, S. Kenderdine, M. Docherty (Eds.), Virtual Systems and Multimedia. XII, 215 pages. 2008.

Vol. 4816: B. Falcidieno, M. Spagnuolo, Y. Avrithis, I. Kompatsiaris, P. Buitelaar (Eds.), Semantic Multimedia. XII, 306 pages. 2007.

Vol. 4813: I. Oakley, S.A. Brewster (Eds.), Haptic and Audio Interaction Design. XIV, 145 pages. 2007.

Vol. 4810: H.H.-S. Ip, O.C. Au, H. Leung, M.-T. Sun, W.-Y. Ma, S.-M. Hu (Eds.), Advances in Multimedia Information Processing – PCM 2007. XXI, 834 pages. 2007.

Vol. 4809: M.K. Denko, C.-s. Shih, K.-C. Li, S.-L. Tsao, Q.-A. Zeng, S.H. Park, Y.-B. Ko, S.-H. Hung, J.-H. Park (Eds.), Emerging Directions in Embedded and Ubiquitous Computing. XXXV, 823 pages. 2007.

Vol. 4808: T.-W. Kuo, E. Sha, M. Guo, L.T. Yang, Z. Shao (Eds.), Embedded and Ubiquitous Computing. XXI, 769 pages. 2007.

Vol. 4806: R. Meersman, Z. Tari, P. Herrero (Eds.), On the Move to Meaningful Internet Systems 2007: OTM 2007 Workshops, Part II. XXXIV, 611 pages. 2007.

Vol. 4805: R. Meersman, Z. Tari, P. Herrero (Eds.), On the Move to Meaningful Internet Systems 2007: OTM 2007 Workshops, Part I. XXXIV, 757 pages. 2007.

Vol. 4804: R. Meersman, Z. Tari (Eds.), On the Move to Meaningful Internet Systems 2007: CoopIS, DOA, ODBASE, GADA, and IS, Part II. XXIX, 683 pages. 2007.

Vol. 4803: R. Meersman, Z. Tari (Eds.), On the Move to Meaningful Internet Systems 2007: CoopIS, DOA, ODBASE, GADA, and IS, Part I. XXIX, 1173 pages. 2007.

Vol. 4802: J.-L. Hainaut, E.A. Rundensteiner, M. Kirchberg, M. Bertolotto, M. Brochhausen, Y.-P.P. Chen, S.S.-S. Cherfi, M. Doerr, H. Han, S. Hartmann, J. Parsons, G. Poels, C. Rolland, J. Trujillo, E. Yu, E. Zimányie (Eds.), Advances in Conceptual Modeling – Foundations and Applications. XIX, 420 pages. 2007.

Vol. 4801: C. Parent, K.-D. Schewe, V.C. Storey, B. Thalheim (Eds.), Conceptual Modeling - ER 2007. XVI, 616 pages. 2007.

Vol. 4797: M. Arenas, M.I. Schwartzbach (Eds.), Database Programming Languages. VIII, 261 pages. 2007.

Vol. 4796: M. Lew, N. Sebe, T.S. Huang, E.M. Bakker (Eds.), Human–Computer Interaction. X, 157 pages. 2007.

Vol. 4794: B. Schiele, A.K. Dey, H. Gellersen, B. de Ruyter, M. Tscheligi, R. Wichert, E. Aarts, A. Buchmann (Eds.), Ambient Intelligence. XV, 375 pages. 2007.

Vol. 4777: S. Bhalla (Ed.), Databases in Networked Information Systems. X, 329 pages. 2007.

Vol. 4761: R. Obermaisser, Y. Nah, P. Puschner, F.J. Rammig (Eds.), Software Technologies for Embedded and Ubiquitous Systems. XIV, 563 pages. 2007.

Vol. 4747: S. Džeroski, J. Struyf (Eds.), Knowledge Discovery in Inductive Databases. X, 301 pages. 2007.

Vol. 4744: Y. de Kort, W. IJsselsteijn, C. Midden, B. Eggen, B.J. Fogg (Eds.), Persuasive Technology. XIV, 316 pages. 2007.

Vol. 4740: L. Ma, M. Rauterberg, R. Nakatsu (Eds.), Entertainment Computing – ICEC 2007. XXX, 480 pages. 2007.

Vol. 4730: C. Peters, P. Clough, F.C. Gey, J. Karlgren, B. Magnini, D.W. Oard, M. de Rijke, M. Stempfhuber (Eds.), Evaluation of Multilingual and Multi-modal Information Retrieval. XXIV, 998 pages. 2007.

Vol. 4723: M. R. Berthold, J. Shawe-Taylor, N. Lavrač (Eds.), Advances in Intelligent Data Analysis VII. XIV, 380 pages. 2007.